THE FUNDAMENTAL HOLMES

No figure stands taller in the world of First Amendment law than Oliver Wendell Holmes Jr. This is the first anthology of Justice Holmes's writings, speeches, and opinions concerning freedom of expression. Prepared by a noted free speech scholar, the book contains eight original essays designed to situate Holmes's works in a historical and biographical context. The volume is enriched by extensive commentaries concerning its many entries, which consist of letters, speeches, book excerpts, articles, state court opinions, and U.S. Supreme Court opinions. The edited materials – spanning Holmes's 1861–64 service in the Civil War to his 1931 radio address to the nation – offer a unique view of the thoughts of the father of the modern First Amendment. The book's epilogue, which includes a major discovery about Holmes's impact on American statutory law, explores Holmes's free speech legacy. In the process, the reader comes to know Holmes and his jurisprudence of free speech as never before.

Ronald K. L. Collins is the Harold S. Shefelman Scholar at the University of Washington School of Law. He is a noted authority on free speech law. His last book, *The Trials of Lenny Bruce* (with David Skover), was selected by the *Los Angeles Times* as one of the best books of the year. Collins is the coauthor (with Sam Chaltain) of the forthcoming *We Must Not Be Afraid to Be Free: Stories of Free Speech in America*. His scholarly articles have appeared in the *Harvard Law Review, Stanford Law Review*, and *Supreme Court Review*, among other places. He is also a Fellow at the First Amendment Center.

Photo of Holmes's study in his home in Washington, D.C. Holmes frequently read in the leather chair to the right of his desk. The crossed swords over the mantle and other military paraphernalia all belonged to his grandfather, Charles Jackson, and had been used in the Indian Civil Wars. Courtesy of Historical & Special Collections, Harvard Law Library.

The Fundamental Holmes

A FREE SPEECH CHRONICLE AND READER

Selections from the Opinions, Books, Articles, Speeches, Letters, and Other Writings by and about Oliver Wendell Holmes Jr.

Edited with essays, notes, and comments by

Ronald K. L. Collins
Harold S. Shefelman Scholar
University of Washington School of Law

CAMBRIDGE
UNIVERSITY PRESS

CAMBRIDGE UNIVERSITY PRESS
Cambridge, New York, Melbourne, Madrid, Cape Town, Singapore,
São Paulo, Delhi, Dubai, Tokyo, Mexico City

Cambridge University Press
32 Avenue of the Americas, New York, NY 10013-2473, USA

www.cambridge.org
Information on this title: www.cambridge.org/9780521143899

First published 2010

Printed in the United States of America

A catalog record for this publication is available from the British Library.

Library of Congress Cataloging in Publication data

Holmes, Oliver Wendell, 1841–1935.
[Selections. 2010]
The fundamental Holmes : a free speech chronicle and reader-selections from
the opinions, books, articles, speeches, letters, and other writings by and about
Oliver Wendell Holmes, Jr. / edited by Ronald K. L. Collins.
   p.   cm.
Includes bibliographical references and index.
ISBN 978-0-521-19460-0 (hardback) – ISBN 978-0-521-14389-9 (pbk.)
1. Law – United States.   2. Freedom of expression – United States.
I. Collins, Ronald K. L.   II. Title.
KF213.H6C65   2010
342.7308′5 – dc22   2009050317

ISBN 978-0-521-19460-0 Hardback
ISBN 978-0-521-14389-9 Paperback

To
Susan Abby Cohen

[W]hen men have realized that time has upset many fighting faiths, they may come to believe even more than they believe the very foundations of their own conduct that the ultimate good desired is better reached by free trade in ideas – that the best test of truth is the power of the thought to get itself accepted in the competition of the market, and that truth is the only ground upon which their wishes safely can be carried out. That, at any rate, is the theory of our Constitution. It is an experiment, as all life is an experiment. Every year, if not every day, we have to wager our salvation upon some prophecy based upon imperfect knowledge.

– Justice Oliver Wendell Holmes, dissenting in
Abrams v. United States (1919)

Contents

Timeline: Holmes's Life and Free Speech Jurisprudence, 1841–1935

1841

March 8: Born in Boston to Oliver Wendell Holmes Sr. and Amelia Lee Jackson.

1857

Autumn: Enters Harvard College.

1861

April: Withdraws, without permission, from senior class at Harvard and enlists as a private in the New England Guards, a Boston unit of the Massachusetts Volunteer Militia, commonly known as the Fourth Battalion of Massachusetts Volunteers.

May 25: Tour of duty ends. Returns to Harvard after a short duty of service and after his battalion breaks up.

July 17: Graduates from Harvard College.

July 23: Commissioned first lieutenant in Company A of Twentieth Regiment Massachusetts Volunteers, a three-year regiment.

October 21: Wounded at the Battle of Ball's Bluff in Virginia.

1862

September 17: Shot through the neck and wounded at Antietam Creek, Maryland.

1863

May 3: Wounded (shot in heel) at Fredericksburg, Virginia.

1864

July 17: End of military service, discharged at Petersburg, Virginia.

September: Enters Harvard Law School.

1866

Summer: Graduates from Harvard Law School.

1867

March 4: Admitted to the Massachusetts Bar. Enters private practice at Chandler, Shattuck, and Thayer.

1870
Spring: Serves as Harvard College lecturer in constitutional law.
October: Becomes coeditor of the *American Law Review*.
1871
April 28:   President and Fellows of Harvard appoint Holmes the university lecturer on jurisprudence at Harvard College.
1872
June 17:   Marries Fanny Bowditch Dixwell.
1872–73   Fills post of lecturer in jurisprudence at Harvard Law School.
1873   "Gas-Stokers' Strike" article published in the *American Law Review*.
December: *Kent's Commentaries* (12th ed.) published with Holmes as editor.
1880
November–December: Gives Lowell Lectures on the common law.
1881
February: *The Common Law* published shortly before his fortieth birthday.
1882
September: Starts teaching at Harvard Law School.
December: Resigns Harvard post and accepts appointment to Supreme Judicial Court of Massachusetts.
1884
May 30:   Memorial Day Address at Keene, New Hampshire.
June 27:   *Cowley v. Pulsifer* decided (majority opinion).
1887–89   Mother and sister die.
1892
January 6:   *McAuliffe v. Mayor of New Bedford* decided (majority opinion).
1893
June 21:   *Hanson v. Globe Newspaper Co.* decided (majority opinion).
1894   "Privilege, Malice, and Intent" published in the *Harvard Law Review*.
October 7:   Oliver Wendell Holmes Sr. dies at the age of eighty-five.
1895
January 1:   *Commonwealth v. Davis* decided (majority opinion).
May 30:   Delivers Memorial Day address "The Soldier's Faith."
1896
October 26: *Vegelahn v. Guntner* decided (dissent).
1897
January 8:   Delivers "The Path of the Law" lecture at Boston University, which is later published in the *Harvard Law Review*.
1899
August 2:   Becomes chief justice of Massachusetts Supreme Judicial Court.
1901
January 1:   *Commonwealth v. Peaslee* decided (majority opinion).

1902

August 11:   At the age of sixty-one, nominated to the U.S. Supreme Court by President Theodore Roosevelt, recess appointment.

December 4:   Unanimously confirmed by Senate.

December 8:   First day as associate justice, U.S. Supreme Court.

1903

March 13:   Remarks at a meeting of the Second Army Corps Association, Washington, D.C.

1904

May 16:   Votes with the majority upholding the Alien Immigration Act, in *United States ex rel. Turner v. Williams*, in which a First Amendment claim was raised.

1905

April 17:   *Lochner v. New York* decided (dissent) (economic due process).

1907

April 15:   *Patterson v. Colorado* decided (majority opinion).

1909

January 18:   *Moyer v. Peabody* decided (majority opinion) (habeas corpus).

May 17:   *Peck v. Tribune Co.* decided (majority opinion).

1912

Early that year: Befriended by Harvard Professor Felix Frankfurter.

January 9:   *Gandia v. Pettingill* decided (majority opinion).

1915

February 23:   *Fox v. Washington* decided (majority opinion).

1916

June 1:   Brandeis confirmed by the Senate (47–22).

July: Felix Frankfurter introduces Holmes to Harold Laski. *Harvard Law Review* tribute to Holmes on the occasion of his seventy-fifth birthday.

1918   "Natural Law" published in the *Harvard Law Review*.

June 10:   *Toledo Newspaper Co. v. United States* decided (dissent).

December 3:   Draft of Holmes's dissent in *Baltzer v. United States* distributed.

1919

March 3:   *Schenck v. United States* decided (majority opinion).

March 10:   *Debs v. United States* and *Frohwerk v. United States* decided (majority opinions).

November 10:   *Abrams v. United States* decided (dissent).

1921

March 7:   *United States ex rel. Milwaukee Social Democratic Publishing Co. v. Burleson* decided (dissent).

December 19:   *American Column & Lumber Co. v. United States* decided (dissent).

1922

February 27:   *Leach v. Carlile* decided (dissent).

1924

June 2:   Receives the Roosevelt Medal of Freedom.

1925

June 8:   *Gitlow v. New York* decided (dissent).

1929

April 30:   Wife Fanny Holmes dies at the age of eighty-nine.

May 27:   *United States v. Schwimmer* decided (dissent).

1931

March 8:   National radio address on occasion of his ninetieth birthday.

August: Suffers mild heart attack.

1932

January 12:   Retires from the Supreme Court.

1935

March 6:   Dies of bronchial pneumonia, two days before his ninety-fourth birthday.

March 8:   Funeral service at All Souls Unitarian Church. Buried at Arlington National Cemetery.

Prologue: The Father of the Modern First Amendment

He liked the idea of risk.
– Louis Menand[1]

Holmes's footprint on the American law of free speech is gigantic. Like Atlas, he is a titan in that world. No one else quite casts a shadow so long. Although James Madison is the grand pater of the historical First Amendment, its modern father figure is surely Justice Oliver Wendell Holmes Jr. (1841–1935). His thought can be found in bold relief in many Supreme Court opinions on freedom of expression, in every contemporary history of the subject, in every casebook and textbook used in law schools and in colleges, and in every serious scholarly treatment of the matter. This is so because "Holmes laid the foundations . . . for the expansive modern view of free speech. . . . "[2] Having done so, he then "left a profound imprint on the law of free speech."[3] Without exaggeration, then, it would be impossible to have any serious discussion of modern free speech theory or law without some consideration of his views.

But from what well does Holmes's fame spring? Does it derive mainly from three opinions – *Schenck v. United States, Abrams v. United States,*

---

[1] Louis Menand, "Bettabilitarianism," *New Republic*, November 11, 1996, at 56 (reviewing *The Collected Works of Justice Holmes*). *See also* Oliver Wendell Holmes Jr., "Remarks at the Dinner of the Chicago Bar Association," October 21, 1902, reproduced in Sheldon M. Novick, ed., *The Collected Works of Justice Holmes* (Chicago: University of Chicago Press, 1995), at 3:532–33 ("If [a judge] aims at the highest, he must take risks."); Max Lerner, *Ideas are Weapons* (New York: Viking Press, 1939), at 56–57, 63 (noting the "gambler" aspect of Holmes's character).

[2] Richard A. Posner, ed., *The Essential Holmes* (Chicago: University of Chicago Press, 1992), at xii.

[3] Richard A. Posner, "Foreword, Symposium: The Path of the Law 100 Years Later: Holmes's Influence on Modern Jurisprudence," 63 *Brooklyn Law Review* 7, 8 (1997).

and *Gitlow v. New York* – issued late in the long life span of this great jurist and scholar? If so, did the ideas for those landmark opinions jet out of his psyche with a singular thrust of insight, or were there some seeds that had been stirring in the soil of his mind for years or even decades before? As with so many other great figures in law, the answer is a combination of both, and yet other things, too.

Fame in the free speech arena did not come to Holmes either early or easily. It is revealing that most commentators have confined their commentary to that corpus of Holmes's free speech jurisprudence that centered on a handful of his later opinions in cases decided between 1919 and 1925.[4] This is so notwithstanding the fact that, by the time the justice sat down to author his two legendary wartime opinions – *Schenck* and *Abrams* – he had already been writing on free speech for several decades in almost a dozen state and federal cases, not to mention his various scholarly publications.

Generally speaking, two things are characteristic of Holmes's pre-1919 Supreme Court opinions: He seldom voted to sustain a claim of free speech or free press, and he seldom, if ever, wrote judicial opinions with the verve so characteristic of his most memorable First Amendment opinions. And yet that pre-1919 body of work did play a role in the evolution of his thought bearing on freedom of expression. In some illuminating ways, Holmes's early writings shed important light on his later First Amendment jurisprudence as evidenced, for example, by his 1896 dissent in *Vegelahn v. Gunter*, a labor-picketing case. In that state court opinion, rendered nearly a quarter century prior to *Schenck* and *Abrams*, Judge Holmes stressed the importance of "free competition"[5] in ideas, be they economic or political ones. In such writings, we see a few jurisprudential seeds germinating. So, too, with Holmes's pre-1919 scholarly writings, wherein his theories of liability, foreseeability, proximity, conspiracy, and social policy are a part of the thinking that would later blossom in his great free speech opinions.

Still, the path to those opinions – especially the analytical toll road from *Schenck* to *Abrams* – was not always linear or consistent. As a scholar, jurist, essayist, public speaker, and habitual letter writer, he did not run from contradictions. On the one hand, he much admired the philosopher with a grand sweep of theories. "[T]he chief end of man is to form general

---

[4] *Cf.* Silas Bent, *Justice Oliver Wendell Holmes: A Biography* (New York: Vanguard Press, 1932), at 179–242 (discussing certain state court opinions by Holmes).
[5] 167 Mass. 92, 106 (1886) (Holmes, J., dissenting).

ideas,"[6] is how he once phrased it. To discover those unifying principles or "general propositions"[7] made life meaningful. In that sense, he was a philosopher with a keen eye to first principles. On the other hand, the same Holmes could add, with no less confidence, "no general proposition is worth a damn."[8] In that sense, he was a pragmatist with an ardent interest in context. Holmes was also like Faust's Mephistopheles; sometimes he liked to "provoke, dazzle and puzzle."[9] This side of him invited "stimulating paradoxes."[10] Or as he once told Harold Laski: "There is nothing like a paradox to take the scum off your mind."[11]

It is against that conceptual setting that we come upon Holmes's oft-repeated maxim in *Schenck v. United States* about "falsely shouting fire in a theatre," and his celebrated clear-and-present-danger test from the same opinion.[12] Few phrases in the law have enjoyed more generalized application; few propositions have been invoked with greater certitude; and few have been summoned forth more often in the absence of critical thinking. Too many times, they have become almost talismanic in our jurisprudence of free speech. Despite the occasional value of such general propositions, it is easy to forget Holmes's admonition: "Too broadly generalized conceptions are a constant source of fallacy."[13] More to the point, he also held that it "is one of the misfortunes of the law that ideas become

---

[6] Letter from Holmes to Morris R. Cohen in Felix S. Cohen, "The Holmes-Cohen Correspondence," 9 *Journal of the History of Ideas* 1, 8 (1948).

[7] Letter from Holmes to Sir Frederick Pollock, in Mark DeWolfe Howe, ed., *The Holmes-Pollock Letters* (Cambridge, MA: Harvard University Press, 1941), at 2:13.

[8] *Ibid.*

[9] Mathias Reimann, "Lives in the Law: Horrible Holmes," 100 *Michigan Law Review* 1676, 1683 (2002). On Holmes as a pragmatist, compare Max Fisch, "Justice Holmes, The Prediction Theory of Law, and Pragmatism," 39 *Journal of Philosophy* 85 (1942) (portraying Holmes as pragmatist) with Patrick J. Kelley, "Was Holmes a Pragmatist? Reflections on a New Twist to an Old Argument," 14 *Southern Illinois Law Journal* 427 (1990) (portraying Holmes as positivist). Perhaps the best single treatment of Holmes as a pragmatist thinker is to be found in Thomas Grey's opus, "Holmes and Legal Pragmatism," 41 *Stanford Law Review* 787, 792 (1988), wherein he engages in a "binocular effort to present pragmatism through the lens of Holmes while at the same time presenting Holmes through the lens of pragmatism."

[10] Thomas C. Grey, "Plotting the Path of the Law," 63 *Brooklyn Law Review* 19, 32 (1997).

[11] Holmes to Laski, December 22, 1921, in *Holmes-Laski Letters: The Correspondence of Mr. Justice Holmes and Harold J. Laski, 1916–1935* (Cambridge, MA: Harvard University Press, 1953), at 1:389.

[12] 249 U.S. 47, 52 (1919).

[13] *Lorenzo v. Worth*, 170 Mass. 598, 600 (1898).

encysted in phrases and thereafter for a long time cease to provoke further analysis."[14]

In the jurisprudential swirl of things, let us not forget that the man who wrote with magisterial eloquence about the importance of tolerating "noxious" legislation in the name of state experimentation[15] was likewise the one who readily struck down state legislation in the name of experimentation in search of elusive truths.[16] So, too, the jurist who championed judicial restraint in *Lochner v. New York* (1905)[17] was also the jurist who allowed the Fourteenth Amendment to be tapped to strike down another law enacted by the same state in *Gitlow v. New York* (1925). In other words, Holmes was very much the inventor (or one of the main ones) of the "double standard in constitutional adjudication that is so conspicuous a feature in modern constitutional law: laws restricting economic freedom are scrutinized much less stringently than those restricting speech and other noneconomic freedoms."[18] So, Holmes had his enigmatic side.[19] He could be of two minds even as he forged ahead in first developing common law principles and then in transforming them into constitutional ones adorned with majestic phrases bearing on the law of the First Amendment.

As one peeks behind the curtain of Holmes's great trio of First Amendment cases, one sees a wizard far less enamored of the plight of those on

---

[14] *Hyde v. United States*, 225 U.S. 347, 390 (1912) (Holmes, J., dissenting).

[15] *See Truax v. Corrigan*, 257 U.S. 312, 344 (1921) (Holmes, J., dissenting). *Accord Baldwin v. Missouri*, 281 U.S. 586, 595 (Holmes, J., dissenting) (Fourteenth Amendment economic due process).

[16] *See Abrams v. United States*, 250 U.S. 616, 630 (Holmes, J., dissenting).

[17] 198 U.S. 45, 74 (1905) (Holmes, J. dissenting) (economic due process).

[18] *The Essential Holmes, supra* note 2, at xii. Compare G. Edward White, *Justice Oliver Wendell Holmes: Law and the Inner Self* (New York: Oxford University Press, 1993), at 281 ("To the extent that he did consider constitutional questions during his Massachusetts tenure, . . . Holmes gave no indication of treating economic and noneconomic issues differently."); Felix Frankfurter, *Mr. Justice Holmes and the Supreme Court* (Cambridge, MA: Harvard University Press, 1938), at 50 ("the liberty of man to search for truth was of a different order that some economic dogma. . . .").

[19] In the most extended single book treatment of Holmes's overall free speech jurisprudence, H. L. Pohlman offers the following assessment: "Justice Holmes had a coherent and a moderately protective doctrine of free speech. He was not speech's greatest defender, but he was hardly hostile to it or insensitive to its value." *Justice Oliver Wendell Holmes: Free Speech and the Living Constitution* (New York: New York University Press, 1991), at 254. For an assessment of a different order, see G. Edward White's useful summary and thoughtful critique of Holmes's free speech jurisprudence in *Justice Oliver Wendell Holmes, supra* note 18, at 412–54, 607.

whose behalf he sometimes wrote so passionately. This is evidenced not only by Holmes's dismal free speech record while on the Massachusetts high court, and his equally disappointing pre–*Debs v. United States* (1919) voting record in the U.S. Supreme Court, but also by some of his personal comments about those whose free speech cause he occasionally championed. Take, for example, Holmes's memorable dissent in *United States v. Schwimmer* (1929),[20] wherein the eighty-eight-year-old jurist came to the legal defense of a pacifist immigrant. Holmes, his liberal reputation notwithstanding, had little sympathy for the radical likes of Rosika Schwimmer and her crowd. He thought such "dame[s]" to be "damned fools" who harbored "silly" ideas grounded in a "hyperaethereal respect for human life."[21] Hardly the words of a Brandeis progressive. The point, however, is not to denounce Holmes but to place the man and his free speech jurisprudence in a fuller and more illuminating frame.[22]

When new light is cast on Holmes and his work, it appears both convincing and disappointing, one and the same. "Brilliantly insightful here, analytically unpersuasive there, rhetorically robust elsewhere" is the impression sometimes left with the attentive reader. It makes one wonder whether his influence was due more to his rhetoric than to his reasoning. Was the charm of his word craft[23] and phrasemaking, often penned in longhand at a stand-up desk, so great as to overwhelm the minds of his audience? Did his hyperbole hide the incongruities of his jurisprudence? That is, was he a "great judge *because* he was a great literary artist"?[24] It is easier

---

[20] That dissent inspired the title of a recent book published by the Pulitzer Prize–winning columnist Anthony Lewis. The title *Freedom for the Thought We Hate* (New York: Basic Books, 2007) comes from Holmes's dissent in *Schwimmer*.

[21] Holmes to Harold Laski, April 13, 1929, in *Holmes-Laski Letters: The Correspondence of Mr. Justice Holmes and Harold J. Laski, 1916–1935* (Cambridge, MA: Harvard University Press, 1953), *supra* note 11, at 2:1146. *See also* Ronald Collins and David Hudson, "Remembering 2 Forgotten Women in Free-Speech History," First Amendment Center, http://www.firstamendmentcenter.org/analysis.aspx?id=19957.

[22] Although some who see him as an "[a]theist, Darwinian, eugenicist, moral relativist, aesthete, and man of the world" (*The Essential Holmes, supra* note 2, at xvi) have roundly condemned him.

[23] *See* Richard A. Posner, *Law and Literature*, rev. ed. (Cambridge, MA: Harvard University Press, 1998), at 266–73; Bernard Schwartz, *Main Currents in American Legal Thought* (Durham, NC: Carolina Academic Press, 1993), at 394–96. See also Appendix 1 to this volume.

[24] *The Essential Holmes, supra* note 2, at xvii (emphasis in original). In 2002, Holmes received a posthumous Burton Award for being "the best judicial writer of the twentieth century" as judged by law school deans.

to answer that question if we have before us other works by Holmes – books,[25] opinions, articles, and speeches – by which to compare how he offers up his thoughts. Some were wooden, others unimaginative, and still others poorly reasoned. But when he wished, he could write in such a way as to make words "feathered arrows . . . that carried to the heart of the target. . . . "[26] Though he could be self-indulgent at times, he nonetheless had an uncanny ability to compact his thought into the confines of a powerful paragraph or a poignant sentence or a poetic phrase. By that gauge, were his metaphors, like the shouting "fire" in *Schenck*, more misleading than informative? Or maybe not? Then again, was the inspiring rhetoric in his *Abrams* dissent akin to the heroic rhetoric in his 1895 "Soldier's Faith" speech? If so, then Holmes was a "writer-philosopher" capable of infusing "literary skill and philosophical insight into his legal work."[27]

In all of the foregoing ways and others, we stand to experience a far richer understanding of Holmes's free speech jurisprudence if we do not cabin ourselves to a few First Amendment opinions penned by the octogenarian while he sat on the Supreme Court. In addition, there is more to Holmes's thinking than mere words or ideas or principles or even his pragmatism. There is the *man*. His understanding of freedom of expression, like his constitutional jurisprudence generally, simply cannot be removed from the cauldron of his own life experiences:

- The son of a great physician and poet descended from a great family[28]
- A Harvard-educated man
- An impressionable student exposed to the poetic thoughts of Ralph Waldo Emerson and the scientific theories of his day[29]
- An educated man who read Greek, French, and German
- The editor of the *American Law Review* and *Kent's Commentaries*
- A lawyer who argued cases in the state and federal high courts

[25] In *The Common Law* (1881), Holmes prefaced a relatively dull written work with one of the most famous passages in law: "The life of the law has not been logic: it has been experience."
[26] Francis Biddle, *Mr. Justice Holmes* (New York: Charles Scribner's Sons, 1943), at 2.
[27] Posner, *The Essential Holmes, supra* note 2, at xvi.
[28] Consider the father-son relationship as discussed in Peter Gibian, "Style and Stance from Holmes Senior to Holmes Junior," in *The Legacy of Oliver Wendell Holmes, Jr.*, ed. Robert W. Gordon (Palo Alto, CA: Stanford University Press, 1992), at 186–215.
[29] *See* Joseph A. Russomanno, "The Firebrand of My Youth: Oliver Wendell Holmes and the Influence of Emerson," 5 *Communications Law and Policy* 33 (2000).

- An intellectual who in his spare time read books voraciously (some 3,475),[30] including books on history, philosophy, anthropology, economics, and language
- The author of scholarly works, including *The Common Law*
- A state high-court jurist (1882–1902)
- A man with an amazing circle of friends and colleagues (e.g., Sir Frederick Pollock, Learned Hand, Zechariah Chafee, Harold Laski, Felix Frankfurter, Louis Brandeis) who likewise played a crucial role in the development of his thought
- A gifted speaker who delivered many powerful "occasional addresses" and the like
- A voluminous letter writer who often revealed his thinking in more candid, condescending, passionate, and philosophical ways[31] in the countless letters he penned[32]
- A man who relished and collected prints and engravings by great artists
- A man with an enormous ambition who wished to be seen as a great cultural figure[33]

It was undeniable: Holmes's ambition made him; his rivalrous mindset invigorated him; his passion (for life and sometimes romantic love) delighted him; his wit charmed others; his mind impressed many; and his heroic spirit when expressed in speeches left still others awestruck. Then again, Holmes could be cold, detached, elitist, and even puritanical at times. In his near century of living, no single life experience influenced his thinking about free speech and other matters more than his military service during the Civil War. At the age of twenty, in July 1861, he enlisted in the Union Army. That three-year experience – first grounded in the earth of the calamity of the Battle of Ball's Bluff, where he almost

---

[30] *See* John S. Monagan, *The Grand Panjandrum: Mellow Years of Justice Holmes* (Lanham, MD: University Press of America, 1988), at 103–08.

[31] *See* G. Edward White "Holmes as Correspondent," 43 *Vanderbilt Law Review* 1707 (1990) (an informative and insightful analysis of Holmes's letter writing). *See also* Henry Steele Commager, "Justice Holmes in His Letters," *New York Times*, March 23, 1941, Book Review, at 1.

[32] Remarkably, to this day many, even thousands, of his letters remain unpublished. There are thirty-two thousand items in the Harvard Law School collection of Holmes papers; they span the years 1861–1935. The story of the posthumous publication of many of Holmes's writings is complicated. See Robert M. Mennel and Christine L. Compston, eds., *Holmes and Frankfurter: Their Correspondence, 1912–1934* (Hanover, NH: University Press of New England, 1996), at xxix–xlii.

[33] *See* G. Edward White, "Holmes's 'Life Plan': Confronting Ambition, Passion, and Powerlessness," 65 *New York University Law Review* 1409 (1990).

died – remained with Holmes and shaped his views of life and law. Recall, for example, those lasting lines from his *Abrams* dissent:

> [W]hen men have realized that time has upset many fighting faiths, they may come to believe even more than they believe the very foundations of their own conduct that the ultimate good desired is better reached by free trade in ideas – that the best test of truth is the power of the thought to get itself accepted in the competition of the market. . . .

Earlier, on the occasion of an 1884 Memorial Day Address, he noted that his life and those of his fellow Civil War soldiers had been "set apart by its experience," one that touched the hearts of all who fought "with fire."[34] Or as he put it a decade or so later in his "Soldier's Faith" remarks: "I believe that struggle for life is the order of the world, at which it is vain to repine."[35] That contact with war was the "maturing force in Holmes's life."[36] Indeed, both literally and metaphorically, it left him a marked man. In a still larger sense, the Civil War also left its mark on the mind of America. Although that war alone did not make America modern, it nonetheless helped usher in "the birth of modern America."[37] There was a transformation in ideas, a different lens by which to view life and law, and also a different way of conceptualizing freedom. Holmes, ever the soldier, played a vital role in the transformation.

Hence, an effort has been made in the pages that follow to develop a picture of Holmes's free speech jurisprudence that offers up his own emerging thoughts against the backdrop of his various life experiences.

The measure of a great man, Holmes once wrote, is this: "The men whom I should be tempted to commemorate would be the originators of transforming thought." He was referring to John Marshall, that "great ganglion in the nerves of society. . . ."[38] To put it another way, a great thinker is one whose ideas are so immense (or swollen) as to transform our own opinions about the things that matter most to us. If that is indeed the

[34] Memorial Day Address, May 30, 1884, reproduced in *The Collected Works of Justice Holmes*, supra note 1, at 3:462, 467.

[35] *Ibid.*, at 3:486, 487.

[36] Max Lerner, *The Mind and Faith of Justice Holmes* (New York: Little, Brown, 1946), at 5. More about this matter is set out in the introductory essay to Part I, wherein "The Memorial Day Address," "The Soldier's Faith," and Holmes's remarks to the Second Army Corps Association are excerpted. *See generally* Mark DeWolfe Howe, ed., *Touched with Fire: Civil War Letters and the Diary of Oliver Wendell Holmes, Jr.* (New York: Fordham University Press, 2000).

[37] Louis Menand, *The Metaphysical Club: A Story of Ideas in America* (New York: Farrar, Straus & Giroux, 2001), at ix.

[38] "John Marshall," February 4, 1901, reproduced in *The Collected Works of Justice Holmes*, supra note 1, at 3:501, 502.

touchstone, then Holmes was a great jurist. This is not, of course, to say that his great ideas were good or wise or liberal, only transformative. Holmes changed the currents of our thinking about many things, especially the law of free speech in America.

How did he do it? Where did he begin? How did his thoughts develop? What were his values? What was his sense of those whose freedom he sometimes safeguarded? How did his star ascend, and how much of that was made possible by the continued efforts of a close circle of influential admirers? And how in the end might we view Holmes's jurisprudence of free speech? These and related issues are the focus of this book, which ventures to answer such questions largely by way of Holmes's own words offered alongside his various life experiences.

⌇

In what follows, I typically present the materials in a chronological fashion. Sometimes, however, as in Part I, chronological preferences yield to substantive ones. Thus, my discussion of Holmes's Civil War views, both at the time and years afterward, prefaces the remainder of the materials. In addition, although some of the writings and cases presented do not explicitly concern free speech matters or doctrines – this is especially so in some of what is set out in Parts I and II – they are included because they are a part of Holmes's larger look at such matters. I have selected them because they inform the reader of the wellspring from which Holmes's free speech jurisprudence flowed. For example, his writings and speeches on topics ranging from war to natural law to common law notions of the crimes of attempt and conspiracy do provide the reader with many key ideas by which to understand what Holmes would later write in his most famous opinions concerning the First Amendment. Finally, citations to cases, statutes, and secondary sources listed within a book or article have been omitted unless there is some important reason to include them.

The biography is determinative or often so. One cannot understand Holmes in any meaningful way without having some basic grasp of his life. I believe that the presentation of Holmes's free speech writings, without more, is insufficient to adequately inform readers. Accordingly, I preface each of the six parts of this book with biographical essays sketching the time period in which the materials offered were written. Obviously, these sketches are meant not to be comprehensive historical or topical accounts but to provide the reader with some historical backdrop and general overview of the subject matter. In a similar vein, I provide certain materials concerning the cases selected, including a statement of the facts, the names of the lawyers arguing the matter, the dates of oral arguments and the decision, the vote, and the authors of the majority and separate opinions. For both cases and other materials, I likewise offer introductory essays to help set up what follows. I also offer commentaries (by me and learned others) following the materials to supplement the primary texts. At the risk of seeming unduly scholarly, specific citations to the works drawn on are included, if only to allow the reader to check such sources. In all of this, I have been the beneficiary of Holmes's first significant biographer, Mark DeWolfe Howe, as well as his major modern biographers, especially G. Edward White, Liva Baker, and Sheldon M. Novick. I have tried to incorporate the biographical backdrop in such a way as not to overwhelm the reader with the essays, commentaries, and citations. My hope is that by the end of the book the reader has some sense of Holmes the man and mind along with some informed sense of Holmes's free speech jurisprudence. The aim is to succeed in doing this without producing a laborious book. Of course, there are always trade-offs, so I leave to my readers' judgments whether I have included too much or too little.

⁂

I am indebted to Daniel O'Neil, of Massachusetts, who offered valuable assistance in developing this book and who did so with patience, excellence, and a measure of commitment well beyond what was expected of him. So let the record show my grateful indebtedness to Dan. And thanks also go out to Rachel Weizman for all her research and editorial help.

Countless hours of home time were devoted to this project. Hence, I owe a debt, yet again, to my wife, Susan A. Cohen, to whom this book is lovingly dedicated. Selflessly, she has stayed with me, supported me, encouraged me, and allowed me a measure of freedom without which my life would be impossible.

Consistent with its venerable centuries-old practice, Cambridge University Press sent out an early version of my manuscript to learned reviewers for anonymous critiques. In my decades of writing books and articles, I have never received such objective, informed, and worthwhile criticisms, which were tendered with a welcome collegial spirit. Thus, my work has been improved thanks to the generous efforts of Professors Paul Horwitz and Timothy Zick. Any lingering mistakes or omissions are, however, my sole responsibility. I am also indebted to my editor, John Berger, who was supportive from the outset and who (as only he can) steered my ship of text to safe harbor.

Alan F. Rumrill, of the Historical Society of Cheshire County, was helpful in providing me with information related to Justice Holmes's 1884 Memorial Day address delivered in Keene, New Hampshire. I also benefited greatly from the treasure trove of information available online from the Harvard Law School's Oliver Wendell Holmes Jr. Digital Collection and from a variety of other resources too numerous to list.

To those living and past, it is impossible to do any serious work on Holmes without incurring some real indebtedness to the works of others, such as Liva Baker, Silas Bent, Francis Biddle, Zechariah Chafee, Mark DeWolfe Howe, Sheldon Novick, and G. Edward White. And then there are Albert Alschuler, Stephen Feldman, Felix Frankfurter, Robert Gordon, Gerald Gunther, Michael H. Hoffheimer, Morton J. Horwitz, Frederic Rogers Kellogg, Max Lerner, Louis Menand, John S. Monagan, H. L. Pohlman, Richard Polenberg, Richard Posner, David Rabban, and Geoffrey R. Stone. Not to be overlooked are the authors of some of the finest articles on Holmes and his jurisprudence: David S. Bogen, Edward Corwin, Ernst Freund, Thomas C. Grey, Harry Kalven, Patrick J. Kelley, Hans Linde, H. L. Mencken, James M. O'Fallon, Fred D. Ragan, Robert D. Richardson, Yosal Rogat, Frank Strong, Adrian Vermeule, John Wigmore, and Edmond Wilson. Finally, in the Civil War category, the works of certain authors were indispensable, including those of George A. Bruce, Byron Farwell, Drew Gilpin Faust, Mark DeWolfe Howe, Louis Menand, Richard F. Miller, James McPherson, Francis Winthrop Palfrey, Dorst Patch, Stephen W. Sears, Saul Touster, and Hiller Zobel. No doubt I have unintentionally overlooked some names, which can readily be found in the source materials.

❧

As my life clock clicks sixty, I look back to when Holmes first lit my imagination afire with thoughts, all sorts of crackling thoughts. No doubt, it began when I was a law student in the early 1970s, when I read his opinions in my big blue constitutional casebook edited by Gunther and Dowling. That experience pointed me to a book that had a profound impact on my life – *The Mind and Faith of Justice Holmes*, edited by Max Lerner. That work, first published in 1943, turned my mind around again and again, leaving me to wrestle with its words. And then I met Max, a giant of a mind and a true free spirit, who became a dear friend with whom I spent many a delightful day drunk in discourse. When his Holmes book was republished and expanded in 1989, Max signed and inscribed a copy for me with these words: "To Ron, whose idea it was, with affection and gratitude."[39] Holding that book in my hands two decades later reminds

[39] Max was similarly kind when it came to other projects on which we both worked. *See* Max Lerner, *Nine Scorpions in a Bottle* (New York: Arcade Publishing, 1994), at xii. Liva Baker was another friend of mine, one who became a Holmes biographer. *See* her *The Justice from Beacon Hill: The Life and Times of Oliver Wendell Holmes* (New

me of just how much I miss Max and all those marvelous discussions we had in the sun of southern California, discussions about life, law, love, and so many other things that matter.[40] His mark on me remains, for I have returned to Holmes... though not always as much the admirer that Max was. Why? Well, I have come to see Holmes through other lenses, including the wide one employed by Louis Menand in his various insightful treatments of Holmes. So, too, with Judge Richard A. Posner in his always-instructive writings and in his reader titled *The Essential Holmes.* Then there is Professor G. Edward White's monumental biographical work, which consistently offers a nuanced and therefore complex look at Holmes. And after reading Albert Alschuler's engaging and thought-provoking *Law without Values,*[41] I surely agree with the Posnerian view that Holmes "wasn't perfect" or moral, or humanitarian; "he was only great." Judge Posner goes a step further and maintains that Holmes's "massive distinction has not been dented by his many detractors."[42] I respectfully disagree. Holmes's overall distinction has surely been dented, many times and on many fronts. On that score, I think wise old Max Lerner was closer to the target's eye: "There will be... dips and rises in his reputation. A figure like Holmes becomes a way of looking into the mirror of ourselves and our time."[43]

York: HarperCollins, 1991). Although I did not work with Liva on the Holmes biography, we nonetheless shared many long conversations about the justice and his views on free speech. Liva described Max as one of those bright young intellectuals who "joined the cult of Holmes's admirers." *Ibid.,* at 9. Although that is not entirely true – Max was always suspicious of anything cultlike – it is close enough to the mark to accept as a general possibility. Still, late in his life Lerner declared: "Holmes never walked on water for us." Max Lerner, *The Mind and Faith of Justice Holmes* (New Brunswick, NJ: Transaction Publishers, 1989), at 457.

[40] *See* Ronald Collins, "Max Lerner's Immortality," *Forward,* June 19, 1992, at 6 (national edition).

[41] Published by the University of Chicago Press in 2000. Any serious study of Holmes should include some reflection on the powerful points made in Professor Alschuler's book, if only to prevent one from being unduly charmed (and that is the word) by Holmes and his word power. That said, for a thoughtful reply, actually a partial one, to Alschuler, *see* Mathias Reimann's review essay of Alschuler's book, "Lives in the Law: Horrible Holmes," *supra* note 9. For an earlier reply to similar criticisms of Holmes, *see* Mark DeWolfe Howe, "The Positivism of Mr. Justice Holmes," 64 *Harvard Law Review* 529 (1951). *See generally,* G. Edward White, "The Rise and Fall of Justice Holmes," 39 *University of Chicago Law Review* 51 (1971).

[42] The last set of quotations, including the "wasn't perfect" one, come from *The Essential Holmes, supra* note 2, at xxx.

[43] *The Mind and Faith of Justice Holmes, supra* note 39, at 470.

One more matter: it is well to bear in mind the epigraph to this book, which is referenced again in the Epilogue, wherein Holmes cautioned that his constitutionalism was "an experiment, as all life is an experiment."[44] And so, if Holmes is the pater of the modern First Amendment, he is also the father of experiment, of risk taking,[45] of taking chances though the heavens may fall. Yes, Louis Menand was right: "He did not believe that the experimental spirit will necessarily lead us, ultimately, down the right path. Democracy is an experiment, and it is in the nature of experiments sometimes to fail. He had seen it fail once."[46] In a legal world where *balancing* and *security* are today's watchwords, one wonders whether the cramped law of *Schenck*, which survives,[47] or the invigorated law of the *Abrams* dissent, which grows, will prevail when the day of danger next befalls us.

In that experimental vein, then, I invite you to ponder what you read – challenge it, grapple with it, look through it, think beyond it, agree with it, or even repudiate it. For the splendid spirit of the First Amendment thrives not on lockstep agreement but on an ever-rebellious tug-of-war in the minds and hearts of all Americans.

Ronald Collins
Bethesda, Maryland
April 2010

---

[44] *Abrams v. United States*, 250 U.S. 616, 630 (1919) (Holmes, J., dissenting).
[45] Perhaps I should say he took calculated risks, though I am unsure. After all, Holmes voluntarily served three stints in the military at a time when death was everywhere in the air, though he did have the good sense not to test his luck a fourth time. See Part I of this volume.
[46] *Metaphysical Club, supra* note 37, at 433.
[47] *See* Ronald Collins and David Skover, "What Is War? Reflections on Free Speech in 'Wartime,'" 36 *Rutgers Law Journal* 833, 848–53 (2005) (noting that *Schenck* and its progeny have never been formally overruled and that *Brandenburg v. Ohio* is readily distinguishable because it is not a wartime case).

Part I   On Life and War

Today it is easy to have striking assessments of Oliver Wendell Holmes Jr. But could one have sensed such things by tracing back to the early arc of his life? I think so. There were many signs that a mantle of greatness would one day be reserved for this grandson of a revered minister on his father's side and the chief justice of the Massachusetts Supreme Judicial Court on his mother's side. Born into Boston's upper-crust society on March 8, 1841, young Wendell was the son of Dr. Oliver Wendell Holmes Sr. (an outgoing physician, Harvard professor, inventor, rhetorician, poet, and famed writer) and Amelia Jackson Holmes (a self-effacing affectionate woman, also an abolitionist).[1] Ever since his Boston birth, young Holmes showed signs of pursuing the Puritan concept (he was of Calvinist heritage) of a calling. After studying Greek, Latin, German, French, ancient history, and math in

---

[1] The senior Holmes was one of the founders of *Atlantic Monthly*. His published works included *The Autocrat at the Breakfast Table* (1858) and a biography of Ralph Waldo Emerson (1885). Such writings, including his essays and poems, made him one of the most famous writers of his time. See G. Edward White, *Justice Oliver Wendell Holmes: Law and the Inner Self* (New York: Oxford University Press, 1991), at 9–14. He was also a famous physician. See *Oliver Wendell Holmes: Physician and Man of Letters*, eds. Scott H. Podolsky and Charles S. Bryan (Sagamore Beach, MA: Science History Publications, 2009). For a thoughtful account of the relationship between Dr. Holmes and his son, see G. Edward White, "Holmes's 'Life Plan': Confronting Ambition, Passion, and Powerlessness," 65 *New York University Law Review* 1409, 1410–29 (1990). In contrast to his rather assertive and loquacious father, Holmes's mother was a quiet and mild-mannered woman best known for being a devoted mother and wife. See *Justice Oliver Wendell Holmes: Law and the Inner Self, supra*, at 14–17. Holmes had a younger sister (Amelia) and brother (Edward) who died at comparatively young ages (thirty-eight and forty-six, respectively) and who didn't seem to figure much in his life.

a private school, the scholastic lad entered Harvard College in the autumn of 1857 – this was the college of his father and his ancestors.[2]

It was in that peculiar atmosphere, the world of the Boston Brahmin as his father coined it, that Holmes was exposed to great men and great ideas. One of those men was Ralph Waldo Emerson (1803–82), the famed essayist, philosopher, poet, and Harvard professor. During Holmes's first year at college, his parents gave him a gift of five volumes of Emerson's works. In Emerson, Holmes found an inspirational and rebellious sentiment then to his intellectual liking: "Whoso would be a man," Emerson wrote, "must be a nonconformist."[3] The man and his work impressed the young Holmes, so much so that he published a piece in *Harvard Magazine* in 1858 that tracked one of Emerson's essays. A few years later, Holmes wrote another essay, this one on Plato.[4] What intrigued Wendell most about the great Greek philosopher was his teacher – Socrates. The ever-skeptical, pipe-smoking young Holmes was drawn to this man whose "peculiar power lay not so much in a profound perception of truth as in a natural spirit of argumentative questioning," a man who was likewise incredulous toward "the unscientific use of language," and a man who to his dying moments had "no clear idea" of any categorical truth. Holmes admired Socrates and his "keen and caustic spirit of enquiry," a trait he found missing in Plato.[5] Although he found some admirable traits in the great Greek, Holmes's newfound love for science and scientific methods made him rather critical of the "unscientific" philosopher who in his view was unduly charmed by "immutable ideas" and thus unmindful of the importance of "mutable matters." When the proud student shared his essay with Emerson, the dedicated Platonist replied: "When you strike at a king, you must *kill* him."[6]

---

[2] Not long before that, on March 6, 1857, the Supreme Court rendered its decision in *Dred Scott v. Sandford*, 60 U.S. (19 How.) 393 (1857).

[3] Ralph Waldo Emerson, "Self-Reliance," in *Essays, Orations and Lectures* (London: William Tegg, 1848), at 28. On Emerson's influence on Holmes, see Louis Menand, *The Metaphysical Club: A Story of Ideas in America* (New York: Farrar, Straus & Giroux, 2001), at 24–26.

[4] "Plato," in *The Collected Works of Justice Holmes*, ed. Sheldon M. Novick (Chicago: University of Chicago Press, 1995), at 1:145–53.

[5] *Ibid.* at 146, 147. Holmes also translated and published the final portion of *The Apology of Socrates*. See *ibid.* at 142.

[6] See *Justice Oliver Wendell Holmes, supra* note 1, at 35–43 (italics in original). *See also* Liva Baker, *The Justice from Beacon Hill* (New York: HarperCollins, 1991), at 89–90. From Emerson, Holmes learned other lessons, including the idea of the "power of the self to shape and even transcend experience." *Justice Oliver Wendell Holmes, supra* note 1, at 43.

Such admonitions, though duly noted, did not stop Wendell from bran-dishing his editorial sword while he served as editor of the *Harvard Maga-zine*. There were, for example, editorials insisting on "free will in matters of religion." To that end, Holmes lent his name to the following line, one that drew disfavor among a faculty already fed up with his disrespectful ways: "A hundred years ago we burnt men's bodies for not agreeing with our religious tenets; we still burn their souls."[7] These kinds of statements, along with others on everything from women in college to abolition, fur-ther tested the patience of the faculty and college president, who finally contacted Dr. Holmes in an attempt to reign in the freethinking young editor.

Despite the cerebral joys experienced at the feet of a few men like Emerson, Holmes found relatively little at Harvard to stimulate his inquis-itive mind. By and large, the college and its faculty were too staid in tradition, dogma, and Christian truth. At a time when the whole world seemed up for grabs, and when all previous "human understanding of the universe was changing as scientists jettison[ed] centuries-old traditions and expos[ed] the futility of metaphysical speculation,"[8] most of Wendell's professors championed formalism, dogmatism, and Christian truths. When Charles Darwin's *The Origin of Species* (1859) was released, it was seen more as heresy than science in many Harvard quarters.[9] Holmes's phi-losophy professor dismissed it outright; his chemistry professor lamented its likely impact on undergraduate morals; and the eminent paleontol-ogist and glaciologist Louis Agassiz, who oversaw the Lawrence Scien-tific School, "publicly disavowed Darwin's disturbing conclusions." Only Holmes's botany professor, Asa Gray, sided with Darwin.[10] For someone who was invigorated by the intellectual freedom endorsed by Emerson and the skepticism practiced by Socrates, science's new day was an excit-ing time – but it was not a time then in sync with Harvard's curriculum and culture. And Holmes knew it.

[7] Quoted in *Justice from Beacon Hill, supra* note 6, at 88. Decades later a similar passage found its way into an opinion written by Justice Louis Brandeis and joined in by Holmes: "Men feared witches and burnt women. It is the function of speech to free men from the bondage of irrational fears." *Whitney v. California*, 274 U.S. 357, 376 (1927) (Brandeis, J., concurring).

[8] *Justice from Beacon Hill, supra* note 6, at 83.

[9] *See Justice Oliver Wendell Holmes, supra* note 1, at 41 (discussing traditional versus new sciences). In later years, Professor White notes, "Holmes would continue to employ 'science' in both its [traditional] systematic and its [modern] empiricist guises in his mature scholarship. He would also merge it with historicism." *Ibid.* at 42.

[10] *See Justice from Beacon Hill, supra* note 6, at 83.

"After three years of uneven attention to his studies and occasional disciplinary problems..., Holmes finally, in the spring of his senior year, found a subject that inspired him. Unfortunately, from the perspective of his father, the subject had nothing to do with his education. It was the issue of slavery and the coming of the Civil War that captured Holmes's attention."[11] Both in public conversation and in his writings for the *Harvard Magazine*, Wendell became more outspoken. "Do men own other men by God's law?" he asked in one article. In more and more ways, he was becoming not only an abolitionist but also an Emersonian abolitionist.[12] By his senior year he had already participated in antislavery discussion groups and had joined in antislavery rallies.

Holmes's abolitionist enthusiasm and that of his colleagues was not, however, then the norm at Harvard. For one thing, Louis Agassiz's public statements about the inferiority of blacks were being used, particularly in the South, as a defense of pro-slavery positions. And though Dr. Holmes was not a defender of slavery, he both knew and befriended Agassiz and welcomed compromise with the South.[13] Moreover, the elder Holmes was "not particularly supportive of the abolitionist movement to outlaw slavery, which had sprung up in the Boston area in the late 1850s and early 1860s. Holmes Sr. felt no particular outrage at those southern states that practiced slavery, but Amelia Jackson did, and abolitionism became an important cause for Wendell Holmes and his mother."[14] So, in April 1861, Holmes and some of his Harvard classmates joined the Fourth Battalion of the Massachusetts Volunteer Infantry without bothering to notify Harvard. His father was unhappy. When the Fourth Battalion dismantled not long afterward, Holmes sought to return to Harvard.[15] To that end, Dr. Holmes

[11] G. Edward White, *Oliver Wendell Holmes, Jr.* (New York: Oxford University Press, 2006), at 10.

[12] Oliver Wendell Holmes, "Books," 4 *Harvard Magazine* 408, 410 (1858). *See also Metaphysical Club, supra* note 3, at 25. According to Menand, Holmes was, "in the context of his times, a student radical." *Ibid.* at 26. Then there was Holmes's personal defense of Wendell Phillips, the fiery abolitionist who was Dr. Holmes's cousin. *See* Irving H. Bartlett, *Wendell Phillips: Brahmin Radical* (Boston: Beacon Press, 1961), at 225–35; James Brewer Stewart, *Wendell Phillips: Liberty's Hero* (Baton Rouge: Louisiana State University Press, 1986), at 209–24.

[13] *See Justice from Beacon Hill, supra* note 6, at 94; Edward Lurie, *Louis Agassiz: A Life in Science* (Baltimore: Johns Hopkins University Press, 1988), at 194, 202–03, 204, 227–28, 235, 305–06. His views on the inequality of the races notwithstanding, Agassiz was a committed defender of the Union.

[14] *Oliver Wendell Holmes, Jr. supra* note 11, at 10.

[15] *See* M. A. DeWolfe Howe, *Holmes of the Breakfast-Table* (New York: Oxford University Press, 1939), at 101–04 (quoting and discussing letter from Harvard President Cornelius Fenton to Dr. Holmes on the need of Wendell to satisfy his examination requirements). (The author of this book was Mark DeWolfe's father.)

"helped persuade the Harvard authorities to allow Wendell and several of his volunteer classmates – who had found, to their dismay, that the Fourth Battalion was not going to see any military action outside of Boston – to return to Harvard and take their examinations."[16]

In July 1861, Holmes and his colleagues received their diplomas from Harvard.[17] In an autobiographical sketch for the college album, Holmes wrote: "[A]t present I am trying for a commission in one of the Massachusetts regiments . . . and hope to go south before very long. If I survive the war I expect to study law as my profession or at least for a starting point."[18] Shortly afterward, the skinny, long-bodied, and bookish young man enlisted for a three-year commission in the Twentieth Regiment of the Massachusetts Volunteer Infantry.[19] "[I]n my day," Holmes recalled sixty-five years later, "I was a pretty convinced abolitionist." While his father wrote poems of peace and sought compromise,[20] a far more resolute Wendell went off to war to fight the good fight. His life would never be the same.

∽

As you go through the woods you stumble constantly,
and, if after dark, as last night on picket, perhaps
tread on the swollen bodies already fly blown
and decaying, of men shot in the head,
back or bowels – many of the wounds
are terrible to look at . . . .

– Oliver Wendell Holmes Jr.[21]

[16] *Oliver Wendell Holmes, Jr., supra* note 11, at 11; *Justice Oliver Wendell Holmes: Law and the Inner Self, supra* note 1, at 44.

[17] See *Justice Oliver Wendell Holmes: Law and the Inner Self, supra* note 1, at 4, 491, n. 1 (noting that the Harvard commencement was in July, not in June as commonly thought); *accord*, Mark DeWolfe Howe, *Justice Holmes: The Shaping Years –, 1841–1870* (Cambridge, MA: Harvard University Press, 1957), at 77.

[18] *Class Book of 1861 Album*, at 329 (Harvard Archives). The sketch is reproduced in full in Frederick C. Fiechter Jr., "The Preparation of an American Aristocrat," 6 *New England Quarterly* 3 (1933).

[19] See George A. Bruce, *The Twentieth Regiment of Massachusetts Volunteer Infantry, 1861–1865* (Boston: Houghton, Mifflin, 1906); Richard F. Miller, *Harvard's Civil War: A History of the Twentieth Massachusetts Volunteer Army* (Hanover, NH: University Press of New England, 2005).

[20] Letter from OWH to Harold Laski, November 5, 1926, in *Holmes-Laski Letters: The Correspondence of Mr. Justice Holmes and Harold J. Laski*, ed. Mark DeWolfe Howe (Cambridge, MA: Harvard University Press, 1953), at 2:893. On Dr. Holmes, see Edwin P. Hoyt, *The Improper Bostonian: Dr. Oliver Wendell Holmes* (New York: William Morrow, 1979), at 143–51; Oliver Wendell Holmes, "The Flower of Liberty," 8 *Atlantic Monthly* 550 (November 1861).

[21] Letter from OWH to parents, June 2, 1862 ("written on field of battle"), reproduced in Mark DeWolfe Howe, ed., *Touched with Fire: Civil War Letters and Diary of Oliver Wendell Holmes, Jr.* (New York: Fordham University Press, 2000), at 51.

To get a sense of how the Civil War influenced Holmes, both personally and philosophically, one must have some idea of the enormity of that war. First, there is its numerical toll, which is hard for a modern mind to comprehend. Professor Drew Gilpin Faust offers a poignant summary:

> In the middle of the nineteenth century, the United States embarked on a new relationship with death, entering into a civil war that proved bloodier than any other conflict in American history, a war that presaged the slaughter of World War I's Western Front and the global carnage of the twentieth century. The number of soldiers who died between 1861 and 1865, an estimated 620,000, is approximately equal to the total American fatalities in the Revolution, the War of 1812, World War I, World War II, and the Korean War combined. The Civil War's rate of death, its incidence in comparison with the size of the American population, was six times that of World War II. A similar rate, about 2 percent, in the United States today would mean six million fatalities.[22]

Beyond the staggering body count, there was the horrifying spectacle of death that Holmes and other Civil War soldiers experienced firsthand. Ambrose Bierce, who endured four years of combat as a Union soldier, offered a moving account of what his eyes beheld on a battlefield similar to the ones on which Holmes fought:

> Men? There were enough; all dead, apparently, except one, who lay near where I had halted my platoon . . . a Federal sergeant, variously hurt, who had been a fine giant in his time. He lay face upward, taking his breath in convulsive, rattling snorts, and blowing it out in sputters of froth which crawled creamily down his cheeks, piling itself alongside his neck and ears. A bullet had clipped a groove in his skull, above the temple; from this the brain protruded in bosses, dropping off in flakes and strings. . . . One of my men, whom I knew for a womanish fellow, asked if he should put his bayonet through him. Inexpressibly shocked by the cold-blooded proposal, I told him I thought not; it was unusual, and too many were looking.[23]

From October 1861 through July 1864, Holmes lived through this "harvest of death," as it was called. He saw not only musket bullets and cannon shrapnel tear into his friends' flesh, but he also witnessed piles of

---

[22] Drew Gilpin Faust, *This Republic of Suffering: Death and the American Civil War* (New York: Vintage Books, 2008), at xi.

[23] Ambrose Bierce, "What I Saw at Shiloh," in *Phantoms of a Blood-Stained Period: The Complete Civil War Writings of Ambrose Bierce*, eds. Russell Duncan and David J. Klooster (Amherst: University of Massachusetts Press, 2002), at 103.

limbs stacked next to surgeons' tables and beheld the specter of numerous corpses dumped and piled into trenches. And then there was the crisis of meaning – what grand principle (divine, philosophical, or political) could begin to justify the carnage of war? What conceivable purpose could explain the staggering costs of war? It is against that backdrop that we come to the Holmes who donned a soldier's uniform before he donned a judge's robe. The soldier's experience would shape the judge's jurisprudence.

In his book *The Mind and Faith of Justice Holmes*, Max Lerner made several telling points about the impact the Civil War had on the mind of Holmes. "The experience of the Civil War was the maturing force in Holmes's life," wrote Lerner. "From it derive four of the great elements in his thinking." They were the following:

- That "life is risk, that our fates depend often on a throw of dice, and that law must embody this aleatory quality,"
- That "life is battle, and the best meaning of effort comes out under fire,"
- That "one must be a good soldier with 'a splendid carelessness for life' in a cause," and
- That "one must have a fighting faith – that 'to act with enthusiasm and faith' is the condition of acting greatly."[24]

These elements, as we will see, play out time and again in Holmes's writings – letters, articles, books, and judicial opinions – in ways at once rhetorically powerful and analytically forceful. The idea of struggle, rooted in the blood-soaked fields of battlegrounds seeded by human casualties, became central to his thought, including his thoughts on freedom of expression. At first, the struggle was seen through a romantic lens – the rush of going off to war with friends to fight for a noble cause and to do one's duty proudly. "Our hearts were touched by fire," Holmes later recalled. And then he altered the metaphor but to the same effect: "[W]e have seen with our own eyes . . . the snowy heights of honor. . . . "[25] It was akin to a holy crusade or, as Holmes labeled it, "the Christian Crusade" in defense of "the cause of the whole civilized world."[26] That was their creed, and theirs was a noble war fought by honorable and brave men wed to the

---

[24] Max Lerner, *The Mind and Faith of Justice Holmes* (New Brunswick, NJ: Transaction Publishers, 1989), at 5 (bullets added).

[25] An address delivered for Memorial Day, May 30, 1884, at Keene, New Hampshire, before John Sedgwick, Post No. 4, Grand Army of the Republic, in *Collected Works of Justice Holmes, supra* note 4, at 3:467.

[26] Letter from Holmes to Charles Eliot Norton, April 17, 1864, reproduced in part in *Touched with Fire, supra* note 21, at 122 n. 1.

highest of principles. It was that faith that made hellish fighting possible. "If one didn't believe that this was such a crusade," Holmes wrote, "it would be hard to keep the hand to the sword. . . ."[27] And so Wendell, at the age of twenty, went into battle. It began in earnest in October 1861 at a place called Ball's Bluff,[28] where a Confederate ambush took a heavy toll of the 1,700 Union soldiers who faced a barrage of musketry and cannon fire in front of them and a deadly body of bullet-hailed water (the Potomac River) behind them, which made retreating near impossible. Holmes was one of those wounded. The first shot, a spent ball, hit him just below his rib cage, on his belly. "I felt as if a horse had kicked me," he wrote in his pocketbook diary.[29] A second shot struck him, entering his left side and then came out behind the right breast. He thought this was the end, and he was prepared for it. And all of this after but an hour of battle. This time death passed him by – one of his fellow soldiers squeezed the bullet ball from his chest and gave it to him as a battle souvenir. With that spent bullet in his pocket, he returned home to Boston (to 21 Charles Street) to convalesce.

By March 1862, the young man was back in action, now as a captain. He was in Washington for a short while, awaiting his orders. When those orders came, Holmes and his regiment boarded steamers to Hampton Roads, Virginia. There they would join General George McClellan's army. In the months ahead, Holmes saw more battles, including one at Fair Oaks. It was there that Captain Holmes led his troops into battle with sword and pistol flying. "If I am killed," he wrote to his parents, "you will find a memorandum on the back of a picture I carry."[30] Once again, there were heavy casualties on both sides, though Holmes survived to fight another day. Shortly afterward, there was an effort to take Richmond, the Confederacy's capital. The campaign produced more miserable face-to-face fighting and

---

[27] *Ibid.* For one account of Holmes's civil war years, see Hiller B. Sobel, "The Three Civil Wars of Oliver Wendell Holmes: Notes for an Odyssey," *Boston Bar Journal*, December 1982, at 13–22; "Part II," *Boston Bar Journal*, January 1983, at 18–23; "Part III," *Boston Bar Journal*, February 1983, at 18–25.

[28] See Byron Farwell, *Ball's Bluff: A Small Battle and its Long Shadow* (McLean, VA: EPM, 1990); Joseph Dorst Patch, *The Battle of Ball's Bluff* (Leesburg, VA: Potomac Press, 1958); *Twentieth Regiment of Massachusetts Volunteer Infantry, supra* note 19, at 16–77; *Harvard's Civil War, supra* note 19, at 51–83; Louis-Philippe-Albert d'Orléans, Comte de Paris, *History of the Civil War in America*, ed. Henry Coppée, trans. Louis Fitzgerald Tasistro (Philadelphia: Porter & Coates, 1875), at 1:367–421.

[29] Qtd. in *Touched with Fire, supra* note 21, at 23. Holmes destroyed the diary, leaving only a few pages and passages.

[30] Letter of June 2, 1862, to parents, qtd. in *Justice Holmes: The Shaping Years, supra* note 18, at 1:119.

the specter of soldiers armed with sabers, bayonets, muskets, and cannon, all charging at one another. There was the damp and cold land caked with mud and polluted water, and then there was that "spasmodic pain" caused by dysentery. If a bullet or shell didn't claim a man's life, sickness was always there to demand its fatal share. The "immense anxiety," the unimaginable "hardships," and the "hard fighting" weighed heavily on the young soldier.[31] The romance of war faded, particularly when victory eluded them. Try as they did, the Union forces could still not conquer Richmond.

In August, the Peninsula Campaign headed north to defend Washington against Confederate attacks planned by General Stonewall Jackson, or so it was feared. When that threat failed to materialize, Union forces regrouped. At about that time, when he was out on a short leave, Holmes stayed at the National Hotel in Washington, this as the Army of the Potomac prepared for new engagements. On September 7, 1862, Union troops left Washington en masse under the leadership of General McClellan. As the troops moved northward, they were greeted with excited jubilation in some Maryland towns – it invigorated them at a time when defeat seemed entirely possible. Victory was on the Union side as corps commanders like "Fighting Joe" Hooker prevailed, leaving behind a cornfield spotted with dead bodies. "Hooker licked the Rebs nicely," Holmes wrote home. Hell, however, awaited them. It came in a conflict near Sharpsburg, Maryland. This clash, known as the Battle of Antietam, was fought on September 17, 1862, the anniversary of the signing of the federal Constitution.[32]

At first, the assault on the Confederate position seemed successful as Rebel troops began to fall back, but then – as if out of nowhere – Union forces were attacked from the rear. They had walked into an ambush. "Four hours of action . . . left a carpet of blue-clad corpses strewn across the fields" along with a "carpet of butternut and gray-clad corpses in the appropriately named Blood Lane."[33] The hand of tragedy was a heavy one – the combined casualties for the blue and gray, not counting the missing, for the "twelve

---

[31] Letter from OWH to his mother, July 4, 1862, reproduced in *Touched with Fire, supra* note 21, at 57.

[32] *See* James M. McPherson, *Crossroads of Freedom: Antietam* (New York: Oxford University Press, 2002), at 102, 104–05; Letters from OWH to parents, September 5 and 17, 1862, in *Touched with Fire, supra* note 21, at 61–62.

[33] *Crossroads of Freedom, supra* note 32, at 122. *See also* Francis Winthrop Palfrey, *The Antietam and Fredericksburg* (New York: Charles Scribner's Sons, 1882), at 82–90; Stephen W. Sears, *George B. McClellan: The Young Napoleon* (New York: Da Capo Press, 1999), at 305–11.

hours of combat came to 22,719."[34] In this maelstrom of agony, Holmes was
wounded, this time in the back of his neck: "Unusual luck," he wrote to his
parents the following day, "ball entered at the rear, passing straight through
the central seam of [my] coat and waistcoat collar coming out [toward] the
front on the left hand side – yet it don't seem to have smashed my spine or I
suppose I should be dead or paralysed or something. . . . "[35] Thereafter, he
was left for dead, though he was found that evening wandering aimlessly,
having faded in and out of consciousness. His life had been spared – again.
Miraculously, he survived another close call when shortly afterward he was
taken to a farmhouse to recuperate temporarily, this as Rebels shelled the
space around it.

Meanwhile, word of his injury was telegraphed to his parents. "[M]y
household was startled from its slumbers by the loud summons of a
telegraphic messenger," Dr. Holmes recalled. "Capt. Holmes wounded
shot through the neck thought not mortal," was the message. Hurriedly,
the elder Holmes left Boston in search of his wounded son. Looking for
the place where his son had been transported, he went to Philadelphia,
Baltimore, Frederick, Antietam, Middletown, Keedysville, Harrisburg, and
then to Hagerstown, where on September 25 he boarded a railroad car
filled with wounded soldiers. Then it happened: "In the first car, on the
fourth seat to the right, I saw my Captain; there I saw him, . . . my first-
born. . . . 'How are you boy?' / 'How are you dad?'"[36]

Holmes returned to Boston to recover, and, after some convalescence,
it was back to duty, this time in the Fredericksburg area of Virginia. Here,
too, the fighting was fierce, both close up and as far as a brass telescope
could carry an eye's sight. "For the Twentieth Massachusetts the ninety
days after Antietam were among the most tumultuous of its existence."[37]
When December arrived, it brought not only a bitter cold but also bitter

---

[34] Stephen W. Sears, *Landscape Turned Red: The Battle of Antietam* (New York: Houghton
Mifflin Co., 1983), at 296. Cf. *Justice Oliver Wendell Holmes: Law and the Inner Self*,
supra note 1, at 57.

[35] Letter from OWH to parents, September 18, 1862, reproduced in *Touched with Fire, supra*
note 21, at 64.

[36] *Harvard's Civil War, supra* note 19, at 179–80 (quoting Oliver Wendell Holmes, *Pages
from an Old Volume of Life: A Collection of Essays, 1857–1881* (Boston: Houghton Mifflin,
1883), at 67). Apparently, young Holmes disfavored such visits. See his letter to his parents,
September 22, 1862, reproduced in *Touched with Fire, supra* note 21, at 67 (not wanting
to "meet any affectionate parent half way").

[37] *Harvard's Civil War, supra* note 19, at 181. See also James Ford Rhodes, *History of the
Civil War* (New York: Macmillan, 1917), at 68 (quoting Dr. Holmes on OWH's battle
injuries).

setbacks as Holmes's regiment failed to drive beyond Fredericksburg and toward Chancellorsville. What had begun as a hopeful victory with the Union bombardment of Fredericksburg – later judged by some to be an act of wanton destruction – ended in crushing defeat, massive slaughter, and pervasive losses so ghastly that the living began to question the purposes of both God and country.[38] Too ill to fight (he was sick with dysentery), Holmes could only wait in "helplessness and hopelessness" as his fellow soldiers died and as Union troops suffered a "great bloodletting." It was during these "anxious and forlornest weeks" that soldier Holmes began to get "indifferent... to the sight of death – perhaps because one gets aristocratic and don't value much a common life...."[39]

Though death was everywhere and beckoning everyone, the resolve of soldiers on both sides had not diminished. Into the eternal breach they went, thousands and thousands of them. "I see no further progress," thought Holmes as Christmas of 1862 neared. "I don't think either of you," he told his parents in a letter, "realize the unity or determination of the South. I think you are hopeful because (excuse me) you are ignorant." And so the terrifying war played out, with the only hope being that civilization and progress might "conquer in the long run... and will stand a better chance in the proper province...."[40] The war and all smacked of Darwinism. By that evolutionary measure, life could be cruel, as when men fought with savage fervor hand to hand and used the butts of their muskets to kill one another.

The seeming futility of it all began to war with Holmes's survival instincts, which became even stronger after he was wounded on May 3, 1863, in a battle near Chancellorsville.[41] Shrapnel from a spherical case lodged in his foot. Though there was some fear he might lose a limb, he was fortunate. Once more, he returned home to the family's brick house to recuperate; this time he took several months off. Back home, where he hobbled on crutches, life came back to normal and then some.

---

[38] See George C. Rable, "It Is Well That War Is So Terrible: The Carnage at Fredericksburg," in *The Fredericksburg Campaign: Decision on the Rappahannock*, ed. Gary W. Gallagher (Chapel Hill: University of North Carolina Press, 1995), at 48–79.

[39] Letter from OWH to his mother, December 12, 1862, reproduced in *Touched with Fire*, *supra* note 21, at 77–78. See also *Justice from Beacon Hill, supra* note 6, at 139. The "great bloodletting" line is by Rable, "It Is Well," *supra* note 38, at 48.

[40] Letter from OWH to his father, December 20, 1862, reproduced in *Touched with Fire*, *supra* note 21, at 80.

[41] See *Harvard's Civil War, supra* note 19, at 217–42; *Justice from Beacon Hill, supra* note 6, at 143.

"He lied on the couch," his doctor reported, "and receives lots of pretty company." He even appeared "jolly."[42]

Holmes grew weary of close-up conflict. Thus, when he returned to service he did so as an aide to a general, Horatio G. Wright of the Sixth Corps. This may have seemed like a safe position, but it didn't play out that way. The carnage didn't stop. The various conflicts in northern Virginia were ghastly in unimagined ways. At one point, for example, while Holmes fiddled with his horse's bridle, cannon fire took off the head of one of his fellow soldiers; the infantryman's blood and brains splattered everywhere.[43] On May 5, 1864, the Army of the Potomac engaged the Army of Northern Virginia in an area covered with thickets. This was the Battle of the Wilderness, a two-day conflict that was one of the bloodiest and most puzzling of the Civil War. It was during this gruesome conflict that Henry L. Abbott – a Harvard man, a Copperhead, and one of Holmes's closest friends – was shot. "Abbott wounded *severely* don't know where,"[44] Holmes wrote to his parents on May 6. A bullet ball had torn into his abdomen. According to an eyewitness account from the time, he "lay on a stretcher, quietly breathing his last – his eyes were fixed and the ashen color of death was on his face."[45] Ironically, and saddened as he surely was, the quality that Holmes so admired in this platoon leader was the "splendid carelessness of death" with which Abbott forged headstrong into battle.

The horror of this battle fought in fog and rain burrowed into Holmes's being. The morning following the battle, Holmes wrote in his diary: "Day spent in straightening out Corps, burying dead. . . . In the corner of the woods . . . the dead of both sides lay piled in trenches 5 or 6 deep – wounded often writhing under superincumbent dead – The trees were in slivers from the constant peppering of bullets."[46] On May 16, 1864, a worn and depressed Holmes wrote home: "Before you get this you will know how immense the butcher's bill has been. . . . [T]hese nearly two weeks have contained all of the fatigue & horror war can furnish. . . . [N]early every

---

[42] Qtd. in *Justice from Beacon Hill, supra* note 6, at 143.

[43] *See* Sheldon M. Novick, *Honorable Justice: The Life and Times of Oliver Wendell Holmes* (New York: Dell Publishing, 1989), at 82; *Metaphysical Club, supra* note 3, at 53.

[44] Letter from OWH to his parents, May 6, 1864, reproduced in *Touched with Fire, supra* note 21, at 105.

[45] Qtd. in George R. Agassiz, ed., *Meade's Headquarters, 1863–65: Letters of Colonel Theodore Lyman from the Wilderness to Appomattox* (Boston: Atlantic Monthly, 1922), at 97; Robert Garth Scott, *Into the Wilderness: Army of the Potomac* (Bloomington: Indiana University Press, 1992), at 166.

[46] OWH diary entry, May 13, 1864, reproduced in *Touched with Fire, supra* note 21, at 117 (asterisk note omitted).

Regimental officer I knew or cared for is dead or wounded.... "[47] By late June, the pressure had not let up: "These last few days have been very bad.... I tell you many a man has gone crazy since this campaign began from the terrible pressure on mind and body...."[48] Between May and June the fighting around places like Spotsylvania and Chancellorsville was so fierce that it claimed the lives of fifty thousand men (Yanks and Rebs) in a single week of brutal battle.[49] The fighting – day and night – was hellish; the devastation horrendous.

Captain Holmes had seen enough bloodshed. The life that first energized him, then desensitized him, had changed him. "I am not the same man," he admitted. "[I] may not have the same ideas ... & certainly am not so elastic as I was.... "[50] On July 8, 1864, he told his mother to "prepare for a stratler"[51] – he was ready to leave the service. When Holmes's military service ended, on July 17, 1864, he no longer romanticized the brutish ways of war. Although he remained wed to the idea of duty, he was far more guarded in his idealism; one might even say he became somewhat cynical. Here is how he put it in an earlier letter penned on a cigar box, one that his father had sent him: "I started in this thing as a boy," he noted, but now

I am a man and I have been coming to the conclusion for the last six months that my duty has changed – I can do a disagreeable thing or face a great danger coolly enough when I *know* it is a duty – but a doubt demoralizes me as it does any nervous man – and now I honestly think the duty of fighting has ceased for me – ceased because I have laboriously and with much suffering of mind and body *earned* the right ... to decide for myself how I can best do my duty to the country and, if you choose, to God.[52]

The war was behind him. But the memories – born on the battle-fields – served as reminders of a passion and agony so intense that life seemed meaningless without those "high and dangerous" moments. In the end, the "war in retrospect became ... an overreaching, 'official' memory that helped Holmes avoid recalling some more specific and more candid

---

[47] Letter from OWH to his parents, May 16, 1864, reproduced in *Touched with Fire, supra* note 21, at 122–23.

[48] Letter from OWH to his parents, June 24, 1864, reproduced in *ibid.* at 148.

[49] *Justice Oliver Wendell Holmes: Law and the Inner Self, supra* note 1, at 61–65; *Honorable Justice, supra* note 43, at 84–89.

[50] Letter from OWH to his parents, May 30, 1864, reproduced in *Touched with Fire, supra* note 21, at 135.

[51] Qtd. in *Justice from Beacon Hill, supra* note 6, at 150.

[52] Reproduced in *Touched with Fire, supra* note 21, at 142–43 (italics in original).

memories."[53] However understood, he would, for a time, share those memories with others, in prose that would deservedly claim a place alongside any of the great American speeches. And then, he would stop speaking and reading about the war.

❧

After the Civil War the world never seemed quite right again.
– Oliver Wendell Holmes Jr.[54]

Thirty some years after Holmes hung up his military uniforms, his view of the Civil War was nowhere near as glum as when he left. In his own words around 1895: "War, when you are at it, is horrible and dull. It is only when time has passed that you see that its message was divine."[55] Two years later he admitted: "My memory of those stirring days has faded to a blurred dream."[56] Even so, he delivered his "divine" message, if it can be called that, in several remarkable speeches he gave between 1884 and 1903. Thereafter, though the war motif continued to occupy and influence Holmes's thinking and likewise found expression in some of his letters and judicial opinions, it largely ceased to be a topic he selected for public speech making.[57]

Following Holmes's early war correspondence and diary entries, set out herein, are four addresses (delivered in 1884, 1895, 1899, and 1903, respectively). In them, we see how much the memory of the Civil War affected Holmes. Veterans groups and others could not help but be moved by his eloquent remarks delivered with his signature baritone voice. War taught the young line officer the importance of duty, that obligation borne of both pragmatic concerns and a kind of romanticized Darwinism, which we see in bold relief in Holmes's remarks to the Second Army Corps Association, also set out here. That idea of duty was likewise linked to honor and chivalry, and all were mixed in a cauldron of a destiny at once determined and yet unknown.

---

[53] *Justice Oliver Wendell Holmes: Law and the Inner Self, supra* note 1, at 85.
[54] Recollection by Lewis Einstein of statement made by Holmes in Lewis Einstein, "Introduction," in *The Holmes-Einstein Letters: Correspondence of Mr. Justice Holmes and Lewis Einstein*, ed. James Bishop Peabody (New York: St. Martin's Press, 1964), at xvi.
[55] "The Soldier's Faith." See below.
[56] OWH, Address, Remarks at a Meeting of the Twentieth Regimental Association, December 11, 1897, reproduced in *Collected Works of Justice Holmes, supra* note 4, at 3:519.
[57] He did give a relatively brief address on the subject in 1911. *See* his "The Class of '61 at the Fiftieth Anniversary of Graduation," June 28, 1911, reproduced in *Collected Works of Justice Holmes, supra* note 4, at 3:504–05.

In the public eye, young Holmes's Civil War honor made him some-what of a celebrity in his own right. He was now more than just the "son of Dr. Holmes." He was more than a shadow. That honor, buttressed by an ambition to establish himself professionally, would permit him to define himself to the point that one day he would no longer use the designation *Jr.* to identify himself. In other words, his character, both personally and professionally, was linked to what he had done and accomplished between 1861 and 1864. As the note materials following the various entries indicate, the Civil War also influenced Holmes's overall philosophy as well as his First Amendment jurisprudence. The more one is steeped in the Civil War experience as Holmes both lived and portrayed it, the more one realizes just how indispensable it was to the views he would express in 1919 – views that found expression, of course, in wartime.

Holmes best summed up the gist of what follows, both in this chapter and in others, in three words – "life is war."[58]

The first night I made up my mind to die.

Letter to Amelia Lee Jackson Holmes
October 23, 1861[59]

My Dear Mother

Here I am flat on my back after our first engagement – wounded but pretty comfortable – I can't write an account now but I felt and acted very cool and did my duty I am sure – I was out in front of our men encouraging 'em on when a spent shock knocked the wind out of me and I fell – then I crawled to the rear a few paces and rose by the help of the 1st Sergt; & the Colonel who was passing said "That's right Mr. Holmes – Go to the Rear" but I felt that I couldn't without more excuse so up I got and rushed to the front where hearing the Col. cheering the men on I waved my sword and asked if none would follow me when down I went again by the Colonel's side – The first shot (the spent ball) struck me on the belly below where the ribs separate & bruised & knocked the wind out of me – The second time I hope only one ball struck me entering the left & coming out behind the right breast in wh. case I shall probably recover and this view is seconded by finding a ball in my clothes by

---

[58] OWH, "Edward Avery and Erastus Worthington, Answer to Resolutions of the Bar," Dedham, May 27, 1898, reproduced in *Collected Works of Justice Holmes, supra* note 4, at 3:522.

[59] Written from "20th Regiment Hospital, Camp Benton, Wed: Oct, 23, 1861," reproduced in *Touched with Fire, supra* note 21, at 13–19 (original editor's notes deleted).

the right hand wound – I may be hit twice in which case the chance is not so good – But I am now so well that I have good hopes – The first night I made up my mind to die & was going to take a little bottle of laudanum[60] a soon as I was sure of dying with any pain – but the doctors told me not to take it. And now seem to think I have a fair chance and all my friends whatever happens I am very happy in the conviction I did my duty handsomely – Lt Putman is dead Capt. Putman lost his right arm. Hallowell fought like a brick but wasn't hurt – Schmidt badly wounded – Lowell wounded – Colonel Major & Adjunct probably prisoners Babo & Wesselhoeft probably dead – Sergt Merchant shot dead (in the head) From a third to half of our company killed wounded and prisoners

. . . Men are concentrating in all directions and fighting still going on – They begun by cutting up the 20th only 8 officers out of 22 in our Regt got home unhurt I hope we'll lick 'em yet though – I was hit in the beginning of the fight,

Yours Always
O. W. Holmes, Jr.

God bless you

I can't send a good-looking note lying on my back – But I believe [Lieutenant Whittier] has written you.[61]

COMMENTARY

> *When the battle is fought and won,*
> *What shall be told of you?*
> – Dr. Oliver Wendell Holmes[62]

Holmes's diary and "the approach of death" – Holmes kept a pocketbook diary, including one from his time at Ball's Bluff. That account of his wounding "was apparently written by him some time after the event but while he was on active duty. It was found on loose sheets in the small diary which he kept from May to July, 1864." *Touched with Fire, supra* at 23. Here are some entries from his Ball's Bluff diary, beginning with the following introduction to it: "There

---

[60] This was an alcoholic herbal preparation of opium, which was potent and used as a painkiller. – *Ed.*

[61] The reference is to a long letter dated October 22 from Edward N. Whittier describing the battle of Ball's Bluff. – *Ed.*

[62] Qtd. in *Holmes of the Breakfast-Table, supra* note 15, at 99.

are a great many things of course – thoughts, occupations & events – of which I wish I'd kept Memoranda during my past life – But I wish especially that after the military affairs – battles etc. in which I have been concerned I had noted many of those facts which so rapidly escape the memory in the midst which settles over a fought field.

"Wound at Ball's Bluff

"Not to speak of while the fight was actually going on, I have been struck by the intensity of the mind's action and its increased suggestiveness, after one has received a wound –

"At Ball's Bluff, Tremlett's boy George told me, I was hit at 4½ P.M., *the heavy firing having begun about an hour before, by the watch* – I felt as if a horse had kicked me and went over – 1st Sergt grabbed me and lugged me to the rear a little way & opened my shirt and ecce! the [two] holes in my breasts & the bullet, which he gave me – George says he squeezed it from the right opening – Well – I remember the sickening feeling of water in my face – I was quite faint – and seeing poor Sergt Merchant lying near – shot through the head and covered with blood – and then the thinking begun – (Meanwhile hardly able to speak – at least, coherently) – Shot through the lungs? Let[']s see – I spit – Yes – already the blood was in my mouth."

The account continues, including the travails of getting the injured Holmes to the bottom of the bluff and then to the ferryboat to take him over to the hospital on Harrington's Island for safety. During that time, recalled Holmes, "bullets struck in the bank of the island over our heads as we were crossing. . . ." Later, as he reflected on the deeper meanings of it all, he wrote: "Of course when I thought I was dying the reflection that the majority vote of the civilized world declared that with my opinions I was *en route* for Hell came up with painful distinctness – Perhaps the first impulse was tremulous – but then I said – by Jove, I die like a soldier anyhow – I was shot in the breast doing my duty up to the hub – afraid? No, I am proud – then I thought I couldn't be guilty of a deathbed recantation – father and I talked of that and were agreed that it generally meant nothing but a cowardly giving way to fear – Besides, thought I, can I recant if I want to, has the approach of death changed my beliefs much & to this I answered – No – Then came in my Philosophy – I am to take a leap in the dark – but now as ever I believe that whatever shall happen is best – for it is in accordance with a general law – and *good* & *universal* (or *general law*) are synonymous terms in the universe – (I can now add that our phrase *good* only means certain general truths seen through the heart & will instead of being merely contemplated intellectually – I doubt if the intellect accepts or recognizes that classification of good and bad.)" *Touched with Fire, supra*, at 23–24, 27–28 (italics in original).

In such diary entries, we can see the formative direction of Holmes's thought, which would develop in later speeches and judicial opinions. On the one hand, there is the emphasis on blind *duty*. On the other hand, there is an equally strong commitment to buck "the majority vote of the civilized world." Duty and dissent – these two ideas would continue to play out in Holmes's jurisprudence. Note also the reference to a "general law" that acts as an omnipresent force. This, too, will surface in Holmes's later writings, leaving readers to wonder what exactly such phrases meant for him.

We do in silence what the world shall sing!

How Our Brothers Fought[63]

How fought our brothers, and how they died, the story
You bid me tell, who shared with them the praise,
Who sought with them the martyr's crown of glory,
The bloody birthright of heroic days!

But, all untuned amid the din of battle,
Not to our lyres the inspiring strains belong;
The cannon's roar, the musket's deadly rattle,
Have drowned the music, and have stilled the song.

Let others celebrate our high endeavor,
When peace once more her starry flag shall fling
Wide o'er the land our arms made free forever,
We do in silence what the world shall sing!

COMMENTARY

From horrors to heroics – Holmes read this poem shortly after he returned to Boston from Petersburg, Virginia, where he was mustered out of duty on July 17, 1864. The poem was recited on the evening of July 20, 1864, at the Young's Hotel. The Harvard class of 1861 had gathered there for a reunion. During the event, Holmes's fellow surviving soldiers – ten of their class had died in the war – sat silently as Holmes read his lines with Tennysonian sentimentality. The verses he wrote and read "stand as Holmes's first attempt to romanticize the events of the past three years, to suppress the horrors and deal in heroics."

---

[63] By Oliver Wendell Holmes Jr. Reprinted from Harvard College Class of 1861, *First Triennial Report* (Cambridge, MA: Privately printed, 1864), reproduced in *Collected Works of Justice Holmes, supra* note 4, at 1:172.

Liva Baker, *The Justice from Beacon Hill: The Life and Times of Oliver Wendell Holmes* (New York: HarperCollins, 1991), at 152–53.

> *We equally believed that those who stood against us held just as sacred conviction that were the opposite of ours, and we respected them as every men with a heart must respect those who give all for their belief.*
>
> *In our youth our hearts were touched with fire.*

Memorial Day Address[64]

Not long ago I heard a young man ask why people still kept up Memorial Day, and it set me thinking of the answer. Not the answer that you and I should give to each other – not the expression of those feelings that, so long as you and I live, will make this day sacred to memories of love and grief and heroic youth – but an answer which should command the assent of those who do not share our memories, and in which we of the North and our brethren of the South could join in perfect accord.

So far as this last is concerned, to be sure, there is no trouble. The soldiers who were doing their best to kill one another felt less of personal hostility, I am very certain, than some who were not imperiled by their mutual endeavors. I have heard more than one of those who had been gallant and distinguished officers on the Confederate side say that they

---

[64] An address delivered for Memorial Day, May 30, 1884, at Keene, New Hampshire, before John Sedgwick, Post No. 4, Grand Army of the Republic, reprinted from the *Boston Daily Advertiser*, in Oliver Wendell Holmes Jr., *Dead, Yet Living* (Boston: Ginn, Heath, 1884), reproduced in *Collected Works of Justice Holmes*, *supra* note 4, at 3:462–67. In preparing the foregoing text, I also consulted a newspaper reproduction of the speech, which is slightly different in a few details from what is set out in *Collected Works* and elsewhere. See "Decoration Day in Keene," *New Hampshire Sentinel*, June 4, 1884. Holmes might have ventured to New Hampshire to honor the memory of General John Sedgwick, the commander of Second Corps whom Holmes first met in 1862. The following year, Holmes wrote to his parents of how General Sedgwick "rather likes me." Letter from OWH to his parents, March 18, 1863, reproduced in *Touched with Fire*, *supra* note 21, at 85. In 1864, Holmes had served under Sedgwick; in May of that year, Sedgwick was killed at the Battle of Spotsylvania Court House. See Gary J. Aichele, *Oliver Wendell Holmes, Jr.: Soldier, Scholar, Judge* (Boston: Twayne Publishers, 1989), 59–64. Holmes was with Sedgwick shortly before he died and recounted the details of Sedgwick's untimely demise in his diary from the time. See OWH, May 9, 1864, diary entry reproduced in *Touched with Fire*, *supra* note 21, at 109–10. Later, in 1868, a post in Keene, New Hampshire, was named in Sedgwick's honor. While he was in Keene, Holmes was awarded an engraved Twentieth Massachusetts Infantry pin-backed medal, which is now at the Holmes archives at Harvard Law School.

had had no such feeling. I know that I and those whom I knew best had not. We believed that it was most desirable that the North should win; we believed in the principle that the Union is indissoluble; we, or many of us at least, also believed that the conflict was inevitable, and that slavery had lasted long enough. But we equally believed that those who stood against us held just as sacred convictions that were the opposite of ours, and we respected them as every man with a heart must respect those who give all for their belief. The experience of battle soon taught its lesson even to those who came into the field more bitterly disposed. You could not stand up day after day in those indecisive contests where overwhelming victory was impossible because neither side would run as they ought when beaten, without getting at last something of the same brotherhood for the enemy that the north pole of a magnet has for the south – each working in an opposite sense to the other, but each unable to get along without the other. As it was then, it is now. The soldiers of the war need no explanations; they can join in commemorating a soldier's death with feelings not different in kind, whether he fell toward them or by their side.

But Memorial Day may and ought to have a meaning also for those who do not share our memories. When men have instinctively agreed to celebrate an anniversary, it will be found that there is some thought or feeling behind it which is too large to be dependent upon associations alone. The Fourth of July, for instance, has still its serious aspect, although we should no longer think of rejoicing like children that we have escaped from an outgrown control, although we have achieved not only our national but our moral independence and know it far too profoundly to make a talk about it, and although an Englishman can join in the celebration without a scruple. For, stripped of the temporary associations which gave rise to it, it is now the moment when by common consent we pause to become conscious of our national life and to rejoice in it, to recall what our country has done for each of us, and to ask ourselves what we can do for our country in return.[65]

So to the indifferent inquirer who asks why Memorial Day is still kept up we may answer, it celebrates and solemnly reaffirms from year to year a national enthusiasm and faith. It embodies in the most impressive form our belief that to act with enthusiasm and faith is the condition of acting

---

[65] This line calls to mind President John F. Kennedy's famous 1961 inaugural address in which he said, "And so my fellow Americans, ask not what your country can do for you – ask what you can do for your country." – *Ed.*

greatly. To fight out a war, you must believe something and want something with all your might. So must you do to carry anything else to an end worth reaching. More than that, you must be willing to commit yourself to a course, perhaps a long and hard one, without being able to foresee exactly where you will come out. All that is required of you is that you should go somewhither as hard as ever you can. The rest belongs to fate. One may fall – at the beginning of the charge or at the top of the earthworks; but in no other way can he reach the rewards of victory.

When it was felt so deeply as it was on both sides that a man ought to take his part in the war unless some conscientious scruple or strong practical reason made it impossible, was that feeling simply the requirement of a local majority that our neighbors should agree with them? I think not: I think the feeling was right – in the South as in the North. I think that, as life is action and passion, it is required of a man that he should share the passion and action of his time at peril of being judged not to have lived.

If this be so, the use of this day is obvious. It is true that I cannot argue a man into a desire. If he says to me, Why should I seek to know the secrets of philosophy? Why seek to decipher the hidden laws of creation that are graven upon the tablets of the rocks, or to unravel the history of civilization that is woven in the tissue of our jurisprudence, or to do any great work, either of speculation or of practical affairs? I cannot answer him; or at least my answer is as little worth making for any effect it will have upon his wishes if he asked why I should eat this, or drink that. You must begin by wanting to. But although desire cannot be imparted by argument, it can be by contagion. Feeling begets feeling, and great feeling begets great feeling. We can hardly share the emotions that make this day to us the most sacred day of the year, and embody them in ceremonial pomp, without in some degree imparting them to those who come after us. I believe from the bottom of my heart that our memorial halls and statues and tablets, the tattered flags of our regiments gathered in the Statehouses, and this day this with its funeral march and decorated graves, are worth more to our young men by way of chastening and inspiration than the monuments of another hundred years of peaceful life could be.

But even if I am wrong, even if those who come after us are to forget all that we hold dear, and the future is to teach and kindle its children in ways as yet unrevealed, it is enough for us that to us this day is dear and sacred.

Accidents may call up the event of the war. You see a battery of guns go by at a trot, and for a moment you are back at White Oak Swamp, or Antietam, or on the Jerusalem Road. You hear a few shots fired in the distance, and for an instant your heart stops as you say to yourself, The skirmishers are at it, and listen for the long roll of fire from the main line. You meet an old comrade after many years of absence; he recalls the moment when you are nearly surrounded by the enemy, and again there comes up to you that swift and cunning thinking on which once hung life or freedom – Shall I stand the best chance if I try the pistol or the saber on that man who means to stop me? Will he get his carbine free before I reach him, or can I kill him first? These and the thousand other events we have known are called up, I say, by accident, and, apart from accident, they lie forgotten.

But as surely as this day comes round we are in the presence of the dead. For one hour, twice a year at least – at the regimental dinner, where the ghosts sit at table more numerous than the living, and on this day when we decorate their graves – the dead come back and live with us.

I see them now, more than I can number, as once I saw them on this earth. They are the same bright figures, or their counterparts, that come also before your eyes; and when I speak of those who were my brothers, the same words describe yours.

I see a fair-haired lad, a lieutenant, and a captain on whom life had begun somewhat to tell, but still young, sitting by the long mess-table in camp before the regiment left the State, and wondering how many of those who gathered in our tent could hope to see the end of what was then beginning. For neither of them was that destiny reserved. I remember, as I awoke from my first long stupor in the hospital after the battle of Ball's Bluff, I heard the doctor say, "He was a beautiful boy,"[66] and I knew that one of those two speakers was no more. The other,[67] after passing harmless through all the previous battles, went into Fredericksburg with strange premonition of the end, and there met his fate.

I see another youthful lieutenant as I saw him in the Seven Days, when I looked down the line at Glendale. The officers were at the head of their companies. The advance was beginning. We caught each other's eye and saluted. When next I looked, he[68] was gone.

I see the brother of the last – the flame of genius and daring in his face – as he rode before us into the wood of Antietam, out of which came only dead and deadly wounded men. So, a little later, he rode to his death at the head of his cavalry in the Valley.

[66] Lieutenant William L. Putnam of the Twentieth Massachusetts Regiment. – *Ed.*
[67] Captain Charles F. Cabot of the Twentieth Massachusetts Regiment. – *Ed.*
[68] Lieutenant James. J. Lowell of the Twentieth Massachusetts Regiment. – *Ed.*

In the portraits of some of those who fell in the civil wars of England, Vandyke[69] has fixed on canvas the type who stand before my memory. Young and gracious faces, somewhat remote and proud, but with a melancholy and sweet kindness. There is upon their faces the shadow of approaching fate, and the glory of generous acceptance of it. I may say of them, as I once heard it said of two Frenchmen, relics of *ancien régime*, "They were very gentle. They cared nothing for their lives." High breeding, romantic chivalry – we who have seen these men can never believe that the power of money or the enervation of pleasure has put an end to them. We know that life may still be lifted into poetry and lit with spiritual charm. . . .

There is one who on this day is always present on my mind. [Henry Abbott[70]] entered the army at nineteen, a second lieutenant. In the Wilderness, already at the head of his regiment, he fell, using the moment that was left him of life to give all of his little fortune to his soldiers. I saw him in camp, on the march, in action. I crossed debatable land with him when we were rejoining the Army together. I observed him in every kind of duty, and never in all the time I knew him did I see him fail to choose that alternative of conduct which was most disagreeable to himself. He was indeed a Puritan in all his virtues, without the Puritan austerity; for, when duty was at an end, he who had been the master and leader became the chosen companion in every pleasure that a man might honestly enjoy. His few surviving companions will never forget the awful spectacle of his advance alone with his company in the streets of Fredericksburg. In less than sixty seconds he would become the focus of a hidden and annihilating fire from a semicircle of houses. His first platoon had vanished under it in an instant, ten men falling dead by his side. He had quietly turned back to where the other half of his company was waiting, had given the order, "Second Platoon, forward!" and was again moving on, in obedience to superior command, to certain and useless death, when the order he was obeying was countermanded. The end was distant only a few seconds; but if you had seen him with his indifferent carriage, and sword swinging from his finger like a cane, you would never have suspected that he was doing more than conducting a company drill on the camp parade ground. He was little more than a boy, but the grizzled corps commanders knew

---

[69] The reference is most likely to Sir Anthony Van Dyck (1599–1641), a noted Flemish painter. – *Ed.*

[70] For an account of Henry Abbott and the role he played in Holmes's life and thought, see *Metaphysical Club, supra* note 3, at 40, 53–54. See also comments following this address. – *Ed.*

and admired him; and for us, who not only admired, but loved, his death
seemed to end a portion of our life also. . . .

I have spoken of some of the men who were near to me among others
very near and dear, not because their lives have become historic, but
because their lives are the type of what every soldier has known and seen
in his own company. In the great democracy of self-devotion private and
general stand side by side. Unmarshalled save by their own deeds, the army
of the dead sweep before us, "wearing their wounds like stars." It is not
because the men I have mentioned were my friends that I have spoken of
them, but, I repeat, because they are types. I speak of those whom I have
seen. But you all have known such; you, too, remember!

It is not of the dead alone that we think on this day. There are those
still living whose sex forbade them to offer their lives, but who gave instead
their happiness. Which of us has not been lifted above himself by the sight
of one of those lovely, lonely women, around whom the wand of sorrow
has traced its excluding circle – set apart, even when surrounded by loving
friends who would fain bring back joy to their lives? I think of one whom
the poor of a great city know as their benefactress and friend. I think of one
who has lived not less greatly in the midst of her children, to whom she
has taught such lessons as may [not] be heard elsewhere from mortal lips.
The story of these and of their sisters we must pass in reverent silence. All
that may be said has been said by one of their own sex:

> But when the days of golden dreams had perished,
> And even despair was powerless to destroy,
> Then did I learn how existence could be cherished,
> Strengthened, and fed without the aid of joy.
>
> Then did I check the tears of useless passion,
> Weaned my young soul from yearning after thine
> Sternly denied its burning wish to hasten
> Down to that tomb already more than mine.[71]

Comrades, some of the associations of this day are not only triumphant,
but joyful. Not all of those with whom we once stood shoulder to shoulder –
not all of those whom we once loved and revered – are gone. On this day
we still meet our companions in the freezing winter bivouacs[72] and in
those dreadful summer marches where every faculty of the soul seemed to

---

[71] This is from a poem by Ellis Bell titled "Remembrance." *See Littell's Living Age*, compiled
by E. Littell (Boston: E. Littell, January–March 1850), at 24:569. – *Ed.*
[72] A temporary encampment for soldiers. – *Ed.*

depart one after another, leaving only a dumb animal power to set the teeth and to persist – a blind belief that somewhere and at last there was rest and water. On this day, at least, we still meet and rejoice in the closest tie which is possible between men – a tie which suffering has made indissoluble for better, for worse.

When we meet thus, when we do honor the dead in terms that must sometimes embrace the living, we do not deceive ourselves. We attribute no special merit to a man for having served when all were serving. We know that, if the armies of our war did anything worth remembering, the credit belongs not mainly to the individuals who did it, but to average human nature. We also know very well that we cannot live in associations with the past alone, and we admit that, if we would be worthy of the past, we must find new fields for action or thought, and make for ourselves new careers.

But, nevertheless, the generation that carried on the war has been set apart by its experience. Through our great good fortune, in our youth our hearts were touched with fire. It was given to us to learn at the outset that life is a profound and passionate thing. While we are permitted to scorn nothing but indifference, and do not pretend to undervalue the worldly rewards of ambition, we have seen with our own eyes, beyond and above the gold fields, the snowy heights of honor, and it is for us to bear the report to those who come after us. But, above all, we have learned that whether a man accepts from Fortune her spade, and will look downward and dig, or from Aspiration her axe and cord, and will scale the ice, the one and only success which it is his to command is to bring to his work a mighty heart.

Such hearts – ah me, how many – were stilled twenty years ago; and to us who remain behind is left this day of memories. Every year – in the full tide of spring, at the height of the symphony of flowers and love and life – there comes a pause, and through the silence we hear the lonely pipe of death. Year after year lovers wandering under the apple boughs and through the clover and deep grass are surprised with sudden tears as they see black veiled figures stealing through the morning to a soldier's grave. Year after year the comrades of the dead follow, with public honor, procession and commemorative flags and funeral march – honor and grief from us who stand almost alone, and have seen the best and noblest of our generation pass away.

But grief is not the end of all. I seem to hear the funeral march become a paean. I see beyond the forest the moving banners of a hidden column. Our dead brothers still live for us, and bid us think of life, not death – of life to which in their youth they lent the passion and joy of the spring. As

I listen, the great chorus of life and joy begins again, and amid the awful orchestra of seen and unseen powers and destinies of good and evil our trumpets sound once more a note of daring, hope, and will.

COMMENTARY

Walt Whitman receives a copy – In 1891, Justice Holmes self-published a collection of his speeches, which included his 1884 Memorial Day Address. He sent a copy of the slim volume to Walt Whitman. After receiving it, the poet replied: "When I came from the country yesterday, dear Judge Holmes, there greeted me that little white book with contents like the Puritan which it describes, . . . full of high and mystical beauty." Whitman to OWH, October 24, 1891, Harvard Law School, Box 51, Folder 18, quoted in Sheldon M. Novick, *Honorable Justice: The Life of Oliver Wendell Holmes* (New York: Dell Publishing, 1989), at 196.

The heroic and the ideal – "Holmes's speeches on the Civil War, characterized by grace and restrained warmth and a felicity of phrase, contain some of the best of his writing. . . . Their theme is the heroic and the ideal – what men can believe when they surrender themselves to something beyond themselves, and what they can do when they stretch their capacities to the breaking-point." Max Lerner, *The Mind and Faith of Justice Holmes* (New Brunswick, NJ: Transaction Publishers, 1989), at 5.

A touchstone of his thought – When Holmes's close friend Henry Abbott was killed at the Battle of the Wilderness, the loss of this courageous soldier weighed heavily on young Wendell. To Holmes, Abbott had been much more than a soldier. "That a man widely recognized as the most distinguished soldier in his unit had continually singled him out as a worthy comrade was a source of self-esteem for which he could feel grateful. But Abbott had also impressed on Holmes, possibly by his conversation but certainly by his example, the belief that nobility of character consists in doing one's job with indifference to ends, and his death seems to have set the seal on this belief. . . . [A]fter the war Abbott's death became a touchstone of [Holmes's] thought." Louis Menand, *The Metaphysical Club* (New York: Farrar, Straus & Giroux, 2001), at 54.

Empty affirmations of militarism – Other commentators have been far less kind toward Holmes and the drift of his 1884 remarks. For example, the cultural historian T. Jackson Lears maintains that "Holmes's language made war appear a kind of Pentecost, from which disciples went forth to preach a stoic gospel. But that gospel lacked content. Holmes was left with an empty affirmation of militarism as a substitute for religious faith." This view of things, added Lears, "can be traced to the *fin-de-siècle* cult of experience." And that experience was grounded in the glorification of war. "To some, war-making alone seemed to offer a restoration of purpose in a universe barren of supernatural or even ethical meaning." Hence, the Civil War experience, as glorified by Holmes, could be understood as a kind of "secular conversion, a collective initiation into larger life." T. Jackson Lears, *No Place of Grace: Antimodernism and the Transformation of American Culture, 1880–1920* (New York: Pantheon Books, 1981), at 123, 124.

"For Holmes," contends Professor Alschuler, "war was not life gone awry. It was life at its most meaningful." Albert W. Alschuler, *Law without Values: The Life, Work, and Legacy of Justice Holmes* (Chicago: University of Chicago Press, 2002), at 51 (footnote omitted).

Free speech implications – Holmes's "touched with fire" remarks do not point to any external absolutes or truth. There is no categorical right; there are only soldiers fighting to say that their categorical something is so. "[T]hose who stood against us," says Holmes early in his address, "held just as sacred conviction that were the opposite of ours, and we respected them as every men with a heart must respect those who give all for their belief. The experience of battle soon taught its lesson even to those who came into the field more bitterly disposed." And that lesson was that struggle – "each working in an opposite sense to the other, but each unable to get along without the other" – was key to life and the life experience. So, too, with free speech. If no man could claim moral superiority in the contest of the battlefield, then by the same logic he could neither claim certainty in the competition of the marketplace. Struggle, competition, combat – this is the (militaristic) vernacular of both Holmes's overall philosophy and his corresponding notion of freedom of speech. By this measure, one might think that his free speech jurisprudence was grounded in majority will, a sort of spoils-to-the-victor mind-set. Although Holmes held that view in matters of economic constitutionalism,[73] when it came to free speech, he was willing to place his thumb on the scales so as to permit a measure of minority expression – or so it came to pass with his 1919 opinion in *Abrams v. United States* (see Part VI).

The battle and its fallen men – For additional information concerning this speech and its various historical references, see "Oliver Wendell Holmes, Jr.: 'In Our Youth Our Hearts Were Touched with Fire,'" http://people.virginia .edu/~mmd5f/memorial.htm.

---

[73] See, e.g., his dissent in *Lochner v. New York*, 198 U.S. 45, 65 (1905).

I do not know what is true. I do not know the meaning of the universe. But in the midst of doubt, in the collapse of creeds, there is one thing I do not doubt, . . . and that is that the faith is true and adorable which leads a soldier to throw away his life in obedience to a blindly accepted duty, in a cause which he little understands, in a plan of campaign of which he has little notion, under tactics of which he does not see the use.

The Soldier's Faith[74]

. . . [A]lthough the generation born about 1840, and now governing the world, has fought two at least of the greatest wars in history, and has witnessed others, war is out of fashion, and the man who commands attention of his fellows is the man of wealth. Commerce is the great power. The aspirations of the world are those of commerce.[75] Moralists and philosophers, following its lead, declare that war is wicked, foolish, and soon to disappear.

The society for which many philanthropists, labor reformers, and men of fashion unite in longing is one in which they may be comfortable and may shine without much trouble or any danger. The unfortunately growing hatred of the poor for the rich seems to me to rest on the belief that money is the main thing (a belief in which the poor have been encouraged by the rich), more than on any other grievance. Most of my hearers would rather that their daughters or their sisters should marry a son of one of the great rich families than a regular army officer. . . . I have heard the question asked whether our war was worth fighting, after all. There are many, poor and rich, who think that love of country is an old wife's tale, to be replaced

74 "An Address Delivered on Memorial Day, May 30, 1895, at a Meeting Called by the Graduating Class of Harvard University." Printed in Oliver Wendell Holmes Jr., *The Soldier's Faith* (Boston: Little, Brown, 1895), and reproduced in *Collected Works of Justice Holmes*, supra note 4, at 3:486–91. This address was given in Harvard's Memorial Hall, "which is laid out like a church." Its walls contain the "names of the Harvard dead, arranged by classes, each listing the date and place of death." Hiller B. Sobel, "The Three Civil Wars of Oliver Wendell Holmes: Notes for an Odyssey," 27 *Boston Bar Journal* 18, 19–20 (1983). The phrase "a soldier's faith" appeared earlier in, among other places, a poem by Lord Byron. *See* J. W. Lake, ed., *The Works of Lord Byron* (Philadelphia: Lippincott, Grambo, 1852), at 536. Finally, Dr. Holmes had recited a powerful hymn in this same memorial hall twenty-one years earlier.

75 In the decades following the Civil War, some observers believed that "too many American youths – especially among the upper classes – had succumbed to the vices of commerce. . . . Military heroism repudiated calculating gain and affirmed the inevitability of loss – including the ultimate loss, death itself. The soldier's willingness to risk all for a cause he believed noble (even if he was mistaken) seemed a powerful antidote to the self-seeking calculus governing commerce." Jackson Lears, *Rebirth of a Nation: The Making of Modern America* (New York: HarperCollins, 2009), at 27, 29. – *Ed.*

by interest in a labor union, or, under the name of cosmopolitanism, by a rootless self-seeking search for a place where the most enjoyment may be had at the least cost.

Meantime we have learned the doctrine that evil means pain, and the revolt against pain in all its forms has grown more and more marked. From societies for the prevention of cruelty to animals up to socialism, we express in numberless ways the notion that suffering is a wrong which can be and ought to be prevented, and a whole literature of sympathy has sprung into being which points out in story and in verse how hard it is to be wounded in the battle of life, how terrible, how unjust it is that any one should fail.

Even science has had its part in the tendencies which we observe. It has shaken established religion in the minds of very many. It has pursued analysis until at last this thrilling world of colors and passions and sounds has seemed fatally to resolve itself into one vast network of vibrations endlessly weaving an aimless web, and the rainbow flush of cathedral windows, which once to enraptured eyes appeared the very smile of God, fades slowly out into the pale irony of the void.

And yet from vast orchestras still comes the music of mighty symphonies. Our painters even now are spreading along the walls of our Library glowing symbols of mysteries still real, and the hardly silenced cannon of the East proclaim once more that combat and pain still are the portion of man. For my own part, I believe that the struggle for life is the order of the world, at which it is vain to repine. I can imagine the burden changed in the way it is to be borne, but I cannot imagine that it ever will be lifted from men's backs. I can imagine a future in which science shall have passed from the combative to the dogmatic stage, and shall have gained such catholic acceptance that it shall take control of life, and condemn at once with instant execution what now is left for nature to destroy. But we are far from such a future, and we cannot stop to amuse or to terrify ourselves with dreams. Now, at least, and perhaps as long as man dwells upon the globe, his destiny is battle, and he has to take the chances of war. If it is our business to fight, the book for the army is a war-song, not a hospital-sketch. It is not well for soldiers to think much about wounds. Sooner or later we shall fall; but meantime it is for us to fix our eyes upon the point to be stormed, and to get there if we can.

Behind every scheme to make the world over, lies the question, What kind of world do you want? The ideals of the past for men have been drawn from war, as those for women have been drawn from motherhood. For all our prophecies, I doubt if we are ready to give up our inheritance. Who is there who would not like to be thought a gentleman? Yet what has that name been built on but the soldier's choice of honor rather than life? To be a soldier or descended from soldiers, in time of peace to be ready to give one's life rather than suffer disgrace, that is what the word has meant; and if we try to claim it at less cost than a splendid carelessness for life, we are trying to steal the good will without the responsibilities of the place. We will not dispute about tastes. The man of the future may want something different. But who of us could endure a world, although cut up into five-acre lots, and having no man upon it who was not well fed and well housed, without the divine folly of honor, without the senseless passion for knowledge outreaching the flaming bounds of the possible, without ideals the essence of which is that they can never be achieved? I do not know what is true. I do not know the meaning of the universe. But in the midst of doubt, in the collapse of creeds, there is one thing I do not doubt, that no man who lives in the same world with most of us can doubt, and that is that the faith is true and adorable which leads a soldier to throw away his life in obedience to a blindly accepted duty, in a cause which he little understands, in a plan of campaign of which he has little notion, under tactics of which he does not see the use.

Most men who know battle know the cynic force with which the thoughts of common sense will assail them in times of stress; but they know that in their greatest moments faith has trampled those thoughts under foot. If you wait in line, suppose on Tremont Street Mall, ordered simply to wait and do nothing, and have watched the enemy bring their guns to bear upon you down a gentle slope like that of Beacon Street, have seen the puff of the firing, have felt the burst of the spherical case-shot as it came toward you, have heard and seen the shrieking fragments go tearing through your company, and have known that the next or the next shot carries your fate; if you have advanced in line and have seen ahead of you the spot you must pass where the rifle bullets are striking; if you have ridden at night at a walk toward the blue line of fire at the dead angle of Spotsylvania, where for twenty-four hours the soldiers were fighting on the two sides of an earthwork, and in the morning the dead and dying lay piled in a row six deep, and as you rode you heard the bullets splashing in the mud and earth about you; if you have been in the picket-line at night in a black and unknown wood, have heard the splat of the bullets upon the trees, and as you moved have felt your foot slip upon a dead man's body; if you have had a blind fierce gallop against the enemy, with your blood up and a pace that left no time for fear – if, in short, as some, I hope many, who hear me, have known, you have known the vicissitudes of terror and triumph in war; you know that there is such a thing as the faith I spoke of. You know your own weakness and are modest; but you know that man has in him that unspeakable somewhat which makes him capable of miracle, able to lift himself by the might of his own soul, unaided, able to face annihilation for a blind belief.

From the beginning, to us, children of the North, life has seemed a place hung about by dark mists, out of which comes the pale shine of dragon's scales and the cry of fighting men, and the sound of swords. Beowulf, Milton, Durer, Rembrandt, Schopenhauer, Turner, Tennyson, from the first war song of the race to the stall-fed poetry of modern English drawing rooms, all have had the same vision, and all have had a glimpse of a light to be followed. "The end of worldly life awaits us all. Let him who may, gain honor ere death. That is best for a warrior when he is dead."[76] So spoke Beowulf a thousand years ago. . . .

When I went to the war I thought that soldiers were old men. I remembered a picture of the revolutionary soldier which some of you may have seen, representing a white-haired man with his flint-lock slung across his back. I remembered one or two examples of revolutionary soldiers whom I have met, and I took no account of the lapse of time. It was not long after, in winter quarters, as I was listening to some of the sentimental songs in vogue, such as –

> Farewell, Mother, you may never
> See your darling boy again,[77]

that it came over me that the army was made up of what I should now call very young men. I dare say that my illusion has been shared by some of those now present, as they have looked at us upon whose heads the white shadows have begun to fall. But the truth is that war is the business of youth and early middle age. You who called this assemblage together, not we, would be the soldiers of another war, if we should have one. . . .

War, when you are at it, is horrible and dull. It is only when time has passed that you see that its message was divine. I hope it may be long before we are called again to sit at that master's feet. But some teacher of the kind we all need. In this snug, over-safe corner of the world we need it, that we may realize that our comfortable routine is no eternal necessity of things, but merely a little space of calm in the midst of the tempestuous untamed streaming of the world, and in order that we may be ready for danger. We need it in this time of individualist negations, with its literature of French and American humor, revolting at discipline, loving flesh-pots,

---

[76] Lesslie Hall, trans., *Beowulf: An Anglo Saxon Epic Poem* (Boston: E. C. Heath, 1897), at 48. – *Ed.*

[77] These lines are similar to those found in an 1864 Confederate song by George Frederick Root titled "Just before the Battle, Mother." – *Ed.*

and denying that anything is worthy of reverence – in order that we may remember all that buffoons forget. We need it everywhere and at all times. For high and dangerous action teaches us to believe as right beyond dispute things for which our doubting minds are slow to find words of proof. Out of heroism grows faith in the worth of heroism. The proof comes later, and even may never come. Therefore I rejoice at every dangerous sport which I see pursued. . . .

We do not save our traditions, in our country. The regiments whose battle-flags were not large enough to hold the names of the battles they had fought vanished with the surrender of Lee, although their memories inherited would have made heroes for a century. It is the more necessary to learn the lesson afresh from perils newly sought, and perhaps it is not vain for us to tell the new generation what we learned in our day, and what we still believe. That the joy of life is living, is to put out all one's powers as far as they will go; that the measure of power is obstacles overcome; to ride boldly at what is in front of you, be it fence or enemy; to pray, not for comfort, but for combat; to keep the soldier's faith against the doubts of civil life, more besetting and harder to overcome than all the misgivings of the battlefield, and to remember that duty is not to be proved in the evil day, but then to be obeyed unquestioning; to love glory more than the temptations of wallowing ease, but to know that one's final judge and only rival is oneself: with all our failures in act and thought, these things we learned from noble enemies in Virginia or Georgia or on the Mississippi, thirty years ago; these things we believe to be true.

> "Life is not lost," said she, "for which is bought
> Endless renown."[78]

We learned also, and we still believe, that love of country is not yet an idle name.

> Deare countrey! O how dearly deare
> Ought thy remembraunce, and perpetual band
> Be to thy foster child, that from thy hand
> Did commun breath and nouriture receave!
> How brutish is it not to understand
> How much to her we owe, that all us gave;
> That gave unto us all, whatever good we have![79]

---

[78] See "The Faerie Queene," in *The Poetical Works of Edmund Spencer*, ed. Rev. George Gilfillan (Edinburgh: Ballantyne, 1850), at 2:310 (bk. 3, canto 19). – *Ed.*

[79] See *ibid.* at 1:101 (bk. 2, canto 10). – *Ed.*

As for us, our days of combat are over. Our swords are rust. Our guns will thunder no more. The vultures that once wheeled over our heads must be buried with their prey. Whatever of glory must be won in the council or the closet, never again in the field. I do not repine. We have shared the incommunicable experience of war; we have felt, we still feel, the passion of life to its top.

Three years ago died the old colonel[80] of my regiment, the Twentieth Massachusetts. He gave the regiment its soul. No man could falter who heard his "Forward, Twentieth!" I went to his funeral. From a side door of the church a body of little choir-boys came in alike a flight of careless doves. At the same time the doors opened at the front, and up the main aisle advanced his coffin, followed by the few grey heads who stood for the men of the Twentieth, the rank and file whom he had loved, and whom he led for the last time. The church was empty. No one remembered the old man whom we were burying, no one save those next to him, and us. And I said to myself, The Twentieth has shrunk to a skeleton, a ghost, a memory, a forgotten name which we other old men alone keep in our hearts. And then I thought: It is right. It is as the colonel would have it. This also is part of the soldier's faith: Having known great things, to be content with silence. Just then there fell into my hands a little song sung by a warlike people on the Danube, which seemed to me fit for a soldier's last word, another song of the sword, but a song of the sword in its scabbard, a song of oblivion and peace.

A soldier has been buried on the battle-field.

> "And when the wind in the tree-tops roared,
> The soldier asked from the deep dark grave:
> 'Did the banner flutter then?'
> 'Not so, my hero,' the wind replied.
> 'The fight is done, but the banner won,
> Thy comrades of old have borne it hence,
> Have borne it in triumph hence.'
> Then the soldier spake from the deep dark grave:
> 'I am content.' ...
>
> ...

---

[80] William Raymond Lee (1807–91). Colonel Lee was in command of the regiment in which Holmes fought at Ball's Bluff and elsewhere. Years before this 1895 address, when Lee retired from his regiment in 1862, Holmes honored his "gallant commander." See *Justice Holmes: The Shaping Years, supra* note 17, at 1:146. – Ed.

Then he heareth the lovers laughing pass,
and the soldier asks once more:
'Are these not the voices of them that love,
That love – and remember me?'
'Not so, my hero,' the lovers say,
'We are those that remember not;
For the spring has come and the earth has smiled,
And the dead must be forgot.'
Then the soldier spake from the deep dark grave:
'I am content.'"[81]

COMMENTARY

The speech that caught the president's ear – Holmes's 1895 Memorial Day address[82] attracted the attention of President Theodore Roosevelt, who would later nominate the Massachusetts jurist to the Supreme Court. Apparently, the president was quite taken by the militarist bent of the remarks. *See* Albert W. Alschuler, *Law without Values: The Life, Work, and Legacy of Justice Holmes* (Chicago: University of Chicago Press, 2002), at 47.

War and commerce – "The Soldier's Faith" speech began with words critical of war, which "is out of fashion." More important, war was said to be "wicked" and "foolish." Its time had passed. This mainstay of the past had been replaced by the "great power" of "Commerce." Money is the measure of all; it was "the main thing." For some, the conflict was between the worshippers of commerce (the soft) and those who revered the kind of manliness associated with military sacrifice. For others, the conflict was between the rich and the poor. Theirs was a war not waged on a battlefield. Rather, it was a conflict between associations that vied for economic power. Hence, the old ideal of "love of country," for which men died, was replaced by "interest in a labor union," which men protested for. Consistent with the coin of commerce, the new ideal was the "most enjoyment" at the "least cost." The heroic ideal of the value of pain and suffering was likewise out of vogue among "philanthropists, labor reformers, and men of fashion." They opposed war; they shunned danger.[83]

---

[81] *See* Frederick Harrison, "I Am Content," reproduced in *United Service: A Monthly Review of Military and Naval Affairs*, 3rd ser. (New York: L. R. Hamersly, 1903), at 3:785. – *Ed.*

[82] Similar sentiments and phrases, including "the soldier's faith," can be found in an earlier speech Holmes gave. *See* OWH, Address, Speech to the Twentieth Regiment, Massachusetts Volunteers, December 10, 1892, reproduced in *Collected Works of Justice Holmes, supra* note 4, at 3:512–13.

[83] For a thoughtful discussion of this overall subject, see T. Jackson Lears, "The Destructive Element: Modern Commercial Society and the Martial Ideal," in *No Place of Grace:*

"Even science" had lent its aid to bringing about "the pale irony of the void." Thus did Holmes prepare his audience for what was to follow.

But that rhetorical course did not continue. Holmes's conceptual path pointed elsewhere, to a time and place far removed from the present. By returning to that time and place in his remarks, Holmes set out to reawaken an old Spartan faith. Unlike his earlier Memorial Day address of 1884, on this occasion he did not speak to war veterans. He addressed young people about to graduate from college. It was their minds, tethered to the gospel of commerce, which Holmes hoped to change. And it was in their hearts that he likewise hoped to rekindle sparks of respect for the highest of ideals, that of struggle. "For my own part," he told them, "I believe that the struggle for life is the order of the world, at which it is vain to repine." Our "destiny is battle"; our highest ideals are "drawn from war." With the fervor inspired by the bugler's call, the waving of the regimental flag, and the drumbeat of battle, Holmes marched his audience into his world, a world of blind heroism: "I do not know the meaning of the universe. But in the midst of doubt, in the collapse of creeds, there is one thing I do not doubt, that no man who lives in the same world with most of us can doubt, and that is that the faith is true and adorable which leads a soldier to throw away his life in obedience to a blindly accepted duty, in a cause which he little understands, in a plan of campaign of which he has little notion, under tactics of which he does not see the use."

The message was aimed at the romantic heart, not the survivalist mind. In a world bereft of certainty, bloated by comfort, and intoxicated by greed, he hoped to revive the great Phoenix of the soldier's faith. And that faith was inextricably tied to duty, which in turn was linked to the value of struggle as a core principle of life. In the broad sweep of it, the fog of Holmes's impassioned rhetoric dimmed a glaring truth – it was the fight, more than what is fought for, that was to be valued. That idea, we will see, won newfound expression in Holmes's later thoughts bearing on the First Amendment. (See comments following the Memorial Address of 1884, and comments following *Abrams* in Part IV.)

A self-defeating quest – In a world grown fat by the pursuit of money, Holmes (a man of means) called for a more vibrant contact with life. His "quest for authenticity" led him back to his war experience. This "militarist obsession with authenticity," argues T. Jackson Lears, "like other cults of risk-taking, became a circular and self-defeating quest for intense experience – a characteristic mode of adjustment to a secular culture of consumption." T. Jackson

Antimodernism and the Transformation of American Culture, 1880–1920 (New York: Pantheon Books, 1981), at 98–139.

Lears, *No Place of Grace: Antimodernism and the Transformation of American Culture, 1880–1920* (New York: Pantheon Books, 1981), at 138.

The pursuit of peril – In the same month and year when Holmes delivered his address, the American essayist Hamilton Wright Mabie preached a gospel that likely would have won a nod of approval from Holmes: "In our slippered ease…we sometimes forget of what perilous stuff we are made, and how unseperable from human life are those elements of tragedy which from time to time startle us in our repose.…A stable world is essential to progress, but a world without the element of peril would comfort the body and destroy the soul." See his "A Comment on Some Recent Books," *Chap-Book*, May 15, 1895, at 368–69. Preserving such an element of peril was an idea that both reflected Holmes thinking in 1895 and that later influenced his jurisprudence of free speech. Interestingly, if this philosophy of peril was intended to replicate the conflict of actual battle, then one can begin to understand why in his 1919 *Abrams* dissent (see Part VI) Holmes protected speech up to the point of its producing an actual "clear and imminent danger" to the safety of the nation. Some would argue (see comments following *Abrams*) that such a rule takes the peril principle perilously close to self-destruction.

An issue of both epistemology and sensibility – "The younger Holmes had volunteered to fight…because of certain moral principles, but 'the war did more than make him lose those beliefs. It made him lose his belief in beliefs.' This was more than just a loss of faith; it was an issue of both epistemology and sensibility, of how we know the world and how we envision our relationship to it." Drew Gilpin Faust, *This Republic of Suffering: Death and the American Civil War* (New York: Vintage, 2008), at 193–94 (quoting Louis Menand, *The Metaphysical Club* (New York: Farrar, Straus & Giroux, 2001), at x, 4).
  "The war experience may have laid the foundations of Holmes's aloof detachment, his disengagement from causes and distrust of enthusiasms, and the bleakly skeptical foundations of his general outlook.…From his war service on, he would repeatedly speak of personal and social life in military terms, as a fight carried on by soldiers blindly following incomprehensible orders." Robert W. Gordon, "Introduction: Holmes's Shadow," in *The Legacy of Oliver Wendell Holmes, Jr.*, ed. Robert Gordon (Palo Alto, CA: Stanford University Press, 1992), at 1.

Creeds, tolerance, and skepticism – It is apparent from many of Holmes's later letters that he disdained political or religious zealots, be they antiwar socialists or antislavery abolitionists. This is not to say that such disdain led him to deny First Amendment protection for such views. Quite the opposite. It was precisely because no one ideology could claim a hold on truth that he felt free to permit, and even encourage, a battle of beliefs. By that measure, the pursuit of truth is more valued for the pursuit than for the acquisition of truth.

During the Civil War, when there was a newfound and newly defined confidence in immortality, soldiers could be encouraged to risk their own demise. (*See This Republic of Suffering, supra*, at 175.) To take away that confidence, as Holmes's epistemology would allow, was to take away one of the very things that made war's pain and suffering possible, justifiable, and even noble. It is ironic, then, that Holmes's own epistemology would tend to make one skeptical of the soldier's faith, a faith that might well seem as misplaced as that of the Christian soldier.

Holmes's agnostic creed – "Holmes remained at heart a Puritan faithful to Plymouth Rock. Perhaps he came nearer to being a great Roman stoic, for he was not religious in any orthodox sense. He did not believe in personal survival nor did he find it desirable. In his creed he attached a kind of religious meaning to his own agnosticism, regarding this in the light of proper humility before the great mystery which could never be fathomed. The assumption that eternal truth had been established seemed to him to imply a kind of arrogance, and arrogance was the only sin he could never forgive. His own lack of belief was very far from being a mere negation. It carried with it the thought that life was in itself an end, but that real life must always wrestle in a struggle either of the mind or the body, for nothing that one came by easily was ever worth having." "Introduction," in *The Holmes-Einstein Letters: Correspondence of Mr. Justice Holmes and Lewis Einstein, 1903–1935*, ed. James Bishop Peabody (New York: St. Martin's Press, 1964), at xx.

War and Holmesian metaphysics – "When one considers 'The Soldier's Faith' in terms of Holmesian metaphysics, the address becomes more than a jingoistic tract. Holmes was not glorifying conquest and brutality and slaughter, but rather juxtaposing them against the 'heroism' of stoic exposure to death in pursuit of 'gentlemanly' ideals." By that measure, the "carnage of the war and the leveling character of wartime death may have served as a reminder that the social terms by which humans evaluated one another were ultimately meaningless. The randomness of death or survival may have been taken as 'proof' of the mystery of 'the ultimate.'" Moreover, "the war was a particularly fertile breeding ground for heroism; it was an environment in which one could affirm what it meant to live all the more fully because one was continually facing death." G. Edward White, *Justice Oliver Wendell Holmes: Law and the Inner Self* (New York: Oxford University Press, 1993), at 83. That said, even some of Holmes's contemporaries saw the speech as glorifying war. *See, e.g.,*

Wendell Garrison, "Sentimental Jingoism," *Nation*, December 19, 1895, at 440; E. L. Godkin, "Force as a Moral Influence," *Evening Post* (New York), December 17, 1895.

Holmes responds – Writing to his friend Sir Frederick Pollock, Holmes took exception to such criticisms: "Fancy my speech of last Memorial Day being treated as a jingo document! Greatly to my disgust it was put over in the *Harvard Magazine* and only came out a few days ago, . . . but now it seems to some of the godly as I were preaching a doctrine of blood! My classmate Wendell P. Garrison, Editor of *The Nation* . . . a most watery person but one who is, was, and ever will be flat, walked into me with a blunt knife . . . and I surmise that [Edwin] Godkin[84] backed him in a No. 2 which was too clever for poor Wendell. I met the great Edward Atkinson [a wealthy Boston entrepreneur and supporter of the Free-Soil Party] this morning and he shook his head & said: 'I don't like it. It's bad morals and bad politics.' To which I civilly replied that I didn't care, but on reflection called his attention to my speech being on Memorial Day, not now." Holmes to Pollock, December 27, 1895, reproduced in Mark DeWolfe Howe, ed., *The Holmes-Pollock Letters* (Cambridge, MA: Harvard University Press, 1941), at 1:66, 67. Years later, Holmes added: "I tried in my speech 'The Soldier's Faith' to bring home by example that men are eternally idealists – (a speech that fools took as advice to young men to wade in gore)." Holmes to Clara Stevens, September 3, 1909, Holmes Papers, Harvard Law School Library, quoted in *Justice Oliver Wendell Holmes: Law and the Inner Self*, *supra*, at 83–84.

The cult of sacrifice and its consequences – The historian Jackson Lears has recently observed that, between 1870 and 1890, the "recoil from comfort led in . . . disturbing directions . . . , toward places in the psyche where not even morality mattered. To Americans whose very sense of selfhood seemed fragmented and frail, aggressive action promised strength and psychic wholeness. To Americans who felt cut off from firsthand experience, it promised immersion in 'real life.' The Christian and even the nationalist frameworks dropped away; risk became its own reward. Courage and endurance became ends in themselves. This was not quite a cult of death, but when combined with the cult of sacrifice, it came very close. Nihilism – and eventually fascism – fluttered at the edges of militarism. . . . Perhaps the most prominent purveyor of this world view was Oliver Wendell Holmes, Jr." *Rebirth of a Nation*, *supra*, at 29–30.

---

[84] Editor of the *New York Evening Post* from 1883 to 1900. – *Ed.*

"Bravery," it has been argued, "is one way to deal with the puzzle of death. Like Hegel, Holmes sees the will to stake honor over life as a great purgative that annihilates idle doubt and boredom. War is a mechanism for producing meaning." John Durham Peters, *Courting the Abyss: Free Speech and the Liberal Tradition* (Chicago: University of Chicago Press, 2005), at 151–52.

A *mystical tone* – Notwithstanding all that has been written about Holmes as cynic, skeptic, positivist, eugenics advocate, and even nihilist, there are still segments of his writings that smack of something beyond, though in curious ways. It can be found at the end of his infamous essay *The Path of the Law* (see Part III) and elsewhere, as in a 1911 speech he gave to a Harvard graduating class. "Commerce has outsoared the steeples that once looked down on the marts, but still their note makes music of the din. For those of us who are not churchmen the symbol still lives. Life is a roar of bargain and battle, but in the very heart of it there rises a mystical spiritual tone that gives meaning to the whole. It transmutes the dull details into romance." OWH, "The Class of '61, at the Fiftieth Anniversary of Graduation," June 28, 1911, reproduced in *The Collected Works of Justice Holmes, supra*, at 3:505.

In an 1889 tribute to Sidney Bartlett, a respected lawyer, Holmes wrote: "[T]he rule for fulfilling the mysterious ends of the universe – it seems to me that the beginning of self-sacrifice and of holiness – is to do one's task with one's might. If we do that, I think we find that our motives take care of themselves. We find that what may have begun as a means becomes an end in itself; that self-seeking is forgotten in labors which are the best contribution that we can make to mankind; that our personality is swallowed up in working to ends outside ourselves." OWH, "Sidney Bartlett," March 23, 1889, reproduced in Sheldon M. Novick, ed., *The Collected Works of Justice Holmes* (Chicago: University of Chicago Press, 1995), at 3:480–81.

Many of Holmes's critics – particularly the less judicious and less nuanced ones who paint him to be simply a monstrous Nietzschean or something akin to that – frequently overlook this side of his writings. Then again, it has been said, and not without some merit, that Holmes "sometimes concluded his after-dinner speeches with a dash of Emersonian idealism, [though] his preferred sensibility was one of True Grit." David A. Hollinger, "The 'Tough Minded' Justice Holmes, Jewish Intellectuals, and the Making of an American Icon," in *The Legacy of Oliver Wendell Holmes, Jr.*, ed. Robert W. Gordon (Stanford, CA: Stanford University Press, 1992), at 217.

Eugenics – The following passage in "The Soldier's Faith" has been seen by some as a Holmesian defense of eugenics: "I can imagine a future in which science shall have passed from the combative to the dogmatic stage, and shall have gained such catholic acceptance that it shall take control of life, and condemn at once with instant execution what now is left for nature to destroy." See also Holmes's opinion in *Buck v. Bell*, 274 U.S. 200 (1927), and Holmes's letter to Felix Frankfurter, September 3, 1921, reproduced in Robert M. Mennel and Christine L. Compston, eds., *Holmes and Frankfurter: Their Correspondence, 1912–1934* (Hanover, NH: University Press of New England, 1996), at 124–25. For a discussion of this matter, see *Law without Values, supra*, at 27–29; Edmund Wilson, *Patriotic Gore* (New York: Oxford University Press, 1962), at 767–69; and Sheldon Novick, "Holmes's Philosophy and Jurisprudence: Origin and Development of Principal Themes," in *The Collected Works of Justice Holmes, supra*, at 1:32–36.

The flag – Flags, Holmes suggested, are symbols by which a nation attempts to preserve its traditions, or least preserve respect for them. The traditions to which he referred were, of course, related to the glorious wars of the past. Thus, they, too, deserve respect. Or as Holmes later put it: "The flag is but a bit of bunting to one who insists on prose. Yet, ... its red is our life blood, its stars our world, its blue our heaven. It owns our land. At will it throws away our lives." "John Marshall," February 4, 1901, reproduced in *The Collected Works of Justice Holmes, supra*, at 502. Six years later, when he was on the Supreme Court, Holmes signed on to an opinion in which the Court upheld a state law criminalizing the display of an American flag for commercial purposes. *See Halter v. Nebraska*, 205 U.S. 34 (1907) (see introduction to Part IV). Some eight decades later, the Court took a different view of the matter and upheld the right to desecrate a flag. *See Texas v. Johnson*, 491 U.S. 397 (1989). Both the majority and the dissent quoted Holmes in support of their positions. *See Johnson*, 491 U.S. at 418–19, 421–22.

People dwell on the sorrows of war

Address at a Banquet for Admiral Dewey
October 14, 1899[85]

... The law does not mean sympathetic advice [that] you may neglect if you choose, but stern monition that the club and bayonet are at hand ready to drive you to prison or the rope if you go beyond the established lines.... As

---

[85] Manuscript, Holmes Papers, Harvard Law School, reproduced in *Collected Works of Justice Holmes, supra* note 4, at 3:523–24. These remarks were to honor Admiral George Dewey (1837–1917), whose victories at Manila Bay in the Spanish-American War greatly excited Holmes. See *Justice from Beacon Hill, supra* note 6, at 324.

the public force gets more organized and complete the need of actually calling it forth grows correspondingly less. But the silence of unquestioned power and the dumbness of anarchy are as far apart as the infinite and zero.

The possibility of having to face death in battle, which throughout all history has been the background of men's outlook upon life, has given shape and color to what at this day we most value in men. . . .

When I hear people talk about civil life as needing and teaching a courage equal to that of war, I feel very sure that I am listening to a noncombatant who never has known what it is to expect a bullet in his bowels in thirty seconds or to sail an iron clad over a mine.

People dwell on the sorrows of war. I know what they are. I saw my share of them when I was young with the Army of the Potomac. I shudder at them. I abhor the Jingo spirit. I would do all that might be done honorably to avoid them. But the horrors of war after all are bodily suffering, the loss of property, and the loss of life. There are spiritual losses that are a thousand times worse. It is worse to be a coward than to lose an arm. It is better to be killed than to have a flabby soul. The true teaching of life is a tender hard heartedness which has passed beyond sympathy and which expects every man to abide his lot as he is able to shape it. . . .

COMMENTARY

A *tender hard-heartedness* – His use of words with contradictory meanings aside, and his abhorrence of the jingo spirit notwithstanding, Holmes had little sympathy for pacifists and antiwar zealots. To kill people with opposing views – those "heretics" – "seem[ed] to be logical," Holmes once wrote, even though he preferred a system of law to prevent such situations. See the letter from OWH to Harold Laski, October 26, 1919, reproduced in *Holmes-Laski Letters: The Correspondence of Mr. Justice Holmes and Harold J. Laski*, Mark DeWolfe Howe, ed. (Cambridge, MA: Harvard University Press, 1953), at 2:217–18.

They obey their destiny without any sight of the promised land.

Remarks to the Second Army Corps Association[86]

When I was a small boy and was allowed to see the celebrations of the day – it may have been on the introduction of the Cochituate water into Boston, or the funeral of John Quincy Adams, or I know not what – I

[86] Address, Washington, D.C., March 13, 1903, manuscript, Holmes Papers, Harvard Law School, reproduced in *Collected Works of Justice Holmes, supra* note 4, at 3:539–41.

was most impressed by the part played by a carload of veterans. I got the notion, which has persisted, that the glory of life was to be carried in a civic procession, in a barge, as a survivor – I did not inquire too curiously of what. Now I am beginning to realize that somber joy, and to feel something like the old gentleman of whom I overheard Judge Hoar tell, who remembered George Washington before dinner – and after dinner remembered Christopher Columbus. Take this Club. In my day, after having been saved from extinction by two members of the Class of 1860, it used to meet, I think rather oftener than elsewhere in my room, at Danforth's in Linden Street, which had the advantage of being outside of the College Yard. If I am not mistaken, the last meeting that I attended before this was there in 1860 or 1861. In those days the Club used to listen to essays by its members before the business of the bottle began. – Without yet going back to Columbus it may connect you with the past if I mention that at that time my grandmother was alive and remembered moving out of Boston when the British troops came in, before the Revolution. – I spoke of the introduction of Cochituate water.... [These events were] all before the war, when I was a boy. Some things that happened after it would seem rather ancient history to most of you.... The war itself, though it started the changes that almost have made a new art of warfare – such as the field telegraph – breech loaders and ironclads – sounds nowadays pretty remote in its methods. We fought in two close ranks, the rear rank firing over the shoulders of the front. A regiment would be wiped out if it tried it now. Yet I remember seeing what I suppose was the germ of that which made it impossible, in the shape of a little go cart with a gunbarrel on top that it was said would grind out a stream of bullets like a hose, on the Peninsula, at Malvern Hill. I never heard that it succeeded and at that time I supposed that it stood on the plane of Christian Commission Crackers[87] that I also saw, with Come to Jesus printed on their side.

But after all our interests are in the present and the future – not in the past.... I have been reading lately a golden book, or rather books, for there are ten volumes of it: *Fabre's Souvenirs Entomologiques*.[88] It is a seed book. There I am very sure is the source of that echo from behind phenomena that for a moment we think we hear in Maeterlinck's *Bees*.[89] I think it must

---

[87] This was a voluntarily charitable organization whose mission was to provide communication between Union soldiers on the battlefield or in hospitals and their families. – Ed.

[88] Jean Henri Fabre (1823–1915) was a French entomologist. – Ed.

[89] *The Life of the Bee*, by Maurice Maeterlinck, was published in 1901. – Ed.

have inspired one of the most noticeable traits in Bergson's philosophy.[90] It is simply the exquisitely told tale of a life long watch of beetles and wasps but from it we learn the faith I spoke of if we had it not before. I heard the doctrine years ago from Dr. Bartol.[91] He spoke of the hen hatching her eggs in obedience to a destiny she did not understand. Fabre tells us of grubs born and having passed their whole lives in the heart of an oak that when, after three years, the time for metamorphosis comes, build a chamber that as grubs they do not need with a broad passage for the beetle that is to be. They obey their destiny without any sight of the promised land. The law of the grub and the hen is the law also for man. We all have cosmic destinies of which we cannot divine the end, if the unknown has ends. Our business is to commit ourselves to . . . life, to accept at once our functions and our ignorance and to offer our heart to fate. When one is drawing near the end it is a great happiness to be assured for a moment by friends such as I see around me that one has borne one's part and has not failed in the faith.

COMMENTARY

The destiny of grubs – At a time when patriotism and religious sentiment provided most Civil War soldiers with some sense of comfort from the senseless agony of annihilation, the Holmes of this period, *circa* 1903, saw life through a different prism. His sense of duty was tied to an unknown destiny, which causes one to embrace life and "function" to his or her fullest and then to leave a "broad passage for the beetle that is to be." That is "the faith" to which Holmes subscribed. He was very much interested in what he labeled "our influence on those who come after us. . . . " OWH, Remarks at a Dinner of the Alumni of the Boston University Law School, June 3, 1890, reproduced in *The Collected Works of Justice Holmes*, Sheldon M. Novick, ed. (Chicago: University of Chicago Press, 1995), at 3:511. By that measure, life was like the common law, forever evolving as it built more and more on the past.

Free speech implications – In light of what has been presented in this section, the Civil War experience seems to have produced in Holmes a mind-set

[90] Henri-Louis Bergson (1859–1941) was a noted French philosopher. Among other things, he compared the flux of consciousness with the inert physical world. His *Time and Free Will* and *Matter and Memory* were published in French in 1889 and 1896, respectively. – *Ed.*

[91] Cyrus Augustus Bartol (1813–1900), known as the "poet of the pulpit," graduated from Harvard Divinity School in 1835 and became a Unitarian minister, author, and member of the Transcendental Club. – *Ed.*

characterized by the following assumptions relevant to his free speech jurisprudence:

- Life, like war, consists of conflict, which can strengthen us.
- There is no certainty in life, only the ongoing pursuit of knowledge.
- We must be prepared to relinquish our "truths" to make way for new ones.
- The hope – and it is no more than a hope – is that evolution will produce a better species ("better" in an evolutionary sense, that is).
- Truth, whatever it is, may or may not be transcendent.
- Freedom, including freedom of expression, belongs to the victors, the majority – their collective will governs (this idea changes in Holmes post-*Abrams* thought).

Part II General Conceptions: The Early Writings

My interest is in ideas – and the law being the door by which I entered, I stick to that.

The man of action has the present, but the thinker controls the future; he is the most subtle, the most far-reaching power. His ambition is the vastest, as it is the most ideal.
– Oliver Wendell Holmes Jr.[1]

If nothing else, young Holmes was curious and ambitious; by mixing the two he forged his own identity, one that would in time eclipse that of his famous father. What is striking about Wendell's post–Civil War formative years is the breadth of interest in, and knowledge of, almost everything, from poetry, philosophy, and literature to economics, science, and law. There was a certain curious bent in him that pursued knowledge wherever he might discover it. In that quest, he turned to books (he was an enthusiastic reader) and friends (he had a circle of learned acquaintances), and in time to the law and its institutions of learning and practice. As with his college education, Holmes found the law school experience (with its faculty of three professors) largely disappointing. While he was there, however, he read many works, one of which was relevant to his early understanding of freedom of speech; the book was *Commentaries on the Laws of England,* by Sir William Blackstone. It was the first book on his

---

[1] The first quote is from a letter from OWH to Lady Ellen Askwith, June 28, 1916, qtd. in Mark DeWolfe Howe, *Justice Oliver Wendell Holmes: The Proving Years, 1870–1882* (Cambridge, MA: Harvard University Press, 1963), at 2:31–32. The second quote is from the address "Sidney Bartlett," March 23, 1889, reproduced in Sheldon M. Novick, ed., *The Collected Works of Justice Holmes* (Chicago: University of Chicago Press, 1995), at 3:480–81.

law school reading list.[2] In that seminal work, Holmes probably read one of its most memorable lines: "The liberty of the press consists in laying no previous restraint upon publications, and not in the freedom from censure for criminal matters when published. . . . [And if anyone] publishes what is improper, mischievous or illegal, he must take the consequences of his own temerity."[3]

Another book on his law school reading list – the fourth one he read[4] – was James Kent's *Commentaries on American Law*. Here he found a view of free speech principles more liberal than the one offered by William Blackstone. "The liberal communication of sentiment, and entire freedom of discussion, in respect to the character and conduct of public men, and of candidates for public favour," wrote Kent, "is deemed essential to the judicious exercise of the right of suffrage, and of that control over their rulers, which resides in the free people of these United States."[5] In that famous treatise, Holmes would find an important free speech case, *Commonwealth v. Blanding* (1825), authored by Chief Justice Isaac Parker of the Massachusetts Supreme Judicial Court. And in that libel case, in which the defendant attempted to prove truth as a defense, the chief justice announced the law as governed by article 16 (the press clause) of the Massachusetts Constitution. "[I]t is well understood . . . and received as a commentary on this provision for liberty of the press, that it was intended to prevent all such previous restraints upon publications as had been practiced by other governments, and in early times here, to stifle the efforts of patriots towards enlightening their fellow subjects upon their rights and the duties of the rulers. The Liberty of the press was to be unrestrained, but he who used it was to be responsible in case of its abuse."[6]

---

[2] *See* Eleanor N. Little, "The Early Reading of Justice Oliver Wendell Holmes," 8 *Harvard Library Bulletin* 163, 168 (1954); David S. Bogen, "The Free Speech Metamorphosis of Mr. Justice Holmes," 11 *Hofstra Law Review* 97, 107–08 n. 50 (1982). Although I do not always agree with all of his conclusions, I nonetheless think that Professor Bogen's article is among the finest works of scholarship on Holmes, and I am indebted to him for several of his insights, which I draw on here and elsewhere.

[3] Sir William Blackstone, *Commentaries on the Laws of England*, 7th ed. (London: Strahan & Woodfall, 1775), at 4:151–52.

[4] *See* "The Early Reading of Justice Oliver Wendell Holmes," *supra* note 2, at 168.

[5] James Kent, *Commentaries on American Law*, 12th ed. (Boston: Little, Brown, 1873), at 2:17–18. *See also* "The Free Speech Metamorphosis of Mr. Justice Holmes, *supra* note 2, at 108–10.

[6] *Commonwealth v. Blanding*, 20 Mass. (3 Pick.) 304, 313 (1825). Years later, Holmes cited *Blanding* approvingly, first in his opinion in *Cowley v. Pulsifer*, 137 Mass. 392, 393 (1884) (see Part III) and then in his opinion for the Supreme Court in *Patterson v. Colorado*, 205 U.S. 454, 462 (1907) (see Part IV).

But Holmes's education was not confined to books and legal treatises. In the final months of his time at law school, Holmes ventured
to Europe, where he set out to meet the British philosopher and Member
of Parliament, John Stuart Mill, among others. In a letter of introduction,
Dr. Holmes stressed that his son "is more familiar with Mill's writings than
most fellows of his years."7 By that time, young Holmes had already read
Mills's *Considerations on Representative Government* and his *An Examination of Sir William Hamilton's Philosophy* and Mill's *Utilitarianism*.8 The
two met and even dined.9

By March 1867, Holmes had been admitted to the bar and soon thereafter
practiced law with the Beacon Hill firm of Chandler, Shattuck,10 and
Thayer,11 where he had worked earlier as an apprentice.12 Much of his
attention was devoted to admiralty law, commercial law, and banking and
insurance law in the three or so years he was with the firm. Even so,
he managed to argue his first case13 before the Massachusetts Supreme
Judicial Court a mere eight months after he had been admitted to the bar.

---

7 Qtd. in Francis Biddle, *Mr. Justice Holmes* (New York: Charles Scribner's Sons, 1942),
at 29. *See also* "The Free Speech Metamorphosis of Mr. Justice Holmes, *supra* note 2, at
113–14.
8 *See* "The Early Reading of Justice Oliver Wendell Holmes," *supra* note 2, at 169, 171.
9 *See* Sheldon M. Novick, *Honorable Justice: The Life of Oliver Wendell Holmes* (New
York: Dell Publishing, 1989), at 105–06. For an account of young Holmes's pilgrimage
to Europe and the impact that Mill and others had on his "maturing mind," *see* Mark
DeWolfe Howe, *Justice Oliver Wendell Holmes: The Shaping Years* (Cambridge, MA:
Harvard University Press, 1957), at 1:208–44.
10 George O. Shattuck, a Harvard law graduate and classmate of James Bradley Thayer.
Shattuck was a highly able lawyer. He was thirty-seven when he hired Holmes, then
twenty-five. Of him, Holmes once said: "I owe to Mr. Shattuck more than I have ever
owed to anyone else in the world, outside my immediate family." *Holmes-Laski Letters:
The Correspondence of Mr. Justice Holmes and Harold J. Laski, 1916–1935* (Cambridge,
MA: Harvard University Press, 1953), at 2:930. *See generally Justice Oliver Wendell Holmes:
The Shaping Years, supra* note 9, at 1:248–61.
11 James Bradley Thayer (1831–1902) was a lawyer and graduate of Harvard College and the
Law School. In 1873 he became a professor of law at Harvard. In 1893 he published his
The Origin and Scope of the American Doctrine of Constitutional Law (Boston: Little,
Brown). *See Justice Oliver Wendell Holmes, supra* note 9, at 1:247–48.
12 *See Honorable Justice, supra* note 9, at 116–22. The firm was later Shattuck and Thayer. By
1873 Holmes was a partner working with George Shattuck and William Adams Munroe.
Before that, Holmes had also experimented with a solo practice. *See* G. Edward White,
Justice Oliver Wendell Holmes: Law and the Inner Self (New York: Oxford University
Press, 1993), at 128.
13 *Richardson v. New York Central*, 98 Mass. 85 (1867). Holmes lost this conflicts of law
case, though he was subsequently vindicated when, years later, the case was materially
modified, if not overruled, in *Riggint v. Central New England & Western Railroad*, 160
Mass. 571 (1909). For an account, see *Justice Oliver Wendell Holmes: The Shaping Years,
supra* note 9, at 2:275–76.

His practice of law notwithstanding, Holmes had more analytical interests, which kept him engaged in discourse with a circle of scholarly lawyers – John Gray, John Ropes,[14] and Melville Bigelow. It wasn't long afterward that Gray and Ropes founded the *American Law Review*, with Holmes serving as a book reviewer. The more Holmes wrote, the more he liked it. Soon, he was on the review's staff broadening his scholarly horizon by writing digests and commentaries of state and English court decisions – this in addition to writing reviews of new law texts and treatises.[15]

Mindful of Holmes's scholarly bent, James Bradley Thayer invited him to assist in updating Chancellor James Kent's *Commentaries on American Law*, a respected treatise that traced back to 1826. It was a daunting project that required considerable time and effort. Holmes was paid $3,000 for a two-year period. Once he reconceived his assignment, the undertaking changed from merely updating citations to drafting original commentaries. Thayer agreed to this change in direction, and Holmes energetically threw himself into the project while working in his firm. Day by day, his life as a lawyer became that of a legal scholar. He became a regular feature at the Social Law Library, the local reference library. There he wrote and researched the law, both for the *American Law Review* and for the *Commentaries*. By 1870 he was the coeditor of the *Review* and was starting to make his mark on the law. As he began to write more and more,[16] he leaned more toward the academic side of life. In 1870–71, he taught constitutional law to Harvard College students and became a university lecturer on jurisprudence. This explosion in intellectual energy continued when Holmes became the editor of the *American Law Review*. Soon enough he would be teaching at the Harvard Law School, this after having left the

---

[14] Gray and Ropes were both Harvard graduates and highly competent lawyers with scholarly bents. For Holmes's memorial tribute to John Gray – a longtime friend and man he greatly admired and respected – see his "John Chipman Gray," delivered at a meeting of the Massachusetts Historical Society, March 12, 1915, reproduced in *Collected Works of Justice Holmes*, *supra* note 1, at 3:441–42. Years later, Gray and Ropes's *War Letters: 1862–1865* (Boston: Houghton Mifflin, 1927) was published.

[15] *See Honorable Justice*, *supra* note 9, at 116, 119; Harry C. Shriver, ed., *Justice Oliver Wendell Holmes: His Book Notices and Uncollected Letters and Papers* (New York: Central Book, 1936); *Collected Works of Justice Holmes*, *supra* note 1, at 1:181–335 (collecting Holmes's writings for the *American Law Review*).

[16] In 1871 Holmes reviewed Thomas Cooley's *Constitutional Limitations* for the *American Law Review*. For a discussion of this, *see* "Free Speech Metamorphosis of Mr. Justice Holmes," *supra* note 2, at 116–19 ("Holmes may not have been impressed by Cooley's [restrictive] view of speech because the view had little practical importance...." In the context of the times, "the 'bogeyman' of punishment for 'harmless publications' feared by Cooley would have seemed, to Holmes, simply a bad dream. Cooley set forth no instances of unconstitutional state laws and cited no authority for this argument.").

Shattuck law firm and venturing out to open his own solo firm, albeit with some help from his brother, Edward, who was also a lawyer.[17]

About this time, Holmes married his longtime sweetheart Fanny Bowditch; they first met when he was eleven. But the joys of the marital occasion were tempered when, a month after their June 1872 marriage, Fanny came down with a serious attack of rheumatic fever that left her bedridden for months afterward. Perhaps this prompted the thirty-one-year-old lawyer-scholar to immerse himself even more in his erudite endeavors. With that vigor, and some later proofreading assistance from Fanny, Holmes's passion for achievement produced the December 1873 publication of the twelfth edition of *Kent's Commentaries*, which he edited. This period also saw the publication of an important note Holmes published in the *American Law Review*, a piece titled "The Gas-Stokers' Strike," which appears later in this chapter. In this piece, we see early on in Holmes's jurisprudence the idea of competition in the marketplace (though Holmes did not use those precise words). This competitive ideal found a place in Holmes's thought, both as a legal and as a philosophical principle. It was part of the fabric of social Darwinism, an idea then in vogue in the circles in which Holmes traveled. Those circles included the likes of William James, Charles Pierce, and others. Similarly, pragmatism – buttressed by a commitment to professionalism, a confidence in science, and a dedication to disinterested inquiry – was a part of the thinking to which Holmes was first exposed and that he then embraced; in short time it, too, found its own special expression in his developing thought.[18]

June 23, 1874, was a special day at Harvard, for it was the occasion of the dedication of Memorial Hall. This was the hall where the names of Harvard's fallen Civil War soldiers were enshrined on the walls. It was a heavily attended and moving ceremony capped by a poem by Dr. Holmes that ended with these lines: "Firm were their hearts in danger's Hour / Sweet was their manhood's morning Flower / Their hopes with rainbow hues were bright, – How swiftly winged the sudden night! / O' Mother! on thy marble page / Thy children read, from age to age The mighty word that upward leads / Through noble thought to nobler deeds / Truth, heavenborn Truth, their fearless guide / Thy saints have lived, thy heroes died /

---

[17] In March 1873, however, Holmes returned to the fold and formed a partnership: Shattuck, Holmes, and Munroe.

[18] See "Free Speech Metamorphosis of Mr. Justice Holmes," *supra* note 2, at 119–22; *Justice Oliver Wendell Holmes: Law and the Inner Self, supra* note 12, at 92–111; Louis Menand, *The Metaphysical Club: A Story of Ideas in America* (New York: Farrar, Straus & Giroux, 2001), at x–xii, 58–61, 64, 337–75 (338–47 sets out a particularly thoughtful account of Holmesian thinking during this general period); Yosal Rogat, "The Judge as Spectator," 31 *University of Chicago Law Review* 213, 229–43 (1964).

Our love has reared their earthly shrine, Their glory be forever thine!"[19] It would be the kind of event and statement of sentiment that Wendell, the Civil War veteran, would attend and address in later years.[20] For now, his mind and body were elsewhere. With his intellectual sails filled with the air of excitement, Wendell (accompanied by Fanny) had already departed for Europe for an extended trip. The vacation appealed both to Holmes's intellectual side and to his more passionate side – his ladies'-man side. Though he dabbled and thus gave vent to that side of his personality, and sometimes did so in an adventurous way, it did not last.[21] In the long run, his ambition and cerebral passion won out. On that score, the aspiring lawyer was determined to make a name for himself in the world of law and ideas.

Holmes's ambition may well have been fed in 1878 when he was considered for a federal judgeship in connection with a district court vacancy that had just opened up. His close friend John C. Gray had previously written to the State Department in support of Holmes's candidacy: "Mr. Holmes, has been solicited by several members of the bar, not his personal friends, to be a candidate for the office, and he has consented to accept it, should it be tendered to him, though he does not want to take any personal step himself."[22] When President Rutherford Hayes reviewed the matter he seemed favorably disposed: "I rather think Holmes is the man," he is reported to have said.[23] Although Holmes wanted the position and felt some "mild excitement" regarding the prospect, he did harbor some doubts. "[I] hardly know whether to be glad or sorry," he wrote to Frederick Pollock.[24] As it turned out, the federal judgeship never came his way, which allowed him to continue his law practice and his scholarly pursuits.

❧

[19] "The Dedication of Memorial Hall," *New York Times,* June 24, 1874, at 5.

[20] Holmes, "A Soldier's Faith," May 30, 1895 (see Part I). The speech was given in Harvard's Memorial Hall.

[21] *See* G. Edward White, "Holmes's 'Life Plan': Confronting Ambition, Passion, and Powerlessness," 65 *New York University Law Review* 1409, 1437–39 (1990); *Justice Oliver Wendell Holmes: Law and the Inner Self, supra* note 12, at 226–27. For an account of Holmes's curious relationship with Clare Castletown, *see ibid.* at 230–52, 601–02. *See also* Morton J. Horwitz, *The Transformation of American Law, 1870–1960* (New York: Oxford University Press, 1991), at 142–43*.

[22] Letter from John C. Gray to William M. Evarts, Department of Justice, General Records, Archives, reproduced in *Justice Holmes: The Proving Years, supra* note 1, at 2:130–31.

[23] George F. Hoar, *Autobiography of Seventy Years* (New York: Charles Scribner's Sons, 1903), at 2:416–19 (Hoar was then Massachusetts's junior senator).

[24] Letter from OWH to Frederick Pollock, December 9, 1878, reproduced in Mark DeWolfe Howe, ed., *Holmes-Pollock Letters: The Correspondence of Mr. Justice Holmes and Sir Frederick Pollock, 1874–1932* (Cambridge, MA: Harvard University Press, 1942), at 10–11.

In January 1879, Holmes traveled with George Shattuck to Washington, D.C., to argue his first case before the U.S. Supreme Court: *United States v. Oakes A. Ames & Oliver M. Ames, 2nd, Executors of Oakes Ames*.[25] It was a complicated equity case. Following Holmes's analytical direction, the Court ruled 8–1 in his client's favor.[26] This achievement reflected Holmes's mastery of the law. It confirmed his reputation as a scholarly lawyer, one unlike the vast majority of his colleagues either in or outside of Boston. Consistent with that reputation, Holmes was later invited to give a series of twelve prestigious lectures hosted by the Lowell Institute, which planned to offer a course on the common law in the fall of 1880. It would change his life far more than the federal judgeship would have had it been offered to him.

The Lowell Institute, with its links to the Athenaeum library, the banking world, Unitarian thinkers, and Beacon Hill Boston, "had quickly become a leading New England dispenser of culture. An invitation to lecture there was coveted by every scholar in the town."[27] The lectures, which had previously been given by illustrious speakers such as his father, Dr. Holmes (in 1853), and Professor Louis Agassiz (in 1846–47),[28] were held in Boston and given on Tuesday and Friday evenings, beginning on November 23, 1880, and ending on December 31, 1880. Huntington Hall on Trenton Street, where the lectures were held, "was nearly full, with young men reported to outnumber older, although the latter were also liberally represented." Louis Brandeis, the twenty-four-year-old progressive lawyer, was there, as was the chief justice of Massachusetts's high court, for whom Brandeis had worked, along with some state lawmakers.[29]

Holmes delivered the twelve lectures "without reference to his manuscript, as if, a member of the audience later recalled, 'he were narrating offhand some interesting story, or telling of the happening of some event of absorbing interest.' . . . The *Boston Advertiser*, in which the entire series had been covered in some detail, reported that 'no other course in the institute in recent years has been attended by so large a proportion of

---

[25] *United States v. Ames*, 99 U.S. 35 (1879).

[26] *Justice Holmes: The Proving Years*, *supra* note 1, at 128–29.

[27] Liva Baker, *The Justice from Beacon Hill: The Life and Times of Oliver Wendell Holmes* (New York: HarperCollins, 1991), at 252.

[28] *See* Edwin P. Hoyt, *The Improper Bostonian: Dr. Oliver Wendell Holmes* (New York: William Morrow, 1979), at 153–54; Edward Lurie, *Louis Agassiz: A Life in Science* (Baltimore: Johns Hopkins University Press, 1988), at 126–28.

[29] *The Justice from Beacon Hill*, *supra* note 27, at 252. In the summer of 1879, Brandeis spent a weekend with the Holmeses at their country residence and later dined with them frequently. *See* Philippa Strum, *Louis D. Brandeis: Justice for the People* (Cambridge, MA: Harvard University Press, 1984), at 35.

young men – an evidence both of the interest they have in the law and the power of Mr. Holmes to interest them.'" The lectures (or eleven of the twelve) were compiled and published by Little, Brown, and Company in 1881 under the title *The Common Law* and sold for $4. Holmes celebrated the event with a bottle of fine champagne, the cork of which he saved for years as a little memento of this glorious event.[30]

In the book, Holmes analyzed several topics that would later affect his free speech jurisprudence. Those topics included discussions of the law of attempts and conspiracy, the law of defamation, objective versus subjective standards of liability, and Holmes's overall theory of common law judging. In Lecture II, the second lecture of *The Common Law*, Holmes even discussed a hypothetical concerning the law of criminal attempts and the "lighting a match with intent to set fire to a haystack . . . although the defendant blew out the match on seeing that he was watched." That hypothetical and the other previously mentioned topics all went into the mix that would later produce *Schenck v. United States* (1919) and its Holmesian progeny (see Parts V and VI).

The year following the publication of *The Common Law*, Holmes achieved another one of his life goals: he was nominated to be a justice on the Massachusetts Supreme Judicial Court (see Part III). That turn of fate gave him a chance to put some of his theoretical ideas into practice, especially those set forth in *The Common Law*.[31]

↭

The article "Privilege, Malice, and Intent" was published while Holmes was on the Massachusetts high court. Though chronologically it should come later in this volume, it is included here to more sharply contrast it with some of the things Holmes posited in *The Common Law*. In the 1894 essay, Holmes returned to one of the main themes of *The Common Law*, namely, the importance of an objective standard in the law. The issue arose in connection with two unfair competition rulings rendered recently by English courts.[32] In both cases, the courts employed a subjective standard to decide whether the combination of economic forces – in one case, that

---

[30] *The Justice from Beacon Hill, supra* note 27, at 252–53.

[31] *See Justice Oliver Wendell Holmes: Law and the Inner Self, supra* note 12, at 148–95.

[32] *See Mogul Steamship Co. v. McGregor*, 23 Q.B.D. 598 (1892) (subjective standard employed: court upheld right of merchants to combine); *Temperton v. Russell*, 1 Q.B. 715 (1893) (subjective standard employed: court disallowed union from striking). *See also* Morton J. Horwitz, "The Place of Justice Holmes in American Legal Thought," in *The Legacy of Oliver Wendell Holmes, Jr.*, ed. Robert W. Gordon (Stanford, CA: Stanford University Press, 1992), at 55–59.

of merchants, in another, that of union workers – was privileged under the relevant law. "This treatment of the labor cases," however, "suggested some difficulties for the jurisprudential theories Holmes had advanced in *The Common Law*."[33] Hence, the law's evolutionary bent, buttressed by objective concepts of liability, could not account for a satisfactory analysis of such cases. In response, Holmes revised what he wrote in *The Common Law* and did so in a way that counseled judges to engage in a balancing of interests and thereby make certain social policy determinations. This conceptual move, it has been argued, marks the "beginning of modernism in American legal thought."[34] Moreover, this general move toward legal realism would find yet bolder expression in Holmes's subsequent essay "The Path of the Law" essay (see Part III), and it would later help to inform his 1919 free speech decisions as well (see Parts V and VI).

By the end of 1881, the Holmesian jurisprudential edifice was well under way, and Holmes's reputation as a respected legal scholar was likewise being fortified. He was not yet a national figure, but he was a figure of increasing stature. Meanwhile, life at Harvard was good; life at their new residence at 10 Beacon Street in Boston was Spartan but satisfying; and life overall was as pleasing as one of Fanny's embroidered panels, the same ones that had recently been on exhibit at the Boston Art Museum.[35] And all of this for a man of forty, a man who would live yet another half century and who had much more wind left in his sails.

The struggle for life . . . is equally the law of human existence.

THE GAS-STOKERS' STRIKE[36]

The famous strike of the gas-stokers[37] in December last, by which all London was plunged for several nights into partial darkness, at last found its way into the courts. The company prosecuted five men for conspiracy. The

---

[33] *Justice Oliver Wendell Holmes: Law and the Inner Self, supra* note 12, at 216.

[34] "Place of Justice Holmes in American Legal Thought," *supra* note 32, at 57.

[35] *See* John S. Monagan, *The Grand Panjandrum: Mellow Years of Justice Holmes* (Lanham, MD: University Press of America, 1988), at 49–50.

[36] Note, "The Gas-Stokers' Strike," 7 *American Law Review* 582 (July 1873). This unsigned note was written in partial response to two articles: John Morley, "The Five Gas-Stokers," 13 *Fortnightly Review* 138 (January 1873), and Henry Crompton, "Class Legislation," 13 *Fortnightly Review* 205 (February 1873). Both articles were critical of the British judge's ruling in the case, though Holmes's interest in his note was more focused on responding to Crompton. – *Ed.*

[37] A person who feeds and tends a furnace. – *Ed.*

trial lasted only one day; the facts were simple and undisputed, substantially as follows: The stokers were hired by the company under special contracts, which require a certain notice to be given of an intention to leave work; the time of this notice varies in the contracts of different classes of workmen, ranging from one week to thirty days. Most of the stokers were combined together into a trade-union association. One of them, a member of the association, was discharged by the company, for what cause [was unknown]; but it was not claimed that the discharge was in violation of the contract. His fellow [union] members . . . demanded his reinstatement, but in vain. They were thereupon . . . refused altogether to go to work unless their demand was complied with. There was no violence towards officers of the company; but there was some violence, accompanied by a good deal of threatening, towards members of the [union] who had not been advised of the intention of the conspirators, and who at first hesitated to fall in with [their plans]. The court charged that the defendants had a perfect right to form a trade-union, and that the fact that their action was in restraint of trade, which would have made it an offense at common law, could not be considered in this action; but that the company alleged that the defendants either agreed to do an unlawful act or to do a lawful act by unlawful means; and he asked the jury whether there was a combination between the defendants either to hinder or prevent the company from carrying on [its] business by means of the men simultaneously breaking [their contract] . . . with the company. This was an illegal act, and, what was more, a criminal act. If they did agree to interfere with their employers' business, by simultaneously breaking such contracts, they were then agreeing to do that which would bring them within the definition of [criminal] conspiracy.

The jury [was] out only twenty minutes, and then brought in a verdict of guilty, but with a recommendation to mercy. This, however, the court disregarded, and sentenced the accused to imprisonment for one year. In imposing the sentence the judge said that he had told the jury that "on the question whether they were to find the defendants guilty or not, they ought not to be influenced by the suggestion that what they were attempting to do would be dangerous to the public. But it did not seem to him now, when he was called on to consider what kind of conspiracy they had been guilty of, that he could throw aside what was one of the obvious results of the conspiracy into which they entered, and what must have been in their minds; and he could not doubt that the obvious result was great danger to the public . . . ; that the danger was present to their minds; and it was by the acting on that knowledge and on the effect they thought it would have upon their masters' minds, and trading upon their knowledge of the danger, that they entered into this conspiracy, in order to force their masters to follow their will. . . .

"The prisoners were the principals – the chief actors; two of them were delegates chosen by the men, and therefore evidently men to whom they looked up. They took a leading part in the conspiracy. Therefore, notwithstanding their good character they had unfortunately put themselves into the position of being properly convicted of a dangerous and wicked conspiracy. The time had come when serious a punishment, and not a nominal or light one, must be inflicted – a punishment that would teach men in their position that, although without offence they might be members of a trade union, or might agree to go into an employment, or to leave it without committing an offence, yet that they must take care when they agreed together that they must not agree to do it by illegal means. If they did that they were guilty of conspiracy, and if they misled others they were guilty of a wicked conspiracy." . . . [38]

. . . It has always seemed to us a singular anomaly that believers in the theory of evolution and in the natural development of institutions by successive adaptations to the environment should be found laying down a theory of government intended to establish its limits once for all by a logical deduction from axioms. But the objection [that] we wish to express at the present time is that this presupposes an identity of interest between the different parts of the community [that] does not exist in fact. Consistently with his views, Mr. Spencer[39] is forever putting cases to show that the reaction of legislation is equal to its action. By changing the laws, he argues, you do not get rid of any burden, but only change the mode of bearing it; and if the change does not make it easier to bear for society, considered as a whole, legislation is inexpedient. This tacit assumption of the solidarity of interests of society is very common, but seems to us to be false. The struggle for life, undoubtedly, is constantly putting the interests of men at variance with those of the lower animals. And the struggle does not stop in the ascending scale with the monkeys, but is equally the law of human existence. Outside of legislation this is undeniable. It is mitigated by sympathy, prudence, and all the social and moral qualities. But in the last resort a man rightly prefers his own interest to that of his neighbors. And this is true in legislation as in any other form of corporate action. All that

[38] According to the compiler of Holmes's papers, the first three paragraphs of this note were authored by Holmes's cousin and friend John Torrey Morse Jr. *See Collected Works of Justice Holmes, supra* note 1, at 1:325 n. 1. – *Ed.*

[39] Herbert Spencer (1820–1903) was an English philosopher and political theorist who ventured to apply Darwin's theory of evolution to social and political contexts, among other areas. He coined the phrase "survival of the fittest" in his book *Principles of Biology* (1864). In May 1866, the young Holmes tried unsuccessfully to visit Spencer while in England. Years later, Justice Holmes referred to Spencer in a famous passage in his dissent in *Lochner v. New York*, 198 U.S. 45, 75 (1905) ("The 14th Amendment does not enact Mr. Herbert Spencer's Social Statics."). – *Ed.*

can be expected form modern improvements is that legislation should easily and quickly, yet not too quickly, modify itself in accordance with the will of the *de facto* supreme power in the community, and that the spread of an educated sympathy should reduce the sacrifice of minorities to a minimum. But whatever body may possess the supreme power for the moment is certain to have interests inconsistent with others who have competed unsuccessfully. The more powerful interests must be more or less reflected in legislation; which, like every other device of man or beast, must tend in the long run to aid the survival of the fittest. The objection to class legislation is not that it favors a class, but either that it fails to benefit the legislators, or that it is dangerous to them because a competing class has gained in power, or that it transcends the limits of self-preference which are imposed by sympathy. Interference with contracts by usury laws and the like is open to the first objection, that it only makes the burden of borrowers heavier. The law brought to bear upon gas-stokers is perhaps open to the second, that it requires to be backed by a more unquestioned power than is now possessed by the favored class; and some English statutes are also very probably open to the third. . . . But it is no sufficient condemnation of legislation that it favors one class at the expense of another; for much or all legislation does that; and [nonetheless] when the bona fide object is the greatest good for the greatest number. Why should the greatest number be preferred? Why not the greatest good of the most intelligent and most highly developed? The greatest good of a minority of our generation may be the greatest good of the greatest number in the long run. But if the welfare of all future ages is to be considered, legislation may as well be abandoned for the present. If the welfare of the living majority is paramount, it can only be on the ground that the majority [has] the power in [its] hands. . . . [L]egislation in this country . . . is necessarily made a means by which a body, having the power, put burdens [that] are disagreeable to them on the shoulders of somebody else. Communism would no more get rid of the difficulty than any other system, unless it limited or put a stop to the propagation of the species. And it may be doubted whether that solution would not be as disagreeable as any other.

COMMENTARY

Pro labor view? – Holmes was thirty-two when the Gas Stokers piece was published in the *American Law Review*. He was a Boston lawyer then, his practice being mainly the representation of companies. By that measure, one would have thought he would be pro-business and therefore unsympathetic to labor unions, strikes, and boycotts. But Holmes broke class ranks in his note, writing as if it were a dissent to a contrary opinion of the law. That opinion did not focus on the civil liability, if any, of the strikers for breach of contract, but rather on the invocation of penal law to punish them for their collective acts of striking. As indicated in his note, the British judge who presided over the trial of the London strikers agreed with the jury that the peaceful strikes were unlawful but disagreed with its recommendation of "mercy" – he sentenced the defendants to a year in prison. For Holmes, this view of the common law was untenable. The ideas he advanced in the note, however, had little or nothing to do with liberal, or pro-labor, or humanitarian values, which were not his trade in thought. The fact is that Holmes had a low opinion of worker strikes. *See, e.g.*, his opinion in *Plant v. Woods*, 176 Mass. 492, 505, 57 N.E. 1011, 1016 (1900).

Law as the prerogative of the powerful – "Holmes . . . suggested that the prosecution of the gas-stokers should be condemned, if at all" on the grounds "that it was initiated and carried through by those who were unaware that the de facto power of labor had reached such proportions that the erstwhile ruling class must recognize that their own power was no longer supreme."

"A notable aspect of this [view] is its implicit qualification – perhaps rejection – of the Austinian concept of sovereignty. Holmes, who never formulated either a political or legal theory of sovereignty, in this brief comment, however, made it clear that he was anxious to look beyond the concept of a theoretically 'sovereign state' to those forces which actually determine the incidence of public power and authority. The 'legislators,' in Holmes's mind, were not the members of Parliament or the English judges who enforced the Statutes of the Realm and the common law of England. There were the persons and the class whose actual, *de facto* power was so real that the Parliament and the Courts felt a political obligation to give effect to their wishes." For Holmes, then, "the ultimate issue of where sovereignty resides turns upon the answer to a question of fact. The lawmakers, whether they be judges or members of a legislature, must always seek to calculate the existing allocation of power and, having made their calculation, give effect as law, to the demands of that group which, as survivor in the Darwinian struggle, has proven itself to be fittest." Mark DeWolfe Howe, *Justice Oliver Wendell Holmes: The Proving Years, 1870–1882* (Cambridge, MA: Harvard University Press, 1963), 2:45.

Law and the clash of groups – "Holmes['s] perspective of law as civilization was that of a generation which had sat at the feet of Charles Darwin, Herbert Spencer, and Walter Bagehot.[40] Life was a struggle for existence, and Holmes

---

[40] Walter Bagehot (1826–77) was a noted essayist, journalist, editor at the *Economist*, and author of several books, including *The English Constitution* (1867), a widely read treatise. – Ed.

had a healthy respect for the survivors, whether men or institutions." Max Lerner, *The Mind and Faith of Justice Holmes* (New Brunswick, NJ: Transaction Publishers, 1989), at 44. In Holmes's mind, "life was a continual clash of groups – nations, races, classes – representing great conflicting principles, struggling for survival in a world of limited resources. The task of the judge was to choose fairly between contending forces. Political truth," as we will see in Part VI, "was to be worked out in the competition of the marketplace and not imposed by armies of police." Sheldon M. Novick, ed., *The Collected Works of Justice Holmes* (Chicago: University of Chicago Press, 1995), 1:17.

Darwinian and Malthusian thinking – Mark DeWolfe Howe, one of Holmes's most esteemed biographers, points to this 1873 note as evidence of Holmes's Darwinian mind-set or, more accurately, his Malthusian mind-set. *See Justice Oliver Wendell Holmes: The Proving Years, supra*, 2:48. Years later, in a letter to a friend, Holmes admitted: "I am a devout Malthusian as you know." OWH to Harold Laski, September 16, 1924, reproduced in *Holmes-Laski Letters: The Correspondence of Mr. Justice Holmes and Harold Laski*, Mark DeWolfe Howe, ed. (Cambridge, MA: Harvard University Press, 1953), at 1:658. A key component of such Malthusian thinking is the idea that "to the apparently narrow principle of self-interest which prompts each individual to exert himself in bettering his condition, we are indebted for all the noblest exertions of human genius, for everything that distinguishes the civilized from the savage state." Thomas Robert Malthus, *Principles of Population*, 8th ed. (London: 1878), at 480.

The right of association – Long before the Supreme Court addressed the question of First Amendment protection for freedom of association in *NAACP v. Alabama*, 357 U.S. 449 (1958), Holmes wrote of its importance in various scholarly and judicial works, though his reasons for valuing it were different from those articulated by Justice Harlan in the 1958 case. Holmes firmly "believed that the right of association was to the long-term advantage of society. At every opportunity, he applauded man's tendency to combine. In his theoretical writings, his correspondence, and in his judicial opinions, he repeatedly characterized modern society as based on the individual's right to form groups by way of the right to contract. Capitalists had the right to form ever-larger corporations and laborers the analogous to form corresponding unions." H. L. Pohlman, *Justice Oliver Wendell Holmes: Free Speech and the Living Constitution* (New York: New York University Press, 1991), at 40.

Repairing the competitive ideal – Although Holmes either discounted the possibility of injury resulting from labor strikes or believed such injuries to be trumped by a public policy favoring a striker's privilege, his views arose in a historical context in which he may well have believed that real competition was being harnessed by laws favoring business. Hence, the question of "the nature and limits of economic struggle had moved to the center of his consciousness due to two major developments. The first arose from the question of economic concentration. To what extent was the rapid organization and concentration of economic power in both England and America legitimate and to be supported by law? In this connection, were there ways in which common law judges could (or should) distinguish fair from unfair competition based on the size or power of the units of competition? A second and more immediate question involved the growing struggle between labor and capital. To what extent was labor organization the same (or different from) business concentration? Should legal rules pertaining to business competition be applied to economic struggles between labor and capital?" Morton J. Horwitz, *The Transformation of American Law: 1870–1960* (New York: Oxford University Press, 1992), at 130–31.

If in the Holmesian sphere there is indeed a place for legal intervention in the competition being waged in the marketplace, and if that intervention is justified in the name of fostering a greater measure of fair competition, then what, if anything, does that imply in First Amendment terms if there was an anticompetitive advantage in the modern media world? *Consider* Jerome A. Barron, *Freedom of the Press for Whom? The Right of Access to the Media* (Bloomington: Indiana University Press, 1973); Jerome A. Barron, "Access Reconsidered," 76 *George Washington Law Review* 826 (2008); C. Edwin Baker, *Media Concentration and Democracy: Why Ownership Matters* (New York: Cambridge University Press, 2007). *But see* both Holmes's comments about communism and his dissent in a later antitrust case, *Northern Securities Company v. United States*, 193 U.S. 197, 400 (1904).

Competitive clashes and content-based laws – To say, as Holmes implied in the Gas Stokers Note, that government cannot categorically favor one group over another is akin to saying that it cannot favor one message over another. In modern First Amendment parlance, the latter is known as the rule barring content-based discrimination. *See Police Department of Chicago v. Mosley*, 408 U.S. 92, 95–96 (1972). So we can see, nearly a century before the idea found express recognition in First Amendment case law, the seeds of a modern doctrine in Holmes's note commenting on a British case.

Preview of opinions to come – The Gas Stokers Note previews what Holmes would write a quarter of a century or so later in two labor cases, *Vegelahn v. Gunter* (1896) and *Plant v. Woods* (1900) (see Part III) and likewise sets the stage for the "free trade in ideas" theme of his famous dissent in *Abrams v. United States* (1919) (see Part VI).

The life of the law has not been logic:
it has been experience.

THE COMMON LAW[41]

Lecture I: Early Forms of Liability

The object of this book is to present a general view of the Common Law. To accomplish the task, other tools are needed besides logic. It is something to show that the consistency of a system requires a particular result, but it is not all. The life of the law has not been logic: it has been experience.[42] The felt necessities of the time, the prevalent moral and political theories, intuitions of public policy, avowed or unconscious, even the prejudices which judges share with their fellow-men, have had a good deal more to do than the syllogism in determining the rules by which men should be governed. The law embodies the story of a nation's development through many centuries, and it cannot be dealt with as if it contained only the axioms and corollaries of a book of mathematics. In order to know what it is, we must know what it has been, and what it tends to become. We must alternately consult history and existing theories of legislation. But the most difficult labor will be to understand the combination of the two into new products at every stage. The substance of the law at any given time pretty nearly corresponds, so far as it goes, with what is then understood to be convenient; but its form and machinery, and the degree to which it is able to work out desired results, depend very much on its past.

In Massachusetts to-day, while, on the one hand, there are a great many rules which are quite sufficiently accounted for by their manifest good sense, on the other, there are some which can only be understood by references to

---

[41] Excerpted from Oliver Wendell Holmes Jr. *The Common Law* (Boston: Little, Brown, 1881) (footnotes omitted). Harvard University Press printed a new edition in 2009 with an introduction by G. Edward White. *The Common Law* was first published on March 3, 1881, shortly before Holmes's fortieth birthday.

[42] This famous line first appeared in an 1880 book review Holmes wrote. *See* Book review of Christopher C. Langdell's *A Selection of Cases on the Law of Contracts*, 14 *American Law Review* 233, 234 (1880), reproduced in *Collected Works of Justice Holmes, supra* note 1, at 3:102–03. For an insightful explanation of Holmes's notion of experience, see *Metaphysical Club, supra* note 18, at 341–47–75. – *Ed.*

the infancy of procedure among the German tribes, or to the social condition of Rome under the Decemvirs.[43]

I shall use the history of our law so far as it is necessary to explain a conception or to interpret a rule, but no further. In doing so there are two errors equally to be avoided both by writer and reader. One is that of supposing, because an idea seems very familiar and natural to us, that it has always been so. Many things [that] we take for granted have had to be laboriously fought out or thought out in past times. The other mistake is the opposite one of asking too much of history. We start with man full grown. It may be assumed that the earliest barbarian whose practices are to be considered had a good many of the same feelings and passions as ourselves.

The first subject to be discussed is the general theory of liability civil and criminal. The Common Law has changed a good deal since the beginning of our series of reports, and the search after a theory [that] may now be said to prevail is a study of tendencies. I believe that it will be instructive to go back to the early forms of liability, and to start from them. . . .

It remains to be proved that, while the terminology of morals is still retained, and while the law does still and always, in a certain sense, measure legal liability by moral standards, it nevertheless, by the very necessity of its nature, is continually transmuting those moral standards into external or objective ones, from which the actual guilt of the party concerned is wholly eliminated.

Lecture II: The Criminal Law

. . . For the most part, the purpose of the criminal law is only to induce external conformity to rule. All law is directed to conditions of things manifest to the senses. And whether it brings those conditions to pass immediately by the use of force, as when it protects a house from a mob by soldiers, or appropriates private property to public use, or hangs a man in pursuance of a judicial sentence, or whether it brings them about immediately through men's fears, its object is equally an external result. In directing itself against robbery or murder, for instance, its purpose is to put a stop to the actual physical taking and keeping of other men's goods, or the actual poisoning, shooting, stabbing, and otherwise putting to death of other men. If those things are not done, the law forbidding them is equally satisfied, whatever the motive.

---

[43] A commission of ten men who wrote a code of law, circa 451 BC, defining the principles of Roman law. –Ed.

Considering this purely external purpose of the law together with the fact that it is ready to sacrifice the individual so far as necessary in order to accomplish that purpose, we can see more readily than before that the actual degree of personal guilt involved in any particular transgression cannot be the only element, if it is an element at all, in the liability incurred. So far from its being true, as is often assumed, that the condition of a man's heart or conscience ought to be more considered in determining criminal than civil liability, it might almost be said that it is the very opposite of truth. For civil liability, in its immediate working, is simply a redistribution of an existing loss between two individuals; and it will be argued in the next Lecture that sound policy lets losses lie where they fall, except where a special reason can be shown for interference. The most frequent of such reasons is, that the party who is charged had been to blame.

It is not intended to deny criminal liability, as well as civil, is founded on blameworthiness. Such a denial would shock the moral sense of any civilized community; or, to put it another way, a law which punished conduct [that] would not be blameworthy in the average member of the community would be too severe for that community to bear. It is only intended to point out that, when we are dealing with that part of the law which aims more directly than any other at establishing standards of conduct, we should expect there more than elsewhere to find that the tests of liability are external, and independent of the degree of evil in the particular person's motives or intentions. The conclusion follows directly from the nature of the standards to which conformity is required. These are not only external, as was shown above, but they are general application. They do not merely require that every man should get as near he can to the best conduct possible for him. They require him at his own peril to come up to a certain height. They take no account of incapacities, unless the weakness is so marked as to fall into well-known exceptions, such as infancy or madness. They assume that every man is as able as every other to behave as they command. If they fall on any one class harder than on another, it is on the weakest. For it is precisely to those who are most likely to err by temperament, ignorance, or folly, that the threats of the law are the most dangerous.

The reconciliation of the doctrine that liability is founded on blameworthiness with the existence of liability where the party is not to blame, will be worked out more fully in the next Lecture. It is found in the conception of the average man, the man of ordinary intelligence and reasonable prudence. Liability is said to arise out of such conduct as would be blameworthy in him. But he is an ideal being, represented by the jury when they are appealed to, and his conduct is an external or objective standard when applied to any given individual. That individual may be morally without stain, because he has less than ordinary intelligence or prudence. But he is required to have those qualities at his peril. If he has them, he will not, as a general rule, incur liability without blameworthiness. . . .

If an act is done of which the natural and probable effect under the circumstances is the accomplishment of a substantive crime, the criminal law, while it may properly enough moderate the severity of punishment if the act has not that effect in the particular case, can hardly abstain altogether from punishing it, on any theory. It has been argued that an actual intent is all that can give the act a criminal character in such instances. But if the views which I have advanced as to murder and manslaughter are sound, the same principles ought logically to determine the criminality of acts in general. Acts should be judged by their tendency under the known circumstances, not by the actual intent which accompanies them.

It may be true that in the region of attempts, as elsewhere, the law began with cases of actual intent, as those cases are the most obvious ones. But it cannot stop with them, unless it attaches more importance to the etymological meaning of the word attempt than to the general principles of punishment. Accordingly there is at least color of authority for the proposition that an act is punishable as an attempt, if, supposing it to have produced its natural and probable effect, it would have amounted to a substantive crime.

But such acts are not the only punishable attempts. There is another class in which actual intent is clearly necessary, and the existence of this class as well as the name (attempt) no doubt tends to affect the whole doctrine. Some acts may be attempts or misdemeanors [that] could not have affected the crime unless followed by other acts on the part of the wrong-doer. For instance, lighting a match with intent to set fire to a haystack has been held to amount to a criminal attempt to burn it, although the defendant blew out the match on seeing that he was watched. So the purchase of dies for making counterfeit coin is a misdemeanor, although of course the coin would not be counterfeited unless the dies were used. In such cases the law goes on a new principle, different from that governing most substantive crimes. The reason for punishing any act must generally be to prevent some harm [that] is foreseen as likely to follow that act under the circumstances in which it is done. In most substantive crimes the ground on which that likelihood stands is the common working of natural causes as shown by experience. But when an act is punished the natural effect of which is not harmful under the circumstances, that ground alone will not suffice. The probability does not exist unless there are grounds for expecting that the act done will be followed by other acts in connection with which its effect will be harmful, although not so otherwise.

But as in fact no such acts have followed, it cannot, in general, be assumed, from the mere doing of what has been done, that they would have followed if the actor had not been interrupted. They would not have followed it unless the actor had chosen, and the only way generally available to show that he would have chosen to do them is by showing that he intended to do them when he did what he did. The accompanying intent in that case renders the otherwise innocent act harmful, because it raises a probability that it will be followed by such other acts and events as will all together result in harm. The importance of the intent is not to show that the act was wicked, but to show that it was likely to be followed by hurtful consequences.

It will be readily seen that there are limits to this kind of liability. The law does not punish every act [that] is done with the intent to bring about a crime. If a man starts from Boston to Cambridge for the purpose of committing a murder when he gets there, but is stopped by the draw and goes home, he is no more punishable than if he had sat in his chair and resolved to shoot somebody, but on second thoughts had given up the notion. On the other hand, a slave who ran after a white woman, but desisted before he caught her, has been convicted of an attempt to commit rape. We have seen what amounts to an attempt to burn a haystack; but it was said in the same case, that, if the defendant had gone no further than to buy a box of matches for the purpose, he would not have been liable.

Eminent judges have been puzzled [as to] where to draw the line, or even to state the principle on which it should be drawn, between the two sets of cases. But the principle is believed to be similar to that on which all other lines are drawn by the law. Public policy, that is to say, legislative considerations, are at the bottom of the matter; the considerations being, in this case, the nearness of the danger, the greatness of the harm, and the degree of apprehension felt. When a man buys matches to fire a haystack, or starts on a journey meaning to murder at the end of it, there is still a considerable chance that he will change his mind before he comes to the point. But when he has struck the match, or cocked and aimed the pistol, there is very little chance that he will not persist to the end, and the danger becomes so great that the law steps in. With an object [that] could not be used innocently, the point of intervention might be put further back, as in the case of the purchase of a die for coining.

The degree of apprehension may affect the decision, as well as the degree of probability that the crime will be accomplished. No doubt the fears peculiar to a slaveowning community had their share in the conviction [that] has just been mentioned.

There is one doubtful point [that] should not be passed over. It has been thought that to shoot at a block of wood thinking it to be a man is not an attempt to murder, and that to put a hand into an empty pocket, intending to pick it, is not an attempt to commit larceny, although on the latter question there is a difference of opinion. The reason given is, that an act which could not have affected the crime if the actor had been allowed to follow it up to all results to which in the nature of things it could have led, cannot be an attempt to commit that crime when interrupted. At some point or other, of course, the law must adopt this conclusion, unless it goes on the theory of retribution for guilt, and not of prevention of harm.

But even to prevent harm effectually it will not do to be too exact. I do not suppose that firing a pistol at a man with intent to kill him is any the less an attempt to murder because the bullet misses its aim. Yet there the act has produced the whole effect possible to it in the course of nature. It is just as impossible that that bullet under those circumstances should hit that man, as to pick an empty pocket. But there is no difficulty in saying that such an act under such circumstances is so dangerous, so far as the possibility of human foresight is concerned, that it should be punished. No one can absolutely know, though many would be pretty sure, exactly where the bullet will strike; and if the harm is done, it is a very great harm. If a man fires at a block, no harm can possibly ensue, and no theft can be committed in an empty pocket, besides that the harm of successful theft is less than that of murder. Yet it might be said that even such things as these should be punished, in order to make discouragement broad enough and easy to understand. . . .

. . . The whole evil [that] the law seeks to prevent is the natural and manifestly certain consequence of the act under the known circumstances. In such a case, if the law of larceny is consistent with the theories here maintained, the act should be passed upon according to its tendency, and the actual intent of the wrong-doer [is] not in any way considered. Yet it is possible, to say the least, that even in such a case the intent would make all the difference. I assume that the act was without excuse and wrongful, and that it would have amounted to larceny, if done for the purpose of depriving the owner of his horse. Nevertheless, if it was done for the sake of an experiment, and without actual foresight of the destruction, or evil design against the owner, the trespasser might not be held a thief. . . .

In the characteristic type of substantive crime acts are rendered criminal because they are done under circumstances in which they will probably cause some harm [that] the law seeks to prevent.

The test of criminality in such cases is the degree of danger shown by experience to attend that act under those circumstances.

In such cases the *mens rea*, or actual wickedness of the party, is wholly unnecessary, and all reference to the state of his consciousness is misleading if it means anything more than that the circumstances in connection with which the tendency of his act is judged are the circumstances known to him. Even the requirement of knowledge is subject to certain limitations. A man must find out at his peril things [that] a reasonable and prudent man would have inferred from the things actually known. . . .

In some cases it may be that the consequence of the act, under the circumstances, must be actually foreseen, if it is a consequence [that] a prudent man would not have foreseen. The reference to the prudent man, as a standard, is the only form in which blameworthiness as such is an element of crime. . . .

Lecture III: Torts – Trespass and Negligence

. . . An act is always a voluntary muscular contraction, and nothing else. The chain of physical sequences [that] it sets in motion or directs to the plaintiff's harm is no part of it, and very generally a long train of such sequences intervenes. An example or two will make this extremely clear.

When a man commits an assault and battery with a pistol, his only act is to contract the muscles of his arm and forefinger in a certain way, but it is the delight of elementary writers to point out what a vast series of physical changes must take place before the harm is done. Suppose that, instead of firing a pistol, he takes up a hose [that] is discharging water on the sidewalk, and directs it at the plaintiff, he does not even set in motion the physical causes which must co-operate with his act to make a battery. Not only natural causes, but a living being, may intervene between the act and its effect. *Gibbons v. Pepper* [1695], which decided that there was no battery when a man's horse was frightened by accident or a third person and ran away with him, and ran over the plaintiff, takes the distinction that, if the rider by spurring is the cause of the accident, then he is guilty. In *Scott v. Shepherd* [1773], trespass was maintained against one who had thrown a squib into a crowd, where it was tossed from hand to hand in self-defence until it burst and injured the plaintiff. Here even human agencies were a part of the chain between the defendant's act and the result, although they were treated as more or less nearly automatic, in order to arrive at the decision.

Now I repeat that, if principle requires us to charge a man in trespass when his act has brought force to bear on another through a comparatively short train of intervening causes, in spite of his having used all possible care, it requires the same liability, however numerous and unexpected the events between the act and the result. If running a man down is a trespass when the accident can be referred to the rider's act of spurring, why is it not a tort in every case, seeing that it can always be referred more remotely to his act of mounting and taking the horse out?

Why is a man not responsible for the consequences of an act innocent in its direct and obvious effects, when those consequences would not have followed but for the intervention of a series of extraordinary, although natural events? The reason is that, if the intervening events are of such a kind that no foresight could have been expected to look out for them, the defendant is not to blame for having failed to do so. It seems to be admitted by the English judges that, even on the question whether the acts of leaving dry trimmings in hot weather by the side of a railroad, and then sending an engine over the track, are negligent – that is, are a ground of liability – the consequences which might reasonably be anticipated are material. Yet these are acts [that], under the circumstances, can hardly be called innocent in their natural and obvious effects. The same doctrine has been applied to acts in violation of statute [that] could not reasonably have been expected to lead to the result complained of.

But there is no difference in principle between the case where a natural cause or physical factor intervenes after the act in some way not to be foreseen, and turns what seemed innocent to harm, and the case where such a cause or factor intervenes, unknown, at the time; as for the matter of that, it did in the English cases cited. If a man is excused in the one case because he is not to blame, he must be in the other. The difference taken in *Gibbons v. Pepper* is not between results which are and those which are not the consequences of the defendant's acts: it is between consequences which he was bound as a reasonable man to contemplate, and those which he was not. Hard spurring is just so much more likely to lead to harm than merely riding a horse in the street that the court thought that the defendant would be bound to look out of the consequences of the one, while it would not hold him liable for those resulting merely from the other; because the possibility of being run away with when riding quietly, though familiar is comparatively slight. If, however, the horse had been unruly, and had been taken into a frequented place for the purpose of being broken, the owner might have been liable, because "it was his fault to bring a wild horse into a place where mischief might probably be done."

To return to the example of the accidental blow with a stick lifted in self-defence, there is no difference between hitting a person standing in one's rear and hitting one who was pushed by a horse within range of the stick just as it was lifted, provided that it was not possible, under the circumstances, in the one case to have known, in the other to have anticipated, the proximity. In either case there is wanting only the element [that] distinguishes voluntary acts from spasmodic muscular contractions as a ground of liability. In neither of them, that is to say, has there been an opportunity of choice with reference to the consequence complained of – a chance to guard against the result which has come to pass. A choice [that] entails a concealed consequence is as to that consequence no choice.

The general principle of our law is that loss from accident must lie where it falls, and this principle is not affected by the fact that a human being is the instrument of misfortune. But relatively to a given human being anything is accident which he could not fairly have been expected to contemplate as possible, and therefore to avoid. In the language of the late Chief Justice [Samuel] Nelson of New York: "No case or principle can be found or if found can be maintained, subjecting an individual to liability for an act done without fault on his part. . . . All the cases concede that an injury arising from inevitable accident, or, which in law or reason is the same thing, from an act that ordinary human care and foresight are unable to guard against, is but the misfortune of the sufferer, and lays no foundation for legal responsibility."[44] If this were not so, any act would be sufficient, however remote, which set in motion or opened the door for a series of physical sequences ending in damage; such as riding the horse, in the case of the runaway, or even coming to a place where one is seized with a fit and strikes the plaintiff in an unconscious spasm. Nay, why need the defendant have acted at all, and why is it not enough that his existence has been at the expense of the plaintiff? The requirement of an act is the requirement that the defendant should have made a choice. But the only possible purpose of introducing this moral element is to make the power of avoiding the evil complained of a condition of liability. There is no such power where the evil cannot be foreseen. Here we reach the argument from policy. . . .

A man need not, it is true, do this or that act – the term act implies a choice – but he must act somehow. Furthermore, the public generally profits by individual activity. As action cannot be avoided, and tends to the public good, there is obviously no policy in throwing the hazard of what is at once desirable and inevitable upon the actor.

The state might conceivably make itself a mutual insurance company against accidents, and distribute the burden of its citizens' mishaps among all its members. There might be a pension for paralytics, and state aid for those who suffered in person or estate from tempest or wild beasts. As between individuals it might adopt the mutual insurance principle *pro tanto*,[45] and divide damages when both were in fault . . . or it might throw all loss upon the

[44] *Harvey v. Dunlop*, 39 N.Y.C.L. Rep. 193 (Hill & Dennio Rep. 1843). – *Ed.*
[45] Latin for "only to that extent." – *Ed.*

actor irrespective of fault. The state does none of these things, however, and the prevailing view is that its cumbrous and expensive machinery ought not to be set in motion unless some clear benefit is to be derived from disturbing the status quo. State interference is an evil, where it cannot be shown to be a good. Universal insurance, if desired, can be better and more cheaply accomplished by private enterprise. The undertaking to redistribute losses simply on the ground that they resulted from the defendant's act would not only be open to these objections, but, as it is hoped the preceding discussion has shown, to the still graver one of offending the sense of justice. Unless my act is of a nature to threaten others, unless under the circumstances a prudent man would have foreseen the possibility of harm, it is no more justifiable to make me indemnify my neighbor against the consequences, than to make me do the same thing if I had fallen upon him in a fit, or to compel me to insure him against lightning. . . .

[S]crutiny of the early books will show that liability in general, then as later, was founded on the opinion of the tribunal that the defendant ought to have acted otherwise, in other words, that he was to blame. . . .

Supposing it now to be conceded that the general notion upon which liability to an action is founded is fault or blameworthiness in some sense, the question arises, whether it is so in the sense of personal moral shortcoming. . . . Suppose that a defendant were allowed to testify that, before acting, he considered carefully what would be the conduct of a prudent man under the circumstances, and, having formed the best judgment he could, acted accordingly. If the story was believed, it would be conclusive against the defendant's negligence judged by a moral standard [that] would take his personal characteristics into account. But supposing any such evidence to have got before the jury, it is very clear what the jury would say, Gentlemen, the question is not whether the defendant thought his conduct was that of a prudent man, but whether you think it was. Some middle point must be found between the horns of this dilemma.

The standards of the law are standards of general application. The law takes no account of the infinite varieties of temperament, intellect, and education [that] make the internal character of a given act so different in different men. It does not attempt to see men as God sees them, for more than one sufficient reason. In the first place, the impossibility of nicely measuring a man's power and limitations is far clearer than that of ascertaining his knowledge of law, which has been thought to account for what is called the presumption that every man knows the law. But a more satisfactory explanation is, that, when men live in society, a certain average of conduct, a sacrifice of individual peculiarities going beyond a certain point, is necessary to the general welfare. If, for instance, a man is born hasty and awkward, is always having accidents and hurting himself or his neighbors, no doubt his congenital defects will be allowed for in the courts of Heaven, but his slips are no less troublesome to his neighbors than if they sprang from guilty neglect. His neighbors accordingly require him, at his proper peril, to come up to their standard, and the courts [that] they establish decline to take his personal equation into account.

The rule that the law does, in general, determine liability by blameworthiness, is subject to the limitation that minute differences of character are not allowed for. The law considers, in other words, what would be blameworthy in the average man, the man of ordinary intelligence and prudence, and determines liability by that. If we fall below the level in those gifts, it is our misfortune; so much as that we must have at our peril, for the reasons just given. But he who is intelligent and prudent does not act at his peril, in theory of law. On the contrary, it is only when he fails to exercise the foresight of which he is capable, or exercises it with evil intent, that he is answerable for the consequences.

There are exceptions to the principle that every man is presumed to possess ordinary capacity to avoid harm to his neighbors, which illustrate the rule, and also the moral basis of liability in general. When a man has a distinct defect of such a nature that all can recognize it as making certain precautions impossible, he will not be held answerable for not taking them. A blind man is not required to see at his peril; and although he is, no doubt, bound to consider his infirmity in regulating his actions, yet if he properly finds himself in a certain situation, the neglect of precautions requiring eyesight would not prevent his recovering for an injury to himself, and it may be presumed, would not make him liable for injuring another. So it is held that, in cases where he is the plaintiff, an infant of very tender years is only bound to take the precautions of which an infant is capable; the same principle may be cautiously applied where is a defendant. . . .

Lecture IV: Fraud, Malice, and Intent – The Theory of Torts

. . . I next take up the law of slander. It has often been said that malice is one of the elements of liability, and the doctrine is commonly stated in this way: that malice must exist, but that it is presumed by law from the mere speaking of the words; that again you may rebut this presumption of malice by showing that the words were spoken under circumstances which made the communication privileged – as, for instance, by a lawyer in the necessary course of his argument, or by a person answering in good faith to inquiries as to the character of a former servant – and then, it is said, the plaintiff may meet this defence in some cases by showing that the words were spoken with actual malice.

All this sounds as if at least actual intent to cause the damage complained of, if not malevolence, were at the bottom of this class of wrongs. Yet it is not so. For although the use of the phrase "malice" points as usual to an original moral standard, the rule that it is presumed upon proof of speaking certain words is equivalent to saying that the overt conduct of speaking those words may be actionable whether the consequence of damage to the plaintiff was intended or not. And this falls in with the general theory, because the manifest tendency of slanderous words is to harm the person of whom they are spoken. Again, the real substance of the defence is not that the damage was not intended – that would be no defence at all; but that, whether it was intended or not – that is, even if the defendant foresaw it and foresaw it with pleasure – the manifest facts and circumstances under which he said it were such that the law considered the damage to the plaintiff of less importance than the benefit of free speaking.

It is more difficult to apply the same analysis to the last stage of the process, but perhaps it is not impossible. It is said that the plaintiff may meet a case of privilege thus made out on the part of the defendant, by proving actual malice, that is, actual intent to cause the damage complained of. But how is this actual malice made out? It is by showing that the defendant knew the statement [that] he made was false, or that his untrue statements were grossly in excess of what the occasion required. Now is it not very evident that the law is looking to a wholly different matter from the defendant's intent? The fact that the defendant foresaw and foresaw with pleasure the damage to the plaintiff, is of no more importance in this case than it would be where the communication was privileged. The question again is wholly a question of knowledge, or other external standard. And what makes even knowledge important? It is that the reason for which a man is allowed in the other instances to make false charges against his neighbors is wanting. It is for the public interest that people should be free to give the best information they can under certain circumstances without fear, but there is no public benefit in having lies told at any time; and when a charge is known to be fatal, or is in excess of what is required by the occasion, it is not necessary to make that charge in order to speak freely, and therefore it falls under the ordinary rule, that certain charges are made at the party's peril in case they turn out to be false, whether evil consequences were intended or not. The defendant is liable, not because his intent was evil, but because he made false charges without excuse.

It will be seen that the peril of conduct here begins farther back than with deceit, as the tendency of slander is more universally harmful. There must be some concomitant circumstances. There must at least be a human being in existence whom the statement designates. There must be another human being within hearing who understands the statement, and the statement must be false. But it is arguable that the latter of these facts need not be known, as certainly the falsity of the charge need not be, and that a man must take the risk of even an idle statement being heard, unless he made it under known circumstances of privilege. It would be no great curtailment of freedom to deny a man immunity in attaching a charge of crime to the name of his neighbor, even when he supposes himself alone. But it does not seem clear that the law would go quite so far as that.

The next form of liability is comparatively insignificant. I mean the action for malicious prosecution. A man may recover damages against another for maliciously and without probable cause instituting a criminal, or, in some cases, a civil prosecution against him upon a false charge. The want of probable cause refers, of course, only to the state of the defendant's knowledge, not to his intent. It means the absence of probable cause in the facts known to the defendant when he instituted the suit. But the standard applied to the defendant's consciousness is external to it. The question is not whether he thought the facts to constitute probable cause, but whether the court thinks they did.

Then as to malice. The conduct of the defendant consists in instituting proceedings on a charge which is in fact false, and which has not prevailed. That is the root of the whole matter. If the charge was true, or if the plaintiff has been convicted, even though he may be able now to prove that he was wrongly convicted, the defendant is safe, however great his malice, and however little ground he had for his charge.

Suppose, however, that the charge is false, and does not prevail. It may readily be admitted that malice did originally mean a malevolent motive, an actual intent to harm the plaintiff by making a false charge. The legal remedy here, again, started from the moral basis, the occasion for it, no doubt, being similar to that which gave rise to the old law of conspiracy, that a man's enemies would sometimes seek his destruction by setting the criminal law in motion against him. As it was punishable to combine for such a purpose, it was concluded, with some hesitation, that, when a single individual wickedly attempted the same thing, he should be liable on similar grounds. I must fully admit that there is weighty authority to the effect that malice in its ordinary sense is to this day a distinct fact to be proved and to be found by the jury.

But this view cannot be accepted without hesitation. It is admitted that, on the one side, the existence of probable cause, believed in, is a justification notwithstanding malice; that, on the other, "it is not enough to show that the case appeared sufficient to this particular party, but it must be sufficient to induce a sober, sensible and discreet person to act upon it, or it must fail as a justification for the proceeding upon general grounds." On the one side, malice alone will not make a man liable for instituting a groundless prosecution; on the other, his justification will depend, not on his opinion of the facts, but on that of the court. When his actual moral condition is disregarded to this extent, it is a little hard to believe that the existence of an improper motive should be material. Yet that is what malice must mean in this case, if it means anything. For the evil effects of a successful indictment are of course intended by one who procures another to be indicted. I cannot but think that a jury would be told that knowledge or belief that the charge was false at the time of making it was conclusive evidence of malice. And if so, on grounds which need not be repeated, malice is not the important thing, but the facts known to the defendant.

Nevertheless, as it is obviously treading on delicate ground to make it actionable to set the regular processes of the law in motion, it is, of course, entirely possible to say that the action shall be limited to those cases where the charge was preferred from improper motives, at least if the defendant thought that there was probable cause. Such a limitation would stand almost alone in the law of civil liability. But the nature of the wrong is peculiar, and, moreover, it is quite consistent with the theory of liability here advanced that it should be confined in any given instance to actual wrong-doing in a moral sense. . . .

Many of the cases [that] have been put thus far are cases where the proximate cause of the loss was intended to be produced by the defendant. But it will be seen that the same result may be caused by a choice at different points. For instance, a man is sued for having caused his neighbor's house to burn down. The simplest case is, that he actually intended to burn it down. If so, the length of the chain of physical causes intervening is of no importance, and has no bearing on the case.

But the choice may have stopped one step farther back. The defendant may have intended to light a fire on his own land, and may not have intended to burn the house. Then the nature of the intervening and concomitant physical causes becomes of the highest importance. The question will be the degree of danger attending the contemplated (and therefore chosen) effect of the defendant's conduct under the circumstances known to him. If this was very plain and very great, as, for instance, if his conduct consisted in lighting stubble near a haystack close to the house, and if the manifest circumstances were that the house was of wood, the stubble very dry, and the wind in a dangerous quarter, the court would probably rule that he was liable. If the defendant lighted an ordinary fire in a fireplace in an adjoining house, having no knowledge that the fireplace was unsafely constructed, the court would probably rule that he was not liable. Midway, complicated and doubtful cases would go to the jury.

But the defendant may not even have intended to set the fire, and his conduct and intent may have been simply to fire a gun, or, remoter still, to walk across a room, in doing which he involuntarily upset a bottle of acid. So that cases may go to the jury by reason of the remoteness of the choice in the series of events, as well as because of the complexity of the circumstances attending the act or conduct. The difference is, perhaps, rather dramatic than substantial.

But the philosophical analysis of every wrong begins by determining what the defendant has actually chosen, that is to say, what his voluntary act or conduct has been, and what consequences he has actually contemplated as flowing from them, and then goes on to determine what dangers attended either the conduct under the known circumstances, or its contemplated consequence under the contemplated circumstances.

Take a case like the glancing of Sir Walter Tyrrell's arrow.[46] If an expert marksman contemplated that the arrow would hit a certain person, *cadit quaestio*.[47] If he contemplated that it would glance in the direction of another person, but contemplated no more than that, in order to judge of his liability we must go to the end of his foresight, and, assuming the foreseen event to happen, consider what the manifest danger was then. But if no such event was foreseen, the marksman must be judged by the circumstances known to him at the time of shooting.

The theory of torts may be summed up very simply. At the two extremes of the law are rules determined by policy without reference of any kind to morality. Certain harms a man may inflict even wickedly; for certain others he must answer, although his conduct has been prudent and beneficial to the community.

But in the main the law started from those intentional wrongs which are the simplest and most pronounced cases, as well as the nearest to the feeling of revenge which leads to self-redress. It thus naturally adopted the vocabulary and in some degree the tests, of morals. But as the law has grown, even when its standards have continued to model themselves upon those of morality, they have necessarily become external, because they have considered, not the actual condition of the particular defendant, but whether his conduct would

---

[46] As the story goes, Sir Walter Tyrrell accidentally killed the unpopular King William Rufus (1056–1100) with an arrow shot during a hunting trip in 1100. – *Ed.*

[47] *Cadit quaestio*, Latin for "the question falls," meaning that a matter has been resolved. – *Ed.*

have been wrong in the fair average member of the community, whom he is expected to equal at his peril.

In general, this question will be determined by considering the degree of danger attending the act or conduct under the known circumstances. If there is danger that harm to another will follow, the act is generally wrong in the sense of the law.

But in some cases the defendant's conduct may not have been morally wrong, and yet he may have chosen to inflict the harm, as where he has acted in fear of his life. In such cases he will be liable, or not, according as the law makes moral blameworthiness, within the limits explained above, the ground of liability, or deems it sufficient if the defendant has had reasonable warning of danger before acting. This distinction, however, is generally unimportant, and the known tendency of the act under the known circumstances to do harm may be accepted as the general test of conduct.

The tendency of a given act to cause harm under given circumstances must be determined by experience. And experience either at first hand or through the voice of the jury is continually working out concrete rules, which in form are still more external and still more remote from a reference to the moral condition of the defendant, than even the test of the prudent man [that] makes the first stage of the division between law and morals. It does this in the domain of wrongs described as intentional, as systematically as in those styled unintentional or negligent.

But while the law is thus continually adding to its specific rules, it does not adopt the coarse and impolitic principle that a man acts always at his peril. On the contrary, its concrete rules, as well as the general questions addressed to the jury, show that the defendant must have had at least a fair chance of avoiding the infliction of harm before he becomes answerable for such a consequence of his conduct. And it is certainly arguable that even a fair chance to avoid bringing harm to pass is not sufficient to throw upon a person the peril of his conduct, unless, judged by average standards, he is also to blame for what he does. . . .

CORRESPONDENCE

To Frederick Pollock
Boston, March 5, 1881

My dear Pollock:

" . . . I now send you by mail . . . a little book *The Common Law*. When a man is engaged all day at his office in practice it is a slow business to do work of this sort by night, but my heart has been deeply in it.... You are happy in being able to afford time to philosophy. I have to make my living by my profession and therefore have been compelled to approach philosophy indirectly through the door of a specialty, but all roads lead to Rome and I don't doubt that a man with the philosophic craving would find stuff to work upon if he was a hatter.... I should like it very much if my book was noticed in England...."

Mark DeWolfe Howe, ed., *Holmes-Pollock Letters: The Correspondence of Mr. Justice Holmes and Sir Frederick Pollock 1874–1932* (Cambridge, MA: Harvard University Press, 1941), at 1:16.

COMMENTARY

Jurisprudential principles – In *The Common Law* "there was something of a symbiotic relationship between the orthodox theory of rights and Holmes's advocacy of external standards. The process of 'line drawing' first advanced in *The Common Law* was ultimately dependent on external criteria. For Holmes, some conception of 'the average,' 'the normal' – in short, some conception of custom – lay in the background of his early thought. Natural rights conceptions, by contrast, he originally identified with the dominant Germanic emphasis on subjective theories of will. He therefore wrote *The Common Law* on the assumption that the shift to an external standard was equivalent to an attack on natural-rights theory itself." Morton J. Horwitz, "The Place of Holmes in American Legal Thought," in *The Legacy of Oliver Wendell Holmes, Jr.*, ed. Robert W. Gordon (Stanford, CA: Stanford University Press, 1992), at 31, 62–63.

Moreover, by "1881 Holmes had completely worked out a comprehensive and integrated way of looking at the world. From that perspective, he had achieved, in the most important book on law ever written by an American, a general statement of the common law conceived as a system resting on relatively few principles,... [which Holmes later applied] in his Supreme Court decisions, for he characteristically solved constitutional law problems by using common-law formulas." Yosal Rogat, "The Judge as Spectator," 31 *University of Chicago Law Review* 213, 214 (1964).

Then again, though "rejecting conceptualism, Holmes nevertheless seemed quite confident in *The Common Law* that there was an underlying rational basis for the distribution of different legal rules and doctrines along the spectrum.... With some exceptions,... the evolution of the law by and large proceeded according to functional rationality." "The Place of Holmes in American Legal Thought," *supra*, at 54. But as we will see in his "Privilege,

Malice, and Intent" article herein and in Part III, Holmes's views on objective standards and the rationality of the law evolved and even changed. *But see* "The Judge as Spectator," *supra*, 31 *University of Chicago Law Review* at 214 ("Holmes rarely changed his mind"). For an extended commentary on *The Common Law*, *see* Mark DeWolfe Howe, *Justice Oliver Wendell Holmes: The Proving Years, 1870–1882* (Cambridge, MA: Harvard University Press, 1963), at 2:117–283; and, for a critical reply to it, *see* Rogat, "The Judge as Spectator," *supra*. See also David Rabban "The Historiography of the Common Law," 28 *Law and Social Inquiry* 1161 (2006).

Judge-made law and will of the dominant forces in society – "Holmes believed that judge-made law was an expression – limited and shaped by precedent – of public opinion, the 'unconscious will' of the dominant forces in society. This will was essentially selfish: 'in the last resort, a man rightly prefers his interest to that of his neighbors.' To the extent that a dominant class accomplished its selfish purposes (moderated only by 'sympathy and socially feelings'), it would survive. Law, therefore, was both an instrument and a reflection of human evolution. Holmes concluded that the common law was evolving toward greater consciousness of its own purposes – the purposes of the law-making power – and towards a more scientific design of the legal instruments for their accomplishment." Sheldon M. Novick, "The Unrevised Holmes and Freedom of Expression," 1991 *Supreme Court Review* 303, 306 (footnotes omitted). *See also* Holmes's "Law in Science and Science in Law," 12 *Harvard Law Review* 443 (1899).

The fire analogy – Recall that, in Lecture II of *The Common Law*, Holmes wrote, "[L]ighting a match with intent to set fire to a haystack has been held to amount to a criminal attempt to burn it, although the defendant blew out the match on seeing that he was watched." Later in the same lecture, he added: "When a man buys matches to fire a haystack . . . there is still a considerable chance that he will change his mind before he comes to the point. But when he has struck the match . . . there is very little chance that he will not persist to the end, and the danger becomes so great that the law steps in."

Many years later, in *Commonwealth v. Peaslee* (1901) (see Part III), he employed a fire analogy, and later in *Schenck v. United States* (1919) (see Part V) Holmes returned to a fire metaphor by way of his famous adage about "a man falsely shouting fire in a theatre and causing a panic."

The basic idea of such analogies may have been sparked by something Dr. Holmes wrote in his book *The Poet at the Breakfast-Table* (Boston: James R. Osgood, 1872), at 3–6. In the opening chapter of this fantastical work, a legislator recalls a nightmare he had about "a certain imaginary Committee of Safety of a certain imaginary Legislature . . . proceeding to burn down his haystack, in accordance with an Act to make the Poor Richer by making the Rich Poorer." When asked who the "they" in the nightmare might be, the response was, "Why, those chaps" are the ones who "are setting folks on to burn us all up in our beds." The "Political firebugs," he added, "[w]ant to substitoot the match-box for the ballot-box. [Their plan is to] scare all our old women half to death." And if this fiery minority did not get its way, then it would level everything and trample "us under foot. . . . That means FIRE, I take it, and knocking you down and stomping on you. . . . *Sounded like a threat; meant, of course, for a warning*. But I don't believe it was in the piece as they spoke it – couldn't have been. . . . I've heard of political gatherings where they barbecued an ox, but I can't think there's a party in this country that wants to barbecue a city. But it isn't quite fair to frighten the old women [with such threats or false warnings]. . . . It's no matter what you say when you talk to yourself, *but when you talk to other people, your business is to use words with reference to the way in which those other people are like to understand them. These pretend inflammatory speeches, so reported as to seem full of combustibles*, even if they were as threatening as they have been represented, would do no harm if read or declaimed in a man's study to his books, or by the sea-shore to the waves. *But they are not so wholesome moral entertainment for the dangerous classes. Boys must not touch off their squibs*[48] *and [fire]crackers too near the powder magazine. This kind of speech doesn't help on the millennium much*" (emphasis added).

The idea of competition – Even before *The Common Law*, Holmes had flagged the idea that the law permits competitive injury to property to advance certain policy preferences.[49] In *The Common Law*, "competition was the most prominent example . . . of a legal system allowing a person to injure another's property, even intentionally, with impunity. . . . But the problem of competitive injury was only a minor theme in *The Common Law*." Later, in his "Privilege, Malice, and Intent" article (1994), Holmes gave the idea a more robust treatment. "The Place of Holmes in American Legal Thought," in *The Legacy of Oliver Wendell Holmes, Jr., supra*, at 55.

If policy considerations allowed for competitive injury to property, then such considerations might also allow for other types of injury to society and government provided that the gravity of the harm did not exceed the benefit to the public writ large. By this measure, Holmes paved the way for his later First Amendment jurisprudence in which the competitive principle was key.

---

[48] Small hissing fireworks – *Ed.*
[49] Holmes later made this point more explicitly. *See, e.g.*, his opinion in *Rideout v. Knox*, 148 Mass. 368, 372 (1889).

The clear-and-present-danger test – When in 1922 Zechariah Chafee, a Harvard law professor and friend of Holmes, wrote to him about the origins of the clear and present danger test announced in *Schenck v. United States* (1919) (see Part V), Holmes replied that he had thought "hard on [the] matter of attempts in my *Common Law* and a Mass. case – [and] later in the *Swift* case..."[50] Letter from Zechariah Chafee to OWH, June 12, 1922, Chafee Papers, Box 14, Folder 12, Harvard Law School Library, quoted in David M. Rabban, *Free Speech in Its Forgotten Years* (New York: Cambridge University Press, 1997), at 285.

Summary of Holmes's views on the common law of attempts – Professor Edward Bloustein sums up Holmes's pre-*Schenck* views on the law of criminal attempts as reflected in *The Common Law* and his Massachusetts Supreme Judicial Court cases (see Part III) this way: "sometimes an action carries the promise of harmful consequences without any further action by the original actor or anyone else. Shooting a gun into a crowd or setting a house afire in a crowded slum are obvious examples. Other acts, however, portend harm only if the original actor or someone else were to undertake another related act. Loading a gun [and] assembling the combustibles for a fire are two such acts. The proof of the likelihood of harm that justifies holding a man liable in the first category is found in 'common experience,' what any 'prudent man' would know, and is independent of whether the actor foresaw or intended the harm. Liability in the second category also turns on the probability of harm, but because an intervening act – firing the gun or lighting the fire – is necessary to cause the harm, the actual intention to accomplish the result must be shown to establish the criminal attempt.

"But, now, what about the proof of such intention? Where no intervening act is necessary to accomplish the harm, a fiction is indulged, and the actor 'is presumed to intend the natural consequences of his own acts,' even if he did not really intend them. What this means is that, in order to enforce the policy of conformity to general external standards of conduct, the law treats the person who is unaware of what might normally be expected from his acts as if he had expected them. We disguise for ourselves the somewhat harsh principle that innocence and ignorance are no defense to liability by indulging in the presumption of bad intentions, even in their absence.

"No such presumption or fiction is indulged by Holmes regarding those attempts in which an intervening act, or intervening acts, are necessary to effectuate the threatened harm. Quite to the contrary. Here, Holmes says that

---

[50] *Swift v. United States*, 196 U.S. 375, 396 (1904), per Holmes for the Court, discussed in commentary following *Commonwealth v. Peaslee* (Mass. 1900) (see Part III). – *Ed.*

'actual intent is clearly necessary,' not to 'show that the act was wicked, but to show that it was likely to be followed by hurtful consequences.' Intent, in such a case, 'raises a probability that [the suspect act] will be followed by such other acts and events as will all together result in harm.' In the one case, harm is foretold in the act itself, whether it is intended or not. In the other, harm is only probable where the suspect act is undertaken with the intention that it produce harm and in anticipation of the intervening acts that would bring it about." Edward J. Bloustein, "Criminal Attempts and the 'Clear and Present Danger' Theory of the First Amendment," 74 *Cornell Law Review* 1118, 1124–25 (1989) (footnotes omitted). For additional discussion of this matter, *see Free Speech in Its Forgotten Years, supra,* at 285–93 (discussing Holmes's notion of attempts and his subsequent Espionage Act opinions); David S. Bogen, "The Free Speech Metamorphosis of Mr. Justice Holmes," 11 *Hofstra Law Review* 97, 154–60 (1982) (discussing two categories of attempts). For another discussion of Holmes's views on the law of attempts, see Yosal Rogat and James M. O'Fallon, "Mr. Justice Holmes: A Dissenting Opinion – The Speech Cases," 36 *Stanford Law Review* 1349, 1361–66 (1984).

Holmes's theory of legal liability – "Some commentators have linked Holmes's theory of free speech to his doctrine of criminal attempt. But the problem with this interpretation is that it is too narrow. Holmes's doctrine of attempts is relevant, but it is not the whole story. To understand his theory of free speech, his entire theory of legal liability must be examined. . . .

  "Holmes's theory of legal liability is composed of more than one branch. No doubt the main branch consisted of the external test that he applied to harmful acts. If an agent, knowing facts that would have warned a rational person of danger, acted anyway, that agent was liable no matter what he or she foresaw or intended. The degree of liability would depend on the degree of danger that the rational person perceived and on what the agent knew about his or her circumstances. Certain harmful acts, however, were ordinarily privileged from liability because of their long-term advantages. But even here liability could be imposed if the agent's actual purpose was malicious, harmful in regard to another person or the public in general. Abuses of privilege constituted a subordinate but important branch of Holmes's theory of legal liability, especially the abuse of the right of association as defined by the law of conspiracy. Attempts were a different branch. In the case of an attempt, liability could be imposed on a non-harmful act, but only if the agent actually intended harm and had done something proximate to it. What is crucial to remember is that two subordinate branches required actual illicit intent." H. L. Pohlman, *Justice Oliver Wendell Holmes: Free Speech and the Living Constitution*

(New York: New York University Press, 1991), at 20, 46 (footnote omitted and emphasis added).

Privileged expression and the law of defamation – "Holmes was at pains from the first to explain some apparent exceptions to the external standard. One such was the class of legally recognized privileges to do harm. There were numerous cases in which defendants could have foreseen, and in fact had foreseen, that their conduct would injure someone, and yet were not held liable for the harm that followed. Slanders and libels by definition were foreseeably harmful, yet often the defendant could avoid liability by claiming that the speech or writing in question was 'privileged'; in other words that, in the circumstances, he or she was privileged to cause foreseeable harm. The real substance of the defense of privilege was not that the injury was unforeseen, but that 'the law considered the damage to the plaintiff of less importance than the benefit of free speaking.'" "The Unrevised Holmes and Freedom of Expression," *supra*, 1991 *Supreme Court Review* at 307 (quoting *The Common Law*, footnote omitted). Examples of this can be found in some of the cases set out in Part III.

What followed: The path beyond scholasticism – "Much was to follow from the appearance of *The Common Law*: Holmes'[s] professional life was not the same again. The book's appearance led him, in a round-about fashion, to a career niche that he had coveted and that he found fulfilling, a judgeship. It also led him, in another fashion, away from original scholarship, as if he feared he could not again in that realm reach the level of performance he had achieved in his Lowell Lectures. In a sense *The Common Law* freed Holmes to become 'writer' again: to devote more of his time to the arts of speechwriting and correspondence, no longer obsessed with the necessity of building professional reputation and confirming it with 'professional' writing." *Justice Oliver Wendell Holmes: Law and the Inner Self, supra*, at 195.

> *My object is not to decide cases, but to make a little clearer the method to be followed in deciding them.*

PRIVILEGE, MALICE, AND INTENT[51]

The law of torts as now administered has worked itself into substantial agreement with a general theory. I should sum up the first part of the theory in a

---

[51] Oliver Wendell Holmes Jr., "Privilege, Malice, and Intent," 8 *Harvard Law Review* 1 (1894), reproduced in *The Collected Works of Justice Holmes, supra* note 1, at 3:371–80. All but one of Holmes's footnotes has been omitted. – Ed.

few words, as follows. Actions of tort are brought for temporal damage. The law recognizes temporal damage as an evil [that] its object is to prevent or to redress, so far as is consistent with paramount considerations to be mentioned. When it is shown that the defendant's act has had temporal damage to the plaintiff for its consequence, the next question is whether that consequence was one [that] the defendant might have foreseen. If common experience has shown that some such consequence was likely to follow the act under the circumstances known to the actor, he is taken to have acted with notice, and is held liable, unless he escapes upon the special grounds to which I have referred, and which I shall mention in a moment. The standard applied is external, and the words malice, intent and negligence, as used in this connection, refer to an external standard. If the manifest probability of harm is very great, and the harm follows, we say that it is done maliciously or intentionally; if not so great, but still considerable, we say that the harm is done negligently; if there is no apparent danger, we call it mischance.

Furthermore, so far as liability for an act depends upon its probable consequences without more, the liability usually is not affected by the degree of the probability if it is sufficient to give the defendant reasonable warning. In other words, for this purpose commonly it does not matter whether the act is called malicious or negligent. To make out a *prima facie* case of trespass or libel, if the likelihood of bringing force to bear on the plaintiff's person or of bringing him into contempt goes to the height expressed by the word negligence, as above explained, it need not go higher. There are exceptions, at least in the criminal law. The degree of danger under the known circumstances may make the difference between murder and manslaughter.[52] But the rule is as I have stated. The foregoing general principles I assume not to need further argument.[53]

But the simple test of the degree of manifest danger does not exhaust the theory of torts. In some cases, a man is not liable for a very manifest danger unless he actually intends to do the harm complained of. In some cases, he even may intend to do the harm and yet not have to answer for it; and, as I think, in some cases of this latter sort, at least, actual malice may make him liable when without it he would not have been. In this connection I mean by malice a malevolent motive for action, without reference to any hope of a remoter benefit to oneself to be accomplished by the intended harm to another. The question whether malice in this sense has any effect upon the extent of a

---

[52] Here, among other references, Holmes cited to "Compare *Hanson v. Globe Newspaper*, 159 Mass. 293," which is set out in Part III. – *Ed.*
[53] See *The Common Law*, chaps. 2–4.

defendant's rights and liabilities, has arisen in many forms. It is familiar in regard to the use of land in some way manifestly harmful to a neighbor. It has been suggested, and brought to greater prominence, by boycotts, and other combinations for more or less similar purposes, although in such cases the harm inflicted is only a means, and the end sought to be attained generally is some benefit to the defendant. But before discussing that, I must consider the grounds on which a man escapes liability in the cases referred to, even if his act is not malicious.

Privileges and Policies

It will be noticed that I assume that we have got past the question [that] is answered by the test of the external standard. There is no dispute that the manifest tendency of the defendant's act is to inflict temporal damage upon the plaintiff. Generally, the result is expected, and often at least it is intended. And the first question that presents itself is why the defendant is not liable without going further. The answer is suggested by the commonplace, that the intentional infliction of temporal damage, or the doing of an act manifestly likely to inflict such damage and inflicting it, is actionable if done without just cause.[54] When the defendant escapes, the court is of opinion that he has acted with just cause. There are various justifications. In these instances, the justification is that the defendant is privileged knowingly to inflict the damage complained of.

But whether, and how far, a privilege shall be allowed is a question of policy. Questions of policy are legislative questions, and judges are shy of reasoning from such grounds. Therefore, decisions for or against the privilege, which really can stand only upon such grounds, often are presented as hollow deductions from empty general propositions like *sic utere tuo ut alienum non laedas*,[55] which teaches nothing but a benevolent yearning, or else are put as if they themselves embodied a postulate of the law and admitted of no further deduction, as when it is said that, although there is temporal damage, there is no wrong; whereas, the very thing to be found out is whether there is a wrong or not, and if not, why not.

When the question of policy is faced it will be seen to be one [that] cannot be answered by generalities, but must be determined by the particular character of the case, even if everybody agrees what the answer should be. I do not try to mention or to generalize all the facts which have to be taken into account; but

[54] Here, among other citations, Holmes referred to *Mogul Steamship Co. v. McGregor*, 23 Q.B.D. 598, 613, 618 (1889). – *Ed.*

[55] Latin for "do not use your property in such a way as to injure another." – *Ed.*

plainly the worth of the result, or the gain from allowing the act to be done, has to be compared with the loss which it inflicts. Therefore, the conclusion will vary, and will depend on different reasons according to the nature of the affair. . . .

Not only the existence but the extent or degree of the privilege will vary with the case. Some privileges are spoken of as if they were absolute, to borrow the language familiar in cases of slander. . . .

So it has been thought that refusing to keep a man in one's service, if he hired a house of the plaintiff, or dealt with him, was absolutely privileged. Here the balance is struck between the benefit of unfettered freedom to abstain from making that contract, on the one side, and the harm [that] may be done by the particular use of that freedom, on the other.

It is important to notice that the privilege is not a general one, maliciously to prevent making contracts with the plaintiff, but is attached to the particular means employed. It is a privilege to abstain from making a certain kind of contract oneself, whether maliciously, in order to prevent others from contracting with the plaintiff, or for a more harmless motive. Still more important it is, and more to the point of this paper, that, in spite of many general expressions to the contrary, the conclusion does not stand on the abstract proposition that malice cannot make a man liable for an act otherwise lawful. It is said that if this were not so a man would be sued for his motives. But the proposition is no more self-evident than that knowledge of the circumstances under which an act is done cannot affect liability, since otherwise a man would be sued for his knowledge, a proposition which is obviously untrue. In a proper sense, the state of a man's consciousness always is material to his liability, and when we are considering the extent of a man's privilege knowingly to inflict pecuniary loss upon his neighbor, it would not be surprising to find that in some cases motives made all the difference in the world. I pass to the inquiry, whether privilege, sometimes at least, is not dependent upon the motives with which the act complained of is done. . . .

Motives

The gratification of ill-will, being a pleasure, may be called a gain, but the pain on the other side is a loss more important. Otherwise, why allow a recovery for a battery? There is no general policy in favor of allowing a man to do harm to his neighbor for the sole pleasure of doing harm.

But there is no need to stay in such thin air. Let us suppose another case of interference with business by an act [that] has some special grounds of policy in its favor. Take the case of advice not to employ a certain doctor, given by one in a position of authority. To some extent it is desirable that people should be free to give one another advice. On the other hand, commonly it is not desirable that a man should lose his business. The two advantages run against one another, and a line has to be drawn. So absolute a right of way may not be given to advice as to abstaining from some contracts [that] have been mentioned. In such a case, probably it would be said that if the advice was believed to be good, and was given for the sake of benefiting the hearers, the defendant would not be answerable. But if it was not believed to be for their benefit, and was given for the sake of hurting the doctor, the doctor would prevail. If the advice was believed to be good, but was volunteered for the sake of doing harm only, courts might differ, but some no doubt would think that the privilege was not made out. What the effect of bad faith without malice would be is outside my subject.

It will be seen that the external standard applied for the purpose of seeing whether the defendant had notice of the probable consequences of his act has little or nothing to do with the question of privilege. The defendant is assumed to have had notice of the probable consequences of his act, otherwise the question of privilege does not arise. Generally the harm complained of is not only foreseen but intended. If there is no privilege, the difference between notice of consequences and malice is immaterial. If the privilege is absolute, or extends to malicious acts, of course it extends to those which are not so. If the privilege is qualified, the policy in favor of the defendant's freedom generally will be found to be qualified only to the extent of forbidding him to use for the sake of doing harm what is allowed him for the sake of good. Suppose, for instance, advice is given which manifestly tends to injure the plaintiff, but without thinking of him in fact, and that the advice would be privileged unless given in bad faith or maliciously, if expressly directed against the plaintiff. The advice could not be given maliciously as against the plaintiff unless he either was thought of, or was embraced in a class which was thought of.

Perhaps one of the reasons why judges do not like to discuss questions of policy, or to put a decision in terms upon their views as law-makers, is that the moment you leave the path of merely logical deduction you lose the illusion of certainty which makes legal reasoning seem like mathematics. But the certainty is only an illusion, nevertheless. Views of policy are taught by experience of the interests of life. Those interests are fields of battle. Whatever decisions are made must be against the wishes and opinion of one party, and the distinctions on which they go will be distinctions of degree. Even the economic postulate of the benefit of free competition, which I have mentioned above, is denied by an important school. . . .

Acts [that] would be privileged if done by one person for a certain purpose may be held unlawful if done for the same purpose in combination. It is easy to see what trouble may be found in distinguishing between the combination of great powers in a single capitalist, not to speak of a corporation, and the other form of combination. It is a question of degree at what point the combination becomes large enough to be wrong, unless the knot is cut by saying that any combination however puny is so. Behind all is the question whether the courts are not flying in the face of the organization of the world [that] is taking place so fast, and of its inevitable consequences. I make these suggestions, not as criticisms of the decisions, but to call attention to the very serious legislative considerations [that] have to be weighed. The danger is that such considerations should have their weight in an articulate form as unconscious prejudice or half conscious inclination. To measure them justly needs not only the highest powers of a judge and a training which the practice of the law does not insure, but also a freedom from prepossessions which is very hard to attain. It seems to me desirable that the work should be done with express recognition of its nature. The time has gone by when law is only an unconscious embodiment of the common will. It has become a conscious reaction upon itself of organized society knowingly seeking to determine its own destinies.

Partial Summation

To sum up this part of the discussion, when a responsible defendant seeks to escape from liability for an act [that] he had notice was likely to cause temporal damage to another, and which has caused such damage in fact, he must show a justification. The most important justification is a claim of privilege. In order to pass upon that claim, it is not enough to consider the nature of the damage, and the effect of the act, and to compare them. Often the precise nature of the act and its circumstances must be examined. It is not enough, for instance, to say that the defendant induced the public, or a part of them, not to deal with the plaintiff. We must know how he induced them.... But in all such cases the ground of decision is policy; and the advantages to the community, on the one side and the other, are the only matters really entitled to be weighed....

Probability of Harm

I now pass to an entirely different class of cases. In these, intent to produce the harm complained of has an importance of its own, as distinguished from notice of danger on the one side, and from actual malice on the other. To begin at a little distance, one of the difficulties which must occur to every one in thinking of the external standard of liability is: if notice so determined is the general ground, why is not a man who sells fire-arms answerable for assaults committed with pistols bought of him, since he must be taken to know the probability that, sooner or later, some one will buy a pistol of him for some unlawful end? I do not think that the whole answer to such questions is to be found in the doctrine of privilege. Neither do I think that any instruction is to be got from the often-repeated discussions as to cause. It is said that the man whose wrong-doing is nearest to the injury is the only cause of it. But, as is pointed out in [in Massachusetts case law], a man whose act is nearest to the injury is as much a cause when his act is rightful, as when it is wrongful. Yet an intervening act may not exonerate the defendant.

The principle seems to be pretty well established, in this country at least, that every one has a right to rely upon his fellowmen acting lawfully, and, therefore, is not answerable for himself acting upon the assumption that they will do so, however improbable it may be. There may have been some nibbling at the edges of this rule in strong cases, for instance, where only the slight negligence of a third person intervenes, or where his negligence plays only a subordinate part, but the rule hardly will be disputed. It applies in favor of wrong-doers as well as others. The classical illustration is, that one who slanders another is not liable for the wrongful repetition of the slander without his authority, but the principle is general. If the repetition were privileged, and so rightful, and also were manifestly likely to happen, the law might be otherwise.

But the case is different when a defendant has not stopped at the point of saying, I take it for granted that my neighbors will keep to the law, and I shall not let myself be checked in doing what I like, by the danger which there would be, if they acted unlawfully; when, instead, he not only has expected unlawful conduct, but has acted with the intent to bring about consequences which could not happen without the help of such unlawful acts on the part of other....

So when the wrongful act expected is that of a third person, and not of the plaintiff, the defendant may be liable for the consequences of it. There is no doubt, of course, that a man may be liable for the unlawful act of another, civilly as well as criminally, and this now is pretty well agreed when the act is a breach of contract as well as when it is a tort. He is liable, if having authority he commands it; he may be liable if he induces it by persuasion. I do not see that it matters how he knowingly gives the other a motive for unlawful action, whether by fear, fraud, or persuasion, if the motive works. But, in order to take away the protection of his right to rely upon lawful conduct, you must show that he intended to bring about consequences to which that unlawful act was necessary. Ordinarily, this is the same as saying that he must have intended the unlawful act. To sum the matter up in a rule, where it is sought to make a man answerable for damage, and the act of a third person is nearer in time than the defendant's to the harm, if the third person's act was lawful, it stands like the workings of nature, and the question is whether it reasonably was to be anticipated or looked out for; but if the third person's act was unlawful, the defendant must be shown to have intended the act, or at least to have expected it, and to have intended consequences which could not happen without the act.

Although actual intention is necessary in this class of cases, malice commonly is not so, except so far as the question of liability for an intervening wrong-doer is complicated with a question of privilege. The damage is assumed to be inflicted unlawfully, since the act of the third person [that] is nearest to it is assumed to be unlawful. If the defendant has no notice that the third person's act will or may be unlawful, he is free on general principles. But ... if he knows that the act will be unlawful, it seems plain that persuasion to do it will make him liable as well when not malicious as when malicious. I cannot believe that bona fide advice to do an unlawful act to the manifest harm of the plaintiff ought to be any more privileged than such advice, given maliciously, to do a lawful act. Of course, I am speaking of effectual advice. It seems to me hard for the law to recognize a privilege to induce unlawful conduct. But, whether there is such a privilege or not, what I am driving at is, that apart from privilege there is no defence; that is to say, that malice is not material, on any other ground than that of privilege, to liability for the wrongful act of another man.

Questions of Privilege

At this point, then, we have come again upon the question of privilege. When the purpose of the defendant's act is to produce the result complained of by means of illegal acts of third persons, his privilege will be narrower than when he intends to induce only legal acts. As I have said, I do not suppose that the privilege extended to honest persuasion to do harm to the plaintiff by lawful conduct, would extend to similar persuasion to do it by unlawful conduct. Take acts of which the privilege is greater. Could a man refuse to contract with A unless he broke his contract with B? There are cases by respectable courts [that] look as if he could not ... [56]

---

[56] Here, among other references, Holmes cited *Temperton v. Russell* (1893), 1 Q.B.D. 715: "In this case, there was the additional element of combination." – *Ed.*

In questions of privilege, the nature of the defendant's act, the nature of the consequences, and the closeness of the bond between them, may vary indefinitely. We may imagine the conduct to be of the most highly privileged kind, like the use of land, and to consist of imposing conditions upon the letting of rooms or the removal of a building cutting off a view. We may imagine the conditions to be stated with intent, but without any persuasion or advice, that they should be satisfied, and we may imagine them to be illegal acts anywhere from murder down to breach of a contract to take the *Herald* for a month. Interesting cases of such a kind might be framed for a moot court, although I hardly expect to meet one in practice. But, as I have said, my object is not to decide cases, but to make a little clearer the method to be followed in deciding them.

CORRESPONDENCE

To Frederick Pollock
Boston, April 2, 1894

Dear Pollock:
. . . I have known and done almost nothing but law. The next *Harv. Law Rev.* will have an article of mine, "Privilege Malice & Intent," a supplement to the doctrine of the external standard. Little more than platitudes, yet things not generally known. . . .

Yours ever,
O. W. Holmes

Mark DeWolfe Howe, ed., *Holmes-Pollock Letters: The Correspondence of Mr. Justice Holmes and Sir Frederick Pollock 1874–1932* (Cambridge, MA: Harvard University Press, 1941), at 1:50.

COMMENTARY

Testing the logic of – The Common Law – As noted previously, while "rejecting conceptualism, Holmes nevertheless seemed quite confident in *The Common Law* that there was an underlying rational basis for the distribution of different legal rules and doctrines along the spectrum. Viewed from the vantage point of a legal anthropologist, one could demonstrate how the doctrines developed and how their placement on the continuum was related to the function that the doctrine was called on to serve. With some exceptions, therefore, the evolution of law by and large proceeded according to functional rationality.

By the time we come to 'Privilege, Malice and Intent' and 'The Path of the Law' [see Part III], however, all that is left are the contradictions between the poles. There is no longer an organic customary principle to mediate the contradictions. . . . For Holmes, the customary theory of law had collapsed. Law is the product of social struggle. Nothing stands between the state and the individual. . . . In 'Privilege, Malice and Intent,' Holmes posits the existence of a fundamental contradiction between accepted notions of property and competition and, for the first time, expresses doubt whether there is any methodology capable of rationally reconciling the two.

"The specific subject of the most important part of his essay was a series of late-nineteenth-century labor cases in which English courts had limited the right of unions to engage in various forms of economic struggle. The problem had been 'suggested, and brought to greater prominence,' he wrote, by cases dealing with 'boycotts, and other combinations for more or less similar purposes. . . .' It was the legal response to the struggle between labor and capital that produced Holmes's essay." Morton J. Horwitz, *The Transformation of American Law, 1870–1960* (New York: Oxford University Press, 1994), at 130 (footnotes omitted). Holmes, of course, had confronted a similar clash between labor and capital and had addressed the matter in his 1873 Gas Stokers Note. Not long after his "Privilege, Malice, and Intent" essay he would return to the matter yet again in his opinions in *Vegelahn v. Gunter* (1896) and *Plant v. Woods* (1900) (see Part III).

Though, as previously noted, Holmes told Pollock that his article was little more than "a supplement to the doctrine of the external standard," "Privilege, Malice, and Intent" nonetheless represented a "significant shift in [Holmes's] views on the sources of common law rules from those he advanced in *The Common Law*." Thus, in that work Holmes "argued that even where the law spoke of rules or doctrines that appeared to be subjective, those rules, in application, evaluated conduct against an objective, external standard." But in his "Privilege" essay he found that position hard to reconcile with the way the English courts had treated competition and labor cases. The treatment of those cases "suggested some difficulties for the jurisprudential theories Holmes had advanced in *The Common Law*." Such difficulties might be resolved, he reasoned, if judges openly engaged in policy decisions. G. Edward White, *Justice Oliver Wendell Holmes: Law and the Inner Self* (New York: Oxford University Press, 1993), at 215–17 (footnotes omitted). *See also* Morton J. Horwitz, "The Place of Justice Holmes in American Legal Thought," in *The Legacy of Oliver Wendell Holmes, Jr.*, ed. Robert W. Gordon (Stanford, CA: Stanford University Press, 1992), at 31, 59 ("Clearly Holmes's acceptance of the malice test in 'Privilege, Malice, and Intent' marks a major retreat from the idea that he had always regarded as his major contribution to legal theory.").

Two classes of cases: Foreseeability and privilege – In the period leading up to "Privilege, Malice, and Intent," Holmes examined two categories of cases that might give rise to liability. "The First were cases in which some third person had intervened between the defendant's act and the plaintiff's injury." Sheldon M. Novick, "The Unrevised Holmes and Freedom of Expression," 1991 *Supreme Court Review* 303, 308. For example, there was the case of the doctor who falsely told a patient that the material used to make buggy-whip snaps was dangerous because of arsenic contamination. This information was communicated by third parties to some of the employees in the buggy-whip factory who then quit their jobs. The manufacturer then sued the doctor in tort for slander. The court, per Holmes, held that the doctor was not legally responsible for a repetition of the slanderous words, as it did not appear that the repetition was privileged or authorized. "[T]he law," declared Holmes, "will look no further back than to the wrongdoer who is the proximate cause of the consequence complained of." *Elmer v. Fessenden*, 151 Mass. 359, 362, 24 N.E. 208, 209 (1890), cited approvingly by Holmes in his opinion for the Court in *American Banana Co. v. American Fruit Co.*, 213 U.S. 347, 358 (1909). In the *Elmer* case "and in a series of tort and contract cases, Holmes followed the long-established doctrine that liability would not be imposed on the defendant if the wrongful acts of a third party intervened between the defendant's conduct and the plaintiff's injury. (This would later prove to be an important line of cases for Holmes's First Amendment jurisprudence, because political dissidents would be prosecuted, not for directly interfering with the war effort, but for inciting others to do so.)" "The Unrevised Holmes and Freedom of Expression," *supra*, 1991 *Supreme Court Review* at 308 (footnote omitted).

"The second class of cases that had to be reconciled with [Holmes's] 'external standard' were those in which a defense of privilege had been raised. Holmes had addressed these briefly in *The Common Law*. In such cases, the defendant admittedly could foresee that her conduct would cause injuries, and yet still asked to be excused from liability. A privilege, if properly asserted, could then be defeated only by a showing of actual malice." "The Unrevised Holmes and Freedom of Expression," *supra*, 1991 *Supreme Court Review* at 309–10 (footnotes omitted).

Privileged acts – In this essay, and in subsequent cases such as his dissent in *Vegelahn v. Guntner* (1896) (see Part III), Holmes espoused the idea that certain acts that would otherwise be legally actionable might nonetheless be privileged under law for various policy reasons. "In the case of privileged action, the defendant harmed another and knew facts that warned of the danger, but the defendant was free of liability because he or she acted with 'just cause.' Of course, for Holmes the question whether a certain harmful act should be privileged was strictly a policy one, even if it was presented in the language of just cause.... In his judgment, 'plainly the worth of the result, or the gain from allowing the act to be done, has to be compared with the loss it inflicts.' His favorite example was that of a wealthy businessman opening up a store in a small town knowing that he will drive his only competitor – a deserving widow – out of business. Such action, though harmful in the short-term, was privileged by law because of the long-term advantages of a free market." Another example Holmes gave was that of an employer who provides truthful but damaging information about a former employee who seeks work elsewhere. "Here again it was thought that society benefits ... if employers were given access to information concerning prospective employees, even if the employees were occasionally harmed." H. L. Pohlman, *Justice Oliver Wendell Holmes: Free Speech and the Living Constitution* (New York: New York University Press, 1991), at 31–32 (footnotes omitted).

Both of Holmes's examples – the competitive businessman and the employer providing information – reflect his views as to what is commercially best for the marketplace. In the case of the former, the idea is that competition will produce the best prices and practices for the public, whereas in the case of the latter, the idea is that the free distribution of truthful information will provide the best employees. Competition and information – these two ideas would later assume a central role in Holmes's free speech jurisprudence.

Limits on privilege – The reason someone commits an otherwise-injurious act, even if privileged, was also important to Holmes. "The law could and often would withdraw the privilege if the agent's actual purpose was malevolent." *Justice Oliver Wendell Holmes: Free Speech and the Living Constitution*, *supra*, at 32. Thus, in the employer information context, assume that the employer expressed truthful but nonetheless harmful information about his former employee and conveyed that to a prospective employer. Such information, in Holmes's mind, would be privileged and therefore protected if done to help the employer but would not be privileged if done to harm the employee. Why? Holmes's answer, as he put it in "Privilege, Malice, and Intent," was simple: "The gratification of ill-will, being a pleasure, may be called a gain, but the pain on the other side is a loss more important."

"Holmes sought in the concept of 'malice' a mediating force that custom could not provide. In so doing," and as previously noted, "he retreated substantially from his insistence on objective standards in the law. The basic notion of [this article] is that sometimes, though rarely the privilege to injure expresses a clear right on one side with no corresponding right on the other. Such a situation represents an easy, though infrequent case, where an external standard can decide whether the defendant is privileged to invade the plaintiff's right. But once rights are regarded as relative, Holmes declared, 'It is entirely conceivable that motive . . . should be held to affect all, or nearly all, claims of privilege,' and there 'is no general policy in favor of allowing a man to do harm to his neighbor for the sole pleasure of doing harm.'" "The Place of Justice Holmes in American Legal Thought," in *The Legacy of Oliver Wendell Holmes, Jr., supra*, at 58 (endnote omitted). Five years after his "Privilege" article, Holmes returned to this topic and reaffirmed his revised views in "Law in Science and Science in Law," 12 *Harvard Law Review* 443 (1899).

Holmes's revised views notwithstanding, if information is indeed helpful to the market and/or to the public generally, an argument could be made that the speaker's motives ought not to determine whether such information is protected. After all, it might be said that, on balance, the benefit to the public may well exceed any harm to a particular individual. If such were the calculation in the first instance when harmful information is expressed for nonmalicious purposes, then by the same logic it might also govern when the benefit to the public remains quite apart from the speaker's intent.

Hints of clear-and-present-danger formula – "Holmes continued to insist that all liability at common law was based on 'foreseeability' of harms that the dominant forces in society wished to prevent. This was still an old-fashioned sort of foreseeability; it was not a matter of mathematical probabilities, but rather a projection into the future of the lines of lawful conduct and the expected course of natural events – 'a manifest tendency to inflict temporal damage.' Holmes also continued to insist that certain behavior, like free speaking, was privileged as a matter of social policy, despite its manifest tendency to do harm in particular cases, because overall the behavior complained of created benefits that outweighed the harm.

"The new element in this theory was simply the recognition that actual intent to cause harm or induce unlawful conduct would defeat a claim of privilege. This new element, Holmes claimed, also was a matter of social policy, to discourage otherwise privileged speech that posed too great a risk of harm.

"The doctrine of 'clear and present danger' had been born. Another twenty-five years would elapse before Holmes would apply the doctrine in First Amendment cases. In the intervening years, he tested it in his judicial laboratory." "The Unrevised Holmes and Freedom of Expression," *supra*, 1991 *Supreme Court Review* at 312–13 (footnotes omitted).

The move away from natural rights law and the birth of modernism in the law – The "law permits competitive injury to property on grounds of 'policy without reference to any kind of morality.' Competition was the most prominent example in *The Common Law* of a legal system allowing a person to injure another's property, even intentionally, with impunity.

"But the problem of competitive injury was only a minor one in *The Common Law*. By the time Holmes wrote 'Privilege, Malice, and Intent,' the general question of the nature and limits of economic struggle had moved to the center of his consciousness as a result of two major developments. The first arose from the question of economic concentration. To what extent was the rapid organization and concentration of economic power in both England and America legitimate and to be supported by law? ... A second and more immediate question involved the growing struggle between labor and capital. To what extent was labor organization the same as (or different from) business concentrations? Should legal rules pertaining to business competition be applied to economic struggles between labor and capital?

"In his section on 'privilege' Holmes first spelled out those reasons of public policy that he had said in *The Common Law* justified allowing injury from competition as well as other privileges to injure. Judicial determinations of when to allow privileges to inflict harm could not be arrived at by 'merely logical deduction' from absolute conceptions of rights, Holmes declared. Since rights were in conflict, decisions must inevitably be based on 'distinctions of degree.' The two rights 'run against one another, and a line has to be drawn.'

"Notice the structure of his argument: A balancing test must replace syllogistic reasoning because there is a conflict between property and competition. Whenever the rights of capital conflict with those of labor, 'a line has to be drawn' based on 'distinctions of degree.' While this analysis of when to permit a privilege to inflict injury was simply a reaffirmation of the external standard proposed in *The Common Law*, it did constitute a far more developed attack on prevailing theories of absolute property rights. Above all, it is the first time, I believe, that a fully articulated balancing test has entered American legal theory. Because of this development, perhaps it is the moment we should identify as the beginning of modernism in American legal thought. Between 1910 and 1920 in virtually all fields of law a balancing test overthrew the earlier system of legal reasoning based on logical deduction from general premises, marking the demise of the late-nineteenth-century system of legal formalism."
"The Place of Justice Holmes in American Legal Thought," in *The Legacy of Oliver Wendell Holmes, Jr., supra*, at 56–57 (endnotes omitted).

Part III   The State Court Years: Fettered Freedom

After years of scrambling, Holmes came out on high ground.
  – Sheldon Novick[1]

Here was a chance to see reality unfold before him, so that per-haps he might discover the rhythmic unplanned mystery that lay behind. . . . The past was but a guide to the future. . . .
  – Francis Biddle[2]

The secret was first revealed in the local newspapers. Holmes, then forty-one, was a Harvard law professor. When the nomination to the Massachusetts Supreme Judicial Court came, he was the youngest person to have ever been selected for the seat. This was the same court before which he had argued many cases,[3] and this was the same court on which his grandfather Justice Charles Jackson had once sat (1814–25). He would fill his new office "with dignity and ability," predicted the *Boston Globe*. He possessed "qualifications far in advance of his years," proclaimed the *Boston Daily Advertiser*.

At Harvard, Holmes taught torts, suretyship and mortgage, agency and carriers, constitutional law, and jurisprudence. But after nine months it

---

[1] Sheldon M. Novick, *Honorable Justice: The Life of Oliver Wendell Holmes* (New York: Bantam Doubleday Dell, 1989), at 169.

[2] Francis Biddle, *Mr. Justice Holmes* (New York: Charles Scribner's Sons, 1943), at 67 (referring to Holmes taking his seat on the Massachusetts high court). Of course, just how much of a glorious chance his career on the state court would offer him was another matter, as is suggested by the end of this introduction.

[3] By this time, Holmes had already argued thirty-two cases before that tribunal, four-teen of which he won. *See* Mark DeWolfe Howe, *O.W. Holmes, Jr., Counselor-at-Law* (Philadelphia: Brandeis Lawyers Society, 1948), at 18.

was over; he left abruptly in the middle of the term. Christopher Columbus Langdell, James Bradley Thayer,[4] John Chipman Gray, and James Barr Ames, his esteemed colleagues, were offended. But no matter.[5] Oliver Wendell Holmes saw his star rising. Hence, he did two things on December 15, 1882: He officially resigned from Harvard Law School, and he then took the oath of office to become an associate justice on the state high court. After having been passed over twice, the tall and slender scholar with a bristling mustache was not about to forsake this invitation to greatness. The career move would allow Holmes to make more money (from $4,500 annually at Harvard to $6,000 a year at the court); to garner more prestige; and, best of all, to bring his cloistered ideas into the light of the law. It was a new day for Holmes; it was a new life struggle, one he welcomed. And Louis Brandeis, the progressive Boston lawyer, welcomed it, too. "As one of the bar I rejoice," he wrote to Holmes. "As a part of the Law School I mourn," he added. "As your friend I congratulate you."[6]

Could he do it? Could the aspiring Holmes leave his mark on the law? He would have twenty years to try, first as an associate justice and then as chief justice of the Massachusetts Supreme Judicial Court. He would author 1,290 majority opinions and 23 dissenting opinions during his state court tenure. Would the number and quality be enough to earn him the kind of legacy earned by Chief Justice Lemuel Shaw (1781–1861), who had earlier presided honorably over that court? Would that happen? Although greatness would come his way, it was not yet known how or how fast it would happen. And in the swirl of life and law in the early 1880s, Holmes paid relatively little regard to what would one day make his words

---

[4] Thayer, critical of Holmes's hasty departure from the law school, believed that Holmes was "wanting sadly in the noblest region of human character – selfish, vain, thoughtless of others." Qtd. in Mark DeWolfe Howe, *Justice Oliver Wendell Holmes: The Shaping Years, 1841–1870* (Cambridge, MA: Harvard University Press, 1957), at 1:282, 316 n. 113 (noting original source).

[5] Psychologically speaking, the judgeship was so important to Holmes that "when the opportunity came he reached spontaneously and perhaps impulsively, and surely did not give serious attention to the feelings of others who might be affected by the decision." G. Edward White, *Justice Oliver Wendell Holmes: Law and the Inner Self* (New York: Oxford University Press, 1993), at 600.

[6] Louis Brandeis to OWH, December 9, 1882, reproduced in Melvin Urofsky and David Levy, eds., *Letters of Louis D. Brandeis* (Albany: State University of New York Press, 1971), at 1:65

memorable – the First Amendment. Still, he was busily paving the way to greatness, even if he didn't know quite where it would all lead.[7]

⤚

The standard fare of the seven-member court on which Holmes sat was mostly mundane by today's standards. Torts, contracts, equity, family law, criminal law, and property law were the fields of substantive law that Holmes would till the most. The cases that came before him involved disgruntled spouses, injured sailors, irate liquor dealers, indignant cigar makers, wronged pond owners, damaged mannequins, and men killed while using outhouses near railroad tracks. Although there were many cases, most were of no moment.[8] And his job wasn't all appellate work confined to the high court located in Boston. For, as did other justices, Holmes had to travel to rural areas to preside over trials in county courthouses. "The great Constitutional questions that Holmes would decide were still far in the future."[9]

Between 1883 and 1902, Holmes authored at least eight opinions (some dissents) that informed his later First Amendment jurisprudence. In these opinions, and others mentioned in the note materials, we see Holmes wrestling with free speech–related concepts such as the following:

- The fair reporting privilege
- The right-privilege distinction
- Regulation of public employee speech
- The meaning of malice in defamation and other actions
- The right of association, including labor strikes and boycotts
- Free trade in ideas
- Public fora and public expression
- Free speech and the proximity of harm

These opinions, though not conceptually complete in First Amendment terms, reveal the development of some of Holmes's key thoughts bearing

---

[7] The information set out in the opening paragraphs was drawn from Liva Baker, *The Justice from Beacon Hill* (New York: HarperCollins, 1991), at 265–70, 274; *Mr. Justice Holmes, supra* note 2, at 67–69; *Honorable Justice, supra* note 1, at 166–70; Harry C. Shriver, ed., *Judicial Opinions of Oliver Wendell Holmes* (New York: Dennis & Co., 1940), at 325 (noting twenty-three dissents); and *Justice Oliver Wendell Holmes: Law and the Inner Self, supra* note 5, at 253–55.

[8] *See Justice Oliver Wendell Holmes: Law and the Inner Self, supra* note 5, at 256–57, 258. *But consider* Mark Tushnet, "The Logic of Experience: Oliver Wendell Holmes on the Supreme Judicial Court," 63 *Virginia Law Review* 975 (1977).

[9] *Honorable Justice, supra* note 1, at 171.

on his free speech jurisprudence. In that regard, consider, for example, the following statements extracted from some of his state court opinions:

- "It used to be said sometimes that the privilege was founded on the fact of the court being open to the public" *Cowley v. Pulsifer* (1884).
- "There is an important distinction to be noticed between the so-called privilege of fair criticism upon matters of public interest and the privilege existing in the case, for instance, of answers to inquiries about the character of a servant" *Burt v. Anderson Newspaper Co.* (1891).
- "Of course it does not matter that the defendant did not intend to injure the plaintiff, if that was the manifest tendency of his words" *Hanson v. Globe Newspaper Co.* (1893).
- "The policy of allowing free competition justifies the intentional inflicting of temporal damage, including the damage of interference with a man's business by some means, when the damage is done, not for its own sake, but as an instrumentality in reaching the end of victory in the battle of trade" *Vegelahn v. Guntner* (1896).
- "The degree of proximity held sufficient may vary with the circumstances, including among other things the apprehension which the particular crime is calculated to excite" *Commonwealth v. Peaslee* (1901).

Though such opinions, first drafted using quill pens, were often workmanlike and free of the grand ideas and arresting imagery that became associated with Holmes in his later life, they do show a mind laboring through common law doctrines that would one day be reworked into constitutional law. This process was cumbersome and disjointed, and the work product was not always entirely faithful to what he had previously written in *The Common Law* and elsewhere. Yet as Holmes became accustomed to his judicial work,[10] he became more adept at discerning those unarticulated grounds of public policy – those unconscious forces that actually drove the law, including the law of free speech. So, as he discovered the law, he likewise rewrote it – at least he tried. At other times, he preferred to ride a bicycle (he learned to do so in his fifties) or go with his wife, Fanny, and their coachman for a horse-drawn carriage ride out in the country.

⚓

Holmes's years on the Massachusetts high court were times of intellectual excitement, professional achievement, familial deaths, and even touches of forbidden romance. Between 1884 and 1894, he buried his brother

---

[10] Holmes kept a bench book for the court terms 1882–83 through 1898–99 that is stored in the Harvard Law School Library Archives.

Edward; his mother, Amelia; and his father, Dr. Holmes. His younger brother Ned, as he was known, had been afflicted with asthma and malaria and was in poor health when he died at the young age of thirty-eight of heart disease. Four years later, his beloved mother passed. She had been in declining health for some time. Her "mental health gradually but steadily deteriorated until she became childlike. She lingered a winter and a summer, but a second winter proved too much, and in February 1888 at the age of seventy, died, giving [Wendell] 'a tug that goes far down to the roots.'"[11] And then came his father's death in 1894.[12] The eighty-five-year-old doctor had lived a long and illustrious life, which was recounted in the newspapers and at the private memorial service held at King's Chapel per the doctor's direction to his son. Though his father's death was, in his own words, "a very great event in my life,"[13] Holmes was nonetheless prepared to go on with his own life and make his own mark. Ironically, he did so by moving back with Fanny to 296 Beacon Street, his father's home.[14]

After having been on the state high court for some years, Holmes, then age sixty-one, took his life in a new direction, one more attuned to personal passion. His "social and intellectual life had a distinctive, and seemingly contradictory, tenor. Following a pattern he had initiated very early in his professional career, Holmes did not participate extensively in social affairs in Boston, where he had lived his entire life. He absorbed himself in his judicial work and in intellectual pursuits, such as extensive reading and frequent letter writing, during his leisure time; he and his wife rarely entertained or socialized. At the same time, however, Holmes developed a series of 'flirtatious' relationships with women in Boston, and especially [with a particular woman] in England, [where] he frequently traveled in

[11] *The Justice from Beacon Hill, supra* note 7, at 286–87 (on Edward), and 293 (on Amelia). "Like all her family, [Mrs. Holmes] was a private person and left no journals or letters. She was not a 'come-outer' and except for her brief but effective management of the local branch of the U.S. Sanitary Commission during the Civil War, she seems to have devoted herself entirely to her family, shielding her husband from the liabilities of fame and lavishing on her children the gentle love of which a sense of security is born – the sort of security with which all things are possible and without which nothing is possible." *Ibid.* at 293.

[12] *See* Edwin P. Hoyt, *The Improper Bostonian: Dr. Oliver Wendell Holmes* (New York: William Morrow, 1979), at 281–85; Obituary, "Oliver Wendell Holmes Dead," *New York Times*, October 8, 1894, at 1.

[13] Letter from OWH to James Bryce, November 5, 1894, OWH Papers, Harvard Law School, Box 38, Folder 3, quoted in *Honorable Justice, supra* note 1, at p. 201.

[14] Not long afterward, Fanny "suffered a return of her rheumatic fever. She became terribly ill and, either through illness or the treatment given, lost her hair." *Honorable Justice, supra* note 1, at 201 (footnote omitted).

the summers after 1887."[15] For reasons at once complex and uncertain, nothing ultimately came of it, and Holmes went back to back to forging his legacy in the law. He wore eyeglasses now; it was a sign of both a renewed dedication to his work and the onset of old age. As his passion for romance diminished, his passion for greatness in the law increased. And so the boldness of his heart came to be replaced with a boldness of ideas, some of which were exceptionally daring.

⊰

It was after a dozen or so years on the bench, and three months after he issued his much-noticed dissent in *Vegelahn v. Guntner,* when Holmes delivered a lecture to commemorate the opening of a new hall at Boston University School of Law. The address, delivered on January 8, 1897, was titled "The Path of the Law."[16] That lecture, it has been said, "pushed American thought into the twentieth century."[17] Though some of its core ideas traced back to what Holmes had written in *The Common Law,*[18] the lecture was intellectually defiant. With analytic bravado and rhetorical flare, Holmes introduced his metaphorical bad man to the mind of American law. This man was concerned with neither morals nor abstractions. "If you want to know the law and nothing else," Holmes told the young law students fixed on his every word, "you must look at it as a bad man, who cares only for the material consequences which such knowledge enables him to predict, not as a good one, who finds his reasons for conduct, whether inside the law or outside of it, in the vaguer sanctions of conscience." By this realist norm, the job of the bad man's lawyer was to

[15] G. Edward White, "Justice Holmes and the Modernization of Free Speech Jurisprudence: The Human Dimension," 80 *California Law Review* 391, 407–08 (1992) (footnotes omitted). *See also* G. Edward White, "Holmes's 'Life Plan': Confronting Ambition, Passion and Powerlessness," 65 *New York University Law Review* 1409, 1440–57 (1990) (discussing, among other things, Holmes's "search for intimacy" and his involvement with Lady Clare Castletown); *Justice Oliver Wendell Holmes: Law and the Inner Self, supra* note 5, at 225–52 (same); John S. Monagan, *The Grand Panjandrum: Mellow Years of Justice Holmes* (Lanham, MD: University Press of America, 1988), at 71–95 (quoting extensively letters between OWH and Castletown). See also the introductory text and note 21 in Part II of this volume.

[16] On November 15, 1996, the Brooklyn Law School held a conference to commemorate the hundredth anniversary of the address. *See* "Symposium: The Path of the Law 100 Years Later: Holmes's Influence on Modern Jurisprudence," 63 *Brooklyn Law Review* 1 (1997).

[17] Morton J. Horwitz, *The Transformation of American Law, 1870–1960: The Crisis of Legal Orthodoxy* (New York: Oxford University Press, 1992), at 142.

[18] *Consider Justice Oliver Wendell Holmes: Law and the Inner Self, supra* note 5, at p. 218 ("the two works have often been contrasted, and the current scholarly view appears to be that Holmes'[s] jurisprudential views evolved considerably between the late 1870s and 1897.").

predict how his client might best dodge the "dangers" of law's "force." This "businesslike understanding of the matter" was not, Holmes assured his audience, "the language of cynicism."[19] Rather, it was a detached scientific look at the law stripped of everything save realism. Although Holmes referred to his *Vegelahn* dissent in the lecture, the free speech implications of "The Path of Law" have been largely overlooked. A number of his First Amendment ideas, however, might well derive from this seminal essay, ideas related to historical intent, skepticism, privileged communications, the relationship between moral norms and constitutional liberty, and the conceptualization of First Amendment doctrine.

With "The Path of the Law," Holmes brought some provocative blaze into the humdrum world of his life on the bench. Lighting an occasional bushfire to stimulate the legal mind seemed to excite him; it also permitted him to move beyond the pettiness of his work to engage the grandeur of his imagination. By the time his career on the Massachusetts Supreme Judicial Court drew near its end, Holmes could speak candidly, as he did on March 7, 1900, at a Boston Bar Association dinner: "I look into my book in which I keep a docket of the decisions of the full court which fall to me to write, and I find about a thousand cases. A thousand cases, many of them upon trifling or transitory matters, to represent nearly a lifetime! . . . Alas, gentlemen, that is life. . . . We cannot live our dreams. We are lucky enough if we can give a sample of our best, and if in our hearts we can feel that it has been nobly done."[20] And in his years on that court, Justice Holmes had indeed given samples of his best, though he was by no measure done trying to live out his dreams of greatness.

It is desirable that the trial of causes should take place under the public eye, not because the controversies of one citizen with another are of public concern, but because it is of the highest moment that those who administer justice should always act under the sense of public responsibility, and that every citizen should be able to satisfy himself with his own eyes as to the mode in which a public duty is performed.

[19] *Cf.* Albert Alschuler, *Law without Values* (Chicago: University of Chicago Press, 2000), at 132–80 (concluding that "The Path of the Law" was a "dark, elegant, engaging, and destructive essay. . . . ").

[20] Speech at a dinner given to Chief Justice Holmes by the Bar Association of Boston, March 7, 1900, reproduced in Mark DeWolfe Howe, comp., *The Occasional Speeches of Justice Oliver Wendell Holmes* (Cambridge, MA: Harvard University Press, 1962), at 122–23.

Cowley v. Pulsifer

137 Mass. 392, 50 Am. Rep. 318 (1884)
Vote: 5–0[21]
Argued: March 10, 1884
Decided: June 27, 1884
For the plaintiff: C. Cowley, *pro se*
For the defendants: S. Lincoln

Holmes, J.

This is an action against the owners and publishers of the *Boston Herald* for a libel printed in that newspaper. The alleged libel was a report of the contents of a petition for the removal of the plaintiff, an attorney at law, from the bar. The report was fair and correct, but the petition included allegations which would be actionable unless justified. In their answer the defendants rely upon privilege; and the main question raised by the plaintiff's exceptions is whether the publication was privileged [under the common law], as ruled by the court below.

The petition had been presented to the clerk of the Supreme Judicial Court...had been marked by him, "Filed February 23, 1883," and then or subsequently had been handed back to the petitioner, but it did not appear that it ever had been presented to the court or entered on the docket.

We are of opinion that the foregoing circumstances do not constitute a justification, and that the defendants do not bring themselves within the privilege admitted by the plaintiff to attach to fair reports of judicial proceedings, even if preliminary or ex parte....

We begin by recalling the familiar distinction between the privilege of the petitioner in respect of filing his petition, and the privilege of the same or any other person in respect of subsequently printing it in the newspapers, or otherwise publishing it to strangers who have no interest in the matter. This distinction, we believe, has always been recognized...*Commonwealth v. Blanding*, 3 Pick. 304, 317 [(1825)].

The privilege set up by the defendants is not that which attaches to judicial proceedings, but that which attaches to fair reports of judicial proceedings.

---

[21] The Massachusetts high court was (and is) a seven-member court, but sometimes only five justices sat on a case, as indicated by the vote in this case and others in this section. – Ed.

Now what is the reason for this latter? The accepted statement is that of Mr. Justice Lawrence in *Rex v. Wright* [1799]: "Though the publication of such proceedings may be to the disadvantage of the particular individual concerned, yet it is of vast importance to the public that the proceedings of courts of justice should be universally known. The general advantage to the country in having these proceedings made public, more than counter-balances the inconveniences to the private persons whose conduct may be the subject of such proceedings." See also . . . *Commonwealth v. Blanding*, 3 Pick. 314.

The chief advantage to the country [that] we can discern, and that which we understand to be intended by the foregoing passage, is the security which publicity gives for the proper administration of justice. It used to be said sometimes that the privilege was founded on the fact of the court being open to the public. This, no doubt, is too narrow . . . but the privilege and the access of the public to the courts stand in reason upon common ground. It is desirable that the trial of causes should take place under the public eye, not because the controversies of one citizen with another are of public concern, but because it is of the highest moment that those who administer justice should always act under the sense of public responsibility, and that every citizen should be able to satisfy himself with his own eyes as to the mode in which a public duty is performed.

If these are not the only grounds upon which fair reports of judicial proceedings are privileged, all will agree that they are not the least important ones. And it is clear that they have no application whatever to the contents of a preliminary written statement of a claim or charge. These do not constitute a proceeding in open court. Knowledge of them throws no light upon the administration of justice. Both form and content depend wholly on the will of a private individual, who may not be even an officer of the court. It would be carrying privilege farther than we feel prepared to carry it, to say that, by the easy means of entitling and filing it in a cause, a sufficient foundation may be laid for scattering any libel broadcast with impunity.

We waive consideration of the tendency of a publication like the present to create prejudice, and to interfere with a fair trial. Neither shall we discuss the question what limitations there are, if any, to the requirement that the proceeding must have been acted on and decided. For apart from the distinction between what takes place in open court and the contents of papers filed in the clerk's office, it might be said that these considerations apply with equal force to a report of proceedings in court published from day to day as they take place, and that nevertheless it has been held that reports might be so published, and that it is not necessary to wait until a trial is completed. The practice of publishing reports in this manner is universal with us, and we may concede that it might happen that the proceedings of the first day stopped with the reading of the pleadings, or, in this case, of the petition, and that a fair report under those circumstances would be privileged, without considering whether a publication of the first day's proceedings could be made actionable by relation if the subsequent ones should be omitted.

For the purposes of the present case, it is enough to mark the plain distinction between what takes place in open court, and that which is done out of court by one party alone, or more exactly, as we have already said, the contents of a paper filed by him in the clerk's office. This distinction, although not established by them, derives an indirect sanction from the cases [that] have turned on the question whether the proceeding – for instance, the examination of a bankrupt – took place in a public court.

It is further to be noticed that the language of Chief Justice Shaw in *Barrows v. Bell* [1856], clearly implies that the privilege claimed by the defendants does not protect them. He says that a fair statement of the proceedings, "when they have been acted upon and decided, made with an honest view of giving useful information, and where the publication will not tend to obstruct the course of justice and interfere with a fair trial, is not a libelous publication." In the English Chancery it is held to be a contempt of court to publish a pleading of one party in a newspaper, or, it would seem, the whole proceedings, before the matter has come on to be heard. A contempt of court cannot be privileged, and we see no reason to doubt that an action could be maintained for such a publication. Nor do we see any reason for confining the liability to proceedings in equity. "If one exhibit a scandalous bill, if the court hath jurisdiction of such matters, an action lies not: otherwise it is, if the court have not jurisdiction; or having, if the party publish his bill abroad, the said bill being false." *Weston v. Dobniet* [(1618)].

We have placed only a qualified reliance on the cases cited, because some of them were decided too early to be conclusive, and those on the question of contempt have been placed on grounds not perhaps convincing with regard to the present question. But they lend strong support to our decision.

It may be objected that our reasoning tacitly assumes that papers properly filed in the clerk's office are not open to the inspection of the public. We do not admit that this is true, or that the reasons for the privilege accorded to the publication of proceedings in open court would apply to the publication of such papers, even if all the world had access to them. But we do not pause to discuss the question, because we are of opinion that such papers are not open to public inspection....

To Frederick Pollock
Washington, December 15, 1912

Dear F. P.:

. . . Early in my judicial experience I wrote a decision on the extent of the privilege in publishing legal proceedings, *Cowley v. Pulsifer*. . . . I remember that *The Nation* pitched into it and don't remember much else. In a divorce case once I remember saying that if reporters saw fit to withdraw out of hearing I thought it would be a very proper and considerate thing, and I let the woman testify in a very low voice. I think some of my predecessors had heard cases *in camera* but I don't think I ever did. . . . "

Yours ever,
O. W. Holmes

Mark DeWolfe Howe, ed., *Holmes-Pollock Letters: The Correspondence of Mr. Justice Holmes and Sir Frederick Pollock, 1874–1932* (Cambridge, MA: Harvard University Press, 1941), at 1:204 (footnote omitted).

COMMENTARY

An earlier Massachusetts precedent – In *Cowley*, we see Holmes citing, with approval, a case he learned in his law school days (see Part II), *Commonwealth v. Blanding*, 20 Mass. (3 Pick.) 304, 313 (1825), authored by Chief Justice Isaac Parker. He cited *Blanding* for the proposition that charges of misconduct are not privileged communications under the common law unless made in a legal proceeding. Years later, Holmes again cited *Blanding* approvingly in his opinion for the Court in *Patterson v. Colorado*, 205 U.S. 454, 462 (1907) (see Part IV), though for proposition related to prior restraints.

Subsequent libel case – In *Bigelow v. Sprague*, 140 Mass. 425, 5 N.E. 144 (1886), Holmes writing for the Court ruled, among other things, that in a libel action each individual copy of a publication can be used to establish an indictment. The opinion contained no discussion of any free speech constitutional questions.

Holmes's general approach to the law of defamation – "Holmes's libel and slander decisions are important because they show that he thought that speech alone could constitute a harmful act subject to liability on general principles. An agent who libeled another was punishable irrespective of motive or intent. Liability was grounded on the harmful act and that alone. In an early article,[22] Holmes wrote: 'So in slander and libel, the distinction between malice in law and malice in fact seems to give the result, that the usual ground of liability in such actions is simply doing overt acts; viz., making the false statements complained of, irrespective of intent.' In *The Common Law* [see Part II], he returned to the same theme, arguing that 'the rule that it [libel] is presumed upon proof of speaking certain words is equivalent to saying that the overt conduct of speaking those words may be actionable whether the consequence of damage the plaintiff was intended or not.' This conclusion 'falls within the general theory,' he added, 'because the manifest tendency of [defamatory] words is to harm the person of whom they are spoken.' Libel was a harmful speech act to which the external standard of liability was applied. A publisher knew facts that would have warned a rational and prudent person of danger and was therefore liable if his or her actions harmed another. No internal facts of intent or motive had to be proved of the defendant." H. L. Pohlman, *Justice Oliver Wendell Holmes: Free Speech and the Living Constitution* (New York: New York University Press, 1991), at 53–54 (footnotes omitted).

The privilege exception – "Holmes's libel decisions are also important because they reveal his doctrine of privilege at work. [W]hether a certain privilege against libel should be recognized and, if it should, whether the privilege held if the agent libeled another maliciously were policy questions. Early in his judicial career," as we see in *Cowley v. Pulsifer*, "Holmes read any privilege against libel narrowly. In 1884, he refused to widen the privilege attached to fair reports of judicial proceedings." *Justice Oliver Wendell Holmes: Free Speech and the Living Constitution, supra*, at 55 (footnote omitted).

Common law privileges narrowly construed – "All of Holmes's state court defamation opinions were, of course, written well before the First Amendment became applicable to the states through the Fourteenth Amendment – that would not happen for another forty years after he wrote for the Supreme Judicial Court in *Cowley. See Gitlow v. New York* (1925) (in Part VI). Thus, it is unfair to chastise Holmes for not deeming dispositive the consequences for free expression of the common law rules he articulated in cases like *Cowley, Hanson v. Globe Newspaper Co.*, and *Burt v. Advertiser Newspaper Co.* Still, Holmes understood full well that the common law privilege asserted by the defendant in *Cowley* was intended by the common law to serve the public

---

[22] "Primitive Notions in American Law," 10 *American Law Review* 422 (1876). – *Ed.*

interest – it was premised on the notion that, as he put it, "it is of the highest moment that those who administer justice should always act under the sense of public responsibility, and . . . every citizen should be able to satisfy himself with his own eyes as to the mode in which a public duty is performed." Nevertheless, he concluded that interest was not served by affording a privilege to the accurate repetition of the contents of documents contained in public court files. On its face, therefore, it is difficult to imagine the Holmes who authored *Cowley* coming to a different conclusion would the case have arisen in 1926 and the First Amendment issue been put squarely before him. Holmes was more keenly sensitive to the power of words to cause harm and generally approved of the strict liability tort that the common law had fashioned to afford a remedy for such harm. He was thus inclined to construe narrowly those privileges that had previously been recognized as exceptions to the general rule of strict liability." Lee Levine, Commentary.[23]

Contemporary law – Although *Cowley v. Pulsifer* is often quoted and retains some staying power in common law cases involving press or public access to pretrial court documents, in more recent times, it has been interpreted more liberally so as to allow greater press access to court procedures and documents. *See, e.g., Republican Co. v. Appeals Court,* 442 Mass. 218, 812 N.E.2d 887 (2004). *See generally* Arthur R. Miller, "Confidentiality, Protective Orders, and Public Access to the Courts," 105 *Harvard Law Review* 427, 440 (1991).

A person publishes libelous matter at his peril.

Burt v. Advertiser Newspaper Co.

154 Mass. 238, 28 N.E. 1 (1891)
Vote: 5–0
Argued: January 21–22, 1891
Decided: June 29, 1891
For the plaintiff: R. M. Morse Jr. and F. J. Stinson
For the defendant: A. Hemenway and Blackman and Sheldon

Plaintiff sued in tort for alleged libels appearing in articles of the Boston Daily Advertiser *in 1889. The articles discussed Burt's involvement with corrupt New York customhouse practices, which involved cheating the government*

---

[23] Mr. Levine is a noted media lawyer, casebook coauthor, and a founding partner in the Washington, D.C., firm of Levine, Sullivan, Koch and Schulz. He kindly prepared this comment and others for inclusion in this part of the book.

by undervaluing sugar. The first article stated, "One Burt is the broker of the Havemeyer sugar people, and boasts that he makes more than fifty thousand dollars a year in that interest by his influence in securing re-appraisals in the valuations of sugar imported by that great house." The second article stated that Burt "had the entire sugar appraising division in his control" and associated Burt with customhouse workers who had been discharged for corruption. The third article cleared Burt's brother's name of any wrongdoing but added that Burt "has for years, undisturbed, carried on the practices which now, when exposed, hold the New York custom-house up as a national disgrace." The fourth article discussed potential perjury in discharged customhouse employees reversing their original statements to law enforcement authorities concerning corrupt customhouse practices by submitting new affidavits "intended, evidently, to shield Broker Burt." The lower court found for the plaintiff, and the defendant appealed.

Holmes, J.

In this [libel] case there must be a new trial. We shall state the grounds on which we come to this conclusion, and shall discuss such of the rulings as dealt with questions which are likely to come up again. Some matters not likely to recur we shall pass over. The first question which we shall consider is raised by the presiding judge's refusal to rule that the articles were privileged. The requests referred to each article as a whole. Each article contained direct and indirect allegations of fact touching the plaintiff, and highly detrimental to him, charging him with being a party to alleged frauds in the New York customhouse. Some or all of these allegations we must take to be false. Therefore the ruling asked was properly refused.

We agree with the defendant that the subject was of public interest, and that in connection with the administration of the custom-house the defendant would have a right to make fair comments on the conduct of private persons affecting that administration in the way alleged. But there is an important distinction to be noticed between the so-called privilege of fair criticism upon matters of public interest and the privilege existing in the case, for instance, of answers to inquiries about the character of a servant. In the latter case a bona fide statement, not in excess of the occasion, is privileged, although it turns out to be false. In the former what is privileged, if that is the proper term, is criticism, not statement; and however it might be if a person merely quoted or referred to a statement as made by others, and gave it no new sanction, if he takes upon himself in his own person to allege facts otherwise libelous, he will not be privileged if those facts are not true. The reason for the distinction lies in the different nature and degree of the exigency and of the damage in the two cases. In these, as in many other instances, the law has to draw a line between conflicting interests, both intrinsically meritorious. When private inquiries are made about a private person, a servant, for example, it is often impossible to answer them properly without stating facts, and those who settled the law thought it more important to preserve a reasonable freedom in giving necessary information than to insure people against occasional unintended injustice, confined, as it generally is, to one or two persons. But what the interest of private citizens in public matters requires is freedom of discussion rather than of statement. Moreover, the statements about such matters [that] come before the courts are generally public statements, where the harm done by a falsehood is much greater than in the other case. If one private citizen wrote to another that a high official had taken a bribe, no one would think good faith a sufficient answer to an action. He stands no better, certainly, when he publishes his writing to the world through a newspaper, and the newspaper itself stands no better than the writer.

The distinction to which we have referred has been brought out more clearly in England than it has been in our own decisions. Thus in *Davis v. Shepstone* [(1886)], Lord Herschell says: "It is one thing to comment upon or criticise, even with severity, the acknowledged or proved acts of a public man, and quite another to assert that he has been guilty of particular acts of misconduct. In the present case the appellants, in the passages which were complained of as libelous, charged the respondent, as now appears, without foundation, with having been guilty of specific acts of misconduct, and then proceeded, on the assumption that the charges were true, to comment upon his proceedings in language in the highest degree offensive and injurious. Not only so, but they themselves vouched for the statements by asserting that, though some doubt had been thrown upon the truth of the story, the closest investigation would prove it to be correct. In their lordships' opinion there is no warrant for the doctrine that defamatory matter thus published is regarded by the law as the subject of any privilege."

The foregoing language is applicable to the case at bar. The defendant in all the articles makes statements of fact on its own behalf, and in the second fairly may be understood to intimate that the private sources of information alleged by words, "we say this on authority," apply, not merely to the existence of corruption in the New York custom-house, but to the plaintiff's connection with it. The articles published by the defendant, so far as they contained false statements, were not privileged.

We should add, however, with reference to another trial, that there was evidence that some of the charges in the articles were true, and so far as the jury might find them to be so, inasmuch as the matter under discussion was a matter of public concern, the defendant would be justified not only in making those charges, but in free and open comment and criticism in regard to them.

The next question, the first which is raised by the bill of exceptions, is whether the court below rightly excluded a letter from the secretary of the treasury of the United States, and an *ex parte* report on the same subject, made to the treasury department, containing similar charges against the plaintiff, coupled with evidence that the writer of the articles had these documents before him, and believed the statements contained in them. The evidence was offered to show that the defendant acted in good faith, and, as it is commonly said, to negatively express malice, in support of its plea of privilege, also as bearing on damages, and generally for any purpose for which it might be admissible.

We already have considered how the defendant stands in respect of privilege. It is said that the report tended to prove that the defendant had reasonable cause to believe the charges to be true, and that it tended to show that the plaintiff was less damaged than he otherwise would have been by reason of the fact that similar charges had been made and published before. As to the former of these suggestions, it is enough to say that it is not a justification that the defendant had reasonable cause to believe its charges to be true. A person publishes libelous matter at his peril. . . .

Exceptions sustained.

COMMENTARY

What constitutes "fair criticism"? – In *Burt*, "Holmes concluded that a newspaper's common law privilege of fair criticism on matters of public interest was less extensive than an employer's privilege of criticizing an employee when a prospective employer asked for a reference. False statements by an employer often were privileged, but false statements by a newspaper could not be." Albert W. Alschuler, *Law without Values: The Life, Work, and Legacy of Justice Holmes* (Chicago: University of Chicago Press, 2000), at 70 (footnote omitted).

Nineteenth-century attitudes toward press freedom – "The *Burt* case furnishes a good example of nineteenth-century common law attitudes toward freedom of the press in defamation cases. Not even a showing that a reasonable editor would have believed the false facts about James Burt to be true would have helped the *Advertiser*: Strict liability was the standard in defamation cases." G.

Edward White, "The Integrity of Holmes' Jurisprudence," *Boston Bar Journal*, December 1982, at 28.

Holmes's theory of foreseeable harm – "As a judge, Holmes repudiated a theory of responsibility for foreseeable harm when the plaintiff's injury was the result of foreseeable misconduct by someone other than the defendant." In the *Burt* case, "Holmes articulated the principle in [broad] terms: 'Wrongful acts of independent third persons, not actually intended by the defendant, are not regarded by the law as natural consequences of his wrong.' Holmes offered no normative defense of this limitation on his general principle of foresight-based liability, and . . . prior decisions did not support so broad – and senseless – a restriction. Holmes, however, seemed to regard his restriction of the foreseeability principle as an original and constructive contribution. It was a central theme of several of his Massachusetts opinions. . . . " *Law without Values, supra*, at 119 (footnotes omitted). See also Holmes's opinions in *Elmer v. Fessenden*, 151 Mass. 359 (1890); *Clifford v. Atlantic Cotton Mills*, 146 Mass. 47 (1888); *Tasker v. Stanley*, 153 Mass. 148 (1891); *Hayes v. Inhabitants of Hyde Park*, 153 Mass. 514 (1891), *Graves v. Johnson*, 256 Mass. 211 (1892). *See generally* Patrick J. Kelley, "Holmes on the Supreme Judicial Court: The Theorist as Judge," in *The History of the Law in Massachusetts: The Supreme Judicial Court – 1692–1992*, ed. Russell K. Osgood (Boston: Supreme Judicial Court Historical Society, 1992), at 333–35.

Qualifying constitutional guarantees – "Good faith was not exculpatory because the publisher knew facts that should have warned of the dangerous character of his or her business. The danger was so obvious," Holmes reasoned, "that the law had developed a concrete external rule: 'A person publishes libelous matter at his peril.' Holmes had no inclination to treat libel differently because freedom of speech was involved; his theory of legal liability qualified the import of constitutional guarantees. He concluded that, apart from any statutory reforms, liability for libel or slander was no more or less than 'the usual liability in tort for the natural consequences of a manifestly injurious act.'" H. L. Pohlman, *Justice Oliver Wendell Holmes: Free Speech and the Living Constitution* (New York: New York University Press, 1991), at 54 (quoting *Burt v. Advertiser Newspaper Co.*).

Holmes and the future of defamation law – Holmes's opinion in *Burt* touches on several elements of the defamation tort that would, a century later, occupy the attention of the Supreme Court as well – the press's freedom to report on matters of "public interest," the relevance of a publisher's "good faith" to its potential liability, the extent to which "fair comment or expressions of opinion can be actionable, and the press's liability for the foreseeable republication of defamatory statements. That Holmes's resolution of many of these issues at common law would be largely repudiated by the Court as a matter of constitutional law may be less significant than the recognition that the issues endured and that, ultimately, the law responded to the matter. As a result, the law of defamation, as it exists today, would hardly be recognized by Holmes. It holds – contrary to *Burt* – that whether a publication addresses a subject of public concern is, more often than not, dispositive; if it does, it is indeed a "a justification that the defendant had reasonable cause to believe its charges to be true." See *Gertz v. Robert Welch, Inc.*, 418 U.S. 323 (1964); *Dun & Bradstreet, Inc. v. Greenmoss Builders, Inc.*, 472 U.S. 749 (1985). And although Holmes appeared to take some pains in *Burt* to emphasize that "fair comment" based on accurate, disclosed facts – however vituperative – is privileged at common law, a rule that endures to this day (*see Restatement [Second] of Torts § 566*), the Supreme Court has now largely endorsed a regime of significantly enhanced protections for such expressions of "opinion." See *Milkovich v. Lorain Journal Co.*, 497 U.S. 1 (1990). For these reasons, among others, although a person "still publishes libelous matter at his peril," he or she is far more likely to find freedom to do so vindicated in a court of law. In the last analysis, this says less about Holmes (although he proved himself a vigorous proponent of a strict liability tort with few and only narrow exceptions) than it does about our evolving conception of freedom of expression, a conception borne of our collective experience, both before and after the great man served on the Supreme Judicial Court of Massachusetts." Lee Levine, Comment.

The petitioner may have a constitutional right to talk politics, but he has no constitutional right to be a policeman.

MCAULIFFE V. MAYOR OF CITY OF NEW BEDFORD[24]

155 Mass. 216, 29 N.E. 517 (1892)
Vote: 5–0
Argued: October 29, 1891
Decided: January 6, 1892
For the petitioner: J. W. Cummings and E. Higginson
For the respondent: T. F. Desmond

The mayor of New Bedford, Massachusetts, removed a police officer from the city police force after the officer, in violation of police regulations, engaged in

---

[24] Although this important and well-known opinion appears in Judge Posner's collection of materials, it is surprisingly absent from Max Lerner's otherwise impressive array of Holmes's writings. – *Ed.*

political soliciting and had supported various political candidates for office. According to statutory law, police officers could hold their positions during good behavior and could be removed by the mayor for cause after a hearing. The mayor gave the officer a hearing but only a half an hour's notice. The officer was present at the hearing but gave no evidence. Another hearing took place at which the officer was present with counsel. The petitioner argued that he did not have a proper hearing and that his right to express his political opinions was violated.

Holmes, J.

This is a petition for mandamus to restore the petitioner to the office of policeman in New Bedford. He was removed by the mayor upon a written complaint, after a hearing, the mayor finding that he was guilty of violating the thirty-first rule of the police regulations of that city. The part of the rule which the petitioner seems certainly to have violated is as follows: "No member of the department shall be allowed to solicit money or any aid, on any pretense, for any political purpose whatever." There was also evidence that he had been a member of a political committee, which likewise was prohibited. Both parties agree that . . . members of the police force held office "during good behavior, and until removed by the mayor for cause deemed by him sufficient, after due hearing." It is argued by the petitioner that the mayor's finding did not warrant the removal; that the part of the rule violated was invalid, as invading the petitioner's right to express his political opinions; and that a breach of it was not a cause sufficient, under the statutes.

One answer to this argument, assuming that the statute does not make the mayor the final judge of what cause is sufficient, and that we have a right to consider it, is that there is nothing in the constitution or the statute to prevent the city from attaching obedience to this rule as a condition to the office of policeman, and making it part of the good conduct required. The petitioner may have a constitutional right to talk politics, but he has no constitutional right to be a policeman. There are few employments for hire in which the servant does not agree to suspend his constitutional rights of free speech as well as of idleness by the implied terms of his contract. The servant cannot complain, as he takes the employment on the terms which are offered him. On the same principle the city may impose any reasonable condition upon holding offices within its control. This condition seems to us reasonable, if that be a question open to revision here. . . .

Petition dismissed.

COMMENTARY

Right-privilege distinction – "One of the principal intellectual architects of the right-privilege distinction was Oliver Wendell Holmes. Holmes, of course, was also one of the earliest judicial exponents of vigorous protections for freedom of speech, so it was particularly interesting to see how, in the mind of Holmes, a civil liberty such as free speech took on entirely distinct hues in the context of conditions attached to largess." Rodney A. Smolla, *Free Speech in an Open Society* (New York: Alfred A. Knopf, 1992), at 180.

Legal liability and free speech protection – "The case did not concern the constitutionality of free speech because public employment was a privilege, not a right. Since removal from public office was not equivalent to legal liability, the police officer was not protected by the right of free speech.... Holmes's theory of legal liability defined the scope of free speech. It was thus hard for him to perceive a case as one of free speech if legal liability was not involved." H. L. Pohlman, *Justice Oliver Wendell Holmes: Free Speech and the Living Constitution* (New York: New York University Press, 1991), at 118.

But what if legal liability came in the form of criminal sanctions against a policeman like officer McAuliffe? "If the Massachusetts legislature passed a statute providing penalties for speaking on behalf of political candidates, Holmes seemed to think this would raise problems under the Constitution of Massachusetts; why should it be different if the legislature dismissed one of its employees for stating his or her political views? The question is currently treated as a complicated one of First Amendment law, resting on a distinction between the government as proprietor and the government as regulator. Holmes's *McAuliffe* opinion seems to have assumed the existence of that distinction but did not explore its ramifications." G. Edward White, *Justice Oliver Wendell Holmes: Law and the Inner Self* (New York: Oxford University Press, 1993), at 286 (footnote omitted).

Nuance: Appraising official motivation – "Viewed from one perspective, depriving a man of a job because the state does not like a speech he had made is a powerful form of censorship, possibly more painful and effective than a criminal fine. From another perspective, however, it may not represent the pursuit of censorship but the pursuit of some other objective with respect to public employment. Moreover, although Justice Holmes was too simplistic in his wit, he did have an insight. The sanction in such a case is *partial*. The state is not making an effort to prevent the speech altogether; the speaker can continue to speak, albeit at the cost of his job; and if someone else makes the same speech, the state need not intervene. The problem is: Does this 'degree of freedom' afford the speaker the normative judgment as to the propriety of the state's action? Or to restate the problem in terms familiar to our analysis: Is the jurisdiction of partial sanctions identical with that of direct total sanctions? And if not, how does one determine what that jurisdiction should be? What accommodations, that is, should constitutional law make for the fact that the sanction is only partial?

"To some extent the answer must turn on an appraisal of official motivation, at least as it can be garnered from the face of the legal measure. If the objective of the partial sanction is to censor speech or to restrict associational liberty, it should be judged precisely as a direct criminal sanction would be. If, however, the prejudice to speech or association can be said to be a by-product of the pursuit of some other legitimate state objective, we are again confronted with the puzzling question of how to delimit the use of the partial sanction.

"A further complexity of the partial sanction problem is that it permits a double view of what liberty is being infringed. To recur to Holmes's policemen, the imposition of the partial sanction can be seen as (i) infringing the privilege of working as a policeman by adding this condition to it, or (ii) as infringing the right to speak by attaching disabilities such as the loss of employment to it. There would seem to be no canon for detecting 'which side is up,' but the question is whether it alters the analysis of propriety any, if we shift from the perspective of infringing employment to the perspective of infringing speech." Harry Kalven Jr., A Worthy Tradition: Freedom of Speech in America, ed. Jamie Kalven (New York: Harper & Row, 1988), at 302 (emphasis in original).

Criticism – "Holmes did not seem concerned that the government would abuse its power to place conditions on the receipt of benefits to achieve harsh or unjust results. For Holmes these were economic transactions, governed by market forces, and not subject to moral concerns. The government was entitled to charge what the market would bear. . . . Conscientious and consistent application of [Holmes's] right-privilege distinction would make [government employees' free speech] disputes easy to solve: The government would always win." Free Speech in an Open Society, supra, at 181.

Response – "Holmes's opinion in McAuliffe might seem to our generation to be extremely insensitive to the value of free speech. It should be noted, however, that even today public employment does justify 'reasonable' regulations limiting a public employee's right of free speech." Free Speech in an Open Society, supra, at 118, 129 n. 83 (citing U.S. Public Workers v. Mitchell, 330 U.S. 75

(1947); *CSC v. Letter Carriers*, 413 U.S. 548 (1973); and *Broadrick v. Oklahoma*, 413 U.S. 601 (1973)). For more contemporary discussions of the right-privilege distinction in free speech jurisprudence, see *Rumsfeld v. Forum for Academic & Institutional Rights*, 547 U.S. 47 (2006) (federal statute constitutionally withhold funding from universities if they refuse to give military recruiters access to school resources). *See generally* Judith Areen, "Government as Educator: A New Understanding of First Amendment Protection of Academic Freedom and Governance," 97 *Georgetown Law Journal* 945, 974–82 (2009).

Such cases notwithstanding, the Court has fortified the reasonableness strand of Holmes's *McAuliffe* opinion. *See Keyishian v. Board of Regents*, 385 U.S. 589, 605–06 (1967) ("the theory that public employment which may be denied altogether may be subjected to any conditions, regardless of how unreasonable, has been uniformly rejected"); *accord Schware v. Board of Bar Examiners*, 353 U.S. 232 (1957) (striking down certain bar admission restraints of political associations); *United States v. Robel*, 389 U.S. 258 (1967) (invalidating federal law prohibiting members of communist organizations from employment in defense facilities). *See generally* Thomas I. Emerson, *The System of Freedom of Expression* (New York: Vintage, 1970), at 564–67; Laurence Tribe, *American Constitutional Law*, 2nd ed. (Mineola, NY: Foundation Press, 1988), at 1017–18.

More recently, the Supreme Court observed: "As the Court's decisions have noted, for many years 'the unchallenged dogma was that a public employee had no right to object to conditions placed upon the terms of employment – including those which restricted the exercise of constitutional rights.' *Connick v. Myers* (1983).... That dogma has been qualified in important respects. *See* [*Connick*]. The Court has made clear that public employees do not surrender all their First Amendment rights by reason of their employment. Rather, the First Amendment protects a public employee's right, in certain circumstances, to speak as a citizen addressing matters of public concern." *Garcetti v. Ceballos*, 547 U.S. 410 (2006) (denying police officer's whistle-blower rights).

Did Holmes change his mind on the right-privilege distinction? – Holmes's dissent in *United States ex rel. Milwaukee Social Democratic Publishing Co. v. Burleson*, 255 U.S. 407, 436 (1921) suggests that he might have come to view this matter differently some thirty years later. See commentary following *Burleson*, in Part VI.

Of course it does not matter that the defendant did not intend to injure the plaintiff, if that was the manifest tendency of his words.

HANSON V. GLOBE NEWSPAPER CO.

159 Mass. 293, 34 N.E. 462 (Mass. 1893)
Vote: 4–3
Argued: January 18, 1893
Decided: June 20, 1893
For the plaintiff: D. Loring
For the defendant: G. M. Palmer

A newspaper published an account of a police court proceeding in which the paper described an H. P. Hanson, a real estate and insurance broker of South Boston, as having "emerged from the seething mass of humanity that filled the dock and indulged in a wordy bout with policeman B., etc." The facts in the newspaper account actually pertained to another Mr. Hanson, one A. P. H. Hanson. The plaintiff was also a real estate and insurance broker in South Boston, and his name was used by mistake. The lower court found that the article was not "of or concerning the plaintiff," and the plaintiff could not recover. The majority affirmed. Holmes dissented and was joined by two other justices.

Holmes, J., dissenting.

I am unable to agree with the decision of the majority of the court, and, as the question is of some importance, in its bearing on legal principles, and as I am not alone in my views, I think it proper to state the considerations which have occurred to me. . . .

The facts are that libelous matter was published in an article by the defendant about "H. P. Hanson, a real-estate and insurance broker of South Boston;" that the plaintiff bore that name and description, and, so far as appears, that no one else did; but that the defendant did not know of his existence, and intended to state some facts about one Andrew P. H. Hanson, also a real-estate and insurance broker of South Boston, concerning whom the article was substantially true.

The article described the subject of it as a prisoner in the criminal dock, and states that he was fined, and this makes it possible to speak of the article as one describing the conduct of a prisoner. But this mode of characterization seems to us misleading. In form it describes the plight and conduct of "H.

P. Hanson, a real-estate and insurance broker of South Boston." In order to give it any different subject, or to give the subject any further qualifications or description, you have to resort to the predicate, to the very libelous matter itself. It is not necessary to say that this never can be done, but it must be done with great caution. The very substance of the libel complained of is the statement that the plaintiff was a prisoner in the criminal dock, and was fined. The object of the article, which is a newspaper criminal court report, is to make that statement. The rest of it amounts to nothing, and is merely an attempt to make the statement amusing. If an article should allege falsely that A. murdered B. with a knife, it would not be a satisfactory answer to an action by A. that it was a description of the conduct of the murderer of B., and was true concerning him. The public, or all except the few who may have been in court on the day in question, or who consult the criminal records, have no way of telling who was the prisoner, except by what is stated in the article; and the article states that it was "H. P. Hanson, a real-estate and insurance broker of South Boston."

If we are right so far, the words last quoted, and those words alone, describe the subject of the allegation, in substance as well as in form. Those words also describe the plaintiff, and no one else. The only ground, then, on which the matters alleged of and concerning that subject can be found not to be alleged of and concerning the plaintiff, is that the defendant did not intend them to apply to him; and the question is narrowed to whether such a want of intention is enough to warrant the finding, or to constitute a defense, when the inevitable consequence of the defendant's acts is that the public, or that part of it which knows the plaintiff, will suppose that the defendant did use its language about him.

On general principles of tort the private intent of the defendant would not exonerate it. It knew that it was publishing statements purporting to be serious, which would be hurtful to a man, if applied to him. It knew that it was using, as the subject of those statements, words which purported to designate a particular man, and would be understood by its readers to designate one. In fact, the words purported to designate, and would be understood by its readers to designate, the plaintiff. If the defendant had supposed that there was no such person, and had intended simply to write an amusing fiction, that would not be a defense; at least, unless its belief was justifiable. Without special reason it would have no right to assume that there was no one within the sphere of its influence to whom the description answered. The case would be very like firing a gun into a street, and, when a man falls, setting up that no one was known to be there. So, when the description which points out the plaintiff is supposed by the defendant to point out another man, whom in fact it does not describe, the defendant is equally liable as when the description is supposed to point out nobody. On the general principles of tort the publication is so manifestly detrimental that the defendant publishes it at the peril of being able to justify it, in the sense in which the public will understand it.

But, in view of the unfortunate use of the word "malice" in connection with libel and slander, a doubt may be felt whether actions for these causes are governed by general principles. The earliest forms of the common law known to me treat slander like any other tort, and say nothing about malice. Probably the word was borrowed at a later, but still early, date, from the *malitia* of the canon law. By the canon law, one who maliciously charged another with a grave sin incurred excommunication, *ipso facto*. Naturally, *malitia* was defined as *cogitatio malae mentis*. Naturally, also, for a time, the common law followed its leader. Three centuries ago it seems to have regarded the malice alleged in slander and libel as meaning the malice of ethics and the spiritual law.

In the famous case where a parson in a sermon repeated out of *Foxe's Book of Martyrs* the story "that one Greenwood, being a perjured person, and a great persecutor, had great plagues inflicted upon him, and was killed by the hand of God, whereas in truth he never was so plagued, and was himself present at that sermon," and afterwards sued the parson for the slander, Chief Justice Wray instructed the jury "that it being delivered but as a story, and not with any malice or intention to slander any, he was not guilty of the words maliciously, and so was found not guilty."

But that case is no longer law. The law constantly is tending towards consistency of theory. For a long time it has been held that the malice alleged in an action of libel means no more than it does in other actions of tort. Indeed, one of the earliest cases to state modern views was a case of libel. Accordingly, it recently was laid down by this court that the liability was the usual liability in tort for the natural consequences of a manifestly injurious act. A man may be liable civilly, and formally, at least, by the common law of England, even criminally, for publishing a libel without knowing it, and, it seems, might be liable civilly for publishing it by mistake, intending to publish another paper. So when, by mistake, the name of the plaintiff's firm was inserted under the head. "First Meetings under the Bankruptcy Act," instead of under "Dissolution of Partnership." So a man will be liable for a slander spoken in jest, if the bystanders reasonably understand it to be a serious charge. Of course it does not matter that the defendant did not intend to injure the plaintiff, if that was the manifest tendency of his words. And, to prove a publication concerning the plaintiff, it lies upon him "only to show that that construction which they've put upon the paper is such as the generality of readers must take it in, according to the obvious and natural sense of it." In *Smith v. Ashley*, the jury were instructed that the publisher of a newspaper article written by another, and supposed and still asserted by the defendant to be a fiction, was not liable, if he believed it to be so. Under the circumstances of the case, "believed" meant "reasonably believed." Even so qualified, it is questioned by Mr. Odgers if the ruling would be followed in England. But it has no application to this case, as here the defendant's agent wrote the article, and there is no evidence that he or the defendant has any reason to believe that "H. P. Hanson" meant any one but the plaintiff.

The foregoing decisions show that slander and libel now, as in the beginning, are governed by the general principles of the law of tort, and if that be so the defendant's ignorance that the words which it published identified the plaintiff is no more an excuse than ignorance of any other fact about which the defendant has been put on inquiry. To hold that a man publishes such words at his peril when they are supposed to describe a different man is hardly a severer application of the law than when they are uttered about a man believed, on the strongest grounds, to be dead, and thus not capable of being the subject of a tort. It has been seen that by the common law of England such a belief would not be an excuse.

I feel some difficulty in putting my finger on the precise point of difference between the minority and majority of the court. I understand, however, that a somewhat unwilling assent is yielded to the general views which I have endeavored to justify; and I should gather that the exact issue was to be found in the statement that the article was one describing the conduct of a prisoner brought before the municipal court of Boston, coupled with the later statement that the language, taken in connection with the publicly known circumstances under which it was written, showed at once that the article referred to A. P. H. Hanson, and that the name of H. P. Hanson was used by mistake. I have shown why it seems to me that these statements are misleading. I only will add, on this point, that I do not know what the publicly known circumstances are. I think it is a mistake of fact to suppose that the public generally know who was before the municipal criminal court on a given day. I think it a mistake of law to say that because a small part of the public have that knowledge the plaintiff cannot recover for the harm done him in the eyes of the greater part of the public, probably including all his acquaintances, who are ignorant about the matter; and I think it, also, no sufficient answer to say that they might consult the criminal records, and find out that probably there was some error. If the case should proceed further on the facts, it might appear that in view of the plaintiff's character and circumstances his acquaintances would assume that there was a mistake, that the harm to him was merely nominal, and that he had been too hasty in resorting to an action to vindicate himself. But that question is not before us. . . .

Even if the plaintiff and A. P. H. Hanson had borne the same name, and the article identified its subject only by a proper name, very possibly that would not be enough to raise the question, for, as every one knows, a proper name always purports to designate one person, and no other, and although through the imperfection of our system of naming, the same combination of letters and sounds may be applied to two or more, the name of each, in theory of law, is distinct, although there is no way of finding out which person was named, but by inquiring which was meant. . . .

Morton and Barker, J.J., agree with this opinion.

CORRESPONDENCE

To Frederick Pollock
Beverly Farms, July 22, 1919

My dear Pollock:

. . . I don't know your [House of Lords] libel case, *Hulton v. Jones*, but it coincides with a dissent of mine from Mass.,[25] and also with a decision of the Supreme Court of U.S. that I wrote in *Peck v. Tribune Co.* [see Part IV] – in principle at least. As I said in the last: – "If the publication was libelous the defendant took the risk." But that hardly reaches the necessary height as the publisher knows that his act will be detrimental if it hits and the plaintiff has no share in bringing about the situation. . . .

Yours ever,
O. W. Holmes

Mark DeWolfe Howe, ed., *Holmes-Pollock Letters: The Correspondence of Mr. Justice Holmes and Sir Frederick Pollock, 1874–1932* (Cambridge, MA: Harvard University Press, 1941), at 2:19.

Washington, February 20, 1925

Dear Pollock:

Your letter must have crossed one from me to you. I don't know about the bother you mention in libel suits. They were not common in Massachusetts and still rarer before us though I once had pleasure in giving a unanimous

---

[25] *Hanson v. Globe Newspaper Co.* (1893).

decision, *Peck-Tribune Co.*, 214 U.S. 185 [(1909), see Part IV], that in principle backed up a dissent of mine in Massachusetts, *Hanson v. Globe Newspaper Co.*. . . . in which I thought the majority failed to grasp the first principles of liability in tort. A judge of the Court of Appeals of the District has just sent me a decision in which they followed my decision seemingly in ignorance of *Peck-Tribune Co.* and quote English cases that later they said had adopted the same views that I did. The article in the *Globe* described the plaintiff H. P. Hanson as in the prisoner's dock, whereas the real man was A. P. H. Hanson. The majority held the defendant not liable as they intended the latter. In the *Peck case* a certificate to the merits of Duffy's Par Malt Whiskey by Mrs. A. Schuman was surmounted by a portrait of the plaintiff who was not Mrs. Schuman and was a teetotaler – we overruled the lower U.S. Courts and held she could recover. We also dismissed the suggestion that there was no consensus of opinion that drinking whiskey was disreputable (this was long before the 18th amendment), answering that liability was not a question of majority vote. . . .

Yours ever,
O.W.H.

Mark DeWolfe Howe, ed., *Holmes-Pollock Letters: The Correspondence of Mr. Justice Holmes and Sir Frederick Pollock, 1874–1932* (Cambridge, MA: Harvard University Press, 1941), at 2:155 (footnotes omitted).

COMMENTARY

Subsequent cases – Two years after *Hanson* came down, the California Supreme Court followed Holmes's thinking. See *Taylor v. Hearst*, 107 Cal. 262, 40 P. 392 (1895). Later, Holmes wrote to the same effect for the Court in another libel case. See *Peck v. Tribune* (1909) (see Part IV). *See generally Washington Post Co. v. Kennedy*, 3 F.2d 207 (D.C. Cir. 1925).

Defamation and principles of liability – His *Hanson* dissent exemplifies "Holmes's general presumption that libel was subject to the extended principle of liability. . . . Firing a gun in a crowded street was, in Holmes's mind, much like publishing a newspaper in a crowded city. While in the former case, there was considerable likelihood that somebody's body would be harmed, in the later case there was as much likelihood that someone's reputation would be hurt. The gunman knew facts that should have warned of the risk and was liable if harm occurred regardless of actual foresight, intent, or purpose. The publisher was in the same position. Both," reasoned Holmes, "had engaged in conduct manifestly dangerous according to the standard of the rational and prudent person." H. L. Pohlman, *Justice Oliver Wendell Holmes: Free Speech and the Living Constitution* (New York: New York University Press, 1991), at 54–55 (footnotes omitted).

"Historically, whether a publication is about the plaintiff had nothing to with the defendant's intent. 'The test is not whom the story intends to name, but who a part of the audience may reasonably think is named – not who is meant but who is hit.' Conversely, a showing that the defendant did or did not have the plaintiff in mind was not permitted, because the unexpressed intention of the defendant was irrelevant. . . . This rule permitting liability without fault for unintentional defamation has doubtless been attenuated by the rule in [*Gertz v. Welch*, 418 U.S. 323, 347 (1974)] abolishing liability without fault, at least with respect to statements of public interest issued by broadcasters and publishers." Robert D. Sack, *Sack on Defamation: Libel, Slander, and Related Problems* (New York: Practising Law Institute, 2001), at 1:2–117–2–118 (footnotes omitted).

Following Holmes and rejecting him – "*Hanson*, like *Cowley v. Pulsifer*, reflects Holmes's palpable sympathy for the subjects of defamatory falsehoods and his desire to afford them a robust cause of action against their defamers at common law. Although Judge Knowlton's opinion for the court in *Hanson* cites an impressive body of law establishing that the subjective intent of the defendant is indeed a factor that should weigh heavily in determining whether a publication has been made "of and concerning" the plaintiff, and although the trial judge in *Cowley*, sitting without a jury, had made a finding of fact "that the alleged libel declared on by the plaintiff was *not* published by the defendant of and concerning" him, Holmes was deterred neither by precedent nor by the deference traditionally afforded the trier of fact in reaching a contrary conclusion. In one sense, Holmes's view of the role of a defendant's subjective intent in the law of defamation prevailed – in the years that followed, common law courts generally followed his lead and held that the meaning of an allegedly defamatory statement, including whether it is "of and concerning" the plaintiff, was to be determined on the face of the publication, without regard to the publisher's state of mind. In another sense, however, Holmes would ultimately find himself on the wrong side of history. Beginning in 1964 with *New York Times Co. v. Sullivan*, 376 U.S. 254 (1964), the Supreme Court undertook to remake the law of defamation in the name of the First Amendment by holding in a series of decisions that a publisher's subjective intent with respect to the truth or falsity of a defamatory statement made all the difference. And as something of an ironic (albeit certainly unintentional) exclamation point, the Court in *Sullivan* not only rejected the rule of strict liability that Holmes had embraced but also held further that the jury verdict in Sullivan's favor could not stand because the publication at issue in that case was not 'of and concerning' him as a matter of constitutional law." Lee Levine, Comment.

For the legislature absolutely or conditionally to forbid public speaking in a highway or public park is no more an infringement of the rights of a member of the public than for the owner of a private house to forbid it in his house.

Commonwealth v. Davis[26]

162 Mass. 510, 39 N.E. 113 (1895)
Vote: 5–0
Argued: November 26, 1894
Decided: January 1, 1895
For the defendant: J. W. Pickering
For the Commonwealth: M. J. Sughrue

William F. Davis, a so-called preacher, was indicted and convicted in the lower court for delivering a sermon to his "congregation" on Boston Common without a permit in violation of a city ordinance. Davis challenged his conviction as violative of his free speech rights under the Massachusetts Constitution.

Holmes, J.

The only question raised by these exceptions [that] was not decided in the former case of *Commonwealth v. Davis* [1886] is one concerning the construction of the present ordinance. That such an ordinance is constitutional is implied by the former decision, and does not appear to us open to doubt. To say that it is unconstitutional means that, even if the legislature has purported to authorize it, the attempt was vain. The argument to that effect involves the same kind of fallacy that was dealt with in *McAuliffe v. New Bedford* [*supra*]. It assumes that the ordinance is directed against free speech generally (as in *Des Plaines v. Poyer*, the ordinance held void was directed against public picnics and open-air dances generally), whereas in fact it is directed toward the modes in which Boston Common may be used. There is no evidence before us to show that the power of the legislature over the common is less than its power over any other park dedicated to the use of the public, or over public streets, the

---

[26] Although this important and well-known opinion appears in Max Lerner's collection of materials, it is surprisingly absent from Judge Posner's otherwise impressive array of Holmes's writings. – *Ed.*

legal title to which is in a city or town [*Lincoln v. Boston*]. As representative of the public, it may and does exercise control over the use which the public may make of such places, and it may and does delegate more or less of such control to the city or town immediately concerned. For the legislature absolutely or conditionally to forbid public speaking in a highway or public park is no more an infringement of the rights of a member of the public than for the owner of a private house to forbid it in his house. When no proprietary rights interfere, the legislature may end the right of the public to enter upon the public place by putting an end to the dedication to public uses. So it may take the less step of limiting the public use to certain purposes.

If the legislature had power, under the constitution, to pass a law in the form of the present ordinance, there is no doubt that it could authorize the city of Boston to pass the ordinance, and it is settled by the former decision that it has done so. As matter of history, we suppose, there is no doubt that the town, and, after it, the city, always regulated the use of the common, except so far as restrained by statute. It is settled also that the prohibition in such an ordinance, which would be binding if absolute, is not made invalid by the fact that it may be removed in a particular case by a license from a city officer, or a less numerous body than the one which enacts the prohibition. It is argued that the ordinance really is directed especially against free preaching of the gospel in public places, as certain western ordinances, seemingly general, have been held to be directed against the Chinese. But we have no reason to believe, and do not believe, that this ordinance was passed for any other than its ostensible purpose, namely, as a proper regulation of the use of public grounds. . . .

COMMENTARY

An earlier case – In an earlier Boston Common case, one involving a tort claim against a municipality, Holmes declared, "the ordinance set out in the declaration is . . . a police regulation of the use of a public place by the public, made by the city under its power to make needful and salutary by-laws. . . . [I]t will save future litigation if we . . . intimate that, as the subject matter was within the city's authority to regulate by by-law, and as the by-law, so far as appears, is reasonable," it is therefore legitimate. *Lincoln v. City of Boston*, 148 Mass. 578, 583, 20 N.E. 329, 331 (1889).

Supreme Court review and reconsideration – The *Davis* case was reviewed and affirmed in *Davis v. Massachusetts*, 167 U.S. 43 (1897). Writing for a unanimous Court, Justice Edward White declared: "The fourteenth amendment to the constitution of the United States does not destroy the power of the states to enact police regulations as to the subjects within their control . . . and does not have the effect of creating a particular and personal right in the citizen to use public property in defiance of the constitution and laws of the state." The Supreme Court, however, later effectively repudiated the *Davis* holding. *See Hague v. CIO*, 307 U.S. 496 (1939) (striking down local permit requirement for public meetings and distributing printed materials in public streets); *Schneider v. State*, 308 U.S. 147 (1939) (handbill-permit ordinance declared void). *See also Cox v. Louisiana*, 379 U.S. 536 (1965) (striking down, on narrow grounds, state statute that prohibited the obstruction of public passages insofar as said law was applied discriminatorily).

Deference to legislative branch – "During his twenty years' service on the Supreme Judicial Court of Massachusetts, he wrote only one opinion declaring Massachusetts legislation unconstitutional. Although Holmes viewed the legislature as an unprincipled battlefield, he believed that judges should not deprive the victors of their spoils." Albert W. Alschuler, *Law without Values: The Life, Work, and Legacy of Justice Holmes* [Chicago: University of Chicago Press, 2002), at 58, 229 n. 34 (citing *Lorden v. Coffey*, 178 Mass. 489, 60 N.E. 124 (1901) (assessment for street improvements held unconstitutional)]. On Holmes's overall record of dissents while sitting on the state high court, *see* Harry C. Shriver, *Judicial Opinions of Oliver Wendell Holmes* (New York: 1940), at 325 (noting twenty-three dissents in Holmes's twenty years on the state court).

Criticisms – Harvard Law professor Zechariah Chafee Jr., a friend and admirer of Holmes who would later influence his free speech jurisprudence, was critical of Holmes's opinion in *Davis*. *See* Zechariah Chafee, *Free Speech in the United States* (Cambridge, MA: Harvard University Press, 1941), at 418–19 (arguing that Holmes showed no concern for the rightful need of the public to use public places for First Amendment activities). The fullest repudiation of Holmes's thinking in this case has come from the late Harry Kalven Jr., a noted First Amendment scholar. In a seminal 1965 article, he wrote: "[I]n an open democratic society . . . the streets, the parks, and other public places are an important facility for public discussion and political process. They are in brief a public forum that the citizen can commandeer; the generosity and empathy with which such facilities are made available is an index of freedom." Harry Kalven Jr., "The Concept of the Public Forum: *Cox v. Louisiana*," 1965 *Supreme Court Review* 1, 12 (1965). *See also* Geoffrey R. Stone, "Fora Americana: Speech in Public Places," 1974 *Supreme Court Review* 233 (1974) ("In the absence of an effective and meaningful opportunity to reach the relevant audience, the theoretical right of expression would be hollow.").

Finally, in neither *McAuliffe* (*supra*) nor *Davis* "did Holmes seriously consider the risk of inhibiting speech or the social interest in free expression. He therefore recognized no rights; he saw only privileges which government need not grant at all, privileges to which it seemingly could attach any conditions whatsoever. [Moreover, although] in *McAuliffe* Holmes suggested that the power to remove the policeman from office might be subject to judicial review for arbitrariness, no similar qualifying language appears in *Davis*." Yosal Rogat and James M. O'Fallon, "Mr. Justice Holmes: A Dissenting Opinion – The Speech Cases," 36 *Stanford Law Review* 1349, 1354–55 (1984) (footnote omitted).

If the policy on which our law is founded is too narrowly expressed in the term free competition, we may substitute free struggle for life.

VEGELAHN V. GUNTHER

167 Mass. 92, 44 N.E. 1077 (1896)
Vote: 5–2
Argued: March 24, 1896
Decided: October 26, 1896
For the plaintiff: B. Hale
For the defendant: T. H. Russell

Following a demand for a nine-hour day and higher wages, a group of workers went on strike at Vegelahn's factory. The workers placed two strikers in front of the business from 6:30 a.m. until 5:30 p.m. everyday. The plaintiff sought to enjoin the protest, alleging that the workers prevented him from running his business and intimidated others who sought factory employment. Sitting in equity court, Holmes had earlier granted a temporary injunction. The case then came before the full court for a final decree. The majority reversed and approved the injunction. In the majority opinion, the court reasoned that the picketers were unlawfully interfering with the rights of both employer and employees. Holmes dissented along with Chief Justice Walbridge Field, who wrote a separate opinion.

Holmes, J., dissenting

In a case like the present, it seems to me that, whatever the true result may be, it will be of advantage to sound thinking to have the less popular view of the law stated, and therefore, although, when I have been unable to bring my brethren to share my convictions, my almost invariable practice is to defer to them in silence, I depart from that practice in this case, notwithstanding my unwillingness to do so, in support of an already rendered judgment of my own.

In the first place, a word or two should be said as to the meaning of the report. I assume that my brethren construe it as I meant it to be construed, and that, if they were not prepared to do so, they would give an opportunity to the defendants to have it amended in accordance with what I state my meaning to have been. There was no proof of any threat or danger of a patrol exceeding two men, and as, of course, an injunction is not granted except with reference to what there is reason to expect in its absence, the question on that point is whether a patrol of two men should be enjoined. Again, the defendants are enjoined by the final decree from intimidating by threats, express or implied, of physical harm to body or property, any person who may be desirous of entering into the employment of the plaintiff, so far as to prevent him from entering the same. In order to test the correctness of the refusal to go further, it must be assumed that the defendants obey the express prohibition of the decree. If they do not, they fall within the injunction as it now stands, and are liable to summary punishment. The important difference between the preliminary and the final injunction is that the former goes further, and forbids the defendants to interfere with the plaintiff's business "by any scheme organized for the purpose of preventing any person or persons who now are or may hereafter be desirous of entering the [plaintiff's employment] from entering it." I quote only a part, and the part which seems to me most objectionable. This includes refusal of social intercourse, and even organized persuasion or argument, although free from any threat of violence, either express or implied. And this is with reference to persons who have a legal right to contract or not to contract with the plaintiff, as they may see fit. Interference with existing contracts is forbidden by the final decree. I wish to insist a little that the only point of difference which involves a difference of principle between the final decree and the preliminary injunction, which it is proposed to restore, is what I have mentioned, in order that it may be seen exactly what we are to discuss. It appears to me that the opinion of the majority turns in part on the assumption that the patrol necessarily carries with it a threat of bodily harm. That assumption I think unwarranted, for the reasons which I have given. Furthermore, it cannot be said, I think, that two men, walking together up and down a sidewalk, and speaking to those who enter a certain shop, do necessarily and always thereby convey a threat of force. I do not think it possible to discriminate, and to say that two workmen, or even two representatives of an organization of workmen, do; especially when they are, and are known to be, under the injunction of this court not to do so. I may add that I think the more intelligent workingmen believe as fully as I do that they no more can be permitted to usurp the state's prerogative of force than can their opponents in their controversies. But, if I am wrong, then the decree as it stands reaches the patrol, since it applies to all threats of force. With this I pass to the real difference between the interlocutory and the final decree.

I agree, whatever may be the law in the case of a single defendant, that when a plaintiff proves that several persons have combined and conspired to injure his business, and have done acts producing that effect, he shows temporal damage and a cause of action, unless the facts disclose or the defendants prove some ground of excuse or justification; and I take it to be settled, and rightly settled, that doing that damage by combined persuasion is actionable, as well as doing it by falsehood or by force.

Nevertheless, in numberless instances the law warrants the intentional infliction of temporal damage, because it regards it as justified. It is on the question of what shall amount to a justification, and more especially on the nature of the considerations which really determine or ought to determine the answer to that question, that judicial reasoning seems to me often to be inadequate. The true grounds of decision are considerations of policy and of social advantage, and it is vain to suppose that solutions can be attained merely by logic and general propositions of law which nobody disputes. Propositions as to public policy rarely are unanimously accepted, and still more rarely, if ever, are capable of unanswerable proof. They require a special training to enable any one even to form an intelligent opinion about them.

In the early stages of law, at least, they generally are acted on rather as inarticulate instincts than as definite ideas, for which a rational defense is ready.

To illustrate what I have said in the last paragraph: It has been the law for centuries that a man may set up a business in a small country town, too small to support more than one, although thereby he expects and intends to ruin some one already there, and succeeds in his intent. In such a case he is not held to act "unlawfully and without justifiable cause," as was alleged in *Walker v. Cronin* and *Rice v. Albee*. The reason, of course, is that the doctrine generally has been accepted that free competition is worth more to society than it costs, and that on this ground the infliction of the damage is privileged. Yet even this proposition nowadays is disputed by a considerable body of persons, including many whose intelligence is not to be denied, little as we may agree with them.

I have chosen this illustration partly with reference to what I have to say next. It shows without the need of further authority that the policy of allowing free competition justifies the intentional inflicting of temporal damage, including the damage of interference with a man's business by some means, when the damage is done, not for its own sake, but as an instrumentality in reaching the end of victory in the battle of trade. In such a case it cannot matter whether the plaintiff is the only rival of the defendant, and so is aimed at specially, or is one of a class all of whom are hit. The only debatable ground is the nature of the means by which such damage may be inflicted. We all agree that it cannot be done by force or threats of force. We all agree, I presume, that it may be done by persuasion to leave a rival's shop, and come to the defendant's. It may be done by the refusal or withdrawal of various pecuniary advantages, which, apart from this consequence, are within the defendant's lawful control. It may be done by the withdrawal of, or threat to withdraw, such advantages from third persons who have a right to deal or not to deal with the plaintiff, as a means of inducing them not to deal with him either as customers or servants.

I pause here to remark that the word "threats" often is used as if, when it appeared that threats had been made, it appeared that unlawful conduct had begun. But it depends on what you threaten. As a general rule, even if subject to some exceptions, what you may do in a certain event you may threaten to do – that is, give warning of your intention to do – in that event, and thus allow the other person the chance of avoiding the consequence. So, as to "compulsion," it depends on how you "compel." In *Sherry v. Perkins*, it was found as a fact that the display of banners which was enjoined was part of a scheme to prevent workmen from entering or remaining in the plaintiff's employment, "by threats and intimidation." The context showed that the words as there used meant threats of personal violence and intimidation by causing fear of it.

I have seen the suggestion made that the conflict between employers and employed was not competition. But I venture to assume that none of my brethren would rely on that suggestion. If the policy on which our law is founded is too narrowly expressed in the term free competition, we may substitute free struggle for life. Certainly, the policy is not limited to struggles between persons of the same class, competing for the same end. It applies to all conflicts of temporal interests.

So far, I suppose, we are agreed. But there is a notion, which latterly has been insisted on a good deal, that a combination of persons to do what any one of them lawfully might do by himself will make the otherwise lawful conduct unlawful. It would be rash to say that some as yet unformulated truth may not be hidden under this proposition. But, in the general form in which it has been presented and accepted by many courts, I think it plainly untrue, both on authority and principle.... It is plain from the slightest consideration of practical affairs, or the most superficial reading of industrial history, that free competition means combination, and that the organization of the world, now going on so fast, means an ever-increasing might and scope of combination. It seems to me futile to set our faces against this tendency. Whether beneficial on the whole, as I think it, or detrimental, it is inevitable, unless the fundamental axioms of society, and even the fundamental conditions of life, are to be changed.

One of the eternal conflicts out of which life is made up is that between the effort of every man to get the most he can for his services, and that of society, disguised under the name of capital, to get his services for the least possible return. Combination on the one side is patent and powerful. Combination on the other is the necessary and desirable counterpart, if the battle is to be carried on in a fair and equal way. . . .

If it be true that workingmen may combine with a view, among other things, to getting as much as they can for their labor, just as capital may combine with a view to getting the greatest possible return, it must be true that, when combined, they have the same liberty that combined capital has, to support their interests by argument, persuasion, and the bestowal or refusal of those advantages which they otherwise lawfully control. I can remember when many people thought that, apart from violence or breach of contract, strikes were wicked, as organized refusals to work. I suppose that intelligent economists and legislators have given up that notion today. I feel pretty confident that they equally will abandon the idea that an organized refusal by workmen of social intercourse with a man who shall enter their antagonist's employ is unlawful, if it is dissociated from any threat of violence, and is made for the sole object of prevailing, if possible, in a contest with their employer about the rate of wages. The fact that the immediate object of the act by which the benefit to themselves is to be gained is to injure their antagonist does not necessarily make it unlawful, any more than when a great house lowers the price of goods for the purpose and with the effect of driving a smaller antagonist from the business. . . .

CORRESPONDENCE

To Frederick Pollock
February [September?] 23, 1902

Dear Fred:

I am just back from this week's circuit and must vent a line of unreasoning – rage I was going to say – dissatisfaction is nearer. There have been stacks of notices of me all over the country and the immense majority of them seem to be hopelessly devoid of personal discrimination or courage. They are so favorable that they make my nomination [to the U.S. Supreme Court] a popular success but they have the flabbiness of American ignorance. There were one or two notable exceptions. And now as to my judicial career they don't know much more than that I took the labor side in *Vegelahn v. Guntner* and as that frightened some money interests, and such interests count for a good deal as soon as one gets out of the cloister, it is easy to suggest that the Judge has partial views, is brilliant but not very sound, has talent but is not great, etc., etc. It makes one sick when he has broken his heart in trying to make every word living and real to see a lot of duffers, generally I think not even lawyers, talking with the sanctity of print in a way that at once discloses to the knowing eye that literally they don't know anything about it.

Believe me I am not exaggerating.

. . . This is a confidential ebullition of spleen to an intimate which will do me good. I ought to be doing other things but first stopped for a moment to unpack my heart.

Yours,

O.W.H.

Mark DeWolfe Howe, ed., *Holmes-Pollock Letters: The Correspondence of Mr. Justice Holmes and Sir Frederick Pollock, 1874–1932* (Cambridge, MA: Harvard University Press, 1941), at 1:106 (footnote omitted).

COMMENTARY

The historical context: Labor unrest – "In the early 1890s, the United States seemed to many to be sliding into class warfare. In 1892, New Orleans had suffered a general strike; in Buffalo, railroads were halted by a switchmen's strike; in Idaho, a copper miners' strike turned violent, and there were shootings and deaths. In the coal fields of east Tennessee, miners went on strike, and in the Monongahela River valley of western Pennsylvania the Carnegie Steel Company went to war against its union, hiring a private army of Pinkerton guards who fought pitched battles with striking steel workers. More violence was promised to come. In the summer of 1893, the inflated market for railroad bonds collapsed, there was a panic, and the United States plunged into a depression. Labor struggles became desperate." Sheldon M. Novick, "The Unrevised Holmes and Freedom of Expression," 1991 *Supreme Court Review* 303, 312–13 (1991) (footnotes omitted).

"Earlier, . . . a similar injunction issued in Chicago drew nationwide publicity. A May 1894 strike at the Pullman Palace Car Company broadened in June to a boycott of Pullman cars on all railroads. Railroad companies, with the assistance of Untied States Attorney General Richard W. Olney, asked federal judge Peter S. Grosscup for an injunction against Eugene V. Debs and other boycott leaders preventing them from obstructing interstate commerce and the mails. Judge Grosscup, coincidentally one of Boston University's first law graduates in 1873, issued the injunction that same day. On July 4, 1894, President Cleveland sent federal troops to Chicago to keep order. Federal authorities prosecuted Debs and others for criminal conspiracy and for contempt of court. Debs was jailed on the contempt charge. The United States Supreme Court upheld Judge Grosscup's injunction and contempt order on May 27, 1895. "Back in Massachusetts, five days later, Vegelahn's petition for a permanent injunction came before Holmes, sitting as a single justice, on June 1, 1895. Holmes ruled that 'persuasion and social pressure' by the striking workmen to discourage prospective replacement workers from accepting jobs was lawful. He refused an injunction against picketing for these purposes. He granted an injunction only against 'threats of personal injury or unlawful harm' and 'persuasion to break existing contracts.' Vegelahn appealed, and the parties argued *Vegelahn v. Guntner* before the full bench on March 24, 1896, before Holmes's trip to England." David J. Seipp, "125th Anniversary Essay: Holmes's Path," 77 *Boston University Law Review* 515, 538 (1997) (footnotes omitted).

Holmes's reading list – About the time of the labor strife in America leading up to the *Vegelahn* case, Holmes familiarized himself with some of the topical themes of his day and thus took to reading Karl Marx, G. W. F. Hegel, Herbert Spencer, and William Morris. Although he had not yet "read Malthus or Darwin, . . . he had absorbed Malthusian and evolutionary thinking from the atmosphere of his earliest years, and had emerged from these studies a confirmed Malthusian evolutionist." "The Unrevised Holmes and Freedom of Expression," *supra*, at 315 (footnote omitted); Sheldon Novick, *Honorable Justice: The Life of Oliver Wendell Holmes* (New York: Dell, 1989), at 201–02.

Painful dissent – "Dissenting in *Vegelahn* had been 'painful'" for Holmes, "but he had to 'face the music once in a while. . . . Shortly after the decision was handed down, a local labor leader approached Holmes to compliment him on his dissent. Holmes, who prided himself on his own impartiality, replied: 'You wait – you'll hate me like Hell the next time.'" Liva Baker, *The Justice from Beacon Hill: The Life and Times of Oliver Wendell Holmes* (New York: HarperCollins, 1991), at 320. To Clare Castletown he wrote: "My dissent in the boycott case gets the adhesion of some who know what they are talking about and the abuse of a good many fools and incompetents including some newspapers." Concerned about how critically his *Vegelahn* dissent was being received by some Boston power brokers, Holmes added: "I dare say I may have to pay for it, practically, before I die." Similarly, he is said to have told another friend, "I have just handed down an opinion that shuts me off forever from judicial promotion." Quoted in G. Edward White, *Justice Oliver Wendell Holmes: Law and the Inner Self* (New York: Oxford University Press, 1993), at 289, 549 nn. 178–80.

A dissent becomes law – Holmes's dissent in *Vegelahn v. Guntner* drew widespread attention both in the United States and in England. It became law in England in the case of *Ware and De Freville, Ltd. v. Motor Trade Association*, 3 K.B. 40 (1921), and its reasoning was likewise reflected in *American Steel Foundries v. Tri-City Central Trades Council*, 257 U.S. 184, 212–13 (1921) (8–1 vote, per C.J. Taft for the Court). Though not citing the *Vegelahn* dissent, the majority (joined by Holmes) declared that there was nothing in existing law that "limits our conclusion here . . . that the members of a local labor union and the union itself do not have sufficient interest in the wages paid to the employees of any employer in the community to justify their use of lawful and peaceable persuasion to induce those employees to refuse to accept such reduced wages and to quit their employment."

Two conflicting principles – "*Vegelahn* required a judge to decide between two established principles of public policy that had come into conflict: combination and conspiracy to injure another's business was a cause for action; on the other hand, ruining another's business was what competition was all about, and hadn't society generally accepted the idea that free competition was 'worth more than its costs'? On that ground, the infliction of damage was, as lawyers said, 'privileged,' or in other words public policy considerations outweighed strict measurements of liability." Hence, as Liva Baker also notes, "Combination and conspiracy could be justified if public policy and 'social advantage' made them desirable. Holmes assumed his brethren would agree that the conflict between labor and capital was competition in the usual sense." *The Justice from Beacon Hill: The Life and Times of Oliver Wendell Holmes, supra*, at 319. Holmes's "statement of 'the law' was in fact a statement of economic theory in the arena of labor relations. By framing the case as a 'justification' case and by noting that in such cases the true grounds of decision were policy considerations, he had exposed the majority reasoning as based on the policy that combinations of labor were not justifiable even though combinations of capital were. . . . Just as labor-based strikes had come to be an accepted feature of labor relations, so, Holmes predicted, would peaceful picketing and boy-cotts. Freed from the confines of a majority opinion, he indulged his passion for theorizing." *Justice Oliver Wendell Holmes: Law and the Inner Self, supra,* at 288–89.

More on struggle and strikes – Four years after *Vegelahn* was handed down, Holmes once again dissented in a strike and boycott case, *Plant v. Woods,* 176 Mass. 492, 57 N.E. 1011 (1900). Wrote Holmes: "While I think the strike a lawful instrument in the universal struggle for life, I think it pure phantasy to suppose that there is a body of capital of which labor as a whole secures a larger share by that means. . . . Organization and strikes may get a larger share for the members of the organization, but if they do, they get it at the expense of the less organized and less powerful portion of the laboring class. They do not create something out of nothing. It is only by divesting our minds of questions of ownership and other machinery of distribution, and by looking solely at the question of consumption – asking ourselves what is the annual product, who consumes it, and what changes would or could we make – that we can keep in the world of realities. But, subject to the qualifications I have expressed, I think it lawful for a body of workmen to try by combination to get more than they now are getting, although they do it at the expense of their fellows, and to that end strengthen their union by the boycott and the strike. . . . "

According to Professor White, "Holmes's opinions in *Vegelahn* and *Plant v. Woods,* and his essay on 'Privilege, Malice, and Intent' [see Part II], indicated that he saw capital and labor as similarly situated actors in the world of political economy. Just as there was nothing inappropriate in labor combining to seek an advantage in the marketplace, there was nothing inappropriate in a legislative majority, sympathetic to the 'plight' of laborers, giving them special dispensations. The worth of the legislative policy need not concern Holmes, and his views on political economy suggested that he would be indifferent toward it, since he felt that capital and labor equally contributed to the flow of good to the consuming masses, where the central issues of political economy played themselves out." *Justice Oliver Wendell Holmes: The Search for the Inner Self, supra,* at 328. For an insightful discussion of *Vegelahn* and Holmes's other writings related to this topic, see Frederic R. Kellogg, *Oliver Wendell Holmes, Jr., Legal Theory, and Judicial Restraint* (New York: Cambridge University Press, 2007), at 127–36. *Cf. Sherry v. Perkins,* 147 Mass. 212, 17 N.E. 307 (1888) (Holmes joins opinion holding that a banner displayed by the defendants protesting outside of the plaintiff's business was "injurious to the plaintiff's business and property").

Holmes returns to the question of labor-management competition – Later, while he was on the U.S. Supreme Court, Holmes participated in deciding several labor-management disputes, typically ones in which management challenged a law creating certain rights for labor that management claimed violated its constitutional right to freedom of contract. In one of those cases, *Coppage v. New York*, 236 U.S. 1, 27 (1915), a majority of the Court sided with management, but Holmes dissented: "I think the judgment should be affirmed. In present conditions a workman not unnaturally may believe that only by belonging to a union can he secure a contract that shall be fair to him.... If that belief, whether right or wrong, may be held by a reasonable man, it seems to me that it may be enforced by law in order to establish the equality of position between the parties in which liberty of contract begins. Whether in the long run it is wise for the workingmen to enact legislation of this sort is not my concern, but I am strongly of opinion that there is nothing in the Constitution of the United States to prevent it, and that *Adair v. United States* ... and *Lochner v. New York* ... should be overruled. I have stated my grounds in those cases and think it unnecessary to add others that I think exist. *See further Vegelahn v. Guntner* ... [and] *Plant v. Woods*.... I still entertain the opinions expressed by me in Massachusetts." *See also Truax v. Corrigan*, 257 U.S. 312, 342 (Holmes, J., dissenting) (due-process challenge to anti-injunction statute).

The law of conspiracy – "Holmes understood conspiracy as an abuse of [common law] privilege. Certainly he believed that the right of association was to the long-term advantage of society. At every opportunity he applauded man's tendency to combine.... Hence Holmes understood man's inclination to form larger, social, economic, and political groups to be an inevitable and beneficial characteristic of modern society. The law privileged it for this reason.... As long as the purpose of [combination] was not malicious in character, the law gave ... no remedy. This was true even if the competitors foresaw the harm that their combination would cause.... Consequently, all acts of combination were privileged, even if they caused damage, unless the purpose of the agents was to harm other persons or the public. In contrast, if the purpose of the agents who combined was malicious, they were then outside of the privilege, subject to liability under the law of conspiracy." H. L. Pohlman, *Justice Oliver Wendell Holmes: Free Speech and the Living Constitution* (New York: New York University Press, 1991), at 40, 41.

The question of intent – What Professor Pohlman's interpretation indicates is that, for Holmes, the exact same words or conduct might be protected or unprotected depending on the intent of the speaker or actor. But how likely is it, in the rough and tumble of labor disputes, that the legitimate intent to improve the plight of workers can be nicely separated from the illegitimate intent to harm the employer? From that vantage point, even Holmes's speech-protective arguments in cases such as *Vegelahn* and *Plant* might be readily undermined by pretrial discovery suggesting that the labor protestors' intent was less than laudatory.

The aftermath – "The *Vegelahn* decision came down just eight days before the election pitting William McKinley against William Jennings Bryan. Bryan was the champion of labor and Boston's Democratic newspapers rejoiced at Holmes's powerful dissent. Holmes himself, a loyal Republican, feared that Bryan would combine farmers and workers into an electoral victory. Employers used pressure of all sorts to ensure McKinley's election. When McKinley won, Holmes wrote of his great relief and added, 'the great body of people who voted for Brian [*sic*] did not want to destroy society any more than I do. They only thought that salvation lay along a different path.'" David J. Seipp, "125th Anniversary Essay: Holmes's Path," 77 *Boston University Law Review* 515, 540–41 (1997) (footnotes omitted) (quoting letter from OWH to Clare Castletown, November 9, 1896).

Labor's hero? – As indicated by the correspondence set out herein, when Holmes was nominated to be a U.S. Supreme Court justice in 1902, many newspapers devoted considerable attention to his purported pro-labor views. This was largely because of his *Vegelahn* dissent. It was, of course, ironic, considering that Holmes was no progressive supporter of unions or a defender of labor. That did not, however, stop newspapers from publishing stories praising him as a hero of the labor movement. "Justice Holmes," said one account, "is disposed to give the largest freedom to labor interests consistent with law and order. As labor and trust questions are becoming more and more matters of judicial concern, his views on these topics are likely to be of great importance. It is a good thing to have on the Supreme bench a justice who is distinctively known as a friend of labor.... [H]is presence in the Supreme Court ought to have a moderating effect on [labor leaders'] denunciation of the Federal courts." "Justice Holmes and Organized Labor," *Washington Post*, August 15, 1902, at 6 (reprinted from the *New York Tribune*). To the same effect, the *Los Angeles Times* reported that "his appointment pleases the labor element of the Bay State on account of his many impartial rulings affecting labor.... He has in him a spirit of humanity, and in some of his opinions, notably [his dissents], he has pointed the way to a higher standard of equity than that which hidebound traditions recognize. He is a man, as well as a Judge." "New Supreme Court Justice," *Los Angeles Times*, August 13, 1902, at 3. The *New York Times* also devoted more than half of its early coverage of the Holmes nomination to a discussion of the *Vegelahn* case. *See* "Justice Holmes's Career," *New York Times*, August 12, 1902, at 1.

"Pet of the proletariat"? – On another occasion, and in response to an opinion he rendered in a referendum case involving women and the right to vote [*Advisory Opinion of the Justices*, 160 Mass. 586, 593 (1894)], Holmes wrote to Pollock: "among the respectable there are some who regard me as a dangerous radical! If I had seen fit to clothe my views in different language, I dare say I could have been a pet of the proletariat.…" Letter from OWH to Frederick Pollock, April 2, 1894, reproduced in *Holmes-Pollock Letters, supra,* at 1:50.

Even President Theodore Roosevelt, a Republican, expressed a similar view shortly before nominating Holmes, stressing the judge's "sympathy for the class from which he has not drawn his clients." Letter from Theodore Roosevelt to Henry Cabot Lodge, July 10, 1902, quoted in G. Edward White, *Justice Oliver Wendell Holmes: Law and the Inner Self* (New York: Oxford University Press, 1993), at 300.

"Holmes's opinions in labor cases," notes Professor Alschuler, "revealed no sympathy whatever for the laboring class. They revealed only his fondness for battle. Although, as he saw it, unions could accomplish nothing for workers as a group, that was no reason not to have a good fight." Albert W. Alschuler, *Law without Values* (Chicago: University of Chicago Press, 2000), at 67.

To an imagination of any scope the most far-reaching form of power is . . . the command of ideas.

THE PATH OF THE LAW (1897)[27]

When we study law we are not studying a mystery but a well known profession. We are studying what we shall want in order to appear before judges, or to advise people in such a way as to keep them out of court. The reason why it is a profession, why people will pay lawyers to argue for them or to advise them, is that in societies like ours the command of the public force is intrusted to the judges in certain cases, and the whole power of the state will be put forth, if necessary, to carry out their judgments and decrees. People want to

---

[27] 10 *Harvard Law Review* 457 (1897), published simultaneously under the title "Law and the Study of Law" in 9 *Juridical Review* 105 (1897). This essay derived from an address Judge Holmes, then fifty-five, gave on January 8, 1897, to commemorate the opening of a new hall at Boston University's School of Law. "The speech was first published by Boston University in pamphlet form and appeared again, under the title 'The Path of the Law,' in the short-lived *Boston Law School Magazine* in February 1897. Subsequently it was published in the *Harvard Law Review*; in the *Juridical Review of Edinburgh*, Scotland; and in Holmes's *Collected Legal Papers*." David J. Seipp, "125th Anniversary Essay:

know under what circumstances and how far they will run the risk of coming against what is so much stronger than themselves, and hence it becomes a business to find out when this danger is to be feared. The object of our study, then, is prediction, the prediction of the incidence of the public force through the instrumentality of the courts.

The means of the study are a body of reports, of treatises, and of statutes, in this country and in England, extending back for six hundred years, and now increasing annually by hundreds. In these sibylline leaves are gathered the scattered prophecies of the past upon the cases in which the axe will fall. These are what properly have been called the oracles of the law. Far the most important and pretty nearly the whole meaning of every new effort of legal thought is to make these prophecies more precise, and to generalize them into a thoroughly connected system. . . . It is to make the prophecies easier to be remembered and to be understood that the teachings of the decisions of the past are put into general propositions and gathered into textbooks, or that statutes are passed in a general form. The primary rights and duties with which jurisprudence busies itself again are nothing but prophecies. One of the many evil effects of the confusion between legal and moral ideas, about which I shall have something to say in a moment, is that theory is apt to get the cart before the horse, and consider the right or the duty as something existing apart from and independent of the consequences of its breach, to which certain sanctions are added afterward. But, as I shall try to show, a legal duty so called is nothing but a prediction that if a man does or omits certain things he will be made to suffer in this or that way by judgment of the court – and so of a legal right.

The number of our predictions when generalized and reduced to a system is not unmanageably large. They present themselves as a finite body of dogma [that] may be mastered within a reasonable time. It is a great mistake to be frightened by the ever-increasing number of reports. The reports of a given jurisdiction in the course of a generation take up pretty much the whole body of the law, and restate it from the present point of view. We could reconstruct

Holmes's Path," 77 *Boston University Law Review* 515, 516 (1997) (footnotes omitted). For an account of the events surrounding the presentation of Holmes's lecture, see also *ibid.* at 545–47. Although I have retained the old-fashioned spellings of words such as "intrusted" and "criticise," I have deleted passages and added bracketed subheadings to assist the modern reader interested in Holmes's thought as it pertains to freedom of expression. The bracketed subtitles are mine, though I refer the reader to those suggested by Professor Thomas Grey in his thoughtful article, "Plotting the Path of the Law," 63 *Brooklyn Law Review* 19 (1997). If my purposes here were not to focus in on the free speech implications of this essay, I would readily adopt Grey's subtitling. Finally, I have deleted most of the article's notes and have added some of my own. – *Ed.*

the corpus from them if all that went before were burned. The use of the earlier reports is mainly historical, a use about which I shall have something to say before I have finished.

I wish, if I can, to lay down some first principles for the study of this body of dogma or systematized prediction which we call the law, for men who want to use it as the instrument of their business to enable them to prophesy in their turn, and, as bearing upon the study, I wish to point out an ideal which as yet our law has not attained.

[The Limits of Law]

The first thing for a businesslike understanding of the matter is to understand its limits, and therefore I think it desirable at once to point out and dispel a confusion between morality and law, which sometimes rises to the height of conscious theory, and more often and indeed constantly is making trouble in detail without reaching the point of consciousness. You can see very plainly that a bad man has as much reason as a good one for wishing to avoid an encounter with the public force, and therefore you can see the practical importance of the distinction between morality and law. A man who cares nothing for an ethical rule which is believed and practised by his neighbors is likely nevertheless to care a good deal to avoid being made to pay money, and will want to keep out of jail if he can.

I take it for granted that no hearer of mine will misinterpret what I have to say as the language of cynicism. The law is the witness and external deposit of our moral life. Its history is the history of the moral development of the race. The practice of it, in spite of popular jests, tends to make good citizens and good men. When I emphasize the difference between law and morals I do so with reference to a single end, that of learning and understanding the law. For that purpose you must definitely master its specific marks, and it is for that that I ask you for the moment to imagine yourselves indifferent to other and greater things.

[On the bad-man theory of law,] I do not say that there is not a wider point of view from which the distinction between law and morals becomes of secondary or no importance, as all mathematical distinctions vanish in presence of the infinite. But I do say that that distinction is of the first importance for the object which we are here to consider – a right study and mastery of the law as a business with well understood limits, a body of dogma enclosed within definite lines. I have just shown the practical reason for saying so. If you want to know the law and nothing else, you must look at it as a bad man, who cares only for the material consequences which such knowledge enables him to predict, not as a good one, who finds his reasons for conduct, whether inside the law or outside of it, in the vaguer sanctions of conscience. The theoretical importance of the distinction is no less, if you would reason on your subject aright. The law is full of phraseology drawn from morals, and by the mere force of language continually invites us to pass from one domain to the other without perceiving it, as we are sure to do unless we have the boundary constantly before our minds. The law talks about rights, and duties, and malice, and intent, and negligence, and so forth, and nothing is easier, or, I may say, more common in legal reasoning, than to take these words in their moral sense, at some state of the argument, and so to drop into fallacy. For instance, when we speak of the rights of man in a moral sense, we mean to mark the limits of interference with individual freedom which we think are prescribed by conscience, or by our ideal, however reached. Yet it is certain that many laws have been enforced in the past, and it is likely that some are enforced now, which are condemned by the most enlightened opinion of the time, or which at all events pass the limit of interference, as many consciences would draw it. Manifestly, therefore, nothing but confusion of thought can result from assuming that the rights of man in a moral sense are equally rights in the sense of the Constitution and the law. No doubt simple and extreme cases can be put of imaginable laws which the statute-making power would not dare to enact, even in the absence of written constitutional prohibitions, because the community would rise in rebellion and fight; and this gives some plausibility to the proposition that the law, if not a part of morality, is limited by it. But this limit of power is not coextensive with any system of morals. For the most part it falls far within the lines of any such system, and in some cases may extend beyond them, for reasons drawn from the habits of a particular people at a particular time. I once heard the late Professor Agassiz[28] say that a German population would rise if you added two cents to the price of a glass of beer. A statute in such a case would be empty words, not because it was wrong, but because it could not be enforced. No one will deny that wrong statutes can be and are enforced, and we would not all agree as to which were the wrong ones.

[What Is Law?]

The confusion with which I am dealing besets confessedly legal conceptions. Take the fundamental question, What constitutes the law? You will find some

[28] Jean Louis Rodolphe Agassiz (1807–73) was a noted nineteenth-century naturalist. Agassiz was appointed professor of zoology and geology at Harvard in 1847, where in 1859 he established the Museum of Comparative Zoology. Among other things, he posited that there were several species of humans, an argument later used by slave owners to justify slavery. – Ed.

text writers telling you that it is something different from what is decided by the courts of Massachusetts or England, that it is a system of reason, that it is a deduction from principles of ethics or admitted axioms or what not, which may or may not coincide with the decisions. But if we take the view of our friend the bad man we shall find that he does not care two straws for the axioms or deductions, but that he does want to know what the Massachusetts or English courts are likely to do in fact. I am much of this mind. The prophecies of what the courts will do in fact, and nothing more pretentious, are what I mean by the law.

Take again a notion which as popularly understood is the widest conception which the law contains – the notion of legal duty, to which already I have referred. We fill the word with all the content which we draw from morals. But what does it mean to a bad man? Mainly, and in the first place, a prophecy that if he does certain things he will be subjected to disagreeable consequences by way of imprisonment or compulsory payment of money. But from his point of view, what is the difference between being fined and taxed a certain sum for doing a certain thing? That his point of view is the test of legal principles is proven by the many discussions which have arisen in the courts on the very question whether a given statutory liability is a penalty or a tax. On the answer to this question depends the decision whether conduct is legally wrong or right, and also whether a man is under compulsion or free. Leaving the criminal law on one side, what is the difference between the liability under the mill acts or statutes authorizing a taking by eminent domain and the liability for what we call a wrongful conversion of property where restoration is out of the question. In both cases the party taking another man's property has to pay its fair value as assessed by a jury, and no more. What significance is there in calling one taking right and another wrong from the point of view of the law? It does not matter, so far as the given consequence, the compulsory payment, is concerned, whether the act to which it is attached is described in terms of praise or in terms of blame, or whether the law purports to prohibit it or to allow it. If it matters at all, still speaking from the bad man's point of view, it must be because in one case and not in the other some further disadvantages, or at least some further consequences, are attached to the act by law. . . .

I mentioned, as other examples of the use by the law of words drawn from morals, malice, intent, and negligence. It is enough to take malice as it is used in the law of civil liability for wrongs what we lawyers call the law of torts – to show that it means something different in law from what it means in morals, and also to show how the difference has been obscured by giving to principles which have little or nothing to do with each other the same name. Three hundred years ago a parson preached a sermon and told a story out of Fox[e]'s

Book of Martyrs of a man who had assisted at the torture of one of the saints, and afterward died, suffering compensatory inward torment. It happened that Fox was wrong. The man was alive and chanced to hear the sermon, and thereupon he sued the parson. Chief Justice Wray instructed the jury that the defendant was not liable, because the story was told innocently, without malice. He took malice in the moral sense, as importing a malevolent motive.[29] But nowadays no one doubts that a man may be liable, without any malevolent motive at all, for false statements manifestly calculated to inflict temporal damage. In stating the case in pleading, we still should call the defendant's conduct malicious; but, in my opinion at least, the word means nothing about motives, or even about the defendant's attitude toward the future, but only signifies that the tendency of his conduct under known circumstances was very plainly to cause the plaintiff temporal harm.[30]

. . . Morals deal with the actual internal state of the individual's mind, what he actually intends. . . . [For example, the] parties are bound by the contract as it is interpreted by the court, yet neither of them meant what the court declares that they have said. In my opinion no one will understand the true theory of contract or be able even to discuss some fundamental questions intelligently until he has understood that all contracts are formal, that the making of a contract depends not on the agreement of two minds in one intention, but on the agreement of two sets of external signs – not on the parties' having *meant* the same thing but on their having said the same thing. . . .

[Two Pitfalls]

This is not the time to work out a theory in detail, or to answer many obvious doubts and questions [that] are suggested by these general views. I know of none [that] are not easy to answer, but what I am trying to do now is only by a series of hints to throw some light on the narrow path of legal doctrine, and upon two pitfalls which, as it seems to me, lie perilously near to it. Of the first of these I have said enough. I hope that my illustrations have shown the danger, both to speculation and to practice, of confounding morality with law, and the trap which legal language lays for us on that side of our way. For my own part, I often doubt whether it would not be a gain if every word of moral significance could be banished from the law altogether, and other words adopted which should convey legal ideas uncolored by anything outside the law. We should

[29] This example was drawn from the case of *Brook v. Sir Henry Montague*, Cro. Jac. 90 (1605). Holmes also used it in his dissent in *Hanson v. Globe Newspaper Co.* (1893). – *Ed.*
[30] *Hanson v. Globe Newspaper Co.*, 159 Mass. 293, 301.

lose the fossil records of a good deal of history and the majesty got from ethical associations, but by ridding ourselves of an unnecessary confusion we should gain very much in the clearness of our thought.

So much for the limits of the law. The next thing [that] I wish to consider is what are the forces which determine its content and its growth. You may assume, with Hobbes and Bentham and Austin, that all law emanates from the sovereign, even when the first human beings to enunciate it are the judges, or you may think that law is the voice of the Zeitgeist, or what you like. It is all one to my present purpose. Even if every decision required the sanction of an emperor with despotic power and a whimsical turn of mind, we should be interested [nonetheless], still with a view to prediction, in discovering some order, some rational explanation, and some principle of growth for the rules which he laid down. In every system there are such explanations and principles to be found. It is with regard to them that a second fallacy comes in, which I think it important to expose.

The fallacy to which I refer is the notion that the only force at work in the development of the law is logic. In the broadest sense, indeed, that notion would be true. The postulate on which we think about the universe is that there is a fixed quantitative relation between every phenomenon and its antecedents and consequents. If there is such a thing as a phenomenon without these fixed quantitative relations, it is a miracle. It is outside the law of cause and effect, and as such transcends our power of thought, or at least is something to or from which we cannot reason. The condition of our thinking about the universe is that it is capable of being thought about rationally, or, in other words, that every part of it is effect and cause in the same sense in which those parts are with which we are most familiar. So in the broadest sense it is true that the law is a logical development, like everything else. The danger of which I speak is not the admission that the principles governing other phenomena also govern the law, but the notion that a given system, ours, for instance, can be worked out like mathematics from some general axioms of conduct. This is the natural error of the schools, but it is not confined to them. I once heard a very eminent judge say that he never let a decision go until he was absolutely sure that it was right. So judicial dissent often is blamed, as if it meant simply that one side or the other were not doing their sums right, and if they would take more trouble, agreement inevitably would come.

[Law & Certainty]

This mode of thinking is entirely natural. The training of lawyers is a training in logic. The processes of analogy, discrimination, and deduction are those

in which they are most at home. The language of judicial decision is mainly
the language of logic. And the logical method and form flatter that longing for
certainty and for repose which is in every human mind. But certainty generally
is illusion, and repose is not the destiny of man. Behind the logical form lies
a judgment as to the relative worth and importance of competing legislative
grounds, often an inarticulate and unconscious judgment, it is true, and yet
the very root and nerve of the whole proceeding. You can give any conclusion
a logical form. You always can imply a condition in a contract. But why do you
imply it? It is because of some belief as to the practice of the community or of
a class, or because of some opinion as to policy, or, in short, because of some
attitude of yours upon a matter not capable of exact quantitative measurement,
and therefore not capable of founding exact logical conclusions. Such matters
really are battle grounds where the means do not exist for the determinations
that shall be good for all time, and where the decision can do no more than
embody the preference of a given body in a given time and place. We do not
realize how large a part of our law is open to reconsideration upon a slight
change in the habit of the public mind. No concrete proposition is self evident,
no matter how ready we may be to accept it, not even Mr. Herbert Spencer's
"Every man has a right to do what he wills, provided he interferes not with a
like right on the part of his neighbors."

[Privileges & Social Policies]

Why is a false and injurious statement privileged, if it is made honestly in giving
information about a servant? It is because it has been thought more important
that information should be given freely, than that a man should be protected
from what under other circumstances would be an actionable wrong. Why is a
man at liberty to set up a business which he knows will ruin his neighborhood?
It is because the public good is supposed to be best served by free competition.
Obviously such judgments of relative importance may vary in different times
and places. Why does a judge instruct a jury that an employer is not liable to
an employee for an injury received in the course of his employment unless he
is negligent, and why do the jury generally find for the plaintiff if the case is
allowed to go to them? It is because the traditional policy of our law is to confine
liability to cases where a prudent man might have foreseen the injury, or at
least the danger, while the inclination of a very large part of the community
is to make certain classes of persons insure the safety of those with whom they
deal. Since the last words were written, I have seen the requirement of such
insurance put forth as part of the programme of one of the best known labor
organizations. There is a concealed, half conscious battle on the question of

legislative policy, and if any one thinks that it can be settled deductively, or once for all, I only can say that I think he is theoretically wrong, and that I am certain that his conclusion will not be accepted in practice *semper ubique et ab omnibus* ["what has been held always, everywhere, by everybody"].

Indeed, I think that even now our theory upon this matter is open to reconsideration, although I am not prepared to say how I should decide if a reconsideration were proposed. Our law of torts comes from the old days of isolated, ungeneralized wrongs, assaults, slanders, and the like, where the damages might be taken to lie where they fell by legal judgment. But the torts with which our courts are kept busy today are mainly the incidents of certain [well-]known businesses. They are injuries to person or property by railroads, factories, and the like. The liability for them is estimated, and sooner or later goes into the price paid by the public. The public really pays the damages, and the question of liability, if pressed far enough, is really a question how far it is desirable that the public should insure the safety of one whose work it uses. It might be said that in such cases the chance of a jury finding for the defendant is merely a chance, once in a while rather arbitrarily interrupting the regular course of recovery, most likely in the case of an unusually conscientious plaintiff, and therefore better done away with. On the other hand, the economic value even of a life to the community can be estimated, and no recovery, it may be said, ought to go beyond that amount. It is conceivable that some day in certain cases we may find ourselves imitating, on a higher plane, the tariff for life and limb. . . .

[Judges & Policy Considerations]

I think that the judges themselves have failed adequately to recognize their duty of weighing considerations of social advantage. The duty is inevitable, and the result of the often proclaimed judicial aversion to deal with such considerations is simply to leave the very ground and foundation of judgments inarticulate, and often unconscious, as I have said. When socialism first began to be talked about, the comfortable classes of the community were a good deal frightened. I suspect that this fear has influenced judicial action both here and in England, yet it is certain that it is not a conscious factor in the decisions to which I refer. I think that something similar has led people who no longer hope to control the legislatures to look to the courts as expounders of the constitutions, and that in some courts new principles have been discovered outside the bodies of those instruments, which may be generalized into acceptance of the economic doctrines which prevailed about fifty years ago, and a wholesale prohibition of what a tribunal of lawyers does not think about right. I cannot but believe that if the training of lawyers led them habitually to consider more definitely and explicitly the social advantage on which the rule they lay down must be justified, they sometimes would hesitate where now they are confident, and see that really they were taking sides upon debatable and often burning questions.

[The Study of Law]

So much for the fallacy of logical form. Now let us consider the present condition of the law as a subject for study, and the ideal toward which it tends. We still are far from the point of view which I desire to see reached. No one has reached it or can reach it as yet. We are only at the beginning of a philosophical reaction, and of a reconsideration of the worth of doctrines which for the most part still are taken for granted without any deliberate, conscious, and systematic questioning of their grounds. The development of our law has gone on for nearly a thousand years, like the development of a plant, each generation taking the inevitable next step, mind, like matter, simply obeying a law of spontaneous growth. It is perfectly natural and right that it should have been so. Imitation is a necessity of human nature.... Most of the things we do, we do for no better reason than that our fathers have done them or that our neighbors do them, and the same is true of a larger part than we suspect of what we think. The reason is a good one, because our short life gives us no time for a better, but it is not the best. It does not follow, because we all are compelled to take on faith at second hand most of the rules on which we base our action and our thought, that each of us may not try to set some corner of his world in the order of reason, or that all of us collectively should not aspire to carry reason as far as it will go throughout the whole domain. In regard to the law, it is true, no doubt, that an evolutionist will hesitate to affirm universal validity for his social ideals, or for the principles which he thinks should be embodied in legislation. He is content if he can prove them best for here and now. He may be ready to admit that he knows nothing about an absolute best in the cosmos, and even that he knows next to nothing about a permanent best for men. Still it is true that a body of law is more rational and more civilized when every rule it contains is referred articulately and definitely to an end which it subserves, and when the grounds for desiring that end are stated or are ready to be stated in words.

At present, in very many cases, if we want to know why a rule of law has taken its particular shape, and more or less if we want to know why it exists at all, we go to tradition.... The rational study of law is still to a large extent the study of history. History must be a part of the study, because without it we cannot know the precise scope of rules [that] it is our business to know. It is a part of the rational study, because it is the first step toward an enlightened scepticism, that is, towards a deliberate reconsideration of the worth of those rules. When you get the dragon out of his cave on to the plain and in the daylight, you can count his teeth and claws, and see just what is his strength. But to get him out is only the first step. The next is either to kill him, or to tame him and make him a useful animal. For the rational study of the law the blackletter man may be the man of the present, but the man of the future is the man of statistics and the master of economics. It is revolting to have no better reason for a rule of law than that so it was laid down in the time of Henry IV. It is still more revolting if the grounds upon which it was laid down have vanished long since, and the rule simply persists from blind imitation of the past. I am thinking of the technical rule as to trespass *ab initio*, as it is called, which I attempted to explain in a recent Massachusetts case....

... [Among other things, Holmes then spoke of the question of whether "criminal law in its present form does more good than harm." He spoke of the law and theory of torts. In that context, he noted the following: "I think that commonly malice, intent, and negligence mean only that the danger was manifest to a greater or less degree, under the circumstances known to the actor, although in some cases of privilege malice may mean an actual malevolent motive, and such a motive may take away a permission knowingly to inflict harm, which otherwise would be granted on this or that ground of dominant public good."]

Everywhere the basis of principle is tradition, to such an extent that we even are in danger of making the role of history more important than it is.... Why should any merely historical distinction be allowed to affect the rights and obligations of business men? ...

[Here Holmes spoke critically of the way "in which tradition not only overrides rational policy, but overrides it after first having been misunderstood and having been given a new and broader scope than it had when it had a meaning."]

I trust that no one will understand me to be speaking with disrespect of the law, because I criticise it so freely. I venerate the law, and especially our system of law, as one of the vastest products of the human mind. No one knows better than I do the countless number of great intellects that have spent themselves in making some addition or improvement, the greatest of which is trifling when compared with the mighty whole. It has the final title to respect that it exists, that it is not a Hegelian dream, but a part of the lives of men. But one may criticise even what one reveres. Law is the business to which my life is devoted, and I should show less than devotion if I did not do what in me lies to improve it, and, when I perceive what seems to me the ideal of its future, if I hesitated to point it out and to press toward it with all my heart.

... We must beware of the pitfall of antiquarianism, and must remember that for our purposes our only interest in the past is for the light it throws upon the present. I look forward to a time when the part played by history in the explanation of dogma shall be very small, and instead of ingenious research we shall spend our energy on a study of the ends sought to be attained and the reasons for desiring them. As a step toward that ideal it seems to me that every lawyer ought to seek an understanding of economics. The present divorce between the schools of political economy and law seems to me an evidence of how much progress in philosophical study still remains to be made. In the present state of political economy, indeed, we come again upon history on a larger scale, but there we are called on to consider and weigh the ends of legislation, the means of attaining them, and the cost. We learn that for everything we have we give up something else, and we are taught to set the advantage we gain against the other advantage we lose, and to know what we are doing when we elect.

[The Study of Jurisprudence]

There is another study which sometimes is undervalued by the practical minded, for which I wish to say a good word, although I think a good deal of pretty poor stuff goes under that name. I mean the study of what is called jurisprudence. Jurisprudence, as I look at it, is simply law in its most general-ized part. Every effort to reduce a case to a rule is an effort of jurisprudence, although the name as used in English is confined to the broadest rules and most fundamental conceptions. One mark of a great lawyer is that he sees the application of the broadest rules. There is a story of a Vermont justice of the peace before whom a suit was brought by one farmer against another for breaking a churn. The justice took time to consider, and then said that he has looked through the statutes and could find nothing about churns, and gave judgment for the defendant. The same state of mind is shown in all our common digests and textbooks. Applications of rudimentary rules of contract or tort are tucked away under the head of Railroads or Telegraphs or go to swell treatises on historical subdivisions, such as Shipping or Equity, or are gathered under an arbitrary title which is thought likely to appeal to the practical mind, such as Mercantile Law. If a man goes into law it pays to be a master of it, and to be a master of it means to look straight through all the dramatic incidents and to discern the true basis for prophecy. Therefore, it is well to have an accurate notion of what you mean by law, by a right, by a duty, by malice, intent, and negligence, by ownership, by possession, and so forth....

The advice of the elders to young men is very apt to be as unreal as a list of the hundred best books. At least in my day I had my share of such counsels, and high among the unrealities I place the recommendation to study the Roman law . . . I assume that, if it is well to study the Roman Law, it is well to study it as a working system. That means mastering a set of technicalities more difficult and less understood than our own, and studying another course of history by which even more than our own the Roman law must explained. . . . The way to gain a liberal view of your subject is not to read something else, but to get to the bottom of the subject itself. The means of doing that are, in the first place, to follow the existing body of dogma into its highest generalizations by the help of jurisprudence; next, to discover from history how it has come to be what it is; and finally, so far as you can, to consider the ends which the several rules seek to accomplish, the reasons why those ends are desired, what is given up to gain them, and whether they are worth the price. . . .

[Conclusion]

. . . Theory is my subject, not practical details. The modes of teaching have been improved since my time, no doubt, but ability and industry will master the raw material with any mode. Theory is the most important part of the dogma of the law, as the architect is the most important man who takes part in the building of a house. The most important improvements of the last twenty-five years are improvements in theory. It is not to be feared as unpractical, for, to the competent, it simply means going to the bottom of the subject. For the incompetent, it sometimes is true, as has been said, that an interest in general ideas means an absence of particular knowledge. I remember in army days reading of a youth who, being examined for the lowest grade and being asked a question about squadron drill, answered that he never had considered the evolutions of less than ten thousand men. But the weak and foolish must be left to their folly. The danger is that the able and practical minded should look with indifference or distrust upon ideas the connection of which with their business is remote. I heard a story, the other day, of a man who had a valet to whom he paid high wages, subject to deduction for faults. One of his deductions was, "For lack of imagination, five dollars." The lack is not confined to valets. The object of ambition, power, generally presents itself nowadays in the form of money alone. Money is the most immediate form, and is a proper object of desire. "The fortune," said Rachel, "is the measure of intelligence." That is a good text to waken people out of a fool's paradise. But, as Hegel says, "It is in the end not the appetite, but the opinion, which has to be satisfied." To an imagination of any scope the most far-reaching form of power is not money, it is the command of ideas. If you want great examples, read Mr.

Leslie Stephen's *History of English Thought in the Eighteenth Century*, and see how a hundred years after his death the abstract speculations of Descartes had become a practical force controlling the conduct of men. Read the works of the great German jurists, and see how much more the world is governed today by Kant than by Bonaparte. We cannot all be Descartes or Kant, but we all want happiness. And happiness, I am sure from having known many successful men, cannot be won simply by being counsel for great corporations and having an income of fifty thousand dollars. An intellect great enough to win the prize needs other food besides success. The remoter and more general aspects of the law are those [that] give it universal interest. It is through them that you not only become a great master in your calling, but connect your subject with the universe and catch an echo of the infinite, a glimpse of its unfathomable process, a hint of the universal law.

COMMENTARY

Fame and notoriety – "The Path of the Law," it has been argued, is "the single most important essay ever written by an American on the law." Sanford Levinson, "Strolling Down the Path of the Law (and toward Critical Legal Studies?): The Jurisprudence of Richard Posner," 91 *Columbia Law Review* 1221, 1228 (1991). "This lecture has been so influential in shaping the thinking of American lawyers," say some, "that it might be described as almost part of the Constitution." Phillip E. Johnson, *Reason in the Balance: The Case against Naturalism in Science, Law and Education* (Downers Grove, IL: InterVarsity Press, 1995), at 140. And Judge Posner views the essay as "the best article-length work on law ever written." Richard Posner, ed., *The Essential Holmes* (Chicago: University of Chicago Press, 1990), at x. Others, as previously noted, view the lecture-essay as a "dark" and "destructive" one that is "incoherent," inconsistent, cynical, and "exaggerated." Albert W. Alschuler, *Law without Values* (Chicago: University of Chicago Press, 2000), at 132–80. For Henry Hart, the essay was "the signpost which so many have followed straight down the path to the deadly bog of behaviorism." "Holmes' Positivism – An Addendum," 64 *Harvard Law Review* 929, 932 (1951). *See generally* Steven J. Burton, ed., *The Path of the Law and Its Influence: The Legacy of Oliver Wendell Holmes, Jr.* (New York: Cambridge University Press, 2000).

The prediction principle and its constitutional counterpart – Holmes tells us at the outset that the object of his study is prediction. He then adds, "[A] legal duty so called is nothing but a prediction that if a man does or omits certain things he will be made to suffer in this or that way by judgment of the court; and so of a legal right." His jurisprudence thus requires that the law allow a "bad man" to predict what would happen to him should he do X. Hence, law is deficient if it lacks this essential predictive element. This principle, adopted by Holmes in the common law context, has an analogous contemporary counterpart of sorts in the constitutional context by way of the void-for-vagueness doctrine, which, though a rule of due process, is nonetheless used quite often in free speech cases. *See, e.g., Winters v. New York*, 333 U.S. 507, 509 (1948) ("A failure of a statute limiting freedom of expression to give fair notice of what acts will be punished and such a statute's inclusion of prohibitions against expressions, protected by the principles of the First Amendment violates an accused's rights under procedural due process and freedom of speech or press."). See also *Exxon Shipping Co. v. Baker*, 128 S. Ct. 2605, 2627 (2008) ("a penalty should be reasonably predictable in its severity, so that even Justice Holmes's 'bad man' can look ahead with some ability to know what the stakes are in choosing one course of action or another").

Historical intent: Con and pro – "We must beware of the pitfall of antiquarianism," warned Holmes, "and must remember that for our purposes our only interest in the past is for the light it throws upon the present. I look forward to a time when the part played by history in the explanation of dogma shall be very small, and instead of ingenious research we shall spend our energy on a study of the ends sought to be attained and the reasons for desiring them." Such comments greatly discount the likelihood that Holmes would have placed much, if any, stock in trying to identify and then explain the "framers' intent" when it came to discerning the "meaning" of the First Amendment. Then again, in *Patterson v. Colorado* (1907) (see Part IV), Holmes turned to history to discern the "main purpose" of the First Amendment. Likewise, in his dissent in *Abrams v. United States* (1919) (see Part VI), he invoked history to refute the notion that "the First Amendment left the common law as to seditious libel in force."

The perils of certainty – In Holmes's mind, there was no denying it: "certainty is generally illusion, and repose is not the destiny of man." Certainty was possible but rare in human affairs. As Holmes would write some two decades later, "Certitude is not the test of certainty. We have been cocksure of many things that were not so." "Natural Law," 32 *Harvard Law Review* 40, 41 (1918). The implications for free speech law – as they pertain to politics, philosophy, science, art, and even morals – are great. For if the law is to privilege certain expression (see the subsequent commentaries) in the name of skepticism, then any cherished value can all too readily be called into question.

Enlightened skepticism – Holmes's study of law was grounded in enlightened skepticism, that is, "a deliberate reconsideration of the worth" of long-held law and rules. As his free speech jurisprudence matured, that idea found a central place in his thinking. By that measure, nothing was sacred simply because time had made it so. Or, as Holmes put it: "It is revolting to have no better reason for a rule of law than that so it was laid down in the time of Henry IV. It is still more revolting if the grounds upon which it was laid down have vanished long since, and the rule simply persists from blind imitation of the past."

Consider the implications of such views for First Amendment jurisprudence. In 1963 the state of New York prosecuted the comedian Lenny Bruce for obscenity for using dirty words in a nightclub after midnight. The law had long been on the books and may have been applied previously in similar settings. But by the time the ribald social critic and comedian was prosecuted, the culture had pretty much abandoned any such view of law. Even so, Bruce was convicted, though he was posthumously pardoned in 2003. This example raises the question of whether a Holmesian judge would have handled the case differently and whether such a judge would have dismissed the criminal complaint or interpreted the relevant statute as to preclude prosecution or set aside the law as contrary to contemporary constitutional free speech norms. More fundamentally, there is the question of whether such an unenforced law is even law for Holmes. Consider *Law without Values, supra*, at 141–44.

The role and rule of judges – Holmes "understood judges to have a representative function independent of the legislature. They were to represent the long-term interests and values of the sovereign American people. Therefore, when federal and state officials began to impose liability on speech that failed to satisfy Holmes's theory of liability, he refused to go along. He did not think that the American people really wanted to punish speech that was not liable according to his general theory of liability." H. L. Pohlman, *Justice Oliver Wendell Holmes: Free Speech and the Living Constitution* (New York: New York University Press, 1991), at 254. If that is indeed the case, it seems odd to argue that the judicial branch, a relatively apolitical entity, should be able to trump legislative judgments, as the latter is that branch of government most associated with the will of the people. Moreover, if state judges exercise a quasi-legislative function, it seems fair to hold them politically accountable in those states where judges are subject to elections of one kind or another.

Certainty and prediction – If indeed "certainty is generally illusion," how is it possible to develop a body of law based on "systematized prediction"? Just how definite do judges have to be to put Holmes's bad man on notice? Notice that Holmes's discussion of the law is judge-centric. Where do lawmakers and administrative agents fit into all of this? (*See Law without Values, supra*, at 143–46.) In this regard, consider that the law of the First Amendment, as set out in its text, is lawmaker-centric – "Congress shall make no law. . . . " This is not to deny the role of judicial review in the First Amendment context but to suggest that one judicial function in this area might be to develop a body of law that would discourage legislators from making impermissible laws in the first place.

Falsehoods, legal privileges, and public policies – Holmes asks, "Why is a false and injurious statement privileged, if it is made honestly [by an employer] in giving information about a [former employee]?" His answer: "It is because it has been thought more important that information should be given freely, than that a man should be protected from what under other circumstances would be an actionable wrong." Notice that neither the statement's falsity nor the injury it causes precludes protection for Holmes's common law judge. Notice also the example he gives is that of a businessperson, an employer giving information about a former employee. Would that same privilege that protects an employer likewise protect, say, a newspaper in honestly providing mistaken information to the public on a matter of public interest? See Holmes's opinion in *Burt v. Advertiser Newspaper Co.* (1891), *supra*.

Another related public policy is that of competition: "Why is a man at liberty to set up a business," asks Holmes, "which he knows will ruin his neighborhood? It is because the public good is supposed to be best served by free competition." This idea, developed in various ways, finds both earlier expression in his essay "Gas-Stokers' Strike" (1873), *The Common Law* (1881), and *Vegelahn v. Gunter* (1896), and later in his dissent in *Abrams v. United States* (1919).

Law, morals, the marketplace, and free speech – In "The Path of the Law," Holmes returns to several of the themes developed in *The Common Law* and builds on them. In this essay, Holmes goes to great lengths to separate law from morals. Consider, again, the following from the foregoing essay: "I often doubt whether it would not be a gain if every word of moral significance could be banished from the law altogether, and other words adopted which should convey legal ideas uncolored by anything outside the law. We should lose the fossil records of a good deal of history and the majesty got from ethical associations, but by ridding ourselves of an unnecessary confusion we should gain very much in the clearness of our thought." Such banishment notwithstanding, Holmes nonetheless grants that the "law is the witness and external deposit of our moral life. Its history is the history of the moral development of the race. The practice of it, in spite of popular jests, tends to make good citizens and good men." Morality, from that perspective, has utilitarian value, not intrinsic value. And because law "emanates from the sovereign" and not God, its rules need not always be moral in any normative sense.

Some laws, like those of obscenity, may derive primarily or entirely from a set of commonly held moral principles, however understood. As the Court said in *Chaplinsky v. New Hampshire*, 315 U.S. 568, 571–72 (1942): "It has been well observed that [lewd and obscene] utterances are no essential part of any exposition of ideas, and are of such slight social value as a step to truth that any benefit that may be derived from them is clearly outweighed by the social interest in order and morality. . . . " The majority – that is, the popular sovereign – has willed such laws to be owing to its power to impose its morals on the minority. In that regard, then, there is a fusion between law and morals, one based on power. But if sexual expression, including pornographic expression, is a form of speech, then it should be allowed a spot in the marketplace. After all, if the competition principle we see both in Holmes's early and later writings is to govern, then should not moral expression battle with its immoral counterparts for our minds and libidos? Judging from Holmes's opinion for the Court in *Fox v. Washington* (1915) (see Part IV), he seems to have had a different, less speech-protective view.

Sovereign will – There is also the question whether the laws, as on the books, always reflect the will of the current sovereign. That is, as noted previously, such laws may have as their only meaningful justification nothing more than antiquated notions of moral behavior. In doubtful cases, how much deference should a Holmesian judge give to the moral precepts of the past? The positivist methodology Holmes urged "was one in which judges, having used history to expose the ends that served as the justification for legal rules, then modified the rules if those ends were no longer socially desirable" in the judge's opinion. G. Edward White, *Justice Oliver Wendell Holmes: Law and the Inner Self* (New York: Oxford University Press, 1993), at 221.

The foolish – Holmes was enough of an elitist to have little or no concern for the plight of the thoughtless masses: "the weak and foolish must be left to their folly," is how he put it in "The Path of Law." If certain ideas placed in the marketplace helped them, all the better; if not, so be it. His experiment with free speech, the one heralded in his *Abrams v. United States* (1919) dissent, was willing to allow for that possibility.

The command of ideas – "The Path of the Law" is nothing if not a victory for the legal imagination, for a "command of ideas" so strong as to invite its readers to

reconsider antiquated notions of law. In Holmes's day, cases, including constitutional ones, were routinely categorized in fact-specific terms, such as tavern-
owner cases or motor-car cases. But, Holmes realized, sometimes a given policy
better explained the result in various factually dissimilar cases. By that criterion,
if one were to identify a given policy that suggested a desirable result in free
expression cases, the law might be reconceptualized accordingly. For example,
the modern trend is to classify cases such as *Buckley v. Valeo*, 424 U.S. 1 (1976)
and its progeny as campaign-finance cases. But, taking a cue from Holmes,
there could be a larger principle or policy at work in such cases that might
better explain them, which would point to the need to reformulate that legal
doctrine.

From shock value to standard value – "Since 1897 this speech has impressed
generations of law students. Generations of legal scholars have proclaimed it
as a forerunner of their own work. Holmes himself, however, would be deeply
disappointed to find that 'The Path of the Law' is seen today as a sober, classic
text. Holmes meant for 'The Path of the Law' to shock American lawyers, and
it no longer shocks us." "125th Anniversary Essay: Holmes's Path," *supra*, at 516
(footnotes omitted).

> *Some preparations may amount to an attempt. It is a question of degree.*
> *If the preparation comes very near to the accomplishment of the act, the*
> *intent to complete it renders the crime so probable that the act will be*
> *[unlawful].*

COMMONWEALTH V. PEASLEE

177 Mass. 267, 59 N.E. 55 (1901)
Vote: 7–0
Argued: November 7, 1900
Decided: January 1, 1901
For the plaintiff: P. White
For the Commonwealth: W. Scott Peters

Holmes, C. J.

This is an indictment for an attempt to burn a building and certain goods
therein, with intent to injure the insurers of the same.... The defense is that
the overt acts alleged and proved do not amount to an offense. It was raised by
a motion to quash, and also by a request to the judge to direct a verdict for the
defendant. We will consider the case in the first place upon the evidence, apart

from any question of pleading, and afterwards will take it up in connection with the indictment as actually drawn.

The evidence was that the defendant had constructed and arranged combustibles in the building in such a way that they were ready to be lighted, and if lighted would have set fire to the building and its contents. To be exact, the plan would have required a candle which was standing on a shelf six feet away to be placed on a piece of wood in a pan of turpentine and lighted. The defendant offered to pay a younger man in his employment if he would go to the building, seemingly some miles from the place of the dialogue, and carry out the plan. This was refused. Later the defendant and the young man drove towards the building, but when within a quarter of a mile the defendant said that he had changed his mind, and drove away. This is as near as he ever came to accomplishing what he had in contemplation.

The question on the evidence, more precisely stated, is whether the defendant's acts come near enough to the accomplishment of the substantive offense to be punishable. The statute does not punish every act done towards the commission of a crime, but only such acts done in an attempt to commit it. The most common types of an attempt are either an act which is intended to bring about the substantive crime, and which sets in motion natural forces that would bring it about in the expected course of events, but for the unforeseen interruption, as, in this case, if the candle had been set in its place and lighted, but had been put out by the police, or an act which is intended to bring about the substantive crime, and would bring it about but for a mistake of judgment in a matter of nice estimate or experiment, as when a pistol is fired at a man, but misses him, or when one tries to pick a pocket which turns out to be empty. In either case the would-be criminal has done his last act.

Obviously new considerations come in when further acts on the part of the person who has taken the first steps are necessary before the substantive crime can come to pass. In this class of cases there is still a chance that the would-be criminal may change his mind. In strictness, such first steps cannot be described as an attempt, because that word suggests an act seemingly sufficient to accomplish the end, and has been supposed to have no other meaning. That an overt act, although coupled with an intent to commit the crime, commonly is not punishable if further acts are contemplated as needful, is expressed in the familiar rule that preparation is not an attempt. But some preparations may amount to an attempt. It is a question of degree. If the preparation comes very near to the accomplishment of the act, the intent to complete it renders the crime so probable that the act will be a misdemeanor, although there is still a *locus penitentiae* [an opportunity to undo what one has done], in the need of a further exertion of the will to complete the crime. As was observed in a recent case, the degree of proximity held sufficient may vary with circumstances, including, among other things, the apprehension which the particular crime is calculated to excite....

A mere collection and preparation of materials in a room for the purpose of setting fire to them, unaccompanied by any present intent to set the fire, would be too remote. If the accused intended to rely upon his own hands to the end, he must be shown to have had a present intent to accomplish the crime without much delay, and to have had this intent at a time and place where he was able to carry it out. We are not aware of any carefully considered case that has gone further than this. We assume, without deciding, that that is the meaning of the indictment; and it would have been proved if, for instance, the evidence had been that the defendant had been frightened by the police as he was about to light the candle. On the other hand, if the offense is to be made out by showing a preparation of the room, and a solicitation of some one else to set the fire, which solicitation, if successful, would have been the defendant's last act, the solicitation must be alleged as one of the overt acts. It was admissible in evidence, on the pleadings as they stood, to show the defendant's intent, but it could not be relied on as an overt act unless set out.... If the indictment had been properly drawn, we have no question that the defendant might have been convicted....

COMMENTARY

Later in the U.S. Supreme Court – In dissent in *Northern Securities Co. v. United States*, 193 U.S. 197, 409 (1904), an antitrust case, Holmes wrote: "Not every act done in furtherance of an unlawful end is an attempt or contrary to the law. There must be a certain nearness to the result. It is a question of proximity and degree." (citing *Commonwealth v. Peaslee*). Earlier, in his opinion for the Court in *Swift v. United States*, 196 U.S. 375, 396 (1904), Holmes expressed a similar idea: "Where acts are not sufficient in themselves to produce a result which the law seeks to prevent – for instance, the monopoly– but require further acts in addition to the mere forces of nature to bring that result to pass, an intent to bring it to pass is necessary in order to produce a dangerous probability that it will happen. *Com. v. Peaslee*.... But when that intent and the consequent dangerous probability exist, this statute, like many others, and like the common law in some cases, directs itself against that dangerous probability as well as against the completed result."

Proximity of harm, and objective and subjective standards – In *Commonwealth v. Kennedy*, 170 Mass. 18, 20–22 (1897), an attempted-murder case, Holmes addressed the question of how proximate an accused's intentional actions had to be before liability could be assigned. Said Holmes for the court: "As the aim of the law is not punish sins, but to prevent certain external results, the act done must come pretty near to accomplishing that result before the law will notice it. . . . Every question of proximity must be determined by its own circumstances." To that end, a court must, Holmes ruled, consider both a defendant's subjective intent and an external objective standard.

"In the *Kennedy* opinion, Holmes delivered an interesting dictum, which like other elements of his analysis would reappear later in First Amendment cases. Where there was an apprehension of truly grave crimes, Holmes said, liability might 'begin at a point more remote from the possibility of accomplishing what is expected than might be the case with lighter crimes.' This germ of the modern analysis of risk, with separate components of probability and magnitude of harm, eventually was imported into the clear-and-present-danger standard." Sheldon Novick, "The Unrevised Holmes and Freedom of Expression," 1991 *Supreme Court Review* 303, 317 (1991) (citations and notes omitted).

Such examples, however, were to be contrasted with those in which some future wrongful act must occur for criminal liability to attach. Or to reiterate what Holmes wrote in *Peaslee*: "If the preparation comes very near to the accomplishment of the act, the intent to complete it renders the crime so probable that the act will be a misdemeanor although there is still a *locus penitentiae* in the need of a further exertion of the will to complete the crime." Referring back to his *Kennedy* opinion, Holmes then added: "the degree of proximity held sufficient may vary with the circumstances, including among other things the apprehension which the particular crime is calculated to excite."

"It is interesting to note that Holmes here again foreshadows, not just the clear-and-present-danger doctrine of *Schenck v. United States*, which was held to be a matter of proximity and 'degree,' but also the more refined analysis of risk which eventually was incorporated into the clear-and-present-danger standard." "The Unrevised Holmes and Freedom of Expression," *supra*, at 318–19 (footnotes and citations omitted). Professor Novick also offers a succinct restatement of Holmes's general views in this area: "It was Holmes's conviction that it all cases of otherwise privileged behavior [where an act is not in and of itself punishable], it was a fundamental principle that two things must be proved before liability could be imposed: the foreseeability of harm by an objective standard, and the subjective intent to bring it about." "The Unrevised Holmes and Freedom of Expression," *supra*, at 320.

The fire analogy – David Rabban has observed: "Holmes may well have been thinking of the solicitation to light a fire in *Peaslee* when he wrote in *Schenck* that the first amendment would not protect 'falsely shouting fire in a theatre.'" *Peaslee* also contains language similar to *The Common Law*. *See* David Rabban, "The Emergence of Modern First Amendment Doctrine," 50 *University of Chicago Law Review* 1207, 1283 (1983). *But see* L. A. Powe Jr., "Searching for the False Shout of 'Fire,'" 19 *Constitutional Commentary* 345, 348–51 (2002). See also commentary following *The Common Law* (in Part II) and commentary following *Schenck v. United States* (in Part V).

Overview of Holmes's state court years – "Holmes had learned two lessons," Professor White has observed, "from his experience on the Supreme Judicial Court of Massachusetts. The first lesson was that cases inevitably presented conflicts between desirable social principles, and judges simply had to choose. That choice was an act of policymaking, not an inevitable unfolding of common law principles. The second lesson was that since such choices were arbitrary, and since the process of line-drawing could not be generalized, judging was a far more modest and less creative activity than Holmes had expected. These lessons fostered two judicial habits in Holmes: the habit of deferring especially arbitrary choices to some other body, such a legislature or jury, that arguably reflected community sentiment; and the habit of not agonizing over the reasoning that justified an arbitrary choice. By the time Holmes left the Massachusetts court in 1902, his opinions were already notable for their brevity, assertiveness, and their cryptic language. It was as if Holmes recognized that his decisionmaking process was largely arbitrary and decided to get on with it." G. Edward White, "The Integrity of Justice Holmes' Jurisprudence," 10 *Hofstra Law Review* 663 (1982).

Part IV   Supreme Court Opinions: The Early Years

September 6, 1901, is one of the most important dates in American constitutional history, though few think of it as such. On that day, Leon Czolgosz attempted to assassinate President William McKinley at the Pan-American Exposition in Buffalo, New York. Though the president would live several more days, the two shots the anarchist fired ultimately killed him[1] and thereby put in motion a string of events that led to Oliver Wendell Holmes Jr. becoming the fifty-eighth justice on the Supreme Court. But for the death of the president, the seat vacated by Justice Horace Gray[2] would not have gone to Holmes, as President McKinley had other plans.

As the summer of 1901 came to an end, it became apparent to McKinley and others that Justice Gray was ill and was likely to retire soon. So the president turned to his friend John Davis Long, then secretary of the navy, for advice. Though Long had nominated Holmes to the Massachusetts bench when he was governor, he did not recommend him for the Supreme Court. Instead, Long urged the president to select Alfred Hemenway, his law partner. And Hemenway was prepared to accept the position if and when offered. But as it turned out, Horace's delay in retiring combined with McKinley's assassination changed everything. Thereafter, Henry Cabot Lodge, a U.S. senator from Massachusetts and one of Theodore Roosevelt's close friends, recommended Holmes for Gray's seat when the ailing justice stepped down in July 1902. Roosevelt acted on Lodge's suggestion and nominated Holmes. By December the Senate confirmed him unanimously.[3]

---

[1] President McKinley died on September 14, 1901.

[2] Louis Brandeis had clerked for Gray while the latter was on the Massachusetts high court.

[3] On the nomination episode, see G. Edward White, *Justice Oliver Wendell Holmes: Law and the Inner Self* (New York: Oxford University Press, 1993), at 299–307. See also Aida D. Donald, *Lion in the White House: A Life of Theodore Roosevelt* (New York: Basic

As ironic as it was, Oliver Wendell Holmes owed his justiceship to a crazed anarchist.

Holmes and his wife left Boston and relocated to a new life in Washington, D.C. By December 8, 1902, the new justice was sitting in the old Senate chamber in the Capitol hearing cases. A month later he delivered his first opinion, *Otis v. Parker*,[4] which drew two dissents. About eight months after that, he and Fanny moved into their new red-brick home located at 1720 Eye Street, N.W.[5] In that home, which quickly came to resemble a well-stocked library, Holmes penned opinions, letters, and addresses for nearly three decades. His work was fairly solitary until 1905, when he began to use secretaries (today known as law clerks). Even with his secretaries – the likes of Francis Biddle, Thomas Corcoran, Arthur Sutherland, Alger Hiss, and Mark DeWolfe Howe – his Court work was almost entirely the product of his own efforts. His secretary for each Court term did little more than summarize Court petitions, balance the Holmes's checkbooks, and keep Mrs. Holmes company. In the later years, after Fanny's death, the well-suited young men read to Holmes.[6]

After being on the Court for a few years, Holmes told a friend that the "last term of the Court was interesting."[7] He was referring to the 1904–05 term, his third term on the Court. In that term, the justices had handed down rulings in some 110 cases. One of those rulings was in *United States ex rel. Turner v. Williams*.[8] The case involved an appeal by John Turner, a visiting English-born anarchist, who was to be deported pursuant to the 1903 Anarchist Exclusion Act.[9] Although there was no evidence that Turner

---

Books, 2007), at 166–67; H.W. Brands, *T.R.: The Last Romantic* (New York: Basic Books, 1997), at 440-42.

[4] *Otis v. Parker*, 187 U.S. 606 (1903) (denying Fourteenth Amendment liberty-of-contract substantive due-process claim).

[5] Today, the home is gone and Café Asia is located at the address where Holmes lived for more than thirty years.

[6] *See* Sheldon M. Novick, *Honorable Justice: The Life of Oliver Wendell Holmes* (New York: Dell Publishing, 1989), at 245–46, 288–89.

[7] Letter from OWH to Patrick A. Sheehan, reproduced in David Burton, ed., *Holmes-Sheehan Correspondence: The Letters of Justice Oliver Wendell Holmes and Canon Patrick Augustine Sheehan* (Port Washington, NY: Kennikat Press, 1976), at 14. Holmes's dissent that term in *Northern Securities Co. v. United States*, 193 U.S. 197, 401 (1904) infuriated President Theodore Roosevelt when it denied the applicability of the Sherman Anti-Trust Act to a corporation that controlled several railway lines. It was in this dissent that Holmes wrote one of his more memorable lines: "Great cases, like hard cases, make bad law."

[8] *United States ex rel. Turner v. Williams*, 194 U.S. 279 (1904).

[9] The legislation was prompted by the assassination of President McKinley by an anarchist.

had advocated the use of force or violence, he was arrested after giving a political lecture at the Murray Hill Lyceum in New York. Thereafter, he was held in detention at Ellis Island while he pursued an appeal to the Supreme Court. Supported by the Free Speech League,[10] and with Clarence Darrow as co-counsel in the case, the petitioner argued that the government's attempt to deport him violated his First Amendment rights. In his brief, Darrow argued that the "fundamental basis of free opinion demands that convictions shall be freely spoken to the end that the truth shall be known. Upon this freedom all progress depends."[11]

The Court, per Chief Justice Melville Fuller, disagreed 9–0. In rejecting Turner's claim, Fuller declared:

> If the word "anarchists" should be interpreted as including aliens whose anarchistic views are professed as those of political philosophers, innocent of evil intent, it would follow that Congress was of opinion that the *tendency* of the general exploitation of such views is so dangerous to the public weal that aliens who hold and advocate them would be undesirable additions to our population, whether permanently or temporarily, whether many or few; and, in the light of previous decisions, the act, even in this aspect, would not be unconstitutional, as applicable to any alien who is opposed to all organized government.[12]

In this passage the Court, with Holmes's approval, invoked the bad-tendency test, which traced back to Blackstone[13] and the common law,[14] to justify the suppression of speech. It was that highly deferential test that would resurface, as we will see, in Holmes's own free speech jurisprudence. In another passage from the *Turner* Court's opinion, Fuller added:

> We are not to be understood as depreciating the vital importance of freedom of speech and of the press, or as suggesting limitations on the spirit of liberty, in itself unconquerable, but this case does not involve those considerations. The flaming brand which guards the realm where no human government is needed still bars the entrance; and as long as

---

[10] The group was formed in 1902 by libertarians concerned about the suppression of dissent. Theodore Schroeder, a noted free speech lawyer who challenged Anthony Comstock and the laws named after him, was one of the chief organizers of the group along with Gilbert E. Roe, another free speech lawyer. *See* David M. Rabban, *Free Speech in Its Forgotten Years* (New York: Cambridge University Press, 1997), at 25–26. *See generally* Theodore Schroeder, *Free Speech for Radicals* (New York: Burt Franklin, 1916).

[11] Quoted in *Free Speech in Its Forgotten Years*, *supra* note 10, at 135.

[12] 194 U.S. at 294 (emphasis added).

[13] William Blackstone, *Commentaries on the Laws of England*, adapted by Robert Malcolm Kerr (Boston: Beacon Press, 1962), at 158–62.

[14] *See The Queen v. Hicklin*, 3 L.R.-Q.B. 360, 371 (1868).

human governments endure they cannot be denied the power of self-preservation, as that question is presented here.[15]

This self-survival instinct, when invoked by the sovereign state, was one that Holmes not only understood but also wholeheartedly endorsed.

The next term brought a case in which Holmes was directly involved – *Lochner v. New York*.[16] This was a liberty-of-contract Fourteenth Amendment due-process challenge to a New York law that limited the number of hours a baker could work each day (ten) and each week (sixty). By a 5–4 vote, with Holmes in spirited dissent,[17] the Court struck down the law with Holmes dissenting. In a famous passage, he wrote: "[A] constitution is not intended to embody a particular economic theory, whether of paternalism and the organic relation of the citizen to the State or of *laissez faire*. It is made for people of fundamentally differing views, and the accident of our finding certain opinions natural and familiar or novel and even shocking ought not to conclude our judgment upon the question whether statutes embodying them conflict with the Constitution of the United States." And then he added a thought that would carry over, at least initially, into his First Amendment jurisprudence: "General propositions do not decide concrete cases. The decision will depend on a judgment or intuition more subtle than any articulate major premise. . . . I think that the word liberty in the Fourteenth Amendment is perverted when it is held to prevent the natural outcome of a dominant opinion, unless it can be said that a rational and fair man necessarily would admit that the statute proposed would infringe fundamental principles as they have been understood by the traditions of our people and our law."[18] Those "fundamental principles" to which he referred were not natural rights or inalienable rights or anything like that; Holmes was quite skeptical of such matters. The test was little more than that of majority opinion of the citizenry.[19]

Holmes's vote in the *Turner* case and his dissent in *Lochner* reveal his unwillingness to use either the First Amendment or the Fourteenth Amendment to set aside the will of majorities. Much of that same mind-set informed his vote in *Halter v. Nebraska*,[20] an early flag-desecration case in which the Court upheld (8–1) a Nebraska law that made

[15] 194 U.S. at 294.
[16] 198 U.S. 45 (1905).
[17] Holmes had written a similar opinion in his first year on the Court. *See Otis v. Parker*, 187 U.S. 606 (1903).
[18] 198 U.S. at 75–76 (Holmes, J., dissenting).
[19] See *Justice Oliver Wendell Holmes, supra* note 3, at 328.
[20] 205 U.S. 34 (1907).

it unlawful to use the flag or images of it for commercial purposes. In dismissing the petitioners' Fourteenth Amendment claims, the majority, with Holmes joining, declared that it "cannot hold that any privilege of American citizenship or that any right of personal liberty is violated by a state enactment forbidding the flag to be used as an advertisement on a bottle of beer. It is familiar law that even the privileges of citizenship and the rights inhering in personal liberty are subject, in their enjoyment, to such reasonable restraints as may be required for the general good."[21] In other words, "free expression, as an aspect of personal liberty, was subordinate to any state actions promoting the common good,"[22] however loosely defined.

It is against that jurisprudential backdrop that we come to Holmes's first free speech opinion while on the Supreme Court, his much overlooked majority opinion in *Patterson v. Colorado*.[23] The controversy involved a cartoon and some articles published in a newspaper; they were critical of the Colorado Supreme Court and its handling of a case then before it. The petitioner, Thomas Patterson, was held in contempt. He challenged the contempt citation as an abridgement of his Fourteenth Amendment rights. As noted in the extended commentary following *Patterson*, "Holmes's understanding of free expression corresponded with the standard nineteenth[-] and early-twentieth[-]century renditions of legal doctrine. The government could not impose prior restraints but could punish speech with bad tendencies because doing so would promote the common good – even if the expression asserted the truth."[24]

A few years later, Holmes authored two freedom-of-the-press opinions – *Peck v. Tribune Co.* (1909)[25] and *Gandia v. Pettingill* (1912)[26] (included herein). Both involved the law of defamation. In the scheme of things, these two opinions would bring him little or no recognition. Nonetheless, they are jurisprudential signposts that reveal how Holmes developed his common law views in ways that expanded the notion of privileged communications, but only in judicious increments. Such opinions echo back to Holmes's dissent in *Hanson v. Globe* (see Part III) and were grounded, as Holmes put it in *Peck*, in "the usual principles of tort." Even so, the modern

---

[21] 205 U.S. at 42.
[22] Stephen M. Feldman, *Free Expression and Democracy in America: A History* (Chicago: University of Chicago Press, 2008), at 236.
[23] 205 U.S. 454 (1907).
[24] *Free Expression and Democracy in America, supra* note 22, at 237.
[25] 214 U.S. 185.
[26] 222 U.S. 452.

law of defamation, colored by constitutional considerations, bears some resemblance to Holmesian jurisprudence if only because, as evidenced by his *Gandia* opinion, Holmes saw the connection between debate concerning public officials and public matters, and privileged communications. Such communications, he thought, were legitimate subjects entitled to common law protection absent a showing of malice. That said, neither his *Peck* opinion nor his *Gandia* one brought Holmes any lasting fame or recognition. At best, they were backdrop, a picture of his past.

❧

For all that he had accomplished by this time – his impressive scholarly work culminating in the publication of *The Common Law*, his two decades on the state high court, his renowned addresses to veterans' groups and others, his honorary doctorate from Oxford University, and his ever-burgeoning reputation as a great justice – Holmes was not satisfied. "I have not as much recognition as I should like,"[27] he complained to a friend. A year or so later, his passion for greatness had not abated. More than ever, he was focusing on "being the greatest legal thinker in the world."[28] That ambition was, however, countered by a sobering realization, namely, the specter of death. He was nearly seventy, and he was beginning to feel it. "Sadness comes with age," he told Canon Patrick Sheehan. "[M]y friends here die," he added, "I really do feel gloomy." This was all the more reason for him to continue his life work and ambition in earnest. "[M]y interest in life is still so keen, I still want to do so much more work, that in the main I feel pretty cheerful."[29]

In Washington, Oliver Wendell Holmes, the handsomely dressed man in striped trousers, lived a pleasant life. He was very much an avowed capitalist then – he reaped a generous income both from his inheritance and lucrative railroad bonds, and he enjoyed the comforts of the privileged life even if he experienced them somewhat modestly. He liked, for example, a restful evening in the quiet of his four-story home with its scholarly study, replete with a writing stand that was handed down to him from his grandfather. There, he could lean back on a worn, leather chair and savor

---

[27] Letter from OWH to Clara Stevens, March 6, 1909, Holmes Papers, Microfilm Edition of the Oliver Wendell Holmes Jr. Papers (1985), qtd. in G. Edward White, "Holmes's 'Life Plan': Confronting Ambition, Passion and Powerlessness," 65 *New York University Law Review* 1409, 1462 (1990).

[28] Letter from OWH to Nina Gray, December 2, 1910, Holmes Papers, *supra* note 27, qtd. in "Holmes's 'Life Plan,'" *supra* note 27, at 1466.

[29] Letter from OWH to Patrick Sheehan, August 14, 1910, reproduced in *Holmes-Sheehan Correspondence*, *supra* note 7, at 36–37.

a good Cuban cigar. Or he and Fanny could go out for a carriage ride about the town, with their coachman (who later became a chauffeur when they got a car) attending to the driving.[30] Having foregone retirement, the distinguished justice with the winged moustache relished the fruits of his lifetime of labors, made sweeter still by his family inheritance. And then there were all the accolades that came his way time and again. Because his ambition was so great, he enjoyed the various ceremonial honors that came his way. "[A]s I grow older I grow calm," is how he put it to those of the Harvard Law School Association gathered for dinner one evening in New York.[31] That calmness was his compass. It allowed him to appreciate a Sunday-afternoon adventure in the country with Fanny at their summer home, Beverly Farms. As analytical as his legal mind could be, there was a side of him that liked spotting the blossom of wildflowers.

It was a time when Holmes could be patient and take the long view of life that comes with delayed wisdom and the serenity of contentment. But with that wisdom and serenity came sober realizations about things like battles with the "new races" or the depletion of the "world's resources" or the conflicts between workers and capitalists. He dismissed the idea that the "nostrums now so strenuously urged" could save his country. In a world where "most men think dramatically,"[32] the most important battle was the battle for the mind, for ideas. For that experiment to succeed, however, men and women of differing views had to learn patience. Absent that, both the society and its laws would be mired in ruinous fights.

"When twenty years ago a vague terror went over the earth and the word socialism began to be heard," he added in his address to his dinner guests, "I thought and still think that fear was translated into doctrines that had no proper place in the Constitution or the common law." Judges had to be above such unfounded fears – we need "to learn to transcend our own

---

[30] See John S. Monagan, *The Grand Panjandrum: Mellow Years of Justice Holmes* (Lanham, MD: 1988), at 32–33, 38–39. As Monagan recounts it, "[T]he chauffeur was designated as an independent contractor rather than as an employee because [Holmes] thereby ... insulate[d] himself from an employer's liability for the negligent operation of the vehicle by a servant." *Ibid.* at 32 (relying on account of James H. Rowe, one of Holmes's secretaries).

[31] "Law and the Court," Speech at Dinner of the Harvard Law School Association of New York, February 15, 1913, reproduced in Sheldon M. Novick, ed., *The Collected Works of Justice Holmes* (Chicago: University of Chicago Press, 1995) at 3:505, 507; *Honorable Justice, supra* note 6, at 310. If one had to list ten of Holmes's most important addresses, this 1913 one might well be included within that list. In one famous line in this speech, Justice Holmes said of the Supreme Court: "We are very quiet here, but it is the quiet of a storm center. . . . " *Ibid.* at 505.

[32] "Law and the Court," *supra* note 31, at 506, 507.

convictions, and to leave room for that which we hold dear to be done away with. . . . "[33] *Transcend our convictions* – this was the Holmes who went into the Civil War with strong beliefs and left without them. *That which we hold dear to be done away with* – this was the Holmes who remembered his fallen friends and the faith of the soldier whose cause was no more. From this caldron of agony came a new value – toleration. Men must learn to live with that they loathe. That he could speak such words with such tranquility was a tribute to the man of the moment. His speech done, the Justice sat down and delighted in the rounds of applause and in the pleasure of a good glass of wine.

If the white-haired jurist was calm in his take on life, it was borne not of weakness but of a confidence in his capitalist country. It was strong enough to tolerate criticism, including the kind that railed against its very existence. Besides, he had no real fear of sudden ruin or calamity. No – life was good in America. To make it even better, Holmes had a cadre of young and bright friends.[34] This began with Felix Frankfurter,[35] the clever young man with Harvard Law School credentials whom he had met the year before. Frankfurter in turn introduced Holmes to the likes of Walter Lippmann, Harold Laski, and Morris R. Cohen, among others. In them, these liberal and impressionable young men, the aging jurist found "a secret fountain of faith."[36] Frankfurter and his friends would play a key role in Holmes's life and legacy. They lionized him, promoted him, and even influenced his thinking on free speech, though Holmes was reluctant to admit it. So great was that admiration that, in 1916, the *Harvard Law Review*, thanks to the efforts of Professor Frankfurter, published a Festschrift honoring the justice on the occasion of his seventy-fifth birthday. The contributors included Frankfurter along with revered figures in the law: Judge Learned Hand, Frederick Pollock, Dean Roscoe Pound, and Dean John Wigmore.

[33] *Ibid.* at 507.

[34] See *Grand Panjandrum, supra* note 30, at 113–23.

[35] For an informative account of Frankfurter's early relationship with Holmes, see *Justice Oliver Wendell Holmes: Law and the Inner Self, supra* note 3, at 356–63.

[36] Letter from OWH to Baroness Moncheur, December 30, 1915, OWH Papers, Harvard Law School, quoted in *Honorable Justice, supra* note 6, at 318–19. To illustrate the level of admiration these young men had for Holmes, consider the following public statement by Walter Lippmann: "When you enter [the home of Justice Holmes], it is as if you had come to into the living stream of high romance. You meet the gay soldier who can talk of Falstaff and eternity in one breath, and tease the universe with a quip. . . . A sage with the bearing of a cavalier, his presence is an incitement to high risks. . . . He wears wisdom like a gorgeous plume, and likes to tickle the sanctities between the ribs." Walter Lippmann, "To Justice Holmes," 6 *New Republic* 156 (1916).

"Very few things in life have given me such pleasure,"[37] Holmes wrote to Frankfurter. These were thankful times, times when a man could gaze beyond the sunset and still see the wondrous specter of stars.

And then there was another Harvard man who would come to figure greatly in Holmes's life and jurisprudence – Louis D. Brandeis. Holmes had known him dating back to his days as an editor of the *American Review*, when had he published an article by the young Brandeis.[38] Earlier still, Brandeis had attended Holmes's common law lectures. Since those times in the late nineteenth century, the two had stayed in touch. So when in 1916 Brandeis was nominated to the Supreme Court, Holmes immediately recognized him as an intellectual and personal ally, notwithstanding the fact that Holmes did not share Brandeis's progressive idealism, which often clashed with the capitalist values Holmes lived by.

Though Brandeis's confirmation hearing was contentious, he prevailed (by a vote of 47–22), much to the delight of Felix Frankfurter and Harold Laski, among many other progressives. One telegram after another congratulated Brandeis, but one was especially important to him – the one from Holmes. Its message was simple: "WELCOME."[39] In a few years they would become a constitutional pair, and nowhere would that mutuality of thought be quite as apparent as in their votes and opinions in First Amendment cases. But that time – beginning in 1918–19 – had yet to arrive.

❧

"Certitude is not the test of certainty." This famous line from Holmes's 1918 article "Natural Law"[40] is as good as any concise statement of the skepticism that had overtaken him by this time in his career. In this article, set out herein, Holmes did his behavioralist best to show how "one's experiences" became dogmas, how "deep-seated preferences" were associated with irrefutable truths. "The jurists who believe in natural law," wrote Holmes, "seem to me to be in that naïve state of mind that accepts what has been familiar and accepted by them and their neighbors as something that must be accepted by all men everywhere." Such skepticism, which extended to the "most fundamental of supposed pre-existing rights," revealed both something profound about Holmes's notion of truth and likewise something about the role of free speech in a diverse and democratic society.

---

[37] Letter from OWH to Felix Frankfurter, April 13, 1916, OWH Papers, Harvard Law School, Box 29, Folder 4, quoted in *Honorable Justice, supra* note 6, at 319.

[38] *See* Louis D. Brandeis, "Liability of Trust-Estates on Contracts Made for Their Benefit," 15 *American Law Review* 449 (1881).

[39] *See* Melvin I. Urofsky, *Louis Brandeis: A Life* (New York: Pantheon, 2009), at 458–59.

[40] Oliver Wendell Holmes Jr., "Natural Law," 32 *Harvard Law Review* 40 (1918).

By the summer of 1918, Holmes had adopted a "bettabilitarian" approach to life. This approach allowed its followers to think they didn't know anything but nonetheless bet with some confidence about life and its outcomes.[41] Soon Holmes's skepticism and his bettabilitarian approach to life and law would find its way into his free speech jurisprudence of 1919 and what followed it.

We leave undecided the question whether there is to be found in the 14th Amendment a prohibition similar to that in the 1st. The main purpose of [our free speech, free press] provisions is "to prevent all such previous restraints upon publications as had been practised by other governments," and they do not prevent the subsequent punishment of such as may be deemed contrary to the public welfare. The preliminary freedom extends as well to the false as to the true; the subsequent punishment may extend as well to the true as to the false.

PATTERSON V. COLORADO

205 U.S. 454 (1907)
Vote: 7–2
Argued: March 5–6, 1907
Decided: April 15, 1907
For the plaintiff: Thomas M. Patterson, Henry M. Teller, Charles S.
Thomas, Sterling B. Toney, James H. Blood, Harvey Riddell,
S. W. Belford, and John A. Rush
For the defendant: I. B. Melville and Horace G. Phelps

The Denver Amendment to the Colorado State Constitution of 1902 sought to wrestle power out of the hands of the state government, then dominated by the Republican Party (in close union with big businesses, such as utility companies). Under this law, home rule would allow for municipal ownership of utilities and monopolies. New seats were also created on the Colorado Supreme Court. In a bold move, the lame-duck governor named Republicans to fill the seats, and the state senate quickly ratified the nominees before the seats had even come into existence. The court would eventually be a critical part of the Republicans maintaining control over the state legislature and governorship. Later, it would hold that parts of the home-rule amendment were unconstitutional.

---

[41] Letter from OWH to Lewis Einstein, August 16, 1918, reproduced in James Bishop Peabody, ed., *The Holmes-Einstein Letters: Correspondence of Mr. Justice Holmes and Lewis Einstein, 1903–1935* (New York: St. Martin's Press, 1964), at 169, 170.

Thomas MacDonald Patterson, whose term as U.S. Senator expired two days before this case was argued before the U.S. Supreme Court, was the principal owner of the Rocky Mountain News *and the* Denver Times. *The papers put out a series of articles (and a cartoon) lambasting the state court's actions. For example, the headline for June 24, 1905, read: "Supreme Court Holds That the People Cannot Amend Constitution so as to Express Their Will." They also suggested that utility monopolies controlled enough political machinery to influence the state courts' outcomes.*

One of the cases mentioned in the series had not yet been decided, and Patterson was charged with contempt for trying to influence pending legal actions. The action was brought by the state attorney general on behalf of the state supreme court justices. Patterson was fined $1,000 and appealed the case, arguing it before the Supreme Court himself. "In his brief to the Supreme Court, Patterson argued that the state supreme court had violated his federal and state constitutional rights by precluding him from demonstrating the truth of his accusations. He stressed that the American conception of popular sovereignty, contained in the federal and in all the state constitutions, protected truthful criticism of 'public officials as to their official conduct.' Only through public discussion, Patterson reasoned, 'are the people who possess sovereign power informed of the merits or demerits of those who are chosen to rule over them.' Patterson did not link this right of truthful public discussion to the First Amendment, but to 'those general rights not specifically named in the constitution, which are reserved by the people.'"[42]

Holmes and a majority of the Court were unconvinced. Justices John Marshall Harlan and David Brewer dissented. This was Holmes's first free speech opinion while sitting on the Supreme Court.

Mr. Justice Holmes delivered the opinion of the Court.

This is a writ of error to review a judgment upon an information for contempt. The contempt alleged was the publication of certain articles and a cartoon, which, it was charged, reflected upon the motives and conduct of the supreme court of Colorado in cases still pending, and were intended to embarrass the court in the impartial administration of justice. There was a motion to quash on grounds of local law and the state Constitution and also of the 14th Amendment to the Constitution of the United States. This was overruled and thereupon an answer was filed, admitting the publication [and] denying the contempt. . . .

---

[42] *Free Speech in Its Forgotten Years, supra* note 10, at 133.

The answer went on to narrate the transactions commented on, at length, intimating that the conduct of the court was unconstitutional and usurping, and alleging that it was in aid of a scheme, fully explained, to seat various Republican candidates, including the governor of the state, in place of Democrats who had been elected, and that two of the judges of the court got their seats as a part of the scheme. Finally the answer alleged that the respondent published the articles in pursuance of what he regarded as a public duty, repeated the previous objections to the information, averred the truth of the articles, and set up and claimed the right to prove the truth under the Constitution of the United States. Upon this answer the court, on motion, ordered judgment finding the plaintiff in error for contempt....

The defense upon which the plaintiff in error most relies is raised by the allegation that the articles complained of are true, and the claim of the right to prove the truth. He claimed this right under the Constitutions both of the state and of the United States, but the latter ground alone comes into consideration here.... We do not pause to consider whether the claim was sufficient in point of form, although it is easier to refer to the Constitution generally for the supposed right than to point to the clause from which it springs. We leave undecided the question whether there is to be found in the 14th Amendment a prohibition similar to that in the 1st. But even if we were to assume that freedom of speech and freedom of the press were protected from abridgments on the part not only of the United States but also of the states, still we should be far from the conclusion that the plaintiff in error would have us reach. In the first place, the main purpose of such constitutional provisions is "'to prevent all such previous restraints upon publications as had been practised by other governments,'" and they do not prevent the subsequent punishment of such as may be deemed contrary to the public welfare. The preliminary freedom extends as well to the false as to the true; the subsequent punishment may extend as well to the true as to the false. This was the law of criminal libel apart from statute in most cases, if not in all.

In the next place, the rule applied to criminal libels applies yet more clearly to contempts. A publication likely to reach the eyes of a jury, declaring a witness in a pending cause a perjurer, would be none the less a contempt that it was true. It would tend to obstruct the administration of justice, because even a correct conclusion is not to be reached or helped in that way, if our system of trials is to be maintained. The theory of our system is that the conclusions to be reached in a case will be induced only by evidence and argument in open court, and not by any outside influence, whether of private talk or public print.

What is true with reference to a jury is true also with reference to a court. Cases like the present are more likely to arise, no doubt, when there is a jury, and the publication may affect their judgment. Judges generally perhaps are less apprehensive that publications impugning their own reasoning or motives will interfere with their administration of the law. But if a court regards, as it may, a publication concerning a matter of law pending before it, as tending toward such an interference, it may punish it as in the instance put. When a case is finished courts are subject to the same criticism as other people; but the propriety and necessity of preventing interference with the course of justice by premature statement, argument, or intimidation hardly can be denied. It is objected that the judges were sitting in their own case. But the grounds upon which contempts are punished are impersonal. No doubt judges naturally would be slower to punish when the contempt carried with it a personal dishonoring charge, but a man cannot expect to secure immunity from punishment by the proper tribunal, by adding to illegal conduct a personal attack. It only remains to add that the plaintiff in error had his day in court and opportunity to be heard. We have scrutinized the case, but cannot say that it shows an infraction of rights under the Constitution of the United States, or discloses more than the formal appeal to that instrument in the answer to found the jurisdiction of this court.

Writ of error dismissed.

COMMENTARY

First Amendment law circa 1907 – When the *Patterson* case was handed down, the view of the law was that the Bill of Rights, including the First Amendment, was little more than a codification of English common law principles. Hence, any speech "injurious to public morals or private reputation" could be abridged without violating the Constitution. *See Robertson v. Baldwin*, 165 U.S. 275, 281 (1897).

Justice Harlan in dissent – John Marshall Harlan was one of the two dissenters in *Patterson*. As to whether the First Amendment should be binding on the states, he argued that "the privileges of free speech and of a free press, belonging to every citizen of the United States, constitute essential parts of every man's liberty, and are protected against violation by that clause of the 14th Amendment forbidding a state to deprive any person of his liberty without due process of law. It is, I think, impossible to conceive of liberty, as secured by the Constitution against hostile action, whether by the nation or by the states, which does not embrace the right to enjoy free speech and the right to have a free press."

Applying the First Amendment to the states – Recall that, formally speaking, Thomas Patterson failed to raise a First Amendment claim, though he did raise a general Fourteenth Amendment liberty claim with a free speech argument attached to it. Hence, the Court could not have rendered a First Amendment ruling because the matter was not squarely before it. Even so, Holmes declared: "We leave undecided the question whether there is to be found in the 14th Amendment a prohibition similar to that in the 1st." Justice Harlan, writing in dissent, discussed the First Amendment and argued that it should be applied to the states, saying "the privileges of free speech and of a free press, belonging to every citizen of the United States, constitute essential parts of every man's liberty, and are protected against violation by . . . the 14th Amendment."

Holmes's dilemma and how he resolved it – Holmes would have "preferred to dismiss Harlan's fourteenth amendment argument by simply asserting that the due process clause did not impose substantive limits on the states, a position he had espoused since his early days on the Court. [See his opinion in *Lochner v. New York*, 198 U.S. 45, 74 (1905) (dissenting)] Had he taken this tack, however, Holmes would have been unable to receive the support of the Court; much to his chagrin, they had no reluctance to read the conceptions of justice and 'natural rights' into the due process clause. Yet Holmes hesitated to make a statement that might be viewed as a retreat from his traditional narrow reading of the fourteenth amendment. He decided, therefore, to finesse the problem, and satisfy his more activist brethren, by arguing that the most extreme position on incorporating the first amendment would still give no protection to Patterson. . . . " David S. Bogen, "The Free Speech Metamorphosis of Mr. Justice Holmes," 11 *Hofstra Law Review* 97, 128–29 (1982). *See also* Yosal Rogat and James M. O'Fallon, "Mr. Justice Holmes: A Dissenting Opinion – The Speech Cases," 36 *Stanford Law Review* 1349, 1357 (1984) ("Holmes'[s] deprecatory view of the first amendment came close to eliminating the claims of free expression altogether.").

In 1920, Justice Louis Brandeis, in a separate opinion not joined in by Holmes, argued that the liberty protected by the Fourteenth Amendment should include freedom of speech. *See Gilbert v. Minnesota*, 254 U.S. 325, 343. Nonetheless, as late as 1922, the Court, with Holmes's approval, had ruled that the Fourteenth Amendment imposed no meaningful restrictions on the states when it came to matters of free speech. *See Prudential Insurance Co. v. Cheek*, 259 U.S. 530, 543 (1922). Of course, in time Holmes joined his colleagues in the majority in announcing that the free speech guarantee of the First Amendment should be applicable to the states. See *Gitlow v. New York* (1925) (see Part VI) and Holmes's vote in *Stromberg v. California*, 283 U.S. 359, 368–69 (1931).

Professor White has offered an interesting take on Holmes and his "fatalistic response to the ultimate powerlessness of comprehensive ideas," such as the incorporation of the Bill of Rights into the Fourteenth Amendment: "the oft-noted inconsistency between Holmes's deferential posture to legislation when challenged under the fourteenth amendment's due process clause, and his adoption of a more stringent standard of review when challenges were based on first amendment grounds, can be seen as potentially dissolving when one considers that the ultimate justification Holmes advanced for the former position was that legislatures, as well as judges, were powerless to prevent beliefs from being accepted, or rejected, in the marketplace of ideas by the currently 'dominant forces of the community.'" G. Edward White, "Holmes's 'Life Plan': Confronting Ambition, Passion and Powerlessness," 65 *New York University Law Review* 1409, 1477 (1990) (footnote omitted). For a criticism of Holmes's stance on incorporation, see Herbert F. Goodrich, "Does the Constitution Protect Free Speech?" 19 *Michigan Law Review* 487, 493, 496, 500 (1921).

Blackstone and the bad-tendency test – Key to Sir William Blackstone's notions of free speech was the idea that speech that had a tendency to "create animosities" or "disturb the public peace" could be punished after publication. This was known as the "bad tendency" test. Holmes echoed Blackstone when in *Patterson* he said: "In the first place, the main purpose of such constitutional provisions is 'to prevent all such previous restraints upon publications as had been practised by other governments,' and they do not prevent the subsequent punishment of such as may be deemed contrary to the public welfare." *See* William Blackstone, *Commentaries on the Law of England* (1769), at 4:151–52. That view of free speech was endorsed, with a nod from Holmes, in *United States ex rel. Turner v. Williams*, 194 U.S. 279, 293–95 (1904). *See* Geoffrey R. Stone, "The Origins of the 'Bad Tendency' Test: Free Speech in Wartime," 2002 *Supreme Court Review* 411 (2002).

"Holmes believed that Blackstone's reasoning, developed in the context of the common law of criminal libel, was particularly applicable to contempts of court. 'Publications criticizing judicial behavior in pending cases,' he asserted, 'tend to obstruct the administration of justice,' whether or not the allegations are true." David M. Rabban, *Free Speech in its Forgotten Years* (New York: Cambridge University Press, 1997), at 134 (footnote omitted).

Justice Holmes adopted Blackstone's views, "treating as irrelevant the fact that Blackstone's *Commentaries* did not take into account the text of the Constitution of the United States." G. Edward White, "Justice Holmes and the Modernization of Free Speech Jurisprudence: The Human Dimension," 80 *California Law Review* 391, 398–99 (1992). Years later, Holmes had a different view of such matters: "[I]n the earlier *Paterson* [*sic*] case, if that was the name of it, I had taken Blackstone and Parker of Mass. as well founded, wrongly. I surely was ignorant." Letter from Oliver Wendell Holmes Jr. to Zechariah Chafee Jr., June 12, 1922, Box 14, Folder 12, Zechariah Chafee Jr. Papers, Manuscript Division, Harvard Law School Library. *See generally* David S. Bogen, "The Free Speech Metamorphosis of Mr. Justice Holmes," 11 *Hofstra Law Review* 97, 101–02 (1982). The reference to "Parker of Mass." is to Chief Justice Isaac Parker and his opinion in *Commonwealth v. Blanding,* 20 Mass. (3 Pick.) 304 (1825) (see Part II).

Minimal scrutiny – In *Patterson,* Holmes reduced the constitutional issues "to whether Colorado's punishment of the editor was a reasonable exercise of its police powers." That question answered itself. The editor had criticized the motives of state judges in cases pending before them. The "'propriety and necessity of preventing interference with the course of justice by premature statement, argument, or intimidation,' Holmes declared, 'hardly can be denied.' In the vocabulary of the time, *Patterson* was a simple 'police power' case in which a 'bad tendency' of a communication had been identified: the standard of judicial scrutiny was minimal." "Justice Holmes and the Modernization of Free Speech Jurisprudence: The Human Dimension," *supra,* at 400 (footnotes omitted).

The suppression of truth – "The combination of the prior-restraints limitation on First Amendment claims with the bad tendency test employed as an evaluative standard for police-power limitations on free speech made Holmes'[s] *Patterson* opinion very restrictive. Under its reasoning a state could suppress even true speech if it concluded that the words had a tendency to promote socially injurious acts. If a newspaper said that a particular decision of the governor of the state, or one of its courts, was reactionary and contrary to the public welfare, then that comment could apparently, after *Patterson,* be made the basis for a contempt conviction simply because it might tend to undermine respect for elected officials or tend to interfere with the administration of justice." "Justice Holmes and the Modernization of Free Speech Jurisprudence: The Human Dimension," *supra,* at 400–01. *See also* Stephen M. Feldman, *Free Expression and Democracy in America: A History* (Chicago: University of Chicago Press, 2008), at 237.

Subsequent law – In *Bridges v. California,* 314 U.S. 252, 262 (1941), a 5–4 decision with Justice Hugo Black writing for the majority, the Court held that for contempt sanctions against the media for out-of-court publications to be constitutional there must be a showing of a clear and present danger to the fair administration of justice. This ruling effectively trumped the holding in

Patterson and employed a more exacting test (for the *Abrams* dissent's clear-and-present-danger formulation, see Part VI).

> *A libel is harmful on its face. If a man sees fit to publish manifestly hurtful statements concerning an individual, without other justification than exists for an advertisement or piece of news, the usual principles of tort will make him liable, if the statements are false or are true only of some one else. No falsehood is thought about or even known by all the world. No conduct is hated by all.*

PECK V. TRIBUNE CO.

214 U.S. 185 (1909)
Vote: 9–0
Argued: April 29–30, 1909
Decided: May 17, 1909
For the petitioner: S. C. Irving, Rufus S. Simmons, and Frank J. R. Mitchell
For the respondent: John Barton Payne and William G. Beale

Mr. Justice Holmes delivered the opinion of the Court.

This is an action on the case for a libel. The libel alleged is found in an advertisement printed in the defendant's newspaper, *The Chicago Sunday Tribune*, and, so far as is material, is as follows: "Nurse and Patients Praise Duffy's. Mrs. A. Schuman, One of Chicago's Most Capable and Experienced Nurses, Pays an Eloquent Tribute to the Great Invigorating, Life-Giving, and Curative Properties of Duffy's Pure Malt Whisky." Then followed a portrait of the plaintiff, with the words, "Mrs. A. Schuman," under it. Then, in quotation marks, "After years of constant use of your Pure Malt Whisky, both by myself and as given to patients in my capacity as nurse, I have no hesitation in recommending it as the very best tonic and stimulant for all local and run-down conditions," etc., etc., with the words, "Mrs. A. Schuman, 1576 Mozart St., Chicago, Ill.," at the end, not in quotation marks, but conveying the notion of a signature, or at least that the words were hers. The declaration alleged that the plaintiff was not Mrs. Schuman, was not a nurse, and was a total abstainer from whisky and all spirituous liquors. There was also a count for publishing the plaintiff's likeness without leave. The defendant pleaded not guilty. At the trial, subject to exceptions, the judge excluded the plaintiff's testimony in support of her allegations just stated, and directed a verdict for the defendant. His action was sustained by the Circuit Court of Appeals.

Of course, the insertion of the plaintiff's picture in the place and with the concomitants that we have described imported that she was the nurse and made the statements set forth. . . . Therefore the publication was of and concerning the plaintiff, notwithstanding the presence of another fact, the name of the real signer of the certificate, if that was Mrs. Schuman, that was inconsistent, when all the facts were known, with the plaintiff's having signed or adopted it. Many might recognize the plaintiff's face without knowing her name, and those who did know it might be led to infer that she had sanctioned the publication under an alias. There was some suggestion that the defendant published the portrait by mistake, and without knowledge that it was the plaintiff's portrait, or was not what it purported to be. But the fact, if it was one, was no excuse. If the publication was libelous, the defendant took the risk. As was said of such matters by Lord Mansfield, "Whenever a man publishes, he publishes at his peril."[43] The reason is plain. A libel is harmful on its face. If a man sees fit to publish manifestly hurtful statements concerning an individual, without other justification than exists for an advertisement or a piece of news, the usual principles of tort will make him liable if the statements are false, or are true only of someone else.

The question, then, is whether the publication was a libel. It was held by the circuit court of appeals not to be, or, at most, to entitle the plaintiff only to nominal damages, no special damage being alleged. It was pointed out that there was no general consensus of opinion that to drink whisky is wrong, or that to be a nurse is discreditable. It might have been added that very possibly giving a certificate and the use of one's portrait in aid of an advertisement would be regarded with irony, or a stronger feeling, only by a few. But it appears to us that such inquiries are beside the point. It may be that the action for libel is of little use, but, while it is maintained, it should be governed by the general principles of tort. If the advertisement obviously would hurt the plaintiff in the estimation of an important and respectable part of the community, liability is not a question of a majority vote.

We know of no decision in which this matter is discussed upon principle. But obviously an unprivileged falsehood need not entail universal hatred to constitute a cause of action. No falsehood is thought about or even known by all the world. No conduct is hated by all. That it will be known by a large number, and will lead an appreciable fraction of that number to regard the plaintiff with contempt, is enough to do her practical harm. Thus, if a doctor were represented as advertising, the fact that it would affect his standing with other of his profession might make the representation actionable, although advertising is not reputed dishonest, and even seems to be regarded by many

---

[43] Quoting *The King v. Woodfall*, 98 English Rep. 914, 916 (K.B. 1909). – *Ed.*

with pride. It seems to us impossible to say that the obvious tendency of what is imputed to the plaintiff by this advertisement is not seriously to hurt her standing with a considerable and respectable class in the community. Therefore it was the plaintiff's right to prove her case and go to the jury, and the defendant would have got all that it could ask if it had been permitted to persuade them, if it could, to take a contrary view.

It is unnecessary to consider the question whether the publication of the plaintiff's likeness was a tort *per se*. It is enough for the present case that the law should at least be prompt to recognize the injuries that may arise from an unauthorized use in connection with other facts, even if more subtlety is needed to state the wrong than is needed here. In this instance we feel no doubt.

Judgment reversed.

CORRESPONDENCE

To Frederick Pollock
Beverly Farms, July 22, 1919

My dear Pollock:

. . . I don't know your [House of Lords] libel case, *Hulton v. Jones* [(1910)], but it coincides with a dissent of mine from Mass.,[44] and also with a decision of the Supreme Court of U.S. that I wrote in *Peck v. Tribune Co.* – in principle at least. As I said in the last: – "If the publication was libelous the defendant took the risk." But that hardly reaches the necessary height as the publisher knows that his act will be detrimental if it hits and the plaintiff has no share in bringing about the situation. . . .

Mark DeWolfe Howe, ed., *Holmes-Pollock Letters: The Correspondence of Mr. Justice Holmes and Sir Frederick Pollock, 1874–1932* (Cambridge, MA: Harvard University Press, 1941), at 2:19 (footnote omitted).

COMMENTARY

Continuity with the past – The *Peck* "case presents another continuity with Holmes's past as a judge on the Massachusetts Court. He had written a dissent in *Hanson v. Globe* [see Part III], and now a similar approach to the problem of libel was adopted by the Supreme Court. In both cases he used the external

---

[44] *Hanson v. Globe Newspaper Co.*, 159 Mass. 293, 34 N.E. 462 (1893).

standard to determine liability for a tort." Max Lerner, *The Mind and Faith of Justice Holmes* (Boston: Little, Brown, 1946), at 353 (footnote omitted).

Preserving a social value? – "Here, as elsewhere, there is a hardness and lack of sentimentality in Holmes's thinking about the law that links him with the great common law judges. If one pushes this hardness back, and asks the *cui bono*, the answer seems to be that there is a social value to be conserved – the protection from invasion of the privacy of the individual personality. Thus, although the case is not constitutional law, this becomes at least a marginal civil liberties case, and Holmes manages to link Lord Mansfield with John Stuart Mill." *The Mind and Faith of Justice Holmes, supra,* at 353.

Free speech and hurtful words at common law – "The common law was strongly protective of reputation. Under traditional common-law doctrine in the United States, the plaintiff did not have to prove fault, falsity, or damage. The plaintiff merely had to establish publication by the defendant of a defamatory statement, of and concerning the plaintiff, to a third party. Defamation was a strict liability tort. The plaintiff was not required to plead or prove fault by the defendant. No showing of negligent, reckless, or intentional publication of falsehood was required. Nor was the plaintiff required to prove that the allegedly defamatory statements were false. The onus was instead on the defendant to plead and prove truth as a justification or defense to the libel. Damages were presumed; the law assumed that damages flowed naturally from the defamation.

"These rules were the quintessential example of a legal regime recognizing the existence of 'words which by their very utterance inflict injury' requiring remedies without additional proof of harm. Justice Holmes captured this orthodoxy in *Peck v. Tribune Co.*, embracing the common-law aphorism that: 'Whatever a man publishes he publishes at his peril.' As Holmes saw it, the reason for this was 'plain,' residing in the common-law's common-sense presumption that hurtful words cause hurt." Rodney Smolla, "Free Speech in an Era of Terrorism: Words 'Which by Their Very Utterance Inflict Injury': The Evolving Treatment of Inherently Dangerous Speech in Free Speech Law and Theory," 36 *Pepperdine Law Review* 317, 343–44 (2009) (footnotes omitted).

Modern free speech law contrasted – Modern First Amendment developments would overtake "the common-law 'super tort' of defamation. The most significant development was the historic opinion of the Supreme Court in *New York Times Co. v. Sullivan* [376 U.S. 254 (1964)]. The rules emanating from *New York Times* and its progeny turned the common law principles on their head, diminishing the protection of reputation in the United States. The balance between protection of reputation and freedom of speech that was struck by the common law was recalibrated, diminishing protection of reputation and concomitantly enhancing protection of freedom of speech. In the *New York Times* case, the Court held that in defamation actions brought by public officials for defamatory speech germane to the official's performance in or fitness for office, the public official plaintiff must demonstrate that the defendant published the defamation with 'actual malice,' defined as knowledge of falsity or reckless disregard for truth or falsity. In a series of decisions following the *New York Times* decision, the constitutional rules evolved to include 'public figures' as among the plaintiffs who must demonstrate actual malice. While there have been hundreds of decisions elaborating on the public figure[–]private figure dichotomy, this basic division of American defamation law is now relatively settled and stable.

"The tort of defamation in the United States has thus been dramatically modified. The changes have been accomplished principally by: (1) requiring proof of fault in all defamation actions in the United States involving 'matters of public concern,' including proof of, at minimum, negligence in all such private-figure cases and 'actual malice' in all such public official and public figure cases; (2) placing the burden of pleading and proving falsity on the plaintiff in all defamation issues involving matters of public concern; (3) modifying the common-law doctrine of 'fair comment' to impose a stricter requirement that all defamation actions be predicated on false statements of fact; and (4) modifying rules governing damages." "Free Speech in an Era of Terrorism," *supra*, at 344–45 (footnotes omitted). *See also Herbert v. Lando*, 441 U.S. 153, 158–59 (1979).

The citizens of Porto Rico had a serious interest, and anything bearing on such action was a legitimate subject of statement and comment.

Gandia v. Pettingill

222 U.S. 452 (1912)
Vote: 9–0
Argued: December 14, 1911
Decided: January 9, 1912
For the plaintiff: Frederic D. McKenney, John Spalding Flannery,
William Hitz, and H. H. Scoville
For the defendant: Willis Sweet and George H. Lamar

Mr. Justice Holmes delivered the opinion of the Court.

This is an action for libels and comes here upon a bill of exceptions after a verdict for the plaintiff. The alleged libels consist of a series of articles in a Porto

Rican newspaper, *La Correspondencia*. These articles stated that the plaintiff, Pettingill, while United States Attorney for Porto Rico, carried on a private practice also, and even acted as a lawyer on behalf of persons bringing suit against the government of Porto Rico. It seems that, if the plaintiff had been an officer of the local government, he would have been forbidden the practice by the local law, and the articles convey the idea that if the practice is not prohibited also by the law for United States officials, it ought to be, especially as the island is charged with a salary for the attorney. The conduct of Mr. Pettingill in the above particulars is described as a monstrous immorality, a scandal, etc., etc. In the view that we take it is not necessary to state the charges here in detail, but it should be observed that in the declaration the plaintiff alleged that while United States Attorney he had a large private practice, and implied, as in his evidence he stated, that a part of this practice consisted of suits against the local government. So there was no issue on the matter of fact.

So far as the facts were concerned, the publication of them alone was not libelous. For, apart from the question whether attributing to the plaintiff conduct that was lawful, as the plaintiff says, could be a libel, he was a public officer in whose course of action connected with his office the citizens of Porto Rico had a serious interest, and anything bearing on such action was a legitimate subject of statement and comment. It was so, at least, in the absence of express malice, – a phrase needing further analysis, although not for the purposes of this case. Therefore the only questions open for consideration were the motives of the publication and whether the comment went beyond reasonable limits, which, of course, the defendant denied. But so far as we see from reading the charge, the judge did not approach the case from this point of view. For after saying to the jury that fair comment upon the actions of public officials was privileged, he went on: 'But you are instructed that in this case . . . [the articles] are what is known in law as libelous per se. . . . Therefore, in any event you must find for the plaintiff upon that issue, and give him such damages as you may believe, from all the facts and circumstances in the case, he is entitled to;' and after that proceeded to direct them only as to the conditions for finding punitive damages also. It is at least doubtful whether this instruction meant that the comments were excessive as matter of law. It rather would seem from the previous explanations given to the jury of the independence of United States officials notwithstanding the source of their salaries, and the instructions that the plaintiff's acts were lawful, that the defendant, in order to justify himself, would have to prove that they were wrong in law, and that his inability to do so might be considered as aggravation of the damages to be allowed, that the latter considerations alone were the ground for what we have quoted from the charge.

However this may be, what we have said is enough to show that the mind of the jury was not directed to what was the point of the case. We do not see how, making reasonable allowance for the somewhat more exuberant expressions of meridional speech, it could be said as matter of law that the comments set out in the declaration went beyond the permitted line, and we think it at least doubtful whether the plaintiff would not have got all if not more than all that he could ask if he had been allowed to go to the jury on that issue. In the absence of express malice of excess the defendant was not liable at all, and in the case of mere excess without express malice, the damages, if any, to which he was entitled, were at most only such as could be attributed to the supposed excess. But what really hurt the plaintiff was not the comment, but the fact. The witnesses for the plaintiff said that the people of Porto Rico considered the acts charged immoral, and the statute referred to showed that such was their conception of public duty. It was peculiarly necessary therefore to instruct the jury that so far as the publication of facts disapproved by the community was concerned, the plaintiff could not recover for it, however technically lawful his conduct might have been, except as we have stated above. Instructions were requested on the point, and the refusal to give them was excepted to, as also was the corresponding charge. Without nice criticism of the form of the requests, it is enough to say that they were so nearly correct as to call the judge's attention to the matter, and to require a different explanation of the defendant's rights.

An exception was taken to the judge's sending the jury out before the counsel for the defendant had stated all of his exceptions to the charge. The judge had told the counsel that he would not instruct the jury otherwise than as he had, and he allowed all the exceptions to be taken in open court after the jury had retired. No doubt it is the stricter practice to note the exceptions before the jury retires (the judge, of course, having power to prevent counsel from making it an opportunity for a last word to them). But in this case they were noted at the trial, in open court, and in the circumstances stated the defendant suffered no wrong, so that we should not sustain an exception upon this ground.

Judgment reversed.

COMMENTARY

Holmes's reputation – For all his scholarly writings, public addresses, state court opinions, and Supreme Court opinions like his dissent in *Lochner v. New York* (1905), at this time there was still a sense that Holmes had not yet come into the limelight of his ambitions. Consider Alexander Bickel's assessment: "Nearly thirty years after the publication of *The Common Law* and his first judicial appointment, the public hardly knew him.... [I]n his seventieth year, even among his professional peers, the general acknowledgement of greatness was still to come for Holmes, and he himself felt its absence rather painfully. He was . . . often charged with obscurity and with a disinclination to take particular facts into account. . . . Holmes in 1910 [two years before the *Gandia* case] . . . was almost all that he would be, lacking only the magnificence of very great age. But no one yet was writing that to know him was 'to have had a revelation of the possibilities . . . of human personality.' No one was yet regarding him as 'a significant figure in the history of civilization and not merely a commanding American figure.' And Benjamin Cardozo's later judgment of Holmes as 'probably the greatest legal intellect in the history of the English-speaking judiciary' had not yet been rendered." Alexander M. Bickel and Beno C. Schmidt, *The Judiciary and Responsible Government, 1910–1921* (New York: Macmillan, 1984), at 9:70–71 (footnotes omitted).

Holmes and privileged communications – "Holmes's liable decisions are . . . important," Professor Pohlman argues, "because they reveal his doctrine of privilege at work. [W]hether a certain privilege against libel should be recognized and, if it should, whether the privilege held if the agent libeled another maliciously were policy questions. Early in his judicial career, Holmes read the privilege against libel narrowly. In 1884 [in *Cowley v. Pulsifer* (see Part III)], he refused to widen the privilege attached to fair reports of judicial proceedings. . . . In 1891 [in *Burt v. Advertiser Newspaper Co.* (see Part III)], Holmes upheld a privilege of fair criticism on matters of public interest, but excluded from the privilege statements of fact. . . . The privilege was confined to comment and criticism. A publisher was strictly liable for factual claims. Holmes may have later widened this narrow conception of the privilege of fair criticism on matters of public interest." In *Gandia v. Pettingill* "Holmes reasoned that that the charge of liable failed for a number of reasons: (1) the facts as presented were true; (2) the conduct attributed to the attorney was lawful and therefore could not constitute a libel; (3) the plaintiff 'was a public officer in whose course of action connected with his office the citizens of Porto Rico had a serious interest, and *anything bearing on such action was a legitimate subject of statement* and debate.' This language seemed to privilege statements of fact, not just criticism and comment on the facts. But in any case, Holmes held that the privilege was made out unless the defendants acted maliciously. In 'the absence of express malice or excess the defendant was not liable at all.' Accordingly, the actual purpose of the agent became crucial in the law of libel only to override a privilege.

"Holmes libel decisions therefore show that in his judgment speech alone could constitute a harmful act subject to liability on ordinary principles. He also thought that harmful speech was privileged if it was a report of official court proceedings, if it contained only comment and criticism, or if it concerned the activities of a public officer. But there was more than a hint that if a publisher acted with malicious purpose, the privilege was withdrawn." H. L. Pohlman, *Justice Oliver Wendell Holmes: Free Speech and the Living Constitution* (New York: New York University Press, 1993), at 55–56 (footnotes omitted, emphasis in original).

Public versus private speech – Holmes's opinion in *Gandia* suggests that, as early as 1912, if not earlier, he realized the significance for free speech purposes between speech on public matters versus speech on private matters. See *Justice Oliver Wendell Holmes: Free Speech and the Living Constitution*, *supra*, at 96 n. 144.

> *In this present case the disrespect for law that was encouraged was disregard of it – an overt breach and technically criminal act.*

Fox v. Washington

236 U.S. 273 (1915)
Vote: 9–0
Submitted: January 19, 1915
Decided: February 23, 1915
For the petitioner: Gilbert E. Roe[45]
For the respondent: W. V. Tanner and Fred G. Remann

A group of anarchists known as "Homeites" had taken to suntan in the nude in the woods of the Key Peninsula, near Tacoma in Washington State. Four individuals were arrested for indecent exposure. Jay Fox, the editor of The Agitator *published a piece called "The Nudes and the Prudes"[46] in which he promoted boycotts of those who interfered with the nude sunbathing, and the State of Washington prosecuted him under a statute that prohibited printing or circulating publications that encouraged a commission of a crime.*

Mr. Justice Holmes delivered the opinion of the Court.

This is an information for editing printed matter tending to encourage and advocate disrespect for law, contrary to a statute of Washington. The statute

---

[45] While Jay Fox's petition was being prepared for review in the Supreme Court, Theodore Schroeder (who formed the Free Speech League in 1902) advised Fox's attorney on how to brief the case. When the lawyer balked, Fox fired him and hired, per Schroeder's suggestion, a most able advocate – Gilbert E. Roe, Schroeder's colleague and collaborator. Roe was a free speech lawyer of some note. See the commentary following *Debs v. United States* in Part V of this volume.

[46] The piece is set out at the end of this case.

is as follows: "Every person who shall willfully print, publish, edit, issue, or knowingly circulate, sell, distribute or display any book, paper, document, or written or printed matter, in any form, advocating, encouraging or inciting, or having a tendency to encourage or incite the commission of any crime, breach of the peace, or act of violence, or which shall tend to encourage or advocate disrespect for law or for any court or courts of justice, shall be guilty of a gross misdemeanor." The defendant demurred on the ground that the act was unconstitutional. The demurrer was overruled and the defendant was tried and convicted. With regard to the jurisdiction of this court, it should be observed that the supreme court of the state, while affirming that the Constitution of the United States guarantees freedom of speech, held not only that the act was valid in that respect, but also that it was not bad for uncertainty . . . so that we gather that the Constitution of the United States, and especially the 14th Amendment, was relied upon, apart from the certificate of the chief justice to that effect.

The printed matter in question is an article entitled, "The Nude and the Prudes," reciting in its earlier part that "Home is a community of free spirits, who came out into the woods to escape the polluted atmosphere of priest-ridden, conventional society;" that "one of the liberties enjoyed by the Home-ites was the privilege to bathe in evening dress, or with merely the clothes nature gave them, just as they chose;" but that "eventually a few prudes got into the community and proceeded in the brutal, unneighborly way of the outside world to suppress the people's freedom," and that they had four per-sons arrested on the charge of indecent exposure, followed in two cases, it seems, by sentences to imprisonment. "And the perpetrators of this vile action wonder why they are being boycotted." It goes on: "The well-merited indig-nation of the people has been aroused. Their liberty has been attacked. The first step in the way of subjecting the community to all the persecution of the outside has been taken. If this was let go without resistance the progress of the prudes would be easy." It then predicts and encourages the boycott of those who thus interfere with the freedom of Home, concluding: "The boycott will be pushed until these invaders will come to see the brutal mistake of their action and so inform the people." Thus by indirection, but unmistakably, the article encourages and incites a persistence in what we must assume would be a breach of the state laws against indecent exposure; and the jury so found.

So far as statutes fairly may be construed in such a way as to avoid doubtful constitutional questions they should be so construed and it is to be presumed that state laws will be construed in that way by the state courts. We understand the state court by implication, at least, to have read the statute as confined to encouraging an actual breach of law. Therefore the argument that this act is both an unjustifiable restriction of liberty and too vague for a criminal law must fail. It does not appear and is not likely that the statute will be construed to prevent publications merely because they tend to produce unfavorable opinions of a particular statute or of law in general. In this present case the disrespect for law that was encouraged was disregard of it – an overt breach and technically criminal act. It would be in accord with the usages of English to interpret disrespect as manifested disrespect, as active disregard going beyond the line drawn by the law. That is all that has happened as yet, and we see no reason to believe that the statute will be stretched beyond that point.

If the statute should be construed as going no farther than it is necessary to go in order to bring the defendant within it, there is no trouble with it for want of definiteness. It lays hold of encouragements that, apart from statute, if directed to a particular person's conduct, generally would make him who uttered them guilty of a misdemeanor if not an accomplice or a principal in the crime encouraged, and deals with the publication of them to a wider and less selected audience. Laws of this description are not unfamiliar. Of course we have nothing to do with the wisdom of the defendant, the prosecution, or the act. All that concerns us is that it cannot be said to infringe the Constitution of the United States.

Judgment affirmed.

COMMENTARY

Holmes's anti–free speech side – One of Holmes's biographers, G. Edward White, has noted, "Taken together, *Patterson* and *Fox* apparently left very little room for the First Amendment to serve as a restraint on state legislation restricting efforts to criticize public officials or majoritarian views. The decisions were consistent with judicial orthodoxy in free speech cases prior to the United States' involvement in World War I. They were not consistent with a later characterization of Holmes as having a 'solicitude for individual expression.'" G. Edward White, *Justice Oliver Wendell Holmes: Law and the Inner Self* (New York: Oxford University Press, 1993), at 352 (quoting Max Lerner).

Broad application of bad-tendency test – "In *Fox*, the Court applied the test quite broadly, since the speaker had not encouraged others to engage in public nudity but rather to boycott the businesses of those who had taken a 'prudish' stance toward it. This suggested that any negative characterization of persons who criticized others for purportedly engaging in an activity that a state had forbidden – such as working on Sunday or dropping out of school at the age of twelve – had 'bad tendencies' and could be made the basis of criminal prosecutions." G. Edward White, "Justice Holmes and the Modernization of Free Speech Jurisprudence: The Human Dimension," 80 *California Law Review* 391, 402 (1992).

The incitement question – It has been argued that "an incitement theory was inconsistent with the facts in *Fox*. Fox's article does not on its face incite a breach of the laws against exposure; it merely threatens certain people with a "boycott." Fox could have been convicted for encouraging disrespect for the law only by advocating the ostracism of the "public minded" citizens who reported violations of the law. But this is not the same as "affirmatively encouraging violations of law," Yosal Rogat and James M. O'Fallon, "Mr. Justice Holmes: A Dissenting Opinion – The Speech Cases," 36 *Stanford Law Review* 1349, 1360 (1984).

Free speech versus price-fixing principles – "Holmes seemed to take the position that a law may on its face validly provide for the punishment of constitutionally immune acts by punishing those who publish material which merely tends to encourage disrespect for law, so long as a court thinks it is 'not likely' to be applied to those acts. Yet eight months earlier, the Court in *International Harvester Co. of America v. Kentucky*[47] had for the first time struck down a criminal statute for uncertainty, holding unconstitutional a Kentucky statute regulating price-fixing combinations. Holmes, writing for the Court, saw those affected as having to 'guess on peril of indictment' and 'divine prophetically,'[48] whether their behavior was unlawful. Because a 'vague' law may inhibit constitutionally protected behavior, a court should consider the importance of the actions that may be inhibited. The two decisions reveal something of Holmes' attitude toward these two activities. Although he considered the risk of inhibiting lawful price-fixing schemes in *International Harvester*, Holmes did not consider the risk of inhibiting lawful criticism of a statute in *Fox*. Nor did he consider the relative unimportance of the state's interest in prosecuting Fox, though, as even clothing manufacturers would agree, it was not a matter of national security. He said, in typical fashion, 'Of course we have nothing to do with the wisdom of the defendant, the prosecution, or the act.' At this time, four years before his *Schenck* opinion, Holmes certainly showed no special concern about the expression of dissident social views."[49] "Mr. Justice Holmes: A Dissenting Opinion – The Speech Cases," *supra*, at 1360.

[47] 234 U.S. 216 (1914).
[48] 234 U.S. at 223.
[49] On the same day that *Fox* was decided, a unanimous Court rejected the claim that motion pictures were within the ambit of first amendment protection, upholding censorship programs in Ohio and Kansas. *Mutual Film Corp. v. Industrial Commission of Ohio*, 236

Intent and Holmes's theory of free speech – "*Fox* is important," it has been argued, "because it shows Holmes using the criteria of the intent branch of his theory in a case involving free speech three years before he came up with his famous phrase 'clear and present danger.' It therefore focuses attention on the criteria that he used to decide cases of free speech rather than on a rhetorical phrase. The case also indicates how he used his theory of liability to assess the constitutionality of statutes restricting speech. His theory of liability therefore forms a backdrop to his opinions in the World War I cases. It reveals the underlying basis of these more important decisions and thereby their consistency with each other and with Holmes's earlier views." H. L. Pohlman, *Justice Oliver Wendell Holmes: Free Speech and the Living Constitution* (New York: New York University Press, 1991), at 64.

Fox and the incorporation doctrine – "*Fox* has some bearing on the relationship between free speech and the liberty protected by the Fourteenth Amendment against state action. Though it is correct that the First Amendment was not explicitly applied against the states until *Gitlow v. New York*, there were earlier hints that the Supreme Court, or at least certain members of the Court, were moving in this direction. They usually took the form of statements that even if free speech was applied against the states, the defendant's actions would not be protected. This was essentially the view Holmes expressed in *Patterson v. Colorado* (1907) [herein]. In *Fox*, he went slightly further. He interpreted the statute narrowly according to his theory of liability to avoid constitutional doubts. The intimation was that if the statute was 'construed to prevent publications merely because they tend to produce unfavorable opinions of a particular statute or of law in general,' it would have had constitutional problems. The conclusion is that, a decade before *Gitlow*, Holmes was seriously considering applying the free speech clause of the First Amendment against state action." *Justice Oliver Wendell Holmes: Free Speech and the Living Constitution, supra,* at 64–65.

The legacy of Lochner – "[I]n the *Fox* case, as in his famous dissent in *Lochner v. New York* and in other cases that construed economic regulations, Holmes was eager to emphasize the irrelevance of his own views about legislation while upholding statutes against constitutional attacks based on the Fourteenth Amendment. His colleagues on the Supreme Court, by contrast, showed no such consistency. Most of them, unlike Holmes, regularly invalidated economic legislation as a violation of the liberty protected by the Fourteenth

U.S. 230 (1915); *Mutual Film Corp. of Missouri v. Hodges*, 236 U.S. 248 (1915). Holmes joined these opinions.

Amendment. Yet they unanimously joined Holmes in denying [Gilbert] Roe's assertion that the Washington statute, by punishing unspecified language for its tendency to produce 'disrespect for law,' deprived Fox of his constitutionally protected liberty under the Fourteenth Amendment." David M. Rabban, *Free Speech in Its Forgotten Years* (New York: Cambridge University Press, 1997), at 141.

Social reformers and their free speech dilemma – "It is not clear that the *Patterson* or *Fox* cases would have been decided differently had the late nineteenth-century view of speech as a liberty challenged Holmes'[s] early orthodox view. What is clear, however, is that when early twentieth-century political reformers began to devote greater attention to the question of expanding protections for political dissidents, an earlier tradition of commentary treating speech as a fundamental liberty was available to them. Along with that tradition, however, came part of its intellectual baggage: the identification of liberty with doctrines, such as liberty of contract, that by the early twentieth century had troublesome political implications for reformers.

"The potential use of liberty arguments as a source of protection for the controversial expressions of political dissidents, such as anarchists, labor organizers, and advocates of unconventional and arguably 'obscene' sexual practices, caused a dilemma for early twentieth-century reformers inclined to challenge orthodox free speech jurisprudence. While they were prepared to resist judicial efforts to confine protection for speech to prior restraints, to permit suppression of expressions that had 'bad tendencies,' or to ignore free speech issues altogether, for them to do so on the basis of a broad-ranging conception of liberty would implicitly require acknowledging the primacy of that conception in the arena of economic affairs. In fine, the liberty premise of protection for free speech seemed to legitimate other protections – such a freedom of contract – to which early twentieth-century political reformers were distinctly unsympathetic." *Justice Oliver Wendell Holmes: Law and the Inner Self, supra,* at 416 (endnote omitted).

✧

"The Nude and the Prudes"

Jay Fox, *The Agitator*, July 1, 1911

Clothing was made to protect the body, not to hide it. The mind that associates impurity with the human body is itself impure. To the humanitarian, the idealist, the human body is divine, "the dwelling place of the soul," as the old poets sang.

To the coarse, half-civilized barbarian, steeped in a mixture of superstition and sensualism, the sight of a nude body suggests no higher thoughts, no nobler feelings than those which the sight of one animal of the lower order of creation produces in another.

The vulgar mind sees its own reflections in everything it views. Pollution cannot escape from pollution, and the polluted mind that sees its own reflection in the nude body of a fellow being and arises in early morning to enjoy the vulgar feast, and then calls on the law to punish the innocent victims whose clean bodies around the savage instincts, is not fit company for civilized people, and should be avoided.

These reflections are based on an unfortunate occurrence which took place recently in Home. Home is a community of free spirits, who came out into the woods to escape the polluted atmosphere of priest-ridden, conventional society. One of the liberties enjoyed by Homeites was the privilege to bathe in evening dress or with merely the clothes nature gave them, just as they chose.

No one went rubbernecking to see which suit a person wore who sought the purifying waters of the bay. Surely it was nobody's business. All were sufficiently pure minded to see no vulgarity, no suggestion of anything vile or indecent in the thought or the sight of nature's masterpiece uncovered.

But eventually a few prudes got into the community and proceeded in the brutal, unneighborly way of the outside world to suppress the people's freedom. They had four persons arrested on the charge of "indecent exposure." One woman, the mother of two small children was sent to jail. The one man arrested will also serve a term in prison. And the perpetration of this vile action wonder why they are being boycotted.

The well-merited indignation of the people has been aroused. Their liberty has been attacked. The first step in the way of subjecting the community to all the persecution of the outside has been taken. If this was let go without resistance the progress of the prudes would be easy. But the foolish people who came to live among us only because they found they could take advantage of our cooperation and buy goods cheaper here than elsewhere, have found they got into a hornet's nest. Two of the store refused to trade with them and the members avoid them in every way. To be sure, not all have been brought to see the importance of the situation. But the propaganda of those who do will go on, and the matter of avoiding these enemies in our midst will be punished in the end.

The lines will be drawn and those who profess to believe in freedom will be put to the test of its practice. There is no possible grounds on which a libertarian can escape taking part in the effort to protect the freedom of Home. There is no half way. Those who refuse to aid the defense is aiding the other side. For those who want liberty and will not fight for it are parasites and do not deserve freedom. Those who are indifferent to the invasion, who can see an innocent woman torn from the side of her children and packed off to jail and are not moved to action, cannot be counted among the rebels of authority. Their place is with the enemy.

The boycott will be pushed until these invaders will come to the brutal mistake of their action and so inform the people.

This subject will receive further consideration in future numbers.

J. F.

Misbehavior means something more than adverse comment or disrespect.

TOLEDO NEWSPAPER CO. V. UNITED STATES

247 U.S. 402 (1918)
Vote: 5–2
Argued: March 7–8, 1918
Decided: June 10, 1918
For the petitioner: Lawrence Maxwell, Charles S. Northup, Jay W. Curts, and Joseph S. Graydon
For the respondent: William L. Day and William C. Fitts

In 1914, the fiery, progressive editor of the Toledo News-Bee, *Negley Cochran, began to take aim at the city's streetcar monopoly and its push to raise fares. The city passed an ordinance that halted any increases, and the streetcar company (whose critics had dubbed it "Big Con") fought back in federal court seeking to prevent enforcement of the ordinance. During the months of delays and hearings the paper kept up a barrage of criticism and editorial cartoons, some of it promoting resistance to fare hikes and some aimed at the presiding judge, John Milton Killits. In one example, the paper reprinted the remarks of labor organizer John Quinlivan, including the phrase "Impeach Killits."[50] After the city conceded that the ordinance went too far, and the streetcar issue came to an end, Judge Killits cited Cochran, along with the paper's managing editor and the paper itself, for contempt. Without the benefit of a jury, the judge found the defendants guilty, basing his decision on an 1831 statute.[51]*

Writing for the Court's majority, Justice Edward White argued that "[t]he test . . . is the character of the act done and its direct tendency to prevent and obstruct the discharge of judicial duty" and in this case the newspaper articles

[50] A copy of the story is reproduced at the end of the commentaries following this case.
[51] *See* "Fines Paper and Editor," *New York Times*, January 24, 1915, at 14.

"manifestly intended to interfere with and obstruct the court in the discharge of its duty in a matter pending before it." Justices Clarke and Day did not participate in the vote because of their acquaintance with Judge Killits.

Justice Holmes, dissenting.

... The question is whether [Judge Killits] acted within his powers under the statutes of the United States.

The statute in force at the time of the alleged contempts confined the power of courts in cases of this sort to where there had been "misbehavior of any person in their presence or so near thereto as to obstruct the administration of justice." Before the trial took place an act was passed giving a trial by jury upon demand of the accused in all but the above-mentioned instances. In England, I believe, the usual course is to proceed in the regular way by indictment. I mention this fact and the later statute only for their bearing upon the meaning of the exception in our law. When it is considered how contrary it is to our practice and ways of thinking for the same person to be accuser and sole judge in a matter which if he be sensitive, may involve strong personal feeling, I should expect the power to be limited by the necessities of the case "to insure order and decorum in their presence" as it is stated in *Ex parte Robinson*. And when the words of the statute are read it seems to me that the limit is too plain to be construed away. To my mind they point only to the present protection of the Court from actual interference, and not to postponed retribution for lack of respect for its dignity – not to moving to vindicate its independence after enduring the newspaper's attacks for nearly six months as the Court did in this case. Without invoking the rule of strict construction I think that "so near as to obstruct" means so near as actually to obstruct – and not merely near enough to threaten a possible obstruction. "So near as to" refers to an accomplished fact, and the word "misbehavior" strengthens the construction I adopt. Misbehavior means something more than adverse comment or disrespect.

But suppose that an imminent possibility of obstruction is sufficient. Still I think that only immediate and necessary action is contemplated, and that no case for summary proceedings is made out if after the event publications are called to the attention of the judge that might have led to an obstruction although they did not. So far as appears that is the present case. But I will go a step farther. The order for the information recites that from time to time sundry numbers of the paper have come to the attention of the judge as a daily reader of it, and I will assume, from that and the opinion, that he read them as they came out, and I will assume further that he was entitled to rely upon his private knowledge without a statement in open court. But a judge of the United States is expected to be a man of ordinary firmness of character, and I find it impossible to believe that such a judge could have found in anything that was printed even a tendency to prevent his performing his sworn duty. I am not considering whether there was a technical contempt at common law but whether what was done falls within the words of an act intended and admitted to limit the power of the courts.

The chief thing done was to print statements of a widespread public intent to board the cars and refuse to pay more than three cents even if the judge condemned the ordinance, statements favoring the course, if you like, and mention of the city officials who intended to back it up. This popular movement was met on the part of the railroad by directing its conductors not to accept three-cent fares but to carry passengers free who refused to pay more; so that all danger of violence on that score was avoided, even if it was a danger that in any way concerned the Court. The newspaper further gave one or two premature but ultimately correct intimations of what the judge was going to do, made one mistaken statement of a ruling which it criticized indirectly, uttered a few expressions that implied that the judge did not have the last word and that no doubt contained innuendoes not flattering to his personality. Later there was an account of a local socialist meeting at which a member, one Quinlivan, spoke in such a way that the judge attached him for contempt and thereupon, on the same day that the decree was entered in the principal case, the paper reported as the grounds of the attachment that Quinlivan had pronounced Judge Killits to have shown from the first that he was favorable to the railroad, had criticized somewhat ignorantly a ruling said to put the burden of proof on the city, and had said that Killits and his press were unfair to the people, winding up "impeach Killits." I confess that I cannot find in all this or in the evidence in the case anything that would have affected a mind of reasonable fortitude, and still less can I find there anything that obstructed the administration of justice in any sense that I possibly can give to those words.

In the elaborate opinion that was delivered by Judge Killits to justify the judgment it is said "In this matter the record shows that the Court endured the *News-Bee's* attacks upon suitors before it and upon the Court itself, and carried all the embarrassment inevitable from these publications, for nearly six months before moving to vindicate its independence."

It appears to me that this statement is enough to show that there was no emergency, that there was nothing that warranted a finding that the administration of justice was obstructed, or a resort to this summary proceeding, but that on the contrary when the matter was over, the Judge thought that the "consistently unfriendly attitude against the Court," and the fact that the publications tended "to arouse distrust and dislike of the Court" were sufficient to justify this information and a heavy fine. They may have been, but not, I think, in this form of trial. I would go as far as any man in favor of the sharpest and most summary enforcement of order in court and obedience to decrees, but when there is no need for immediate action contempts are like any other breach of law and should be dealt with as the law deals with other illegal acts. Action like the present in my opinion is wholly unwarranted by even color of law.

Mr. Justice Brandeis concurs in this opinion.

CORRESPONDENCE

To Harold Laski
Washington, D.C., May 25, 1918

Dear Laski

... On Tuesday the C. J. asked me to take two cases which I done gone done and had them distributed (I mean my opinion) on Thursday. On that day came down an opinion] [*Hammer v. Dagenhart*, 247 U.S. 251, 277] that stirred the innards of Brandeis and me and he spurred me to write a dissent. I read one to him that p.m. and in consequence of his criticisms rewrote it and sent it to the printer yesterday and now am awaiting the corrected proof to send round. I incidentally printed another dissent in an important case [*Toledo Newspaper*] in which the opinion has not yet appeared and sent it to the writer – that he might have my views before him – so altogether I have been busy. . . .

Mark DeWolfe Howe, ed., *Holmes-Laski Letters, The Correspondence of Mr. Justice Holmes and Harold J. Laski* (Cambridge, MA: Harvard University Press, 1953), at 1:157 (footnote omitted).

To Frederick Pollock
Washington, June 14, 1918

Dear Pollock:

... My last two cases in Court were marked by two dissents that I imagine the majority thought ill timed and regrettable as I thought the decisions. . . . [52]

[52] *Hammer v. Dagenhart*, 247 U.S. 251, 277 (1918); *Toledo Newspaper Co. v. United States* (1918).

The second case was when a Judge, after the event, punished a newspaper and its editor by a summary proceeding that he ordered instituted and tried himself without a jury, for contempt – such summary proceedings being limited by Statute to misconduct in the presence of the Court or so near thereto as to obstruct the administration of justice. I thought the performance wholly unwarranted and the last thing that could maintain respect for the Courts.

We stood . . . 2 to 5 on the last – two Judges [Day and Clarke] preferring not to sit because of their relations with the Judge etc. One of them at least agreed with me, as Brandeis did openly. . . .

Mark DeWolfe Howe, ed., *Holmes-Pollock Letters: The Correspondence of Mr. Justice Holmes and Sir Frederick Pollock, 1874–1932* (Cambridge, MA: Harvard University Press, 1941), at 1:266–67.

COMMENTARY

Spirit of intolerance – "Curiously, the first important free speech case to come before the White Court, that of *Toledo Newspaper Company v. United States* . . . had nothing to do with the war, though the decision may have been influenced by the prevailing spirit of war intolerance." Ernest Sutherland Bates, *The Story of the Supreme Court* (New York: Bobbs-Merrill, 1936), at 253.

Moving away from the bad-tendency test? – In his *Toledo Newspaper* dissent, "Holmes did not directly address the issues of free speech and press. . . . ; his concern was [more] for the dignity of the court, which he thought had been compromised by [Judge] Killits's behavior. But his pessimistic stance regarding the *News-Bee*, combined with the clear implication he thought Killits had acted foolishly, foreshadowed his positions in a series of freedom-of-expression cases with which he would have to deal shortly." Liva Baker, *The Justice from Beacon Hill: The Life and Times of Oliver Wendell Holmes* (New York: HarperCollins, 1991), at 510.

Both the language of Holmes's opinion and his vote in the case "appeared inconsistent with his endorsement of the bad tendency test in *Fox* [herein]. Moreover, his assumption that the case raised a first amendment issue did not seem to square with his view, previously expressed in *Patterson v. Colorado* [herein], that subsequent punishment for objectionable speech did not violate the First Amendment at all, since the Amendment was confined to prior restraints against publication." Moreover, Holmes's opinion in *Toledo Newspaper* suggested that "the *Patterson* premise that the First Amendment only applied to prior restraints was coming to be abandoned" in his mind. G.

Edward White, *Justice Oliver Wendell Holmes: Law and the Inner Self* (New York: Oxford University Press, 1993), at 414, 417.

Imminent-danger language – Given the significance that the word would come to take on in subsequent free speech jurisprudence, note Holmes's use of the word *imminent*: "suppose that an imminent possibility of obstruction is sufficient. Still I think that only immediate and necessary action is contemplated. . . . " *See* H. L. Pohlman, *Justice Oliver Wendell Holmes: Free Speech and the Living Constitution* (New York: New York University Press, 1993), at 96 n. 144.

Use of majority opinion by government lawyers in 1919 free speech case – When *Debs v. United States*, 249 U.S. 211 (1919) (see Part V), was before the Supreme Court, the government lawyers invoked the *Toledo Newspaper* to support their case against Eugene Debs for violating the Espionage Act. They argued that "the war power of congress can limit free speech as readily as the contempt power of a court." Brief for the United States in *Debs v. United States* at 89–90, quoted in David M. Rabban, *Free Speech in Its Forgotten Years* (New York: Cambridge University Press, 1997), at 279. Despite his dissent in *Toledo Newspaper*, Holmes wrote for the Court in *Debs* and denied his free speech claim.

Subsequent law – *Toledo Newspaper* was effectively undermined in *Nye v. United States* 313 U.S. 33, 51–52 (1941). Herbert Wechsler – who years later successfully argued *New York Times Co. v. Sullivan*, 376 U.S. 254 (1964) – argued the *Nye* case.

◈

PLAINTIFFS'. EXHIBIT No. 3, PAR. 1, COUNT 2.

QUINLIVAN IS READY TO DEFEND KILLITS' CONTEMPT CHARGES

BASIS OF CHARGES AGAINST UNION LEADER

These are the remarks alleged to have been made by John Quinlivan, and on which Judge Killits bases his contempt charges:

"The street car situation of Toledo is in the hands of a friend of the Rail-Light.

"Judge Killits has demonstrated from the first that he was at all times favorable to the Rail-Light.

"Any fair-minded citizen will see that when Killits placed the burden of proof of the Schreiber ordinance on the city that the city was going to be the goat. The Central Labor union should adopt stinging resolutions and let our federal friend know what we think of him.

"The burden of proof should have been placed on the Rail-Light. Killits and the press are preparing to hand the people a lemon. They are unfair to the people.

"Impeach Killits."

That he was thoroughly prepared to face the contempt of court proceedings in federal court on Saturday afternoon, in response to the summons of Federal Judge Killits, was the statement of John Quinlivan, business agent of the Central Labor union, on Saturday afternoon. The case has been set for hearing at 2:30 o'clock.

Quinlivan will be represented by the law firm of Kohn, Northup, McMahon & Ritter. Owing to the absence from the city of Charles S. Northup, a continuance of the hearing probably will be asked until Monday.

Judge Killits stated on Saturday

The charges were based on criticisms Quinlivan is said to have made of Killits' conduct in the hearing of a suit to invalidate an ordinance providing three-cent car fares all day.

SAYS JUDGE MISINFORMED.

Although Quinlivan had not outlined his defense on Saturday he denied that he had made several of the statements attributed to him in the citation by Judge Killits. Quinlivan said the judge apparently had been misinformed, and that the misinformation had been given by persons in the employ of interests that would like to ruin his (Quinlivan's) influence.

The citation was served on Quinlivan by Deputy Marshals Bartley and McKindley on Friday night. Quinlivan was not arrested. The issuance of the citation followed an

Certitude is not the test of certainty. We have been cocksure of many things that were not so.

NATURAL LAW[53]

It is not enough for the knight of romance that you agree that his lady is a very nice girl – if you do not admit that she is the best that God ever made or will make, you must fight. There is in all men a demand for the superlative, so much so that the poor devil who has no other way of reaching it attains it by getting drunk. It seems to me that this demand is at the bottom of the philosopher's effort to prove that truth is absolute and of the jurist's search for criteria of universal validity which he collects under the head of natural law.

I used to say, when I was young, that truth was the majority vote of that nation that could lick all others. Certainly we may expect that the received opinion about the present war will depend a good deal upon which side wins (I hope with all my soul it will be mine), and I think that the statement was correct insofar as it implied that our test of truth is a reference to either a present or an imagined future majority in favor of our view. If, as I have suggested elsewhere, the truth may be defined as the system of my (intellectual) limitations, what gives it objectivity is the fact that I find my fellow man to a greater or less extent (never wholly) subject to the same *Can't Helps*. If I think that I am sitting at a table I find that the other persons present agree with me; so if I say that the sum of the angles of a triangle is equal to two right angles. If I am in a minority of one they send for a doctor or lock me up; and I am so far able to transcend the [?] to me convincing testimony of my sense or my reason as to recognize that if I am alone probably something is wrong with my works.

Certitude is not the test of certainty. We have been cocksure of many things that were not so. If I may quote myself again, property, friendship, and truth have a common root in time. One cannot be wrenched from the rocky crevices into which one has grown for many years without feeling that one is attacked in one's life. What we most love and revere generally is determined by

[53] 32 *Harvard Law Review* 40 (1918). "Suggested by reading François Geny, *Science et Technique en Droit Positif Privé*, Paris, 1915" – so wrote Holmes. Shortly before he drafted this short article, he began to "trudge through volume two of the recently published" book by Geny, a French professor and legal philosopher whose view of the law was similar to that of Holmes. "Geny's philosophy combined empiricism with natural law in a complex and sometimes ambivalent fashion." The French philosopher's writings inspired Holmes, as he noted, to write his essay on natural law. *See* Liva Baker, *The Justice from Beacon Hill* (New York: HarperCollins, 1991), at 516–17. – *Ed.*

early associations. I love granite rocks and barberry bushes, no doubt because with them were my earliest joys that reach back through the past eternity of my life. But while one's experience thus makes certain preferences dogmatic for oneself, recognition of how they came to be so leaves one able to see that others, poor souls, may be equally dogmatic about something else. And this again means scepticism. Not that one's belief or love does not remain. Not that we would not fight and die for it if important – we all, whether we know it or not, are fighting to make the kind of a world that we should like – but that we have learned to recognize that others will fight and die to make a different world, with equal sincerity or belief. Deep-seated preferences cannot be argued about – you cannot argue a man into liking a glass of beer – and therefore, when differences are sufficiently far reaching, we try to kill the other man rather than let him have his way. But that is perfectly consistent with admitting that, so far as appears, his grounds are just as good as ours.

The jurists who believe in natural law seem to me to be in that naïve state of mind that accepts what has been familiar and accepted by all men everywhere. No doubt it is true that, so far as we can see ahead, some arrangements and the rudiments of familiar institutions seem to be necessary elements in any society that may spring from our own and that would seem to us to be civilized – some form of permanent association between the sexes – some residue of property individually owned – some mode of binding oneself to specified future conduct – at the bottom of all, some protection for the person. But without speculating whether a group is imaginable in which all but the last of these might disappear and the last be subject to qualifications that most of us would abhor, the question remains as to the *Ought* of natural law.

It is true that beliefs and wishes have a transcendental basis in the sense that their foundation is arbitrary. You cannot help entertaining and feeling them, and there is an end of it. As an arbitrary fact people wish to live, and we say with various degrees of certainty that they can do so only on certain conditions. To do it they must eat and drink. That necessity is absolute. It is a necessity of less degree but practically general that they should live in society. If they live in society, so far as we can see, there are further conditions. Reason working on experience does tell us, no doubt, that if our wish to live continues, we can do it only on those terms. But that seems to me the whole of the matter. I see no a priori duty to live with others and in that way, but simply a statement of what I must do if I wish to remain alive. If I do live with others they tell me that I must do and abstain from doing various things or they will put the screws on to me. I believe that they will, and being of the same mind as to their conduct I not only accept the rules but come in time to accept them with sympathy and emotional affirmation and begin to talk about duties and rights. But for legal purposes a right is only the hypostasis of a prophecy – the imagination of a substance supporting the fact that the public force will be brought to bear upon those who do things said to contravene it – just as we talk of the force of gravitation accounting for the conduct of bodies in space. One phrase adds no more than the other to what we know without it. No doubt behind these legal rights is the fighting will of the subject to maintain them, and the spread of his emotions to the general rules by which they are maintained; but that does not seem to me the same thing as the supposed *a priori* discernment of a duty or the assertion of a preexisting right. A dog will fight for his bone.

The most fundamental of the supposed preexisting rights – the right to life – is sacrificed without a scruple not only in war, but whenever the interest of society, that is, of the predominant power in the community, is thought to demand it. Whether that interest is the interest of mankind in the long run no one can tell, and as, in any event, to those who do not think with Kant and Hegel it is only an interest, the sanctity disappears. I remember a very tender-hearted judge being of opinion that closing a hatch to stop a fire and the destruction of a cargo was justified even if it was known that doing so would stifle a man below. It is idle to illustrate further, because to those who agree with me I am uttering commonplaces and to those who disagree I am ignoring the necessary foundations of thought. The *a priori* men generally call the dissentients superficial. But I do agree with them in believing that one's attitude on these matters is closely connected with one's general attitude toward the universe. Proximately, as has been suggested, it is determined largely by early associations and temperament, coupled with the desire to have an absolute guide. Men to a great extent believe what they want to – although I see in that no basis for a philosophy that tells us what we should want to want.

Now when we come to our attitude toward the universe I do not see any rational ground for demanding the superlative – for being dissatisfied unless we are assured that our truth is cosmic truth, if there is such a thing – that the ultimates of a little creature on this little earth are the last word of the unimaginable whole. If a man sees no reason for believing that significance, consciousness and ideals are more than marks of the finite, that does not justify what has been familiar in French sceptics; getting upon a pedestal and professing to look with haughty scorn upon a world in ruins. The real conclusion is that the part cannot swallow the whole – that our categories are not, or may not be, adequate to formulate what we cannot know. If we believe that we come out of the universe, not it out of us, we must admit that we do not know what we are talking about when we speak of brute matter. We do know that a certain complex of energies can wag its tail and another can make syllogisms. These are among the powers of the unknown, and, if, as may be, it has still greater powers that we cannot understand, as Fabre[54] in his studies of instinct would have us believe, studies that gave Bergson[55] one of the strongest strands for his philosophy and enabled Maeterlinck[56] to make us fancy for a moment that we heard a clang from behind phenomena – if this be true, why should we not be content? Why should we employ the energy that is furnished to us by the cosmos to defy it and shake our fist at the sky? It seems to me silly.

That the universe has in it more than we understand, that the private soldiers have not been told the plan of campaign, or even that there is one, rather than some vaster unthinkable to which every predicate is an impertinence, has no bearing upon our conduct. We still shall fight – all of us because we want to live, some, at least, because we want to realize our spontaneity and prove our powers, for the joy of it, and we may leave to the unknown the supposed final valuation of that which in any event has value to us. It is enough for us that the universe has produced us and has within it, as less than it, all that we believe and love. If we think of our existence not as that of a little god outside, but as that of a ganglion within, we have the infinite behind us. It gives us our only but our adequate significance. A grain of sand has the same, but what competent person supposes that he understands a grain of sand? That is as much beyond our grasp as man. If our imagination is strong enough to accept the vision of ourselves as parts inseverable from the rest, and to extend our final interest beyond the boundary of our skins, it justifies the sacrifice even of our lives for ends outside of ourselves. The motive, to be sure, is the common wants and ideals that we find in man. Philosophy does not furnish motives, but it shows men that they are not fools for doing what they already want to do. It opens to the forlorn hopes on which we throw ourselves away, the vista of the farthest stretch of human thought, the chords of a harmony that breathes from the unknown.

---

[54] Jean-Henri Fabre (1823–1915) was a French entomologist and author. He studied and wrote about the lives of insects. He is considered the father of modern entomology. – *Ed.*

[55] Henri Bergson (1859–1941) was an influential French philosopher. Bergson maintained that intuition is deeper than intellect. In his *Creative Evolution* (1907) and *Matter and Memory* (1896), he tried to integrate his findings of biological science with his theory of consciousness. – *Ed.*

[56] Maurice Maeterlinck (1862–1949) was a poet, playwright, and essayist. His early writings were characterized by fatalism, mysticism, and death. His plays were an influential part of the Symbolist movement. In 1911 he won the Nobel Prize in Literature. – *Ed.*

To Oliver Wendell Holmes
December 20, 1918

My dear Holmes:

[I]f you mean to imply that no one can accept natural law . . . without maintaining it as a body of rules known to be absolutely true, I do not agree. . . . If you deny that any principles of conduct at all are common to and admitted by all men who try to behave reasonably – well, I don't see how you can have any ethics or any ethical background for law. . . .

Mark DeWolfe Howe, ed., *Holmes-Pollock Letters: The Correspondence of Mr. Justice Holmes and Sir Frederick Pollock, 1874–1932* (Cambridge, MA: Harvard University Press, 1941), at 1:274–75.

To Frederick Pollock
January 24, 1919

Dear F. P.:

. . . I didn't expect you to agree with me altogether. As to Ethics I have called them a body of imperfect social generalizations expressed in terms of emotion. Of course I agree that there is such a body on which to a certain extent civilized men would agree – but how much less than would have been taken for granted fifty years ago, witness the Bolsheviki. . . .

Mark DeWolfe Howe, ed., *Holmes-Pollock Letters: The Correspondence of Mr. Justice Holmes and Sir Frederick Pollock, 1874–1932* (Cambridge, MA: Harvard University Press, 1941), at 2:3.

COMMENTARY

Law and values – Commenting on the Pollock-Holmes correspondence quoted herein, Max Lerner observed: "Note that Holmes here suggests a relativism of attitude, . . . it is a relativism that does not exclude the need for deep convictions as to values," what Holmes called "deep-seated preferences." Drawing on the skepticism and mysticism of "Natural Law," Lerner added: "We have here the behaviorist definition of law, squeezing it dry of all morality and sentiment; and we have also the attempt to bring in the element of faith and energy as a natural part of the human mind. I tend to agree with [Lon] Fuller and some others that Holmes did not adequately bridge the gaps between the two worlds. There was within him a deep conflict between skepticism and belief, between mind and faith, between a recognition that men act in terms of a cold calculation of interests, and a recognition also that they are moved by symbols [that], if you squeeze the life and energy out of them, become merely tinsel and rag. He tried to construct a legal theory, as he tried to construct a philosophy of life for himself, which would allow him to take account of both strains. He was not wholly successful logically in the attempt, but he made a going concern out of it." Max Lerner, *The Mind and Faith of Justice Holmes* (New Brunswick, NJ: Transaction Publishers, 1989), at 372–73.

Holmes's existential side – "The existential side of Holmes is best expressed in his succinct article, Natural Law, which he published one year before he wrote the *Abrams* dissent.... [see Part VI] This essay richly rewards a close reading by anyone who would interpret what Holmes says in *Abrams*." Vincent Blasi, "*Propter Honoris Respectum*: Reading Holmes through the Lens of Schauer: The *Abrams* Dissent," 72 *Notre Dame Law Review* 1343, 1347 n. 19 (1997).

Skepticism and free speech – This wartime-era article penned while Holmes was on the Court, and published not long before the release of the opinions in the *Schenck* through *Abrams* lines of cases, is, as noted earlier, important to students of free speech for at least two reasons: (1) it opens a window into Holmes's notions of truth, and (2) it likewise informs us of his notion of rights, including the right of free speech.

The pursuit of truth, Holmes tells us early on in his article, is "a demand for the superlative" and is akin to the plight of "the poor devil who has no other way of reaching" the absolute than by "getting drunk." As for the right to pursue truth, a legal right embodied in the First Amendment, that is no more than "the hypostasis of a prophecy – the imagination of a substance supporting the fact that public force will be brought to bear on those who do things said to contravene it." Hence, First Amendment rights are not fundamental in any natural law or Declaration of Independence sense. Holmes was dubious of the entire enterprise of rights talk generally. As he declared in *Jackman v. Rosenbaum Company*, 260 U.S. 22, 31 (1922): "Such words as 'right' are a constant solicitation to fallacy." For Holmes, the vitality of so-called rights depended on the public will, which in times of war generally had little toleration for dissent as evidenced by the holdings in *Schenck, Frohwerk, Debs,* and *Abrams* (see Parts V and VI), with Holmes dissenting only in the last case.

Part V   Supreme Court Opinions: "When a nation is at war"

There is nothing that could not be destroyed if it were enough to point to an incidental evil. . . .
   – Oliver Wendell Holmes Jr.[1]

One whose whole outlook on life was profoundly influenced by his Civil War experience was bound to acquiesce in some subordination of private opinion during war which he would find unwarranted in times of peace.
   – Felix Frankfurter[2]

Woodrow Wilson narrowly won reelection in 1916 partly because of a powerful slogan: "He kept us out of war." After he took office, however, the new president concluded that the nation could not remain neutral, and certainly not after three American ships had been sunk by German submarines patrolling the waters around England and France. As commander in chief, he then asked Congress, on April 2, 1917, to declare war on Germany. Some of Wilson's original supporters and others took exception to this move and held to their steadfast ways, and opposed America's entry into the war – but to no avail. For them, it was ironic that the "war 'to make the world safe for democracy' triggered one of the worst invasions of civil liberties in the nation's history."[3] And that was clear from the outset. Wilson left no doubt that his administration would not tolerate much, if any, opposition to the war. He was stern: "if there should be any disloyalty,

---

[1] Letter from OWH to Lewis Einstein, January 29, 1914, reproduced in James Bishop Peabody, ed., *The Holmes-Einstein Letters: Correspondence of Mr. Justice Holmes and Lewis Einstein, 1903–1935* (New York: St. Martin's Press, 1964), at 87–88.

[2] Felix Frankfurter, *Mr. Justice Holmes and the Supreme Court* (Cambridge, MA: Harvard University Press, 1938), at 52.

[3] Melvin I. Urofsky, *Louis Brandeis: A Life* (New York: Pantheon Books, 2009), at 548.

it will be dealt with a firm hand of stern repression."[4] Disloyal speech, he insisted, was "not a subject on which there was room for . . . debate." Those who engaged in it, he argued, "had sacrificed their right to civil liberties."[5] Unable to persuade Congress to go as far as he wished in squelching anti-war expression, he warned that the "authority to exercise censorship over the press . . . is absolutely necessary to the public safety."[6]

What followed was a campaign not only to protect the nation against subversion but also to suppress criticism of the administration's war efforts. To that end, Wilson pushed for and Congress passed a number of laws, which included the following:

- The Selective Service Act of 1917,[7] which among other things provided for criminal sanctions against anyone who obstructed the draft.
- The Espionage Act of 1917,[8] which punished anyone who made or conveyed false reports for the benefit of the enemy, or sought to cause disobedience in the armed services, or obstructed recruitment or enlistment in the armed forces. Going beyond the intended confines of the law as passed, the Justice Department readily "prosecuted more than two thousand dissenters during the war for allegedly disloyal, seditious, or incendiary speech."[9]
- The Trading with the Enemy Act of 1917,[10] which among other things authorized the postmaster general to confiscate and cancel postal matter, including foreign-language and other publications.

[4] Qtd. in Edward M. Coffman, *The War to End All Wars* (New York: Oxford University Press, 1968), at 25, qtd. in Geoffrey R. Stone, *Perilous Times: Free Speech in Wartime* (New York: W. W. Norton, 2004), at 127. *See also* Robert Goldstein, *Political Repression in Modern America* (New York: G. K. Hall, 1978), at 105–07.

[5] 65th Cong., Spec. Sess., in 55 *Congressional Record Supplement* 104, April 2, 1917, qtd. in *Perilous Times, supra* note 4, at 1127.

[6] "Wilson Demands Press Censorship," *New York Times*, May 23, 1917, at 1, qtd. in *Perilous Times, supra* note 4, at 139.

[7] Act of May 18, 1917, 40 Stat. 76. (1917).

[8] Espionage Act of 1917, ch. 30, 40 Stat. 217 (1917). Most of the prosecutions under the act were brought pursuant to title I, which in relevant part provided: "Whoever, when the United State is at war, shall willfully make or convey false reports or false statements with the intent to interfere with the operation or success of the military or naval forces of the United States or to promote the success of its enemies and whoever, when the United States is at war, shall willfully cause or attempt to cause insubordination, disloyalty, mutiny, or refusal of duty, in the military or naval forces of the United States, or shall willfully obstruct the recruiting or enlistment service of the United States, to the injury of service in the United States, shall be punished by a fine not more than $10,000 or imprisonment for not more than twenty years, or both."

[9] *Perilous Times, supra* note 4, at 160.

[10] Ch. 106, 40 Stat. 411 (1917).

- The 1918 Sedition Act,[11] which often made any meaningful and public opposition to the war difficult or impossible. Some of its provisions were so constitutionally suspect that John Lord O'Brian,[12] the assistant attorney general and head of the Justice Department's War Emergency Division, "declined to defend its constitutionality."[13]
- The Immigration Act of 1918,[14] which broadened the government's power to deport aliens urging the forceful overthrow of the government.[15] Notably, in 1918 alone, the government "deported 11,625 individuals under this act."[16]

Such laws and their state counterparts severely restricted free speech, and there would be court challenges, but those hoping to utilize the First Amendment faced a difficult road. There had been little jurisprudence about the Speech Clause, and the few cases on record followed [William] Blackstone's view that free speech meant little more than the absence of prior restraint. While the government could not [lawfully] stop someone from saying or publishing something, it could punish that person afterward, especially if the courts found the speech had a "bad tendency,"[17] that is, it fostered undesirable actions or behavior. Between the Civil War and World War I, both state and federal courts rejected [the few] free-speech claims [that came before them] or ignored them, and no court seemed more unsympathetic than the U.S. Supreme Court.[18] In the patriotic and frenzied mood of the times, such laws were tapped by Woodrow Wilson's Justice Department and others to safeguard the nation, on the one hand, and to squelch oppositional sentiments of all kinds, on the other hand. Or as H. L. Mencken put it: "Between Wilson and his brigade of informers,

---

[11] Sedition Act of 1918, ch. 75, 40 Stat. 553 (1919). Beyond what was prohibited under the 1917 act, its 1918 successor also prohibited "disloyal, profane, scurrilous or abusive language about the Constitution . . . or the military or naval forces . . . [,] the flag . . . [,] or the uniform of the Army or Navy."

[12] O'Brian and Alfred Bettman argued the *Schenck* and *Frohwerk* cases for the government, and O'Brian also argued the *Debs* case.

[13] *Perilous Times*, *supra* note 4, at 182 [citing John Lord O'Brian, "Civil Liberty in War Time," 42 *Reports of New York State Bar Association* 275, 304 (1919)].

[14] Ch. 186, 40 Stat. 1012 (1918) (also known as the Alien Act of 1918).

[15] *See generally Louis Brandeis*, *supra* note 3, at 548–49.

[16] *Perilous Times*, *supra* note 4, at 172.

[17] *See Shaffer v. United States*, 255 F. 886, 887–89 (9th Cir. 1919) (applying bad-tendency test in Espionage Act case and denying free speech claim).

[18] *Louis Brandeis*, *supra* note 3, at 548–49 (endnotes omitted and annotated footnotes added).

spies, volunteer detectives, perjurers and complaisant judges . . . the liberty of the citizens has pretty well vanished in America."[19]

Mindful of all of this, a December 3, 1917, letter by Holmes reveals how the justice viewed the larger picture. "The only limit I can see to the power of the law-maker," he wrote, "is the limit of power as a question of fact. . . . When I talk of law I talk as a cynic. . . . And I understand by human rights what a given crowd will fight for (successfully). Old Agassiz (Louis) once said that in some part of Germany if you added a farthing to the price of a glass of beer there would be a revolution. If that was true, to have beer at the current price was one of the rights of man in that place."[20]

It is against that backdrop that we come to the four Holmes opinions that follow – an unpublished dissent and three majority opinions. In them, we see Justice Holmes grappling with free speech principles in a bolder way than he had done heretofore. Though he was not, to be sure, writing on a blank conceptual slate, in these opinions, we witness the seventy-eight-year-old jurist bringing his ideas into sharper focus. In one of them, *Schenck v. United States*, Holmes announced his famous clear-and-present-danger test – a First Amendment formula that stood to recalibrate First Amendment thinking in significant ways. But before the printer's ink was dry on that landmark opinion, which worried some of his closest allies, Holmes wrote for the Court in *Frohwerk v. United States* and *Debs v. United States*. Here, as in *Schenck*, all the First Amendment rights claimants lost. After *Debs*, some of Holmes's own defenders took public exception to his constitutional handiwork.[21] Interestingly, before all of this, Holmes stood prepared to defend the free speech principle in a case that never made headlines – *Baltzer v. United States*. In it, Holmes issued what has been called a dramatic dissent. The *Baltzer* case produced a curious opinion by Justice Holmes, one that was never officially published but that has survived nonetheless.

These four cases and the ones that follow them (see Part VI) brought Holmes eye to eye with the clash between the necessities of war and the ideal of military heroism, on the one hand, and the ideal of dissident antiwar speech, on the other hand. Could they coexist? Could the honor of military struggle survive in a world where that very honor was devalued and even denied? And if they could, to what extent could both his life

---

[19] H. L. Mencken, *On Politics: A Carnival of Buncombe* (Baltimore: Johns Hopkins University Press, 1956), at 11.

[20] Letter from OWH to Harold Laski, December 3, 1917, reproduced in Mark DeWolfe Howe, ed., *Holmes-Laski Letters: The Correspondence of Mr. Justice Holmes and Harold J. Laski* (Cambridge, MA: Harvard University Press, 1953), at 1:115.

[21] *See, e.g.*, Ernst Freund, "The *Debs* Case and Freedom of Speech," *New Republic*, May 13, 1919, at 13.

experience (grounded in the reality of his Civil War service) and his jurisprudence (shaped by his scholarly writings, judicial opinions, and collegial input) help him to resolve such conflicts? Both played a role, in some ways predictable and in other ways not.

◈

Another influence on Holmes was the company he kept. As previously noted in the introduction to Part IV, Holmes met Felix Frankfurter in 1912, and then in 1916 he was introduced to Harold Laski ("an astonishing young Jew," and "most learned," as Holmes first tagged him[22]). In the process, Holmes developed relationships with still others, including the young progressive crowd affiliated with the *New Republic*. And in July 1919, Laski introduced Holmes to Zechariah Chafee, a Harvard law professor. From the start, the young professor impressed Holmes as being "unusually pleasant and intelligent."[23] Soon enough, this cadre of young men took to the light of Holmes's 1919 free speech opinions and began to praise them or, as with Chafee, to offer important critical comments, either in publications or in correspondence.[24] These men influenced Holmes's thinking, to some degree, and likewise helped to enhance his reputation in the legal community and then in the nation in general. To that end, in the summer of 1919, Laski first proposed and then arranged to have Holmes's collected legal papers published by a respected house, Harcourt, Brace, and Howe. Predictably, there was a "generous review" (by Morris Cohen) in the *New Republic*.[25]

---

[22] Letters from OWH to Frederick Pollock, July 12, 1916, and February 18, 1917, reproduced in Mark DeWolfe Howe, ed., *Holmes-Pollock Letters: The Correspondence of Mr. Justice Holmes and Sir Frederick Pollock, 1874–1932* (Cambridge, MA: Harvard University Press, 1941), at 1:237–38, 243. In a 1917 letter to Laski, Holmes wrote: "You are a splendid young enthusiast and you make me feel more alive." OWH to Harold Laski, November 30, 1917, reproduced in *Holmes-Laski Letters, supra* note 20, at 1:114.

[23] Letter from OWH to Frederick Pollock, June 21, 1920, reproduced in *Holmes-Pollock Letters, supra* note 22, at 2:45 (referring to his meeting with Chafee a year earlier). By this time, Chafee had already published his first article on free speech. *See* Zechariah Chafee Jr., "Freedom of Speech," *New Republic*, November 16, 1918, at 66. *See also* Donald L. Smith, *Zechariah Chafee Jr., Defender of Liberty and Law* (Cambridge, MA: Harvard University Press, 1986), at 17–18.

[24] *See, e.g.,* "The *Debs* Case and Freedom of Speech," *supra* note 21, at 13; "The Call to Toleration," *New Republic*, November 26, 1919, at 360; Gerard Henderson, "What Is Left of Free Speech?" *New Republic*, December 1919, at 50; Zechariah Chafee, "Freedom of Speech in Wartime," 32 *Harvard Law Review* 932 (1919); Zechariah Chafee, "A Contemporary State Trial: The United States versus Jacob Abrams et al.," 33 *Harvard Law Review* 747 (1920); Letter from OWH to Harold Laski, May 13, 1919, reproduced in *Holmes-Laski Letters, supra* note 20, at 2:202–04, quoted following *Debs* opinion herein.

[25] *See* G. Edward White, *Justice Oliver Wendell Holmes: Law and the Inner Self* (New York: Oxford University Press, 1993), at 365–66 (footnotes omitted).

There was another person whose views on free speech caught Justice
Holmes's attention – Billings Learned Hand (1872–1961), a contemplative
federal district court judge. Hand had been on the federal district court for
the Southern District of New York for eight years when *Masses Publishing
Co. v. Patten*[26] (1917) came to his docket. The case concerned an early
test of the new Espionage Act. The matter involved an attempt by the
postmaster general to prevent the mailing of *The Masses*, a confrontational
leftist publication. Its declared policy was "to do as it pleases and conciliate
nobody, not even its readers." Its editor, Max Eastman, went to court to
enjoin the postmaster's action.

After reviewing the evidence and studying the Espionage Act, Judge
Hand issued his ruling on July 24, 1917. He wrote on a slate of little or no
judicial precedent. His published opinion – one based on an interpretation
of the statute and not, strictly speaking, on the First Amendment – would
become a landmark ruling in establishing a boundary between lawful
advocacy and punishable speech.

Hand ruled in Eastman's favor and enjoined the postmaster from excluding *The Masses* from the mail. Quite simply, Hand concluded that the
Espionage Act of 1917 was designed to punish those who actually interfered with the conduct of the war. It was not, by contrast, designed to
punish young and passionate idealists who criticized the war or who pro-
pagandized against capitalism and for communism. Absent a clear directive
from Congress, Hand ruled, it should not be presumed that the freedoms
granted by the First Amendment should be so readily set aside. Or as the
judge put it in his own analytical way:

> Political agitation, by the passions it arouses or the convictions it engen-
> ders, may in fact stimulate men to the violation of the law. Detesta-
> tion of existing policies is easily transformed into forcible resistance of
> the authority which puts them in execution, and it would be folly to
> disregard the causal relation between the two. Yet to assimilate agi-
> tation, legitimate as such, without *direct incitement to violence*, is to
> disregard the tolerance of all methods of political agitation which in
> normal times is a safeguard of free government. The distinction is not
> a scholastic subterfuge, but a hard-bought acquisition in the fight for
> freedom.[27]

---

[26] 244 F. 535 (S.D.N.Y. 1917). *See* Geoffrey R. Stone, "Judge Learned Hand and the Espionage Act of 1917: A Mystery Unraveled," 70 *University of Chicago Law Review* 335
(2003).

[27] 244 F. at 540 (emphasis added).

Reading the Espionage Act narrowly, Judge Hand held that speech could be punished under the statute only when it amounted to a "direct incitement to violent resistance" to the law. By that generously speech-protective standard, what graced the pages of the magazine was patently lawful. Zechariah Chafee hailed the opinion in the pages of the *New Republic*.[28] Moreover, it was an opinion that would, in short time, alert Holmes to how a thoughtful judge might consider a free speech case in wartime.

If there was any pinpoint in time when Holmes began to reconsider views like those he articulated in *Patterson v. Colorado* (1907) and *Fox v. Washington* (1915) (see Part IV), it was perhaps in June 1918, when he hooked up with Judge Hand by a chance encounter.[29] The two met on a train leaving the newly built, white granite Washington Union Station – Holmes en route to Beverly Farms, Massachusetts, and Hand en route to Cornish, New Hampshire. As they rode the boxy Pacific Railroad cars, they began to talk about toleration and then, gradually, about free speech. Holmes was passionate about the law but quite dispassionate about defending the rights of rogues bent on subverting that law. Though Holmes had not yet read Hand's *Masses* opinion, it is possible that if the stiff-collared jurist had read it he might have sided with the appellate court that reversed Hand.[30] Again, the idea of national security, defined very broadly, was foremost on his mind, this in addition to his own views on the common law and speech crimes. And then there was his daring statement in *The Common Law*: "No society has ever admitted that it could not sacrifice individual welfare

---

[28] Zechariah Chafee Jr., "Freedom of Speech," *New Republic*, November 16, 1918, at 67. Wrote Chafee: "The true meaning of freedom of speech seems to be this. One of the most important purposes of society and government is the discovery and spread of truth on subjects of general concern. This is possible only through absolutely unlimited discussion, for . . . once force is thrown into the argument, it becomes a matter of chance whether it is thrown on the false side or the true, and truth loses all its natural advantage in the contest. Nevertheless, there are other purposes of government, such as order, the training of the young, [and] protection against external aggression. Unlimited discussion sometimes interferes with these purposes, which must then be balanced against freedom of speech, but freedom of speech ought to weigh very heavily in the scale. The First Amendment gives binding force to this principle of political wisdom."

[29] The story and related facts are discussed in Gerald Gunther, *Learned Hand: The Man and Judge* (New York: Alfred A. Knopf, 1994), at 161–63.

[30] *Masses Publishing Co. v. Patten*, 245 F. 102 (2nd Cir. 1917). A few years after the *Masses* case, the Supreme Court declared that the postmaster general had broad powers to regulate the uses of mail in time of war. *United States ex rel. Milwaukee Social Democrat Publishing Co. v. Burleson* (1921) (Holmes & Brandeis, J.J., dissenting). *See* Part VI of this volume.

to its own existence. If conscripts are necessary for its army, it seizes them, and marches them, with bayonets in their rear, to death. . . . "[31]

Judge Hand was nowhere as bold, either in temperament or in philosophy. Nonetheless, when Hand later mulled over his train conversation, the ever-guarded judge felt he had granted the justice too much conceptual ground. In a June 22, 1918, letter to Holmes, Hand wrote:

> . . . I gave up rather more easily than I now feel disposed about Tolerance. . . . Here I take my stand. Opinions are the best provisional hypotheses, incompletely tested. The more they are tested, after the tests are well scrutinized, the more assurance we may assume, but they are never absolutes. So we must be tolerant of opposite opinions or varying opinions by the very fact of our incredulity of our own. . . .
>
> . . . [H]ere we may differ, I do say that you may not cut off heads (except for limited periods and then only when you want to very much indeed), because the victims insist on saying things which look against Provisional Hypothesis Number Twenty-Six, the verification of which to date may be found in its proper place in the car catalogue. Generally, I insist, you must allow the possibility that if the heads are spared, other cars may be added under that subtitle which will have, perhaps, an important modification.
>
> All this seems to me . . . perfectly self-evident [and] self-explanatory. . . . [32]

Holmes was taken aback. "Rarely," he wrote to Hand on June 24, 1918, had a "letter hit me so exactly where I live as yours." Even so, Holmes felt that the government was well within its lawful power in doing what it had attempted to do in the *Masses* case. "[F]ree speech stands," he continued, "no differently than freedom from vaccination. The occasions would be rarer when you cared enough to stop it but if for any reason you did care enough you wouldn't care a damn for the suggestion that you were acting on a provisional hypothesis and might be wrong." And then with true military flare he ended: "Therefore take thy place on the one side or the other, if with the added grace of knowing that the Enemy is as good a man as thou, so much the better, but kill him if thou Canst."[33]

---

[31] Oliver Wendell Holmes Jr., *The Common Law* (Cambridge, MA: Harvard University Press, 2009), at 41. *See* Part II in this volume.

[32] Letter from Learned Hand to OWH, June 22, 1918, reproduced in *Holmes-Laski Letters, supra* note 20, at 1:159 n. 1.

[33] Quoted in Liva Baker, *The Justice from Beacon Hill* (New York: HarperCollins, 1991), at 516. *See also Justice Oliver Wendell Holmes, supra* note 25, at 424–25; Bernard Schwartz, "Holmes versus Hand: Clear and Present Danger or Advocacy of Unlawful Action," 1994 *Supreme Court Review* 209 (1994).

Later, while the *Schenck, Frohwerk*, and *Debs* cases were pending before the Supreme Court, "Hand tried to induce Holmes to think about his *Masses* formulation. Holmes told him that he did not have 'the details in my mind' of the *Masses* case, and Hand got only a perfunctory acknowledgement: Holmes had assumed he would 'come to a different result' but praised Hand's forcefulness and 'admirable form.'"[34] Even so, there would be more time and more cases for Holmes to consider how, if at all, his own thinking on the matter might be influenced by Judge Hand's views.[35]

❧

Just as the Civil War, his scholarly writings, and his associations with a learned group of friends helped to color Holmes's view of the law, his thought was likewise influenced by what he read. Holmes was a voracious reader; he had some four thousand books stacked in his home library at 1720 Eye Street, N.W., in Washington, D.C. "Holmes had a lifelong reading habit, one that provided him immense satisfaction. His taste ran to history, biography, philosophy, and the classics, but he also read novels, plays, and poetry, and he sometimes took up a book of prints or paintings."[36] He kept a black book in which he recorded the titles of the books he read alongside of the dates when he read them. In 1919 Holmes was busily reading many things beyond the pages of heavily cited court briefs and the like. Some of those outside readings included works that bore on the subject of the free speech cases then before the Court. The following books, listed in Holmes's black book for that year, may well have informed his thinking:[37]

- E. S. P. Haynes, *The Decline of Liberty in England* (1916)
- Harold J. Laski, *Authority in the Modern State* (1919)
- John Stuart Mill, *On Liberty* (1859)
- Walter Lippman, *The Political Scene: An Essay on the Victory of 1918* (1919)
- John Locke, *Essays on Government* (1690)
- Charles H. McIlwain, *Introduction to the Political Works of James I* (1918)

---

[34] February 25, 1919, letter from OWH to Learned Hand, qtd. in *Learned Hand, supra* note 29, at 164.

[35] For a comparison of the two, see authorities cited in *Learned Hand, supra* note 29, at 707–08 n. 232.

[36] Richard Polenberg, *Fighting Faiths: The Abrams Case, the Supreme Court, and Free Speech* (New York: Viking, 1987), at 224.

[37] *See Justice Oliver Wendell Holmes: Law and the Inner Self, supra* note 25, at 577–78 n. 125 (listing books). *See also Fighting Faiths, supra* note 36, at 224–27 (discussing books OWH read in 1919).

- James Ford Rhodes, *History of the Civil War* (1917)[38]
- Graham Wallas, *The Life of Francis Place* (1918)[39]

Such works gave Holmes a wider perspective with which to measure the cause of freedom and its relationship to the security of the nation. For example, Laski's *Authority in the Modern State* not only was dedicated to Holmes but also set out ideas that would later resonate in the great jurist's opinions:

> In his book Laski insisted that history's greatest truth was that the "only real security for social well-being is the free exercise of men's minds." There is a "real within," the individual conscience, where "the state can have no rights and where it is well that it should have none." No mind was free, Laski wrote, "once a penalty is attached to the thought." The modern state must regard "freedom of thought . . . as absolute . . . whether on the part of the individual or a social group." For the state to claim it knows the one truth was to claim an obnoxious "centralized finality." " . . . Political good refuses the swaddling clothes of finality. It is a shifting conception," Laski writes. It is "in the clash of ideas that we shall find the means of truth. There is no other safeguard of progress."[40]

Unlike Brandeis, Holmes did not tend to cite secondary sources in his opinions. Still, one can discern traces of influence here and there, as in the case of certain similarities between Laski's *Authority in the Modern State*[41] and some of Holmes's First Amendment opinions, which will become more apparent in the materials set out in Part VI.

In what follows here, we see Holmes shaping a free speech jurisprudence influenced by his own thoughts and writings, the thoughts of friends and

---

[38] Among other things, this book denounced Lincoln's "arbitrary interference with freedom of the press in [some Southern] States." *Justice Oliver Wendell Holmes: Law and the Inner Self, supra* note 25, at 577 n. 125 (quoting Rhodes). As Professor Polenberg has noted, p. 68 of the Rhodes book contained both a reference to the Battle of Ball's Bluff (see Part I) and a quotation from a letter written by Oliver Wendell Holmes Sr. about Union casualties and his own son's involvement in the war. *Fighting Faiths, supra* note 36, at 224.

[39] This was a "biography of an early nineteenth-century English reformer who opposed government taxation of newspapers." *Justice Oliver Wendell Holmes: Law and the Inner Self, supra* note 25, at 578 n. 125.

[40] Isaac Kramnick and Barry Sheerman, *Harold Laski: A Life on the Left* (New York: Allen Lane, Penguin Press, 1993), at 127 (quoting from *Authority in the Modern State* (New Haven, CT: Yale University Press, 1919).

[41] For additional comments on how Laski's work, especially his *Studies in the Problem of Sovereignty* (1917), influenced Holmes's First Amendment jurisprudence, see *Harold Laski, supra* note 40, at 126–27.

colleagues, ideas set out in books and articles, and the events of the time. Sometimes he was innovative and other times not; sometimes he was consistent, though not always so; and sometimes the speech-protective character of his jurisprudence seemed liberal, though that, too, came to be questioned in some quarters. All of this, of course, is prelude to what would follow in cases such as *Abrams v. United States* and *Gitlow v. New York* (see Part IV) – but it was a most important prelude.

I think our intention to put out all our powers in aid of success in war should not hurry us into intolerance of opinions and speech that could not be imagined to do harm.

BALTZER V. UNITED STATES

248 U.S. 593 (1918)[42]
Case No.: 320
Vote: 7–2
Argued: Late November 1918
Holmes dissent distributed: December 3, 1918
Government concedes error: December 16, 1918
For petitioner: Mr. Joe Kirby
For respondent: Mr. William C. Rempfer

Emanuel Baltzer and William J. Head[43] *were farmers in Hutchinson County, South Dakota. After the United States entered World War II, they, along with twenty-six others, formed an organization known as the German Socialist Local and sent a petition "of an intimidating nature" to Governor Peter Norbeck of South Dakota. In the petition they objected to the draft law quotas, criticized the war, and asked the governor to renounce the war. Though the petition was not circulated publicly, they were nonetheless convicted under the Espionage Act of 1917. The plaintiffs in error appealed the ruling against them in the District Court for the United States for the District of South Dakota. Baltzer was the first case involving a First Amendment right of petition claim to be heard by the Supreme Court. Although a majority was originally prepared to rule against the petitioners, no such opinion was ever rendered. Rather, the justices granted the motion of the solicitor general, who had confessed error. The Court then reversed and remanded the case. Before doing so, however, Holmes had prepared*

---

[42] Citation to Court's per curiam order.
[43] The other named petitioners included Gottfried Baltzer and Fritrich Leneschmidt.

a dissent, which Brandeis planned to join. That dissent was never officially published and only became publicly available in 1991.[44]

Mr. Justice Holmes dissenting.

The only evidence against the plaintiffs in error is that the petition set forth in the indictment was signed and sent by them to the Governor of the State, and to two other officials probably supposed to have power. It was not circulated publicly. The signing and sending of it is taken to amount to willfully obstructing the recruitment and enlistment service of the United States. Uniting to sign and send it is supposed to amount to a conspiracy to do the same thing and also to a conspiracy to prevent the Governor by intimidation from discharging his duties as an officer of the United States in determining the quota of men to be furnished for the draft by the local board. I can see none of these things in the document. It assumes that the draft is to take place and complains that volunteers have been counted with the result that counties have been exempted. It demands that the Governor should stand for a referendum on the draft and advocates the notion that no more expense should be incurred for the war than could be paid in cash and that war debts should be repudiated. It demands an answer and action or resignation on penalty of defeat at the polls of himself and "your little nation J. P. Morgan." The later phrase was explained by the writer to mean J. P. Morgan's class, as I think it obviously does without explanation. The class is supposed to stand behind the Governor and to be destined to defeat with him if he does not do as he is asked.

It seems to me that this petition to an official by ignorant persons who suppose him to possess power of revision and change that he does not, and demand of him as the price of votes, of course assumed to be sufficient to turn the next election, that he make these changes, was nothing in the world but the foolish exercise of a right. I cannot see how asking a change in the mode of administering the draft so as to make it accord with what is supposed to be required by law can be said to obstruct it. I cannot see how combining to do it is conspiracy to do anything that citizens have not a perfect right to do. It is apparent on the face of the paper that it assumes the power to be in the person addressed. I should have supposed that an article in a newspaper advocating these same things would have left untouched the sensibilities even of those

---

[44] *Baltzer v. United States* (Holmes, J., dissenting), memorandum distributed to the justices on December 3, 1918, Oliver Wendell Holmes Jr. Papers, Harvard Law School Library, reprinted in Sheldon M. Novick, "The Unrevised Holmes and Freedom of Expression," 1991 *Supreme Court Review* 301, 388–90.

most afraid of free speech. As to the repudiation of the war debt that obviously was a statement of policy not something contemplated as happening forthwith by the fiat of the Governor. From beginning to end the changes advocated are changes by law, not in resistance to it, the only threat being that which every citizen may utter, that if his wishes are not followed his vote will be lost.

The petition purported to come from members of the Socialist party all bearing German names. But those facts were not of themselves evidence of an attempt to obstruct. On the other hand they gave notice of probable bias on the part of the writers that would be likely to be appreciated by the world at large. I do not see that the case can be strengthened by argument if the statement of the fact does not convince by itself.

Real obstructions of the law, giving real aid and comfort to the enemy, I should have been glad to see punished more summarily and severely than they sometimes were. But I think that our intention to put out all our powers in aid of success in war should not hurry us into intolerance of opinions and speech that could not be imagined to do harm, although opposed to our own. It is better for those who have unquestioned and almost unlimited power in their hands to err on the side of freedom. We have enjoyed so much freedom for so long that perhaps we are in danger of forgetting that the bill of rights which cost so much blood to establish still is worth fighting for, and that no title of it should be abridged. I agree that freedom of speech is not abridged unconstitutionally in those cases of subsequent punishment with which this court has had to deal from time to time. But the emergency would have to be very great before I could be persuaded that an appeal for political action through legal channels, addressed to those supposed to have power to take such action was an act that the Constitution did not protect as well after as before.

COMMENTARY

The origins and aftermath of Holmes's unpublished dissent – Shortly after the case was argued, the Court "apparently voted 7–2 to uphold [the] convictions. The only votes for reversal seem to have been Holmes's and Brandeis's. After the Court's conference at which the vote was taken, . . . Holmes set to work drafting a dissenting opinion that he sent off to the printer, . . . and as usual he distributed his draft to the other justices. . . .

"This was Holmes at his best, and the draft dissent had an immediate effect. Chief Justice White, plainly very concerned to secure a unanimous Court in the first of these important cases, sent back a brief note: 'Please stall.' Apparently a strategy of delay had been discussed, perhaps at the conference, for Justice

Brandeis also urged delay: 'I gladly join you,' Brandeis's return reads. 'As I said, I think in decency – this case should be held until the many involving the same and similar positions – advanced for January – are heard.'

"The only other return that remains in the Holmes's papers is a brief note from Justice Mahlon Pitney: 'I submit with great respect, that this reads as if it proceeded from the heart rather than the head – Pitney. P.S. A good fault perhaps, but still a fault. P.'

"A delay may have been agreed upon in the Court conference December 7. In the following week, the Justice Department seems to have been warned of the damaging dissent Holmes planned to read. In any event, the government filed a motion asking that the Baltzer case be restored to the docket. On Monday morning, December 16, when the Court routinely heard motions, the matter was finished. Holmes made a note with evident satisfaction: 'After opinion written by me – but before delivery Govt. asked to restore to docket and on Dec. 16 US confessed error.'

"The Chief Justice thereupon wrote a brief per curiam opinion: 'Judgment reversed, upon confession of error; and cause remanded for further proceedings in accordance with law.'

"These extraordinary events put Holmes at the center of the Court's deliberations on freedom of speech." "The Unrevised Holmes and Freedom of Expression," *supra*, at 331–33 (footnotes omitted). *See also* Sheldon Novick, "Justice Holmes and the Art of Biography," 33 *William & Mary Law Review* 1219, 1231 (1992).

Holmes and free speech: A sympathetic view – "Holmes's strongly held views on the First Amendment had prompted him to write a dramatic dissent well before the *Schenck* cases were argued, and Holmes, by the strength of his views, moved the Court a long way toward his own position in *Schenck* – a position he had first stated in *Baltzer*, and then restated so passionately in *Abrams*, when the Court again went further than he was willing to go." Sheldon Novick, "Justice Holmes and the Art of Biography," *supra*, at 1231.

Holmes and free speech: Other views – "While Holmes believed that the [*Baltzer*] case turned on statutory construction, he nonetheless twice alluded to the scope of free expression. Both times, however, he appeared to do no more than express his approval of the bad tendency test, albeit in somewhat convoluted fashion (as was typical of Holmes). First, he reaffirmed the Court's earlier decisions, which had embraced the bad tendency standard.... Second, he wrote: 'I think our intention to put out all our powers in aid of success in war should not hurry us into intolerance of opinions and speech that could not be imagined to do harm.' At first blush, this language might be viewed as expressing a disdain for suppression during wartime, but a closer look reveals an implicit endorsement of the bad tendency approach rather than the articulation of a more speech-protective stance. Expression is to be unprotected, Holmes seemed to say, if it can 'be imagined to do harm.' Indeed, this language might be deemed to be yet another Holmesian reiteration of the bad tendency standard." Stephen M. Feldman, *Free Expression and Democracy in America: A History* (Chicago: University of Chicago Press, 2008), at 264–65 (footnote omitted).

The unpublished *Baltzer* dissent, Professor White maintains, "was evidence that Holmes could wax eloquently about free speech . . . but it was hardly evidence that he had developed the kind of approach to free speech issues that he would exhibit in some of his subsequent opinions." G. Edward White, *Justice Oliver Wendell Holmes: Law and the Inner Self* (New York: Oxford University Press, 1993), at 414 (footnote omitted). For an additional critique of Novick's thesis, and the March 1921 letter that helped to inform it, see *ibid.* at 573 n. 12. *See also* David M. Rabban, *Free Speech in Its Forgotten Years* (New York: Cambridge University Press, 1997), at 294 n. 211; Geoffrey R. Stone, *Perilous Times: Free Speech in Wartime* (New York: W. W. Norton, 2004), at 607 n. 314.

The most stringent protection of free speech would not protect a man in falsely shouting fire in a theatre and causing a panic. The question in every case is whether the words used are used in such circumstances and are of such a nature as to create a clear and present danger that they will bring about the substantive evils that Congress has a right to prevent.

SCHENCK V. UNITED STATES

249 U.S. 47 (1919)
Vote: 9–0
Argued: January 9–10, 1919
Decided: March 3, 1919
For petitioner: Mr. Henry John Nelson and Mr. Henry J. Gibbons
For respondent: John Lord O'Brian and Alfred Bettman

Charles T. Schenck (general secretary of the Socialist Party) and Dr. Elizabeth Baer (a member of the party's executive committee[45]*) were indicted on three*

---

[45] "Baer acted as a recording secretary for the committee's meetings and took minutes in a small black notebook. Despite government insistence at her trial that Baer was also a member of the Executive Committee, she never admitted to any duplicity or importance

counts: (1) conspiracy to violate the Espionage Act of 1917 by causing or attempting to cause insubordination[46] in the military; (2) conspiracy to commit a crime
against the United States by using the mails for unlawful purposes; and (3)
unlawful use of the mails. The charges stemmed from some fifteen thousand
antiwar circulars[47] that were to be sent by the defendants to recently conscripted
soldiers. Some of the recipients of the mailings complained to postal inspectors,
who forwarded the matter to federal prosecutors. A federal district court for the
Eastern District of Pennsylvania found both defendants guilty on all counts.
Though they faced a twenty-year prison sentence, Schenck received a six-month
sentence and Baer ninety days.

   The defendants' lawyers raised three challenges: (1) whether the Espionage
Act "constitutes an abridgement of freedom of speech and right of petition
in contravention of the First Amendment"; (2) whether the defendants "were
lawfully found guilty of conspiracy under all the evidence"; and (3) "whether or
not papers seized under a search warrant" and used as evidence were obtained
in violation of the Fourth Amendment.[48]

   Defense lawyers Nelson and Gibbons devoted much of their constitutional
discussion to argue that the reach of the First Amendment was not confined
to prohibitions against prior restraints as Holmes had suggested in his 1907
opinion for the Court in Patterson v. Colorado (see Part IV). As they put it in
their brief: "How can a speaker or writer be said to be free to discuss the actions of
Government if twenty years in prison stares him in the face if he makes a mistake
and says too much? Severe punishment for sedition will stop political discussion
as effectively as censorship." Assuming the Court were to get past the historical
hurdle of the limited reach of the First Amendment, the lawyers for the defense
urged the justices to adopt the following test: "The fair test of protection by the
constitutional guarantee of free speech is whether an expression is made with

   within the party beyond her role as notetaker." Jeremy Cohen, *Congress Shall Make No
   Law: Oliver Wendell Holmes, the First Amendment and Judicial Decision Making* (Ames:
   Iowa State University Press, 1989), at 41.
[46] The relevant section of the Act provides: "Whoever, when the United States is at war,
   shall willfully . . . cause or attempt to cause insubordination, disloyalty, mutiny, refusal
   of duty, in the military or naval forces of the United States, or shall willfully obstruct the
   recruiting or enlistment service of the United States, to the injury of the service or of the
   United States, shall be punished by a fine of not more than $10,000 or imprisonment for
   not more than twenty years, or both." Another section of the act defined conspiracy. The
   circulars are briefly discussed in Holmes's dissent, and a copy of one is reproduced at the
   end of this section.
[47] The circulars are briefly discussed in Holmes's dissent and the text of one is reproduced
   at the end of this section.
[48] Brief for the Plaintiffs-in-Error, *Schenck v. United States* (case nos. 437, 438), at 994, 1002.

sincere purpose to communicate honest opinion or belief, or whether it masks a primary intent to incite to forbidden action, or whether it does, in fact, incite to forbidden action."

John Lord O'Brian, *the government's lawyer*[49] *in this case and in the Fro-hwerk and Debs cases after it, argued that it was not the defendants' words but their wrongful intentions and actions that rendered them legally culpable. It was one thing to print circulars; it was yet another to send them to men already drafted with the intent to persuade them "to disobey the requirements of the law." He thus argued that speech is punishable if "assuming unlawful intention to be shown . . . the utterances complained of would have the natural and reasonable effect of producing the result aimed at by the statute."*[50]

Mr. Justice Holmes delivered the opinion of the Court.

. . . The defendants . . . set up the First Amendment [as their defense and] have argued some other points . . . of which we must dispose.[51]

It is argued that the evidence, if admissible, was not sufficient to prove that the defendant Schenck was concerned in sending the documents. According to the testimony Schenck said he was general secretary of the Socialist party and had charge of the Socialist headquarters from which the documents were sent. He identified a book found there as the minutes of the Executive Committee of the party. The book showed a resolution of August 13, 1917, that 15,000 leaflets should be printed on the other side of one of them in use, to be mailed to men who had passed exemption boards, and for distribution. Schenck personally attended to the printing. On August 20 the general secretary's report said "Obtained new leaflets from printer and started work addressing envelopes" etc.; and there was a resolve that Comrade Schenck be allowed $125 for sending leaflets through the mail. He said that he had about fifteen or sixteen thousand printed. There were files of the circular in

[49] A Buffalo lawyer, O'Brian served as the head of the War Emergency Division of the Department of Justice. For a more detailed account, see Geoffrey R. Stone, *Perilous Times, supra* note 4, at 212–20, 228–32. Alfred Bettman was the primary author of the government's brief in this case and in *Frohwerk v. United States* and *Debs v. United States*.

[50] Brief for United States, *Schenck v. United States* (case nos. 437, 438), at 1037; *Perilous Times, supra* note 4, at 215.

[51] A copy of the indictment is reproduced in George Anastaplo, *The Constitutionalist: Notes on the First Amendment* (Lanham, MD: Lexington Books, 2005), at 300–04. – *Ed.*

question in the inner office which he said were printed on the other side of the one sided circular and were there for distribution. Other copies were proved to have been sent through the mails to drafted men. Without going into confirmatory details that were proved, no reasonable man could doubt that the defendant Schenck was largely instrumental in sending the circulars about.

...The document in question upon its first printed side recited the first section of the Thirteenth Amendment, said that the idea embodied in it was violated by the Conscription Act and that a conscript is little better than a convict. In impassioned language it intimated that conscription was despotism in its worst form and a monstrous wrong against humanity in the interest of Wall Street's chosen few. It said, "Do not submit to intimidation," but in form at least confined itself to peaceful measures such as a petition for the repeal of the act. The other and later printed side of the sheet was headed "Assert Your Rights." It stated reasons for alleging that any one violated the Constitution when he refused to recognize "your right to assert your opposition to the draft," and went on, "If you do not assert and support your rights, you are helping to deny or disparage rights which it is the solemn duty of all citizens and residents of the United States to retain." It described the arguments on the other side as coming from cunning politicians and a mercenary capitalist press, and even silent consent to the conscription law as helping to support an infamous conspiracy. It denied the power to send our citizens away to foreign shores to shoot up the people of other lands, and added that words could not express the condemnation such cold-blooded ruthlessness deserves, etc., etc., winding up, "You must do your share to maintain, support and uphold the rights of the people of this country." Of course the document would not have been sent unless it had been intended to have some effect, and we do not see what effect it could be expected to have upon persons subject to the draft except to influence them to obstruct the carrying of it out. The defendants do not deny that the jury might find against them on this point.

But it is said, suppose that that was the tendency of this circular, it is protected by the First Amendment to the Constitution. Two of the strongest expressions are said to be quoted respectively from well-known public men. It well may be that the prohibition of laws abridging the freedom of speech is not confined to previous restraints, although to prevent them may have been the main purpose, as intimated in *Patterson v. Colorado*. We admit that in many places and in ordinary times the defendants in saying all that was said in the circular would have been within their constitutional rights. But the character of every act depends upon the circumstances in which it is done.[52] The most stringent protection of free speech would not protect a man in falsely shouting fire in a theatre and causing a panic. It does not even protect a man from an injunction against uttering words that may have all the effect of force. The question in every case is whether the words used are used in such circumstances and are of such a nature as to create a clear and present danger[53] that they will bring about the substantive evils that Congress has a right to prevent.[54] It is a question of proximity and degree.[55] When a nation is at war many things that might be said in time of peace are such a hindrance to its effort that their utterance will not be endured so long as men fight and that no Court could regard them as protected by any constitutional right. It seems to be admitted that if an actual obstruction of the recruiting service were proved, liability for words that produced that effect might be enforced. The statute of 1917 in section 4 punishes conspiracies to obstruct as well as actual obstruction. If the act, (speaking, or circulating a paper,) its tendency and the intent with which it is done are the same, we perceive no ground for saying that success alone warrants making the act a crime. Indeed that case might be said to dispose of the present contention if the precedent covers all *media concludendi*.[56] But as the right to free speech was not referred to specially, we have thought fit to add a few words. . . .

Judgments affirmed.

---

[52] Compare this with what Holmes wrote in *The Common Law* (see Part II): "All acts, taken apart from their surrounding circumstances, are indifferent to the law." *The Common Law, supra* note 31, at 51. – *Ed.*

[53] This precise phrase had been used earlier in an Espionage Act case in which Holmes was not involved. *See* L. A. Powe Jr., "Searching for the False Shout of 'Fire,'" 19 *Constitutional Commentary* 345, 352 n. 61 (2002), discussed in the commentaries following this case. – *Ed.*

[54] Again, this is similar to what Holmes had written in *The Common Law*: "In the characteristic type of substantive crime acts are rendered criminal because they are done under circumstances in which they will probably cause some harm which the law seeks to prevent." *The Common Law, supra* note 31, at 69. *See also ibid.* at 61–62. – *Ed.*

[55] Similar to here, in *Swift v. United States*, 196 U.S. 375, 401–02 (1905), an antitrust case, Holmes wrote: "Whether this particular combination can be enjoined, as it is, apart from its connection with the other elements, if entered into with the intent to monopolize, as alleged, is a more delicate question. The question is how it would stand if the tenth section were the whole bill. Not every act that may be done with intent to produce an unlawful result is unlawful, or constitutes an attempt. It is a question of proximity and degree. The distinction between mere preparation and attempt is well known in the criminal law. *Commonwealth v. Peaslee*, 177 Mass. 267, 272." As noted in Part III of this volume, Holmes also authored the *Peaslee* case which he cited. – *Ed.*

[56] Translated: "All the steps of the argument." – *Ed.*

To Alice Stopford Green
March 26, 1919

My Dear Mrs. Green,

. . . Some of the lower court Judges got rather hysterical and there were some cases in which I should have dissented and in fact had written [dissents], if the Govt. had not wisely dropped [the matter], and the Court had gone the other way.

OWH Papers, Harvard Law School, Box 43, Folder 13, quoted in Sheldon M. Novick, *Honorable Justice: The Life of Oliver Wendell Holmes* (New York: Dell Publishing, 1989), at 471 n. 69.

COMMENTARY

Schenck's historical importance – Decades after *Schenck* was handed down, Chief Justice Frederick Vinson declared: "No important case involving free speech was decided by this Court prior to *Schenck v. United States*." *Dennis v. United States*, 341 U.S. 494, 503 (1951). It is thus the first great First Amendment case rendered by the Supreme Court. Of great cases, Holmes once wrote: "I loath great cases. They are not half as important as many small ones that involve interstitial developments of the law, but they make talk for the newspapers." Letter from OWH to Lewis Einstein, December 19, 1910, reproduced in James Bishop Peabody, ed., *The Holmes-Einstein Letters: Correspondence of Mr. Justice Holmes and Lewis Einstein, 1903–1935* (New York: St. Martin's Press, 1964), at 57–58. Even so, Holmes understood how cases came to be great and thus important. *See Northern Securities Co. v. United States*, 193 U.S. 197, 400 (1904) (Holmes, J., dissenting) ("Great cases, like hard cases, make bad law. . . .").

Brevity and speed – By today's standards, Holmes's opinion in *Schenck* was quite abbreviated. The opinion, which was handed down after an armistice had been signed, consisted of six paragraphs and some 1,650 words. Concerning such Holmesian brevity, Justice Frankfurter once noted: "Mr. Justice Holmes spoke for the Court, in most instances tersely and often cryptically. . . ." *Federal*

---

[57] Additional correspondence relevant to this case can also be found in the materials following *Debs v. United States* herein.

Maritime Board v. Isbrandtsen Co., 356 U.S. 481, 523 (1958) (Frankfurter, J., dissenting). Moreover, the portion of the opinion that discussed the First Amendment was a mere 450 or so words long. The bulk of the opinion was concerned with evidentiary and statutory questions. In other words, "the First Amendment played a minimal role in Justice Holmes's *Schenck* decision." Jeremy Cohen, *Congress Shall Make No Law: Oliver Wendell Holmes, the First Amendment and Judicial Decision Making* (Ames: Iowa State University Press, 1989), at 107. The short opinion was published within eight weeks of when it was argued.

Zechariah Chafee's Harvard Law Review *article* – Several months after *Schenck*, *Frohwerk v. United States*, and *Debs v. United States* came down, Professor Zechariah Chafee published an article on free speech, which discussed the Holmes opinions while also charting out certain historical and policy principles. *See* Zechariah Chafee, "Freedom of Speech in Wartime," 32 *Harvard Law Review* 932 (1919). Urging a balancing approach for the resolution of free speech issues in wartime, Chafee emphasized that the societal interest in free expression "is especially important in wartime," and because of that, "the great interest in free speech should be sacrificed only when the interest in public safety is really imperiled, and not, as most men believe, when it is barely conceivable that it may be slightly affected." *Ibid.* at 957–60. Rejecting the Court's traditional test in free speech cases – "the First Amendment forbids the punishment of words merely for their injurious tendencies" – he argued that even in wartime speech could not be censored "unless it is clearly liable to cause direct and dangerous interference with the conduct of the war." *Ibid.* at 960. By that measure, he added, Judge Hand's *Masses* opinion offered "the fullest attention to the meaning of free speech during the war." *Ibid.* at 961.[58] Incredibly, Chafee then argued that Holmes's opinion in *Schenck* was consistent in principle with such views and values as he was expressing in his article. Ignoring *Frohwerk*, Chafee concluded that the holding in *Debs* was the result of a distortion of the application of the clear-and-present-danger test. In short time, Chafee's article would help to chart the direction of the free speech thinking of both Holmes and Brandeis. For an excellent historical and analytical discussion of the Chafee article and the liberties it took, see David M. Rabban, *Free Speech in Its Forgotten Years* (New York: Cambridge University Press, 1997), at 316–35.

[58] Chafee's *Freedom of Speech* (New York: Harcourt, Brace & Howe, 1920) was dedicated to Judge Hand, "United States District Judge for the Southern District of New York who during the turmoil of the war courageously maintained the tradition of English-speaking freedom and gave it new clearness and strength for the wiser years to come."

The evidence in the record and the continuing debate – The leaflet in the *Schenck* case (reproduced herein) was set forth in the "indictment and may be found in the Briefs and Records of the Supreme Court. But it is *not* found, even in substantial quotations therefrom, in the *Schenck* opinion. . . . The political folly, as well as the constitutional impropriety, of the attempt at suppression in *Schenck* should be evident upon inspecting this leaflet, which calls upon its readers to 'Assert [Their] Rights.' Prominent politicians are quoted in the effort to enlist opposition to the Conscription Act. In short, the defendants (who were anything but original) were continuing the debate that had occupied the Country for several years, culminating in their somewhat naïve appeal, 'Come to the headquarters of the Socialist Party . . . and sign a petition to congress for the repeal of the Conscription Act.'" George Anastaplo, *Reflections on Freedom of Speech and the First Amendment* (Lexington: University Press of Kentucky, 2007), at 103. *See also* Yosal Rogat and James M. O'Fallon, "Mr. Justice Holmes: A Dissenting Opinion – The Speech Cases," 36 *Stanford Law Review* 1349, 1371 (1984) ("The government had presented no evidence of probable or even possible effects.").

What if Schenck's leaflet had been printed in a newspaper? – "Such sentiments as those expressed in the *Schenck* case leaflet could have been published (and may have even been published) at that time without risk in the Country's larger newspapers. An attempt by the Administration to have a press censorship provision included in the Espionage Act had failed, which meant that vigorous criticism of the government continued. Perhaps, therefore, the only practical effect of the *Schenck Case* was to set an unfortunate precedent in First Amendment law." *Reflections on Freedom of Speech and the First Amendment*, *supra*, at 103–04. *See also* Geoffrey R. Stone, *Top Secret: When Our Government Keeps Us in the Dark* (Lanham, MD: Rowman & Littlefield, 2007), at 71.

Replaying the past – In *Schenck* and in the wartime cases immediately following it, Holmes never mentioned speech-protective theories like those articulated by Judge Learned Hand in his opinion in *Masses Publishing Co. v. Patten*, 244 F. 535 (S.D.N.Y. 1917). *See* Gerald Gunther, "Learned Hand and the Origins of the Modern First Amendment Doctrine: Some Fragments of History," 27 *Stanford Law Review* 719 (1975). Instead, he "concentrated on issues of criminal law and accepted most of the positions advocated by the government. Holmes approved punishment based on the indirect tendency of speech, upheld substantial judicial deference to jury evaluations of evidence, and supported greater restrictions on speech during times of war. . . . [H]is analysis bore a remarkable similarity to his prewar decisions, particularly his opinion in *Fox v. Washington*." David M. Rabban, *Free Speech in Its Forgotten Years* (New York: Cambridge University Press, 1997), at 279.

Back to the common law – "When Holmes served on the Court," Professor Novick maintains, "it was close enough in time to [the English political] tradition that it usually understood the broad guarantees of liberty in the Constitution to mean fundamental principles found in the common law, subject to traditional limitations. Holmes followed this approach through his whole career as a judge. . . . [O]n the federal bench, his landmark opinions on the First Amendment were based on his common law jurisprudence. . . . " Sheldon M. Novick, "Holmes's Philosophy and Jurisprudence: Origin and Development of Principal Themes," in *The Collected Works of Justice Holmes*, Sheldon Novick, ed. (Chicago: University of Chicago Press, 1995), at 1:62–63 (footnote omitted).

Three years after *Schenck* came down, Zechariah Chafee wrote to him and asked if he might offer any "light you can give me on the background of your opinion in the *Schenck* case." Specifically, he wondered, if "your test of clear and present danger . . . was at all suggested to you by any writers on the subject or was the result entirely of your reflections"? In response, Holmes admitted to having mistakenly relied on Blackstone and Parker, as he had done in *Patterson v. Colorado* (see Part IV) in confining the protections of the First Amendment to the prohibition against prior restraints. As to the origin of the clear-and-present-danger test, Holmes wrote: "I did think hard on this matter of attempts in my *Common Law* and a Mass. case [*Commonwealth v. Peaslee*] – later in the *Swift* case (U.S.) – and I thought it out unhelped." *Free Speech in Its Forgotten Years, supra*, at 285 (footnotes omitted) (quoting Chafee to Holmes, June 9, 1922, and Holmes to Chafee, June 12, 1922).

As previously set out in Part II, in the *Common Law*, Holmes mentioned the following factors in discussing the law of criminal attempts, all of which proved important to him in developing the clear-and-present-danger test in *Schenck*. Consider the following phrases taken from *The Common Law*:

- "[T]he nearness of the danger, the greatness of the harm"
- The "degree of apprehension"
- "[T]he degree of probability that the crime will be accomplished"
- "[A]cts are rendered criminal because they are done under circumstances in which they will probably cause harm which the law seeks to prevent."

Oliver Wendell Holmes Jr., *The Common Law* (Cambridge, MA: Harvard University Press, 2009), at 61–70 (Lecture II). For a more extended discussion of the relationship between Holmes's understanding of the common law of attempts and its connection to his clear-and-present-danger test, see Yosal Rogat, "The Judge as Spectator," 31 *University of Chicago Law Review* 213, 215–17 (1964); John R. Green, "Liberty under the Fourteenth Amendment," 27 *Washington University Law Quarterly* 616 (1942); Livingston Hall, "The Substantive Law of Crimes, 1887–1936," 50 *Harvard Law Review* 616 (1937); and Note, 41 *Harvard Law Review* 525 (1927).

Holmes and the law of conspiracy – *Schenck* was, among other things, a conspiracy case. As indicated by his opinion in *Vegelahn v. Guntner* (1896) (see Part III) and elsewhere, Holmes found the right to associate (or "combine") to be privileged "unless it was part of a conspiracy. The law of conspiracy qualified the privilege or right of association. In *Hyde v. United States* [225 U.S. 347, 387–88 (1911)] Holmes carefully distinguished conspiracy from attempts. In his view, danger or its proximity was a necessary condition for [two kinds of attempts]: harmful acts that failed to produce a harmful result, and innocent acts that were proximate to a harm and conjoined to an unlawful intent. Moreover, an attempt necessitated an overt act. It was the 'essence of the offence.' Conspiracy was different. In Holmes's words, 'the essence of conspiracy is being combined for an unlawful purpose – and if an overt act is required, it does not matter how remote [a person] may be from accomplishing the purpose, if done to effect it; that is, I suppose, in furtherance of it in any degree.' It is true that Holmes did not equate a conspiracy with the unlawful agreement. A conspiracy 'is the result of the agreement, rather than the agreement itself, just as the partnership, although constituted by a contract, is not the contract, but is a result of it.' But even so, conspiracy could be established without proof of an overt act (other than the act of the conspiracy itself) or any proximity to harm. . . . Holmes understood conspiracy as an abuse of privilege. Certainly he believed that the right of association was to the long-term advantage of society. At every opportunity, he applauded man's tendency to combine. . . . [H]e repeatedly characterized modern society as based on the individual's right to form groups," whether for the benefit of capitalists or union laborers. H. L. Pohlman, *Justice Oliver Wendell Holmes: Free Speech and the Living Constitution* (New York: New York University Press, 1993), at 39–40 (endnotes omitted).

The law of conspiracy and the clear-and-present-danger test – "The real problem with *Schenck* is not why Holmes affirmed the conviction, but why he wrote the opinion that he did. . . . [That is,] why did Holmes announce the clear-and-present-danger doctrine in *Schenck*? . . . [T]he mystery is not why he said 'a few words' about free speech, but why he said the words that he did. What did a clear and present danger have to do with a case of conspiracy? According to Holmes's theory of liability, if persons had conspired to do something unlawful, that sufficed for a conviction. No proximity of harm was required." *Justice Oliver Wendell Holmes: Free Speech and the Living Constitution, supra,* at 66–67 (endnotes omitted).

Bad-tendency test revisited? – "Holmes did not intend [his] 'clear and present danger' language to delineate a new standard for free expression. Rather, he meant to reformulate the customary bad tendency test, adhered to by the Court in the past and by most courts for over one hundred years. If so, one might still wonder why Holmes did not state the bad tendency doctrine in its more typical language. Most likely, Holmes drew his own understanding of the law of criminal attempts to inform his construal of bad tendency." Stephen M. Feldman, *Free Expression and Democracy in America: A History* (Chicago: University of Chicago Press, 2008), at 260. *See also* Geoffrey R. Stone, *Perilous Times, supra* at 195; *Free Speech in Its Forgotten Years, supra,* at 282.

Professor Pohlman, by contrast, has observed: "Holmes's opinion that Schenck was guilty does not make him into an adherent of the bad-tendency doctrine.... If 'an act,' 'its tendency,' and 'the intent with which it is done' are 'the same' – that is, they are illegal or harmful – then liability could be imposed even if the harm did not occur. But that did not mean that Holmes would impose liability on any speech that had a bad tendency. All that Holmes was saying was that conspiring with others was an act whose tendency and accompanying intent were harmful. Liability could therefore be imposed on persons who conspired to obstruct the draft through speech." *Justice Oliver Wendell Holmes: Free Speech and the Living Constitution, supra,* at 67.

Intended effect of defendants' expression? – In an important passage, Holmes stressed that "the document would not have been sent unless it had been intended to have some effect, and we do not see what effect it could be expected to have upon persons subject to the draft except to influence them to obstruct the carrying of it out." Professor Stone finds this to be a "puzzling statement" insofar as the circular "expressly called upon readers to support the repeal of the draft through lawful political means. It did not expressly advocate obstruction of the draft. Of course, the defendants could reasonably have 'expected' that some readers might be moved to refuse induction, and that the defendants sent the pamphlets to men who had already been drafted certainly supports the inference that they might have hoped to inspire some of them to refuse induction. But that was not what they advocated, so it is unclear why this *must* have been their 'intent.'" *Perilous Times, supra,* at 193 (emphasis in original).

In times of war – Recall that Holmes wrote: "We admit that, in many places and in ordinary times, the defendants, in saying all that was said in the circular, would have been within their constitutional rights." But this is war and a different set of rules applies. "When a nation is at war," Holmes stressed, "many things that might be said in time of peace are such a hindrance to its effort that their utterance will not be endured so long as men fight. . . . " As Professor Rabban has observed: "The 'circumstances' of war, Holmes seemed to be saying, are themselves likely 'to create a clear and present danger" that speech will hinder the nation's effort, thereby producing one of 'the substantive evils Congress has a right to prevent.'" *Free Speech in Its Forgotten Years, supra,* at 282.

The war factor alone distinguishes *Schenck*, which has never been overruled, from later more liberal First Amendment cases such as *Brandenburg v. Ohio*, 395 U.S. 444 (1969). *See* Ronald Collins and David Skover, "What Is War? Reflections on Free Speech in 'Wartime,'" 36 *Rutgers Law Journal* 833, 848–53 (2005). It is noteworthy that in an October 23, 2001, memorandum a Justice Department official said the following: "First Amendment speech and press rights may . . . be subordinated to the overriding need to wage war successfully," then Deputy Assistant Attorney General John Yoo wrote, adding later: "The current campaign against terrorism may require even broader exercises of federal power domestically." "Bush Memos: President has Broad Authority to Set Aside Rights," *Associated Press*, March 3, 2009.

Truth and competition – Significantly, the words *truth* and *competition* are nowhere to be found in the *Schenck* opinion. Those two words and the ideas behind them trace back to Holmes's early writings and thereafter to his post-*Schenck* free speech opinions such as *Abrams* (see Part VI). And yet they are strikingly absent in *Schenck*. That is to say, the idea of the pursuit of truth – so key in *Abrams* – is of little or no express moment in *Schenck*. There are no soldiers in Holmes's marketplace of ideas. There can be no competition to win over their minds. Consistent with the soldier's faith, they are to follow orders and fight, and never to think on their own.

In this world of war, the truth or falsity of the defendants' message was irrele-vant. What was important is that their message, directed to draftees, was poten-tially perilous. It could cause great harm. The harm principle (and not the truth principle) is therefore the touchstone of Holmes's thinking in *Schenck*. *See* Richard A. Posner, *Law, Pragmatism, and Democracy* (Cambridge, MA: Harvard University Press, 2003), at 361. Had the same messages, however, been sent to lay citizens, the result might have been different, though even that is questionable because the nation was at war. "When a nation is at war," wrote

Holmes in *Schenck*, "many things that might be said in time of peace are such a hindrance to its effort that their utterance will not be endured so long as men fight and that no Court could regard them as protected by any constitutional right." By that measure, what was most problematic in *Schenck* for Holmes was the parties to whom the expression had been directed (draftees) and the time when the expression occurred (wartime).

Of course, Holmes did refer to truth's opposite when he wrote of "falsely shouting fire in a theatre and causing a panic." But to equate such false statements with the facts in the case is to take great license as suggested by the subsequent comments.

Fire and the law of attempts – In Lecture II of *The Common Law* (in Part II here), Holmes used a fire analogy in his discussion of the law of attempts: "When a man buys matches to fire a haystack, . . . there is still a considerable chance that he will change his mind before he comes to the point. But when he struck the match . . . there is little chance that he will not persist to the end, and the danger becomes so great that the law steps in." *The Common Law, supra*, at 64. *See also* David M. Rabban, "The Emergence of Modern First Amendment Doctrine," 50 *University of Chicago Law Review* 1207, 1283 (1983).

Possible source of fire metaphor – Professor Lucas Powe speculates that Holmes may have come on the idea for his *Schenck* fire metaphor from two well-publicized news events involving falsely yelling fire. The first occurred on August 26, 1911, when someone falsely shouted fire in an opera house; in the resultant panic twenty-six people were killed. *See* "26 Die, 50 Hurt in Theatre Rush," *New York Times*, August 27, 1911, at 1; "26 Are Killed in Panic at Theatre," *Washington Post*, August 27, 1911, at 1. The other occurred during a 1913 Christmas Eve celebration – attended by hundreds of coal-miner strikers and their families – on the second floor of a meeting hall. After someone leaned in a door and yelled fire, the resultant pandemonium left seventy-three people dead. *See* "Fund for Victims of Calumet Panic; Death Toll Is 72," *Chicago Tribune*, December 26, 1913, at 1, 2. *See* L. A. Powe Jr., "Searching for the False Shout of 'Fire,'" 19 *Constitutional Commentary* 345, 348–51 (2002). See also commentary following *The Common Law* in Part II, and commentary following *Commonwealth v. Peaslee*, in Part III.

The metaphor of fire in the theater – It is helpful in judging Holmes's fire metaphor to break it down to its explicit and implicit elements. Again, here is the *Schenck* text, with bracketed numbers inserted: "The most stringent protection of free speech would not protect a man in [1] falsely [2] shouting [3] fire in a [4] theatre and [5] causing a [6] panic."

At the outset, the speech must be false. But in Holmes's statement of the facts, there is no claim that the circulars distributed were false – they were largely matters of political opinion. Next, the metaphorical formula requires that the false words be shouted, as if to cause some alarm. It is this union between falsity and alarm that creates a danger. The alarm is escalated and made more immediate by the mention of fire. Context is important, too, as evidenced by the fact that the words falsely shouted be done so in a theater, presumably a crowed one. In such circumstances, there is little room for reflection. Putting these factors together, the metaphor points to a reflexive and spontaneous action unwed to deliberation. There must, of course, be some causal connection between elements 1–4 and 6, thereby creating a panic. But that is a rhetorical formula at best. For it is virtually impossible to have elements 1–4 without then having elements 5 and 6. Note also that true speech (e.g., shouting fire when there was one) could also cause a panic, though it would be protected.

To return to the facts of *Schenck*, in assessing the gravity and immediacy of the possible harm that might have been caused by the defendants' circulars, Holmes analogizes to a situation clearly fraught with present danger, his fire metaphor. However alluring the metaphor, it has little real application to the *Schenck* facts, if only for the following reasons: (1) the truthfulness of the defendants' speech was not at issue in the case (no falsity); (2) any danger caused by the defendants' mailing of their antiwar leaflets was nowhere as imminent as the danger (e.g., panic) caused by falsely yelling fire in a theater; and (3) the actuality of the harm (as distinguished from probable or potential harm) seems far less in the leaflets scenario than in the theater one. Holmes's rhetorically appealing metaphor aside, what he was actually saying is that at some point the probability and magnitude of potential harm can be so great as to justify restrictions on expression. See *Law, Pragmatism, and Democracy, supra*, at 359–60. At that point, the experimentation heralded in *Abrams* and elsewhere must cease.

Interestingly, by equating the peril of the fire metaphor with the facts of *Schenck*, Holmes invited the mind to skip a few analytical jumps and then a few more. What he was actually suggesting is that allowances must be made in wartime. By contrast, had he applied the logic of the fire metaphor faithfully to the facts before him, the defendants' convictions might have been reversed. See *Perilous Times, supra*, at 195. Not surprisingly, some have observed that "there does appear to be a startling irrelevance to the hypothetical." Lee C. Bollinger, *The Tolerant Society: Freedom of Speech and Extremist Speech in America* (New York: Oxford University Press, 1986), at 190; Yosal Rogat and James M. O'Fallon, "Mr. Justice Holmes: A Dissenting Opinion – The

Speech Cases," 36 *Stanford Law Review* 1349, 1372 (1984). *See generally* Steven L. Winter, "Re-Embodying Law," 58 *Mercer Law Review* 869, 879–84 (2007).

Shouting fire and popular culture – In 1966 Universal Pictures released a movie produced by Alfred Hitchcock titled *Torn Curtain*, starring Paul Newman and Julie Andrews. At one point in the movie, Newman yelled, "Fire!" in a crowed theater, which resulted in pandemonium. More recently, an HBO documentary produced by Liz Garbus and narrated by her father, Martin Garbus, was titled *Shouting Fire: Stories from the Edge of Free Speech*. Books have likewise used the Holmesian phrase for titles. *See, e.g.,* Alan Dershowitz, *Shouting Fire: Civil Liberties in a Turbulent Age* (Boston: Little, Brown, 2002).

Prior restraints and subsequent punishment – In his majority opinion in *Patterson v. Colorado* (1907) (see Part IV), Holmes wrote: "the main purpose of such constitutional provisions is 'to prevent all such previous restraints upon publications as had been practised by other governments,' and they do not prevent the subsequent punishment of such as may be deemed contrary to the public welfare." In *Schenck*, by contrast, Holmes gave a more generous interpretation of the First Amendment: "It well may be that the prohibition of laws abridging the freedom of speech is not confined to previous restraints, although to prevent them may have been the main purpose. . . . "

What does "circumstances" mean? – In *Schenck*, Holmes wrote: "The question in every case is whether the words used are used in such circumstances and are of such a nature as to create a clear and present danger that they will bring about the substantive evils that Congress has a right to prevent." It was unclear whether Holmes was referring to general circumstances (e.g., the general state of affairs in the nation or world) or more particularized circumstances (e.g., the specific context in which the words were expressed). Regarding the latter, the trial record in the case showed "that few inductees ever received the circulars and that none who did, and who testified, were influenced by it." Richard Polenberg, *Fighting Faiths: The Abrams Case, the Supreme Court, and Free Speech* (New York: Viking, 1987), at 215. By contrast, an example of a generalized circumstance would be a state of war, as noted in *Schenck* – "When a nation is at war many things that might be said in time of peace are such a hindrance to its effort that their utterance will not be endured so long as men fight and that no Court could regard them as protected by any constitutional right." 249 U.S. at 52. If that circumstance was determinative, then it may have been of no great consequence whether Charles Schenck's circulars actually reached draftees or that it might have had some real impact on them. Then again, and as Holmes noted, the defendant's guilt would remain by way of conspiring to violate the law even if that conspiracy failed. But if that is the case, there was little or anything in the trial record to show that the defendant's circulars created a proximate and real danger.

Herbert Wechsler, who would later successfully argue *New York Times Co. v. Sullivan*, 376 U.S. 254 (1964), made the following observations concerning *Schenck* and its progeny: "It is worth a moment to pause on these wartime cases which reached the Supreme Court after the peace. In all of them, the challenged speech was addressed to an unquestionably immediate issue, the continuance and conduct of the war. If action was proposed in resistance to the policy of the government, it was immediate action; if there was a danger that the publication would lead to unlawful resistance, it was a danger at that time; if such resistance was intended, it was intended then. Thus the clear and present danger test could have only a minimal operation to place beyond the pale of liability those statements which were patently impotent and were motivated by some other purpose than to promote obstruction of the conduct of the war." Herbert Wechsler, "Symposium on Civil Liberties," 9 *American Law School Review* 881, 882–83 (1941).

Earlier uses of clear-and-present-danger language – As Professor Powe has also observed, in "the summer of 1918, Benjamin W. Shaw, defending (unsuccessfully until appeal) an Espionage Act case, uttered the following during his closing argument to the jury: 'Under all of the facts and circumstances disclosed by the evidence in this case, how can it be said that he wilfully [*sic*] said and did the things alleged? How can the words used under the circumstances detailed in the evidence *have the tendency to create a clear and present danger that they will bring about the substantive evils that Congress has a right to prevent?*" John Fontana, 12 *American State Trials*, ed. John D. Lawson (F. H. Thomas Book Co., 1920) at 897, 932 (emphasis added), quoted in "Searching for the False Shout of 'Fire,'" *supra*, 19 *Constitutional Commentary*, at 352 n. 61.

In addition, the phrase "present danger" had been used in many common law state court cases prior to 1919, including in one authored by Holmes. *See Merrigan v. Boston & A. R. Co.*, 154 Mass. 189, 193, 28 N.E. 149, 150 (1891) ("We believe that it accurately expresses the actual effect of an open gate at a railroad crossing upon the minds of careful people, and it is in accordance with the decisions as to flagmen whose attitude conveys the impression that there is no present danger."). So, too, the phrase "clear and present" had been employed by state courts prior to 1919, though not in any Massachusetts case. *See, e.g., Rhodes v. Webb*, 34 Mo. 464 (1864); *Warlick v. White*, 86 N.C. 139, 141 (1882); and *Walton v. Parish*, 95 N.C. 259, 263 (1886). That same phrase had even been employed in works of fiction. *See, e.g.*, Madame de Staël, *Corinne*, *or Italy* (New York, 1876), at 181 ("clear, and present emotions"). Though too much ought not be made of it, it is noteworthy nonetheless that a copy of this novel was in the Harvard College Library as early as 1879, and the author's works were known to Dr. Holmes. *See, e.g.,* Oliver Wendell Holmes, *The Works of Oliver Wendell Holmes* (Boston: Houghton, Mifflin, 1892), at 429.

Distrust of phrases – Francis Biddle, one of Holmes's former law clerks (or secretaries, as they were then known), said the following about the clear-and-present-danger test: "The phrase has become famous, has been quoted constantly, is today a sort of liberal rudder to hold some direction of objective standard. Its implication has been endlessly discussed; and issues will arise again for further analysis of the authority of its formula. It is improbable that Holmes, who so greatly distrusted phrases and their use to displace the freer play of imaginative thinking, would have been much impressed by such a test as more than an instinctive guide, hardly accurate to chart proximity and degree. But surely it might serve, if not to define a legal principle, at least to suggest a standard of approach, cautious and realistic." Francis Biddle, *Mr. Justice Holmes* (New York: Charles Scribner's Sons, 1943), at 156. Biddle later served as attorney general from 1941 to 1945.

Holmes himself warned of the problem of ideas becoming encrusted in phrases: "It is one of the misfortunes of the law that ideas become encysted in phrases, and thereafter for a long time cease to provoke further analysis." *Hyde v. United States,* 225 U.S. 347, 384 (1912) (Holmes, J., dissenting).

Delusion of certitude? – "The truth is that the 'clear and present danger' test is an oversimplified judgment unless it takes account also of a number of other factors: the relative seriousness of the danger in comparison with the value of the occasion for speech or political activity; the availability of more moderate controls than those which the state has imposed, and perhaps the specific intent with which the speech or activity is launched. No matter how rapidly we utter the phrase 'clear and present danger,' or how closely we hyphenate the words, they are not a substitute for the weighing of values. They tend to convey a delusion of certitude when what is most certain is the complexity of the strands in the web of freedoms which the judge must disentangle." Paul Freund, *On Understanding the Supreme Court* (Boston: Little, Brown, 1949), at 27–28.

The inapplicability of the Schenck *test* – The "'clear and present danger' test is not designed for objections based on offensiveness; for the harm of offense is not deferred or probabilistic, but immediate and certain.... In Holmes's day the right of government to repress offensive speech of a sexual character was so taken for granted that Holmes felt no need to develop a free speech

test broad enough to encompass offensive as well as dangerous speech...."
Richard Posner, "The Speech Market and the Legacy of Schenck," in Eternally
Vigilant: Free Speech in the Modern Era, ed. Lee C. Bollinger and Geoffrey
R. Stone (Chicago: University of Chicago Press, 2002), at 128.

Fortifying the Schenck test – In Schaefer v. United States, 251 U.S. 466, 483,
486 (1920), Justice Louis Brandeis (joined by Holmes) registered a dissenting
opinion in which he elaborated on Schenck. Here is the relevant text, with
emphasis added to show where Brandeis fortified the Holmes formula:

- The question whether in a *particular instance* the words spoken or written
  fall within the permissible curtailment of free speech is, under the rule
  enunciated by this Court, one of degree....
- The nature and possible effect of a writing cannot be properly determined
  by culling here and there a sentence and presenting it separated from the
  context. In making such determination, it should be read as a whole....
- [A]s this court has declared, and as Professor Chafee has shown in his
  'Freedom of Speech in War Time,' 32 *Harvard Law Review*, 932, 963, the
  test to be applied – as in the case of criminal attempts and incitement – is
  not the remote or possible effect.

See also Brandeis's separate opinion (joined by Holmes) in Pierce v. United
States, 252 U.S. 239, 253 (1920).

Schenck reincarnated: A cost-benefit model of First Amendment jurisprudence –
The Schenck majority opinion has been and continues to be cited more often
by the Supreme Court than Holmes's dissent in Abrams (see Appendices 1 and
2). Even so, perhaps Schenck's most remarkable reincarnation has come from
the mind of circuit Judge Richard Posner, who has taken several Holmesian
insights and crafted them into a more scientific model of jurisprudence than
did Holmes. This is most apparent in Posner's article "The Speech Market
and the Legacy of Schenck," supra, at 121.

   Posner's "instrumental approach," as he labels it, is rooted in Holmes's
opinions in Schenck and Abrams. "The case that first put the constitutional
approach to free speech on the map ... is ... Schenck v. United States," which
employed "an instrumental approach." Ibid. at 122 (footnote omitted). According to this approach, "freedom of speech is to be valued to the extent that it
promotes specified goals, such as political stability, economic prosperity, and
personal happiness." In Schenck, adds Posner, Holmes examined the costs or
harm side of the cost-benefit equation, whereas in Abrams, he focused more on
the benefits side of that equation. This instrumental approach attempts, with

Holmesian vigor, to employ scientific criteria to better identify the actual relationship between speech and certain specified goals and consequential harms. Hence, expression should be protected "if the benefits of the speech equal or exceed its costs discounted by their probability and futurity, and reduced by the costs of administering the ban." *Ibid.* at 121, 125–26. More is said about this approach – which is different from a moral approach to analyzing free speech questions – in the Epilogue of this volume.

Modern adoptions of the clear-and-present-danger test – As discussed in the Epilogue, most states have codified the clear-and-present-danger test in one form or another and have applied it in a variety of contexts. These state statutes have in turn generated a considerable number of appellate court decisions.

[Schenck circular]

Long Live the Constitution of the United States (1917)

Wake up, America! Your Liberties Are in Danger!

The 13th Amendment, Section 1, of the Constitution of the United States says: "Neither slavery nor involuntary servitude, except as a punishment for crime whereof the party shall have been duly convicted, shall exist within the United States, or any place subject to their jurisdiction."

The Constitution of the United States is one of the greatest bulwarks of political liberty. It was born after a long, stubborn battle between king-rule and democracy. (We see little or no difference between arbitrary power under the name of a king and under the name of a few misnamed "representatives.") In this battle the people of the United States established the principle that freedom of the individual and personal liberty are the most sacred things in life. Without them we become slaves.

For this principle the fathers fought and died. The establishment of this principle they sealed with their own blood. Do you want to see this principle abolished? Do you want to see despotism substituted in its stead? Shall we prove degenerate sons of illustrious sires?

The Thirteenth Amendment to the Constitution of the United States, quoted above, embodies this sacred idea. The Socialist Party says this idea is violated by the Conscription Act. When you conscript a man and compel him to go abroad and fight against his will, you violate the most sacred right of personal liberty, and substitute for it what Daniel Webster called "despotism in its worst form."

A conscript is little better than a convict. He is deprived of his liberty and of his right to think and act as a free man. A conscripted citizen is forced to surrender as a citizen and become a subject. He is forced into involuntary servitude. He is deprived of the protection given him by the Constitution of the United States. He is deprived of all freedom of conscience in being forced to kill against his will.

Are you one who is opposed to the war, and were you misled by the venal capitalist newspapers, or intimidated or deceived by gang politicians and registrars into believing that you would not be allowed to register your own objection to conscription? Do you know that many citizens of Philadelphia insisted on their right to answer the famous question twelve, and went on record with their honest opinion of honest opposition to the war, notwithstanding the deceitful efforts of our rulers and the newspaper press to prevent them from doing so? Shall it be said that the citizens of Philadelphia, the cradle of American liberty, are so lost to a sense of right and justice that they will let such monstrous wrongs against humanity go unchallenged?

In a democratic country each man must have the right to say whether he is willing to join the army. Only in countries where uncontrolled power rules can a despot force his subjects to fight. Such a man or men have no place in a democratic republic. This is tyrannical power in its worst form. It gives control over the life and death of the individual to a few men. There is no man good enough to be given such power.

Conscription laws belong to a bygone age. Even the people of Germany, long suffering under the yoke of militarism, are beginning to demand the abolition of conscription. Do you think it has a place in the United States? Do you want to see unlimited power handed over to Wall Street's chosen few in America? If you do not, join the Socialist Party in its campaign for the repeal of the Conscription Act. Write to your congressman and tell him you want the law repealed. Do not submit to intimidation. You have a right to demand the repeal of any law. Exercise your rights of free speech, peaceful assemblage and petitioning the government for a redress of grievances. Come to the headquarters of the Socialist Party, 1326 Arch Street, and sign a petition to congress for the repeal of the Conscription Act. Help us wipe out this stain upon the Constitution!

Help us re-establish democracy in America.
Remember, "eternal vigilance is the price of liberty."
Down with autocracy!
Long live the Constitution of the United States! Long live the Republic!

Books on Socialism for Sale at

SOCIALIST-PARTY BOOKSTORE HEADQUARTERS
1326 ARCH ST. Phone, Filbert 3121
(Over)

Assert Your Rights!

Article 6, Section 2, of the Constitution of the United States says: "This Constitution shall be the *supreme law of the land.*"

Article 1 (Amendment) says: "Congress shall make no law respecting an establishment of religion, *or prohibiting the free exercise thereof.*"

Article 9 (Amendment) says: "The enumeration in the Constitution of certain rights, shall not be construed to deny or disparage others retained by the people."

The Socialist Party says that any individual or officers of the law entrusted with the administration of conscription regulations, violate the provisions of the United States Constitution, the Supreme Law of the Land, when they refuse to recognize your right to assert your opposition to the draft.

If you are conscientiously opposed to the war, if you believe in the commandment "thou shall not kill," then that is your religion, and you shall not be prohibited from the free exercise thereof.

In exempting clergymen and members of the Society of Friends (popularly called Quakers) from active military service, the examination boards have discriminated against you.

If you do not assert and support your rights, you are helping to "deny or disparage rights" which it is the solemn duty of all citizens and residents of the United States to retain.

Here in this city of Philadelphia was signed the immortal Declaration of Independence. As a citizen of the "cradle of liberty" you are doubly charged with the duty of upholding the rights of the people.

Will you let cunning politicians and a mercenary capitalist press wrongfully and untruthfully mould your thoughts? Do not forget your rights to elect officials who are opposed to conscription.

In lending tacit or silent consent to the conscription law, in neglecting to assert your rights, you are (whether knowingly or not) helping to condone and support a most infamous and insidious conspiracy to abridge and destroy the sacred and cherished rights of a free people. *You are a citizen, not a subject!* You delegate your power to the officers of the law to be used for your good and welfare, not against you.

They are your servants. Not your masters. Their wages come from the expenses of government *which you pay.* Will you allow them to unjustly rule you? The fathers who fought and bled to establish a free and independent nation here in America were so opposed to the militarism of the old world from which they had escaped; so keenly alive to the dangers and hardships they had undergone in fleeing from political, religious and military oppression, that they handed down to us "certain rights which must be retained by the people."

They held the spirit of militarism in such abhorrence and hate, they were so apprehensive of the formation of a military machine that would insidiously and secretly advocate the invasion of other lands, that they limited the power of Congress over the militia in providing only for the calling forth of "the militia to execute laws of the Union, suppress insurrections and repel invasions." (See general powers of Congress, Article I, Section 8, Paragraph 15.)

No power was delegated to send our citizens away to foreign shores to shoot up the people of other lands, no matter what may be their internal or international disputes.

The people of this country did not vote in favor of war. At the last election they voted against war.

To draw this country into the horrors of the present war in Europe, to force the youth of our land into the shambles and bloody trenches of war-crazy nations, would be a crime the magnitude of which defies description. Words could not express the condemnation such cold-blooded ruthlessness deserves.

Will you stand idly by and see the Moloch of Militarism reach forth across the sea and fasten its tentacles upon this continent? Are you willing to submit to the degradation of having the Constitution of the United States treated as a "mere scrap of paper?"

Do you know that patriotism means a love for your country and not hate for others?

Will you be led astray by a propaganda of jingoism masquerading under the guise of patriotism?

No specious or plausible pleas about a "war for democracy" can becloud the issue. Democracy cannot be shot into a nation. It must come spontaneously and purely from within.

Democracy must come through liberal education. Upholders of military ideas are unfit teachers.

To advocate the persecution of other peoples through the prosecution of war is an insult to every good and wholesome American tradition.

"These are the times that try men's souls."
"Eternal vigilance is the price of liberty."

You are responsible. You must do your share to maintain, support, and uphold the rights of the people of this country.

In this world crisis where do you stand? Are you with the forces of liberty and light or war and darkness?

The First Amendment while prohibiting legislation against free speech as such cannot have been, and obviously was not, intended to give immunity for every possible use of language.

FROHWERK V. UNITED STATES

249 U.S. 204 (1919)
Vote: 9–0
Argued: January 27, 1919
Decided: March 10, 1919
For petitioner: Mr. Joseph D. Shewalter and Mr. Frans E. Lindquist
For respondent: John Lord O'Brian

Jacob Frohwerk was a copy editor for the German-language newspaper Missouri Staats Zeitung. *From July to December 1917, the paper published a number of articles generally critical of the war, but he made no effort to target draftees. Frohwerk was charged under the Espionage Act, convicted, and sentenced to prison, and fined $500. Holmes, speaking for a unanimous Court, upheld the convictions.*

Mr. Justice Holmes delivered the opinion of the Court.

This is an indictment in thirteen counts. The first alleges a conspiracy between the plaintiff in error and one Carl Gleeser, they then being engaged in the preparation and publication of a newspaper, the *Missouri Staats Zeitung*, to violate the Espionage Act of June 15, 1917. It alleges as overt acts the preparation and circulation of twelve articles &c. in the said newspaper at different dates from July 6, 1917, to December 7 of the same year. The other counts allege attempts to cause disloyalty, mutiny and refusal of duty in the military and naval forces of the United States, by the same publications, each count being confined to the publication of a single date. . . . There was a trial and Frohwerk was found guilty on all the counts except the seventh, which needs no further mention. He was sentenced to a fine and to ten years imprisonment on each count, the imprisonment on the later counts to run concurrently with that on the first.

Owing to unfortunate differences no bill of exceptions is before us. Frohwerk applied to this Court for leave to file a petition for a writ of mandamus requiring the judge to sign a proper bill of exceptions, but a case was not stated that would warrant the issuing of the writ and leave was denied. . . . The absence of a bill of exceptions and the suggestions in the application for mandamus have caused us to consider the case with more anxiety than if it presented only the constitutional question which was the theme of the principal argument here. With regard to that argument we think it necessary to add to what has been said in *Schenck v. United States*, only that the First Amendment while prohibiting legislation against free speech as such cannot have been, and obviously was not, intended to give immunity for every possible use of language. We venture to believe that neither Hamilton nor Madison, nor any other competent person then or later, ever supposed that to make criminal the counseling of a murder within the jurisdiction of Congress would be an unconstitutional interference with free speech.

Whatever might be thought of the other counts on the evidence, if it were before us, we have decided in *Schenck v. United States*, that a person may be convicted of a conspiracy to obstruct recruiting by words of persuasion. The Government argues that on the record the question is narrowed simply to the power of Congress to punish such a conspiracy to obstruct, but we shall take it in favor of the defendant that the publications set forth as overt acts were the only means and, when coupled with the joint activity in producing them, the only evidence of the conspiracy alleged. Taking it that way, however, so far as the language of the article goes there is not much to choose between expressions to be found in them and those before us in *Schenck v. United States*.

The first begins by declaring it a monumental and inexcusable mistake to send our soldiers to France, says that it comes no doubt from the great trusts, and later that it appears to be outright murder without serving anything practical; speaks of the unconquerable spirit and undiminished strength of the German nation, and characterizes its own discourse as words of warning to the American people. Then comes a letter from one of the counsel who argued here, stating that the present force is a part of the regular army raised illegally; a matter discussed at length in his voluminous brief, on the ground that before its decision to the contrary the Solicitor General misled this Court as to the law. Later, on August 3, came discussion of the causes of the war, laying it to the administration and saying "that a few men and corporations might amass unprecedented fortunes we sold our honor, our very soul" with the usual repetition that we went to war to protect the loans of Wall Street. Later, after more similar discourse, comes "We say therefore, cease firing."

Next, on August 10, after deploring "the draft riots in Oklahoma and else-where" in language that might be taken to convey an innuendo of a different sort, it is said that the previous talk about legal remedies is all very well for those who are past the draft age and have no boys to be drafted, and the paper goes on to give a picture, made as moving as the writer was able to make it, of the sufferings of a drafted man, of his then recognizing that his country is not in danger and that he is being sent to a foreign land to fight in a cause that neither he nor any one else knows anything of, and reaching the conviction that this is but a war to protect some rich men's money. Who then, it is asked, will pronounce a verdict of guilty upon him if he stops reasoning and follows the first impulse of nature: self-preservation; and further, whether, while technically he is wrong in his resistance, he is not more sinned against than sinning; and yet again whether the guilt of those who voted the unnatural sacrifice is not greater than the wrong of those who now seek to escape by ill advised resistance. On August 17 there is quoted and applied to our own situation a remark to the effect that when rulers scheme to use it for their own aggrandizement loyalty serves to perpetuate wrong. On August 31 with more of the usual discourse, it is said that the sooner the public wakes up to the fact that we are led and ruled by England, the better; that our sons, our taxes and our sacrifices are only in the interest of England. On September 28 there is a sneering contrast between Lord Northcliffe and other Englishmen spending many hundreds of thousands of dollars here to drag us into the war and Count Bernstorff spending a few thousand to maintain peace between his own country and us. Later follow some compliments to Germany and a statement that the Central powers are carrying on a defensive war. There is much more to the general effect that we are in the wrong and are giving false and hypocritical reasons for our course, but the foregoing is enough to indicate the kind of matter with which we have to deal.

It may be that all this might be said or written even in time of war in circumstances that would not make it a crime. We do not lose our right to condemn either measures or men because the country is at war. It does not appear that there was any special effort to reach men who were subject to the draft; and if the evidence should show that the defendant was a poor man, turning out copy for Gleeser, his employer, at less than a day laborer's pay, for Gleeser to use or reject as he saw fit, in a newspaper of small circulation, there would be a natural inclination to test every question of law to be found in the record very thoroughly before upholding the very severe penalty imposed. But we must take the case on the record as it is, and on that record it is impossible to say that it might not have been found that the circulation of the paper was in quarters where a little breath would be enough to kindle a flame and that the fact was known and relied upon by those who sent the paper out. Small compensation would not exonerate the defendant if it were found that he expected the result, even if pay were his chief desire. When we consider that we do not know how strong the Government's evidence may have been we find ourselves unable to say that the articles could not furnish a basis for a conviction upon the first count at least. We pass therefore to the other points that are raised.

It is said that the first count is bad because it does not allege the means by which the conspiracy was to be carried out. But a conspiracy to obstruct recruiting would be criminal even if no means were agreed upon specifically by which to accomplish the intent. It is enough if the parties agreed to set to work for that common purpose. That purpose could be accomplished or aided by persuasion as well as by false statements, and there was no need to allege that false reports were intended to be made or made. It is argued that there is no sufficient allegation of intent, but intent to accomplish an object cannot be alleged more clearly than by stating that parties conspired to accomplish it. The overt acts are alleged to have been done to affect the object of the conspiracy and that is sufficient. . . . Countenance we believe has been given by some Courts to the notion that a single count in an indictment for conspiring to commit two offences is bad for duplicity. This Court has given it none. The conspiracy is the crime, and that is one, however diverse its objects. Some reference was made in the proceedings and in argument to the provision in the Constitution concerning treason, and it was suggested on the one hand that some of the matters dealt with in the Act of 1917 were treasonable and punishable as treason or not at all, and on the other that the acts complained of not being treason could not be punished. These suggestions seem to us to need no more than to be stated. The amendment of the Act of 1917 in 1918 did not affect the present indictment. Without pursuing the matter further we are of opinion that the indictment must stand.

. . . There is nothing before us that makes it possible to say that the judge's discretion was wrongly exercised. Upon the whole case we are driven to the conclusion that the record shows no ground upon which the judgment can be reversed.

Judgment affirmed.

COMMENTARY

In times of war – Unlike *Schenck*, where Holmes gave considerable, even determinative, weight to the fact of war and its impact of First Amendment rights, in *Frohwerk*, Holmes expressed a more sympathetic attitude toward free speech in wartime. "We do not," he said, "lose our right to condemn either measures or men because the country is at war." Even so, his application of the First Amendment in *Frohwerk* tracked what he had done in *Schenck*.

Did poor lawyering account for the result in the case? – Professor David Bogen makes a telling observation about how the *Frohwerk* was argued: "Frohwerk, convicted under the Espionage Act of 1917 for publishing several articles critical of the war and draft, was represented both at trial and on appeal by attorney Joseph Shewalter. In this case it would have been more fitting if the attorney had been the defendant, both because it was Shewalter's articles that furnished the basis of the prosecution and because it was his poor representation that resulted the publisher going to jail. Shewalter failed to get agreement on a bill of exceptions and was unable, despite an extension of time, to get the transcript of the trial typed to meet the date for filing the appeal. Consequently, the sole issue appealed to the Supreme Court was the sufficiency of the indictment. Neither the evidence adduced at trial nor the rulings or charge below were before the Court.... Without the trial transcript, the Supreme Court could not know the situation in which the articles were published.... Thus, Holmes had to assume the charge was proper and supported by the strongest possible evidence consistent with the indictment.... [In other words,] the narrow question before the Court simply did not open up on the conduct of trial or the evidence there presented, so Holmes had little trouble in affirming the conviction." David S. Bogen, "The Free Speech Metamorphosis of Mr. Justice Holmes," 11 *Hofstra Law Review* 97, 164–65 (1982) (footnotes omitted). *Compare* David M. Rabban, *Free Speech in Its Forgotten Years* (New York: Cambridge University Press, 1997), at 282–83.

More metaphors – Once again using a fire metaphor, Holmes claimed that "a little breath would be enough to kindle a flame." Here, the metaphor hardly suits the facts of the case. It is "very hard to see, despite Holmes' 'kindle a flame' metaphor, how printing a circular intended for an audience of German-speaking socialists created a clear and present danger that the war effort would be obstructed." G. Edward White, *Justice Oliver Wendell Holmes: Law and the Inner Self* (New York: Oxford University Press, 1993), at 419. *See also* Yosal Rogat and James M. O'Fallon, "Mr. Justice Holmes: A Dissenting Opinion – The Speech Cases," 36 *Stanford Law Review* 1349, 1373 (1984).

It has been argued that Holmes's flame metaphor reinforced "the conclusion that he had not intended his clear and present danger phrase in *Schenck* to articulate a new and more protective standard for free expression. To the contrary, Holmes's subsequent *Frohwerk* language not only disregarded his clear and present danger phrasing, but it also resonated closely with the bad tendency test. Given the facts of the case and the Court's ready willingness to find the writings unprotected, the 'kindle a flame' language appeared to be just another way to say bad tendency." Stephen M. Feldman, *Free Expression and Democracy in America: A History* (Chicago: University of Chicago Press, 2008), at 262 (endnote omitted). *Accord* David M. Rabban, *Free Speech in Its Forgotten Years, supra,* at 283.

Clear and present danger? – Though it came down only a week after *Schenck,* Holmes made no explicit reference to the clear-and-present-danger test. "Since *Frohwerk* involved a conspiracy," Professor Pohlman has argued, "no actual danger of harm was required. It should therefore not be surprising – even though this fact has drawn some comment – that in his opinion Holmes never referred to the clear-and-present-danger doctrine. The only question was whether Frohwerk joined with others for the unlawful purpose of obstructing the draft and causing insubordination in the military." H. L. Pohlman, *Justice Oliver Wendell Holmes: Free Speech and the Living Constitution* (New York: New York University Press, 1991), at 70, 91 (omitted footnote referring to different view held by Rabban).

Frohwerk's fate – In the early summer of 1919, after his *Frohwerk* opinion came down, Holmes wrote to Frederick Pollock: "I . . . have said whenever it was proper that I thought the President should pardon a lot of poor devils that it was my misfortune to have to write opinions condemning." Letter from OWH to Pollock, June 17, 1919, reproduced in Mark DeWolfe Howe, ed., *Holmes-Pollock Letters: The Correspondence of Mr. Justice Holmes and Sir Frederick Pollock, 1874–1932* (Cambridge, MA: Harvard University Press, 1941), at 2:15.

Without any apparent involvement by Holmes, President Woodrow Wilson commuted Jacob Frohwerk's ten-year sentence to a year. *See* Zechariah Chafee Jr., *Free Speech in the United States* (New York: Atheneum, 1968), at 82 n. 87.

One purpose of [Debs's] speech, whether incidental or not does not matter, was to oppose not only war in general but this war, and that the opposition was so expressed that its natural and intended effect would be to obstruct recruiting.

DEBS V. UNITED STATES

249 U.S. 211 (1919)
Vote: 9–0
Argued: January 27–28, 1919
Decided: March 10, 1919
For petitioner: Seymour Stedman
For respondent: John Lord O'Brian
Amicus: Gilbert E. Roe

Eugene V. Debs was a five-time presidential candidate for the Socialist Party. In 1918 he gave a speech in Canton, Ohio, disapproving of American participation

*in World War I. He was convicted under the insubordination and obstruction
provisions of the Espionage Act. The District Court of the United States for the
Northern District of Ohio sentenced Debs to ten years in a federal penitentiary.
The following is an excerpt from Debs's speech:*

> *I have just returned from a visit over yonder [pointing to the workhouse],
> where three of our most loyal comrades are paying the penalty for their
> devotion to the cause of the working class. [Applause]. They have come to
> realize, as many of us have, that it is extremely dangerous to exercise the
> constitutional right of free speech in a country fighting to make democracy
> safe in the world. [Applause]. I realize that, in speaking to you this after-
> noon, there are certain limitations placed upon the right of free speech.
> I must be exceedingly careful, prudent, as to what I say, and even more
> careful and prudent as to how I say it. [Laughter]. I may not be able to say
> all I think; [Laughter and applause] but I am not going to say anything
> I do not think. [Applause].... [Our three comrades] are simply paying
> the penalty, that all men have paid in all the ages of history for standing
> erect, and for seeking to pave the way to better conditions for mankind.
> [Applause].... They tell us that we live in a great free republic; that our
> institutions are democratic; that we are a free and self-governing people.
> [Laughter]. This is too much, even for a joke. [Laughter]. But it is not a
> subject for levity; it is an exceedingly serious matter.[59]*

Mr. Justice Holmes delivered the opinion of the Court.

...There was a demurrer to the indictment on the ground that the
statute is unconstitutional as interfering with free speech, contrary to the First
Amendment, and to the several counts as insufficiently stating the supposed
offence.... The defendant was found guilty and was sentenced to ten years
imprisonment on each of the two counts, the punishment to run concurrently
on both.

The main theme of the speech was socialism, its growth, and a prophecy
of its ultimate success. With that we have nothing to do, but if a part of the
manifest intent of the more general utterances was to encourage those present
to obstruct the recruiting service and if in passages such encouragement was
directly given, the immunity of the general theme may not be enough to
protect the speech. The speaker began by saying that he had just returned
from a visit to the workhouse in the neighborhood where three of their most
loyal comrades were paying the penalty for their devotion to the working

---

[59] Eugene Debs, Speech in Canton, Ohio, June 16, 1918, quoted in *Perilous Times, supra*
note 4, at 196–97 [quoting Arthur M. Schlesinger Jr., *Writings and Speeches of Eugene
V. Debs* (New York: Hermitage, 1948), at 417–22].

class – these being Wagenknecht, Baker and Ruthenberg,[60] who had been convicted of aiding and abetting another in failing to register for the draft. He said that he had to be prudent and might not be able to say all that he thought, thus intimating to his hearers that they might infer that he meant more, but he did say that those persons were paying the penalty for standing erect and for seeking to pave the way to better conditions for all mankind. Later he added further eulogies and said that he was proud of them. He then expressed opposition to Prussian militarism in a way that naturally might have been thought to be intended to include the mode of proceeding in the United States.

After considerable discourse that it is unnecessary to follow, he took up the case of Kate Richards O'Hare, convicted of obstructing the enlistment service, praised her for her loyalty to socialism and otherwise, and said that she was convicted on false testimony, under a ruling that would seem incredible to him if he had not had some experience with a Federal Court. We mention this passage simply for its connection with evidence put in at the trial. The defendant spoke of other cases, and then, after dealing with Russia, said that the master class has always declared the war and the subject class has always fought the battles – that the subject class has had nothing to gain and all to lose, including their lives; that the working class, who furnish the corpses, have never yet had a voice in declaring war and have never yet had a voice in declaring peace. "You have your lives to lose; you certainly ought to have the right to declare war if you consider a war necessary." The defendant next mentioned Rose Pastor Stokes, convicted of attempting to cause insubordination and refusal of duty in the military forces of the United States and obstructing the recruiting service. He said that she went out to render her service to the cause in this day of crises, and they sent her to the penitentiary for ten years; that she had said no more than the speaker had said that afternoon; that if she was guilty so was he, and that he would not be cowardly enough to plead his innocence; but that her message that opened the eyes of the people must be suppressed, and so, after a mock trial before a packed jury and a corporation tool on the bench, she was sent to the penitentiary for ten years.

There followed personal experiences and illustrations of the growth of socialism, a glorification of minorities, and a prophecy of the success of the international socialist crusade, with the interjection that "you need to know that

---

[60] See *Ruthenberg v. United States*, 245 U.S. 480 (1918). Charles Ruthenberg was the one-time national executive secretary of the Communist Party. Because of his outspoken radicalism, he was deemed the "most arrested red in America." Later in life, one of his cases was the companion case to *Whitney v. California*, 274 U.S. 357 (1927). *See* Ronald Collins and David Skover, "Curious Concurrence: Justice Brandeis's Vote in *Whitney v. California*," 2005 *Supreme Court Review* 333 (2005). – Ed.

you are fit for something better than slavery and cannon fodder." The rest of the discourse had only the indirect though not necessarily ineffective bearing on the offences alleged that is to be found in the usual contrasts between capitalists and laboring men, sneers at the advice to cultivate war gardens, attribution to plutocrats of the high price of coal, &c., with the implication running through it all that the working men are not concerned in the war, and a final exhortation "Don't worry about the charge of treason to your masters; but be concerned about the treason that involves yourselves." The defendant addressed the jury himself, and while contending that his speech did not warrant the charges said "I have been accused of obstructing the war. I admit it. Gentlemen, I abhor war. I would oppose the war if I stood alone." The statement was not necessary to warrant the jury in finding that one purpose of the speech, whether incidental or not does not matter, was to oppose not only war in general but this war, and that the opposition was so expressed that its natural and intended effect would be to obstruct recruiting. It that was intended and if, in all the circumstances, that would be its probable effect, it would not be protected by reason of its being part of a general program and expressions of a general and conscientious belief.

The chief defenses upon which the defendant seemed willing to rely were the denial that we have dealt with and that based upon the First Amendment to the Constitution, disposed of in *Schenck v. United States*. His counsel questioned the sufficiency of the indictment. It is sufficient in form. The most important question that remains is raised by the admission in evidence of the record of the conviction of Ruthenberg, Wagenknecht and Baker, Rose Paster Stokes, and Kate Richards O'Hare. The defendant purported to understand the grounds on which these persons were imprisoned and it was proper to show what those grounds were in order to show what he was talking about, to explain the true import of his expression of sympathy and to throw light on the intent of the address, so far as the present matter is concerned.

There was introduced also an "Anti-war Proclamation and Program" adopted at St. Louis in April, 1917, coupled with testimony that about an hour before his speech the defendant had stated that he approved of that platform in spirit and in substance. The defendant referred to it in his address to the jury, seemingly with satisfaction and willingness that it should be considered in evidence. But his counsel objected and has argued against its admissibility, at some length. This document contained the usual suggestion that capitalism was the cause of the war and that our entrance into it "was instigated by the predatory capitalists in the United States." It alleged that the war of the United States against Germany could not "be justified even on the plea that it is a war in defence of American rights or American 'honor.'" It said

"We brand the declaration of war by our Government as a crime against the people of the United States and against the nations of the world. In all modern history there has been no war more unjustifiable than the war in which we are about to engage." Its first recommendation was, "continuous, active, and public opposition to the war, through demonstrations, mass petitions, and all other means within our power." Evidence that the defendant accepted this view and this declaration of his duties at the time that he made his speech is evidence that if in that speech he used words tending to obstruct the recruiting service he meant that they should have that effect. The principle is too well established and too manifestly good sense to need citation of the books. We should add that the jury were most carefully instructed that they could not find the defendant guilty for advocacy of any of his opinions unless the words used had as their natural tendency and reasonably probable effect to obstruct the recruiting service, &c., and unless the defendant had the specific intent to do so in his mind.

Without going into further particulars we are of opinion that the verdict on the fourth count, for obstructing and attempting to obstruct the recruiting service of the United States, must be sustained. Therefore it is less important to consider whether that upon the third count, for causing and attempting to cause insubordination, &c., in the military and naval forces, is equally impregnable. The jury were instructed that for the purposes of the statute the persons designated by the Act of May 18, 1917, registered and enrolled under it, and thus subject to be called into the active service, were a part of the military forces of the United States. The Government presents a strong argument from the history of the statutes that the instruction was correct and in accordance with established legislative usage. We see no sufficient reason for differing from the conclusion but think it unnecessary to discuss the question in detail.

Judgment affirmed.

CORRESPONDENCE

To Harold Laski
March 16, 1919

Dear Laski,

. . . I sent you yesterday some opinions in the [Eugene] Debs and other similar cases. . . . I greatly regretted having to write them – and (between ourselves) that the Government pressed them to a hearing. Of course I know that don-keys and knaves would represent us as concurring in the condemnation of Debs because he was a dangerous agitator. Of course, too, so far as that is concerned, he might split his guts without my interfering with him or sanc-tioning interference. But on the only questions before us I could not doubt about the law. The federal judges seem to me (again between ourselves) to have got hysterical about the war. I should think the President when he gets through with his present amusements might do some pardoning. I have been interrupted and so perhaps have been less coherent than I should have been.

In relevant part, Laski responded: "I think you would agree that none of the accused ought to have been prosecuted; but since they have been and the statute is there, the only remedy lies in the field of pardon." Laski to Holmes, March 18, 1919.

Holmes-Laski Letters: The Correspondence of Mr. Justice Holmes and Harold J. Laski, ed. Mark DeWolfe Howe (Cambridge, MA: Harvard University Press, 1953), at 2:189, 190, 191.

To Lewis Einstein
Washington, April 5, 1919

My dear Einstein:

. . . Just now I am receiving some singularly ignorant protests against a decision that I wrote sustaining a conviction of Debs, a labor agitator, for obstructing the recruiting service. They make me want to write a letter to ease my mind and shoot off my mouth; but of course I keep a judicial silence.

Early in life I saw much of the abolitionists in whom I believed devoutly, but it gave me lasting disgust for Come-outers. They are so cocksure on the strength of semi-education. They may be one of the disagreeable necessities of progress, but I wonder how many of them could give an intelligent statement of what progress is – or what they mean by it. I asked my secretary what it was and he said increasing complexity. I thought that good for a starter. I was inclined to doubt whether I could confidently call any step one toward progress unless it were to get broader napes to our necks. That we could help and it would be progress to help it along, but the only way I know of to do so would strike horror to the breasts of my fellow citizens including those who regard me as an old fogey to be got rid of as soon as may be. . . .

The Holmes-Einstein Letters: Correspondence of Mr. Justice Holmes and Lewis Einstein, 1903–1935, ed. James Bishop Peabody (New York: St. Martin's Press, 1964), at 184.

To Frederick Pollock
Washington, April 5, 1919

Dear Pollock:

... I am beginning to get stupid letters of protest against a decision that Debs, a noted agitator, was rightly convicted of obstructing the recruiting service so far as the law was concerned. I wondered that the Government should press the case to a hearing before us, as the inevitable result was that fools, knaves, and ignorant persons were bound to say he was convicted because he was a dangerous agitator and that obstructing the draft was a pretence. How it was with the Jury of course, I don't know, but of course the talk is silly as to us. There was a lot of jaw about free speech, which I dealt with somewhat summarily in an earlier case – *Schenck v. U.S.* ... also *Frohwerk v. U.S.* ... As it happens I should go farther probably than the majority in favor of it, and I daresay it was partly on that account that the C. J. assigned the case to me. ...

Holmes-Pollock Letters: The Correspondence of Mr. Justice Holmes and Sir Frederick Pollock, 1874–1932, ed. Mark DeWolfe Howe (Cambridge, MA: Harvard University Press, 1941), at 2:7.

To Frederick Pollock
Washington, April 27, 1919[61]

Dear Pollock:

... Meantime things have gone pretty smoothly. Of course there were people who pitched into the Court for sending Debs to prison under the espionage act, but there was no doubt that the Jury was warranted in finding him guilty or that the act was Constitutional. Now I hope the President will pardon him and some other poor devils with whom I have more sympathy. Those whose cases have come before us seemed to me poor fools whom I should have been inclined to pass over if I could. The greatest bores in the world are the come-outers who are cock-sure of a dozen nostrums. The dogmatism of a little education is hopeless. ...

[61] This letter was sent about six weeks after the *Debs* case came down.

Holmes-Pollock Letters: The Correspondence of Mr. Justice Holmes and Sir Frederick Pollock, 1874–1932, ed. Mark DeWolfe Howe (Cambridge, MA: Harvard University Press, 1941), at 2:11.

To Harold Laski
[May 13, 1919]

Dear Laski:

Yesterday I wrote the within [letter to Herbert Croly] and decided not to send it as some themes may become burning. Instead I trust it confidentially to you and it will answer your inquiry about Freund.[62] I thought it was poor stuff – for reasons indicated within. . . .

[Enclosure]

Supreme Court of the United States
Private
Washington, D.C., May 12, 1919

My dear Mr. Croly:

. . . As long ago as 1908 when I wrote *Harriman v. I.C.C.*, 211 U.S. 407, it seemed to me that we so long had enjoyed the advantages protected by bills of rights that we had forgotten – it used sometimes to seem to me that the *New Republic* had forgotten – that they had had to be fought for and could not be kept unless we were willing to fight for them. Few can sympathize more than I do with Mr. [William] Hard's general way of thinking on the subject [as he set out his views in his *New Republic* article (May 10, 1919) critical of the postmaster general's actions]. As I spoke of it to my secretary and my inclination to write to you he called my attention to the article on the *Debs* case which I had not seen. You had a short paragraph in an earlier number that struck me as exactly right. This article appeared to me less so if I understood its implications. The constitutionality of the act so far as the clauses concerning obstructing the recruiting service are involved was passed upon in *Schenck v. U.S.* and so all that was needed in the *Debs* case was to refer to that decision, and, given the finding of the jury, in my opinion it was impossible to have a

---

[62] Holmes was referring to an article by Ernst Freund, "The Debs Case and Freedom of Speech," *supra* note 21, at 13, which is excerpted in the commentary materials herein.

rational doubt about the law, which for thirty years I have made my brethren smile by insisting to be everywhere a matter of degree.... I hated to have to write the *Debs* case and still more those of the other poor devils before us the same day and the week before. I could not see the wisdom of pressing the cases, especially when the fighting was over and I think it quite possible that if I had been on the jury I should have been for acquittal but I cannot doubt that there was evidence warranting a conviction on the disputed issues of fact. Moreover I think the *clauses under consideration* not only were constitutional but were proper enough while the war was on. When people are putting out all their energies in battle I don't think it unreasonable to say we won't have obstacles intentionally put in the way of raising troops – by persuasion any more than by force. But in the main I am for aeration of all effervescing convictions – there is no way so quick for letting them get flat.... I write this letter only to ease my mind, not impose an answer on you.

Very sincerely yours, O. W. Holmes
Of course it is only for your private eye.

Holmes-Laski Letters: The Correspondence of Mr. Justice Holmes and Harold J. Laski, ed. Mark DeWolfe Howe (Cambridge, MA: Harvard University Press, 1953), at 2:202–04.

To Frederick Pollock
Washington, D.C., December 14, 1919

Dear Pollock:

...As the *Debs case* and the two other were assigned to me, in which the convictions were upheld, I thought it was proper to state what I thought the limits of the [clear-and-present-danger] doctrine. The general principles laid down by me I think correct, and the particular conclusion I adhere to, because even if there were evidence of a conspiracy to obstruct, etc., the overt act laid must be an act done to effect the object of the conspiracy and it seems to me plain that the only object of the leaflets was to hinder our interference with Russia. I ought to have developed this in the opinion. But that is ancient history now....

Holmes-Pollock Letters: The Correspondence of Mr. Justice Holmes and Sir Frederick Pollock, 1874–1932, ed. Mark DeWolfe Howe (Cambridge, MA: Harvard University Press, 1941), at 2:32.

To Harold Laski
Washington, D.C., January 15, 1922

Dear Laski:

. . . I too was glad at the release of Debs – although I can hardly believe him
honest (not that that has anything to do with his being kept in or let out).

*Holmes-Laski Letters: The Correspondence of Mr. Justice Holmes and Harold J.
Laski*, ed. Mark DeWolfe Howe (Cambridge, MA: Harvard University Press,
1953), at 1:399.

COMMENTARY

Bomb threats – A few months after *Debs* came down, anarchists mailed sixteen
bombs from the New York City post office, one of which was addressed to
Holmes. Fortunately, the packages went undelivered for insufficient postage
and were defused. Police guards were thereafter posted near Holmes's residence. The justice claimed to be unconcerned. He told his wife that if he
"worried over all the bullets that [had] missed [him, he] should have a job."
Liva Baker, *The Justice from Beacon Hill* (New York: HarperCollins, 1991),
at 529; Kenneth D. Ackerman, *Young J. Edgar: Hoover, the Red Scare, and
the Assault on Civil Liberties* (New York: Carroll & Graf, 2007), at 150. *See*
"Red Bombs Palmer's House; Dies Himself; Family Is Not Injured," *Washington Post*, June 3, 1919, at 1; "Attempt to Terrorize Has Failed, Says Palmer,"
Washington Post, June 4, 1919, at 1.

Amicus brief – An amicus brief in support of Debs was filed by Gilbert Roe,
the lawyer for the Free Speech League who knew and had worked with
Louis Brandeis before the latter became a justice. In 1917 Roe represented
Max Eastman, the petitioner in *Masses Publishing Co. v. Patten*, 244 F. 535
(S.D.N.Y. 1917, per Hand., J.). Before that he was Eastman's lawyer in a
criminal libel case. *See People v. Eastman*, 89 Misc. 596, 152 N.Y.S. 314 (N.Y.
1915). Earlier still, Roe was the attorney for the petitioner in *Fox v. Washington*
(see Part IV). And in April 1917, he testified before Congress against the
Espionage Act. In his *Debs* brief, Roe, along with the attorney for the petitioner,
challenged the Blackstonian interpretation of freedom of expression. He also
drew on Judge Learned Hand's district court opinion in the *Masses* case.
Having read the briefs in the case, Holmes wrote to Judge Hand: "I read your
Masses decision – I haven't the details in mind and will assume for present

purposes that I should come to a different result – but I did want to tell you after reading it that I thought that few judges indeed could have put their view with such force or in such admirable form." Letter from OWH to Learned Hand, February 25, 1919, quoted in Gerald Gunther, "Learned Hand and the Origins of Modern First Amendment Doctrine," 27 *Stanford Law Review* 719, 758 (1975). *See also* David S. Bogen, "The Free Speech Metamorphosis of Mr. Justice Holmes," 11 *Hofstra Law Review* 97, 147 (1982); David Rabban, *Free Speech in Its Forgotten Years* (New York: Cambridge University Press, 1999), at 55–57, 261–64, 272–74.

Most disgraceful prosecution of unpopular speech – "*Debs v. United States* is perhaps the most serious free speech case in the history of the First Amendment. After all, the man jailed had, in his campaigns for the Presidency, polled almost 1 million votes in 1912 and again in 1920 (while in prison), equivalent to almost 3 million votes today. . . . All this means . . . is that *Debs v. United States* may be the most disgraceful prosecution for unpopular political speech in the history of the Country." George Anastaplo, *Reflections on Freedom of Speech and the First Amendment* (Lexington: University Press of Kentucky, 2007), at 111. One of Anastaplo's professors, the late Harry Kalven, made a similar point. Kalven analogized Debs's speech to what Senator George McGovern said decades later in connection with the Vietnam War: "To put the [*Debs*] case in modern context, it is somewhat as though George McGovern had been sent to prison for his criticism of the war." Harry Kalven Jr., "Professor Ernst Freund and *Debs v. United States*," 40 *University of Chicago Law Review* 235, 237 (1973). *See also* Yosal Rogat and James M. O'Fallon, "Mr. Justice Holmes: A Dissenting Opinion – The Speech Cases," 36 *Stanford Law Review* 1349, 1374 (1984) ("the *Debs* opinion . . . is most incompatible with any meaningful clear and present danger standard.").

Conservative justices applaud Holmes – Holmes's judgments in *Schenck, Frohwerk*, and *Debs* won the approval and applause of his conservative brethren as expressed in their notes to him. Justice James McReynolds wrote: "I agree and may he [Holmes] enjoy many days." "Yes," added Justice Willis Van Devanter, "I think you [Holmes] have happily disposed of a bunch of unattractive cases." And Justice William R. Day likewise agreed: "Right again." Liva Baker, *The Justice from Beacon Hill: The Life and Times of Oliver Wendell Holmes* (New York: HarperCollins, 1991), at 526.

Notably, the editors of the *New Republic* agreed: "Eugene Debs has gone to the West Virginia Penitentiary to begin his ten-year sentence. There is no doubt about the legality of his conviction. His Canton Speech clearly violated the Espionage Act." Editorial, *New Republic*, April 19, 1919, at 362.

Learned Hand's reservations – After *Debs* came down, Judge Hand wrote to Holmes, but his views on free speech in wartime (his direct incitement test) seemed to fall, yet again, on deaf ears. Holmes failed to grasp the logic of Hand's arguments. "I don't quite get your point," he wrote to Hand in April 1919. Writing to Ernest Freund thereafter on May 7, 1919, Hand expressed frustration: "I own I was chagrined that Justice Holmes did not line up on our side; indeed, I have so far been unable to make him see that he and we have any real differences." Quoted in Gerald Gunther, *Learned Hand: The Man and the Judge* (New York: Alfred A. Knopf, 1994), at 164–65. Later, in a January 2, 1921, letter to Chafee, Hand declared: "I am not wholly in love with Holmes's test," which he felt left judges too much wiggle room. "I should prefer a qualitative formula, hard, conventional, difficult to evade." Quoted in David M. Rabban, *Free Speech in Its Forgotten Years* (New York: Cambridge University Press, 1997), at 333–34.

Brandeis weighs in afterward – Sometime after the *Debs* case came down, Brandeis apparently communicated some misgivings about how the case should have been analyzed. "I would have placed the *Debs* case," he told Frankfurter, "on the war power – instead of taking Holmes'[s] line about 'clear and present danger.' Put it frankly on the war power – like [the] *Hamilton* case[63] ... and then the scope of the espionage legislation would be confined to war. But in peace the protection of freedom of speech would be unabated. You might as well recognize that during war ... all bets are off. But we would have a clear line to go on. I didn't know enough in the early cases to put it on that ground." Transcript of conversations between Louis Brandeis and Felix Frankfurter, manuscript in Brandeis Papers, Harvard Law School, Box 114, Folder 14, quoted in *Free Speech in its Forgotten Years*, *supra*, at 363.

Two ways of looking at the evidence in the case – On the one hand, the "speeches for which Debs was convicted did not directly urge the violation of any law, and no one was shown to have broken any law because of the speeches. Further, unlike the circulars in *Schenck*, the speeches were directed to a general audience instead of being targeted to draftees. And, unlike [the lawyer] in *Frohwerk*, Debs'[s] attorneys had preserved for review the full record of the trial with all the circumstances that surrounded the speeches." On the other hand, in "Holmes's view, the proper test for the power of the government to punish speech was the danger posed by that speech, and intent was relevant

---

[63] *Hamilton v. Kentucky Distilleries & Warehouse Co.*, 251 U.S. 146 (1919) (holding that the power to prohibit the liquor traffic as a means of increasing war efficiency is part of the war power of Congress). – *Ed.*

only insofar as it increased the danger of violation of law proceeding from the speech. He saw no difference between his test and Hand's 'direct incitement' because he thought that words that posed a clear and present danger, that were close to illegal action, would surely be 'directly an incitement' even if their form was not that of direct incitement." By that measure, the "most obvious factor that would lead Holmes to believe that a jury could legitimately find that a clear and present danger existed in *Debs* was the apprehension of great danger. The draft and recruiting service were being interfered with in wartime – thus, the normal self-interested reluctance of an individual to join the armed services was sharply reinforced at the very time when the need for soldiers was greatest. . . . " Moreover, "Debs'[s] notoriety – as labor leader and presidential candidate – combined with his skill as a speaker, made it far more likely that his audience would be stirred to action by his speech. . . . " David S. Bogen, "The Free Speech Metamorphosis of Mr. Justice Holmes," 11 *Hofstra Law Review* 97, 170–71 (1982) (footnotes omitted).

The return of the bad-tendency test – "Holmes'[s] analysis of the issues in *Debs* is difficult to square with his 'clear and present danger' language in *Schenck*. . . . " Given the facts in the case, Holmes's application of that test "established the principle that one could be convicted for opposing war generally. *Debs* therefore was not a 'clear and present danger' case unless Holmes was treating that formula as merely codifying the 'tendency' element of criminal attempt law." G. Edward White, *Justice Oliver Wendell Holmes: Law and the Inner Self* (New York: Oxford University Press, 1999), at 420. *Accord* Laurence Tribe, *American Constitutional Law*, 2nd ed. (Mineola, NY: Foundation Press, 1988), at 842 n. 8.

Ernst Freund takes critical look – Ernst Freund was a noted legal American scholar who taught at the University of Chicago Law School when the *Debs* case was handed down. Writing shortly thereafter in the *New Republic* – a magazine that tended to be quite laudatory toward Holmes – Freund took aim at Holmes's handiwork in *Debs* and how he applied the law to the facts of the case: "There was nothing to show actual obstruction or an attempt to interfere with any of the process of recruiting. How can it be denied that the upholding of such a finding upon such evidence involves the question of the limits of permissible speech? If verbal or written opposition to the war . . . can be stretched to mean obstruction, then Congress strikes at utterances as effectively through punishing obstruction as though it had punished utterances directly." Later in his article, he added: "So long as we apply the notoriously loose common law doctrines of conspiracy and incitement to offenses of a political character, we are adrift on a sea of doubt and conjecture. To know what you may do and what you may not do, and how far you may go in criticism, is the first condition of political liberty; to be permitted to agitate at your peril, subject to a jury's guessing at motive, tendency and possible effect," he wrote, "makes the right of free speech a precarious gift." Ernst Freund, "The *Debs* Case and Freedom of Speech," *New Republic*, May 13, 1919, at 13–14, reprinted in 40 *University of Chicago Law Review* 239, 240 (1973). *See also* Chafee's criticism in Zechariah Chafee Jr., *Free Speech in the United States* (Cambridge, MA: Harvard University Press, 1941), at 85.

Toothless test – Years later, and echoing Freund, the much-respected First Amendment scholar Harry Kalven was also openly critical of Holmes's opinion for the Court in *Debs*: "It has been customary to lavish care and attention in the *Schenck* case" and to ignore the *Debs* case. *Debs* "represented the first effort by Justice Holmes to apply what he had worked out about freedom of speech in *Schenck*. The start of the law of the First Amendment is not *Schenck*; it is *Schenck* and *Debs* read together. . . . [Holmes's] almost laconic affirmance of the conviction raises serious question as to what the First Amendment, and more especially, what the clear and present danger formula can possibly have meant at the time. . . . [In *Debs*, Holmes] shows no sensitivity to accommodating a tradition of political dissent . . . and makes no effort to suggest the parameters of improper criticism of the war. In fact the case did not move Justice Holmes to discuss free speech at all; his brief opinion is occupied with two points about [the] admissibility of certain evidence at trial. It was for Holmes a routine criminal appeal." "Professor Ernst Freund and *Debs v. United States*," *supra*, at 235–36, 238.

To much the same effect, Kalven subsequently wrote that Holmes "does not devote even a sentence to the circumstance that the special audience of *Schenck* is no longer present, that he is dealing with a speech to the general public. The jury instruction quoted with apparent approval is keyed to 'natural tendency' and 'reasonably probable effect.' Are these for Holmes synonyms of clear and present danger? Equally troublesome, there is no effort to curb the misunderstanding likely to be aroused by the decision itself. If Eugene Debs can be sent to jail for a public speech, what, if anything, can the ordinary man safely say against the war? Although subsequent World War I cases are to provide close competition, *Debs* marks a low point in the Court's performance in speech cases." Harry Kalven Jr., *A Worthy Tradition* (New York: Harper & Row, 1988), at 136.

Professor Edward Corwin likewise observed that the *Frohwerk* and *Debs* rulings "went far to dispel whatever impression may have been created by [*Schenck*] that there is a constitutional requirement that 'clear and present danger' of some 'substantive evil' be proved where intent to incite a crime is found to exist." Edward Corwin, "Bowing Out 'Clear and Present Danger,'" 27 *Notre Dame Law Review* 325, 331 (1952).

"*Schenck, Frohwerk,* and *Debs,* taken together, suggest that Holmes'[s] 'clear and present danger' test was simply a restatement of 'attempts' language found in his earlier opinions. If this conclusion is accurate," Professor White maintains, "Holmes'[s] Espionage Act decisions did not significantly modify his earlier free speech jurisprudence. The only clear modification in the cases was Holmes' abandonment of the 'prior restraints' interpretation of constitutional provisions affecting speech." *Justice Oliver Wendell Holmes: Law and the Inner Self, supra,* at 420.

It has been argued that Holmes's opinions in *Schenck, Frohwerk,* and *Debs* reveal that "Holmes'[s] celebrated concept of clear and present danger did not emerge as possessing any clear-cut meaning or content." Samuel J. Konefsky, *The Legacy of Holmes and Brandeis* (New York: Collier Books, 1961), at 201.

Schenck *test ineffective in safeguarding free speech rights?* – Though Holmes cited to the *Schenck* precedent in both *Frohwerk* and *Debs,* it proved of no consequence to the rights claimants in those cases. Nonetheless, Professor Chafee maintained that the test was eventually effective in protecting free speech rights. The clear-and-present-danger "test did eventually reverse many convictions, and no doubt it staved off many prosecutions which would otherwise have taken place in peace and during the Second World War." Zechariah Chafee Jr., "Thirty-Five Years with Freedom of Speech," pamphlet (New York: Roger N. Baldwin Civil Liberties Foundation, May 1952), at 8. By contrast, Professor Walter Berns has argued that the *Schenck* precedent was ineffective in protecting subsequent rights claimants who were similarly situated: "[T]o listen to the praise heaped on [the clear and present danger] test by people working for free speech, one would think it had taken its place alongside the writ of *habeas corpus* as a means of restoring freedom. . . . Although Justice Holmes initiated the rule with the support of a unanimous Court, it was not until 1937 that a majority of that body applied it favorably." Hence, in Berns's opinion, the Supreme Court "has overturned one conviction on the basis of the clear and present danger doctrine when that doctrine has been applied to a situation *for which it was designed.*" Walter Berns, *Freedom, Virtue, and the First Amendment* (Chicago: Henry Regnery, 1965), at 50–52.

Machiavellian move? – In light of the foregoing, one wonders whether Holmes applied the clear-and-present-danger rule in the manner he did (in a very restrained way) or declined to invoke it so as to produce the result the conservatives wanted but pave the way for a rule more speech protective than the old bad-tendency test. That is, had Holmes applied the clear-and-present-danger test in a rigorous manner in *Schenck, Frohwerk,* and *Debs,* he surely would not have won the votes of the likes of Van Devanter and his conservative colleagues. By this strategic logic, Holmes was willing to wait for a time when he could invoke the test and apply it in a more invigorating way. Meanwhile, he was willing to lose a pawn to gain a rook, or even an eventual king. *Consider Free Speech in the United States, supra,* at 86.

Debs's prison term and the "gracious act of mercy" – Although there was some pressure to pardon Debs – and Holmes approved of it as indicated by his April 27, 1919, letter herein – President Woodrow Wilson declined to do so. After two and a half years in prison, however, President Warren G. Harding commuted Debs's sentence to time served, and Debs was released from prison. He did so at the behest of Attorney General H. M. Daugherty, whose December 23, 1921, memorandum to the president said in part: "A great lesson has been taught, not only to this country, but to the world and to future generations, by the decision in this case. The [*Debs*] decision was by a unanimous court and is sound. Too much credit cannot be given to the Judiciary and those connected with the Department of Justice, in seeing to it that justice was administered and that the law was interpreted aright, as it was essential it should be interpreted, for the protection and preservation of this nation in its extremity, when assailed by foes within as well as by foes without." Then, adding that America was victorious in the war and that Debs had served two years in prison, the attorney general continued: "Under these circumstances I am of the opinion that the time has come when it is not only proper but expedient that some action be taken in the *Debs* case and his sentence materially reduced. . . . [T]he ends of justice would be served and it would be a gracious act of mercy to release him in the near future. . . . " Quoted in Stephen M. Kohn, *American Political Prisoners: Prosecutions under the Espionage and Sedition Acts* (Westport, CT: Praeger), at 79.

President Harding heeded Daugherty's counsel and commuted Debs's sentence at Christmastime in 1921. *See* "Harding Frees Debs and 23 Others Held for War Violations," *New York Times,* December 24, 1921, at 1; Jeffrey Crouch, *The Presidential Pardon Power* (Lawrence: University Press of Kansas, 2009), at 56–57. *See generally* Nick Salvatore, *Eugene V. Debs: Citizen and Socialist* (Urbana: University of Illinois Press, 1982); Ernest Freeberg, *Democracy's Prisoner: Eugene V. Debs, the Great War, and the Right to Dissent* (Cambridge, MA: Harvard University Press, 2008), at 292–95.

Part VI   Supreme Court Opinions: Experimenting with Freedom

[The Constitution] is an experiment, as all life is an experiment.
– Holmes, dissenting in *Abrams v. United States*

The purpose of the experiment is to keep the experiment going.
– Louis Menand[1]

We now enter Holmes's "liberal" free speech period, that time in his life when many progressives hailed him as their hero. It had much to do with his memorable dissent in *Abrams v. United States* (1919). Both before and after *Abrams*, Holmes fortified his reputation as a liberal constitutional jurist with opinions such his dissents in *Lochner v. New York*[2] and *Truax v. Corrigan*.[3] The *Abrams* dissent buttressed that reputation[4] and won him considerable respect in the First Amendment world.

In *Abrams*, the Supreme Court upheld by a 7–2 vote the convictions of five Russian immigrants charged with violating a 1918 amendment to the Espionage Act of 1917. The defendants had distributed leaflets criticizing

---

[1] Louis Menand, *The Metaphysical Club: A Story of Ideas in America* (New York: Farrar, Straus & Giroux, 2001), at 442.

[2] 198 U.S. 45, 74 (1905) (Holmes, J., dissenting) (economic due process). *See also Hammer v. Dagenhart*, 247 U.S. 251, 277 (1919) (Holmes, J., dissenting) (commerce clause and child labor laws).

[3] 257 U.S. 312, 342 (Holmes, J., dissenting) (due-process challenge to anti-injunction statute).

[4] Of course, Holmes was hardly a "liberal," at least as that term is used today. It has been said that Holmes "is a rather odd hero for civil libertarians: he had a lukewarm appreciation for public debate and saw social policy questions as differences of taste ultimately resolvable by war." John Durham Peters, *Courting the Abyss: Free Speech and the Liberal Tradition* (Chicago: University of Chicago Press, 2005), at 146. Some recent scholarship has even come to question the liberality of one of his chief defenders, Zechariah Chafee. *See* Charles L. Barzun, "Politics or Principle? Zechariah Chafee and the Social Interest in Free Speech," 2007 *Brigham Young University Law Review* 259 (2007).

certain of the government's wartime practices and likewise had called for a general strike. They were sentenced to twenty years in prison. This proved too much for Holmes; he could not accept such an outcome, which surprised his colleagues. Not long after he circulated a draft of his dissent, the seventy-eight-year-old jurist received a visit at his Eye Street home in Washington, D.C. Three of his Court colleagues came to urge him to change his vote. As Holmes's clerk, Stanley Morrison, recounted: "They laid before him their request that in this case, which they thought affected the safety of the country, he should, like the old soldier he had once been, close ranks and forego individual predilections. Mrs. Holmes agreed. The tone of the discussion was at all times friendly, even affectionate. The Justice regretted that he could not do as they wished. They did not press."[5] And so the venerated Civil War veteran stood with Brandeis in dissent.

As we have seen, as early as 1873,[6] Holmes had experimented with various notions of free speech liberty, first as a scholar and later as a jurist. That experimentation, also influenced by his Civil War experience, continued throughout his long tenure on the Supreme Court. Thus, he had more than a half century to experiment with and fine-tune his understanding of freedom of speech. By early November 1919, eight months after *Schenck v. United States,* he came to some closure in his thinking about free speech rights in wartime. There was, however, more at stake in his *Abrams* dissent than idle experimentation. For Holmes wanted to make his mark on American law. In one of his less humble, though candid, moments, the justice had earlier expressed his ambitions in a letter to a friend, an Irish priest: "The thing I . . . want to do is put as many new ideas into the law as I can, to show how particular solutions involve general theory, and to do it with style. I should like to be admitted to be the greatest jurist in the world. . . . "[7] To that end, he penned what became a landmark opinion, a dissent with enormous staying power.

After *Abrams* Holmes became "a kind of popular icon of American liberalism." Ironic as it was given overall views of life and law, "he did not bother to disabuse his public of their view of him; he liked the attention

---

[5] Qtd. in Richard Polenberg, *Fighting Faiths: The Abrams Case, the Supreme Court, and Free Speech* (New York: Viking, 1987), at 236 [citing Dean Acheson, *Morning and Noon: A Memoir* (New York: Houghton Mifflin, 1965), at 119].

[6] *See* "The Gas-Stokers' Strike" and materials following in Part II of this volume.

[7] Letter from OWH to Patrick Sheehan, December 15, 1912, reproduced in David H. Burton, ed., *Holmes-Sheehan Correspondence: The Letters of Justice Oliver Wendell Holmes and Canon Patrick Augustine Sheehan* (Port Washington, NY: Kennikat Press, 1976), at 56.

too well."[8] That attention stemmed primarily from his *Abrams* dissent. Although *Abrams* drew some sharp criticism, as noted in the commentaries following the opinion set out herein, quite often it drew high praise, especially in liberal quarters. It was a "remarkable" dissent, wrote the editors of the *New Republic*; the opinion revealed the justice's "grasp of juristic principles and his political wisdom," they added. And it accomplished this feat with "memorable words."[9] In Zechariah Chafee's more scholarly eyes, Holmes's dissent was nothing less than a "magnificent exposition of the philosophic basis"[10] of the First Amendment. For the ever-admiring Professor Frankfurter, what Holmes had done was "lift the voice of the noble human spirit."[11] Such acclaim, and there was plenty of it, pleased the "damned egotist,"[12] the jurist who seemed to be "driven by an unusual longing for recognition."[13] And so it came to be: the *Abrams* dissent greatly helped to solidify Holmes's reputation as a liberal jurist destined to be remembered. Hence, that dissent remains his most celebrated contribution to the First Amendment's jurisprudence of freedom of expression.[14] "Written against an unacknowledged tradition of judicial hostility to the value of free speech, Holmes's dissent in *Abrams* constituted the most protective construction of the First Amendment in the history of the U.S. Supreme Court."[15]

The praise was so great that many forgot the various opinions and many times Holmes had given short shrift to free speech claims in cases such as *Commonwealth v. Davis* (1895), *Patterson v. Colorado* (1907), and *Fox v. Washington* (1915), not to mention the *Schenck*, *Frohwerk*, and *Debs* cases. Prior to *Abrams*, Holmes had voted to sustain free speech claims only

---

[8] *Metaphysical Club, supra* note 1, at 437.

[9] "The Call to Toleration," *New Republic*, November 26, 1919, at 360–61.

[10] Zechariah Chafee Jr., "A Contemporary State Trial – The United States versus Jacob Abrams et al.," 33 *Harvard Law Review* 749, 769 (1920).

[11] Letter from Felix Frankfurter to OWH, November 12, 1919, reproduced in Robert M. Mennel and Christine L. Compston, eds., *Holmes and Frankfurter, Their Correspondence, 1913–1934* (Hanover, NH: University Press of New England, 1996), at 75.

[12] Qtd. in G. Edward White, *Justice Oliver Wendell Holmes: Law and the Inner Self* (New York: Oxford University Press, 1993), at 296, 550 n. 212 (OWH letter to Clare Castletown, February 2, 1897).

[13] Qtd. in David Rabban, "The Emergence of Modern First Amendment Doctrine," 50 *University of Chicago Law Review* 1207, 1280 n. 459 (1983) (quoting a former OWH law clerk); Mark DeWolfe Howe, *Justice Oliver Wendell Holmes* (Cambridge, MA: Harvard University Press, 1957), at 85.

[14] By contrast, Holmes's most cited and significant contribution to First Amendment law is his opinion for the Court in *Schenck*, if only because of the widespread use of his clear-and-present-danger test.

[15] David M. Rabban, *Free Speech in Its Forgotten Years* (New York: Cambridge University Press, 1997), at 355.

three times since he came to the Court in 1902. In the other eleven such Supreme Court cases in which he participated, he denied the claims. By contrast, in the fourteen post-*Abrams* free speech cases in which Holmes participated, he voted to sustain such claims in all but two of the cases.[16]

Something seemed to change in the man and his thought. Some, as noted in the comments following the *Abrams* opinion herein, thought the change dramatic, one that amounted to a decisive transformation.[17] If so, had Holmes yielded to the many urgings of his friends, colleagues such as Zechariah Chafee, Paul Freund, Learned Hand, and Harold Laski? Or was it simply a matter of the harsh sentences meted out to the *Abrams* defendants that prompted him to vote and write as he did? Or was his *Abrams* opinion but the latest installment in his experimentation with ideas about free speech? Whatever the answer, in his *Abrams* dissent, Holmes marked the pinnacle of his jurisprudential experimentation with free speech issues, though he would write a few more opinions and cast a few more votes to complete the picture of his free speech jurisprudence.

☙

The day after the Court handed down its *Abrams* ruling, the *Washington Post* ran the following headline: "Reds to Be Deported: Palmer Speeds Cases to Drive Out 391 Reds Caught in Raids." The news item began: "Deportation proceedings have been instituted in a number of cities to rid the country of the violent radicals caught in the nation-wide raids, which have been in progress since Friday, Attorney General [Alexander Mitchell] Palmer announced last night."[18] That day, of course, was Armistice Day (November 11, 1919). There were parades and public meetings to mark the occasion. On that day, too, Felix Frankfurter spoke at a rally at Faneuil Hall to urge the Wilson Administration to recognize the Soviet Union and likewise to call a halt to the deportations. But to no avail. By December 19, the administration had deported some 250 aliens to the Soviet Union. Frankfurter and the editors at the *New Republic* complained,[19] though few, including Holmes, much minded. "On the deportation of aliens,"

---

[16] Though the cases mentioned all involved free speech, a number of them were not decided on First Amendment grounds.

[17] *See, e.g.*, Stephen M. Feldman, *Free Expression and Democracy in America: A History* (Chicago: University of Chicago Press, 2008), at 267–81; Stephen M. Feldman, "Free Speech, World War I, and Republican Democracy: The Internal and External Holmes," 6 *First Amendment Law Review* 192, 193–95 (2008); Albert W. Alschuler, *Law without Values: The Life, Work, and Legacy of Justice Holmes* (Chicago: University of Chicago Press, 2000), at 74–79 (noting different views by scholars but concluding that Holmes had indeed changed his position).

[18] "Reds to Be Deported: Palmer Speeds Cases to Drive Out 391 Reds Caught in Raids," *Washington Post*, November 11, 1919, at 1.

[19] *New Republic*, December 21, 1919, at 37.

Holmes wrote back to Frankfurter, the *New Republic*'s editors "ought to remember that the decisions have gone very far in giving the government a right to do as it damn chooses."[20] If Holmes were a constitutional liberal, which is highly questionable, the Republican-voting justice was surely no political liberal.

Holmes's less liberal side did, however, surface from time to time as evidenced by his dissenting vote in *Meyer v. Nebraska*[21] and his majority opinion in *Buck v. Bell*.[22] The *Meyer* case involved a Fourteenth Amendment challenge to a Nebraska law that made it unlawful to teach any language other than English to schoolchildren before the eighth grade. The Court struck down the law by a 7–2 vote with Justices Holmes and George Sutherland in dissent. "We all agree," wrote Holmes, "that it is desirable that all citizens of the United States should speak a common tongue, and therefore that the end aimed at the statute is a lawful and proper one." As Professor White has observed, the "logic of that proposition is not easy to follow" because the laws at issue "did not merely establish English as the common language of ... education" but also "prohibited the teaching of language courses that had previously been offered."[23] Incredibly, Holmes treated the challenges in *Meyer* as more akin to liberty of contract than to the search for truth hailed in *Abrams*. *Buck v. Bell*[24] involved an attempt by the state of Virginia to sterilize Carrie Buck, a young woman who had been committed to the State Colony for Epileptics and Feeble Minded. The law in question allowed for the sterilization of "mental defectives" when in the judgment of institutional authorities the "best interests of the patients and society" would be served by compelled sterilization. The Court, per Justice Holmes with only Justice Pierce Butler in dissent, upheld the law over a Fourteenth Amendment challenge. Declared Holmes:

> We have seen more than once that the public welfare may call upon the best citizens for their lives. It would be strange if it could not call upon those who already sap the strength of the State for these lesser sacrifices, often not felt to be such by those concerned, in order to prevent

---

[20] Letter from OWH to Felix Frankfurter, December 21, 1919, reproduced in *Holmes and Frankfurter, supra* note 11, at 80.

[21] 262 U.S. 390 (1923). The companion case, *Bartels v. Iowa*, 262 U.S. 404 (1923) was similar but also included a prohibition against teaching German.

[22] 274 U.S. 200 (1927).

[23] *Justice Oliver Wendell Holmes: Law and the Inner Self, supra* note 12, at pp. 438–40.

[24] For a full account of the case and its history, see Paul Lombardo, *Three Generations, No Imbeciles: Eugenics, the Supreme Court, and* Buck v. Bell (Baltimore: Johns Hopkins University Press, 2008); *see also Justice Oliver Wendell Holmes: Law and the Inner Self, supra* note 12, at pp. 404–09; Liva Baker, *The Justice from Beacon Hill: The Life and Times of Oliver Wendell Holmes* (New York: HarperCollins, 1991), at pp. 599–604; *see also Law without Values, supra* note 17, at 27–29.

our being swamped with incompetence. It is better for all the world, if instead of waiting to execute degenerate offspring for crime, or to let them starve for their imbecility, society can prevent those who are manifestly unfit from continuing their kind. The principle that sustains compulsory vaccination is broad enough to cover cutting the Fallopian tubes. . . . Three generations of imbeciles are enough.[25]

As Holmes confided to a friend shortly after *Buck* came down, his endorsement of eugenic reform by way of upholding the law over due process and equal protection challenges "gave me pleasure."[26]

Liberal or not, social Darwinist or not, eugenic elitist or not, Holmes basked in the sunlight of the veneration that continued to come his way more and more as he got older. To help that cause further along, Harold Laski had collected Holmes's articles and addresses in a book, *Collected Legal Papers*, published in November 1920. Predictably, the reviews by Thomas Reed Powell, writing for the *Nation*, and Morris R. Cohen, writing in the *New Republic*, were laudatory. It was "an extraordinary book . . . clothed in rare nobility of language," wrote Cohen, Holmes's young friend and admirer. By the following March, the machinery of adoration was in high gear as friends from near and after joined in celebrating the old jurist's eightieth birthday, replete with flowers, telegrams, and well wishes from the likes of Learned Hand, John Wigmore, and Frankfurter. And then there was the special issue of the *Harvard Law Review*, with Holmes's photo as the frontispiece, dedicated to the justice. Dean Roscoe Pound wrote the first essay honoring their Harvard man on the Court.[27] Not to be left out, the *New Republic* lent its congratulatory wreaths as well.[28] A few years later came the Roosevelt Medal for "distinguished service to the American people on the development of public law." On receiving it from President Calvin Coolidge, Holmes commented, "[F]or five minutes you make me believe that the dream of a lifetime has come true."[29] To cap things off, Holmes's picture would later appear on the cover of *Time* magazine.[30]

---

[25] 274 U.S. at 207.

[26] Letter from OWH to Lewis Einstein, May 19, 1927, reproduced in James B. Peabody, ed., *The Holmes-Einstein Letters: Correspondence of Mr. Justice Holmes and Lewis Einstein* (New York: St. Martins Press, 1964), at 267.

[27] Frankfurter had arranged a similar Festschrift to Holmes in a 1916 issue of the *Harvard Law Review*.

[28] *See* Sheldon M. Novick, *Honorable Justice: The Life of Oliver Wendell Holmes* (New York: Bantam Doubleday Dell, 1989), at 337–38 (endnotes omitted).

[29] Qtd. in *Justice Oliver Wendell Holmes: Law and the Inner Self, supra* note 12, at 369.

[30] *Time*, March 15, 1926.

Holmes's experiment with life continued as he grew older, and so, too, did his experiment with freedom of speech.

◈

With the conceptual floodgates broken open in his *Abrams* opinion, Holmes continued to tinker with his experiment in free speech law,[31] but in ways not confined to wartime cases. In the dozen or so years that he remained on the Court after *Abrams*, the justice further fortified his free speech jurisprudence. For example, in the other Holmes-authored cases in this section – the *Burleson* case (1921), *American Column & Lumber Co. v. United States* (1921), *Leach v. Carlile* (1922), *Gitlow v. New York* (1925), and *United States v. Schwimmer* (1929) – we see him voting to vindicate the rights of all of the free speech claimants in theses five cases. Moreover, in those cases, one can detect several speech-protective refinements in his thinking:

- The dissent Holmes filed in *Burleson* both argued that the use of the mails was a legally protected free speech right and maintained that the postmaster general's legal powers must be construed narrowly when it comes to regulating expression.
- *American Column & Lumber Co. v. United States* is a case where we see Holmes discussing free speech principles in the context of an antitrust case and doing so in a way so as not to find a restraint of trade.
- In his *Leach* dissent, Holmes not only endorsed the presumption against prior restraints but did so in the context of commercial expression.
- In *Gitlow*, Holmes tapped his more speech-protective *Abrams* formulation of the clear-and-present-danger test rather than relying on how that test had been developed and applied in *Schenck*, *Frohwerk*, and *Debs*.
- In the *Schwimmer* case, the dissenting Justice stressed the elevated importance and even centrality of free speech principles generally, and likewise reaffirmed his position that we must be willing to tolerate "the thought we hate."

And then there is Justice Brandeis's jurisprudentially expansive and free speech–protective concurrence in *Whitney v. California*,[32] which Holmes joined.

---

[31] This might even be seen as constituting yet another conceptual stage in the development of Holmes's free speech jurisprudence. *See Justice Oliver Wendell Holmes: Law and the Inner Self, supra* note 12, at 445–49, 453, 607.

[32] 274 U.S. 357, 372 (Brandeis, J., concurring). *See* Ronald Collins and David Skover, "Curious Concurrence: Justice Brandeis's Vote in *Whitney v. California*," 2005 *Supreme Court Review* 333.

In *Abrams* and the free speech cases following it – those in which he authored opinions and those in which he simply voted – Holmes moved ever closer to what might loosely be called a libertarian perspective. As we will see in yet-bolder strokes, he "had developed from a judge for whom speech issues seemed incidental or trivial or secondary to common law issues into one who accorded free speech central constitutional importance."[33] Though the bold thrust of his jurisprudence seemed plain, he was sometimes inconsistent or opaque, and he sometimes traded eloquence for soundness. And then there was contradiction, which seemed to be an accepted part of his views on life and law. In that vein, the old white-moustached soldier once explained his views thusly: "[I]n the abstract, I have no very enthusiastic belief" in "favor of free speech," he told Sir Frederick Pollock, "though I hope I would die for it."[34]

❧

Holmes spent much of his time in his Eye Street home, located not far from the White House and west of Farragut Square, working in his second-floor study. There, in that space surrounded by walls of books and adjacent to his secretary's room, he prepared and penned many of the opinions that made him great. At some point in his afternoons he would take a break, put aside his legal papers, and read for pleasure. And then there were the times when he dozed off in his easy chair, letting his book fall to the floor.[35] In this home where books and matters of the mind meant everything, it was a common occurrence for Holmes and his wife, Fanny, to read aloud together, with "Dickie bird" (as he lovingly called her) usually doing the reading. By the mid-1920s they didn't socialize nearly as much as they once did, and over the years, Fanny became rather reclusive, due in real part to her failing health. Then on April 30, 1929, while the *Schwimmer* case was pending, she died. Painful as it was, Holmes took it in strong stride. "I am reconciled," he wrote to Pollock, "to my wife's death as the alternative seemed inevitably a life of nothing but pain.. . . . If I can work on for a year or two more," he added, "it is well enough – and if not, I have lived my life."[36]

---

[33] *Justice Oliver Wendell Holmes: Law and the Inner Self*, *supra* note 12, at 450.

[34] Letter from OWH to Pollock, October 26, 1919 (a few days after *Abrams* was argued), reprinted in *Holmes-Pollock Letters: The Correspondence of Mr. Justice Holmes and Sir Frederick Pollock 1874–1932*, Mark DeWolfe Howe, ed. (Cambridge, MA: Harvard University Press, 1941), at 2:27, 29.

[35] *See* John S. Monagan, *The Grand Panjandrum: Mellow Years of Justice Holmes* (Lanham, MD: University Press of America, 1988), at 36.

[36] Letter from OWH to Harold Laski, May 23, 1929, reproduced in *Holmes-Laski Letters: The Correspondence of Mr. Justice Holmes and Harold Laski, 1916–1935*, Mark DeWolfe Howe, ed. (Cambridge, MA: Harvard University Press, 1953), at 2:1152.

His experiments in life and law were winding down, and with each passing day, more and more of his friends followed Fanny's fate. Life was becoming increasingly lonely as Holmes became more and more disengaged from the struggle. To be sure, there were joyous moments – as when he was lauded in the Senate on the occasion of his eighty-ninth birthday, or when a life-size portrait of him was unveiled at the Harvard Law School. The painting, by Charles Hopkins, hung opposite that of Chief Justice John Marshall. But such occasions were never enough to return him to the vigorous give-and-take of life he had so long known. Now, with his eyesight failing and Fanny dead, he depended on his maid, Annie Mary Donnellan, to care for the household; on his coachman, Charlie Buckley, to chauffeur him around; and on his Harvard-trained secretaries to escort him on short walks or to read to him from a novel or a classical work. Otherwise, he was left to playing his favorite game – solitaire.[37]

⤚

To return to where we began at the opening of this section, recall the epigraph quote: "The purpose of the experiment is to keep the experiment going," says Mr. Menand. That is the modern idea in Holmes; that is what makes him decisively modernist; and that is what separates him from the likes of Thomas Jefferson who preceded him and Hugo Black who succeeded him. Similar to the leading pragmatists of his day, Holmes "believed that ideas are not 'out there' waiting to be discovered, but are tools . . . that people devise to cope with the world in which they find themselves." Thus, "ideas are not [so much] produced by individuals, but by groups of individuals – that ideas are social." For any variety of reasons, Holmes was of the view that "ideas do not develop according to some inner logic of their own, but are entirely dependent, like germs, on their human carriers and the environment." Accordingly, "since ideas are provisional responses to particular and [irreproducible] circumstances, *their survival depends not on their immutability but on their adaptability.*"[38]

Ironically, Holmes's survivalist take on the law of free speech remains popular and radical at the same time. It is popular in its democratic idea of the relativist value of speech, while it is also radical in its dystopian breach from the idea of transcendent truths. In this sense, there is something

---

[37] See *Grand Panjandrum*, *supra* note 35, at 55, 57, 60, 103–05, 114.
[38] *Metaphysical Club*, *supra* note 1, at xi–xii (emphasis added).

uniquely paradoxical about Holmes: He is both the hero[39] and antihero[40] of his times and our day.

It is against that backdrop – the great, the glorious, the mysterious, the monstrous, and the jurist in his twilight years – that we come to the last line of cases in the free speech jurisprudence of Mr. Justice Holmes.

The United States constitutionally may punish speech that produces or is intended to produce a clear and imminent danger that it will bring about forthwith certain substantive evils that the United States constitutionally may seek to prevent. When men have realized that time has upset many fighting faiths, they may come to believe even more than they believe the very foundations of their own conduct that the ultimate good desired is better reached by free trade in ideas – that the best test of truth is the power of the thought to get itself accepted in the competition of the market.

ABRAMS V. UNITED STATES

250 U.S. 616 (1919)
Vote: 7–2
For the majority: Clarke, J.
Argued: October 21, 22, 1919
Decided: November 10, 1919[41]
For petitioner: Harry Weinberger
For respondent: Assistant Attorney General Robert P. Stewart[42]

Jacob Abrams, Mollie Steimer, Samuel Lipman, Hyman Lachowsky, Jacob Schwartz, Gabriel Prober, and Hyman Rosansky, all Russian immigrants, were indicted by a federal grand jury for violating the Sedition Act of 1918. They were

[39] In Justice Benjamin Cardozo's words: Holmes is the "great overlord of the law and its philosophy," he is the celebrated "philosopher and the seer" of our times, and he is "the greatest of our age in the domain of jurisprudence." Benjamin Cardozo, "Mr. Justice Holmes," 44 *Harvard Law Review* 682, 691 (1931).
[40] In Professor Alschuler words: "We have walked Holmes's path and have lost our way." *Law without Values, supra* note 17, at 187.
[41] *Schenck, Frohwerk,* and *Debs* were all handed down in March 1919. *Abrams* came down several months later. "During the period between March and November, debate over the Versailles Peace Treaty prompted many Americans to realize that the war had failed to achieve the idealistic goals that justified their initial support of American intervention." *Free Speech in Its Forgotten Years, supra* note 15, at 342.
[42] "Originally, in March 1919, the brief had been assigned to Alfred Bettman and John Lord O'Brian, who had been instrumental in the enactment of the Sedition Act and its enforcement. But they had resigned in May, when the War Emergency Division closed shop. One wonders what might have happened had they remained in the Department of

tried under the Espionage Act, after tossing leaflets[43] *(one set in English, the other in Yiddish) from a rooftop in New York City. Abrams, along with a set of young Russian-Jewish immigrants, opposed the intervention of American troops in Vladivostok and Murmansk, Russia. To curb the American intervention there, the defendants called for a general strike to prevent shipments of ammunitions to Russia. Several of the defendants were sentenced to terms of up to twenty years.*

In his appellate brief, the lawyer for the petitioners, Harry Weinberger, argued among other things that the "discussion of public questions is absolutely immune under the First Amendment to the Constitution, when that is the only intention in the discussion." The framers, he continued, guaranteed such a right, – "the unabridged liberty of discussion [was] a natural right." Overt acts, not speech, argued Weinberger, could alone be punished: "It is time enough for the rightful purposes of civil government for its officers to interfere when principles break out into overt acts against peace and good order." Hence, "absolute freedom of speech is the only basis upon which the Government can stand and remain free." Counsel for the government, Assistant Attorney General Robert P. Stewart, countered by arguing that "no liberty of the press was conceived of which included the unlimited right to publish a seditious libel. No claim of that sort was ever made by a respectable person."[44]

When the matter came before the Supreme Court, it was first argued on the fifty-eighth anniversary (to the day)[45] *of the Battle of Ball's Bluff, in which Holmes fought. Thereafter, a majority upheld the convictions on two of the four counts charged. "The principal difficulty for the majority was finding the requisite intent – no small problem, since the defendants ... had opposed the wrong war. The difficulty was surmounted by imputing to the defendants the knowledge that strikes would necessarily impede the war effort against Germany, as well as operations in Russia."*[46] *Nineteen days after oral arguments, the*

Justice. Both men, but especially Bettman, had devoted their last months to urging the President to pardon or commute or reduce the sentences of those convicted under the Espionage and Sedition Acts." *Fighting Faiths, supra* note 5, at 230. Moreover, Bettman opposed the prosecution in *Abrams. Free Speech in Its Forgotten Years, supra* note 15, at 350 and n. 33.

43 The text of the leaflets is set out in the materials at the end of this case.
44 *Fighting Faiths, supra* note 5, at 229–33 (quoting briefs for petitioners and respondent).
45 It was a day Holmes always remembered. *See, e.g.,* OWH to Frederick Pollock, October 21, 1895, reproduced in *Holmes-Pollock Letters, supra* note 24, at 1:64; letter from OWH to Lewis Einstein, October 21, 1906, reproduced in James Bishop Peabody, ed., *The Holmes-Einstein Letters: Correspondence of Mr. Justice Holmes and Lewis Einstein, 1903–1935* (New York: St. Martin's Press, 1964), at 27.
46 Laurence Tribe, *American Constitutional Law,* 2nd ed. (Mineola, NY: Foundation Press, 1988), at 843.

Court, per Justice John H. Clarke, rendered its opinion against the defendants. Holmes and Brandeis dissented.

Mr. Justice Holmes, dissenting.

This indictment is founded wholly upon the publication of two leaflets which I shall describe in a moment. The first count charges a conspiracy pending the war with Germany to publish abusive language about the form of government of the United States, laying the preparation and publishing of the first leaflet as overt acts. The second count charges a conspiracy pending the war to publish language intended to bring the form of government into contempt, laying the preparation and publishing of the two leaflets as overt acts. The third count alleges a conspiracy to encourage resistance to the United States in the same war and to attempt to effectuate the purpose by publishing the same leaflets. The fourth count lays a conspiracy to incite curtailment of production of things necessary to the prosecution of the war and to attempt to accomplish it by publishing the second leaflet to which I have referred.

The first of these leaflets says that the President's cowardly silence about the intervention in Russia reveals the hypocrisy of the plutocratic gang in Washington. It intimates that "German militarism combined with allied capitalism to crush the Russian revolution" – [and] goes on that the tyrants of the world fight each other until they see a common enemy-working class enlightenment, when they combine to crush it; and that now militarism and capitalism combined, though not openly, to crush the Russian revolution. It says that there is only one enemy of the workers of the world and that is capitalism; that it is a crime for workers of America, etc., to fight the workers' republic of Russia, and ends "Awake! Awake, you workers of the world! Revolutionists." A note adds[,] "It is absurd to call us pro-German. We hate and despise German militarism more than do you hypocritical tyrants. We have more reason for denouncing German militarism than has the coward of the White House."

The other leaflet, headed "Workers-Wake Up," with abusive language says that America together with the Allies will march for Russia to help the Czecko-Slovaks in their struggle against the Bolsheviki, and that this time the hypocrites shall not fool the Russian emigrants and friends of Russia in America. It tells the Russian [immigrants] that they now must spit in the face of the false military propaganda by which their sympathy and help to the prosecution of the war have been called forth and says that with the money they have lent or are going to lend "they will make bullets not only for the Germans but also for the Workers Soviets of Russia," and further, "Workers in the ammunition factories, you are producing bullets, bayonets, cannon to murder not only the

Germans, but also your dearest, best, who are in Russia fighting for freedom." It then appeals to the same Russian emigrants at some length not to consent to the "inquisitionary expedition in Russia," and says that the destruction of the Russian revolution is "the politics of the march on Russia." The leaflet winds up by saying "Workers, our reply to this barbaric intervention has to be a general strike!" and after a few words on the spirit of revolution, exhortations not to be afraid, and some usual tall talk ends "Woe unto those who will be in the way of progress. Let solidarity live! The Rebels."

No argument seems to be necessary to show that these pronunciamentos in no way attack the form of government of the United States, or that they do not support either of the first two counts. What little I have to say about the third count may be postponed until I have considered the fourth. With regard to that it seems too plain to be denied that the suggestion to workers in the ammunition factories that they are producing bullets to murder their dearest, and the further advocacy of a general strike, both in the second leaflet, do urge curtailment of production of things necessary to the prosecution of the war within the meaning of the Act of May 16, 1918. But to make the conduct criminal that statute requires that it should be "with intent by such curtailment to cripple or hinder the United States in the prosecution of the war." It seems to me that no such intent is proved.

I am aware of course that the word "intent" as vaguely used in ordinary legal discussion means no more than knowledge at the time of the act that the consequences said to be intended will ensue. Even less than that will satisfy the general principle of civil and criminal liability. A man may have to pay damages, may be sent to prison, at common law might be hanged, if at the time of his act he knew facts from which common experience showed that the consequences would follow, whether he individually could foresee them or not. But, when words are used exactly, a deed is not done with intent to produce a consequence unless that consequence is the aim of the deed. It may be obvious, and obvious to the actor, that the consequence will follow, and he may be liable for it even if he regrets it, but he does not do the act with intent to produce it unless the aim to produce it is the proximate motive of the specific act, although there may be some deeper motive behind.

It seems to me that this statute must be taken to use its words in a strict and accurate sense. They would be absurd in any other. A patriot might think that we were wasting money on aeroplanes, or making more cannon of a certain kind than we needed, and might advocate curtailment with success, yet even if it turned out that the curtailment hindered and was thought by other minds to have been obviously likely to hinder the United States in the prosecution of the war, no one would hold such conduct a crime. I admit that my illustration does not answer all that might be said but it is enough to show what I think and to let me pass to a more important aspect of the case. I refer to the First Amendment to the Constitution that Congress shall make no law abridging the freedom of speech.

I never have seen any reason to doubt that the questions of law that alone were before this Court in the cases of *Schenck*, *Frohwerk*, and *Debs* were rightly decided. I do not doubt for a moment that by the same reasoning that would justify punishing persuasion to murder, the United States constitutionally may punish speech that produces or is intended to produce a clear and imminent danger that it will bring about forthwith certain substantive evils that the United States constitutionally may seek to prevent. The power undoubtedly is greater in time of war than in time of peace because war opens dangers that do not exist at other times.

But as against dangers peculiar to war, as against others, the principle of the right to free speech is always the same. It is only the present danger of immediate evil or an intent to bring it about that warrants Congress in setting a limit to the expression of opinion where private rights are not concerned. Congress certainly cannot forbid all effort to change the mind of the country. Now nobody can suppose that the surreptitious publishing of a silly leaflet by an unknown man, without more, would present any immediate danger that its opinions would hinder the success of the government arms or have any appreciable tendency to do so. Publishing those opinions for the very purpose of obstructing, however, might indicate a greater danger and at any rate would have the quality of an attempt. So I assume that the second leaflet if published for the purposes alleged in the fourth count might be punishable. But it seems pretty clear to me that nothing less than that would bring these papers within the scope of this law. An actual intent in the sense that I have explained is necessary to constitute an attempt, where a further act of the same individual is required to complete the substantive crime, for reasons given in *Swift & Co. v. United States*. It is necessary where the success of the attempt depends upon others because if that intent is not present the actor's aim may be accomplished without bringing about the evils sought to be checked. An intent to prevent interference with the revolution in Russia might have been satisfied without any hindrance to carrying on the war in which we were engaged.

I do not see how anyone can find the intent required by the statute in any of the defendant's words. The second leaflet is the only one that affords even a foundation for the charge, and there, without invoking the hatred of German militarism expressed in the former one, it is evident from the beginning to the end that the only object of the paper is to help Russia and stop American intervention there against the popular government – not to impede the United

States in the war that it was carrying on. To say that two phrases taken literally might import a suggestion of conduct that would have interference with the war as an indirect and probably undesired effect seems to me by no means enough to show an attempt to produce that effect.

I return for a moment to the third count. That charges an intent to provoke resistance to the United States in its war with Germany. Taking the clause in the statute that deals with that in connection with the other elaborate provisions of the Act, I think that resistance to the United States means some forcible act of opposition to some proceeding of the United States in pursuance of the war. I think the intent must be the specific intent that I have described and for the reasons that I have given I think that no such intent was proved or existed in fact. I also think that there is no hint at resistance to the United States as I construe the phrase.

In this case sentences of twenty years imprisonment have been imposed[47] for the publishing of two leaflets that I believe the defendants had as much right to publish as the Government has to publish the Constitution of the United States now vainly invoked by them. Even if I am technically wrong and enough can be squeezed from these poor and puny anonymities to turn the color of legal litmus paper; I will add, even if what I think the necessary intent were shown; the most nominal punishment seems to me all that possible could be inflicted, unless the defendants are to be made to suffer not for what the indictment alleges but for the creed that they avow – a creed that I believe to be the creed of ignorance and immaturity when honestly held, as I see no reason to doubt that it was held here but which, although made the subject of examination at the trial, no one has a right even to consider in dealing with the charges before the Court.

Persecution for the expression of opinions seems to me perfectly logical.[48] If you have no doubt of your premises or your power and want a certain result with all your heart you naturally express your wishes in law and sweep away all opposition. To allow opposition by speech seems to indicate that you think the speech impotent, as when a man says that he has squared the circle, or that you do not care whole heartedly for the result, or that you doubt either your power or your premises. But when men have realized that time has upset

---

[47] For a detailed account of the trial and a critique of it, see "A Contemporary State Trial," *supra* note 10. – *Ed.*

[48] The free speech implications of this line are discussed in Martin Redish, *The Logic of Persecution: Free Expression and the McCarthy Era* (Stanford, CA: Stanford University Press, 2005). – *Ed.*

many fighting faiths,[49] they may come to believe even more than they believe the very foundations of their own conduct that the ultimate good desired is better reached by free trade in ideas – that the best test of truth is the power of the thought to get itself accepted in the competition of the market,[50] and that truth is the only ground upon which their wishes safely can be carried out. That at any rate is the theory of our Constitution. It is an experiment, as all life is an experiment. Every year if not every day we have to wager our salvation upon some prophecy based upon imperfect knowledge. While that experiment is part of our system I think that we should be eternally vigilant against attempts to check the expression of opinions that we loathe and believe to be fraught with death, unless they so imminently threaten immediate interference with the lawful and pressing purposes of the law that an immediate check is required to save the country. I wholly disagree with the argument of the Government that the First Amendment left the common law as to seditious libel in force. History seems to me against the notion. I had conceived that the United States through many years had shown its repentance for the Sedition Act of 1798 by repaying fines that it imposed. Only the emergency that makes it immediately dangerous to leave the correction of evil counsels to time warrants making any exception to the sweeping command, "Congress shall make no law abridging the freedom of speech." Of course I am speaking only of expressions of opinion and exhortations, which were all that were uttered here, but I regret that I cannot put into more impressive words my belief that in their conviction upon this indictment the defendants were deprived of their rights under the Constitution of the United States.

Mr. Justice Brandeis concurs with the foregoing opinion.

CORRESPONDENCE

The letter here was written after the Abrams *case was argued, but before Holmes published his dissent in it.*

[49] Holmes had used this expression earlier in private correspondence. *See* letter from OWH to Lewis Einstein, November 9, 1913, reproduced in *Holmes-Einstein Letters, supra* note 45, at 81, 82. – *Ed.*

[50] Holmes employed the phrase "competition of the open market" as early as 1870. *See* OWH, "Codes and the Arrangement of the Law," 5 *American Law Review* 1, 3 (1870), reproduced in Sheldon M. Novick, ed., *The Collected Works of Justice Holmes* (Chicago: University of Chicago Press, 1995), at 1:212–13. Later, in 1913, he spoke of the "beliefs that have triumphed in the battle of ideas." OWH, "Law and the Court," Speech at a Dinner of the Harvard Law School Association of New York, February 15, 1913, reproduced in *ibid.* at 3:505, 507. – *Ed.*

To Harold J. Laski
October 26, 1919

Dear Laski:

... I fear we have less freedom of speech here than they have in England. Little as I believe in it as a theory I hope I would die for it and I go as far as anyone whom I regard as competent to form an opinion, in favor of it. Of course when I say I don't believe in it as a theory I don't mean that I do believe in the opposite as a theory. But on their premises it seems to be logical in the Catholic Church to kill heretics and the Puritans to whip Quakers – and I see nothing more wrong in it from our ultimate standards than I do in killing Germans when we are at war. When you are thoroughly convinced that you are right – wholeheartedly desire and end – and have no doubt of your power to accomplish it – I see nothing but municipal regulations to interfere with you using your power to accomplish it. The sacredness of human life is a formula that is good only inside a system of law – and so of the rest – all which apart from its *banalité* I fear seems cold talk if you have been made to feel popular displeasure. I should not be cold about that – nor do I in any way shrink from saying what I think – but I can't spare the energy necessary to deal with extra legal themes. . . .

Affly yours,
O. W. H.

Holmes-Laski Letters: The Correspondence of Mr. Justice Holmes and Harold J. Laski, Mark DeWolfe Howe, ed. (Cambridge, MA: Harvard University Press, 1953), at 1:217–18.

To Frederick Pollock
Washington, November 6, 1919

Dear F. P:

... Today I am stirred about a case that I can't mention yet to which I have sent around a dissent that was prepared to be ready as soon as the opinion was circulated. I feel sure that the majority will very highly disapprove of my saying what I think, but as yet it seems to me my duty. No doubt I shall hear about it on Saturday at our conference and perhaps be persuaded to shut up, but I can't expect it.

Holmes-Pollock Letters: The Correspondence of Mr. Justice Holmes and Sir Frederick Pollock, Mark DeWolfe Howe, ed. (Cambridge, MA: Harvard University Press, 1942), at 2:29 (footnotes omitted).

To Frederick Pollock
Washington, December 14, 1919

Dear Pollock:

As to the *Abrams* case your puzzle as to a special act of Congress being necessary is answered by the consideration that there are no crimes against the U.S. except by statute. I think it possible that I was wrong in thinking that there was no evidence on the Fourth Count in consequence of my attention being absorbed by the two leaflets that were set forth. But I still am of the opinion that I was right, if I am right in what I devoutly believe, that an actual intent to hinder the U.S. in its war *with* Germany must be proved.

Holmes-Pollock Letters: The Correspondence of Mr. Justice Holmes and Sir Frederick Pollock, Mark DeWolfe Howe, ed. (Cambridge, MA: Harvard University Press, 1942), at 1:32 (emphasis in original).

To Harold Laski
December 27, 1919

My dear Laski:

... Yesterday I received an article on my dissent in the *Abrams* case – written in *The Review*[51] [that] my secretary[52] tells me is a sheet intended to counteract the revolutionary influence of the *New Republic*. It is somewhat surprising to me that even under cover of the anonymous one should think it safe to give an off-hand condemnation of the work of a man who may be supposed to know enough of his job not to fall into obvious errors. He would not accuse me of being uncandid but he notes that I have omitted a most pregnant sentence quoted by [Justice] Clarke. He seemingly does not note that the sentence was from another sheet not mentioned in the indictment whereas I was discussing the leaflet laid as an overt act. It was, I assumed, but I ought to have made it clearer, necessary that the overt act laid should be proved to be done with

[51] "Justice Holmes's Dissent," *The Review*, 636, December 6, 1919.
[52] Law clerks were then known as secretaries. – *Ed.*

intent to forward a conspiracy to interfere with the war with Germany – and I thought it plain on the face of the document that it was written *alio intuitu*.[53] On that question I thought what was said at other times immaterial. The whole piece seemed to me incompetent – and I don't think that my opinion depended at all on the article being adverse. . . .

Holmes-Laski Letters, supra, at 1:229.

To Lewis Einstein
Beverly Farms, July 11, 1925

Dear Einstein,

. . . I had my whack on free speech some years ago in the case of one Abrams, and therefore did no more than lean to that and add that an idea is always an incitement. To show the ardor of the writer is not a sufficient reason for judging him. I regarded my view as simply upholding the right of a donkey to drool. But the usual notion is that you are free to say what you like if you don't shock *me*. Of course the value of the constitutional right is only when you do shock people. . . .

The Holmes-Einstein Letters: Correspondence of Mr. Justice Holmes and Lewis Einstein, 1903–1935, James Bishop Peabody, ed. (New York: St. Martin's Press, 1964), at 244.

COMMENTARY

Waiting for the right case – Writing in 1941, Zechariah Chafee Jr. noted: "Looking backwards . . . we see that Justice Holmes was biding his time until the Court should have before it a conviction so clearly wrong as to let him speak out his deepest thoughts about the First Amendment." Zechariah Chafee Jr., *Free Speech in the United States* (Cambridge, MA: Harvard University Press, 1941), at 86.

The centrality of the Abrams *dissent* – As Professor Lee Bollinger has observed, "[W]ithin the legal community today, the *Abrams* dissent of Holmes stands as one of the central organizing pronouncements for our contemporary vision of free speech." Lee C. Bollinger, *The Tolerant Society: Freedom of Speech and Extremist Speech in America* (New York: Oxford University Press, 1986), at 18. Holmes's dissent, it has been said, "is at the root of modern First Amendment

---

[53] Translated: "From another point of view." – *Ed.*

protections. It has also been called one of the foundation stones of modern liberalism." Sheldon M. Novick, *Honorable Justice: The Life of Oliver Wendell Holmes* (New York: Dell Publishing, 1989), at 473 n. 87. Vincent Blasi, an eminent First Amendment scholar, has labeled Holmes's dissent "canonical." The opinion, he added, "may be the single most influential judicial opinion ever written on" the subject of freedom of speech. Vincent Blasi, "*Propter Honoris Respectum*: Reading Holmes through the Lens of Schauer: The *Abrams* Dissent," 72 *Notre Dame Law Review* 1343 (1997). Much to the same effect, Anthony Lewis has observed: "The Supreme Court's recognition of freedom of expression as a paramount constitutional value began with Justice Holmes's dissent in *Abrams v. United States*. And what a beginning. Holmes boldly asserted, as no judge had before him, that the First Amendment had wiped out the common law of seditious libel." Anthony Lewis, *Make No Law: The Sullivan Case and the First Amendment* (New York: Random House, 1991), at 80.

Praise from the New Republic – An editorial in the *New Republic*, a magazine typically friendly toward Holmes, expressed predictable support for the *Abrams* dissent: "American educators and lawyers no longer act as if the government and Constitution of the United States is, as Justice Holmes says, an experiment which needs for its own safety an agency of self-adjustment and which seeks it in the utmost possible freedom of opinion." "The Call to Toleration," *New Republic*, November 26, 1919, at 360.

Holmesian rhetoric – Of Holmes's dissent in *Abrams*, Felix Frankfurter predicted: "It is not reckless prophecy to assume that his famous dissenting opinion in the *Abrams* case will live as long as English prose retains its power to move." Felix Frankfurter, *Mr. Justice Holmes and the Supreme Court* (Cambridge, MA: Harvard University Press, 1938), 54–55. In Judge Richard Posner's estimation, Holmes "was the most eloquent judge who ever wrote; perhaps his only peers as American masters of prose are Abraham Lincoln and Henry James." Richard Posner, *Cardozo: A Study in Reputation* (Chicago: University of Chicago Press, 1990), at 138–39. Of the "great 'literary' judges," Posner considers Holmes the finest of "legal stylists." Even so, some of Holmes's greatest of literary triumphs are not, in Posner's opinion, "well reasoned" opinions or "logically organized" or attentive to the "factual record," though his "rhetorical tricks" may be popular because readers are charmed by "enchanting rhetoric." Richard Posner, *Law and Literature*, rev. ed. (Cambridge, MA: Harvard University Press, 1998), at 266, 267, 271–72, 367.

It has also been observed that some of the most colorful passages in the *Abrams* dissent are somewhat macabre in their orientation. "The whiff of decay and death presides over the whole *Abrams* passage – fighting, wagering, transience. Judges, like citizens, should be consecrated figures who can touch things fraught with death without being harmed – and if they bear scars, that only adds to their luster. As evolutionary processes are governed by chance, so ethical processes are governed by gambling." John Durham Peters, *Courting the Abyss: Free Speech and the Liberal Tradition* (Chicago: University of Chicago Press, 2005), at 149.

The evolution of Holmes's Darwinian metaphors – In ways reminiscent of some of his earlier writings (e.g., "The Gas-Stokers' Strike," in Part II) and opinions (e.g., *Vegelahn v. Guntner*, in Part III), here we see Holmes qualifying "one Darwinian metaphor (survival of the fittest in the political process) with another more protective of freedom of expression (survival of the fittest in the marketplace of ideas)." Albert W. Alschuler, *Law without Values* (Chicago: University of Chicago Press, 2000), at 52–53. Although he was probably well aware of Darwin's general ideas, it should be noted that Holmes had not read, as far as we know, Darwin until 1907. *See* Mark DeWolfe Howe, *Justice Oliver Wendell Holmes: The Shaping Years, 1841–1870* (Cambridge, MA: Harvard University Press, 1957), at 1:156, 302 n. 46 (citing letter to Clara Sherwood Stevens, April 28, 1907).

Market metaphor: Historical origins – In one way or another, Holmes's marketplace metaphor traced back centuries to the writings of the English poet and political thinker John Milton. In *Areopagitica* (1644), Milton wrote: "And though all the winds of doctrine were let loose to play upon the earth, so Truth be in the field, we do injuriously by licensing and prohibiting to misdoubt her strength. Let her and Falsehood grapple; who ever knew Truth put to the worse in a free and open encounter?" John Milton, *Areopagitica*, with commentary by Sir Richard C. Jebb (Cambridge, UK: Cambridge University Press, 1918), at 58. John Stuart Mill expressed similar ideas in 1859. See his *On Liberty*, David Bromwich and George Kateb, eds. (New Haven, CT: Yale University Press, 2003), at 86–120. *See generally* David S. Bogen, "The Free Speech Metamorphosis of Mr. Justice Holmes," 11 *Hofstra Law Review* 97, 120, 188 (1982) (also listing influence of Charles Sanders). In May 1866, the young Holmes met and then dined with John Stuart Mill. The event is recounted in Mark DeWolfe Howe's *Justice Holmes: The Shaping Years, 1841–1870* (Cambridge, MA: Harvard University Press, 1957), at 226–27. And then there was Harold Laski's recently published *Authority in the Modern State* (New Haven, CT: Yale University Press, 1919), which was dedicated to Holmes and Frankfurter. In that work, Laski wrote that it "is in the clash of ideas that we shall find the means of truth. There is no other safeguard of progress." *See also* Isaac Kramnick and Barry Sheerman, *Harold Laski: A Life* (New York: Allen Lane,

Penguin Press, 1993), at 127; Jeffrey O'Connell and Thomas E. O'Connell, *Friendships across the Ages: Johnson and Boswell; Holmes and Laski* (Lanham, MD: Lexington Books, 2008), at 112–13.

The "marketplace of ideas": Origin of the precise phrase – Although the phrase "marketplace of ideas" is all too frequently attributed to Holmes and his dissent in *Abrams*, the precise phrase was not used in an appellate court opinion until decades later by Justice William O. Douglas in his concurrence in *United States v. Rumely*, 345 U.S. 41, 56 (1953), which cited neither Holmes nor his *Abrams* dissent. Later, Justice William Brennan employed it, sans any reference to Holmes, in a concurrence in *Lamont v. Postmaster General*, 381 U.S. 301, 308 (1965), and later still in *Keyishian v. Board of Regents*, 385 U.S. 589, 603 (1967), wherein he wrote: "The classroom is peculiarly the 'marketplace of ideas.'" The use of the metaphor is discussed further in the Epilogue of this volume. For a discussion of the use of metaphors in the *Abrams* case, *see* Haig A. Bosmajian, *Metaphor and Reason in Judicial Opinions* (Carbondale, IL: Southern Illinois University Press, 1992), at 49–72.

Meanings of the market metaphor – "Holmes'[s] opinion [in *Abrams*] builds strong protection for speech on two foundations: [1] skepticism about prevailing understandings of truth and [2] the metaphor of 'competition in the market.' Truth itself is defined by reference to what emerges through 'free trade in ideas.' The competition of the market is the governing conception of free speech. On his view, politics itself is a market, like any other. Holmes does not appear to place any special premium on political discussion. . . . His reasoning seems to apply to all speech, whether political or not. Finally, the value of speech is instrumental in the sense that it is connected with the emergence of truth. Holmes does not suggest that freedom of speech is a good in itself." Cass Sunstein, *Democracy and the Problem of Free Speech* (New York: Free Press, 1993), at 25.

Critical of the market metaphor as Holmes employed it, Sunstein added: "In all his writings on free speech, Holmes pays little attention to the appropriate conditions under which free trade in ideas will ensure truth, a gap that is probably attributable to his skepticism about whether truth, as an independent value, is at issue at all. Thus Holmes concludes one of his great free speech opinions [*Gitlow*] with the remarkable suggestion that if, "in the long run, the beliefs expressed in the proletarian dictatorship are destined to be accepted by the dominant forces of the community, the only meaning of free speech is that they should be given their chance and have their way.'" *Ibid.* at 26 (footnote omitted).

Consistent with the foregoing opinion, Steven Shiffrin has noted: "The marketplace analogy was an elegant turn employed in a good cause, but there is no excuse for elevating it into a guiding framework. Free speech is an important principle, but there is no reason to assume that what emerges in the 'market' is usually right or that the 'market' is the best test of truth. Societal pressures to conform are strong, and incentives to keep quiet about the corruptions of power are often great. What emerges in the market might better be viewed as a testimonial to power than as a reflection of truth." Steven H. Shiffrin, *Dissent, Injustice, and the Meanings of America* (Princeton, NJ: Princeton University Press, 1999), at 6.

Others, such as Professor Blasi, interpret the market metaphor and its First Amendment significance differently and therefore view it in a more favorable light. *See "Propter Honoris Respectum," supra*, at 1359. *See generally* Steven L. Winter, "Re-Embodying Law," 58 *Mercer Law Review* 869, 884–87 (2007).

Marketplace approach: The lesser of two evils – "It might be argued," Professor Vincent Blasi maintains, "that although an open marketplace of ideas may not lead to truth, any governmental intervention in the market is likely to exacerbate rather than ameliorate the preexisting distortions, thereby adding still another hindrance to the quest for truth. Furthermore, a policy of non-regulation at least leaves open the theoretical possibility that error can be corrected by persistent and persuasive appeals to the public consciousness, whereas a fully implemented policy of selective suppression permits some orthodoxies to be perpetuated in the face of the irrefutable evidence of their falsity. Thus, diversity of expression can be considered a primary value under-lying the First Amendment. . . . " Vincent Blasi, "The Checking Value in First Amendment Theory" 2 *American Bar Foundation Research Journal* 521 (1977).

Marketplace failures – In Blasi's view, "Holmes was a notorious skeptic. To him, 'truth' apparently meant little more than an equilibrium of doubt, folly, and prejudice. The marketplace-of-ideas concept," he added, "is sometimes equated with a rigorous truth-determining process, and when this happens the concept is generally found wanting as a persuasive contemporary rationale for free speech. Few would deny that there are such serious structural distortions in the ideological market that the economist's ideal of perfect competition is hardly approached. Indeed, if the forming of a consensus can ever be likened to the setting of a price – a dubious proposition in itself – the market in ideas is probably best described as one of monolithic competition or oligopoly. Moreover, the market structure with regard to ideas is likely to prove every bit as resilient in the face of trust-busting efforts as have the entrenched market structures in other countries. The case for freedom of expression is an uneasy one if it depends on the claim that the collective decisions that result from the existing or any reasonably foreseeable process of opinion formation are likely to be wise, to ascertain some objectively verifiable reality, or to be 'true' in any other significant sense." "The Checking Value in First Amendment Theory," *supra*, at 521. *See also* his *"Propter Honoris Respectum,"* *supra*, at 1357–58.

The old market metaphor and the new market – "For all the power it has exercised over free speech theory since *Abrams*, the marketplace of ideas metaphor has done little to keep pace with changes in economic theory. Although criticisms of the marketplace of ideas metaphor have mirrored – and in many instances explicitly adopted – criticisms of the neoclassical view of a perfectly efficient market, defenders of the metaphor have not yet responded – as their economist counterparts have – by adopting a view of the 'marketplace' that takes into account the existence of transaction costs and the institutions that mediate them." Employing the new-institutional-economics model of analysis, the author develops an approach to free speech that attempts to do just that. *See* Joseph Blocher, "Institutions in the Marketplace of Ideas," 57 *Duke Law Journal* 821, 887 (2008). For a further discussion of this and related points, *see* the Epilogue.

The marketplace argument and other First Amendment values – "[C]ourts that invoke the marketplace model of the first amendment justify free expression because of the aggregate benefits to society, and not because an individual speaker receives a particular benefit. Courts that focus their concern on the audience rather than the speaker relegate free expression to an instrumental value, a means toward some other goal, rather than a value onto itself. Once free expression is viewed solely as an instrumental value, however, it is easier to allow government regulation of speech if society as a whole 'benefits' from a regulated system of expression." Stanley Ingber, "The Marketplace of Ideas: A Legitimizing Myth," 1984 *Duke Law Journal* 1, 4–5.

Sharp criticism of Holmes's dissent from military quarter – Shortly after *Abrams* was decided, Dean John H. Wigmore (a friend of Holmes and noted scholar in the law of evidence) published an impassioned article in the *Illinois Law Review* highly critical of Holmes's dissent in *Abrams*. Here are some excerpts from that article by Colonel Wigmore followed by Holmes's correspondence referring to the article. Wigmore, it bears noting, served proudly in the Reserve Corps of the Judge Advocate General's Office during World War I:

"The Minority Opinion in *Abrams v. United States*... represents poor law and poor policy; and I wish to point out its dangerous implications.... The specific and concrete actions... urged [by the petitioners in *Abrams*] are reducible to these: (1) A concerted general strike, or cessation of work; (2) particularly by workers in war-munitions factories; (3) with such armed violence that the

American troops remaining in the United States would be kept at home to oppose this violence and to preserve civic order. These three things stare out in plain words. Only the willfully blind could refuse to see them.... What was the attitude of the Supreme Court" as to the matters stated above?

"The majority of seven...held that there was 'competent and substantial evidence before the jury, fairly tending to sustain the verdict of guilty.'.... There is nothing further to say as to the majority opinion. The minority of two held that there was no proof of intent to commit such offenses.... [Justices Holmes's dissent, joined by Justice Brandeis,] is shocking in its obtuse indifference to the vital issues at stake in August, 1918, and in it is ominous in its portent of like indifference to pending and coming issues...."

At this point, Dean Wigmore took exception to the dissent's analysis of the evidence concerning "the intent to provoke *resistance to the United States in war*" and to the "intent to *curtail production of munitions*": "Now, as to this interpretation of the intent of the circulars, and of the danger of the acts urged in the circular, argument is useless. The opposite interpretations of the majority and the minority were due, not to genuine ambiguities in the language, but to differences of temperament and attitude towards the issues involved. A pre-existing attitude of the minority disinclined them to interpret the facts as the majority did. You cannot argue with a state of mind. But you can point out its nature and its portent. Let us look a moment at the military situation of America in August, 1918, to see what issues the Minority Opinion attitude contemplated with such indifference."

Wigmore then went on to argue that the petitioners' circulars calling for a curtailment of munitions production in 1918 constituted "a 'present danger' to the fighting forces": "By March, 1917, intelligent America had realized what was at stake in the European contest. A ruthless military caste had inspired the Germans to dominate the world by force, at any cost to life, treasure, honor, and decency.... The whole spirit and conduct of the German cause, from start to finish, was the egoistic brutal will to bruise, smash, and destroy every other interest, however worthy in itself, which interfered in the slightest with the most trifling will of the German. That was the issue before the civilized world. And it was a supreme moral issue. There was but one side to take: and America took it...."

Wigmore stressed how "gloomy" things looked from March to June 1918 for the forces opposing German aggression. By July of that year, however, there was some hope, thanks to American success stopping the "fifth German offensive": "The civilized world's task was now to use this fortunate breathing space to turn defensive into offensive, and to gain real victory. Two million American troops were in France or on their way; two million more were in training; and two million more were in sight, under the new Man-Power Act of August 30. What remained was to supply them with munitions. On this supply depended the future of this tremendous issue."

"Rifles, machine guns, artillery, and ammunition had been slow in their starting pace. The needful speed was not reached until the summer of 1918. Only by the spring of 1918 were rifles being turned out at the speed of about 200,000 a month. Machine guns were coming at 10,000 a month in April and 25,000 a month in August. Units of artillery rose from 100 a month in May to 300 a month in September. But, for the enlarged American army that was ready to continue the initial success of the Allied offensive of July–October, 1918, the supply never equaled the need, until the end of September. About that date the huge and dogged labors of the munitions workers began to show results. It became plain that safety was in sight. If the pace of the summer were kept up, the American forces soon to be available for the field would be adequately supplied throughout the coming campaign with the needed quantity of munitions. . . .

"It was during this same crucial August, 1918, then, that Abrams and this band of alien parasites, and a hundred other such bands, were doing all in their power to curtail this production and cripple our fighting men. Every load of rifles less meant more hopelessness for the cause of world-morality and world-safety. . . .

" . . . In a period when the fate of the civilized world hung in the balance, how could the Minority Opinion interpret law and conduct in such a way as to let loose men who were doing their hardest to paralyze the supreme war efforts of our country?"

Next, Dean Wigmore proceeded to critique Holmes's view of free speech as it related to the urgencies of the time. The dissent's purported concern for "[t]ruth . . . shows a blindness to the deadly fact that meantime the 'power of the thought' of these circulars might well 'get itself accepted in the competition of the market,' by munitions workers, so as to lose the war; in which case, the academic victory which Truth, 'the ultimate good,' might later secure in the market, would be too 'ultimate' to have any practical value for a defeated America.

"This disquisition of Truth seems sadly out of place. To weigh in juxta-position the dastardly sentiments of these circulars and the great theme of world-justice for which our armies were sacrificing themselves, and then to assume the sacred cause of Truth as equally involved in both, is to mis-use high ideals. [If the dissent were to have become law, it] would have ended by letting our soldiers die helpless in France, through our anxiety to protect the distribution of a leaflet whose sole purpose was to cut off the soldiers' munitions and supplies. How would this advance the cause of Truth? . . . "

Wigmore likewise disagreed with Holmes as to what extent free speech could be limited in times of crisis. When a nation is at war, Wigmore wrote, "all principles of normal internal order may be suspended. As property may be taken and corporal service may be conscripted, so liberty of speech may be limited or suppressed, so far as deemed needful for the successful conduct of the war....

"Hence, *the moral right of the majority to enter upon the war imports the moral right to secure success by suppressing public agitation against the completion of the struggle.* If a company of soldiers in war-time on their way to the front were halted for rest in the public highway, and a disaffected citizen, going among them, were to begin his harangue: 'Boys! This is a bad war! We ought not to be in it! And you ought not to be in it!' – the state would have a moral right to step promptly up to that man and smite him on the mouth. So would any well-meaning citizen, for that matter. And that moral right is the basis of the Espionage Act, in its application to these circulars...."

In peacetime, by contrast, Wigmore felt that the case was "different. Here, the 'free trade in ideas' may be left to signify unlicensed ventilation of the most extreme views, sane or insane, on any subject whatsoever." And on that score, Wigmore argued, America enjoys ample freedom of expression to *discuss* ideas. Even so, he continued, "[T]he constitutional guarantee of freedom of speech is being invoked more and more in misuse. It represents the unfair protection much desired by impatient and fanatical minorities – fanatically committed to some new revolutionary belief, and impatient of the usual process of rationally converting the majority....

"The portent of the Minority Opinion is an unpleasant one. It leaves us to infer that little indeed would be safe from licensed turbulence, if the doctrines of [the dissent] were generally sanctioned by the courts. This 'free trade in ideas' may violently upturn – what? Well, even the entire constitutional fabric itself. Why? Because, calmly says the Minority Opinion, 'that at any rate is the theory of the Constitution. *It is an experiment,* as all life is an experiment....'

"In the transcendental realms of philosophic and historical discussion by closet jurists, these expressions might pass. But when found publicly recorded in an opinion of the Supreme Guardians of that Constitution, licensing propaganda which in the next case before the Court may be directed against the Constitution itself, this language is ominous indeed." John H. Wigmore, "*Abrams v. U.S.*: Freedom of Speech and Freedom of Thuggery in War-Time and in Peace-Time," 14 *Illinois Law Review* 539 (1920) (paragraph indentation omitted in places).

ॐ

Of the differences between Wigmore and Holmes, Professor Richard Polenberg has noted the following: "Where Holmes talked about relativity, freedom, and experimentation, Wigmore talked about continuity, order, and stability. Where Holmes welcomed a certain turbulence in public affairs, Wigmore favored uninterrupted tranquility. Holmes searched for a standard that would preserve the individual's right to freedom of speech while protecting society against a 'clear and present danger.' Wigmore accepted a formula that extinguished free speech in time of war, and that left it flickering dimly in time of peace. Wigmore could well have quoted [a] remark of [Edmund] Burke's: 'What is liberty without wisdom, and without virtue? It is the greatest of all possible evils; for it is folly, vice and madness, without tuition or restraint.'" Richard Polenberg, *Fighting Faiths: The* Abrams *Case, The Supreme Court, and Free Speech* (New York: Viking, 1987), 256 [*quoting* Edmund Burke, *Reflections on the Revolution in France* (1790)].

CORRESPONDENCE

To Felix Frankfurter
Washington, D.C.
April 12, 1920

Dear Frankfurter,

. . . The other day Laski adverted to something Wigmore's and previously, Wigmore had intimated in a letter that something of his would appear, as I inferred, *apropos* of or suggested by the *Abrams* case. Do you know of any such matters? I have seen nothing from his hand for a long time except the letter above mentioned. If you do know of such a piece please let me know what and where it is as I always want to see what Wigmore says. . . .

To Oliver Wendell Holmes
Rochester, New York
April 19, 1920

Dear Justice Holmes,

. . . Which takes me to Wigmore. The poor man has not yet come out of his uniform and thinks the War is still on. So he has let a perfect diatribe against your *Abrams* opinion in the April *Illinois Law Review* – the same number that contains a measured but enthusiastic analysis of your opinion. I'm rather sad about Wigmore – it's the kind of recklessness that he not infrequently manifests. It's [nonetheless] saddening that a mind like his should be so violent and so tempestuous. All through the war he was hell-bent, and humorless beyond words but I had hoped the "militaristic" virus would wear off. It hasn't. You'll be interested in a paper on the *Abrams* case by my colleague Chafee in the forthcoming *Harvard Law Review*. [Chafee, "A Contemporary State Trial – The United States v. Jacob Abrams et al.," 30 *Harvard Law Review* 747 (1920)]

To Felix Frankfurter
Washington, D.C.
April 25, 1920

Dear Frankfurter,

. . . I got Wigmore's piece after you told me where it was and glanced over it on the bench but came to the conclusion that it wasn't reasoning but emotion. He certainly got the military sting good and hard – he was a damned sight more a soldier than I ever was and I shouldn't be surprised to hear him tell me that I didn't understand patriotism as I inferred that he thought I didn't understand the emergencies of war. . . .[54] Absolute beliefs are a rum thing. I always wonder at a man who takes himself seriously all the time. . . . I have been surprised at some of Wigmore's *pronunciamentos* before but I remember noting how tremendously military his bearing was, in uniform. . . .

Holmes and Frankfurter, Their Correspondence, 1913–1934, Robert M. Mennel and Christine L. Compston, eds. (Hanover, NH: University Press of New England 1996), at 85–88 (footnotes omitted).

To Frederick Pollock
Washington, D.C.
April 25, 1920

Dear Pollock:

. . . Wigmore in the *Ill. Law Rev.* goes for me *ex cathedra* as to my dissent in the *Abrams case*. You didn't agree with it, but Wigmore's explosion struck

[54] Although Holmes wrote to a friend that "doubtless" Wigmore knew more about the law than he did, the Civil War veteran added, "but I think I know a little bit more about war." Qtd in Gary J. Aichele, *Oliver Wendell Holmes, Jr.: Soldier, Scholar, Judge* (Boston: Twayne Publishers, 1989), at 151, 193 n. 103. – *Ed.*

me (I only glanced at it) as sentiment rather than reasoning – and in short I thought it bosh. He has grown rather dogmatic in tone, with success, though he doesn't equal another Chicago man, [John M.] Zane, who patronized and condemned me on other matters,[55] and also with one sweep wiped all German jurists off the slate, and with another Hobbes, Bentham, Austin, etc., so that nothing seemed to remain but Zane, and what he stood for he didn't tell. Goodbye till next time.

Holmes-Pollock Letters, supra, at 2:40, 42.

A few years after the Wigmore-Holmes correspondence, Holmes wrote an introduction to a book that his "friend Wigmore" edited. See the letter from OWH to Lewis Einstein, February 5, 1923, *Holmes-Einstein Letters, supra,* at 209.

COMMENTARY

Narrow scope of Holmes's dissent, the question of intent – In *The Common Law* and elsewhere, Holmes had argued for an objective standard of liability. But in *Abrams,* he seems to have opted for a subjective standard: "[A] deed is not done with the intent to produce a consequence unless that consequence is the aim of the deed." In this regard, Holmes took exception to the majority's objective standard. Given this, it "seems surprising that in free expression cases he would insist upon proof of subjective wrongdoing while a majority of the Court did not." Albert W. Alschuler, *Law without Values* (Chicago: University of Chicago Press, 2000), at 75.

Comparing majority and dissenting opinions – Despite all that has been said and written about Holmes's "great" dissent in *Abrams,* one of his biographers maintains that the divide between the majority opinion and the dissent may not have been that wide. "Holmes's dissents were narrowly drawn, and the precise issue dividing him from the majority hardly seems earthshaking on its surface." The point of difference between them was "the precise intent require[d] to be shown before speech could be punished." To put it in a slightly different way: "Because he rested his dissents on the narrowest possible ground, his difference with the majority could be expressed in a single point of doctrine: the question of specific intent." Even so, adds Novick, "the underlying difference between Holmes and the Court was deeper than this point of doctrine. Proof of subjective intent would have required attention to the unique defendants

---

[55] *See Justice Oliver Wendell Holmes, supra* note 12: *Law and the Inner Self* (New York: Oxford University Press, 1993), at 371–72 (discussing Zane's criticisms of Holmes). – *Ed.*

and the particular circumstances of individual cases. In Holmes's view, stated in all the criminal attempt and conspiracy cases from *Kennedy* [see Part II commentary] to *Schenck*, it was only these particular circumstances that the Court had a right to consider in determining whether there had been a clear and present danger of harm." Sheldon M. Novick, ed., "Holmes's Philosophy and Jurisprudence: Origin and Development of Principal Themes," in *The Collected Works of Justice Holmes*, Sheldon Novick, ed. (Chicago: University of Chicago Press, 1995), at 1:90, 91–92. The issue of intent bears directly on the debate, sketched out subsequently, over whether Holmes's view of the law in this area had changed in *Abrams*.

Narrow scope of Holmes's dissent and the range of applicable cases – Recall that Holmes saw his imminence test as having a limited applicability: "It is only the present danger of immediate evil or an intent to bring it about that warrants Congress in setting a limit to the expression of opinion where *private rights are not concerned*" (emphasis added). That qualification suggests that the imminence test would not apply, for example, to defamation cases involving nongovernmental figures. *See* Frederick Schauer, "Uncoupling Free Speech," 92 *Columbia Law Review* 1321 (1992); "*Propter Honoris Respectum*," *supra*, at 1354–55. By the same token, it likewise suggests that speech about government and public matters is entitled to greater protection. *See Free Speech in Its Forgotten Years*, *supra*, at 348.

The Abrams *dissent contrasted with the* Schenck *opinion* – Writing in 1920, Zechariah Chafee noted: "Although a dissenting opinion, it must carry great weight as an interpretation of the First Amendment, because it is only an elaboration of the principle of 'clear and present danger' laid down by [Justice Holmes] with the backing of a unanimous court in Schenck v. United States." Zechariah Chafee, *Freedom of Speech* (Cambridge, MA: Harvard University Press, 1920), at 155. Of course, by this statement, Chafee may have hoped to give Holmes's *Abrams* dissent some added staying power, particularly because that opinion conformed to Chafee's interpretation of *Schenck*. *See Freedom of Speech in Its Forgotten Years*, *supra*, at 330–35, 346. "The strategy," according to the late Harry Kalven Jr., was to "read the burst of eloquence at the end of the *Abrams* dissent into the casual *Schenck* dictum and then to claim that it was there all the time, that it was this intense commitment to a stringent test for freedom of speech that the whole Court underwrote in *Schenck*." Harry Kalven Jr., *A Worthy Tradition* (New York: Harper & Row, 1988), at 146.

So how different was what Holmes wrote in *Schenck* for the Court from what he wrote in dissent, joined by Brandeis, in *Abrams*? At the very least, there were some notable differences in how Holmes worded key criteria in his *Schenck* majority opinion as compared to how he proceeded in his *Abrams* dissent. In the comments following this one, the significance of such textual differences is debated. For now, it is enough to first list the key differences between the two opinions and then discuss them briefly. The differences, by no means comprehensive, between the two are as follows:

1. The *Abrams* dissent appears to be more restrictive concerning the limits it placed on Congress's power to define those substantive evils that would thereafter be subject to a danger test.
2. The power of courts to evaluate congressional power appears greater in *Abrams* than in *Schenck*.
3. In *Abrams*, the danger test appears more demanding than in *Schenck*.
4. The *Abrams* dissent deems the common law crime of seditious libel to be incompatible with the First Amendment, whereas *Schenck* and its progeny were silent on this point.
5. The question of truth as a value to be cherished becomes central in *Abrams*, whereas it was nowhere so in *Schenck* and its progeny.

With regard to the first difference, limits on congressional power, it is instructive to compare what Holmes said in *Schenck* with what he said in *Abrams* concerning the role of Congress in determining "substantive evils":

Schenck: "The question in every case is whether the words used are used in such circumstances and are of such a nature as to create a clear and present danger that they will bring about the substantive evils that Congress has a right to prevent."

Abrams: "[T]he United States constitutionally may punish speech that produces or is intended to produce a clear and imminent danger that it will bring about forthwith *certain* substantive evils that the United States constitutionally may seek to prevent." (Emphasis added.)

The word *certain*, argues Professor Rabban, reveals that Holmes was less willing to defer to legislative determinations in *Abrams* than he was in *Schenck*. *See Free Speech in Its Forgotten Years*, *supra*, at 347. Even granting that, however, one may wonder what exactly the qualifiers *certain* and *constitutionally* add. Do they suggest, for example, that the substantive evils must be *serious* and not trivial as expressly noted by Justice Brandeis in his concurrence in *Whitney v. California*, 247 U.S. 357, 377, 379 (1927)?

On the second difference, enhanced power of judicial review, consider the role of the courts in evaluating those "substantive evils" that give rise to government regulation of speech:

> *Schenck*: "The question in every case is whether the words . . . will bring about the substantive evils that *Congress* has a right to prevent." (Emphasis added.)

> *Abrams*: "[T]he United States constitutionally may punish . . . certain substantive evils that *the United States* constitutionally may seek to prevent." (Emphasis added.)

This shift in language may well reveal a shift in Holmes's perspective regarding the role of courts to evaluate not merely the proximity of the danger but the danger itself. In that regard, the *Abrams* dissent seems to envision a larger role for courts in this process.

Third is the new imminent-danger test. Contrast the italicized language that follows:

> *Schenck*: "The question in every case is whether the words used are used in such circumstances and are of such a nature as to create a *clear and present* danger that they will bring about the substantive evils that Congress has a right to prevent." (Emphasis added.)

> *Abrams*: "[T]he United States constitutionally may punish speech that produces or is intended to produce a clear and *imminent* danger that it will bring about *forthwith* certain substantive evils that the United States constitutionally may seek to prevent." (Emphasis added.)

Note the temporal shift between the two formulas. It seems that in *Abrams* Holmes required a closer temporal link between the speech regulated and the harm feared; the evil to be avoided must be near, very near, before any suppression is allowed under the *Abrams* formula. In this regard, Professor Tribe has argued that in *Abrams* Holmes's "doctrinal approach was to infuse more immediacy into the *Schenck* formulation of the 'clear and present danger' test and thereby sharply distinguish it from the loose predictions of remote consequence which had been sufficient to sustain criminal convictions in previous cases." Laurence Tribe, *American Constitutional Law*, 2nd ed. (Mineola, NY: Foundation Press, 1988), at 843. *But see* Sheldon M. Novick, "The Unrevised Holmes and Freedom of Expression," 1991 *Supreme Court Review* 303, 347 n. 186, 350 n. 195 (rejecting the notion that the "immediate check" language was a new and important gloss on the clear-and-present-danger test).

A century before *Abrams* and its danger test, a similar test was mentioned by one of the judicial members of the New York Council of Revision in 1818. The state legislature had passed a law by which a parent who became a Shaker (a member of a Protestant religious sect) stood to lose all child custody rights. The council held the statute unconstitutional. It ruled that, to impose such a penalty on believers of a particular faith, "the danger to the 'peace and safety of the State' must be not merely speculative, remote and possible, but imminent and certain." Alfred Billings Street, *The Council of Revision of the State of New York* (Albany, NY: William Gould Publishing, 1859), at 387 (quoting Justice Jonas Platt, February 27, 1818). *See* Mark DeWolfe Howe, Book Review, 55 *Harvard Law Review* 695 n. 2 (1942).

Fourth is the First Amendment and seditious libel point. In his *Abrams* dissent, Holmes declared: "I wholly disagree with the argument of the Government that the First Amendment left the common law as to seditious libel in force. History seems to me against the notion." This bold assertion, which would be tested by scholars in future years, was nowhere to be found in *Schenck* and its progeny. *See generally* Leonard W. Levy, *Emergence of a Free Press* (New York: Oxford University Press, 1985), at 281 ("Contrary to Justice Holmes, history favors the notion."). Cf. Justice William Brennan's opinion for the Court in *New York Times Co. v. Sullivan*, 376 U.S. 254, 275–76 (1964) (citing the *Abrams* dissent and then noting a "a broad consensus that the [Sedition] Act, because of the restraint it imposed upon criticism of government and public officials, was inconsistent with the First Amendment").

Fifth is the centrality of truth point. In one of the most famous passages in his dissent, Holmes wrote: "when men have realized that time has upset many fighting faiths, they may come to believe even more than they believe the very foundations of their own conduct that the ultimate good desired is better reached by free trade in ideas – that the best test of truth is the power of the thought to get itself accepted in the competition of the market, and that truth is the only ground upon which their wishes safely can be carried out." This concern with the pursuit of truth becomes central in *Abrams*. In *Schenck*, *Frohwerk*, and *Debs*, by stark contrast, the word *truth* is entirely absent from Holmes's opinions. The question of truth and Holmes's views on the matter are discussed further in the subsequent comments.

For a thoughtful commentary on the several differences between the *Abrams* dissent and what came before it, see *Free Speech in Its Forgotten Years, supra*, at 347–50.

Had Holmes's views between Schenck *and* Abrams *changed?* – Recall that, in his dissent, Holmes declared: "I never have seen any reason to doubt that the questions of law that alone were before this Court in the cases of *Schenck*, *Frohwerk*, and *Debs* were rightly decided." Nonetheless, over the years, there has been considerable debate among scholars as to whether the views espoused and applied by Holmes in his opinions in *Schenck*, *Frohwerk*, and *Debs* are consistent with what he wrote and how he voted in *Abrams*. In other words, did his view on free speech and matters related to it change in some important way?

Laurence Tribe has noted that "Holmes'[s] dissent in *Abrams* is marred by ambiguity and by his insistence [that] *Schenck*, *Frohwerk*, and especially *Debs* had been rightly decided." *American Constitutional Law, supra*, at 843 (footnote omitted). In light of that, there has been controversy over how to interpret the *Abrams* dissent.

First, some argue that Holmes remained consistent and had not changed his jurisprudence. Such scholars maintain that "Holmes's *basic* approach to free speech remained stable throughout his life." That is, the argument goes, "Justice Holmes had a coherent and a moderately protective doctrine of free speech." H. L. Pohlman, *Justice Oliver Wendell Holmes: Free Speech and the Living Constitution* (New York: New York University Press, 1991), at 254, 255.

"Holmes's understanding of his own phrase [clear and present danger] was rooted in considerations he used to define attempts. Speech that could induce unlawful acts, when engaged in for that purpose under circumstances where the danger was extreme, satisfied this 'clear and present danger' test. All of the convictions in the spring of 1919 involved persons of some prominence within a relevant community, challenging the war and conscription in the middle of the war with statements urging their listeners or readers to take some action and jury findings (either actual or assumed, but based on sufficient evidence) that the language was intended to obstruct and capable of doing so. Thus Holmes reasonably believed that, applying his test to the issues presented him, the convictions in *Schenck*, *Frohwerk* and *Debs* were properly upheld. This fact is important to keep in mind [in considering] *Abrams*. It will allow the reader to understand that the differences between the Espionage Act opinions and the legendary dissent in *Abrams*, both in tone and result, are not due to a major change in Holmes'[s] view of the first amendment between *Debs* and *Abrams*. Instead, . . . the change in result can be explained by important factual differences between the early cases and *Abrams*, and the change in tone and fervor were the result not of new thinking but rather of frustration at critics' misunderstanding of the strides made in *Schenck*. . . ." "The Free Speech Metamorphosis of Mr. Justice Holmes," *supra*, at 171–74 (footnotes omitted). *See also ibid.* at 174–86.

Sheldon Novick, relying on "the importance of motive," has also rejected the notion that Holmes's *Abrams* opinion marks a significant shift in his views on free speech. "Such a profound change in Holmes's thinking, when he was seventy-eight years old, had been a judge for thirty-six years, and had already written several opinions on the same question for a unanimous Supreme Court, calls for an explanation. One would expect dramatic evidence to be put forward. But this is not the case. . . . " Sheldon M. Novick, *Honorable Justice: The Life of Oliver Wendell Holmes* (New York: Dell Publishing, 1989), at 473 n. 87. *See also* Sheldon M. Novick, "The Unrevised Holmes and Freedom of Expression," *supra*, at 303, 347–65.

Second, some argue that Holmes changed but did so within a framework previously established. Professor Edward Bloustein offers a nuanced view of this matter, one that places him at somewhat of a middle ground: "I agree that the libertarian creed and analytic structure embodied in *Abrams* constituted a considerable shift in Holmes's opinion, and that he was impelled, among other reasons, by the criticism of his friends and the pressure of events, to abandon his prior position. Rather than focus on what *caused* Holmes to change his mind, [I am more interested in exploring] *the nature of the change*. Holmes's critics suggest that the change in his viewpoint represented a radical transformation of his thinking. I believe that he modified his views in *Abrams* by extending ideas and theories he had previously espoused in *Schenck*, in earlier cases, and in his treatise on *The Common Law*." Later he concluded: "I see [*Abrams*] as an outgrowth of [Holmes's] early philosophic orientation and the views on criminal attempts that he had expressed in *The Common Law*. These influences were clearly at work in the *Schenck* case, but his earlier 'bad tendency' theory of the first amendment adjudication, and his disdain for political radicalism and the patriotic fervor of the immediate post-war period led him to subdue his true conceptual lights. In *Abrams*, stung by the criticism of his role in the *Schenck* line of cases, and imbued with a new awareness of the dangers that repression of speech poses to a democracy, the strength of the long-standing pragmatist tendency of his thought, and the concept of criminal attempts he had developed in *The Common Law*, finally came into their own as elements of his first amendment theory." Edward J. Bloustein, "Criminal Attempts and the 'Clear and Present Danger' Theory of the First Amendment," 74 *Cornell Law Review* 1118, 1119–20, 1150 (1989) (footnotes omitted).

Third, some claim that Holmes changed his jurisprudence in a significant way. Finally, it has been argued that the "clear and present danger test, in its original form, was not at all solicitous of the rights of dissenters. Between

March and November" 1919; however, "Holmes's thinking [underwent] a significant change, and the *Abrams* case [played] a central role in that change." Richard Polenberg, *Fighting Faiths, supra,* at 207–08. *Accord* Fred Ragan, "Justice Oliver Wendell Holmes, Jr., Zechariah Chafee, Jr., and the Clear and Present Danger Test for Free Speech: The First Year, 1919," 58 *Journal of American History* 24 (1971); Gerald Gunther, "Learned Hand and the Origins of Modern First Amendment Doctrine," 27 *Stanford Law Review* 719, 720 (1975); Bernard Schwartz, "Holmes versus Hand: Clear and Present Danger or Advocacy of Unlawful Action," 1994 *Supreme Court Review* 209 (1994), 223–24.

In light of the foregoing and what follows, recall what Holmes said about this matter in his *Abrams* dissent: "I never have seen any reason to doubt that the questions of law that alone were before this Court in the cases of *Schenck, Frohwerk,* and *Debs* were rightly decided." If by that he meant to infer that what he had done in *Abrams* was a part of what he had done in the earlier 1919 cases, then that claim is subject to dispute as indicated by the commentaries below and the ones following it.

"Holmes's actual language in *Abrams*," Professor Rabban maintains, "belies" what he said in his dissent and in correspondence to others. He adds: "in *Abrams* Holmes rephrased [his *Schenck* test] in words that significantly modified its meaning. . . ." *Free Speech in Its Forgotten Years, supra,* at 348–49.

"Since Holmes had not referred to a 'clear and present danger' in *Frohwerk* and *Debs,*" Professor White maintains, "and since he had employed the bad-tendency test in both cases, the trilogy of 1919 cases could have been taken simply as attempt cases, with the 'clear and present danger' phrase serving as one of Holmes' vivid aphorisms. In *Abrams,* however, 'clear and present danger' moved to the center of First Amendment analysis." And that test, adds White, was "reconfigured" by Holmes and then applied to the facts of the case. In addition, "Holmes explicitly linked the 'clear and present danger' test to the idea that thoughts gained or lost acceptance in 'the market' of ideas and were 'corrected' with time, producing 'truth,' an idea now characterized as 'the theory of our Constitution.' Somehow the 'experimental' character of the constitutional scheme of government was linked to the 'experimental' process by which ideas were tested and discarded in the marketplace. And since 'the ultimate good' was reached by allowing this experimental process to go on, only those ideas that directly threatened the existence of the nation should be removed from the process by being suppressed. The First Amendment had become a 'sweeping command' to test all ideas in the marketplace unless they immediately threatened the country." By this process, White argues, Holmes's views transformed from ideas related to the common law of criminal attempts to the "first stage in the modernization of American free speech jurisprudence...." *Justice Oliver Wendell Holmes: Law and the Inner Self, supra*, at 433–36 (footnotes omitted).

Why Holmes changed his views – Assuming Holmes had changed his views in *Abrams* – though a tough call, I am generally inclined to agree with Gunther, Rabban, and White on this score – why did he do so? Though it is difficult to say with certainty, Professor Rabban offers up what may be the best array of explanations: (1) certain factual differences between *Abrams* and the earlier cases; (2) changes in the political climate ("current events") in the nation; (3) Holmes's *"psychological need for approval"* combined with the books that he read at the time; and (4) the criticisms leveled against him by his friends, people like Chafee, Hand, and Freund, among others. *Free Speech in Its Forgotten Years, supra*, at 350–55. *See also* Ronald J. Krotoszynski, Steven G. Gey, et al., *The First Amendment: Cases and Theory* (New York: Wolters Kluwer, 2008), at 42.

Abandon the clear-and-present-danger test? – Notably, one of Holmes's greatest admirers and defenders, Felix Frankfurter, felt that clear and present danger, at least as reformulated by Holmes in *Abrams v. United States*, was unduly speech protective. "It were far better that the phrase be abandoned than that it be sounded once more to hide from the believers in an absolute right of free speech the plain fact that the interest in speech, profoundly important as it is, is no more conclusive in judicial review than other attributes of democracy or than a determination of the people's representatives that a measure is necessary to assure the safety of government itself." Frankfurter, J., concurring in *Dennis v. United States*, 341 U.S. 494, 544 (1951).

By stark contrast, Richard Posner finds Holmes's approach in *Abrams* to be exemplary, though in need of some scientific retooling. *See* Richard Posner, "The Speech Market and the Legacy of *Schenck*," in *Eternally Vigilant: Free Speech in the Modern Era*, Lee C. Bollinger and Geoffrey R. Stone, eds. (Chicago: University of Chicago Press, 2002), at 121. Judge Posner's views of Holmes and his free speech jurisprudence are further discussed in the Epilogue, as are some of the more modern criticisms of the clear-and-present-danger test.

Intelligence and ideas as our directive force – John Dewey (1859–1952), a famous American philosopher and educational reformer, was impressed by Holmes's memorable passage about men's "fighting faiths" and "the best test of truth."

Of that passage, Dewey wrote: "It contains, in spite of its brevity, three out-standing ideas: [1] belief in conclusions of intelligence as the finally directive force in life; [2] in freedom of thought and expression as a condition needed in order to realize this power of direction by thought, and [3] in the experimental character of life and thought. These three ideas state the essence of one type, and, to my mind, the only enduring type, of liberal faith." John Dewey, "Justice Holmes and the Liberal Mind," *New Republic*, January 11, 1928, at 210.

Liberalism as a method of intelligence – Dewey saw Holmes's thought as expressed in *Abrams* as a form of liberalism, but not one of the commonly understood type. Instead, he saw Holmesian as "a method of intelligence, prior to being a method of action, as a method of experimentation based on insight into both social desires and actual conditions. . . . It signifies the adoption of the scientific habit of mind in application to social affairs." By this measure, Holmes's thought had "no social panacea to dole out, no code of fixed ends to be realized." In Holmes, Dewey discerned a "definitely realistic strain" in thought, "as there must be in any working liberalism, any liberalism which is other than a vague and windy hope." "Justice Holmes and the Liberal Mind," *supra*, at 210–11.

An alternative to "false logic" – It is "not logic," argued Dewey, to which Holmes "takes exception, but the false logic involved in applying the classic system of fictitious fixed concepts, and demonstrably exact subsumptions under them, to the decision of social issues which arise out of a living conflict of desires. Such a logic involves distinctions of degree, consideration of the limitation placed upon an idea which represents the value of one type of desire by the presence of ideas which express neighboring, but competing interests. These requirements can be met only by employing the method borrowed, as far as possible from science, of comparison by means of measuring and weighing." He objects to [the] domination of law by classic logic in the interest of a logic in which precision is material or quantitative, not just formal." "Justice Holmes and the Liberal Mind," *supra*, at 211.

Holmesian realism – "At times," wrote Dewey, Holmes's "realism seems almost to amount to a belief that whatever wins out in fair combat, in the struggle for existence, is therefore the fit, the good and the true. But all such remarks have to be understood in the light of his abiding faith that, when all is said and done, intelligence and ideas are the supreme force in the settlement of social issues." "Justice Holmes and the Liberal Mind," *supra*, at 212.

Holmesian faith – "To those whose faith is failing, the work of Justice Holmes is a tonic.... I do not doubt that the day will come when the principles set forth by Justice Holmes... will be accepted commonplaces, and when the result of his own teachings will afford an illustration of the justice of his faith in the power of ideas. When that day comes, the spirit of Justice Holmes will be the first to remind us that life is still going on, is still an experiment, and that then, as now, to repose on any formula is to invite death." "Justice Holmes and the Liberal Mind," *supra*, at 212. For an extended and thoughtful discussion of Dewey and Holmes, *see Freedom of Speech in Its Forgotten Years, supra*, at 335–41.

Bickel on Holmes: Jurisprudence of relativism – According to the famed Yale law professor Alexander Bickel, Holmes's First Amendment thought was a "Whig model" of jurisprudence that "begins not with theoretical rights" like natural law, but rather with "a real society, whose origins in the historical mists it acknowledges to be mysterious. The Whig model assesses human nature as it is seen to be. It judges how readily and how far men can be moved by means other than violent [ones], that is to say, how far they can be moved by government.... The Whig model is obviously flexible, pragmatic, slow moving, highly political. It partakes, in substantial measure, of the relativism that pervades Justice Oliver Wendell Holmes's theory of the First Amendment, although not to its ultimate logical exaggeration." Alexander Bickel, *The Morality of Consent* (New Haven, CT: Yale University Press, 1975), at 4. Among other things, Professor Bickel, aided by Floyd Abrams, successfully argued the *Pentagon Papers* case in the Supreme Court. *See* Floyd Abrams, *Trials of the First Amendment* (New York: Viking, 2005), at 1–33.

"Hell in a basket" free speech jurisprudence – The "theory of truth in the marketplace, determined ultimately by a count of noses – this total relativism – cannot be the theory of our Constitution, or there would be no Bill of Rights in it, and certainly no Supreme Court to enforce it," claimed Professor Bickel. "It amused Holmes to pretend that if his fellow citizens wanted to go to Hell in a basket he would help them. It was his job, he said. But not his sole job, and not always. And Holmes knew that, too." Alexander Bickel, *The Morality of Consent, supra*, at 77. For additional discussion of this point, see the commentary following *Gitlow v. New York* (1925) herein.

Other views of Holmes's dissent with respect to claims about truth – Professor
Vincent Blasi has offered four views of Holmes's *Abrams* dissent, the last one
being his own:

1. *The Instrumental Justification for the Priority of Truth – Its Political Function*: If "the value of truth is that it helps to satisfy our desires, as various
   and conflicting as they may be, truth is performing a function that is, in
   essence, political."
2. *The Instrumental Justification for the Priority of Truth – Its Individualistic
   Function*: "One might [also ascribe to] Holmes a much more individualistic frame of reference. Thus, truth discovered by means of unfettered
   discussion might be instrumental to the satisfaction of desires but only
   at the level of personal judgment, not that of a societal construction
   of norms and understandings. Collective well-being is not what he is
   concerned with, in this view."
3. *The Liberal Process-Oriented Justification for the Priority of Truth*: "An
   alternative, equally misleading reading would portray Holmes not as a
   libertarian but as a 'liberal' more concerned with process than [with]
   consequences.... [T]he procedure of the market becomes itself a truth,
   perhaps not exactly as an end in itself but something at least as important
   as the contingent understandings it produces. This reading invites us to
   reify the market, protect it against distortions, perfect it, treat its purest
   form as an ideal, not to serve any particular political objective but out of
   a blind faith in the efficacy of the cognitive and normative outcomes it
   will generate."
4. *The Political Function of Free Speech Justification for the Priority of Truth*:
   "The *Abrams* opinion, as I read it, is much more about the substantive
   effects of political criticism and challenge than it is about process as a
   measure of fairness or justice or wisdom. Despite his Olympian image,
   Holmes actually built his argument for free speech around a concern
   for political consequences." Unlike his *Schenck* opinion, which stressed
   how certain speech had to be regulated, Holmes's *Abrams* dissent moves
   "in the opposite direction. There is some speech, Holmes suggests, that
   we simply have to have under the First Amendment.... The claim that
   Holmes's argument for truth rests on a vision of the political function of
   free speech is reinforced by his choice of a term in the *Abrams* dissent
   that would otherwise seem out of place. He says: 'truth is the only ground
   upon which their wishes safely can be carried out.' Why the concern for
   safety? To what risk does he refer? I believe he is worried about the risk of

desires being thwarted by wielders of power who claim to control others in the name of values other than truth, or in the name of some notion of truth measured by means other than the open competition of ideas. His injunction three sentences later that we be 'eternally vigilant against attempts to check the expression of opinions' employs the Madisonian rhetoric of political distrust. Holmes is worried, it seems, about the exercise of authority. The credential of the market, in this reading, is that it is the most valuable alternative to authoritative decree. The claim is modest but no less important for that."

"*Propter Honoris Respectum*," *supra*, at 1346–49 (footnotes and critiques omitted).

The plight of the Abrams *defendants and their defenders* – Before the *Abrams* case was heard in the Supreme Court, Jacob Schwartz, one of the original defendants, began his prison term and was beaten with blackjacks while incarcerated. Subsequently, he was transferred to Bellevue Hospital, where he died on October 14, 1918. An unfinished note was found in his cell that read: "Farewell, comrade. When you appear before the court I will be with you no longer. Struggle without fear, fight bravely. I am sorry to leave you. But this is life itself. . . ." *American Political Prisoners*, *supra*, at 187–88. *See also Fighting Faiths*, *supra*, at 88–90, 94–95. Another defendant, Gabriel Prober, was acquitted, but his colleagues were less fortunate.

After the *Abrams* case was decided and the petitioners' convictions upheld, the noted First Amendment scholar Zechariah Chafee signed a petition calling for amnesty for the *Abrams* defendants. Felix Frankfurter and Dean Roscoe Pound, among others, also signed the petition. When J. Edgar Hoover, head of the new General Intelligence Division of the Justice Department, learned of the petition, he "instructed one of his agents to compile 'as complete a resume as you have upon each of these subjects.'" *Fighting Faiths*, *supra*, at 273–74.

"On November 23, 1921, after serving two and a half years of her sentence, [Mollie] Steimer, along with three of her codefendants [Samuel Lipman, Hyman Lachowsky, and Jacob Abrams], was deported to the Soviet Union. In addition to being deported, Steimer was prohibited from ever returning to the United States." Stephen M. Kohn, *American Political Prisoners: Prosecutions under the Espionage and Sedition Acts* (Westport, CT: Praeger), at 112, 134. Steimer's life in Russia proved even more difficult after she was arrested by the secret police in July 1923. *See Fighting Faiths*, *supra*, at 352–59. On the role of Zechariah Chafee in all of this and the campaign against him because of it, *see ibid.* at 272–84.

EXHIBITS AGAINST ABRAMS

16

UNITED STATES V. JACOB ABRAMS ET AL.

Exhibit A.

THE
HYPOCRISY
OF THE
UNITED STATES
AND HER ALLIES

"Our" President Wilson, with his beautiful phraseology, has hynotized the people of America to such an extent that they do not see his hypocrisy.

Know, you people of America, that a frank enemy is always preferable to a concealed friend. When we say the people of America, we do not mean the few Kaisers of America, we mean the "People of America." you people of America were deceived by the wonderful speeches of the masked President Wilson. His shameful, cowardly silence about the intervention in Russia reveals the hypocrisy of the plutocratic gang in Washington and vicinity.

The President was afraid to announce to the American people the intervention in Russia. He is too much of a coward to come out openly and say: "We capitalistic nations cannot afford to have a proletarian republic in Russia." Instead, he uttered beautiful phrases about Russia, which, as you see, he did not mean, and secretly, cowardly, sent troops to crush the Russian Revolution. Do you see how German militarism combined with allied capitalism to crush the russian revolution?

This is not new. The tyrants of the world fight each other until they see a common enemy—WORKING CLASS—ENLIGHTENMENT as soon as they find a common enemy, they combine to crush it.

In 1815 monarchic nations combined under the name of the "Holy Alliance" to crush the French

17

UNITED STATES V. JACOB ABRAMS ET AL.

Revolution. Now militarism and capitalism combined, though not openly, to crush the russian revolution.

What have you to say about it?

Will you allow the Russian Revolution to be crushed? You: Yes, *we mean you the people of America!

THE RUSSIAN REVOLUTION CALLS TO THE WORKERS OF THE WORLD FOR HELP.

The Russian Revolution cries: "WORKERS OF THE WORLD! AWAKE! RISE! PUT DOWN YOUR ENEMY AND MINE!

Yes friends, there is only one enemy of the workers of the world and that is CAPITALISM.

It is a crime, that workers of America, workers of Germany, workers of Japan, etc., to fight THE WORKERS' REPUBLIC OF RUSSIA.

AWAKE! AWAKE, YOU
WORKERS OF THE WORLD!
REVOLUTIONISTS

P. S. It is absurd to call us pro-German. We hate and despise German militarism more than do your hypocritical tyrants. We have more reasons for denouncing German militarism than has the coward of the White House.

18

Exhibit B-I.

Original exhibit was printed in Yiddish and is translated in next exhibit.

———$

Exhibit B-II.

(Translation of Exhibit B-I.)

WORKERS—WAKE UP.

The preparatory work for Russia's emancipation is brought to an end by his Majesty, Mr. Wilson, and the rest of the gang; dogs of all colors!

America, together with the Allies, will march to Russia, not, "God Forbid", to interfere with the Russian affairs, but to help the Czecko-Slovaks in their struggle against the Bolsheviki.

Oh, ugly hypocrites; this time they shall not succeed in fooling the Russian emigrants and the friends of Russia in America. Too visible is their audacious move.

Workers, Russian emigrants, you who had the least belief in the honesty of our government, must now throw away all confidence, must spit in the face the false, hypocritic, military propaganda which has fooled you so relentlessly, calling forth your sympathy, your help, to the prosecution of the war. With the money which you have loaned, or are going to loan them, they will make bullets not only for the Germans but also for the Workers Soviets of Russia. Workers in the ammunition factories, you are producing bullets, bayonets, cannon, to murder not

19

UNITED STATES V. JACOB ABRAMS ET AL.

o

only the Germans, but also your dearest, best, who are in Russia and are fighting for freedom.

You who emigrated from Russia, you who are friends of Russia, will you carry on your conscience in cold blood the shame spot as a helper to choke the Workers Soviets? Will you give your consent to the inquisitionary expedition to Russia? Will you be calm spectators to the fleecing blood from the hearts of the best sons of Russia?

America and her Allies have betrayed (the workers). Their robberish aims are clear to all men. The destruction of the Russian Revolution, that is the politics of the march to Russia.

Workers, our reply to the barbaric intervention has to be a general strike! An open challenge only will let the government know that not only the Russian Worker fights for freedom, but also here in America lives the spirit of revolution.

Do not let the government scare you with their wild punishment in prisons, hanging and shooting. We must not and will not betray the splendid fighters of Russia. Workers, up to fight.

Three hundred years had the Romanoff dynasty taught us how to fight. Let all rulers remember this, from the smallest to the biggest despot, that the hand of the revolution will not shiver in a fight.

Woe unto those who will be in the way of progress. Let solidarity live!

THE REBELS.

The decree as it stands seems to me surprising in a country of free speech that affects to regard education and knowledge as desirable.

AMERICAN COLUMN & LUMBER CO. V. UNITED STATES

257 U.S. 377 (1921)
Vote: 6–3
For the majority: Clark, J.
Reargued: October 12, 13, 1921
Decided: December 19, 1921
For appellants: Louis Claire Boyle and G. Carroll Todd
For respondent: Solicitor General James M. Beck and James A. Fowler

"The 'Open Competition Plan' of the American Hardwood Manufacturers' Association, by means of which members pooled information on sales, prices, supply on hand, and production, was held by the Court to be a combination in restraint of trade in violation of the Sherman" Antitrust Act. The majority opinion labeled this "abnormal conduct on the part of the 365 natural competitors" and done in a "skillfully devised way" so as to "evade the law." The majority concluded "daily reports, weekly reviews and forecasts, and frequent trade meetings were evidence of a purpose to suppress competition by restricting production and harmonizing prices. Despite the absence of a specific agreement to fix prices, the evidence showed concerted action to restrict production and by large price increases."[56] Justice John Clarke wrote for the majority and concluded that the actions of the petitioners "constituted a combination and conspiracy in restraint of interstate commerce within the meaning of the Anti-Trust Act of 1890." Justice Louis Brandeis issued a dissent in which Joseph McKenna joined, as did Justice Holmes. Holmes also wrote separately.

Mr. Justice Holmes, dissenting.

When there are competing sellers of a class of goods, knowledge of the total stock on hand, of the probable total demand, and of the prices paid, of course will tend to equalize the prices asked. But I should have supposed that the Sherman Act did not set itself against knowledge – did not aim at a transitory cheapness unprofitable to the community as a whole because not corresponding to the actual conditions of the country. I should have thought that the ideal of commerce was an intelligent interchange made with

---

[56] This summary of the facts was taken largely from Alfred Lief, comp., *The Social and Economic Views of Mr. Justice Brandeis* (New York: Vanguard Press, 1930), at 89.

full knowledge of the facts as a basis for a forecast of the future on both sides. A combination to get and distribute such knowledge, notwithstanding its tendency to equalize, not necessarily to raise, prices, is very far from a combination in unreasonable restraint of trade. It is true that it is a combination of sellers only, but the knowledge acquired is not secret, it is public, and the buyers, I think I may assume, are not less active in their efforts to know the facts. A combination in unreasonable restraint of trade imports an attempt to override normal market conditions. An attempt to conform to them seems to me the most reasonable thing in the world. I see nothing in the conduct of the appellants that binds the members even by merely social sanctions to anything that would not be practised, if we could imagine it, by an all[-]wise socialistic government acting for the benefit of the community as a whole. The parties to the combination are free to do as they will.

I must add that the decree as it stands seems to me surprising in a country of free speech that affects to regard education and knowledge as desirable. It prohibits the distribution of stock, production, or sales reports, the discussion of prices at association meetings, and the exchange of predictions of high prices. It is true that these acts are the main evidence of the supposed conspiracy, but that to my mind only shows the weakness of the Government's case. I cannot believe that the fact, if it be assumed, that the acts have been done with a sinister purpose, justifies excluding mills in the backwoods from information, in order to enable centralized purchasers to take advantage of their ignorance of the facts.

I agree with the more elaborate discussion of the case by my Brother Brandeis.

COMMENTARY

Brandeis dissenting – Justice Brandeis also registered a far-reaching dissent in which Holmes joined, even though Brandeis did not sign onto Holmes's opinion. In relevant part, Brandeis wrote the following concerning his interpretation of the Sherman Antitrust Act: " . . . It is claimed that the purpose of the Open Competition Plan was to lessen competition. Competition among members was contemplated and was in vigorous operation. The Sherman Law does not prohibit every lessening of competition; and it certainly does not command that competition shall be pursued blindly, that business rivals shall remain ignorant of trade facts, or be denied aid in weighing their significance. It is lawful to regulate competition in some degree. . . . But it was neither the aim of the Plan, nor the practice under it, to regulate competition in any way. Its purpose was to make rational competition possible, by supplying data not otherwise available, and without which most of those engaged in the trade would be unable to trade intelligently.

"The hardwood lumber mills are widely scattered. The principal area of production is the Southern States. But there are mills in Minnesota, New York, New England, and the Middle States. Most plants are located near the sources of supply, isolated, remote from the larger cities and from the principal markets. No official, or other public, means have been established for collecting from these mills and from dealers' data as to current production, stocks on hand, and market prices. Concerning grain, cotton, coal, and oil, the government collects and publishes regularly, at frequent intervals, current information on production, consumption, and stocks on hand; and Boards of Trade furnish freely to the public details of current market prices of those commodities, the volume of sales, and even individual sales, as recorded in daily transactions. Persons interested in such commodities are enabled through this information to deal with one another on an equal footing. The absence of such information in the hardwood lumber trade enables dealers in the large centers more readily to secure advantage over the isolated producer. And the large concerns, which are able to establish their own bureaus of statistics, secure an advantage over smaller concerns. Surely it is not against the public interest to distribute knowledge of trade facts, however detailed. Nor are the other features of the Plan – the market letters and the regional conferences – an unreasonable interference with freedom in trade. Intelligent conduct of business implies, not only knowledge of trade facts, but an understanding of them. To this understanding editorial comment and free discussion by those engaged in the business and by others interested are aids. Opinions expressed may be unsound; predictions may be unfounded; but there is nothing in the Sherman Law which should limit freedom of discussion, even among traders.

" . . . The co-operation which is incident to this plan does not suppress competition. On the contrary, it tends to promote all in competition which is desirable. By substituting knowledge for ignorance, rumor, guess, and suspicion, it tends also to substitute research and reasoning for gambling and piracy, without closing the door to adventure, or lessening the value of prophetic wisdom. In making such knowledge available to the smallest concern, it creates among producers equality of opportunity. In making it available, also, to purchasers and the general public, it does all that can actually be done to protect the community from extortion. If, as is alleged, the Plan tends to substitute stability in prices for violent fluctuations, its influence, in this respect, is not against the public interest. The evidence in this case, far from establishing an illegal restraint of trade, presents, in my opinion, an instance of commendable effort by concerns engaged in a chaotic industry to make possible its intelligent conduct under competitive conditions. . . . "

Free speech, antitrust laws, and the marketplace – In the context of commercial expression, especially where antitrust laws come into play, the Supreme Court has been relatively deferential to attempts to regulate speech. *See, e.g., Indiana Farmer's Guide Publishing Co. v. Prairie Farmer Publishing Co.*, 293 U.S. 268 (1934), and *Associated Press v. United States*, 326 U.S. 1 (1945). The Holmes and Brandeis dissents, by comparison, reveal a certain willingness to sustain statutory free speech claims in the antitrust context, especially where to do so would expand the amount of truthful information available to the interested parties and the public at large and would encourage trade rather than constrain it. *Accord Maple Flooring Manufacturers' Association v. United States*, 268 U.S. 563 (1925) (finding no violation of Sherman Act where trade association members gathered and disseminated information as to the cost of their product, the volume of production, and the actual price that the product brought in past transactions). *Compare Sugar Institute, Inc. v. United States*, 297 U.S. 553 (1936) (although collection and dissemination of trade statistics is permissible and useful to fair competition, the same conduct is unlawful if it is part of a plan to limit production and increase prices). *See generally* Femi Alese, *Federal Antitrust and EC Competition Law Analysis* (London: Ashgate, 2008), at 136–40. For Holmes's views in other antitrust cases, see his dissents in *Northern Securities Co. v. United States*, 193 U.S. 197, 400 (1904), and *Dr. Miles Medical Co. v. John D. Park & Sons Co.*, 220 U.S. 373, 409 (1911); *see also* Spencer Weber Waller, "The Modern Antitrust Relevance of Oliver Wendell Holmes," 59 *Brooklyn Law Review* 1443 (1994).

Of the *American Column* case, a former Federal Trade commissioner has observed that, in that case, "the Supreme Court concluded that the exchange of information by the American Hardwood Manufacturers' Association was a 'systematic effort . . . to cut down production and increase prices.' Unlawful purpose was inferred in part from the quantity and quality of information that the members shared through their association. 'Genuine competitors,' the Court said, 'do not make daily, weekly and monthly reports of the minutest details of their business to their rivals,' as did the members of the Hardwood association. As to the effects of the plan, the Court observed both that hardwood prices had increased 'to an unprecedented extent' in 1919 and that '1919 was a year of high and increasing prices generally.' A number of considerations that are important in modern antitrust analysis are lacking in the [*American Column*] case. We do not see, for example, any discussion by the majority of the potential benefits from information exchanges. Nor did the majority discuss the structure of the industry or the market power (or lack of it) of the trade association and its members. Two of the dissenting justices, Justice Holmes and Justice Brandeis, commented on these aspects of the case." Mary L. Azcuenaga, "Price Surveys, Benchmarking and Information Exchanges," Speech, Eighth Annual Legal Symposium before the American Society of Association Executives, November 8, 1994, Washington, D.C. (Westlaw) (footnotes omitted).

When I consider the ease with which the power claimed by the Postmaster could be used to interfere with very sacred rights, I am of [the] opinion that the refusal to allow the [petitioner] the rate to which it was entitled ... was unjustified by statute and was a serious attack upon liberties that not even the war induced Congress to infringe.

UNITED STATES EX REL. MILWAUKEE SOCIAL DEMOCRATIC PUBLISHING CO. V. BURLESON

255 U.S. 407 (1921)
Vote: 7–2
Argued: January 18, 19, 1921
Decided: March 7, 1921
For plaintiff: Henry F. Cochems
For respondent: William H. Lamar and William L. Frierson

Born in Austria-Hungary, Victor Berger came to the United States in 1878 and became deeply involved in the politics of Milwaukee, Wisconsin. He was one of the founders and leading figures of the Socialist Party and in 1910 became the first socialist ever elected to the House of Representatives. He was also the editor for the Social Democratic Herald, *which later became the* Milwaukee Leader. *In 1917, soon after the Espionage Act had been enacted into law, Postmaster General Albert Burleson denied second-class mailing rates to the* Milwaukee Leader *and blocked first-class mail addressed to the newspaper. This imposed heavy burdens on the newspaper and its continued existence. A postal hearing was held and an order was later entered revoking the second-class mail privilege granted to the* Milwaukee Leader. *On appeal to the postmaster general, the order was approved. The matter was challenged and the trial court ruled against the petitioner. The Court of Appeals of the District of Columbia then affirmed the judgment. While the case was making its way up to the Supreme Court, Victor Berger was separately convicted under the Espionage Act for several antiwar pieces he had published in the* Milwaukee Leader. *Despite the conviction,*

Berger was reelected to Congress in 1918. The members of the House voted to deny him his seat on the basis of the conviction. He was sentenced to twenty years in prison by Judge Kennesaw Mountain Landis, but the conviction was overturned by the Supreme Court because of the judge's personal bias.[57] *Berger then went on to serve two more terms in the House of Representatives. But in the next case that went to the Supreme Court, Berger's paper lost. The majority (with Justice John Clarke writing) upheld the postmaster's order. In his majority opinion, Justice Clarke noted that because "the petition in this case was filed, it has also become settled that the Espionage Act is a valid, constitutional law." He cited the Court's rulings in* Schenck, Frohwerk, Debs, *and* Abrams *as support for that proposition. He also stressed that access to second-class mail was not a right but a privilege – an idea that Justice Louis Brandeis objected to in a separate dissent. Holmes also dissented.*

Mr. Justice Holmes, dissenting.

I have had the advantage of reading the judgment of my Brother Brandeis in this case and I agree in substance with his view. At first it seemed to me that if a publisher should announce in terms that he proposed to print treason and should demand a second-class rate it must be that the Postmaster General would have authority to refuse it. But reflection has convinced me that I was wrong. The question of the rate has nothing to do with the question whether the matter is mailable, and I am satisfied that the Postmaster cannot determine in advance that a certain newspaper is going to be nonmailable and on that ground deny to it not the use of the mails but the rate of postage that the statute says shall be charged.

Of course the Postmaster may deny or revoke the second-class rate to a publication that does not comply with the conditions attached to it by statute, but as my Brother Brandeis has pointed out, the conditions attached to the second-class rate by the statute cannot be made to justify the Postmaster's action except by a quibble. On the other hand the regulation of the right to use the mails by the Espionage Act has no peculiarities as a war measure but is similar to that in earlier cases, such as obscene documents. Papers that violate the Act are declared non-mailable and the use of the mails for the transmission of them is made criminal. But the only power given to the Postmaster is to

---

[57] See *Berger v. United States*, 255 U.S. 22 (1921). Afterward, all charges against Berger were dropped. In another case, Judge Landis declared: "When a country is at peace it is the legal right of free speech to oppose going to war and to oppose even preparation for war. But when once war is declared, this right ceases." Qtd. in *Free Expression and Democracy in America, supra* note 17, at 252.

refrain from forwarding the papers when received and to return them to the senders. He could not issue a general order that a certain newspaper should not be carried because he thought it likely or certain that it would contain treasonable or obscene talk. The United States may give up the postoffice when it sees fit, but while it carries it on the use of the mails is almost as much a part of free speech as the right to use our tongues and it would take very strong language to convince me that Congress ever intended to give such a practically despotic power to any one man. There is no pretence that it has done so. Therefore I do not consider the limits of its constitutional power.

To refuse the second-class rate to a newspaper is to make its circulation impossible and has all the effect of the order that I have supposed. I repeat. When I observe that the only powers expressly given to the Postmaster General to prevent the carriage of unlawful matter of the present kind are to stop and to return papers already existing and posted, when I notice that the conditions expressly attached to the second-class rate look only to wholly different matters, and when I consider the ease with which the power claimed by the Postmaster could be used to interfere with very sacred rights, I am of opinion that the refusal to allow the [petitioner] the rate to which it was entitled whenever its newspaper was carried, on the ground that the paper ought not to be carried at all, was unjustified by statute and was a serious attack upon liberties that not even the war induced Congress to infringe.

COMMENTARY

The government's lawyer – William H. Lamar represented the United States on appeal. He served as an assistant attorney general and solicitor of the Post Office Department. In 1919 before the *Burleson* case was argued in the Supreme Court, he had been targeted for assassination by a campaign of anarchist bombings. *See* Geoffrey R. Stone, *Perilous Times: Free Speech in Wartime* (New York: W. W. Norton, 2004), at 220–22.

Not a wartime case – In his dissent, Justice Louis Brandeis stressed that this case was not a wartime case and thus should be judged by a standard different from the one employed in *Schenck v. United States* and its progeny. "This case arose during the World War; but it presents no legal question peculiar to war. It is important, because what we decide may determine in large measure whether in times of peace our press shall be free." And again toward the end of his dissent, he added: "I say again – because it cannot be stressed too strongly – that the power here claimed is not a war power. There is no question of its necessity to protect the country from insidious domestic foes." 255 U.S. 407, 417, 436 (Brandeis, J., dissenting).

In a similar vein, Zechariah Chafee observed: "No decision of the United States Supreme Court has gone so far in sustaining government powers over the press as its opinion" in the *Burleson* case. "Although the case arose under the Espionage Act, its most important effect will probably be in extending the power of the Postmaster General to penalize discussion in time of peace. . . . The correctness of this decision is far less important than its consequences. It is nowise limited to war cases, and enables the Postmaster General to suppress any newspaper with a few articles [that] are unmailable on any ground." *Free Speech in the United States, supra,* at 298–99, 304.

The reach of the Espionage Act – "Even if the particular issues of the *Leader* were properly held to violate the Espionage Act, this does not affect the main question – if the Postmaster General denies that a newspaper has published non-mailable matter in past issues, may he revoke its second-class permit for all future issues? Nothing in the statutes expressly gives him this drastic power." *Free Speech in the United States, supra,* at 303.

Return to the rights-privilege distinction – According to Professor White, Holmes "confessed that, until he had read Brandeis' dissent, he had been inclined to support the majority's position on the ground that 'if a publisher should announce in terms that he proposed to print treason and should demand a second-class rate it must be that the Postmaster General would have authority to refuse it.' But Holmes had become convinced that '[t]he question of the rate has nothing to do with the question whether the matter is mailable,' and that the Postmaster General could not determine nonmailability in advance. The only thing the Postmaster General was empowered to do under the statute, Holmes felt, was to deny second-class mail privileges, and after the publications were mailed 'to refrain from forwarding the papers . . . and to return them to the senders.' He was not empowered to decide, on the basis of a publication's content, that it could not be carried in the mails. . . .

"Holmes'[s] response to the free speech implications of *Burleson* was in stark contrast to his treatment of arguably similar cases earlier in his career. Holmes had conceded that '[t]he United States may give up the Post Office when it sees fit.' He did not accept the government's argument, however, that 'a citizen uses the mail at second-class rates not as of right – but by virtue of a privilege or permission, the granting of which rests in the discretion of the Postmaster General.' In fact, Holmes spoke in his opinion of 'rights' and 'liberties' in the use of the mails. Yet in his . . . opinion in *McAuliffe v. Mayor of*

New Bedford [see Part III], the Massachusetts case involving a policeman who was fired for engaging in partisan political activity, he had summarily dismissed a First Amendment claim that the government could not condition access to its employment on conformity to its rules where those rules included a ban on the expression of political sentiments. *Burleson* embodied an analogous claim – that the government could condition access to its mailing privileges, which it could withdraw at any point, on a user's not engaging in seditious speech. And yet Holmes, who had announced that there was no constitutional right to be a policeman, suggested in Burleson that there was a constitutional right to use the mails. His shift of position was consonant with the enhanced sensitivity to free speech issues that his Abrams dissent had demonstrated." G. Edward White, "Justice Holmes and the Modernization of Free Speech Jurisprudence: The Human Dimension," 80 *California Law Review* 391, 443– 44 (1992).

The importance of a Holmesian aphorism – Recall that, in his dissent, Holmes declared that "the United States may give up the Postoffice when it sees fit, but while it carries it on the use of the mails is almost as much a part of free speech as the right to use our tongues." It has been observed that this statement "is justifiably famous simply as a rhetorical device . . . Justice Holmes's aphorism . . . is in some ways . . . the perfect embodiment of the notion of an institutional First Amendment. One way to see this is to compare the Post Office to a public educational institution such as a university. At first blush, the two do not seem comparable, but the premise underlying Justice Holmes's statement – that the mere creation and maintenance of a post office entails government responsibilities that are constrained by First Amendment principles – is precisely what underlay some of the early seminal public university First Amendment cases." Anuj C. Desai, "The Transformation of Statutes into Constitutional Law: How Early Post Office Policy Shaped Modern First Amendment Doctrine," 58 *Hastings Law Journal* 671, 713–14 (2007) (footnotes omitted).

Restoration of mail privileges – Postmaster General Albert Burleson's successor, William Hays, restored the *Leader's* second-class mail privilege. *See Free Speech in the United States, supra,* at 305 n. 32.

Subsequent cases – Writing for the Court in *Hannegan v. Esquire,* Justice William O. Douglas declared, "grave constitutional questions are immediately raised once it is said that the use of the mails is a privilege which may be extended or withheld on any grounds whatsoever. See the dissents of Mr. Justice Brandeis and Mr. Justice Holmes in *United States ex rel. Milwaukee Social Democrat Publishing Co. v. Burleson.*" 327 U.S. 146, 156 (1946). *See also*

"The Transformation of Statutes into Constitutional Law," *supra*, at 705–17 (2007).

I do not suppose that anyone would say that the freedom of written speech is less protected by the First Amendment than the freedom of spoken word. Therefore I cannot understand by what authority Congress undertakes to authorize anyone to determine in advance . . . that certain words shall not be uttered. Even those who interpret the Amendment most strictly agree that it was intended to prevent previous restraints. If the execution of this law does not abridge freedom of speech I do not quite see what could be said to do so.

LEACH V. CARLILE

258 U.S. 138 (1922)
For the majority: Justice John Clarke
Vote: 5–2
Submitted: January 18, 1922
Decided: February 27, 1922
For the appellant: Lee D. Mathias and P. W. Sullivan
For appellee: Solicitor General James M. Beck, Assistant Attorney General Crim, and H. S. Ridgely

Fred Leach sold, under a variety of names, an alleged remedy for "sexual weakness and disorders in men" (as the Court of Appeals put it[58]) through the mail. Leach called the tablets Orchic Extract, and they consisted of dried and powdered sheep's testicles. The pills were advertised, sold, and sent through the mail. In 1919 the postmaster general issued a fraud order against the company and refused to deliver mail or payment from money orders. Leach was a repeat offender, having gone through much of the same ordeal in 1917 and 1918. Writing for the 7–2 majority, Justice John Clarke deferred to the decision of the postmaster general. Holmes dissented and was joined by Justice Brandeis.

Mr. Justice Holmes, dissenting.

The statute under which fraud orders are issued by the Postmaster General has been decided or said to be valid so many times that it may be too late to expect a contrary decision. But there are considerations against it that seem to me never to have been fully weighed and that I think it my duty to state.

The transmission of letters by any general means other than the postoffice is forbidden by the Criminal Code. Therefore, if these prohibitions are valid,

[58] *Leach v. Carlile*, 267 F. 61 (7th Cir. 1920) (per Alschuler, J.).

this form of communication with people at a distance is through the postoffice alone; and notwithstanding all modern inventions letters still are the principal means of speech with those who are not before our face. I do not suppose that anyone would say that the freedom of written speech is less protected by the First Amendment than the freedom of spoken words. Therefore I cannot understand by what authority Congress undertakes to authorize anyone to determine in advance, on the grounds before us, that certain words shall not be uttered. Even those who interpret the Amendment most strictly agree that it was intended to prevent previous restraints. We have not before us any question as to how far Congress may go for the safety of the nation. The question is only whether it may make possible irreparable wrongs and the ruin of a business in the hope of preventing some cases of a private wrong that generally is accomplished without the aid of the mail. Usually private swindling does not depend upon the postoffice. If the execution of this law does not abridge freedom of speech I do not quite see what could be said to do so.

Even if it should be held that the prohibition of other modes of carrying letters was unconstitutional . . . it would not get rid of the difficulty to my mind, because the practical dependence of the public upon the postoffice would remain. . . . The decisions thus far have gone largely if not wholly on the ground that if the Government chose to offer a means of transportation which it was not bound to offer it could choose what it would transport; which is well enough when neither law nor the habit that the Government's action has generated has made that means the only one. But when habit and law combine to exclude every other it seems to me that the First Amendment in terms forbids such control of the post as was exercised here. I think it abridged freedom of speech on the part of the sender of the letters and that the appellant had such an interest in the exercise of their right that he could avail himself of it in this case.

Mr. Justice Brandeis concurs in this opinion.

CORRESPONDENCE

To Harold Laski
Washington, D.C.
February 7, 1922

Dear Laski,

. . . I frequently remark that I am paid to listen to people, and that the notion of gratuitously going in search of that kind of trouble is against my grain. In a few minutes I must try to get hold of Brandeis and see whether he thinks it worth while for me to utter a squeak on the matter of fraud orders by the post office which raises doubts in my mind that never have been adequately discussed. The trouble is that it is perhaps too late in the day. This is the moment when I specially need your suggestions – we are adjourned until the end of the month and my cases are written – so I hope to read a little. . . .

Holmes-Laski Letters: The Correspondence of Mr. Justice Holmes and Harold J. Laski, Mark DeWolfe Howe, ed. (Cambridge, MA: Harvard University Press, 1953), at 2:406.

To Felix Frankfurter
Washington, D.C.
February 9, 1922

Dear Frankfurter,

. . . My cases are all written and agreed to by everybody except that in one Clarke may dissent. And I have embodied in a short dissent my views on fraud orders. Whether in view of the decisions it will be worthwhile to publish them I still hesitate and await the conference (this of course strictly between ourselves). . . .

Holmes and Frankfurter: Their Correspondence, 1912–1934, Robert M. Mennel and Christine L. Compston, eds. (Hanover, NH: University Press of New England, 1996), at 135.

To Francis Pollock
Washington, February 26, 1922

My dear Pollock:

. . . I have four cases to fire off, and think I shall express a dissent upon a matter that has been settled without to my mind adequate consideration of the question [in *Leach v. Carlile*]. The U.S. Statutes require letters, etc., to be sent by post, which apart from the requirement is practically the only means of communication at a distance. The Postmaster General stops letters and circulars that he (*i.e.* generally, I suppose, some understaffer) decides to be fraudulent, etc. etc. . . . The Constitution, 1st Amendment, forbids any law abridging the freedom of speech and I can't believe that the stoppage is lawful. I think in fact it has been an instrument of more or less tyranny and used to stop communications that would seem all right to a different mode of thought. . . .

Holmes-Pollock Letters: The Correspondence of Mr. Justice Holmes and Sir Frederick Pollock, 1874–1932, Mark DeWolfe Howe, ed. (Cambridge, MA: Harvard University Press, 1941), at 2:90.

To Harold Laski
Washington, D.C.
March 11, 1922

Dear Laski,

. . . Perhaps I told you that I wrote a short dissent (Brandeis alone concurring) against the constitutionality of the post office fraud orders. It was too deeply settled to be disturbed at once, but it has been on my conscience for years and some day a dissent may bear fruit.

Holmes-Laski Letters, supra, at 2:410.

COMMENTARY

Brandeis and his influence on Holmes – According to Holmes's biographer Sheldon Novick, Brandeis urged Holmes to write dissents in *Gitlow v. New York, United States v. Schwimmer*, and other cases, playing on Holmes's "sense of duty. In response to Brandeis's urging, Holmes wrote a dissenting opinion in a case of censorship of the mails, which for twenty years he had allowed to pass without objection. With each dissent he became more celebrated, but he did not look back with much interest at the parade of strangers who were carrying him at the head of their march." Adds Novick, "In the 1920s, particularly when early efforts to achieve compromise broke down, Brandeis urged Holmes to write dissents, and Holmes did publish dissenting opinions more often than he would have, as in *Leach v. Carlilie . . .* and *Milwaukee Social Democrat Pub. Co. v. Burleson. . . .* I have found no evidence at all that Holmes's substantive thought was affected by Brandeis, who was very much his junior in age and judicial experience." Sheldon M. Novick, *Honorable Justice: The Life of Oliver Wendell Holmes* (New York: Dell Publishing, 1989), at 353, 476 n. 36.

> *If, in the long run, the beliefs expressed in proletarian dictatorship are destined to be accepted by the dominant forces of the community, the only meaning of free speech is that they should be given their chance and have their way.*

GITLOW V. NEW YORK

268 U.S. 652 (1925)
Vote: 7–2
For the majority: Sanford, J.
Argued: April 12, 1923
Reargued: November 23, 1923
Decided: June 8, 1925
For petitioner: Walter H. Pollak and Walter Nelles
For respondent: John Caldwell Myers, W. J. Wetherbee,
and Claude T. Dawes

After the 1919 spate of free speech cases that came before the Court, litigants begin to challenge newly enacted state syndicalism laws,[59] like the one in the Gitlow *case. Benjamin Gitlow was a member of the Left Wing Faction – a splinter group of the Socialist Party. The faction's advocacy of violence caused it to split off, and in 1919 Gitlow published "The Left Wing Manifesto" in the* Revolutionary Age.[60] *The piece advocated a Communist regime brought about by strikes and revolution. He was arrested under New York's Criminal Anarchy Act of 1902 and sentenced to five to ten years in prison.[61] He first appealed his conviction in the New York state courts[62] and then to the U.S. Supreme Court.[63]*

When the Gitlow *case came before the Court for reargument in November 1923, the First Amendment had not yet been held applicable to the states by way of the Fourteenth Amendment. Even so, a majority of the Court had been active in using the Fourteenth Amendment to strike down various kinds of protective legislation as unconstitutional abridgements of liberty of contract. Three days after* Gitlow *was originally argued, the Court in* Adkins v. Children's Hospital[64] *struck down a federal minimum wage law for women as just such an abridgment. Holmes dissented. It was against that backdrop that Holmes wrote the following to Harold Laski about the* Gitlow *case, which had just been argued. "I am*

---

[59] See Clem Work, *Darkest before Dawn: Sedition and Free Speech in the American West* (Albuquerque: University of New Mexico Press, 2006).

[60] The manifesto's cover page is reproduced at the end of the commentaries following this case. For the full text of the lengthy manifesto, see http://1stam.umn.edu/main/primary/primary.htm.

[61] See "Gitlow, Anarchist, Gets Limit Sentence," *New York Times*, February 12, 1920, at 1.

[62] See *People v. Gitlow*, 195 A.D. 773, 187 N.Y.S. 783 (N.Y. App. Div., 1921); *People v. Gitlow*, 234 N.Y. 132, 136 N.E. 317 (N.Y. 1922).

[63] For a detailed account of the facts in the case and its history in the courts, see Zechariah Chafee Jr., *Free Speech in the United States* (Cambridge, MA: Harvard University Press, 1967), at 318–25.

[64] 261 U.S. 525 (1923).

curious to see what the enthusiasts of liberty of contract will say with regard to liberty of speech under a State law punishing advocating the overthrow of the government – by violence. The case was argued this week."[65] That incorporation issue was the one that Holmes himself had left unresolved in his opinion for the Court in Patterson v. Colorado (1907) (see Part IV).

More than a year and a half after the case was reargued, the Court rendered its judgment in Gitlow. Justice Edward Sanford wrote for the majority. Two aspects of his opinion are noteworthy. First, he declared: "For present purposes we may and do assume that freedom of speech and of the press – which are protected by the First Amendment from abridgment by Congress – are among the fundamental personal rights and 'liberties' protected by the due process clause of the Fourteenth Amendment from impairment by the States."[66] Second, he held that Schenck's clear-and-present-danger rule did not apply to the facts in Gitlow. Instead, he resurrected a variation of the old bad-tendency test:

> It is clear that the question in such cases [like Abrams v. United States] is entirely different from that involved in those cases where the statute merely prohibits certain acts involving the danger of substantive evil, without any reference to language itself, and it is sought to apply its provisions to language used by the defendant for the purpose of bringing about the prohibited results. There, if it be contended that the statute cannot be applied to the language used by the defendant because of its protection by the freedom of speech or press, it must necessarily be found, as an original question, without any previous determination by the legislative body, whether the specific language used involved such likelihood of bringing about the substantive evil as to deprive it of the constitutional protection. In such case it has been held that the general provisions of the statute may be constitutionally applied to the specific utterance of the defendant if its natural tendency and probable effect was to bring about the substantive evil which the legislative body might prevent.

Furthermore, Sanford took issue with the clear-and-present-danger formulation, concluding that the calculation of danger could reasonably be set earlier in time. In making that argument, Sanford employed metaphors reminiscent of Holmes's fire metaphor in Schenck. Wrote Sanford:

> And the immediate danger is none the less real and substantial, because the effect of a given utterance cannot be accurately foreseen. The State

---

[65] Holmes-Laski Letters, supra note 36, at 1:495.

[66] See Charles Warren, "The New 'Liberty' under the Fourteenth Amendment," 39 Harvard Law Review 431 (1925–26).

cannot reasonably be required to measure the danger from every such utterance in the nice balance of a jeweler's scale. A single revolutionary spark may kindle a fire that, smouldering for a time, may burst into a sweeping and destructive conflagration. It cannot be said that the State is acting arbitrarily or unreasonably when in the exercise of its judgment as to the measures necessary to protect the public peace and safety, it seeks to extinguish the spark without waiting until it has enkindled the flame or blazed into the conflagration. It cannot reasonably be required to defer the adoption of measures for its own peace and safety until the revolutionary utterances lead to actual disturbances of the public peace or imminent and immediate danger of its own destruction; but it may, in the exercise of its judgment, suppress the threatened danger in its incipiency.

Justice Holmes, joined by Brandeis, dissented in the case, though not on the issue of the presumptive application of the First Amendment to the states.

Holmes, J., dissenting.

Mr. Justice Brandeis and I are of opinion that this judgment should be reversed. The general principle of free speech, it seems to me, must be taken to be included in the Fourteenth Amendment, in view of the scope that has been given to the word "liberty" as there used, although perhaps it may be accepted with a somewhat larger latitude of interpretation than is allowed to Congress by the sweeping language that governs or ought to govern the laws of the United States. If I am right, then I think that the criterion sanctioned by the full Court in *Schenck v. United States* applies: "The question in every case is whether the words used are used in such circumstances and are of such a nature as to create a clear and present danger that they will bring about the substantive evils that [the State] has a right to prevent."

It is true that, in my opinion, this criterion was departed from in *Abrams v. United States*, but the convictions that I expressed in that case are too deep for it to be possible for me as yet to believe that it and *Schaefer v. United States* [251 U.S. 466 (1920)], have settled the law. If what I think the correct test is applied, it is manifest that there was no present danger of an attempt to overthrow the government by force on the part of the admittedly small minority who shared the defendant's views. It is said that this manifesto was more than a theory, that it was an incitement. Every idea is an incitement. It offers itself for belief, and, if believed, it is acted on unless some other belief outweighs it or some failure of energy stifles the movement at its birth. The only difference between the expression of an opinion and an incitement in the narrower sense is the speaker's enthusiasm for the result. Eloquence may set fire to reason.[67] But whatever may be thought of the redundant discourse before us, it had no chance of starting a present conflagration. If, in the long run, the beliefs expressed in proletarian dictatorship are destined to be accepted by the dominant forces of the community, the only meaning of free speech is that they should be given their chance and have their way.

If the publication of this document had been laid as an attempt to induce an uprising against government at once, and not at some indefinite time in the future, it would have presented a different question. The object would have been one with which the law might deal, subject to the doubt whether there was any danger that the publication could produce any result, or in other words, whether it was not futile and too remote from possible consequences. But the indictment alleges the publication, and nothing more.

CORRESPONDENCE

To Frederick Pollock
Washington, D.C.
June 2, 1925

Dear Pollock:

... I am bothered by a case in which conscience and judgment are a little in doubt concerning the constitutionality under the 14th amendment of a State law punishing the publication of a manifesto advocating the forcible overthrow of government.... Such is the effect of putting a doubt into words that I turned aside from this letter and wrote my views which now are waiting to go to the printer. The theme is one which I have written majority and minority opinions heretofore and to which I thought I could add about ten words to what I have said before. So the result is that you get nothing from me this time except wishes for a pleasant journey and successful return which I suppose is approaching....

Holmes-Pollock Letters: The Correspondence of Mr. Justice Holmes and Sir Frederick Pollock, 1874–1932, Mark DeWolfe Howe, ed., (Cambridge, MA: Harvard University Press, 1941), at 2:162.

---

[67] For a discussion of the use of fire metaphors in the *Gitlow* case, see Haig A. Bosmajian, *Metaphor and Reason in Judicial Opinions* (Carbondale: Southern Illinois University Press, 1992), at 186–98. – *Ed.*

To Harold Laski
Beverly Farms
June 14, 1925

Dear Laski:

... The last day of Court I let out a page of slack on the right of an ass to drool about proletarian dictatorship but I was alone with Brandeis. Free speech means to most people you may say anything that I don't think shocking....

Holmes-Laski Letters: The Correspondence of Mr. Justice Holmes and Harold J. Laski, Mark DeWolfe Howe, ed. (Cambridge, MA: Harvard University Press, 1953), at 1:752.

To Frederick Pollock
Beverly Farms, June 18, 1925

Dear Pollock:

... My last performance during the term, on the last day, was a dissent (in which Brandeis joined) in favor of the rights of an anarchist (so-called) to talk drool in favor of the proletarian dictatorship. But the prevailing notion of free speech seems to be that you may say what you choose if you don't shock *me*....

Holmes-Pollock Letters, supra, at 2:163 (emphasis in original).

To Lewis Einstein
Beverly Farms, July 11, 1925

Dear Einstein,

... What you quote from Dizzy [Benjamin Disraeli] comes in apropos as I was just writing a day or two ago to a friend who repeated a criticism of my opinions that they might be literature but were not the proper form of judicial exposition. My notion was that longwinded expositions of the obvious were as out of place in opinions as elsewhere. This however is not intended as a hit at the judgment of the majority in the *Gitlow* case. I had my whack on free speech some years ago in the case of one Abrams, and therefore did no more than lean to that and add that an idea is always an incitement. To show the ardor of the writer is not a sufficient reason for judging him. I regarded my view as simply upholding the right of a donkey to drool. But the usual notion is that you are free to say what you like if you don't shock *me*. Of course the value of the constitutional right is only when you do shock people. . . .

The Holmes-Einstein Letters: Correspondence of Mr. Justice Holmes and Lewis Einstein, 1903–1935, James Bishop Peabody, ed. (New York: St. Martin's Press, 1964), at 243–44.

COMMENTARY

The popular press – Even after Holmes's *Abrams* dissent, the popular press, including the *New York Times*, sympathized with the majority view expressed in *Gitlow*. "Yesterday's decision of the Supreme Court in the *Gitlow* case is, in its essence, simply a reaffirmation of an old principle of law and government. Any constituted Government is entitled to protect itself against overthrow by violence. . . . The vaporings of one anarchist, or of 10,000 anarchists, could make the authorities tremble. But there is such a thing as moral peril in addition to one merely physical. And the Supreme Court is of the opinion that an open incitement to violence against the State is a moral peril against which the State may lawfully protect itself by a stringent statute.

"This is no denial of free speech. But the free speakers must be ready to face their responsibility to the law for what they say. . . . Revolutionists retain their old privilege of perishing gloriously in arms, but they can't incite others to perish and hope to get off themselves scot free." "When Anarchy Is Criminal," *New York Times*, June 9, 1925.

A similar but more colorful view was expressed in an editorial in the *Evening Star*, a paper from Washington, D.C.: "Denial of the freedom of speech is not involved in the enactment and enforcement of laws which are designed to protect the state from subversive radicalism. Advocacy of a different form of government is not denied. But in this case, as in many others that have not come to the point of prosecution and punishment, in large degree in consequence of a policy of tolerance, there was actually a call for action, a summoning of the forces of disruption, a mandate for revolt.

"'I was only theorizing, only pointing out the way to ideal government,' says the anarchist who is held for seditious utterances. 'I was only exercising the right of free speech in expressing my opinion of what government should be, not raising the standard of rebellion.' Such in effect was the defense in the *Gitlow* case. The Supreme Court says now that that is no defense, that incitation to revolution for the overturning of government is a crime against the

United States or against any State that has a specific statute such as that of New York, which is now sustained. This decision will strengthen the defenses of this country against radical subversion. Even though the defendant in this case, who has already served a considerable length of time in prison, should now be pardoned by Gov. Smith of New York, the decision stands as a safeguard for sound government." "The Gitlow Decision," *Evening Star*, June 9, 1925.

Predictably, Professor Chafee, writing in the *New Republic*, offered a different view: "The victories of liberty of speech must be won in the mind before they are won in the courts. In that battle-field of reason we possess new and powerful weapons, the dissenting opinions of Justices Holmes and Brandeis. Out of this long series of legal defeats has come a group of arguments for toleration that may fitly stand beside the *Aeropagitica* and Mill's *Liberty*. The majority opinions determined the cases, but these dissenting opinions will determine the minds of the future." Zechariah Chafee Jr., "The Gitlow Case," *New Republic*, July 1, 1925.

The Gitlow *case and its lawyers* – Before the matter came to the U.S. Supreme Court, the New York Court of Appeals denied Benjamin Gitlow's claims in *People v. Gitlow*, 234 N.Y. 132 (1922). Then Judge Benjamin Cardozo dissented in the case, although not on constitutional grounds. *See generally* Harold Josephson, "Political Justice during the Red Scare: The Trial of Benjamin Gitlow," *in American Political Trials*, Michal R. Belknap, ed. (Westport, CT: Greenwood Press, 1994), at 139 *passim*. On the earlier history of the case, *see* "Gitlow Convicted in Anarchy Trial," *New York Times*, February 6, 1920, at 17; Thomas C. Mackey, "They Are Positively Dangerous Men: The Lost Court Documents of Benjamin Gitlow and James Larkin before the New York City Magistrates' Court, 1919," 69 *New York University Law Review* 421 (1994).

Walter H. Pollak, one of Gitlow's lawyers in the U.S. Supreme Court, had previously worked as a young associate in Cardozo's law firm before Cardozo was elevated to the state high court. Pollak did not, however, represent Gitlow in the state court. Later, Pollak and his colleague Walter Nelles represented Anita Whitney in *Whitney v. California*, 274 U.S. 357 (1927). *See* Ronald Collins and David Skover, "Curious Concurrence: Justice Brandeis's Vote in *Whitney v. California*, 2005 *Supreme Court Review* 333. But for the work of Pollak and Nelles it is unlikely that the procedural posture of the case would have allowed for a First Amendment ruling. One more note: before he died, Pollak hired a young associate named Thomas Emerson, who went on to become a Yale Law School professor and a noted First Amendment scholar. On his death, Zechariah Chafee wrote a tribute in his honor. *See* "Walter Heilprin Pollak," *Nation*, October 12, 1940, at 318–19.

Chief Justice Taft dissenting? – "It appears that at first Taft voted to reverse Git-low's conviction and considered joining Holmes's dissent. On May 4, Holmes sent Taft a draft passage asking whether he should add it to his dissenting opinion (he did)...)....He would not have asked Taft's advice unless Taft were considering joining in the dissenting opinion. But when the opinion of the Court was announced on June 8, 1925, only Brandeis joined Holmes's dissent." Sheldon M. Novick, *Honorable Justice: The Life of Oliver Wendell Holmes* (New York: Dell Publishing, 1989), at 478 n. 68.

Speech, dictatorships, and opinions "fraught with death" – Recall Holmes's statement in his *Gitlow* dissent: "If, in the long run, the beliefs expressed in proletarian dictatorship are destined to be accepted by the dominant forces of the community, the only meaning of free speech is that they should be given their chance and have their way." Commenting on this view of things, Professor Sunstein has observed, "Holmes'[s] skepticism, and his insistence on 'free trade,' give his conception a distinctive flavor of its own. In all his writings on free speech, Holmes pays little attention to the appropriate conditions under which free trade in ideas will ensure truth, a gap that is probably attributable to his skepticism about whether truth, as an independent value, is at issue at all." Cass Sunstein, *Democracy and the Problem of Free Speech* (New York: Free Press, 1993), at 26.

Considering what Holmes wrote in *Abrams* and *Gitlow*, Professor Stanley Fish has noted: "If our commitment to freedom of speech is so strong that it obliges us, as Holmes [declared in *Abrams*], to tolerate 'opin-ions...we...believe fraught with death,...then we are being asked to court our own destruction for the sake of an abstraction that may doom us rather than save us. There are really only three alternatives: [1] either Holmes does not mean it, as suggested by his instant qualification ("unless...an immediate check is required to save the country"), or [2] he means it but doesn't think that opinions fraught with death could ever triumph in a free market (in which case he commits himself to a progressivism he neither analyzes nor declares), or [3] he means it and thinks deadly opinions could, in fact, triumph, but is saying something like '*qué será, será,*' (as it would appear he is in...*Gitlow*...). Each of these readings of what Holmes is telling us in *Abrams* and *Gitlow* is problematic...." Stanley Fish, *There's No Such Thing as Free Speech...And It's a Good Thing, Too* (New York: Oxford University Press, 1993), at 119. Pro-fessor Peters has suggested another possible alternative: Holmes "wanted a strong First Amendment not because he thought more speech was the cure for bad speech, but because he wanted to leave the evolutionary battlegrounds uncluttered – like a Roman official making sure the gladiators all have water and bread before they head into combat." John Durham Peters, *Courting the Abyss: Free Speech and the Liberal Tradition* (Chicago: University of Chicago Press, 2005), at 152.

Extraordinary prose, disturbing implications – The late Professor Harry Kalven was somewhat critical of Holmes's *Gitlow* dissent, which he thought "did not rise to the occasion" in responding to Justice Sanford's legitimate arguments concerning line drawing, judicial evaluations of danger, and the inapplicability of the *Schenck* logic to the *Gitlow* case. *See* Harry Kalven Jr., ed., *A Worthy Tradition: Freedom of Speech in America* (New York: Harper & Row, 1988), at 154–56. "Justice Holmes's dissent in *Gitlow*," added Kalven, "like his *Abrams* peroration, is extraordinary prose to find in a judicial opinion, and I suspect it has contributed beyond measure to the charisma of the First Amendment. But it also carries the disturbing suggestion that the defendants' speech is to be protected precisely because it is harmless and unimportant. It smacks . . . of a luxury civil liberty." *Ibid.*, at 156.

Holmes's dilemma – "By the time *Gitlow* was decided it had become apparent that [Holmes] and other adherents of the 'clear and present danger' principle faced a dilemma. That test had been designed to deal with situations in which a legislature had identified a proscribed end (e.g., obstructing the war effort), and the issue was whether a particular expression closely related to that end. In *Gitlow*, however, the statute had criminalized the form of expression itself. . . . [T]he application of 'clear and present danger' to *Gitlow* seemed to come out of the blue. If the states had more latitude to restrict speech than the federal government," as it had seemed to Holmes and others, "judicial tests developed in cases in which Congress had restricted speech might not necessarily be applicable. On the other hand, if *Schenck* controlled, and the 'clear and present danger' test was a rule of causation, evaluating the closeness of the connection between advocacy and illegal acts, causation would seem to have been satisfied in those instances in which a legislature had outlawed advocacy itself. It was only if the 'clear and present danger' in its reformulated version – the version Holmes insisted had been departed from in *Abrams* and *Schaefer* – was the correct test, that the legislative action in *Gitlow* deserved searching scrutiny. But if so, the same level of judicial scrutiny obtained in state and federal speech cases. Holmes'[s] successive comments, then, appeared to contradict one another. . . . After *Abrams*, Holmes had come to see the 'clear and present danger' test as a substantive evaluation of the seriousness of any threat posed by the speech at issue, even though he couched that inquiry in the 'remoteness' language of causation." G. Edward White,

Justice Oliver Wendell Holmes: Law and the Inner Self (New York: Oxford University Press, 1993), at 441, 443.

What happened to the clear-and-present-danger test? – "Holmes'[s] dissent is too compressed to be clear. He started from the factual situation, and since he saw no present danger from either the publication in question or from the activities of the small group, he argued that the statute could not validly be applied. He did not use the clear and present danger standard to question the constitutionality of the statute itself. Yet he clearly did not agree with Justice Sanford that the Court always had to accept as conclusive a legislative determination of the danger likely from statements which advocated [government opposition]." Yosal Rogat and James M. O'Fallon, "Mr. Justice Holmes: A Dissenting Opinion – The Free Speech Cases," 36 *Stanford Law Review* 1349, 1402 (1964).

Critical questions Holmes left unanswered – Holmes did not deal "with a critical question, namely, whether the Court should simply accept a legislative judgment that some types of speech were dangerous and could therefore be proscribed. There is no indication in his very brief dissent that the New York statute might be unconstitutional. He also did not address Sanford's notion that the courts should accept legislative determination, a position Holmes and Brandeis had long held in economic cases. If a case concerned civil liberties, did that put it into a different category or give judges greater responsibilities? These questions would concern Brandeis in the next speech case to come to the Court." Melvin I. Urofsky, *Louis Brandeis: A Life* (New York: Pantheon Books, 2009), at 634.

Much to the same effect, it has been argued that Holmes "completely avoided discussing the extent to which the Court can independently determine the likelihood of danger from a particular expression. Judging from his opinion, his position might have been that a court *at times* could still consider whether a particular publication presented any reasonable expectation of harm, and that, in terms of the clear and present danger standard, it was unconstitutional to apply the statute to the particular facts of *Gitlow*. In any case, one would think that the desire to influence future decisions, to guide those eager to follow his lead on this question, would have led him to clarify the basis of his position, to demonstrate that it answered the problem posed by the New York law." "Mr. Justice Holmes: A Dissenting Opinion – The Free Speech Cases," *supra*, 36 *Stanford Law Review* at 1402 (emphasis in original).

Rethinking Gitlow – Oregon Supreme Court Justice Hans Linde offered different ways of thinking about how to analyze the First Amendment issue raised in *Gitlow*: "Since New York's law itself defined the prohibited speech," he wrote, "the [*Gitlow*] Court could choose among three positions: It could (1) accept this legislative judgment of the harmful potential of the proscribed words, subject to conventional judicial review; (2) independently scrutinize the facts to see whether a 'danger,' as stated in *Schenck*, justified suppression of the particular expression; or (3) hold that by legislating directly against the words rather than the effects, the lawmaker had gone beyond the leeway left to trial and proof by the holding in *Schenck* and had made a law forbidden by the First Amendment." Hans Linde, "'Clear and Present Danger' Reexamined," 22 *Stanford Law Review* 1163, 1171 (1970). The third option, consistent with the express command of the First Amendment, places the initial constitutional obligation on lawmakers rather than on judges. It was an option Holmes did not exercise.

What became of Benjamin Gitlow? – Six months after the Court affirmed Benjamin Gitlow's conviction, New York Governor Al Smith pardoned him. As reported in the *New York Times*: "Benjamin Gitlow, Socialist and former State Assemblyman, will leave Sing Sing Prison tomorrow morning as soon as Warden Lawes opens the mail, for in it will be a pardon for Gitlow, Governor Smith announced tonight." ("Gitlow Is Pardoned by Governor Smith as Punished Enough," *New York Times*, December 12, 1925, at 1.) Thereafter, in 1928 Gitlow opposed Al Smith and ran as the vice presidential candidate for the Communist Party. Subsequently, he fell out with the Communist Party, which he openly condemned in testimony before the U.S. House Committee on Un-American Activities in the late 1930s. See Benjamin Gitlow, *I Confess: The Truth about American Communism* (New York: E. P. Dutton, 1939); Benjamin Gitlow, *The Whole of Their Lives: Communism in America* (New York: Charles Scribner's Sons, 1948); Ronald Collins and Sam Chaltain, *We Must Not Be Afraid to Be Free* (New York: Oxford University Press, 2011).

Brandeis's famous concurrence – In 1927 the Court handed down a unanimous judgment in the case of *Whitney v. California*, 274 U.S. 357, wherein it upheld the conviction of Charlotte Anita Whitney under a California syndicalism statute that proscribed "advocating, teaching or aiding and abetting the commission of crime, sabotage . . . or unlawful acts of force and violence or unlawful methods of terrorism as a means of accomplishing a change in the industrial ownership or control or effecting any political change." Whitney was convicted of organizing and belonging to an organization that advocated criminal syndicalism. Because of purported procedural reasons,[68] Brandeis joined

[68] *See* "Curious Concurrence," *supra*.

in the judgment but expressed his own views of the law in a concurrence that read like a dissent. Holmes joined that opinion. As far as Holmes's free speech jurisprudence is concerned, his signing on to the Brandeis concurrence is important for at least three reasons.

First is the expansion of the *Schenck* test. Taking his cue from Holmes's *Abrams* dissent, Brandeis announced a clear-and-present-danger test more demanding than what had been announced and applied in *Schenck* and in the *Gitlow* majority's application of that standard. Declared Brandeis, "[T]he necessity which is essential to a valid restriction does not exist unless speech would produce, or is intended to produce, a clear and *imminent* danger of some substantive evil which the state constitutionally may seek to prevent has been settled." He added: "[N]o danger flowing from speech can be deemed clear and present, unless the incidence of the evil apprehended is so *imminent* that it may befall before there is opportunity for full discussion. If there be time to expose through discussion the falsehood and fallacies, to avert the evil by the processes of education, the remedy to be applied is more speech, not enforced silence. Only an *emergency* can justify repression. Such must be the rule if authority is to be reconciled with freedom." 274 U.S. at 373, 376 (emphasis added).

Second is the independent judicial review of legislative determinations. In his concurrence Brandeis made it clear that in First Amendment cases a reviewing court need not automatically and uncritically defer to a legislative determination regarding the purported danger of speech. Said Brandeis: "The Legislature must obviously decide, in the first instance, whether a danger exists which calls for a particular protective measure. But where a statute is valid only in case certain condition[s] exist, the enactment of the statute cannot alone establish the facts which are essential to its validity. Prohibitory legislation has repeatedly been held invalid, because unnecessary, where the denial of liberty involved was that of engaging in a particular business. The powers of the courts to strike down an offending law are no less when the interests involved are not property rights, but the fundamental personal rights of free speech and assembly." *Ibid.*, at 374 (footnote omitted).

Third are the justifications for protecting free speech. Although Holmes's *Abrams* dissent held out the test of truth in the marketplace as a free speech value, Brandeis added two additional values: there was the self-governance or democratic government rationale ("Political discussion is a political duty"), and there was the liberty or self-autonomy rationale ("that freedom to think as you will and to speak as you think").

When it came to the announced test, the values vouchsafed, and the role of judicial review of legislative determinations, Brandeis led Holmes beyond the confining *Schenck* test (which Holmes never renounced) and the lone justification tendered in the *Abrams* dissent for protecting speech, as well as beyond the cramped posture of his *Gitlow* dissent. On Brandeis's role in developing Holmes's free speech jurisprudence, *see* David Rabban, *Free Speech in Its Forgotten Years* (New York: Cambridge University Press, 1997), at 355–71.

A free speech victory – The same day the Court released its *Whitney* ruling, it also rendered a unanimous opinion in the case of *Fiske v. Kansas*, 274 U.S. 38 (1927). The issue in the case was whether printed matter in the forms of leaflets quoting "equivocal language" from the preamble to the Industrial Workers of the World's Constitution amounted to criminal syndicalism unprotected by the due-process clause of the Fourteenth Amendment. The Court, per Justice Edward Sanford (the author of the *Gitlow* and *Whitney* majorities), concluded that the petitioner Harold Fiske had been denied due process. Although not formally a First Amendment case, it was nevertheless the first time that the Court had ruled in favor of a rights claimant in a free speech case involving syndicalism.

Cover Page of "Left Wing Manifesto" (the text was 5 pages of solid 3-column text)

The Revolutionary Age

Devoted to the International Communist Struggle

| Vol. 2, No. 1. | Saturday, July 5, 1919 | Price 5c. |

In This Issue:
Left Wing Convention,
Manifesto and Program

THE RIGHT WINGERS

"Nothing Doing!"

If there is any principle of the Constitution that more imperatively calls for attachment than any other it is the principle of free thought – not free thought for those who agree with us but freedom for the thought that we hate.

United States v. Schwimmer

279 U.S. 644 (1929)
For the majority: Butler, J.
Vote: 6–3
Argued: April 12, 1929
Decided: May 27, 1929
For petitioner: Alfred A. Wheat
For respondent: Olive H. Rabe

Rosika Schwimmer, forty-nine at the time of the case, had worked for years in her native Hungary and elsewhere on behalf of pacifist and feminist causes. She fled Europe in 1921 to escape prosecution for her work and her ethnicity. After living in Chicago for five years, she applied for citizenship in 1926. When asked on a form if she would take up arms in defense of the country, she responded in line with her pacifism, simply answering no. Although the Naturalization Board and the district court denied her claims, the Circuit Court of Appeals[69] reversed the decision, noting that a woman would not be eligible for combat – a theme Holmes picked up in his dissent. With Justice Pierce Butler writing the majority opinion, the Supreme Court upheld the denial of the application, worrying that Schwimmer would "exert her power to influence others." Holmes, the war veteran who was no fan of pacifists, wrote a dissent that is considered his last opinion of enduring import. Justice Brandeis joined his dissent. Justice Edward Sanford wrote a separate dissent.

Mr. Justice Holmes, dissenting.

The applicant seems to be a woman of superior character and intelligence, obviously more than ordinarily desirable as a citizen of the United States. It is agreed that she is qualified for citizenship except so far as the views set forth in a statement of facts "may show that the applicant is not attached to the principles of the Constitution of the United States and well disposed to the good order and happiness of the same, and except in so far as the same may show that she cannot take the oath of allegiance without a mental reservation." The views

[69] *Schwimmer v. United States,* 27 F.2d 742 (7th Cir. 1928).

referred to are an extreme opinion in favor of pacifism and a statement that she would not bear arms to defend the Constitution. So far as the adequacy of her oath is concerned I hardly can see how that is affected by the statement, inasmuch as she is a woman over fifty years of age, and would not be allowed to bear arms if she wanted to. And as to the opinion the whole examination of the applicant shows that she holds none of the now-dreaded creeds but thoroughly believes in organized government and prefers that of the United States to any other in the world. Surely it cannot show lack of attachment to the principles of the Constitution that she thinks that it can be improved. I suppose that most intelligent people think that it might be. Her particular improvement looking to the abolition of war seems to me not materially different in its bearing on this case from a wish to establish cabinet government as in England, or a single house, or one term of seven years for the President. To touch a more burning question, only a judge mad with partisanship would exclude because the applicant thought that the Eighteenth Amendment should be repealed.

Of course the fear is that if a war came the applicant would exert activities such as were dealt with in *Schenck v. United States*. But that seems to me unfounded. Her position and motives are wholly different from those of *Schenck*. She is an optimist and states in strong and, I do not doubt, sincere words her belief that war will disappear and that the impending destiny of mankind is to unite in peaceful leagues. I do not share that optimism nor do I think that a philosophic view of the world would regard war as absurd. But most people who have known it regard it with horror, as a last resort, and even if not yet ready for cosmopolitan efforts, would welcome any practicable combinations that would increase the power on the side of peace. The notion that the applicant's optimistic anticipations would make her a worse citizen is sufficiently answered by her examination [that] seems to me a better argument for her admission than any that I can offer. Some of her answers might excite popular prejudice, but if there is any principle of the Constitution that more imperatively calls for attachment than any other it is the principle of free thought – not free thought for those who agree with us but freedom for the thought that we hate.[70] I think that we should adhere to that principle with regard to admission into, as well as to life within this country. And recurring to the opinion that bars this applicant's way, I would suggest that the Quakers have done their share to make the country what it is, that many citizens agree

---

[70] This line inspired a book title by the same name. *See* Anthony Lewis, *Freedom for the Thought That We Hate* (New York: Basic Books, 2008). – *Ed.*

with the applicant's belief and that I had not supposed hitherto that we regretted our inability to expel them because they believed more than some of us do in the teachings of the Sermon on the Mount.

Justice Brandeis concurs in this opinion.

CORRESPONDENCE

To Harold Laski
Washington, D.C.
April 13, 1929

My dear Laski:

. . . I have returned from the conference pretty well tired with it, though afterwards Brandeis and I drove over to Georgetown and home. . . . A case has gone over for further consideration, of a woman wanting to become a citizen, but who, being as she says, more of a pacifist than Jane Ad[d]ams, has to explain that she would not fight for the Constitution (or, as her counsel said, wouldn't do what the law wouldn't let her do) and so opens to the Government a discourse on the foundation of the Constitution being in readiness to defend itself by force &c. &c. All isms seem to me silly – but this hyperaetheral respect for human life seems perhaps silliest of all. . . .

To Harold Laski
Washington, D.C.
May 30, 1929

My dear Laski:

. . . My wife's death seems like the beginning of my own – but I am confused and hardly know what I think about anything. It hasn't prevented my writing. Frankfurter wrote to me highly praising something that I wrote in the midst of anxieties – and I have just turned off a dissent about the refusal to admit a pacifist to citizenship that Brandeis liked and joined in. There seems to be a distinct compartment in one's mind that works away no matter what is going on with the rest of the machinery. . . .

From Harold Laski
To Oliver Wendell Holmes
Devon Lodge
4.VI.29

My dear Justice:

... I was made very happy by your dissent in ... the Rosika Schwimmer case ... [which] I thought an iniquitous injustice and I was proud of your dissent. I do hope the modern state is not going to become a medieval church. ...

To Harold Laski
Beverly Farms
June 15, 1929

My dear Laski:

... Your last letter received yesterday ... gave me the usual pleasure. [But] I think you were ... not quite right as to Mrs. Schwimmer – I don't think the majority meant any more than that a person couldn't be attached to the principles of the Constitution if he didn't recognize that in case of need it must be supported by force, coupled with a recollection of the anti-draft talk during the late war. I couldn't help suspecting that their view was made easier by her somewhat flamboyant declaration that she was an atheist. I alluded to it discreetly without mentioning it, in what I said. ...

To Harold Laski
Beverly Farms
August 23, 1929

My dear Laski

... I still get letters from lonely enthusiasts who shout over my dissent in the case of a dame who was not allowed to become a citizen because she was a pacifist. I had one this morning (also my D.C. tax bill, bigger than I hoped). I told one of them that it was moral sympathy not legal judgment that led to his encomiums. ...

Holmes-Laski Letters: The Correspondence of Mr. Justice Holmes and Harold J. Laski, Mark DeWolfe Howe, ed. (Cambridge, MA: Harvard University Press, 1953), at 2:1146, 1152–53, 1158, 1177.

COMMENTARY

Mrs. Holmes dies – As noted in the introduction to this section and in his May 30, 1929, letter to Laski, Holmes's wife died during this period. Fanny

(Bowditch Dixwel) Holmes died on April 3, 1929, a few weeks after the oral arguments in *Schwimmer*. To help the grieving Holmes, then eighty-eight years old, Justice Brandeis spoke to his colleague about the *Schwimmer* case and about freedom of conscience. Talk of the case and the principle in it were therapeutic for the grieving jurist, or so Brandeis hoped. Thanks in part to Brandeis, Holmes rallied his energy and wrote a dissent. *See* Lewis J. Paper, *Brandeis: An Intimate Biography of One of America's Truly Great Supreme Court Justices* (Englewood Cliffs, NJ: Prentice Hall, 1980), at 326.

Woman lawyer – Olive Henrietta Rabe represented Rosika Schwimmer in the Supreme Court and in the lower courts. She was the first woman to argue a free expression and loyalty oath case in the Supreme Court. She attended the University of Chicago, where she majored in economics and was elected to Phi Beta Kappa. Rabe began her legal education at the age of twenty-seven at the John Marshall Law School in Chicago (1914–15). While there, she maintained a nearly straight-A average. She then transferred to Northwestern University Law School, again earning impressive grades, including an A in her five-credit constitutional law course. Rabe received her LLB in 1916 and was selected by the faculty for consideration as commencement speaker. For an account of her remarkable life in the law and beyond, see Ronald Collins and David Hudson, "Remembering Two Forgotten Women in Free-Speech History, Parts I & II," First Amendment Center, May 27, 2008, http://www.firstamendmentcenter. org/analysis.aspx?id=19957.

Statutory interpretation – Long before the spate of loyalty cases that flowed from President Harry Truman's Executive Order 9835 (1947), and before the Supreme Court struck down a loyalty law on constitutional grounds in *Speiser v. Randall*, 357 U.S. 513 (1958), lawyers litigated cases like Schwimmer's by first inquiring whether the government was authorized by law to deprive someone of a claimed right. If that point was decided in favor of a rights claimant, then there was no need to reach any larger constitutional (i.e., First Amendment or due-process) question because the claimant would have received the relief prayed for. Hence, though the *Schwimmer* case is a freedom of expression case, it was not a First Amendment case. The issue before the Court was whether the Naturalization Act authorized the Naturalization Board or the courts to deny citizenship to Rosika Schwimmer because of her beliefs, including her beliefs about pacifism. That is, did the act allow the board to deny Schwimmer citizenship simply because she refused to perform an act (bearing arms) that the law did not authorize her to perform as a member of the military?

On examining the statute and its history, the Seventh Circuit concluded that the act did not authorize any such government action. *Schwimmer v. United States*, 27 F.2d 742 (1928). Surprisingly, on that score, Justice Edward T. Sanford (author of the majority opinions denying free-speech claims in *Gitlow v. New York* and in *Whitney v. California*) dissented. He agreed, "in substance, with the views expressed by the Circuit Court of Appeals." By contrast, Holmes's short (634 words) but memorable dissent is devoid of any formal statutory analysis. For all its rhetorical power, his opinion substitutes his views about the respondent and her ideas about the war for any sustained examination of what power Congress had actually delegated to the Naturalization Board.

A *"glorious" piece of writing* – Predictably, the dissent won favor with Harvard Law School professor Felix Frankfurter. "I had assumed that you exhausted my capacity for being thrilled by magisterial utterance on behalf of sanity in your *Abrams* opinion. But you have done it again and anew. It was like real, prewar champagne to read your *Schwimmer* opinion and not because Mrs. Schwimmer matters at all to me," Frankfurter wrote to Holmes. "But the invigoration you give to spacious feeling and the confidence you intensify that man's optimism isn't a menace and may be a fillip to life mean, oh! ever so much to us. It is a glorious piece of writing. We so need the antiseptic play of your humor and wisdom." Frankfurter to Holmes, May 29, 1929, reproduced in Robert M. Mennel and Christine L. Compston, eds., *Holmes and Frankfurter: Their Correspondence, 1912–1934* (Hanover, NH: University Press of New England, 1996), at 240.

Abandonment of clear-and-present-danger test? – Though not a First Amendment case, some of the considerations in determining the purported dangerousness of Rosika Schwimmer's views were similar to those Holmes evaluated in *Schenck* and its progeny. Holmes's dissent, argues Professor White, "can be read to signify an abandonment of the 'clear and present danger' test. While continuing to accept *Schenck* and seeking to distinguish it on the basis of the respective defendants' 'position on motives,' Holmes failed to use any 'clear and present danger' language. Instead, he suggested that the 'principle of free thought,' including 'freedom for the thought that we hate,' was now a more significant constitutional principle than any other, which should apply to aliens – prospective citizens – who should not be punished for expressing their views even if those views are 'hateful' to most Americans." G. Edward White, *Justice Oliver Wendell Holmes: Law and the Inner Self* (New York: Oxford University Press, 1993), at 447–48.

Holmes's dissent in *Schwimmer*, maintains Professor Pohlman, "confirms, in a very eloquent way, the conclusion that he widened the scope of his theory of free speech beyond the core criteria of his theory of liability. . . . Free speech protected speakers not only from civil and criminal liability, but also, to an unclear degree, from a loss of privileges." H. L. Pohlman, *Justice Oliver Wendell Holmes: Free Speech and the Living Constitution* (New York: New York University Press, 1991), at 122–23.

Viewed from a broader perspective, "Holmes's opinions from *Schenck* through *Schwimmer* demonstrate that while the transformation of his ideas on free speech is readily discernible, the expression of that transformation in the form of consistent legal doctrine is not. Although on the surface Holmes appeared to continue to endorse the 'clear and present danger' test as the best means of protecting speech rights, he made very little use of it in later opinions. He employed the formula as an analytical device only once in his later speech cases, the *Gitlow* dissent, which also appeared to endorse a variety of additional tests." G. Edward White, *Justice Oliver Wendell Holmes: Law and the Inner Self, supra*, at 449. *See also* G. Edward White, *Justice Holmes and the Modernization of Free Speech Jurisprudence: The Human Dimension*, 80 *California Law Review* 391, 461–63 (1992).

Changed view of sovereignty? – In *Tiaco v. Forbes*, 228 U.S. 549, 556–57 (1913), Holmes, writing for the Court, declared: "It is admitted that sovereign states have inherent power to deport aliens, and seemingly that Congress is not deprived of this power by the Constitution of the United States." By contrast, Holmes's *Schwimmer* dissent has been described as "abandonment" in free speech cases of his "positivist views on sovereignty. In the past, Holmes had been remarkably deferential to the power of the United States to treat aliens as lacking constitutional rights. Indeed, he had been the principal early-twentieth-century Supreme Court proponent of an ultrapopulist view of sovereignty and a starkly restrictionist view of the rights of those who sought to enter or to remain in the United States. In contrast, Holmes'[s] dissent not only suggested that a constitutional principle of free thought applied to naturalization proceedings, it stated flatly that the 'principle of free thought' was of greater constitutional significance than 'any other.'" G. Edward White, *Justice Oliver Wendell Holmes: Law and the Inner Self, supra*, at 448 (footnote omitted).

Holmes the liberal – The editors of the *New Republic* (June 12, 1929) thought enough of Holmes's *Schwimmer* dissent to publish it in its entirety and prefaced it with these words: "We feel that it sets out, far more ably than any words of ours can do, the attitude which any person who calls himself a liberal ought to take toward this decision."

Sometime after the *Schwimmer* dissent came down, Holmes later told his friend and the noted fiction writer Owen Wister that his opinion was "designed to occasion discomfort in certain quarters." Quoted in Francis Biddle, *Mr. Justice Holmes* (New York: Charles Scribner's Sons, 1943), at 165.

Proposed legislation – Holmes'[s] dissent "led those sympathetic with the pacifist cause to start pushing for congressional modification of the legislation under which Mrs. Schwimmer had been barred." Paul Murphy, *The Meaning of Freedom of Speech: First Amendment Freedoms from Wilson to FDR* (Westport, CT: Greenwood Press, 1972), at 221–22. On that front, the American Civil Liberties Union took the lead. Its June 1929 newsletter described the actions it would take in response to the *Schwimmer* ruling: "The American Civil Liberties Union is planning two courses of action to overcome the Supreme Court decision. One, and the most promising, is to back a bill in Congress to prohibit the denial of citizenship to aliens because of their views on bearing arms. Such a bill, in a form not yet satisfactory, has already been introduced by Representative Anthony J. Griffin."

Rosika Schwimmer writes to Holmes – Rosika Schwimmer was moved by Holmes's dissent. She wrote to him personally, even at "the risk of violating legal etiquette," to express her "deep-felt gratitude" to Holmes. The magnificence of his dissent, she wrote, "helped me to take the blow of refusal without loss of faith in the inherent idealism of your nation." Liva Baker, *The Justice from Beacon Hill: The Life and Times of Oliver Wendell Holmes* (New York: HarperCollins, 1991), at 625–26. Critical as Holmes had privately been of Schwimmer's "silly" opinions, he was judicious in his reply, though kindly so: "You are too intelligent to need explanation of the saying you must never thank a judge. . . . If his decision was of a kind to deserve thanks," he continued, "he would not be doing his duty." And then, with Holmesian detachment, he added: "A case is simply a problem to be solved, although the considerations are more complex than those of mathematics." But he ended his letter on a personal note: "I must add of course that I am gratified by your more than kind expression." *Ibid.*, at 626.

What became of Schwimmer? – Though she never became an American citizen, Rosika Schwimmer was permitted to remain in the United States. During that time, and a year or so before Holmes died, she paid a call on the Justice at his Eye Street home in Washington, D.C.

The evolution of decisional law – In 1946 the Court (5–3) rendered its opinion in *Girouard v. United States*, 328 U.S. 61. *Girouard* was another naturalization case involving a noncombatant. Writing for the majority, Justice William O. Douglas quoted generously from Holmes's *Schwimmer* dissent. And in that spirit, Douglas stressed: "The victory for freedom of thought recorded in our Bill of Rights recognizes that in the domain of conscience there is a moral power higher than the State." By that logic, and the legal arguments accompanying it, the *Schwimmer* holding could not remain since it no longer stated "the correct rule of law." 328 U.S. at 69.

Adieu

> *Death plucks my ear and says, 'Live – I am coming.'*

Radio Address

March 8, 1931[71]

On the occasion of his ninetieth birthday, the aging justice prepared to address his fellow countrymen and countrywomen by way of a nationwide radio broadcast. It was a small part of a larger ceremony, a tribute, arranged "ostensibly by the editors of the Harvard, Yale, and Columbia Law Reviews, but with the background guidance of Felix Frankfurter. Preparations for the ceremony, which was to be held on Sunday, March 8, began on Friday, when a number of newspaper photographers sought to take Holmes' picture with Chief Justice Hughes. . . . " *Later, when the time neared, "a microphone was installed in his study so that he could respond to tributes from Hughes, dean Charles Clark of Yale Law School, and Charles Boston, president of the American Bar Association.[72] A hookup of the broadcast was set up in Langdell Hall at Harvard Law School, and about five hundred people gathered to hear it." The late-evening "broadcast involved a coordination of Boston's and Clark's remarks, which were made from a studio in New York, with remarks of Hughes and Holmes, which originated from Holmes'[s] home in Washington. The Columbia Broadcast System broadcast*

---

[71] This radio address to the nation was delivered on the occasion of Holmes's ninetieth birthday. From a manuscript in the OWH Papers, Box 19, Folder 12, reproduced in *Collected Works of Justice Holmes, supra* note 50, at 3:541. The bracketed pause indicators are from Francis Biddle, *Mr. Justice Holmes* (New York: Charles Scribner's Sons, 1943), at 192–93.

[72] Roscoe Pound, then dean of Harvard Law School, was not included in this list.

the program.”[73] *Surround by his books, some fourteen thousand of them in his home,*[74] *and with Harold Laski nearby, he relaxed in his upholstered leather chair and waited as the fireplace gently warmed the second-floor room. When his turn came, Holmes looked down at the penned remarks he had written, with lines crossed out toward the end. A moment later, he cleared his throat and began to read haltingly. He spoke softly and slowly for one minute and twenty-nine seconds as his Boston-British accent filtered his message into the microphone on his desk, this for the first and last time in his life.*[75]

In this symposium my part is only to sit in silence. [Pause.] To express one’s feelings as the end draws near is too intimate a task. But I may mention one thought that comes to me as a listener in. The riders in a race do not stop short when they reach the goal. There is a little finishing canter before coming to a stand still. There is time to hear the kind voice of friends and to say to oneself: The work is done. But just as one says that, the answer comes: The race is over, but the work is never done while the power to work remains. The canter that brings you to a stand still need not be only coming to rest. It cannot be, while you still live. For to live is to function. That is all there is in living. [Pause] And so I end with a line from a Latin poet who uttered the message more than fifteen hundred years ago – “Death plucks my ear and says, ‘Live – I am coming.’”[76]

COMMENTARY

The triumph of the ancient veteran – “Often he related that as a boy he had gazed admiringly on some venerable survivors of the Revolution riding in a military procession, and had felt that to be carried in triumph as an ancient veteran of a long past war was the most enviable lot that could befall any man. Now that America had suddenly awakened to his greatness he discovered that he had become that ancient veteran for he, too, was being carried in triumph.” “Introduction,” in *The Holmes-Einstein Letters: Correspondence of Mr. Justice*

---

[73] *Justice Oliver Wendell Holmes, supra note 12, at 462.*

[74] Most of them are now stored in the Library of Congress.

[75] *See Justice from Beacon Hill, supra note 24, at 3–7;* Mark DeWolfe Howe, comp. and ed., *The Occasional Speeches of Justice Oliver Wendell Holmes* (Cambridge, MA: Harvard University Press, 1962), at 179 (containing facsimile of hand-penned letter). *See also* Harold J. Laski, “Ever Sincerely Yours, O.W. Holmes,” *New York Times*, February 15, 1948, Sunday Magazine, at 11, 56.

[76] In the audio version, Holmes repeats the word *death*, presumably to clear his throat. – Ed.

Holmes and Lewis Einstein, 1903–1935, James Bishop Peabody, ed. (New York: St. Martin's Press, 1964), at xxii.

Latin poetry – The poem from which the last line of Holmes's radio address had been taken was "The Syrian Dancing Girl." The poem has been attributed to Virgil. *See* Theodore Martin, *Poems: Original and Translated* (London: 1863) (ascribed to Virgil, "The Tavern Dancing Girl"), at 320. "It was a poem in praise of wine, gambling, and other hedonistic pleasures, but Holmes was to use it for different purposes." *Justice Oliver Wendell Holmes: Law and the Inner Self, supra*, at 464. *See also The Justice from Beacon Hill, supra*, at 6 (Latin line from *Copa Surisca*); Mark Kaminsky, ed., *The Uses of Reminiscence* (New York: Routledge, 1984) ("Here's Death twitching my ear, 'Live,' says he, 'for I am coming'"), at 19; Virgil, *Culix*, Hermanno Vsenero, ed. (Berolini, 1891), at 117.

Life and struggle – Some of what Holmes said in his 1931 radio address was prefigured in a speech he gave to the Chicago Bar Association on October 21, 1902. In relevant part, he said: "When a man is satisfied with himself it means that he has ceased to struggle and therefore ceased to achieve. He is dead, and may be allowed the thin delight of reading his own obituary. . . . [O]ne would indeed be morbid if he did not hope . . . that the race is worth running. . . . But while it is a delight to get praise that one hopes one deserves, the fiercest joy is in the doing. Those who run the hardest probably have the least satisfaction with themselves, but they find, I am sure, that they know most of the joy of life when at top speed." *The Collected Works of Justice Holmes, supra*, at 3:532.

"Holmes'[s] capacity to survive dominates any consideration of his life," wrote G. Edward White. "Capacity to survive in the face of physical danger and emotional turmoil; capacity not merely to survive, but to thrive, to live a very long time and to function, mentally and physically, at a very high level. The unreconstructed fatalism of Holmes'[s] prose, his singular preoccupation with his somewhat narrow regimen, his periodic revelations of how little he cared for humankind in general and how mincing and structured was his affection, even for individual humans for which he cared, may tend to conceal the enthusiasm, the love, with which he approached life." *Justice Oliver Wendell Holmes: Law and the Inner Self, supra*, at 488.

Life after the Court years – After he retired from the Court on January 12, 1932, Holmes left that life behind him, though he continued to remain in contact with friends and colleagues. "The justices took turns calling, making the transition from one way of life to another less abrupt, giving time a chance to work. Felix Frankfurter, former [law clerks], family, Washington figures, all followed in their turn to the shrine. On his ninety-first birthday, NBC broadcast the tributes offered at the annual banquet of the Federal Bar Association; Holmes 'listened in' from his study.... He was seen occasionally passing the Capitol on his daily drives, but he did not return to the courtroom and did not keep up with the affairs of the Court. That chapter was closed.... He did, however, contribute a [very] short introduction to Felix Frankfurter's collection of tributes to Brandeis, which was published in 1932 as *Mr. Justice Brandeis*. And the [law clerks] continued to arrive each fall, dispatched from Harvard by Frankfurter, who recognized the continuing value of their companionship to the aging Holmes. They drove him and read to him while he listened or dozed. One of them estimated that they had read four and a half million words during the first eight months of [this period]." *The Justice from Beacon Hill, supra*, at 639.

The road to Arlington: Mrs. Holmes – As newspaper reporters from the time noted: "He drives out to Arlington. There he alights from his motor in a little frequented part of the cemetery. Slowly, he makes his way up the little hill to a grave, the last resting place of Mrs. Holmes, whose gracious personality made her a charming part of official life here until her death, a few years ago. Usually a single flower, a rose, a spray of honeysuckle or perhaps a glowing poppy is in his hand. Placing the floral tribute on her grave, he stands there a few minutes in silent contemplation and then makes his way down the little hill again to the waiting motor." The Poe Sisters, "The Washington Scene," *Washington Post*, January 27, 1935, at A12. *See also* John S. Monagan, *The Grand Panjandrum: Mellow Years of Justice Holmes* (Lanham, MD: University Press of America, 1988), at 61.

The ghost on the battlefield – For all his survival capacities, Holmes was, of course, powerless to alter his ultimate fate, including the fate of his reputation. And that fact weighed on his mind. After having left the Court, he put "a great deal of his energies into remaining in a position that [would secure] him prestige and recognition while at the same time finding that process increasingly difficult and even discouraging.... Holmes believed that when he left the Court he would surrender not only the power to work but the power of place; that he would then be subject to the vicissitudes of fame or obscurity; that *others* would determine his fate." G. Edward White, "Holmes's 'Life Plan': Confronting Ambition, Passion and Powerlessness," 65 *New York University Law Review* 1409, 1474 (1990) (emphasis added). In the summer of 1932, he admitted to Frankfurter, "I'm like a ghost on the battlefield with bullets flying through me." Felix Frankfurter Memorandum, August 8, 1932, quoted in Sheldon M. Novick, *Honorable Justice: The Life of Oliver Wendell Holmes* (New York: Dell Publishing, 1989), at 376.

Struggle and free speech – Nonetheless, even toward the end, the old soldier in Holmes was unwilling to give up the fight, the struggle. To alter the metaphor, but to the same effect, the purpose of life is to stay in the race – to keep functioning until one's last breath is exhausted. Free speech, like life itself, is akin to just such a struggle, to such a race. The more one tries, the more one realizes how much there is to know and how futile is the attempt to know all. There is, by that measure, something Socratic in Holmes's thought. In that sense, the quest is humbling. And yet despite all odds, one continues; one stays in the race. One does one's part. Because to struggle with ideas is to participate in that wondrous experiment called life. There is also this: yesterday's ideas may one day spark a thought in new generation, and thus the runner's torch is passed on. Or as Max Lerner once put it: "Perhaps a youngster will come upon a book of mine and his blood and brain will quicken, as mine used to do – and still does – when I pick up a book with some fire in it." He then quoted Samuel Butler – "'Yet meet we shall, and part, and meet again, / Where dead men meet, on lips of living men.'" Max Lerner, *Wrestling with the Angel: A Memoir of Triumph over Illness* (New York: W. W. Norton, 1990), at 193–94, 204 (quoting Butler's "Life after Death").

Last book – The last book listed in Holmes's record of the books he had read (or were read to him) was *Heaven's My Destination* (1935) by Thornton Wilder. His secretary James Rowe read the book aloud to him before he became deathly ill. The novel, set in the Great Depression, is a tale of a traveling textbook salesman with a Bible Belt enthusiasm (tinged with Gandhian insights) for leading the good life and a passion for getting others to do likewise. When the book came out, some saw it as mocking religion, though others held a contrary view. *See* Thorton Wilder, *Heaven's My Destination* (New York: Perennial, 2003), at x. In a sense, this comic romp of an Evangelical gadfly is a story about, among other things, toleration. To be able to tolerate George Brush, the menacing lead character, is not easy in a world where, as had happened in the novel, some would prosecute him, jail him, throw him out of town, or beat him up, all because of his righteous views. From this vantage point, George Brush is something like a modern-day Socrates of the moral right (with a taste of Tolstoy thrown into the mix). In another sense, he is also rather like the Jehovah's Witnesses who later came to need First Amendment protection. *See, e.g., Cantwell v. Connecticut*, 310 U.S. 296 (1940). Perhaps no American novel so well captures the essence of the First Amendment – both its expression and religion components – as well as this novel does.

Holmes dissenting: "Aged Justice Denies He's Seriously Ill" – "Indomitable as ever he had been on the bench of the United States Supreme Court, former Justice Oliver Wendell Holmes today filed a dissenting opinion against his physicians in his fight against an attack of pneumonia. While attending physicians were agreed that the condition of the 94-year-old jurist was serious, he carried assurance to his friends that there is no cause for alarm. His dissent came in thumbing his nose impudently at one of the friends who came to visit him. To prove that his condition was not alarming, the jurist insisted that friends be permitted to see him. Among them came Prof. Felix Frankfurter. . . . As the professor paused at his bed, Justice Holmes raised a weak hand, put his thumb to his nose, and extended his fingers. [Those gathered around] gasped as the jurist's eyes twinkled and his mouth stretched into a wide grin." "Holmes Refuses to Uphold View of Physicians," *Chicago Daily Tribune*, March 2, 1935, at 3.

Death comes – Late in winter 1934, Holmes caught a cold, which over time led to bronchial pneumonia. He died at 2:15 a.m. on March 6, 1935, two days before his ninety-fourth birthday. His funeral service was held at All Souls' Unitarian Church on March 8, his birthday, "with the justices of the Supreme Court as honorary pallbearers." A poem – "Mysterious Night," by Joseph Blanco White – was read at the service. During it, the reverend Ulysses Pierce quoted a passage from an 1899 memorial speech Holmes gave in which he closed by saying: "At the grave of a hero . . . we end not with sorrow at the inevitable loss, but with the contagion of his courage; and with a kind of desperate joy we go back to the fight." When the service at the church ended, "Holmes's casket was transported to Arlington National Cemetery, where President Franklin Roosevelt met the procession." G. Edward White, *Oliver Wendell Holmes, Jr.* (New York: Oxford University Press, 2006), at 129. "At Arlington National Cemetery, the coffin was placed upon a caisson drawn by artillery horses and accompanied by a guard of honor. The Army Band played 'The Battle Hymn of the Republic,' and the rudderless horse with the boots reversed in the stirrups walked in the procession." *The Grand Panjandrum, supra*, at 146. At the grave site, soldiers fired three-volley salute as the casket was placed in the grave. A single bugler played "Taps."

A soldier's last will – Holmes's estate, the bulk of which was left to the U.S. government, was valued at $568,000, which in modern dollars would be approximately $5 million. In his safety deposit box were stored two musket balls, the very ones that had wounded him in the Civil War. And in his bedroom closet hung his war uniforms. A piece of paper, with Holmes's writing on it, was pinned to one of them. It read: "These uniforms were worn by me in the Civil War and the stains upon them are my blood." *Justice Oliver Wendell Holmes: Law and the Inner Self, supra,* at 472, 488.

Epilogue: The Long Shadow

Is the influence Holmes left transitory? And are we in danger of accepting him too uncritically?
– Max Lerner[1]

Holmes had no offspring. What DNA remains of him lingers in a plot (in section 5, lot 7004) at the Arlington National Cemetery. His headstone reads:

OLIVER WENDELL HOLMES

Captain and Brevet Colonel
20th Mass. Vol. Inf., Civil War
Justice of the Supreme Court of the United States
March 1841 March 1935

After almost ninety-five years of life, that is all that is left of the physical remains of anything Holmes. His legacy was cerebral, not familial.[2] His ideas became his namesake. There is no grand monument to him and no law school named after him.[3] What survives is Holmes's image in Edgardo Simone's bust of him and in portrait paintings in the Supreme Court, Harvard Law School, and

---

[1] Max Lerner, *Nine Scorpions in a Bottle: Great Judges and Cases of the Supreme Court* (New York: Arcade Publishing, 1994), at 124. Adds Lerner: "Despite the strictures of Holmes and the skepticism about him from skeptical minds, there will be in every generation young men to read Holmes's words who will not read the words of warning about him. And their minds will be captured not by the words alone but by the personal image of Holmes that emerges from them." *Ibid.*

[2] Holmes and his wife, Fanny, did, however, raise an orphaned niece, Dorothy Upham.

[3] In 1980 Congress authorized the acquisition of land near the Supreme Court for a memorial park in Holmes's honor. *See* Act of December 18, 1980, 94 Stat. 3130; Act of

elsewhere, along with assorted photographs.[4] His likeness can also be found on a fifteen-cent U.S. postage stamp issued in 1978. Even Hollywood paid its own celluloid tribute to Holmes in a 1950 Metro-Goldwyn-Mayer movie titled *The Magnificent Yankee*, which followed a 1946 play by the same name. As for more tangible things, the remains of his estate are stored at Harvard and in the Library of Congress. Still, the best evidence of Holmes inheres in neither likenesses nor objects but in his ideas. It was those ideas – in torts, contracts, jurisprudence, constitutional law, and First Amendment law – that cast a long shadow over the law. His ideas are all the more memorable because of Holmes's voluminous writings, which include the more than two thousand signed opinions he published during his years on the Massachusetts state court and on the U.S. Supreme Court.[5] That corpus of work and the life behind it have provided the grist for an unprecedented amount of interest in Holmes. It is a fact: in "the last twenty years alone," there have been "four biographies, four symposia, three new collections of his work, two volumes of essays, and various monographs, not to mention a multitude of free-standing law review articles."[6] In 2009, a new edition of *The Common Law* found its way into print, courtesy of Harvard University Press.[7] Moreover, new histories of the First Amendment still profile Holmes,[8] new First Amendment casebooks still discuss him generously,[9] new encyclopedias on the subject still portray him as a major figure in free speech law,[10] and his First Amendment opinions continue to be cited. Federal lawmakers have also seized on Holmes's clear-and-present-danger formula in connection with the Anti-Riot Act of 1968[11]

December 29, 1982, 96 Stat. 1958. As of this date, however, no such memorial park exists, though a memorial plaque did exist at one point and was located near the Court.

[4] The bust is located in the Supreme Court. In the Holmes collection at Harvard Law School, there is also a plaster-cast death mask of the justice as well.

[5] Sheldon M. Novick, *Honorable Justice* (New York: Dell Publishing, 1989), at 406 (noting additional unsigned opinions or memoranda).

[6] Mathias Reimann, "Lives in the Law: Horrible Holmes," 100 *Michigan Law Review* 1676–77 (2002).

[7] Oliver Wendell Holmes Jr., *The Common Law* (Cambridge, MA: Harvard University Press, 2009 [intro by G. Edward White]).

[8] *See, e.g.*, Stephen M. Feldman, *Free Expression and Democracy in America: A History* (Chicago: University of Chicago Press, 2008); Geoffrey R. Stone, *Perilous Times: Free Speech in Wartime* (New York: W. W. Norton, 2004) (for numerous references).

[9] *See* Ronald J., Krotoszynski Jr., et al., *The First Amendment: Cases and Theory* (Boston: Aspen Publishers, 2008), at 32–54.

[10] *See* John R. Vile, David Hudson, and David Schultz, eds., *Encyclopedia of the First Amendment* (Washington, D.C.: CQ Press, 2009), at 1:576–77.

[11] Section 2102 (a) of the Anti-Riot Act of 1968, 18 U.S.C. ch. 102, provides: "As used in this chapter, the term 'riot' means a public disturbance involving (1) an act or acts of violence . . . which act or acts shall constitute a clear and present danger of, or shall result in, damage or injury to the property of any other person or to the person of

and the Armed Services Procurement Authorization Bill of 1970.[12] So, too, lawmakers in virtually all of the states have tapped Holmes's clear-and-present-danger formula to regulate everything from public utility security to criminal advocacy.[13] Even European courts have adopted his test.[14] And now that the United States is at "war" again, Holmes's thoughts and words may prove of some moment in the future.[15] Incredibly, even in the popular culture, Holmes's words have offered inspiration for trendy novels[16] and movies,[17] as well as for articles on marketing management[18] and titles for the covers of *Time*[19] and comic books.[20]

Hence, this much seems clear: certain parts of Holmes's thought endure.[21] They are still very much on our minds, especially when it comes to First Amendment jurisprudence. In this epilogue, I sketch out how Holmes's main

any other individual or (2) a threat or threats of the commission of an act or acts of violence . . . having, individually or collectively, the ability of immediate execution of such threat or threats, while the performance of the threatened act or acts of violence would constitute a clear and present danger of. or shall result in, damage or injury to the property of any other person or to the person of any other individual." As Professor George Anastaplo notes, this law was used in the infamous Chicago Conspiracy Trial of 1969–70. *See* George Anastaplo, *The Constitutionalist: Notes on the First Amendment* (Dallas, TX: Southern Methodist University Press, 1971), at 594–95.

[12] "The Congress views with grave concern the deepening involvement of the United States in the Middle East and the clear and present danger to world peace resulting from such involvement which cannot be ignored by the United States." Armed Services Procurement Authorization Bill, title V, sec. 501 (H.R. 17123), *Congressional Record* 116 (September 29, 1970). State statutes adopting the clear-and-present-danger language are discussed later in this Epilogue.

[13] LexisNexis search of "clear and present danger," May 10, 2009 (listing 329 references). The codification of Holmes's clear-and-present-danger formula is discussed herein.

[14] *See* David G. Barnum, "The Clear and Present Danger Test in Anglo-American and European Law," 7 *San Diego International Law Journal* 263, 280–88 (2006).

[15] *See* Ronald K. L. Collins and David M. Skover, "What Is War? Reflections on Free Speech in 'Wartime,'" 36 *Rutgers Law Journal* 833 (2005).

[16] *See* Tom Clancy, *Clear and Present Danger* (New York: G. P. Putnam's Sons, 1989).

[17] *See* Harrison Ford in *Clear and Present Danger* (1994).

[18] *See* R. Jelinek and M. Ahearne, "The ABC's of ACB: Unveiling a Clear and Present Danger in the Sales Force," *Industrial Marketing Management*, May 1, 2006.

[19] *See* Michael Elliott, "A Clear and Present Danger," *Time*, October 8, 2001.

[20] *See* Kurt Busiek and George Perez, "Avengers: Clear and Present Dangers," *Marvel Comics*, November 1, 2001.

[21] On the one hand, and speaking generally, Holmes has been characterized as the second most important figure in American law, behind only John Marshall. *See* Roger K. Newman, ed., *The Yale Biographical Dictionary of American Law* (New Haven, CT: Yale University Press, 2009), at xi. On the other hand, some have qualified that view, arguing that "Holmes's true greatness is not as a lawyer, judge, or legal theorist in a narrowly professional sense of these words, but as a writer and, in a loose sense . . . as a philosopher, in fact as a 'writer philosopher.' . . . " Richard A. Posner, ed., *The Essential Holmes* (Chicago: University of Chicago Press, 1992), at xvi.

thoughts on free speech have fared in the courts and in the academy. Thereafter, I step back to provide a broader view of the man and his thought. Before
turning to that, however, a few words should be said about the campaign to
glorify Holmes and his views.

The word commonly used is *canonization*, as in "the canonization of Justice Holmes."[22] It is an ironic use of the word to describe a man who had
little or no interest or belief in "the upward and onward,"[23] as he called
it. "In life, there was little heavenly about the irreverent agnostic, the twin-
kling skeptic, the down-to-the-ground judicial realist." It was once said that it
took years "to elevate Mr. Justice Holmes from deity to mortality."[24] Because
Holmes's life and legacy abound in irony, it is entirely understandable that
such words have been used to describe the making of Holmesian memories and
myths.

The canonization began when Holmes was alive, and with his approval and
even encouragement.[25] "Holmes'[s] 'greatness' was . . . the conscious product
of a systematic campaign of publicity, a campaign in which Holmes participated," maintains biographer G. Edward White. "Holmes was fortunate to
have," adds White, "as one of his principal boosters a person who was emi-
nently suited to launch such a campaign and highly motivated to do so."[26] That
person, of course, was Felix Frankfurter – the man who introduced Holmes

---

[22] *See, e.g.,* G. Edward White, "The Canonization of Holmes and Brandeis: Epistemology
and Judicial Reputations," 70 *New York University Law Review* 576 (1995). *See also*
Albert W. Alschuler, *Law without Values: The Life, Work, and Legacy of Justice Holmes*
(Chicago: University of Chicago Press, 2000), at 181–816 ("the Beatification of Oliver
Wendell Holmes").

[23] Letter from OWH to Frederick Pollock, May 26, 1919, reproduced in Mark DeWolfe
Howe, ed., *Holmes-Pollock Letters: The Correspondence of Mr. Justice Holmes and Sir
Frederick Pollock, 1874–1932* (Cambridge, MA: Harvard University Press, 1941), at 2:13.

[24] Fred Rodell, *Nine Men: A Political History of the Supreme Court from 1790 to 1955* (New
York: Random House, 1955), at 179–80 (quoting, in part, Walton Hamilton).

[25] Though there were earlier works praising Holmes, in 1929 Alfred Lief edited the book *The
Dissenting Opinions of Mr. Justice Holmes* (New York: Vanguard Press), followed by his
Representative Opinions of Justice Holmes (New York: Vanguard Press, 1931). And then
there was the tribute to Holmes on the occasion of his ninetieth birthday. *See* 44 *Harvard
Law Review* 677 (1931) (with contributions by Chief Justice Hughes, Judge Benjamin
Cardozo, and Frederick Pollock, among others). There was also Silas Bent's flattering
1932 biography of the justice, which Holmes had nothing to do with and claimed not to
have read at the time, though he described it as "harmless." *See* letter from OWH to Lewis
Einstein, September 30, 1932, reproduced in James Bishop Peabody, ed., *The Holmes-
Einstein Letters: Correspondence of Mr. Justice Holmes and Lewis Einstein, 1903–1935*
(New York: St. Martin's Press, 1964), at 348–49.

[26] G. Edward White, *Justice Oliver Wendell Holmes: Law and the Inner Self* (New York:
Oxford University Press, 1993), at 355–56.

to a bevy of young admirers,[27] who secured favorable coverage in the *New Republic*; who organized tributes in the *Harvard Law Review*; who arranged for laudatory books to be published by Harvard University Press; and who, in all of this and more, set in motion near-perpetual admiration for the "great judge." This campaign, buttressed by the mystique of Holmes's life and the breadth, eloquence, and force of his diverse writings,[28] helped to secure for Holmes a reputation rivaling that of Chief Justice John Marshall, whom he once honored publicly.[29] To be sure, all of that helped to situate Holmes in a place of special importance when it came to his First Amendment jurisprudence.

Although there is always a real danger, as Max Lerner warns, of accepting Holmes's thought too uncritically, that is not how things began. Canonization efforts notwithstanding, there was, as noted in what follows, some dissension in the Holmesian ranks about the adequacy of his danger test. Moreover, Holmes's greatest defender, Felix Frankfurter, began in time to oppose the liberal application of the danger test and did his best to assign a narrow meaning to it. So, too, some notable progressive scholars and judges who were not a part of the admirers' alliance were quite outspoken in their rejection of Holmes's free speech jurisprudence.

⊷

If he ranks with Marshall as a maker of the Constitution, he ranks with Kent and Story as a molder of the thinking of lawyers and law teachers, and the combination is unique.

– Roscoe Pound (1935)[30]

The story of posthumous commentary on or related to Justice Holmes's First Amendment jurisprudence begins with a book by the Harvard Law professor Felix Frankfurter (*Mr. Justice Holmes and the Supreme Court*[31]), published by Harvard University Press; followed by another book (*Free Speech in the United States*) by one of the justice's friends (the Harvard professor Zechariah Chafee), which was also published by Harvard; followed by a review of that

---

[27] Holmes's secretaries, or law clerks, alone "published at least thirty-one books, articles, and book reviews praising him." *Law without Values, supra* note 22, at 184 (footnote omitted).

[28] *See* Richard A. Posner, *Cardozo: A Study in Reputation* (Chicago: University of Chicago Press, 1990), at 61–62.

[29] "John Marshall," February 4, 1904, reproduced in Mark DeWolfe Howe, comp., *The Occasional Speeches of Justice Oliver Wendell Holmes* (Cambridge, MA: Harvard University Press, 1962), at 131–35.

[30] Roscoe Pound as quoted in "Simplicity to Mark Last Rites Tomorrow on Holmes' Birthday," *Washington Post*, March 7, 1935, at 1, 4 (quoting Associated Press story).

[31] Part II of the 1938 book was on "Civil Liberties and the Individual" and discussed some of Holmes's post-*Debs* free speech cases, in an always-flattering way.

book in the *Harvard Law Review* by one of Holmes's secretaries (Mark DeWolfe Howe); followed by the two-volume set of the Holmes-Pollock letters (edited by DeWolfe Howe) and published by Harvard; which in turn was followed by a biography of the justice (*Mr. Justice Holmes*) by another of his secretaries (Francis Biddle) – the last work alone did not bear a Harvard imprint. Except for Frankfurter, there was a varying measure of critical comment in all of those works, though it occurred against a more general backdrop of admiration and approval.

Zechariah Chafee had been writing about freedom of speech ever since Harold Laski urged him to do so for the *New Republic* in 1918. The following year, he published his "Freedom of Speech in Wartime" article in the *Harvard Law Review*. And the year after that, he offered up his first book on the topic, *Freedom of Speech*. Years later, the editors of Harvard University Press urged him to expand and update that book, which he did in *Free Speech in the United States* (1941). From early on, Chafee had sought to liberalize Holmes's danger test in a way that brought it closer to what Chafee perceived as the more libertarian test formulated by Judge Learned Hand in *Masses Publishing Co. v. Patten*.[32] That said, when his 1941 book came out, he heralded Holmes's work:

- His danger test is "of great value for determining the true scope of the First Amendment."
- "The concept of freedom of speech received for the first time an authoritative judicial interpretation in accord with the purpose of the framers of the Constitution."
- The "rule now serves as a guiding principle for the future, and ought to make impossible hereafter a repetition of the worst decisions of the trial courts under the Espionage Act of 1917."
- "The preceding chapters have been written in support of the danger test as marking the true limit of governmental interference with speech and writing under our constitutions. . . . "[33]

Admittedly, he did take some tempered exception to Holmes's handiwork in *Debs v. United States* – his harshest criticism came by way of offering up quotations from Ernst Freund's 1919 *New Republic* article[34] – and likewise

---

[32] 244 F. 535 (S.D.N.Y. 1917), *rev'd* 246 F. 24 (2nd Cir. 1917); David M. Rabban, *Free Speech in Its Forgotten Years* (New York: Cambridge University Press, 1997), at 316, 328.

[33] Zechariah Chafee Jr., *Free Speech in the United States* (Cambridge, MA: Harvard University Press, 1941), at 81–82, 86, 137.

[34] "The Debs Case and Freedom of Speech," *New Republic*, May 3, 1919, at 13.

conceded that the "three decisions in March, 1919, came as a great shock to forward-looking men and women.... Looking backward," he explained, "we see that Justice Holmes was biding his time until the Court should have before it a conviction so clearly wrong as to let him speak out of his deepest thoughts about the First Amendment."[35] The reference, of course, was to Holmes's *Abrams* dissent, of which little or nothing was said about its apparent transformative character in light of what had preceded it.

When Mark DeWolfe Howe, then dean at the University of Buffalo Law School, reviewed Chafee's book, he criticized the inadequacy of Holmes's danger test and Chafee's unwillingness to move beyond it. What troubled Howe was that part of the Holmesian formula related to "the substantive evils that Congress had a right to prevent." Although that formula may well have suited wartime cases involving calls for the violent overthrow of the government, it seemed ill suited to other kinds of cases. Echoing Herbert Wechsler,[36] Howe asked, Was "the immediate evil...of a serious or trivial sort?" On that count, Howe argued, Chafee failed to "reconsider the over-all sufficiency of the Holmes test...as applied to other social interests than security from violence."[37] Unless Holmes's danger test was fortified by what Brandeis had argued in his *Whitney* concurrence,[38] the test – even in its *Abrams* incarnation[39] – would prove ineffectual in many other kinds of different cases and thereby invite government suppression.[40] As Chafee came to consider the criticisms leveled by Howe, Wechsler, and others, he became more doubtful of its utility: "Important as this clear-and-present-danger test is, it is probably

[35] *Free Speech in the United States, supra* note 33, at 86.

[36] Herbert Wechsler, "The Clear and Present Danger Test," 9 *American Law School Review* 881 (1941). Critical of the Court's 1919 clear-and-present-danger line of cases, Wechsler wrote: "If action was proposed in resistance to the policy of government, it was immediate action; if there was danger that the publication would lead to unlawful resistance, it was a danger at that time; if such resistance was intended, it was intended then. Thus the clear and present danger test could at the best have only a minimal operation to place beyond the pale of liability those statements which were patently impotent and were motivated by some other purpose than to promote obstruction of the conduct of the war." *Ibid.,* at 882–83.

[37] Mark DeWolfe Howe, Book Review, 55 *Harvard Law Review* 695, 699 (1942).

[38] In relevant part, the operative language is "whether the evil apprehended was one so substantial as to justify the stringent restriction imposed by the legislature." 247 U.S. 357, 379 (1927) (Brandeis, J., concurring). In short, the evil apprehended must be "relatively serious." 247 U.S. at 377.

[39] *Cf. Free Speech in Its Forgotten Years, supra* note 32, at 347; *Whitney v. California,* 247 U.S. 357, 377, 379 (1927) (Brandeis, J., concurring).

[40] Chafee came to agree. *See* Zechariah Chafee Jr., *Government and Mass Communications* (Chicago: University of Chicago Press, 1947), at 1:52.

not a key which opens all doors" – there were real-world "difficulties" with it.[41] This became more apparent, as he discussed in his subsequent book *Government and Mass Communications*, as he began to consider cases other than criminal advocacy in wartime. Accordingly, he came to favor a "balancing" of interest approach to free speech adjudication.[42]

When it came to Holmes, Francis Biddle was no Felix Frankfurter – he was far more honest, though with nuance and diplomacy. In his biography of the justice, Biddle noted how the clear-and-present-danger test had become "a sort of liberal rudder." Of its analytical worth, he wrote: "It is improbable that Holmes, who so greatly distrusted phrases and their use to displace the freer play of imaginative thinking, would have been much impressed by such a test as more than an instinctive guide, hardly accurate to chart proximity and degree." Then, by way of a curious compliment, he added: "But surely [the test] might serve, if not to define a legal principle, at least to suggest a standard of approach, cautious and realistic." As for the *Abrams* dissent, though Biddle recognized its rhetorical power, he did not think it "added anything to the 'clear and present danger' test suggested in *Schenck*. . . . " [43]

One other book must be mentioned, one published in the same year as Biddle's biography of Holmes. I refer to Max Lerner's *The Mind and Faith of Justice Holmes*, which was also reviewed by Chafee.[44] The book was a collection of Holmes's writings combined with a series of essays and notes prepared by Lerner. No other book on Holmes has had quite the impact on the popular and scholarly minds as did Lerner's.[45] Though Lerner surely praised Holmes,[46] he did not hesitate to criticize him, including certain tenets and applications of his free speech jurisprudence.[47] Even so, in this "pioneering work,"[48] Lerner succeeded in turning Holmes into an Olympian figure in American law and letters – a figure at once dark and enlightening.[49] Hence, one simply could not

---

[41] *Ibid.* (listing two such difficulties).

[42] *See Free Speech in the United States, supra* note 33, at 35; *Government and Mass Communications, supra* note 40, at 50.

[43] Francis Biddle, *Mr. Justice Holmes* (New York: Charles Scriber's Sons, 1943), at 156.

[44] Zechariah Chafee, Book Review, 49 *American Historical Review* 457 (1943).

[45] In the interest of full disclosure, I reiterate that Max was a friend.

[46] He described the *Abrams* dissent as "the greatest utterance on intellectual freedom by an American, ranking in the English tongue with Milton and Mill." *The Mind and Faith of Justice Holmes* (Boston: Little, Brown, 1943), at 306.

[47] *See*, e.g., his criticism of Holmes's *Debs* opinion. *Ibid.*, at 298–99.

[48] David H. Burton, *Taft, Holmes, and the 1920s Court* (Madison, NJ: Fairleigh Dickinson University Press, 1998), at 157.

[49] In 1944 Catherine Drinker Bowen published her quasi-factual portrait of Holmes, *Yankee from Olympus*, which was a largely dramatic and fanciful rendition of Holmes's private life.

ignore Holmes when writing about law in general and First Amendment law in particular. Or as the University of Chicago law professor Max Rheinstein put it in his review of the Lerner book: "Holmes is on the way of becoming one of the great representative figures of his nation, a type of man which has so far been rare in American history."[50]

Thus, although there was a concerted effort to canonize Holmes and glorify his free speech jurisprudence, we see that, early on, his own followers and other admirers came to have their doubts about Holmes's thoughts in this area.

※

Two of the greatest champions of the First Amendment, Hugo Black and Alexander Meiklejohn, were among the first wave of thinkers outside of the Holmes clique who were critical of the justice's free speech jurisprudence. For Black, Holmes's famed clear-and-present-danger test did not by any means "mark the furthermost constitutional boundaries of protected expression. . . . "[51] It was a test, he believed, that "permits courts to sustain anything."[52] For Meiklejohn, Holmes's constitutional formula in *Schenck* "annuls the most significant purpose of the First Amendment. It destroys the intellectual basis of our plan of self government."[53] In the years following Holmes's death through 1951, the year *Dennis v. United States*[54] was decided, some of the great progressives vied to distance their notions of free speech liberty from those espoused by Holmes, whereas conservatives often embraced some of those same views, albeit in diluted form, to deny First Amendment claims. By 1969, the year *Brandenburg v. Ohio*[55] came down, a new generation of free speech progressives returned to Holmes for constitutional guidance.

Slightly more than a decade after Holmes died – while Brandeis was still on the Court and Cardozo new to it, but before the arrivals of Black and Douglas – the Hughes Court declared certain First Amendment rights to be "fundamental," so much so that they could not be abridged without breaching core "principles of liberty and justice which lie at the base of all civil and political

---

[50] Max Rheinstein, Book Review, 29 *Virginia Law Review* 1074, 1076-77 (1943). For an account of other reviews of Lerner's Holmes, see G. Edward White, *The Constitution and the New Deal* (New York: Oxford University Press, 2000), at 274–75.

[51] *Bridges v. California*, 314 U.S. 252, 263 (1941) (per Black., J., for the Court).

[52] Hugo Black, conference notes from *Dennis v. United States* (1951), qtd. in Roger K. Newman, *Hugo Black: A Biography* (New York: Pantheon Books, 1994), at 402.

[53] Alexander Meiklejohn, *Free Speech and Its Relation to Self-Government* (New York: Harper & Brothers, 1948), at 29.

[54] 341 U.S. 494.

[55] 395 U.S. 444.

institutions. . . . "⁵⁶ Such language suggests the primacy of First Amendment rights, and not necessarily because of any link to the search for truth. With such new ideas in place, the Court began to move away from Holmesian constructs. The Court's 1941 ruling in *Bridges v. California*,⁵⁷ for example, illustrates that point. Writing for the majority, Justice Hugo Black first invigorated Holmes's free speech formulas and then moved beyond them:

> What finally emerges from the "clear and present danger" cases is a working principle that the substantive evil must be *extremely serious* and the degree of imminence *extremely high* before utterances can be punished. *Those cases do not purport to mark the furthermost constitutional boundaries of protected expression,* nor do we here. They do no more than recognize a *minimum* compulsion of the Bill of Rights. For the First Amendment does not speak equivocally. It prohibits any law "abridging the freedom of speech, or of the press." It must be taken as a command of the *broadest scope* that explicit language, read in the context of a liberty-loving society, will allow.⁵⁸

This "sudden break"⁵⁹ from the past outraged Felix Frankfurter, who as a Supreme Court justice turned to Holmes's free speech opinions as justifications for limiting First Amendment rights.

By the time *Thomas v. Collins*⁶⁰ came down, a majority of the Court seemed disposed to invigorate the *Abrams* dissent and the measure of free speech freedom it offered. To that end, Justice Wiley Rutledge, writing for a 5–4 divided Court, declared:

> [A]ny attempt to restrict [First Amendment freedoms] must be justified by clear public interest, threatened not doubtfully or remotely, but by clear

⁵⁶ *DeJonge v. Oregon*, 299 U.S. 353, 364 (1937) (right of peaceful assembly). *See also Herndon v. Lowry*, 301 U.S. 242, 258 (1937) ("The power of a state to abridge freedom of speech and of assembly is the exception rather than the rule."); on the "rigorous definition of the clear and present danger test" in *Herndon*, see *Free Speech in Its Forgotten Years, supra* note 32, at 375–77.

⁵⁷ 314 U.S. 252 (1941) (5–4) (setting aside contempt citation of publisher for an out-of-court editorial statement concerning a pending criminal case). In some respects, the outcome in *Bridges* and subsequent contempt-of-court cases was influenced in part by Holmes's dissent in *Toledo Newspaper Co. v. United States*, 247 U.S. 402, 422 (1918). *See also Pennekamp v. Florida*, 328 U.S. 331 (1946) (setting aside contempt-of-court citation on First Amendment grounds); *Craig v. Harney*, 331 U.S. 367 (1947) (same).

⁵⁸ 314 U.S. at 263 (emphasis added).

⁵⁹ 314 U.S. at 279 (Frankfurter, J., dissenting). For the background history of this case and how Black's dissent became a majority opinion, see *Hugo Black: A Biography, supra* note 52, at 289–92.

⁶⁰ 323 U.S. 516 (1945).

and present danger.... Only the gravest abuses, endangering paramount interests, give occasion for permissible limitation ... in the light of our constitutional tradition. And the answer, under that tradition, can be affirmative, to support an intrusion upon this domain, only if grave and impending public danger requires this.[61]

As the precedential momentum of *Bridges* continued in *Thomas* and thereafter in *Pennekamp v. Florida*,[62] Justice Frankfurter took sharp exception to the entire enterprise of attempting to give *Schenck* and its progeny a liberal gloss:

"Clear and present danger" was never used by Mr. Justice Holmes to express a technical legal doctrine or to convey a formula for adjudicating cases. It was a literary phrase not to be distorted by being taken from its context. In its setting it served to indicate the importance of freedom of speech to a free society but also to emphasize that its exercise must be compatible with the preservation of other freedoms essential to a democracy and guaranteed by our Constitution. When those other attributes of a democracy are threatened by speech the Constitution does not deny power to the States to curb it.

In his *Pennekamp* dissent, Frankfurter proceeded to downplay the imminence component of the test Holmes had formulated in *Abrams*:

"The clear and present danger" to be arrested may be danger short of a threat as comprehensive and vague as a threat to the safety of the Republic or "the American way of life." Neither Mr. Justice Holmes nor Mr. Justice Brandeis nor this Court ever suggested in all the cases that arose in connection with the First World War, that only imminent threats to the immediate security of the country would authorize courts to sustain legislation curtailing utterance.[63]

By 1949 the Court was still citing the *Schenck* test,[64] even though it applied it in a far more liberal way than the rule had previously been employed. That fact so much troubled Justice Robert Jackson that, in his dissent in *Terminiello v. Chicago*,[65] he felt obliged to argue that if the clear-and-present-danger test

---

[61] 323 U.S. at 530, 531–32.

[62] 328 U.S. 331 (1946).

[63] 328 U.S. at 353 (Frankfurter, J., dissenting).

[64] Holmes's dissent in *Abrams* had not yet received much attention by the Court, though the danger test was still viewed critically at the time. *See, e.g.*, Paul Freund, *On Understanding the Supreme Court* (Boston: Little, Brown, 1949), at 27.

[65] 337 U.S. 1 (1949) (First Amendment claim sustained, 5–4, with respect to a disorderly conduct charge and angry mob).

were faithfully applied, the First Amendment claim in the case would have to be denied. That is, unless the Court "silently abandoned this long-standing test and substituted for the purposes of this case an unexpressed but more stringent test. . . . "[66]

⋰

Criticisms of Holmes's clear-and-present-danger test were not confined to Supreme Court pronouncements. Perhaps the most significant criticism to come from an academic quarter came from Alexander Meiklejohn, the former president of Amherst College and a leading educational reformer, who likewise took issue with Holmes and his thinking, but for reasons far different than those advanced by Wechsler. (Meiklejohn was a progressive who knew both Holmes and Laski. In 1923, Felix Frankfurter rallied to Meiklejohn's defense when Amherst trustees ousted him.[67]) With the publication of *Free Speech and Its Relation to Self-Government*, Professor Meiklejohn sought to place First Amendment thinking on a new axis, thereby changing the sphere designated by Holmes.

Key to Meiklejohn's thinking was the idea of self-government, citizen rule. The principle of free speech, he maintained,

> is a deduction from the basic American agreement that public issues shall be decided by universal suffrage. Since sovereignty inhered in the people, citizens must be able to both learn about their government and criticize it if they were to engage in the process of self-rule. In that regard, he confronted Holmes head-on in at least two respects. First, he maintained that certain evils must be suffered in the name of free speech and what it represents. That is, if the principle of free expression is to mean anything to self-governing citizens, it must mean that certain substantive evils which, in principle, Congress has a right to prevent, must be endured if the only way of avoiding them is by abridging them by abridging that freedom of speech upon which the entire structure of our free institutions rests.[68]

Second, Holmesian formulas, however liberalized,[69] operated to suppress precisely the kinds of speech most central to self-government. "Taken as it

---

[66] 337 U.S. at 25–26 (Jackson, J., dissenting).

[67] See "Meiklejohn Defiant, Urges Amherst Men to Abolish Trustees," *New York Times*, June 21, 1923, at 1; Cynthia Stokes Brown, ed., *Alexander Meiklejohn: Teacher of Freedom* (Berkeley, CA: Meiklejohn Civil Liberties Institute, 1981), at 14–20; H. N. Hirsch, *The Enigma of Felix Frankfurter* (New York: Basic Books, 1981), at 70–71.

[68] *Free Speech and Its Relation to Self-Government, supra* note 53, at 44.

[69] Brandeis's thinking, as articulated in his *Whitney v. California*, was far more agreeable to Meiklejohn. See *Free Speech and Its Relation to Self-Government, supra* note 53, at 49–50.

stands," Meiklejohn argued, Holmes's "formula tells us that whenever the expression of a minority opinion involves a clear and present danger to the public safety it may be denied the protection of the First Amendment. And that means that whenever crucial and dangerous issues [arise], free and unhindered discussion of them must stop."[70]

The year following the publication of Meiklejohn's popular track, Zechariah Chafee came to Holmes's defense. Chafee had known Meiklejohn for some time, dating back to his years as an undergraduate at Brown University when Meiklejohn was dean there. In a *Harvard Law Review* essay[71] reviewing *Free Speech and Its Relation to Self-Government*, Chafee defended Holmes the jurist while criticizing, albeit modestly, Meiklejohn the philosopher.

- "Mr. Meiklejohn is by no means on the side of lawyers like myself who regard the 'clear and present danger' test of Justice Holmes as substantially sound."
- "No matter how terrible and immediate the dangers may be, [Meiklejohn] keeps saying, the First Amendment will not let Congress or anybody else in the government try to deal with Communists who have not yet committed unlawful acts. . . . Such a view may be courageous, but it won't work."
- "Mr. Meiklejohn [is] a philosopher . . . not a pragmatist."
- "[H]is critique of the clear and present danger test . . . [is] badly misdirected. . . . "
- "The author shows no realization of the long uphill fight which Holmes had to wage in order to give free speech its present protection. First, Holmes worked out a formula which would invalidate a great deal of suppression, and won for it the solid authority of a unanimous Court. Afterwards, again and again, when his test was misapplied by the majority, Holmes restated his position in ringing words which, with the help of Brandeis and Hughes, eventually inspired the whole Court."[72]

After the review was completed, Chafee told Frankfurter that the "book has more errors of law per page than about any I have ever read, but long acquaintance, his great work [as president of] Amherst, and the location of his heart in the right place led me to write as I did."[73] Such affection could not, however, trump fidelity to Holmes and his thought, albeit revised somewhat by Chafee and others.

[70] *Free Speech and Its Relation to Self-Government, supra* note 53, at 45.
[71] Zechariah Chafee Jr., Book Review, 62 *Harvard Law Review* 891 (1949).
[72] *Ibid.*, at 892–910. (footnotes omitted).
[73] Qtd. in Donald L. Smith, *Zechariah Chafee, Jr.: Defender of Liberty and Law* (Cambridge, MA: Harvard University Press, 1986), at 90.

Disfavor with the Holmesian formula was not limited to the likes of Meik-lejohn. One came from the Scholars' quarter, from a man who had taken issue with Holmes as early as 1919, Ernst Freund of the University of Chicago Law School. Thirty years later, the Harvard Law Professor Paul Freund took renewed aim at Holmes's famed free speech formula and called for a more nuanced and less abstract test when considering free speech matters:

> The truth is that the clear-and-present-danger test is an oversimplified judgment unless it takes account also of a number of other factors: the relative seriousness of the danger in comparison with the value of the occasion for speech or political activity; the availability of more moderate controls than those which the state has imposed; and perhaps the specific intent with which the speech or activity is launched. No matter how rapidly we utter the phrase "clear and present danger," or how closely we hyphenate the words, they are not a substitute for the weighing of values. They tend to convey a delusion of certitude when what is most certain is the complexity of the strands in the web of freedoms which the judge must disentangle.[74]

Felix Frankfurter was even more critical in his relentless attacks on the thinking and logical direction of his mentor's formulas and how they were used and applied by liberals.[75] He could not fathom rulings such as the one in *Terminiello v. Chicago*, a 5–4 First Amendment case authored by Justice Douglas. In his majority opinion, Douglas both endorsed and fortified the lib-eralized version of the danger test. He declared: "freedom of speech, though not absolute, . . . is nevertheless protected against censorship or punishment, unless shown likely to produce a clear and present danger of a serious substantive evil that rises far above public inconvenience, annoyance, or unrest."[76]

That slim margin of Holmesian hope evidenced in *Terminiello* did not last as the Court entered the McCarthy era and the fear of the "Red Menace" returned. (During this time, in 1950, Alger Hiss, a former Holmes secretary and then a high-level official in the State Department, was convicted of perjury for lying to the House Committee on Un-American Activities in connection with alleged espionage.) In that climate, the justices heard *American Communications Association v. Douds*,[77] a labor union loyalty case. When it was

---

[74] On Understanding the Supreme Court, *supra* note 64, at 27–28.
[75] See, e.g., his concurrence in *Kovacs v. Copper*, 336 U.S. 77, 89 (1949), and his dissent in *Craig v. Henry*, 331 U.S. 367, 384 (1946).
[76] 337 U.S. 1, 4 (1949) (citations omitted).
[77] 339 U.S. 382 (1950). Justices Douglas, Clark, and Minton did not participate; Justice Frankfurter concurred in part; and Justice Jackson both concurred and dissented in part. Justice Black dissented.

decided, the Court had a new chief justice – Frederick M. Vinson, who took his seat in the summer of 1946 following the *Thomas* ruling. Vinson, a judge of illiberal persuasion, wrote for a plurality and attempted to scale back Holmes's danger test:

> The important question that came to this Court immediately after the First World War was not whether, but how far, the First Amendment permits the suppression of speech which advocates conduct inimical to the public welfare. Some thought speech having a reasonable tendency to lead to such conduct might be punished. Justices Holmes and Brandeis took a different view.... When the effect of a statute or ordinance upon the exercise of First Amendment freedoms is relatively small and the public interest to be protected is substantial, it is obvious that a rigid test requiring a showing of imminent danger to the security of the Nation is an absurdity.[78]

By that logic, the test to be applied should not be the Holmesian danger formula but rather an ad hoc balancing test: "When particular conduct is regulated in the interest of public order, and the regulation results in an indirect, conditional, partial abridgment of speech, the duty of the courts is to determine which of these two conflicting interests demands the greater protection under the particular circumstances presented."[79]

When the liberal justices Frank Murphy and Wiley Rutledge left the Court in 1949, they were replaced by two more conservative jurists, Tom C. Clark and Sherman Minton. That fact combined with the conservative bent of the chief justice and Justices Felix Frankfurter and Stanley Reed did not bode well for the future of the *Abrams* dissent. Attacks on it were no longer academic.

⤙

Although there was, for a time, a trend to either liberalize Holmes's clear-and-present-danger test or replace it with a more protective rule, that trend halted when the Court decided *Dennis v. United States*.[80] Thirty-two years after *Schenck* was handed down, its test was under attack from many quarters for many reasons. The issue in *Dennis* was whether the Smith Act – which made it a crime to "knowingly or willfully advocate, abet, advise, or teach the duty, necessity, desirability, or propriety of overthrowing or destroying any government in the United States by force or violence, or by

[78] 339 U.S. at 397.
[79] 339 U.S. at 399.
[80] 341 U.S. 494 (1951).

assignation" – violated the First Amendment. By a 6–2 margin (with Justice Tom Clark not participating), the Court sustained the constitutionality of the act. There was no majority opinion, and five of the eight justices wrote their own opinions.

Again writing for a plurality, Chief Justice Vinson began with a statement of the basic question before the Court: "In this case we are squarely presented with the application of the 'clear and present danger' test, and must decide what the phrase imports."[81] He answered that question by articulating a new and less speech-protective test, one that relied on what Learned Hand had written in his circuit court opinion in *Dennis*:[82] "Chief Judge Learned Hand, writing for the majority below, interpreted the phrase [clear and present danger] as follows: "In each case [courts] must ask whether the gravity of the 'evil,' discounted by its improbability, justifies such invasion of free speech as is necessary to avoid the danger." We adopt this statement of the rule. As articulated by Chief Judge Hand, it is as succinct and inclusive as any other we might devise at this time. It takes into consideration those factors which we deem relevant, and relates their significances. More we cannot expect from words."[83] For all Hand had done decades earlier to urge Holmes to adopt a more liberal test, when the matter finally came to him, he ratcheted his jurisprudence in the opposite direction.

And then there was Justice Felix Frankfurter, the same man who once characterized Holmes's dissent in *Abrams* as an opinion that "will live as long as English prose retains its power to move."[84] But its logic no longer moved Frankfurter. In fact, he was now disposed to jettison Holmes's jurisprudential handiwork: "The demands of free speech in a democratic society as well as the interest in national security are better served by candid and informed weighing of the competing interests, within the confines of the judicial process, than by announcing dogmas too inflexible for the non-Euclidian problems to be solved. . . . We are to set aside the judgment of those whose duty it is to legislate only if there is no reasonable basis for it."[85]

---

[81] 341 U.S. at 508.

[82] *Dennis v. United States*, 183 F.2d 201, 212 (2nd Cir. 1950). For a discussion of this case and its relation to Holmes's jurisprudence, see Bernard Schwartz, "Holmes versus Hand: Clear and Present Danger or Advocacy of Unlawful Action?" 1994 *Supreme Court Review* 209, 233–36 (1994).

[83] 341 U.S. at 510.

[84] Felix Frankfurter, *Mr. Justice Holmes and the Supreme Court* (Cambridge, MA: Harvard University Press, 1938), at 54–55.

[85] 341 U.S. at 524–25 (Frankfurter, J., concurring).

Justice Robert Jackson, though more nuanced and somewhat more respectful of Holmesian thought, was nonetheless unconvinced that the clear-and-present-danger test was of any value in the case before the Court:

> [The *Schenck* doctrine] has been attacked as one which "annuls the most significant purpose of the First Amendment. It destroys the intellectual basis of our plan of self-government." [Meiklejohn] It has been praised: "The concept of freedom of speech received for the first time an authoritative judicial interpretation in accord with the purpose of the framers of the Constitution." [Chafee] In either event, it is the only original judicial thought on the subject, all later cases having made only extensions of its application. All agree that it means something very important, but no two seem to agree on what it is. . . .

Whatever merit the clear-and-present-danger test had, opined Jackson, its logic was not applicable across the board to free speech cases and controversies:

> I would save it, unmodified, for application as a "rule of reason" in the kind of case for which it was devised. When the issue is criminality of a hot-headed speech on a street corner, or circulation of a few incendiary pamphlets, or parading by some zealots behind a red flag, or refusal of a handful of school children to salute our flag, it is not beyond the capacity of the judicial process to gather, comprehend, and weigh the necessary materials for decision whether it is a clear and present danger of substantive evil or a harmless letting off of steam. It is not a prophecy, for the danger in such cases has matured by the time of trial or it was never present.

For Jackson, the clear-and-present-danger test was a special test for a particular class of cases, nothing more:

> The test applies and has meaning where a conviction is sought to be based on a speech or writing which does not directly or explicitly advocate a crime but to which such tendency is sought to be attributed by construction or by implication from external circumstances. The formula in such cases favors freedoms that are vital to our society, and, even if sometimes applied too generously, the consequences cannot be grave. But its recent expansion has extended, in particular to Communists, unprecedented immunities. Unless we are to hold our Government captive in a judge-made verbal trap, we must approach the problem of a well-organized, nation-wide conspiracy, such as I have described, as realistically as our

predecessors faced the trivialities that were being prosecuted until they were checked with a rule of reason.[86]

Critical of the outcome in the case and the views espoused by the majority, Justice Hugo Black likewise took aim at Holmes's constitutional handiwork: "At least as to speech in the realm of public matters, I believe that the 'clear and present danger' test does not 'mark the furthermost constitutional boundaries of protected expression,' but does 'no more than recognize a minimum compulsion of the Bill of Rights.'"[87]

~◈

After *Dennis*, a reconstituted Court tinkered with First Amendment doctrine or balancing tests or statutory construction in free expression cases involving congressional investigations, the Smith Act, or state loyalty laws.[88] The big doctrinal change, however, did not come until *Brandenburg v. Ohio*,[89] a case decided a half century after *Schenck*. The issue there was whether an Ohio criminal syndicalism statute punishing advocacy of violence as a means of achieving industrial or political reform violated the First Amendment. By a 9–0 margin, the Warren Court sustained the First Amendment claim.

The *Brandenburg* opinion was originally assigned to Justice Abe Fortas. In his draft, Fortas wrote that "advocacy of unlawful action could be proscribed where it incited," in his words, "'imminent lawless action and is attended

---

[86] 341 U.S. at 524–25, 567–69 (Jackson, J. concurring). *See also* Mark DeWolfe Howe, Book Review, 63 *Yale Law Journal* 132 (1953) (critiquing Sidney Hook's *Heresy, Yes – Conspiracy, No* (1953) and Justice Jackson's concurrence in *Dennis*).

[87] 341 U.S. at 580 (Black, J., dissenting). Justice Douglas also dissented but was not critical of the clear-and-present-danger test: "This record, however, contains no evidence whatsoever showing that the acts charged, *viz.*, the teaching of the Soviet theory of revolution with the hope that it will be realized, have created any clear and present danger to the Nation. The Court, however, rules to the contrary." 341 U.S. at 587 (Douglas, J., dissenting). For a useful discussion of Holmes and the general line of clear-and-present-danger cases after Holmes's death, *see* Stephen A. Siegel, "The Death and Rebirth of the Clear and Present Danger Test," in *Transformations in American Legal History*, Daniel W. Hamilton and Alfred L. Brophy, eds. (Cambridge, MA: Harvard University Press, 2009), at 210–45.

[88] *See, e.g., Yates v. United States*, 354 U.S. 298 (1957); *Speiser v. Randall*, 357 U.S. 513 (1958); *Barenblatt v. United States*, 360 U.S. 109 (1959); *Uphaus v. Wyman*, 360 U.S. 72 (1959); *Scales v. United States*, 367 U.S. 203 (1961); *Noto v. United States*, 367 U.S. 290 (1961); *Konisberg V. State Bar*, 366 U.S. 36, 49–50 (1961).

[89] 395 U.S. 444 (1969). *See generally* Tinsley E. Yarbrough, *John Marshall Harlan: Great Dissenter of the Warren Court* (New York: Oxford University Press, 1992) at 190–200.

by present danger that such action may in fact be produced.'"[90] When Fortas's bid for chief justice failed because of a threatened Senate filibuster, he stepped down and the *Brandenburg* opinion was reassigned to Justice William Brennan, who then drafted a per curiam.[91] In it, he recalibrated the danger test: "the constitutional guarantees of free speech and free press do not permit a State to forbid or proscribe advocacy of the use of force or of law violation except where such advocacy is directed to inciting or producing imminent lawless action and is likely to incite or produce such action."[92] This would prove a major refinement in a landmark First Amendment case.

In his *Brandenburg* concurrence, Justice Douglas expressed some lingering doubts both about Holmes's test and about how it had evolved. "Though I doubt if the 'clear and present danger' test is congenial to the First Amendment in time of a declared war," he wrote, "I am certain it is not reconcilable with the First Amendment in days of peace." He then added: "When one reads the opinions closely and sees when and how the 'clear and present danger' test has been applied, great misgivings are aroused. First, the threats were often loud, but always puny, and made serious only by judges so wedded to the *status quo* that critical analysis made them nervous. Second, the test was so twisted and perverted in *Dennis* as to make the trial of those teachers of Marxism an all-out political trial which was part and parcel of the cold war that has eroded substantial parts of the First Amendment."[93] Justice Black went even further: "the 'clear and present danger' doctrine should have no place in the interpretation of the First Amendment."[94]

Nearly a decade after *Brandenburg*, yet another clear-and-present-danger case came before the Court. In *Landmark Communications, Inc. v. Virginia*, the Court was called on to decide the constitutionality of a state law that made it a crime to divulge information regarding proceedings before a state judicial review commission. The commission in question concerned complaints about judges' disability or misconduct. When the *Virginian Pilot* accurately reported on a pending inquiry and identified the judge whose conduct was being investigated, it was charged and convicted of violating the state law and

---

[90] "Holmes Versus Hand," *supra* note 82, at 240 (footnote omitted). Fortas's April 11, 1969, draft of *Brandenburg* is located in the Thurgood Marshall Papers in the Library of Congress.

[91] *Ibid.*

[92] 395 U.S. at 447 (footnote omitted).

[93] 395 U.S. at 452, 454 (Douglas, J., concurring).

[94] 395 U.S. at 449–50 (Black, J., concurring).

thereafter ordered to pay a $500 fine. On appeal, the justices unanimously reversed, with Chief Justice Warren Burger writing for the Court. In relevant part, he wrote:

> The Supreme Court of Virginia relied on the clear-and-present-danger test in rejecting Landmark's claim. We question the relevance of that standard here; moreover we cannot accept the mechanical application of the test which led that court to its conclusion. Mr. Justice Holmes' test was never intended "to express a technical legal doctrine or to convey a formula for adjudicating cases." *Pennekamp v. Florida*, . . . (1946) (Frankfurter, J., concurring). Properly applied, the test requires a court to make its own inquiry into the imminence and magnitude of the danger said to flow from the particular utterance and then to balance the character of the evil, as well as its likelihood, against the need for free and unfettered expression. The possibility that other measures will serve the State's interests should also be weighed.[95]

At least two points are noteworthy about the passage just quoted. First, the Court may conduct an independent inquiry of the purported danger and need not categorically defer, as it did in *Gitlow v. New York* (1925), to a legislative determination. Second, the Court's invocation of and reliance on Justice Frankfurter's concurrence in *Pennekamp* and its own parallel views may be interpreted as a way of transforming Holmes's danger test into a more fluid balancing test, a test less formidable than the one articulated by Holmes in *Abrams* or by the Court in *Brandenburg*.

As the previously mentioned line of cases reveals, the clear-and-present-danger test has been reworked, redefined, renounced, reconceptualized, and revitalized.[96] Even so, the fact remains that *Schenck*, a wartime case, has never been formally overruled. Insofar as it has been implicitly overruled by *Brandenburg*, a non-wartime case, its functional value in First Amendment jurisprudence, as distinguished from other areas of the law discussed below,

---

[95] *Landmark Communications, Inc. v. Virginia*, 435 U.S. 828–29 (1978) (footnote omitted) (6–1, Justices Brennan and Powell not participating). Floyd Abrams successfully argued the case. The *Schenck* test has also received some casual attention in other post-*Brandenburg* Supreme Court cases and elsewhere. *See, e.g., Nebraska Press Association v. Stuart*, 427 U.S. 539, 543, 556, 562 (1976); Benno Schmidt, "*Nebraska Press Association*: An Expansion of Freedom and Contraction of Theory," 29 *Stanford Law Review* 431, 459–60 (1977) (critical of C.J. Burger's reliance on *Dennis*); *Communist Party of Indiana v. Whitcomb*, 414 U.S. 441, 448–51 (1974) (relying on *Brandenburg*); Sheldon M. Novick, "The Unrevised Holmes and Free Expression," 1991 *Supreme Court Review* 303, 377–83 (1991).

[96] *See* Frank Strong, "Fifty Years of 'Clear and Present Danger': From *Schenck* to *Brandenburg* – and Beyond," 1969 *Supreme Court Review* 41 (1969).

is marginal so long as it is not invoked as binding precedent in a wartime or emergency case.[97]

෴

Despite all that has been done to the clear-and-present-danger test, it never ceases to kindle the imagination of creative thinkers. In that regard, few have tapped into that mine of Holmesian thought with more enthusiasm and insight than Judge Richard A. Posner, of the U.S. Court of Appeals for the Seventh Circuit. Beyond his *The Essential Holmes*, which has greatly extended the shelf life of the great jurist's views, Posner has written often and brilliantly on the jurist he admires most, even though he does "not share all of Holmes's beliefs, philosophical and otherwise. . . ."[98] Although Posner is no apologist, he is intrigued enough by Holmes's thought to adopt it and shape it as his own, or so it seems. This is particularly true in the First Amendment context, where Posner has both explained Holmes and lifted his jurisprudence to the next level. The best example of this is Posner's much-overlooked article "The Speech Market and the Legacy of *Schenck*."[99]

Posner urges an instrumentalist approach for resolving certain free speech issues. His approach traces back to Holmes's opinion in *Schenck* and moves away from a moral approach, which Posner sees as "spongy and arbitrary." Posner both defends and formalizes Holmes's thinking in this area and he does so in formulaic terms: "If the benefits of challenged speech are given by B; the cost (a fire, desertion, riot, rebellion, and so on) if the speech is allowed by H (for harm) or O (for offensiveness); the probability that the cost will actually materialize if the speech is allowed by p; the rate at which future costs or benefits are discounted to the present by d (like p a number between 0 and 1); the number of years (or other unit of time) between when the speech occurs and the harm from the speech materializes or is likely to occur if the speech is allowed by n; and the cost of administering a regulation banning the

---

[97] *Free Speech in Its Forgotten Years, supra* note 32, at 371 ("implicitly overruled"). On the wartime precedent, see "What Is War?" *supra* note 15, at 848–53; commentary following *Schenck v. United States* in Part V. *Consider* Adrian Vermeule, "Holmes on Emergencies," 61 *Stanford Law Review* 163 (2008). Even so, *Schenck* and its progeny, including *Abrams*, seem to have been eclipsed by various First Amendment doctrines, like overbreadth, such that their relevance is marginalized accordingly. *See* e.g., *Holder v. Humanitarian Law Project* (no. 08-1498, 2010) (no reference to *Schenk* or *Abrams* in main briefs).

[98] *The Essential Holmes, supra* note 21, at xxvi.

[99] Reproduced in Lee C. Bollinger and Geoffrey R. Stone, eds., *Eternally Vigilant: Free Speech in the Modern Era* (Chicago: University of Chicago Press, 2002), at 121; Richard A. Posner, *Frontiers of Legal Theory* (Cambridge, MA: Harvard University Press, 2001), at 62.

speech by *A*, then the speech should be allowed but only if . . . the benefits of the speech equal or exceed its costs discounted by their probability and by their futurity, and reduced by the costs of administering a ban." By this measure, expression may be banned "if the expected costs of the speech exceed the sum of the benefits of the speech and the costs of administering a prohibition of it." An alternative way of formulating such trade-offs is to posit that the "net benefits of speech are the gross benefits minus the costs, including both the harm and offensiveness caused by the speech and the costs of regulating speech."[100]

In developing his Holmesian-like model, Posner stresses that *B* (benefits) "need have nothing to do with the promotion of social or scientific progress or of political freedom or stability; aesthetic or even sexual pleasure is as much a genuine benefit as democracy or truth, though it need not be as great a benefit." *B* can even have a "negative value," as when "some restrictions on speech actually promote speech," as in the case of "restricting the speech opportunity of the fringe candidates may increase the speech benefits of debate overall."[101] In his cost-benefit analysis, offensiveness is not part of the equation; that is, his "pragmatic" approach is an "argument for banishing considerations of offensiveness from free-speech analysis."[102] Although there are a variety of considerations to take into account, including the problem of measuring the costs and benefits of speech, this instrumentalist approach, Posner argues, is preferable to other approaches if only because it invites rigorous attention to "the *context* of speech that is sought to be suppressed."[103] And though Posner's highly speech-protective reformulation of Holmes's danger test allows for exceptions (he lists eighteen), he believes such a scientific approach preferable to those shaped by "broadly political considerations" and that lack "theoretical coherence."[104] Thus understood, Posner's approach, echoing Holmes, seeks to add what is missing from Supreme Court decisions and normative theories of free speech, namely an empirical dimension.[105]

[100] *Ibid.*, at 121–22, 125–26.
[101] *Ibid.*, at 127.
[102] *Ibid.*, at 128. *See also ibid.* at 136 ("offensiveness is a wild card"). Adds Posner: "In Holmes's day the right of the government to repress offensive speech of a sexual character was so taken for granted that Holmes felt no need to develop a free-speech test broad enough to encompass offensive as well as dangerous speech [*see Fox v. Washington* (1915) in Part IV], though there is a sense, of course, in which the pamphlets in *Abrams* and *Schenck* were, whether or not actually dangerous, 'offensive' to patriotic sentiment." *Ibid.*
[103] *Ibid.*, at 130 (emphasis in original).
[104] *Ibid.*, at 141. For a general discussion of Holmes and how his "man of science" might interact with the law, *see Justice Oliver Wendell Holmes: Law and the Inner Self, supra* note 26, at 222–23.
[105] *Ibid.*, at 151.

I offer the foregoing sketch not necessarily to endorse Posner's theory (though it is a most intriguing idea) but to reveal how a modern-day Holmesian mind dedicated to merging law with science might approach free speech problems in our time.

√

Suppose that a code were made and expressed in language sanctioned by the assent of the courts.

– Oliver Wendell Holmes[106]

Incredibly, commentators have long overlooked one of Holmes's greatest contributions to American law, namely his contribution to state statutory law. Today, forty-six states have codified, in one form or another, Holmes's clear-and-present-danger formula for either civil or criminal liability. This codification, found in 209 state statutes,[107] is not limited to criminal advocacy cases. State lawmakers have tapped Holmes's famous formula for any variety of purposes, including but not limited to the following categories of regulation:

- Parental rights[108]
- Food and drug safety[109]
- Witness protection[110]
- Bullying in schools[111]
- Gun safety[112]
- Therapist and counselor privilege[113]
- Building safety[114]
- Environmental reports[115]

---

[106]OWH, "Codes, and the Arrangement of the Law," 5 *American Law* Review 1, 2 (1870), reproduced in Sheldon M. Novick, ed., *The Collected Works of Justice Holmes* (Chicago: University of Chicago Press, 1995), at 1:212–13.

[107]Some federal statutes likewise use Holmes's clear-and-present-danger formula. *See, e.g.*, Pub. L. No. 110-358, § 102 (October 8, 2008), 122 Stat. 4001 (finding of fact regarding child pornography); 31 U.S.C. Ann. § 1344 (regulation of agencies' passenger carriers); and 18 U.S.C. Ann. § 2102 (defining riot).

[108]Ala. Code, 1975, § 12-15-319.

[109]W. Va. Code, § 60A-8-10; Ohio Revised Codes, § 3717.27.

[110]West's Ann. Calif. Penal Code, § 136.2.

[111]Ark. Code Ann., § 6-18-514.

[112]Ga. Code Ann., § 43-38-11.1.

[113]Conn. Code Ann., § 52-146-p & s.

[114]Ore. Rev. Stat., § 453.685.

[115]Iowa Code Ann., § 455K.5.

- Banking law[116]
- Involuntary commitment[117]
- State-municipal loans[118]
- Treatment of the elderly[119]

Because this body of statutory does not concern free speech cases involving criminal advocacy, *Schenck* and its progeny leading to and beyond *Brandenburg v. Ohio* need not govern the interpretative meaning of the clear-and-present-danger formula. In other words, state courts are largely free, consistent with other legal constraints, to give such statutes whatever interpretative gloss they wish.

Of the 209 state laws that currently employ the clear-and-present-danger language, 40 have done so in matters relating to freedom of expression and/or assembly. Examples of such laws include the following:

- Regulation of the content of student newspapers[120]
- Regulation of speech advocating the overthrow of the government[121]
- Regulation of speech related to the incitement of riots[122]
- Criminal contempt with respect to publication of court proceedings[123]
- Regulation of criminal syndicalism[124]
- Regulation of reading materials of the mentally ill[125]
- Regulation of free assembly[126]
- Regulation of expression in public places where alcohol is served[127]
- Regulation of prison inmate correspondence[128]

Such statutes, by contrast to the previous ones, raise First Amendment concerns, though the meaning assigned to the clear-and-present-danger formula will not always track that of *Schenck* and its progeny. In other instances – say, in cases involving either student or prisoner expression – state courts may

[116]N.Y., McKinney's Banking Law, § 636.
[117]Ark. Code Ann., § 20-47 207.
[118]53 Pa. Stat. § 11701.302.
[119]West's Rev. Codes of Wash. Ann., § 70.124.020.
[120]West's Ann. Calif. Education Code, § 76120; Ark. Code Ann., § 6-18-1204.
[121]Colo. Rev. Stat. Ann., § 18-11-201.
[122]Kan. Stat. Ann., § 21-4105.
[123]N.C. General Stat. Ann., § 5A-11.
[124]Okla. Rev. Codes, § 1266.1.
[125]Okla. Rev. Codes, § 5122.29.
[126]Pa. Stat., § 30360 and § 36203.
[127]West's Rev. Codes of Wash. Ann., § 66.08.050
[128]28 Vt. Stat. Ann., § 802.

use a standard of review less demanding than that of either Holmes's *Abrams* dissent or the *Brandenburg* holding. In still other cases, state courts relying on their own law may assign a different meaning to the phrase or even a meaning more constitutionally stringent than the one employed in *Brandenburg*. However such concerns may be, it is notable that, in the past decade alone, appellate courts in forty-one states have rendered some 422 opinions in variety of cases in which a clear-and-present standard, of one form or another, was employed.[129]

The interpretation of all such Holmesian statutes might likewise bow to the Holmesian maxim that such laws are but a "mere text-book recommended by the government"[130] to aid in assigning meaning to these statutory provisions. For Holmes, that meaning is to be discerned less by grandiose phrases like "clear and present danger" than by the relevant policy considerations that come into play in particular cases.[131]

For all of the popularity and current widespread use of the phrase "marketplace of ideas,"[132] it took a half century before that expression came to be associated in any federal or state appellate court opinion with Justice Holmes and his dissent in *Abrams*.[133] Before that, Justice William O. Douglas was the first to employ the phrase, sans any reference to Holmes or to *Abrams*, in a 1953 concurrence.[134] Thereafter, the phrase received sparse judicial use prior to 1970, being employed in matters like property disputes[135] and local

---

[129]LexisNexis search, August 1, 2009. The search was for the period between August 1, 1999, and August 1, 2009. The subject matter of the state court opinions, virtually all of which are based on the application of a clear-and-present-danger statute, runs the gamut from tax disclosures to mental institution commitment, contempt of court, expungement of criminal records, child safety, incitement of riots, and beyond.

[130]"Codes, and the Arrangement of the Law," reproduced in *Collected Works of Justice Holmes, supra* note 106, at 1:212–13.

[131]*See* Oliver Wendell Holmes, "Privilege, Malice, and Intent," 8 *Harvard Law Review* 1, 3 (1984).

[132]Prior to 1970, federal and state appellate courts combined used Holmes's precise phrase – "get itself accepted in the competition of the market" – only fifteen times. Lexis-Nexis search, May 24, 2009.

[133]*See Red Lion Broadcasting Co. v. Federal Communications Commission*, 395 U.S. 367, 390 (1969) (citing *Abrams* dissent).

[134]*See United States v. Rumely*, 345 U.S. 41, 56 (1953) (Douglas, J. concurring) ("Like the publishers of newspapers, magazines, or books, this publisher bids for the minds of men in the market place of ideas."). This is the first time the phrase appears in any federal or state appellate court opinion.

[135]*See Park v. Sweeten*, 270 S.W.2d 687, 692 (Tex. Ct. Civ. App. 1954).

government[136] cases. In 1954 the Pennsylvania Supreme Court Justice Michael A. Musmanno looked on the seldom-invoked phrase with disdain: "The incredible paradox is that while some political science academicians see something calamitous in a typist or file clerk expressing a preference for mayor, governor or president, they at the same time argue strenuously for free speech for Communists (using the glib phrase of 'a market place of ideas.')."[137] By 1965, the phrase began to gain more legitimacy in the courts when Justice William Brennan invoked it, again without mentioning Holmes, in his concurrence in *Lamount v. Postmaster General*.[138] In other words, for decades after the *Abrams* dissent, courts had little awareness of or interest in the marketplace-of-ideas maxim. And when they first began to see the phrase in appellate court opinions, it was not associated with Holmes.

What this sketch of judicial history suggests is that the great Holmesian idea expressed in *Abrams* depended on rhetorical refinement for its general acceptance in the law. In the half century or so after Justices Douglas and Brennan used the marketplace-of-ideas metaphor, some one thousand appellate courts have echoed it in published opinions.[139] Indicative of that trend toward judicial acceptance of and reliance on that metaphor, in the past decade alone, it has been invoked often by liberals and conservatives alike in Supreme Court opinions involving government speech,[140] campaign contributions,[141] the establishment clause,[142] "true threats,"[143] election law,[144] and in commercial speech cases,[145] among others. Perhaps it is not surprising that Holmes's market metaphor, at least as recast by Douglas and Brennan, should enjoy common acceptance in a highly commercial culture; that culture has, in turn, helped to shape the law of free speech in America.

Nonetheless, although the phrase has won much acceptance in U.S. courts and culture, it has enjoyed a far less enthusiastic acceptance in the

---

[136]*See Clark v. Meade*, 377 Pa. 150, 204, 104 A.2d 465, 476 (1954) (Musmanno, J., dissenting).
[137]*Ibid*.
[138]381 U.S. 301, 308 (1965) (Brennan, J., concurring) ("I think the right to receive publications is such a fundamental right. The dissemination of ideas can accomplish nothing if otherwise willing addressees are not free to receive and consider them. It would be a barren marketplace of ideas that had only sellers and no buyers.").
[139]LexisNexis search, May 24, 2009. References in the legal and social science literature are, of course, substantially greater.
[140]*See Pleasant Grove City v. Summum*, 129 S. Ct. 1125, 1131 (2009).
[141]*See Davis v. FEC*, 128 S. Ct. 2759, 2781 (2008).
[142]*See McCreary County v. ACLU*, 545 U.S. 844, 883 (2005) (O'Connor, J., concurring).
[143]*See Virginia v. Hicks*, 539 U.S. 113, 119 (2003).
[144]*See Clingman v. Beaver*, 544 U.S. 581, 620 (2005).
[145]*See Johanns v. Livestock Marketing Association*, 544 U.S. 550, 574 (2005).

scholarly literature, as has been mentioned previously in the comments following the *Abrams* dissent (Part VI). Noted First Amendment scholars such as C. Edwin Baker,[146] Vincent Blasi,[147] Owen Fiss,[148] Frederick Schauer,[149] Steven Shiffrin,[150] Rodney Smolla,[151] and Cass Sunstein,[152] among others, have criticized the metaphor, sometimes sharply. To be sure, there are also those who view the metaphor as key to any healthy system of freedom of expression.[153] My point, or one of them, is not necessarily to deny or affirm such charges but to note that, though yesterday's progressives rallied to Holmes and his market metaphor, today's progressive scholars often lead the charge against it. There is also another point, which is that courts and commentators have, in more recent decades, moved away from any single theory of or rational for protecting free expression. Hence, even if one doubts the wisdom of the market model as the sole reason for affirming free speech claims, it is hard to deny it any role in the First Amendment scheme of things. By that measure, Holmes has survived his free speech critics.

⁓⌀

Despite the widespread appeal of the clear-and-present-danger idea and the equally popular appeal of the marketplace-of-ideas concept, there is much in Holmes's free speech jurisprudence that has not stood the test of time.[154] Holmes's views on several matters have either been eclipsed or repudiated or

---

[146]C. Edwin Baker, *Human Liberty and Freedom of Speech* (New York: Oxford University Press, 1989), at 6–24, 37–46.

[147]Vincent Blasi, "The Checking Value in First Amendment Theory," 2 *American Bar Foundation Research Journal* 521 (1977).

[148]Owen Fiss, *Liberalism Divided: Freedom of Speech and the Many Uses of State Power* (Boulder, CO: Westview Press, 1996), at 16–17.

[149]Frederick Schauer, *Free Speech: A Philosophical Inquiry* (New York: Cambridge University Press, 1982), at 15–34.

[150]Steven Shiffrin, *Dissent, Injustice, and the Meanings of America* (Princeton, NJ: Princeton University Press, 1999), at 6.

[151]Rodney Smolla, *Free Speech in an Open Society* (New York: Knopf, 1992), at 6–8.

[152]Cass Sunstein, *Democracy and the Problem of Free Speech* (New York: Free Press, 1993), at 25–26.

[153]*See, e.g.*, Melville Nimmer, *Nimmer on Freedom of Speech* (1984), secs. 1–12 ("If acceptance of an idea in the competition of the market is not the 'best test' [what] is the alternative?"). *See also* Kent Greenawalt, "Free Speech Justifications," 89 *Columbia Law Review* 119, 130–41, 153–54 (1989).

[154]*See, e.g.*, Louise Weinberg, "Holmes's Failure," 96 *Michigan Law Review* 691, 719, 722–23 (1997) (noting infatuation with Holmes – "we are always drawn to him, even to his chilling indifference" – and the campaign to build up his reputation, and noting how much of his thought has not been accepted by today's lawyers, judges, and scholars).

seem antiquated. Consider, for example, the following areas of law that have moved beyond the Holmesian cases:

- The law of defamation and judicial proceedings (*Cowley v. Pulsifer*)
- The law of defamation and liability without fault for unintentional defamation (*Hanson v. Globe Newspaper Co.*)
- The right of the press to comment on court proceedings without fear of contempt citations (*Patterson v. Colorado*)
- The right of the press and others to criticize majoritarian views (*Fox v. Washington*)
- The right-privilege distinction in free speech cases (*McAuliffe v. Mayor of City of New Bedford*)
- Free speech rights in public fora (*Commonwealth v. Davis*)
- The evidence needed to establish clear and present danger (*Debs v. United States*)

Furthermore, there are entire areas of modern First Amendment law in which Holmesian tests or doctrines do little, if anything, to inform our thinking (e.g., public forum doctrine, libel law, commercial speech, obscenity, indecency, expressive conduct). It has been more than forty years since the Court has decided a real clear-and-present-danger case. If such a case were to come before the Court, it is far more likely that it would resolve such a matter by way of ad hoc balancing or some variation of rationales,[155] or by turning to today's most widely used doctrinal tools (e.g., overbreadth, content discrimination),[156] which have few if any real links to Holmes's free speech jurisprudence. For all of the enthusiasm over Holmes, it is well to note that Brandeis's concurrence in *Whitney v. California*[157] resonates far more closely with the particulars of contemporary free speech jurisprudence than does Holmes's dissent in *Abrams*. And the centerpiece of contemporary First Amendment jurisprudence – *New York Times Co. v. Sullivan*[158] – owes far more to Meiklejohn's thinking than to Holmes's.

But in a larger sense, these are mere technical or doctrinal points – lawyers' stuff. To dwell on them is, simply, to miss something far more consequential. For when one gets to the cash value of the matter, as William James liked to say, Holmes did a lot more with First Amendment jurisprudence than tinker with the common law of attempts or conspiracy. In his *Abrams* opinion and

---

[155]*See* Geoffrey R. Stone, "Free Speech in the Twenty-First Century: Ten Lessons from the Twentieth Century," 36 *Pepperdine Law Review* 273, 275–76 (2009).
[156]*See* "What Is War?" *supra* note 15, at 854–57.
[157]274 U.S. 357, 372 (1927) (Brandeis, J., concurring, joined by Holmes, J.).
[158]376 U.S. 254 (1964).

the opinions following it, he ushered in an entire new way of thinking about free speech. What was once a matter of degree – his word was *probability* – became a matter of an entirely new order. In that new order, the First Amendment came, in time, to enjoy a centrality that it had not previously experienced. In the process, probability became more doubtful; harm became more tolerable; experimentation became more desirable; truth became less categorical; and free speech freedom became more durable. The result is that though Holmes failed to bring about certain doctrinal changes in discrete areas of First Amendment law, he did, nonetheless, bring about an enormous change in the temperament of the law of free speech.[159] It is undeniable: free speech in America was never the same after 1919. Though gradual, this triumph of the free speech principle was inevitable after Holmes unleashed his *Abrams* dissent on the minds of generations longing to break with the restrictive traditions of the past. He didn't so much liberalize that world as help transform it. The transformation was predicated on a basic transaction: the exchange of certainty for freedom, of faith for science, and of uncompromising principles for a compromising democracy of ideas.[160] The Holmesian hope was to bring such changes about by changing free speech doctrine into a kind of free speech science (much as Judge Posner now hopes to do).

Although the scientific side of Holmes's jurisprudence is still emerging – with sustained help from the law and economics movement – the attitudinal side has blossomed considerably. This temperament in the law of modern free speech explains, in significant part, the newfound protections accorded to hate speech, sexual expression, defamation, commercial speech, and the idea that money is speech, which is why more and more restraints on campaign contributions are struck down in the name of the First Amendment. Technically, such developments do not readily derive from Holmesian precedents. But philosophically, they are cut from Holmesian cloth or are at least threaded together by it.[161]

Not surprisingly, no name in the First Amendment arena stands out more in the minds of students, lawyers, judges, scholars, and others than that of Oliver Wendell Holmes. I have discussed why this might be so. That said, there is still something more here. Part of that something is the man and his time. It

---

[159]For a similar occurrence in philosophy, see William James's *Pragmatism: A New Name for Some Old Ways of Thinking* (New York: Longmans, Green, 1907), excerpted in Louis Menand, ed., *Pragmatism: A Reader* (New York: Vintage, 1997), at 97.

[160]*Compare* Louis Menand, *American Studies* (New York: Farrar, Straus & Giroux, 2002), at 204 (discussing Christopher Lasch's conception of modern life).

[161]*Hustler Magazine, Inc. v. Falwell*, 485 U.S. 46 (1988) is one such example where a unanimous Court ruled that a lewd parody of a private figure was protected expression.

is easy in retrospect to ignore the obvious. One of the main reasons Holmes is considered the father of modern free speech jurisprudence is because he wrote what he did, when he did, and voted as he did in *Abrams* and its progeny. It was, after all, a grand moment when the most revered jurist in America – a Harvard grad, distinguished Civil War hero, respected state judge, author of *The Common Law* and various scholarly articles, and esteemed Supreme Court justice – wagered his reputation on upholding the First Amendment rights of foreign dissidents and communists. If 1919 was indeed a turning point in America's free speech history, it is in good measure because *Holmes* made it so. One can do no better in articulating the point than to quote Holmes himself: "A great man represents a great ganglion in the nerves of society, or, to vary the figure, a strategic point in the campaign of history, and part of his greatness consists in *his* being *there*."[162] Had a lesser justice like Mahlon Pitney or Willis Van Devanter done the same, it is highly questionable whether the impact would be nearly as great as when Holmes lent his name to both the opinion and the vote in *Abrams*.

Beyond such considerations, there is another important one. That something was Holmes's modernity.

✧

[T]he law opens a way to philosophy as well as anything else, if pursued far enough, and I hope to prove it before I die.

– Holmes to Emerson, 1876[163]

Oliver Wendell Holmes, a Civil War hero, was a modern man.[164] He was one of the great intellectuals who first marched into modernity and then down the paths of what it came to represent.[165] His evolution in thought from 1864 through 1927 reflects his cerebral journey. He once said that "many of the infinities of [his] youth have become finites."[166] In that regard, some scholars

---

[162]"John Marshall," February 4, 1901, reproduced in *Collected Works of Justice Holmes*, *supra* note 106, at 3:501–02 (emphasis added only to the word *his*).

[163]Letter from OWH to Ralph Waldo Emerson, April 16, 1876, qtd. in Mark DeWolfe Howe, *Justice Holmes: The Shaping Years* (Cambridge, MA: Harvard University Press, 1957), at 1:203.

[164]There was a sense of this while Holmes was alive. *See* Jerome Frank, *Law and the Modern Mind* (New York: Brentano's, 1930), at 253–60.

[165]Some few, such as H. L. Mencken, contested Holmes's greatness. There is "no evidence," Mencken maintained, in "Holmes's decisions that he ever gave any really profound thought to the great battle of ideas which raged in his time." Moreover, added Mencken, Holmes's opinions revealed "a wide spread and a beautiful inconsistency." H. L. Mencken, "The Great Holmes Mystery," 26 *American Mercury* 123, 124 (1932).

[166]Letter from OWH to Lewis Einstein, September 2, 1912, reproduced in *Holmes-Einstein Letters*, *supra* note 25, at 70.

of the history of ideas understand Holmes (and the drift of his free speech jurisprudence) better than most of their counterparts trained in the law. Louis Menand is one such scholar who appreciates the modernity of the Holmesian mind.[167] In his *The Metaphysical Club: A Story of Ideas in America*, Menand perceptively describes the mind-set of the man who left the Civil War scarred in body and mind, a man who left the battlefield with an entirely new outlook on life and law, and on war and truth. Here are a few sample passages from Menand:

- "He had found that he did not require religious faith."
- "Uncertainty – 'I had to take a leap in the dark' – turned out to be all the certainty he needed."
- "The assurance that he had done his duty was a wholly adequate consolation."
- "'How rapidly the mind adjusts itself': the test of a belief is not its immutability, but adaptability. Our reasons for needing reasons are always changing."
- "Holmes carefully erased every connection between his experiences as a soldier and his views as an abolitionist. This is not because he changed those views. It is because he changed his view of the nature of views. It was the great lesson he thought the war had taught him, and he took pains, in later life, to make sure the record reflected it."[168]

Similarly, Drew Gilpin Faust, in her *This Republic of Suffering: Death and the American Civil War*, sees much of the same in the thought of Holmes and his generation:

- "One product of the horror of the Civil War was the proliferation of irony, of a posture of distance and doubt in relation to experience."
- "[E]mbracing Darwinian notions of 'nature red in tooth and claw,'" Holmes and some of the great thinkers of his day mocked "the doctrines and authority of organized religion."
- "Death itself becomes war's end, the product of its industrialized machinery; there is no more transcendent or glorious purpose. . . ."

[167] Before Menand, there was Edmund Wilson. See his insightful account of Holmes in his *Patriotic Gore: Studies in the Literature of the American Civil War* (New York: Oxford University Press, 1962), at 743–96.

[168] Louis Menand, *The Metaphysical Club: A Story of Ideas in America* (New York: Farrar, Straus & Giroux, 2001), at 37–38. Compare the preface to Thomas W. Higginson, ed., *Harvard Memorial Biographies* (Cambridge, MA: Sever & Francis, 1867), at vi: "The best monument that we can build to these our [fallen Civil War] heroes, is to show that they have renewed our faith, and made nobler the years that are to come."

- On the heels of the Civil War, Holmes and others mapped "the contours of doubt" and thereby "helped delineate the broader topography of belief and unbelief that grew from the war." That experience produced in them a "sense of a failure of knowledge and understanding. . . ."[169]

Perhaps the best statement of Holmesian modernity comes from the pen of the man himself, who in a 1915 article titled "Ideals and Doubts" declared with daring abandon: "To have doubted one's own first principles is the mark of a civilized man."[170] Or as he cast it ten years later: "Scepticism is a saving grace if it takes in enough of oneself."[171] That basic idea finds eloquent expression in something Dr. Holmes, his father, wrote in 1884: "[T]o think of trying to waterproof the American mind against the questions that Heaven rains down upon it shows a misapprehension of our new conditions. If to question everything be unlawful and dangerous, we had better undeclare our independence at once; for what the Declaration means is the right to question everything, even the truth of its own foundation."[172] That belief, grounded in his own brand of skepticism, was the son's creed as well: "It seems to me that the sceptic well may be the most truly religious as well as the most philosophical of men. I would," added Holmes, "undertake to defend that thesis."[173] Not surprisingly, when he spoke of the law, he spoke "as a cynic,"[174] and as someone who could gleefully admit that "if my fellow citizens want to go to Hell I will help them. It's my job."[175] The disinterested and detached Holmesian mind knew "nothing about absolute truth" and loathed those who, "like

[169]Drew Gilpin Faust, *This Republic of Suffering: Death and the American Civil War* (New York: Vintage Books, 2008), at 194, 200, 202, 208.

[170]Oliver Wendell Holmes, "Ideals and Doubts," 10 *Illinois Law Review* 1, 2 (1915), reproduced in *Collected Works of Justice Holmes, supra* note 93, at 3:442, 444.

[171]Letter from OWH to Lewis Einstein, June 1, 1925, reproduced in *Holmes-Einstein Letters, supra* note 25, at 241–42.

[172]Oliver Wendell Holmes Sr., *The Professor at the Breakfast-Table* (London: George Routledge & Sons, 1884), at 291.

[173]Letter from OWH to Lewis Einstein, February 1, 1927, reproduced in *Holmes-Einstein Letters, supra* note 25, at 263–64. For a discussion of Holmes's skepticism, see Yosal Rogat and James M. O'Fallon, "Mr. Justice Holmes: A Dissenting Opinion – The Speech Cases," 36 *Stanford Law Review* 1349, 1367–68 (1984).

[174]Letter from OWH to Harold Laski, December 3, 1917, reproduced in Mark DeWolfe Howe, ed., *Holmes-Laski Letters: The Correspondence of Mr. Justice Holmes and Harold J. Laski* (Cambridge, MA: Harvard University Press, 1953), at 1:115.

[175]Letter from OWH to Harold Laski, March 4, 1920, reproduced in *Holmes-Laski Letters, supra* note 174, at 1:248–49. There were, of course, certain matters about which Holmes was not so skeptical. *See* Yosal Rogat, "The Judge as Spectator," 31 *University of Chicago Law Review* 213, 251–54 (1964).

the clergy, dogmatize on unrealities."[176] Holmes wondered "if there is such a thing" as immutable truths.[177] Or as he once told William James, "[T]here are as many truths as there are men."[178] A real tooth-and-nail devotion to truth, he liked to say, is synonymous with "hard obscure work" and is the antithesis of "wrapping oneself in a toga and talking tall."[179] Skepticism, by stark contrast, was the best of "modern improvements" in that it did not allow grand talk, philosophical posturing, or theological thinking to "sneak in the miraculous at the back door."[180] Hence, for Holmes, "the true end of life is the exercise of one's faculties."[181] Beyond that, he believed that what "is an end in itself is a question for the individual, and no one has a right to dogmatize."[182] Because truth was relational, always in flux, and not knowable with final certainty, a well-functioning system of freedom of expression was vital to human existence, for any variety of reasons. In all of these ways and others, the mark of skepticism left an indelible imprint on Holmes's mind, his philosophical outlook, and his free speech jurisprudence.

Behind the curtain of Holmes's skepticism was a certain fatalism, a peculiar detachment that bowed to the ubiquity of force.[183] As on the battlefield, he was prepared to yield to the commands of the "dominant power." Still, he valued the fight, the valor, and the contest of wills engaged in Darwinian struggle. At times, it is easy to believe that the contest – that glorious fight for life itself – was the be-all and end-all of human existence. It is a remarkable metaphor

[176]Letter from OWH to Lewis Einstein, June 1, 1905, reproduced in *Holmes-Einstein Letters, supra* note 25, at 15–17.

[177]Letter from OWH to Lewis Einstein, November 9, 1913, reproduced in *ibid.*, at 81–82.

[178]Letter from OWH to William James, March 24, 1907, reproduced in *Mind and Faith of Justice Holmes, supra* note 40, at 415–16.

[179]Letter from OWH to Lewis Einstein, August 27, 1906, reproduced in *Holmes-Einstein Letters, supra* note 25, at 25–26.

[180]Letter from OWH to Lewis Einstein, June 1, 1905, reproduced in *Holmes-Einstein Letters, supra* note 25, at 15–16, 18 (the last page reference is to a September 18, 1905, letter from OWH to Einstein). Holmes came to be critical of the thought of his college-days colleague William James. He accused him of turning the lights down to give spiritual "magic" a chance. But James' biographer contests the portrayal. *See* Robert D. Richardson, *William James in the Maelstrom of American Modernism* (Boston: Houghton Mifflin, 2007), at 510.

[181]Letter from OWH to Lewis Einstein, October 21, 1906, reproduced in *Holmes-Einstein Letters, supra* note 25, at 27.

[182]Letter from OWH to Lewis Einstein, August 1, 1908, reproduced in *Holmes-Einstein Letters, supra* note 25, at 38.

[183]One of the most thoughtful accounts of Holmes's skepticism and detachment is found in Yosal Rogat's "The Judge as Spectator," *supra* note 175, at 251–56 (1964). For a more general account of Holmes's overall philosophy, see *The Collected Works of Justice Holmes, supra* note 106, at 1:24–28.

that says much about the man and his life: positioned centrally in Holmes's voluminous study, in a space above the fireplace where family photos rested on a mantle, were a pair of sabers crossed in an X form.[184] In other words, his world of ideas was never far from his world of war.

Although more can and needs to be said about the centrality of the Civil War experience on Holmes and his thought, the foregoing (along with what has been set out in Part I) should suffice to provide readers with a glance out the window through which Holmes came to see a new world, that of modernity. If indeed the Civil War was key to Holmes's philosophical development, then his free speech jurisprudence, particularly as reflected in his *Abrams* dissent, represents a central component of that philosophical stance. That jurisprudence represents the field on which the implications of Holmes's greater philosophy were played out. If the Civil War produced in Holmes a crisis of belief in God, reason, and values, then that crisis likewise manifested itself in his jurisprudence of free speech. Here, too, a few passages from Professor Menand help to sharpen the focus of such matters: "[Holmes] makes the value of an idea not its correspondence to a preexisting reality or metaphysical truth, but simply the difference it makes in the life of the group. Holmes's concept of a 'marketplace of ideas' . . . is the metaphor of probabilistic thinking: the more arrows you shoot at the target, the better sense you will have of the bull's eye. The more individual variations, the greater the chances the group will survive."[185] This view is not one grounded in any notion of rights, let alone inalienable rights.[186] As in war, it is not the soldier that counts; it is his duty to protect his own country and its cause: "We do not (on Holmes's reasoning) permit the free expression of ideas because some individual may have the right one. No individual alone can have the right one. We permit free expression because we need the resources of the whole group to get us the ideas we need. Thinking is a social activity. I tolerate your thought because it is part of my thought – even when my thought defines itself in opposition to yours."[187]

---

[184]*See* John S. Monagan, *The Grand Panjandrum: Mellow Years of Justice Holmes* (Lanham, MD: University Press of America, 1988), at 37 (the swords had been used in the Indian Wars by his Grandfather Charles Jackson).

[185]*Metaphysical Club, supra* note 168, at 431.

[186]As Holmes once put it: "All my life I have sneered at the natural rights of man." Letter from OWH to Harold Laski, September 15, 1916, reproduced in *Holmes-Laski Letters, supra* note 174, at 1:21. *See also* Albert Alschuler, "Historic Proponents and the Critics of Higher Law: From Blackstone to Holmes: The Revolt against Natural Law," 36 *Pepperdine Law Review* 491 (2009).

[187]*Metaphysical Club, supra* note 168, at 431. To this should be added what Holmes wrote in a September 19, 1919, letter to Sir Frederick Pollock: "The whole collectivist tendency seems to be toward underrating or forgetting the safeguards in bills of rights that had to be fought for in their day and that still are worth fighting for. I have had to deal with cases that made my blood boil and yet seemed to create no feeling in the public or even

It has been said that "all agree that Holmes deserves a place at the pantheon of American jurisprudence, but there are some who insist that he should wear a black hat."[188] Consistent with that view, in his *Law without Values*, Professor Alschuler sounds a clarion call to alert vulnerable innocents to steer clear of Holmes and his modernist kind.[189] He warns that Holmes has "walked twentieth-century law down the wrong path."[190] And yet we – particularly many of the legal and cultural elite – march down that path happily. If we do, it is not because we consciously reject such warnings or knowingly accept the creed of *Buck v. Bell* (the eugenics opinion authored by Holmes).[191] Rather, if we embrace the modernist gospel, it is because we are moderns, in some or all ways. Holmes's metaphors and philosophical directions coincide with much in the culture of skepticism, that is, with the life and law of much in our modernist times. By that measure, is it any wonder that his market metaphor should resonate with those who live, work, and rejoice in a highly capitalistic culture? Or is it surprising that his skeptical views should be tapped by the demands of an often-cynical society? Similarly, it should not shock us that Holmes could well be our secular saint of relativism, of the idea that the search for truth is more important than truth itself. Or in the political realm, is it at all strange that Holmes's free speech jurisprudence has been branded as a nothing short of a "nihilistic vision of American democracy"?[192] I raise such questions and offer such statements not to necessarily denounce Holmesian thought outright – though Professor Alschuler makes a case for doing almost that – but to describe it and thereby explain why it has become nearly "canonical" in our lives and in the life of the law of free speech.[193]

in most of my brethren. We have been comfortable so long that we are apt to take it for granted that everything will be all right without our taking any trouble. All of which is but a paraphrase of eternal vigilance is the price of freedom – and I would fain add, to the labor of men, eternal hard work is the price of living. . . . " *Holmes-Pollock Letters*, *supra* note 23, at 2:24–25.

[188] H. L. Pohlman, *Justice Oliver Wendell Holmes: Free Speech and the Living Constitution* (New York: New York University Press, 1991), at 1 (Pohlman, however, does not hold this view).

[189] I happily recognize the influence of my colleague James L. Swanson in the articulation of this thought and other related ones.

[190] *Law without Values, supra* note 22, at 194.

[191] For another view of Holmes and the eugenics question, see *The Essential Holmes, supra* note 21, at 104. *Compare* Stephen A. Siegel, "Justice Holmes, *Buck v. Bell*, and the History of Equal Protection," 90 *Minnesota Law Review* 106 (2005) (critiquing Holmes's equal protection analysis in *Buck*).

[192] Jeffrey Rosen, "Free to Develop Their Faculties," in *A New Literary History of America*, Greil Marcus and Werner Sollors, eds. (Cambridge, MA: Harvard University Press, 2009), at 612–13.

[193] A similar frame of mind, though sometimes satirical, is offered in Ronald Collins and David Skover, *The Death of Discourse* (Boulder, CO: Westview Press, 1996).

This brings us back to the beginning, to the epigraph to this book from the *Abrams* dissent. Recall that quotation concerned Holmes's fascination with risk, with experimentation. Importantly, the great jurist "defended free speech in the language of risk."[194] His belief was that, because life is an experiment, we can never be entirely certain of anything – thus we must tolerate dissent. Holmes's constitutionalism – from his *Lochner* dissent to and beyond his *Abrams* dissent – was tooled to allow for and even encourage social experimentation, including certain experiments that Holmes found personally objectionable. Thus, the same Constitution that denied Fourteenth Amendment economic rights, which if granted would have prevented social experimentation, affirmed Fourteenth Amendment free speech rights to further the cause of cultural experimentation. And where experimentation is the coin of the realm, the only experiments that are wrong are those that the majority deems to be so. That is the governing principle – witness the holding in *Buck v. Bell*. In this regard, Holmes was neither malevolent minded nor utopian minded; he was indifferent. If competitive free speech helped us to become better citizens and more humane people, then fine. But if it did not, that was fine, too. For such are the risks of life.[195]

It is that fight, that unending war within us and within our culture, which the old soldier invited us to engage in, to struggle with, and if need be to die for. That, at any rate, was his fighting faith, and in many respects it has, for better or worse, become ours, too.

[194] *The Metaphysical Club, supra* note 168, at 432–33.
[195] A statement from Professor Thomas Grey seems fitting to add before closing: "I am fascinated by Holmes, a fascination compounded of repulsion and attraction. It is easy to list the man's repulsive aspects: his naïve attraction to pseudo-scientific eugenics, his fatalism, his indifference to human suffering, his egotism and vanity, his near-worship of force and obedience. But even when all that is taken into account, I am drawn on by Holmes' charms of person and of style, charms enhanced for the interpretive suitor by the complexities that shroud his character and thought. And the substance of his most famous teaching, the primacy of experience over logic, still seems to me the central, if obscure, truth of American legal thought; as Cardozo wrote, 'Here is the text to be unfolded. All that is to come will be development and commentary.'" "Holmes and Legal Pragmatism," 41 *Stanford Law Review* 787, 792 (1988) [quoting Benjamin Cardozo, "Mr. Justice Holmes," in *Mr. Justice Holmes*, Felix Frankfurter, ed. (Cambridge, MA: Harvard University Press, 1931), at 3].

Appendix 1: Holmes on Free Speech and Related Matters: Selected Quotations

Modern free speech jurisprudence begins with the words and wisdom of Oliver Wendell Holmes Jr. Whatever one may make of that, it is impossible to deny. Whether Holmes was a liberal or a libertarian, a pragmatist or a nihilist, a defender of individual rights or of majority will, a social Darwinist or a totalitarian, or a "Jekyll-Holmes and Hyde-Holmes"[1] as Albert Alschuler has branded him, is difficult to say absent nuanced elaboration. What is easier to gauge is his enormous impact on how we – laypeople and lawyers alike – think and talk about our system of freedom of expression. This is not necessarily because of the analytical soundness of his opinions but rather, to echo Judge Richard Posner, because of his "rhetorical skill."[2] That is, "Holmes was a great judge because he was a great literary artist." His "specialty was great utterance," said Felix Frankfurter. If "we care for our literary treasures," added Frankfurter, "the expression of his views must become part of our national culture."[3]

The most memorable and important instances of judge-announced law cannot always be reduced, as Holmes well understood, to Kantian formulas thereafter stamped as precedents. They often consist of statements that awaken within us readily recognizable emotions or instantly persuasive ideas or even enticingly provocative thoughts. By that measure, Holmes's many statements on free speech remain touchstones in our free expression discourse. Then again, other lesser-known Holmes statements reveal a jaundiced view

---

[1] Albert Alschuler, *Law without Values* (Chicago: University of Chicago Press, 2000), at 15.

[2] Richard A. Posner, ed., *The Essential Holmes* (Chicago: University of Chicago Press, 1992), at xvii.

[3] Felix Frankfurter, *Mr. Justice Holmes and the Supreme Court* (Cambridge, MA: Harvard University Press, 1938), at 28–29. Frankfurter also noted that "the significance of his genius would evaporate in any analysis of specific decisions." *Ibid.*, at 29.

of our First Amendment freedoms. And Holmes's pre-1919 statements point to a far more crabbed notion of freedom of expression than what came later. Mindful of all of this and more, the selection of sixty quotes offered here is submitted for the reader's examination, duly mindful of his or her right to dissent.

Free Speech and Other Values

1. "[F]ree speech stands no differently than freedom from vaccination."
   – Letter from OWH to Learned Hand, June 24, 1918
2. "I regarded my view in [*Abrams v. U.S.*] as simply upholding the right of a donkey to drool. But the usual notion is that you are free to say what you like if you don't shock *me*. Of course the value of the constitutional right is only when you do shock people. . . . "
   – Letter from OWH to Lewis Einstein, July 11, 1925
3. "[D]ecisions for or against the privilege [to harm another by speech], which really can stand only upon [legislative policy] grounds, often are presented as hollow deductions from empty general propositions."
   – OWH, "Privilege, Malice, and Intent," 8 *Harvard Law Review* 1, 3 (1894)
4. "All my life I have sneered at the natural rights of man – and at times I have thought that the bills of rights in the Constitutions were overworked – [still,] they embody principles that men have died for, and that it is well not to forget in our haste to secure our notion of general welfare. . . . "
   – Letter from OWH to Harold Laski, September 15, 1916
5. "We cannot live our dreams. We are lucky enough if we can give a sample of our best, and if in our hearts we can feel that it has been nobly done."
   – OWH Bar Association Address, Boston, March 7, 1900

Free Speech and the Pursuit of Truth

6. Value choices are "more or less arbitrary. . . . Do you like sugar in your coffee or don't you? . . . So as to truth."
   – OWH to Lady Pollock, September 6, 1902
7. "It has seemed to me that certainty is an illusion."
   – OWH address before the Middlesex Bar Association, December 3, 1902

8. "Certitude is not the test of certainty."
   – OWH, "Natural Law," 32 *Harvard Law Review* 40 (1918)
9. "I do not know what is true. I do not know the meaning of the universe. But in the midst of doubt, in the collapse of creeds, there is one thing I do not doubt... and that is that the faith is true and adorable which leads a soldier to throw away his life in obedience to a blindly accepted duty, in a cause which he little understands, in a plan of campaign of which he has no notion, under tactics of which he does not see the use."
   – OWH, "The Soldier's Faith" address, Harvard University, Memorial Day, 1895
10. "[W]hen men have realized that time has upset many fighting faiths, they may come to believe even more than they believe the very foundations of their own conduct that the ultimate good desired is better reached by free trade in ideas – that the best test of truth is the power of the thought to get itself accepted in the competition of the market, and that truth is the only ground upon which their wishes safely can be carried out. That, at any rate, is the theory of our Constitution. It is an experiment, as all life is an experiment. Every year, if not every day, we have to wager our salvation upon some prophecy based upon imperfect knowledge. While that experiment is part of our system, I think that we should be eternally vigilant against attempts to check the expression of opinions that we loathe and believe to be fraught with death, unless they so imminently threaten immediate interference with the lawful and pressing purposes of the law that an immediate check is required to save the country."
    – OWH dissenting in *Abrams v. United States*, 250 U.S. 616, 630 (1919)

Defamation

11. "So in slander and libel, the distinction between malice in law and malice in fact seems to give the result, that the usual ground of liability in such actions is simply doing certain overt acts; viz., making the false statements complained of, irrespective of intent."
    – OWH, "Primitive Notions in Modern Law," 10 *American Law Review* 422 (1876)
12. "[T]he rule that [libel] is presumed upon proof of speaking certain words is equivalent to saying that the overt conduct of speaking those

words may be actionable whether the consequence of damage to the plaintiff was intended or not."
– OWH, *The Common Law* (1881, 1963 printing), at 110.

13. "It is for the public interest that people should be free to give the best information they can under certain circumstances without fear, but there is no public benefit in having lies told at any time; and when a charge is known to be false, or is in excess of what is required by the occasion, it is not necessary to make that charge in order to speak freely, and therefore it falls under the ordinary rule, that certain charges are made at the party's peril in case they turn out to be false, whether evil consequences were intended or not."
– OWH, *The Common Law* (1881, 1963 printing), at 111

14. "It would be no great curtailment of freedom to deny a man immunity in attaching a charge of crime to the name of his neighbor, even when he supposes himself alone. But it does not seem clear that the law would go quite so far as that."
– OWH, *The Common Law* (1881, 1963 printing), at 112

15. "The publication is so manifestly detrimental that the defendant publishes it at the peril of being able to justify it in the sense in which the public will understand it. [To privilege such a communication] would be very like firing a gun into the street, and, when a man falls, setting up [a defense] that no one was known to be there."
– OWH dissenting in *Hanson v. Globe Newspaper Co.*, 159 Mass 293, 302, 301 (1893)

16. "'Whenever a man publishes [to quote Lord Mansfield], he publishes at his peril.'... The reason is plain. A libel is harmful on its face. If a man sees fit to publish manifestly hurtful statements concerning an individual, without other justification than exists for an advertisement or a piece of news, the usual principles of tort will make him liable, if the statements are false or true only of someone else."
– OWH for the Court in *Peck v. Tribune Co.*, 214 U.S. 185, 186 (1909)

17. The plaintiff "was a public officer in whose course of action connected with his office the citizens of Porto Rico had a serious interest, anything bearing on such action was a legitimate subject of statement and debate. It was so, at least, in the absence of express malice – a phrase needing further analysis, although not for the purposes of this case."
– OWH for the Court in *Gandia v. Pettingill*, 222 U.S. 452, 457 (1911)

Freedom of Expression: Written and Spoken Speech

18. "[N]otwithstanding all modern inventions[,] letters still are the principal means of speech with those who are not before our face. I do not suppose that anyone would say that the freedom of written speech is less protected by the First Amendment than the freedom of spoken words."
    – OWH dissenting in *Leach v. Carlile*, 258 U.S. 138, 140 (1922)

Competition in the Market

19. "[F]ree competition is worth more to society than its costs, and on that ground the infliction of the damage is privileged."
    – OWH dissenting in *Vegelahn v. Gunter*, 167 Mass. 92, 104 (1896)
20. "One of the eternal conflicts out of which life is made up is that between the effort of every man to get the most he can for his services, and that of society, disguised under the name of capital, to get his services for the least possible return. Combination on the one side is patent and powerful. Combination on the other side is the necessary and desirable counterpart if the battle is to be carried on in a fair and equal way."
    – OWH dissenting in *Vegelahn v. Gunter*, 167 Mass. 92, 104 (1896)
21. "[T]he best test of truth is the power of the thought to get itself accepted in the competition of the market, and that truth is the only ground upon which their wishes safely can be carried out."
    – OWH dissenting in *Abrams v. United States*, 250 U.S. 616, 630 (1919)

Commercial Expression

22. "[W]hen habit and law combine to exclude every other [means of distant communication,] it seems to me that the First Amendment...forbids such control of the post as was exercised here. I think [the postal 'fraud order' prohibiting the delivery of mail or payment of money orders to appellant] abridged freedom of speech on the part of the sender of the letters and that the appellant had such an interest in the exercise of their right that he could avail himself of it in this case."
    – OWH dissenting in *Leach v. Carlile*, 258 U.S. 138, 141 (1922)

Postal Censorship

23. "[N]otwithstanding all modern inventions[,] letters still are the principal means of speech with those who are not before our face. I do not suppose that anyone would say that the freedom of written speech is less protected by the First Amendment than the freedom of spoken words."
    – OWH dissenting in *Leach v. Carlile*, 258 U.S. 138, 140 (1922) (see also no. 22)

Prior Restraints

24. "[T]he main purpose of [the federal and state free speech guarantees] is 'to prevent all such previous restraints upon publications as had been practised by other governments,' and they do not prevent the subsequent punishment of such as may be deemed contrary to the public welfare."
    – OWH for the Court in *Patterson v. Colorado*, 205 U.S. 454, 462 (1907)
25. "It well may be that the prohibition of laws abridging the freedom of speech is not confined to previous restraints, although to prevent them may have been the main purpose. . . ."
    – OWH for the Court in *Schenck v. United States*, 249 U.S. 47, 51–52 (1919)
26. "I do not suppose that anyone would say that the freedom of written speech is less protected by the First Amendment than the freedom of spoken words. Therefore I cannot understand by what authority Congress undertakes to authorize anyone to determine in advance, on the grounds before us, that certain words shall not be uttered. Even those who interpret the Amendment most strictly agree that it was intended to prevent previous restraints. We have not before us any question as to how far Congress may go for the safety of the nation. The question is only whether it may make possible irreparable wrongs and the ruin of a business in the hope of preventing some cases of a private wrong that generally is accomplished without the aid of the mail. Usually private swindling does not depend upon the post-office. If the execution of this law does not abridge freedom of speech I do not quite see what could be said to do so."
    – OWH dissenting in *Leach v. Carlile*, 258 U.S. 138, 140–41 (1922)

Public Forum

27. "For the legislature absolutely or conditionally to forbid public speaking in a highway or public park is no more an infringement of the rights of a member of the public than for the owner of a private house to forbid it in his house."
    – OWH for the court in *Commonwealth v. Davis*, 39 N.E. 113 (Mass. 1895)

Free Speech and Popular Will

28. "Patriotism is the demand of the territorial club for priority, and as much priority as it needs for vital purposes, over such tribal groups as the churches and the trade unions. I go whole hog for the territorial club and I don't care a damn if it interferes with some of the spontaneities of the other groups. I think the Puritans were quite right when they whipped the Quakers and if it were conceivable – as every brutality is – that we should go back a century or two, the Catholics would be quite right, if they got the power, to make you and me shut our mouths."
    – Letter from OWH to Felix Frankfurter, March 27, 1917

29. "[I]t seems to me logical in the Catholic Church to kill heretics and the Puritans to whip Quakers – I see nothing more wrong in it from our ultimate standards than I do in killing Germans when we are at war."
    – Letter from OWH to Harold Laski, October 26, 1919 (see also no. 54)

30. "If the people want to go to Hell, I will help them. It's my job."
    – Letter from OWH to Harold Laski, May 13, 1919

31. "I am so skeptical as to our knowledge about the goodness or badness of laws that I have no practical criticism except what the crowd wants."
    – Letter from OWH to Harold Laski, May 13, 1919

32. "If, in the long run, the beliefs expressed in proletarian dictatorship are destined to be accepted by the dominant forces of the community, the only meaning of free speech is that they should be given their chance and have their way."
    – OWH dissenting in *Gitlow v. New York*, 268 U.S. 652, 673 (1925)

Free Speech Dangers

33. "The most stringent protection of free speech would not protect a man in falsely shouting fire in a theatre and causing a panic."
    – OWH for the Court in *Schenck v. United States*, 249 U.S. 47, 52 (1919)

34. "The question in every case is whether the words used are used in such circumstances and are of such a nature as to create a clear and present danger that they will bring about the substantive evils that Congress has a right to prevent. It is a question of proximity and degree."
    – OWH for the Court in *Schenck v. United States*, 249 U.S. 47, 52 (1919)

35. The government "constitutionally may punish speech that produces or is intended to produce a clear and imminent danger that it will bring about forthwith certain substantive evils that the United States constitutionally may seek to prevent. The power undoubtedly is greater in time of war than in time of peace, because war opens dangers that do not exist at other times."
    – OWH dissenting in *Abrams v. United States*, 250 U.S. 616, 627–28 (1919)

36. "I think that we should be eternally vigilant against attempts to check the expression of opinions that we loathe and believe to be fraught with death, unless they so imminently threaten immediate interference with the lawful and pressing purposes of the law that an immediate check is required to save the country."
    – OWH dissenting in *Abrams v. United States*, 250 U.S. 616, 630 (1919)

37. "Every idea is an incitement. It offers itself for belief, and, if believed, it is acted on unless some other belief outweighs it or some failure of energy stifles the movement at its birth. The only difference between the expression of an opinion and an incitement in the narrower sense is the speaker's enthusiasm for the result. Eloquence may set fire to reason. But whatever may be thought of the redundant discourse before us, it had no chance of starting a present conflagration. If, in the long run, the beliefs expressed in proletarian dictatorship are destined to be accepted by the dominant forces of the community, the only meaning of free speech is that they should be given their chance and have their way."
    – OWH dissenting in *Gitlow v. New York*, 268 U.S. 652, 673 (1925)

38. "[S]uppose that an imminent possibility of obstruction is sufficient. Still I think that only immediate and necessary action is contemplated, and that no case for summary proceedings is made out if after the event publications are called to the attention of the judge that might have led to an obstruction although they did not. So far as appears that is the present case."
    – OWH dissenting in *Toledo Newspaper Co. v. United States*, 247 U.S. 402, 424 (1918)

39. "I would go as far as any man in favor of the sharpest and most summary enforcement of order in court and obedience to decrees, but when there is no need for immediate action, contempts are like any other breach of law and should be dealt with as the law deals with other illegal acts."
    – OWH dissenting in *Toledo Newspaper Co. v. United States*, 247 U.S. 402, 426 (1918)

40. "Misbehavior means something more than adverse comment or disrespect."
    – OWH dissenting in *Toledo Newspaper Co. v. United States*, 247 U.S. 402, 426 (1918)

The Thought We Hate

41. "[I]f there is any principle of the Constitution that more imperatively calls for attachment than any other it is the principle of free thought – not free thought for those who agree with us but freedom for the thought that we hate."
    – OWH dissenting in *United States v. Schwimmer*, 279 U.S. 644, 654–55 (1929)

42. "Persecution for the expression of opinions seems to me perfectly logical. If you have no doubt of your premises or your power, and want a certain result with all your heart, you naturally express your wishes in law, and sweep away all opposition. To allow opposition by speech seems to indicate that you think the speech impotent, as when a man says that he has squared the circle, or that you do not care wholeheartedly for the result, or that you doubt either your power or your premises."
    – OWH dissenting in *Abrams v. United States*, 250 U.S. 616, 630 (1919)

43. "I think that we should be eternally vigilant against attempts to check the expression of opinions that we loathe and believe to be

fraught with death, unless they so imminently threaten immediate interference with the lawful and pressing purposes of the law that an immediate check is required to save the country."
– OWH dissenting in *Abrams v. United States*, 250 U.S. 616, 630 (1919)

44. "If, in the long run, the beliefs expressed in proletarian dictatorship are destined to be accepted by the dominant forces of the community, the only meaning of free speech is that they should be given their chance and have their way."
– OWH dissenting in *Gitlow v. New York*, 268 U.S. 652, 673 (1925)

Free Speech and War

45. "No society has ever admitted that it could not sacrifice individual welfare to its own existence. If conscripts are necessary for its army, it seizes them, and marches them, with bayonets in their rear, to death.... If a man is on a plank in the deep sea which will float only one, and a stranger lays hold of it, he will thrust him off if he can. When the state finds itself in a similar position, it does the same thing."
– OWH, *The Common Law* (1881, 1951 printing), at 43–44

46. "[I]n the midst of doubt, in the collapse of creeds, there is one thing I do not doubt...and that is that the faith is true and adorable which leads a soldier to throw away his life in obedience to a blindly accepted duty, in a cause which he little understands, in a plan of campaign of which he has no notion, under tactics of which he does not see the use."
– OWH, "The Soldier's Faith" Address, Harvard University, Memorial Day, 1895

47. "When it comes to a decision by the head of the state upon a matter involving its life, the ordinary rights of individuals must yield to what he deems the necessities of the moment."
– OWH for the Court in *Moyer v. Peabody*, 212 U.S. 78, 85 (1908)

48. "When a nation is at war, many things that might be said in time of peace are such a hindrance to its effort that their utterance will not be endured so long as men fight, and that no Court could regard them as protected by any constitutional right."
– OWH for the Court in *Schenck v. United States*, 249 U.S. 47, 52 (1919)

49. "We do not lose our right to condemn either measures or men because the country is at war."
    – OWH for the Court in *Frohwerk v. United States*, 294 U.S. 204, 208 (1919)

50. "When people are putting out all their energies in battle, I don't think it unreasonable to say we won't have obstacles intentionally put in the way of raising troops – by persons any more than by force."
    – Unsent letter from OWH to Herbert Croly, May 12, 1919

51. "The power [of the government to punish certain speech] undoubtedly is greater in time of war than in time of peace, because war opens dangers that do not exist at other times."
    – OWH dissenting in *Abrams v. United States*, 250 U.S. 616, 627–28 (1919)

52. "If a man thinks that in time of war the right of free speech carries the right to impede by discourse the raising of armies, I am content to ignore his intellect and say you will find that you had better not monkey with the buzzard."
    – Letter from OWH to John Wigmore, June 7, 1919

Suppression of Speech

53. "I go whole hog for the territorial club and I don't care a damn if it interferes with some of the spontaneities of the other groups. I think the Puritans were quite right when they whipped the Quakers and if it were conceivable – as every brutality is – that we should go back a century or two, the Catholics would be quite right, if they got the power, to make you and me shut our mouths."
    – Letter from OWH to Felix Frankfurter, March 27, 1917

54. "[I]t seems to me logical in the Catholic Church to kill heretics and the Puritans to whip Quakers – I see nothing more wrong in it from our ultimate standards than I do in killing Germans when we are at war."
    – Letter from OWH to Harold Laski, October 26, 1919 (see also no. 29)

Government's Power to Restrict Freedom of Speech and the Press

55. "[T]here is nothing in the Constitution or the statute to prevent the city from attaching obedience to this rule [against political

canvassing] as a condition to the office of policeman, and making it part of the good conduct required. The petitioner may have a constitutional right to talk politics, but he has no constitutional right to be a policeman. There are few employments for hire in which the servant does not agree to suspend his constitutional right of free speech, as well as of idleness, by the implied terms of his contract. The servant cannot complain, as he takes the employment on the terms which are offered him."

– OWH for the court in *McAuliffe v. Mayor of New Bedford*, 29 N.E. 517–18 (Mass. 1892)

56. "[T]he only power given to the Postmaster is to refrain from forwarding the papers when received and to return them to the senders. . . . He could not issue a general order that a certain newspaper should not be carried because he thought it likely or certain that it would contain treasonable or obscene talk. The United States may give up the post office when it sees fit, but while it carries it on the use of the mails is almost as much a part of free speech as the right to use our tongues and it would take very strong language to convince me that Congress ever intended to give such a practically despotic power to any one man."

– OWH dissenting in *United States ex rel. Milwaukee Social Democratic Publishing Co. v. Burleson*, 255 U.S. 407, 438 (1921)

57. "[T]he main purpose of [the federal and state free speech guarantees] is 'to prevent all such previous restraints upon publications as had been practised by other governments,' and they do not prevent the subsequent punishment of such as may be deemed contrary to the public welfare."

– OWH for the Court in *Patterson v. Colorado*, 205 U.S. 454, 462 (1907)

58. "But if a court regards, as it may, a publication concerning a matter of law pending before it, as tending toward . . . an interference, it may punish it as in the instance put. When a case is finished courts are subject to the same criticism as other people; but the propriety and necessity of preventing interference with the course of justice by premature statement, argument, or intimidation hardly can be denied."

– OWH for the Court in *Patterson v. Colorado*, 205 U.S. 454, 463 (1907)

59. "In this present case the disrespect for law that was encouraged was disregard of it – an overt breach and technically criminal act. It

would be in accord with the usages of English to interpret disrespect as manifested disrespect, as active disregard going beyond the line drawn by the law."
– OWH for the Court in *Fox v. Washington*, 236 U.S. 273, 277 (1915)

Exceptions to the First Amendment

60. "[T]he First Amendment while prohibiting legislation against free speech as such cannot have been, and obviously was not, intended to give immunity for every possible use of language. . . . We venture to believe that neither Hamilton nor Madison, nor any other competent person then or later, ever supposed that to make criminal the counseling of a murder within the jurisdiction of Congress would be an unconstitutional interference with free speech."
– OWH for the Court in *Frohwerk v. United States*, 249 U.S. 204, 206 (1919)

Appendix 2: Holmes's Supreme Court Voting Record in Free Speech Cases

Table A2.1. *Justice Holmes's Overall Record in Free Speech Cases (Not all First Amendment Cases) During His Tenure on the Supreme Court*

Years on the Court (December 1902–January 1932)	29 years, one month
Number of free speech cases in which OWH voted	29
Number of free speech opinions authored	13
Number of free speech majority opinions authored	06
Number of free speech dissenting opinions	07
Total Supreme Court votes sustaining free speech claim	16
Total Supreme Court votes denying free speech claim	13
Votes sustaining free speech claims after *Debs*:	13 of 15 cases

Table A2.2. *How Justice Holmes Voted in Particular Free Speech Cases (not all First Amendment Cases) during His Tenure on the Supreme Court*

Case	Year	Vote
United States ex rel. Turner v. Williams	1904	Denied
Halter v. Nebraska	1907	Denied
Patterson v. Colorado	1907	Denied[b]
Peck v. Tribune Co.	1909	Denied[b]
Gompers v. Buck Stove & Range Co.	1911	Sustained[c]
Gandia v. Pettingill	1911	Sustained[b]
Lewis Publishing Co. v. Morgan	1913	Denied
Mutual Film Corp. v. Industrial Commission of Ohio	1915	Denied
Fox v. Washington	1915	Denied[b]
Toledo Newspaper Co. v. United States	1918	Sustained[a]
Sugarman v. United States	1919	Denied
Schenck v. United States	1919	Denied[b]
Frohwerk v. United States	1919	Denied[b]
Debs v. United States	1919	Denied[b]
Abrams v. United States	1919	Sustained[a]
Schafer v. United States	1920	Sustained
Pierce v. United States	1920	Sustained
Gilbert v. Minnesota	1920	Denied
United States ex rel. Milwaukee Social Democratic Publishing Co. v. Burleson	1921	Sustained[a]
American Column & Lumber Co. v. United States	1921	Sustained[a]
Leach v. Carlile	1922	Sustained[a]
Gitlow v. New York	1925	Sustained[a]
Whitney v. California	1927	Denied
Fiske v. Kansas	1927	Sustained[c]
New York ex rel. Bryant v. Zimmerman	1928	Sustained
United States v. Schwimmer	1929	Sustained[a]
Stromberg v. California	1931	Sustained
United States v. Macintosh	1931	Sustained
Near v. Minnesota	1931	Sustained

[a] Indicates authorship of dissenting opinion.
[b] Indicates authorship of majority opinion.
[c] Indicates unanimous judgment. Only sustained cases are noted.

About the Editor

Ronald K. L. Collins is the Harold S. Shefelman Scholar at the University of Washington School of Law and a fellow at the First Amendment Center. He previously served as a law clerk to Justice Hans A. Linde on the Oregon Supreme Court and thereafter was a judicial fellow under Chief Justice Warren Burger at the U.S. Supreme Court. He was president of the Supreme Court Fellows Alumni Association in 2008.

Collins has taught constitutional law and commercial law at Temple Law School, Syracuse University Law School, Seattle University Law School, and George Washington University Law School. He has written constitutional briefs that were submitted to the Supreme Court and various other federal and state courts. He has also published some fifty articles in scholarly journals, including the Harvard, Stanford, and Michigan law reviews and in the *Supreme Court Review*. His writings on the First Amendment have appeared in *Columbia Journalism Review, Nation, New York Times, Los Angeles Times, Washington Post*, and elsewhere.

Collins is coauthor (with David Skover) of *The Trials of Lenny Bruce* (2002), *The Death of Discourse* (2nd ed., 2006), and *We Must Not Be Afraid to Be Free: Stories of Free Speech in America* (with Sam Chaltain) (Oxford University Press, 2010). His next book, also with Skover, is *On Dissent* (Cambridge University Press, forthcoming). He is the editor of *Constitutional Government in America* (1981) and *The Death of Contract* (1992).

In 2003, Collins and Skover successfully petitioned the governor of New York to posthumously pardon Lenny Bruce. In 2004, they received the Hugh Hefner First Amendment Award. In September 2006, Collins conducted a public interview with Anthony Lewis at the Nieman Foundation for Journalism at Harvard University, and, in February 2008, he interviewed Lewis for C-SPAN's Book TV. In 2010, he received a Norman Mailer fellowship in fiction writing in connection with a forthcoming novel and collection of short stories.

Collins lives with his family in Bethesda, Maryland.

Index